W9-BJI-687

Así es

THIRD EDITION

Así es

THIRD EDITION

NANCY LEVY-KONESKY
SIMMONS COLLEGE

KAREN DAGGETT
BOSTON COLLEGE

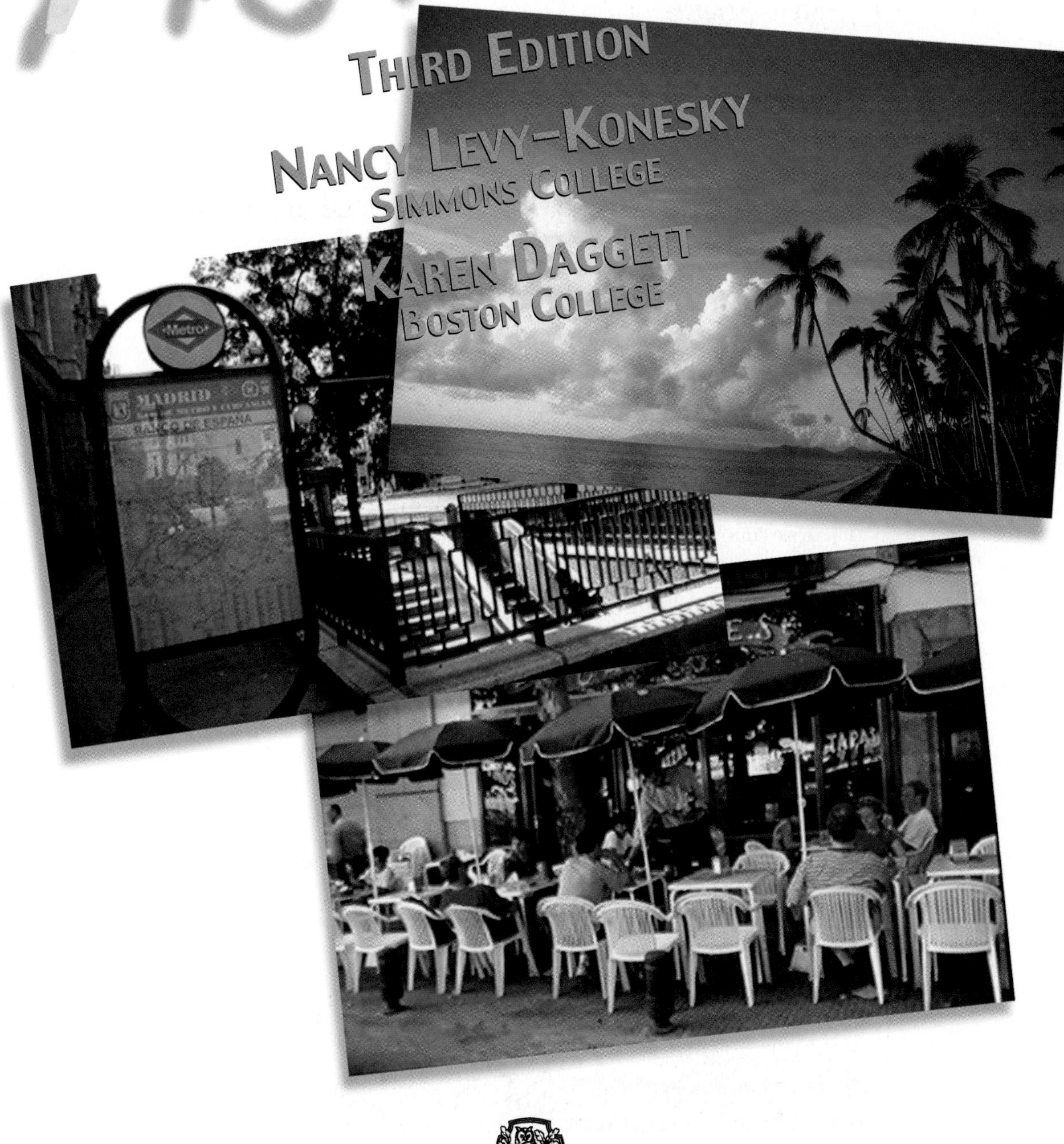

Holt, Rinehart and Winston
A Division of Harcourt College Publishers
Fort Worth Philadelphia San Diego New York Orlando San Antonio
Toronto Montreal London Sydney Tokyo

Publisher	Phyllis Dobbins
Acquisitions Editor	Jeff Gilbreath
Market Strategist	Kenneth S. Kasee
Project Editor	Jon Davies
Art Director	Sue Hart
Production Manager	Angela Williams Urquhart
Cover	Doug Bates/TSI GRAPHICS

ISBN: 0-03-025928-2

Library of Congress Catalog Card Number: 99-63076

Address for Domestic Orders
Holt, Rinehart and Winston, 6277 Sea Harbor Drive, Orlando, FL 32887-6777
800-782-4479

Address for International Orders
International Customer Service
Holt, Rinehart and Winston, 6277 Sea Harbor Drive, Orlando, FL 32887-6777
407-345-3800
(fax) 407-345-4060
(e-mail) hbintl@harcourtbrace.com

Address for Editorial Correspondence
Harcourt College Publishers, 301 Commerce Street, Suite 3700, Fort Worth, TX 76102

Web Site Address
http://www.harcourtcollege.com

Harcourt College Publishers will provide complimentary supplements or supplement packages to those adopters qualified under our adoption policy. Please contact your sales representative to learn how you qualify. If as an adopter or potential user you receive supplements you do not need, please return them to your sales representative or send them to: Attn: Returns Department, Troy Warehouse, 465 South Lincoln Drive, Troy, MO 63379.

Printed in the United States of America

9 0 1 2 3 4 5 6 7 8 048 9 8 7 6 5 4 3 2 1

Holt, Rinehart and Winston
Harcourt College Publishers

AMÉRICA DEL SUR
MAR CARIBE
OCÉANO ATLÁNTICO
OCÉANO PACÍFICO
BELICE
HONDURAS
NICARAGUA
Lago de Nicaragua
EL SALVADOR
GUATEMALA
COSTA RICA
PANAMÁ
Barranquilla
Cartagena
Maracaibo
Caracas
Lago de Maracaibo
Río Magdalena
Río Orinoco
San Cristóbal
VENEZUELA
Medellín
Bogotá
Cali
COLOMBIA
Georgetown
Paramaribo
Cayena
GUAYANA
SURINAM
GUAYANA FRANCESA
Boa Vista
ECUADOR
Quito
Guayaquil
Cuenca
Iquitos
ISLAS GALÁPAGOS (Ecuador)
LOS ANDES
Río Amazonas
AMAZONAS
PERÚ
BRASIL
Lima
Ayacucho
Machu Picchu
Cuzco
BOLIVIA
La Paz
Lago Titicaca
Santa Cruz
Sucre
Potosí
Brasilia
Río Paraná
PARAGUAY
Asunción
Río de Janeiro
São Paulo
Iguazú
TRÓPICO DE CAPRICORNIO
CHILE
Río Uruguay
URUGUAY
Córdoba
Viña del Mar
Valparaíso
Santiago
Buenos Aires
Montevideo
Río de la Plata
ARGENTINA
Concepción
Bahía Blanca
Viedma
ISLAS MALVINAS (Br.)
Estrecho de Magallanes
TIERRA DEL FUEGO
80°
70°
60°
50°
40°
10°
0°
20°
30°
Elevación en metros
4.000+
2.000–4.000
500–2.000
200–500
0–200
Nivel del mar
0 250 500 750 MILLAS
0 500 1.000 KILÓMETROS
ÁFRICA
NIGERIA
CAMERÚN
Malabo
GUINEA ECUATORIAL
GABÓN
0 MILLAS 250
0 KILÓMETROS 500

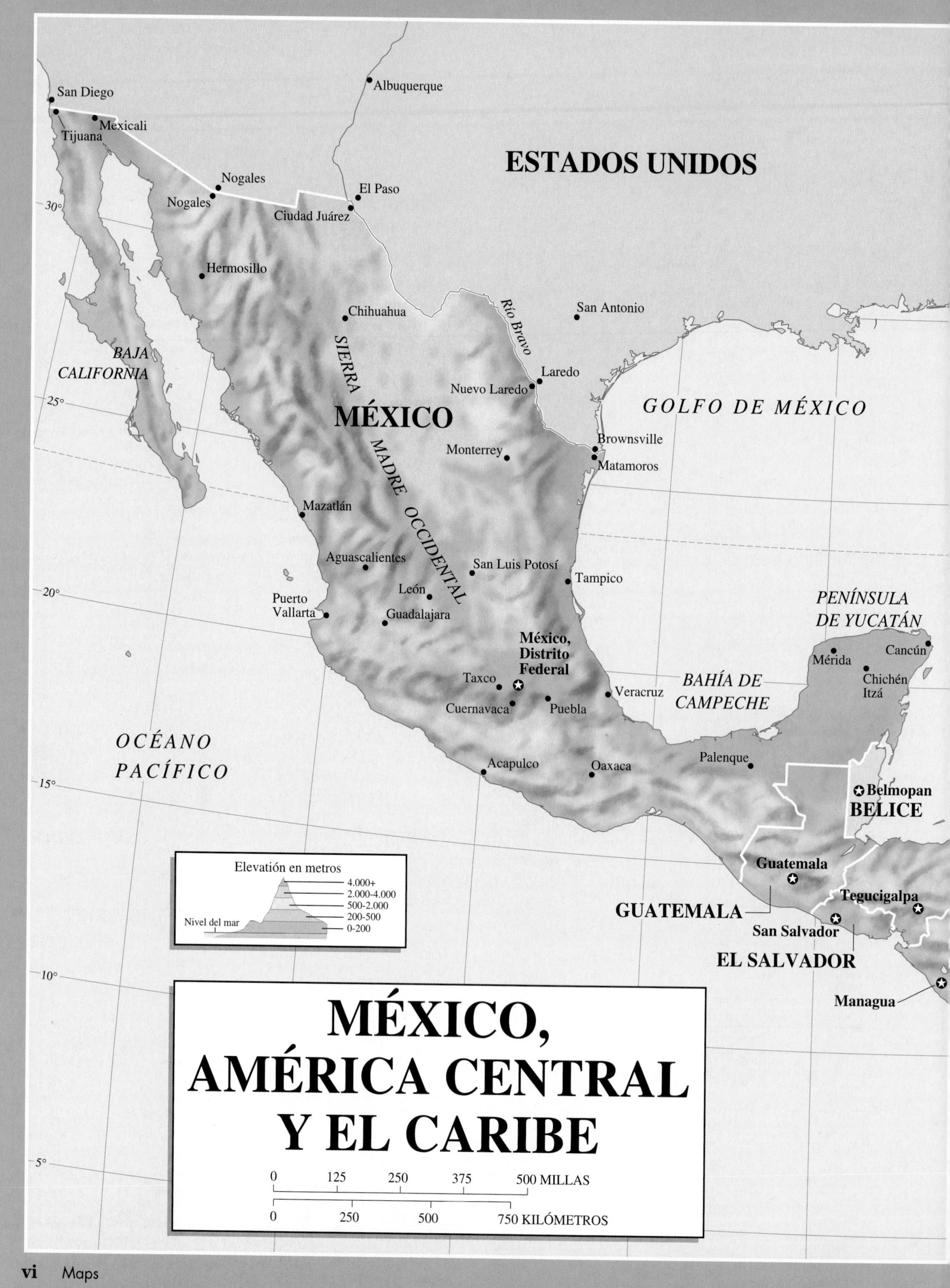

MÉXICO, AMÉRICA CENTRAL Y EL CARIBE

75°
70°
65°
60°
55°
30°
25°
20°
15°
10°
OCÉANO
ATLÁNTICO
TRÓPICO DE CÁNCER
Miami
Nassau
BAHAMAS
La Habana
CUBA
Santiago
REPÚBLICA
DOMINICANA
San Juan
Puerto Príncipe
Santo
Domingo
PUERTO
RICO
MAR CARIBE
Kingston
HAITÍ
JAMAICA
GUADALUPE
DOMINICA
MARTINICA
BARBADOS
HONDURAS
NICARAGUA
TRINIDAD
TOBAGO
Lago de
Nicaragua
Caracas
CANAL DE
PANAMÁ
San José
Colón
Panamá
PANAMÁ
VENEZUELA
COSTA
RICA
GOLFO
DE
PANAMÁ
COLOMBIA
Bogotá

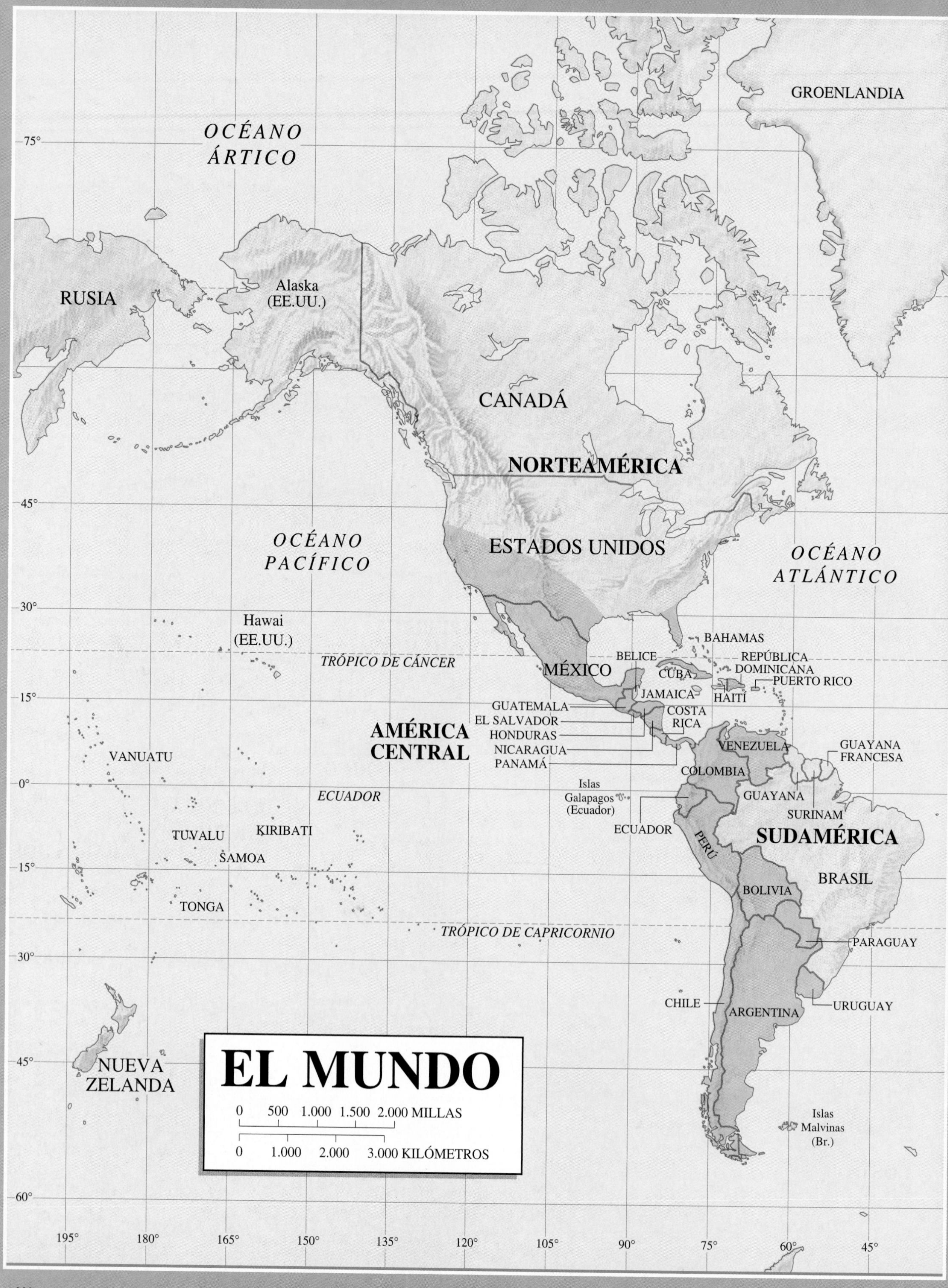
EL MUNDO
0 500 1.000 1.500 2.000 MILLAS
0 1.000 2.000 3.000 KILÓMETROS
OCÉANO ÁRTICO
GROENLANDIA
RUSIA
Alaska (EE.UU.)
CANADÁ
NORTEAMÉRICA
ESTADOS UNIDOS
OCÉANO PACÍFICO
OCÉANO ATLÁNTICO
Hawai (EE.UU.)
TRÓPICO DE CÁNCER
BAHAMAS
BELICE
REPÚBLICA DOMINICANA
CUBA
MÉXICO
PUERTO RICO
JAMAICA
HAITÍ
GUATEMALA
EL SALVADOR
HONDURAS
NICARAGUA
PANAMÁ
COSTA RICA
AMÉRICA CENTRAL
VENEZUELA
GUAYANA FRANCESA
COLOMBIA
GUAYANA
SURINAM
Islas Galapagos (Ecuador)
ECUADOR
PERÚ
SUDAMÉRICA
BRASIL
BOLIVIA
PARAGUAY
CHILE
ARGENTINA
URUGUAY
Islas Malvinas (Br.)
VANUATU
TUVALU
KIRIBATI
SAMOA
TONGA
ECUADOR
TRÓPICO DE CAPRICORNIO
NUEVA ZELANDA
75°
45°
30°
15°
0°
15°
30°
45°
60°
195°
180°
165°
150°
135°
120°
105°
90°
75°
60°
45°

MAR DE NORUEGA
SUECIA
FINLANDIA
NORUEGA
ISLANDIA
REINO UNIDO
REPÚBLICA DE IRLANDA
DINAMARCA
HOLANDA
ALEMANIA
POLONIA
BIELORRUSIA
ESTONIA
LETONIA
LITUANIA
UCRANIA
MOLDAVIA
BÉLGICA
FRANCIA
SUIZA
EUROPA
ESPAÑA
PORTUGAL
ITALIA
RUMANIA
BULGARIA
GEORGIA
ARMENIA
TURQUÍA
GRECIA
1 LA REPÚBLICA CHECA
2 ESLOVAQUIA
3 AUSTRIA
4 HUNGRÍA
5 ESLOVENIA
6 CROACIA
7 BOSNIA Y HERZEGOVINA
8 YUGOSLAVIA
9 ALBANIA
10 MACEDONIA
11 LUXEMBURGO
RUSIA
ASIA
KAZAJSTÁN
TURKMENISTÁN
UZBEKISTÁN
MONGOLIA
COREA DEL NORTE
KIRGUIZISTÁN
TADJIKISTÁN
AFGANISTÁN
REPÚBLICA POPULAR CHINA
JAPÓN
AZERBAIYÁN
IRÁN
IRAK
SIRIA
CHIPRE
LÍBANO
ISRAEL
JORDANIA
KUWAIT
QATAR
BAHREIN
EMIRATOS ÁRABES UNIDOS
ARABIA SAUDITA
OMÁN
YEMEN
PAKISTÁN
NEPAL
BHUTÁN
INDIA
BANGLADESH
MYANMAR
LAOS
VIETNAM
TAILANDIA
CAMBOYA
COREA DEL SUR
TAIWÁN
FILIPINAS
BRUNEI
MALASIA
SINGAPUR
INDONESIA
PAPÚA-NUEVA GUINEA
SRI LANKA
REP. ÁRABE SAHARAUI DEMOCRÁTICA
TÚNEZ
MARRUECOS
ARGELIA
LIBIA
EGIPTO
ISLAS CANARIAS (ESPAÑA)
MAURITANIA
MALÍ
ÁFRICA
NÍGER
CHAD
SUDÁN
ERITREA
SENEGAL
BURKINA FASO
GAMBIA
NIGERIA
GUINEA-BISSAU
SIERRA LEONA
GUINEA
LIBERIA
COSTA DE MARFIL
GHANA
TOGO
BENÍN
CAMERÚN
GABÓN
REP. DEL CONGO
REP. CENTRO-AFRICANA
R.D. DEL CONGO
UGANDA
ETIOPÍA
SOMALIA
JIBUTI
KENIA
RUANDA
BURUNDI
TANZANIA
ANGOLA
ZAMBIA
MALAWI
GUINEA ECUATORIAL
NAMIBIA
BOTSWANA
MADAGASCAR
LESOTO
ZIMBABUE
MOZAMBIQUE
SUDÁFRICA
SUAZILANDIA
ECUADOR
OCÉANO ÍNDICO
TRÓPICO DE CAPRICORNIO
AUSTRALIA
15° 0° 15° 30° 45° 60° 75° 60° 105° 120° 135°
30° 15° 0° 45° 60°
15° 0° 15° 30° 45° 60° 75° 90° 105° 120° 135°

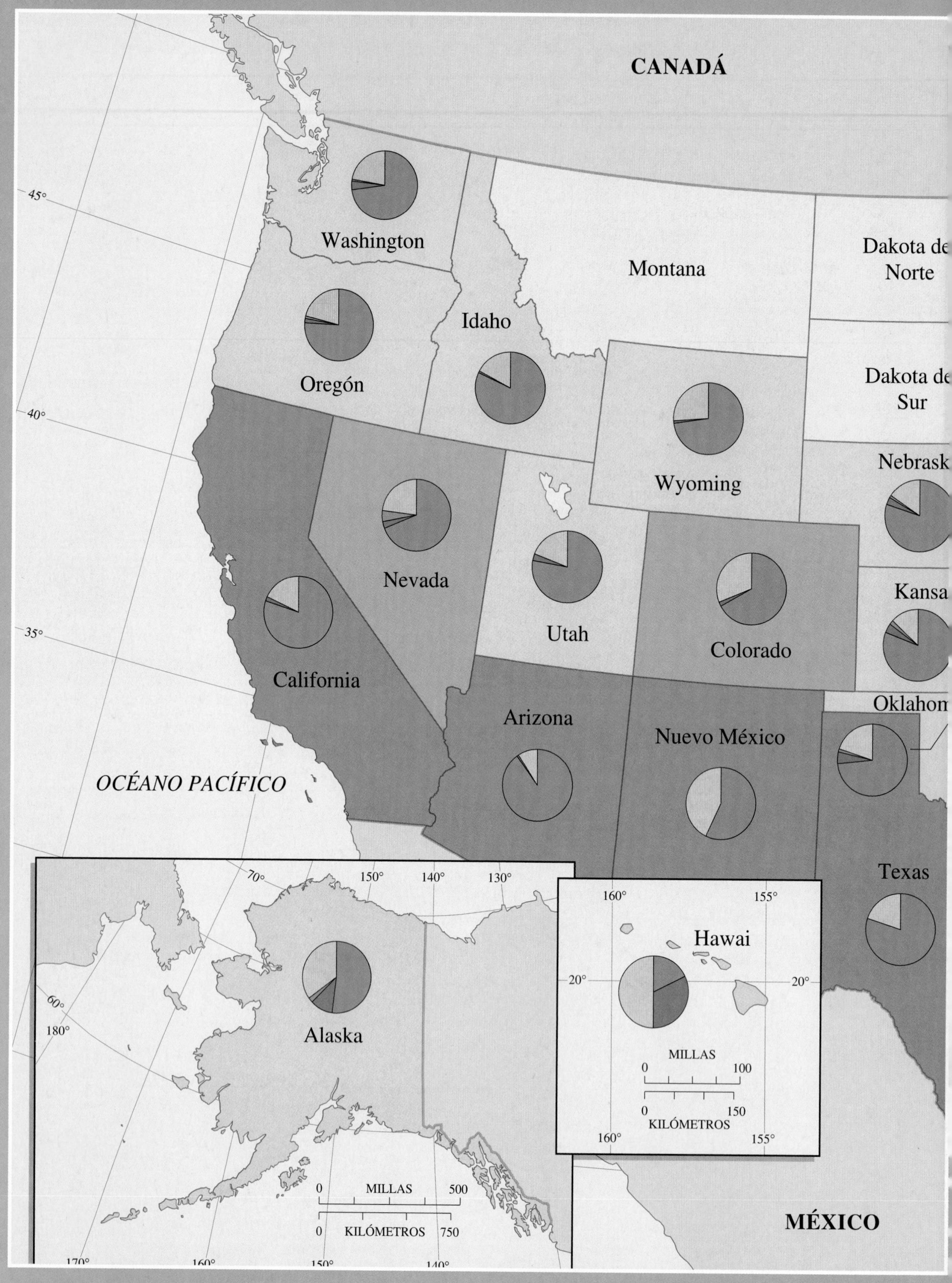

CANADÁ
Washington
Montana
Dakota de Norte
Oregón
Idaho
Dakota de Sur
Wyoming
Nebrask
Nevada
Utah
Colorado
Kansa
California
Arizona
Nuevo México
Oklahom
OCÉANO PACÍFICO
Texas
Alaska
Hawai
MILLAS
0
100
0
150
KILÓMETROS
0
MILLAS
500
0
KILÓMETROS
750
MÉXICO
45°
40°
35°
70°
60°
180°
150°
140°
130°
160°
155°
20°
170°

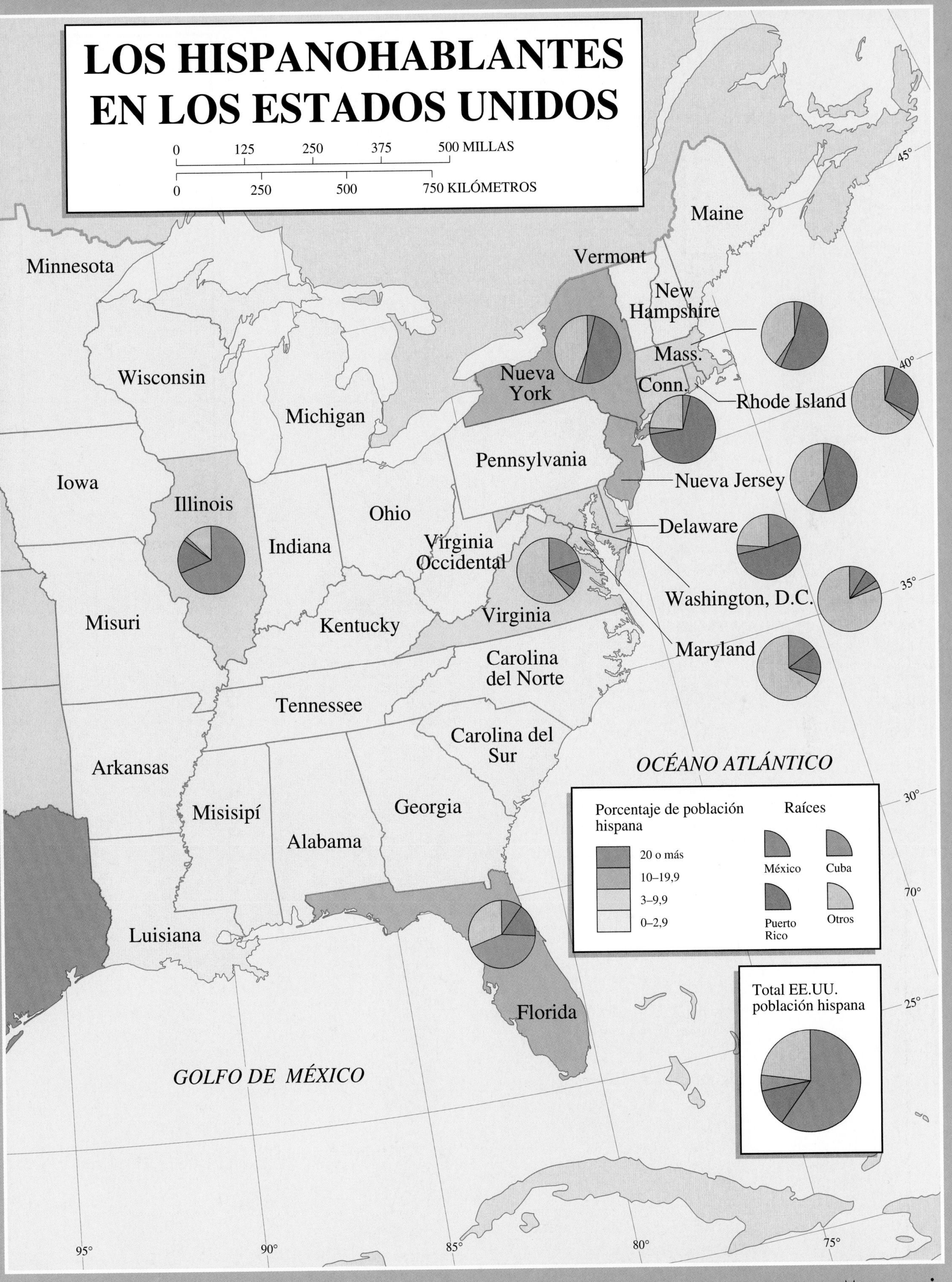

LOS HISPANOHABLANTES EN LOS ESTADOS UNIDOS
0 125 250 375 500 MILLAS
0 250 500 750 KILÓMETROS
Minnesota
Wisconsin
Michigan
Iowa
Illinois
Indiana
Ohio
Misuri
Kentucky
Virginia Occidental
Virginia
Pennsylvania
Nueva York
Vermont
Maine
New Hampshire
Mass.
Conn.
Rhode Island
Nueva Jersey
Delaware
Washington, D.C.
Maryland
Carolina del Norte
Carolina del Sur
Tennessee
Arkansas
Misisipí
Alabama
Georgia
Luisiana
Florida
GOLFO DE MÉXICO
OCÉANO ATLÁNTICO
Porcentaje de población hispana
20 o más
10–19,9
3–9,9
0–2,9
Raíces
México
Cuba
Puerto Rico
Otros
Total EE.UU. población hispana
45°
40°
35°
30°
25°
70°
95°
90°
85°
80°
75°

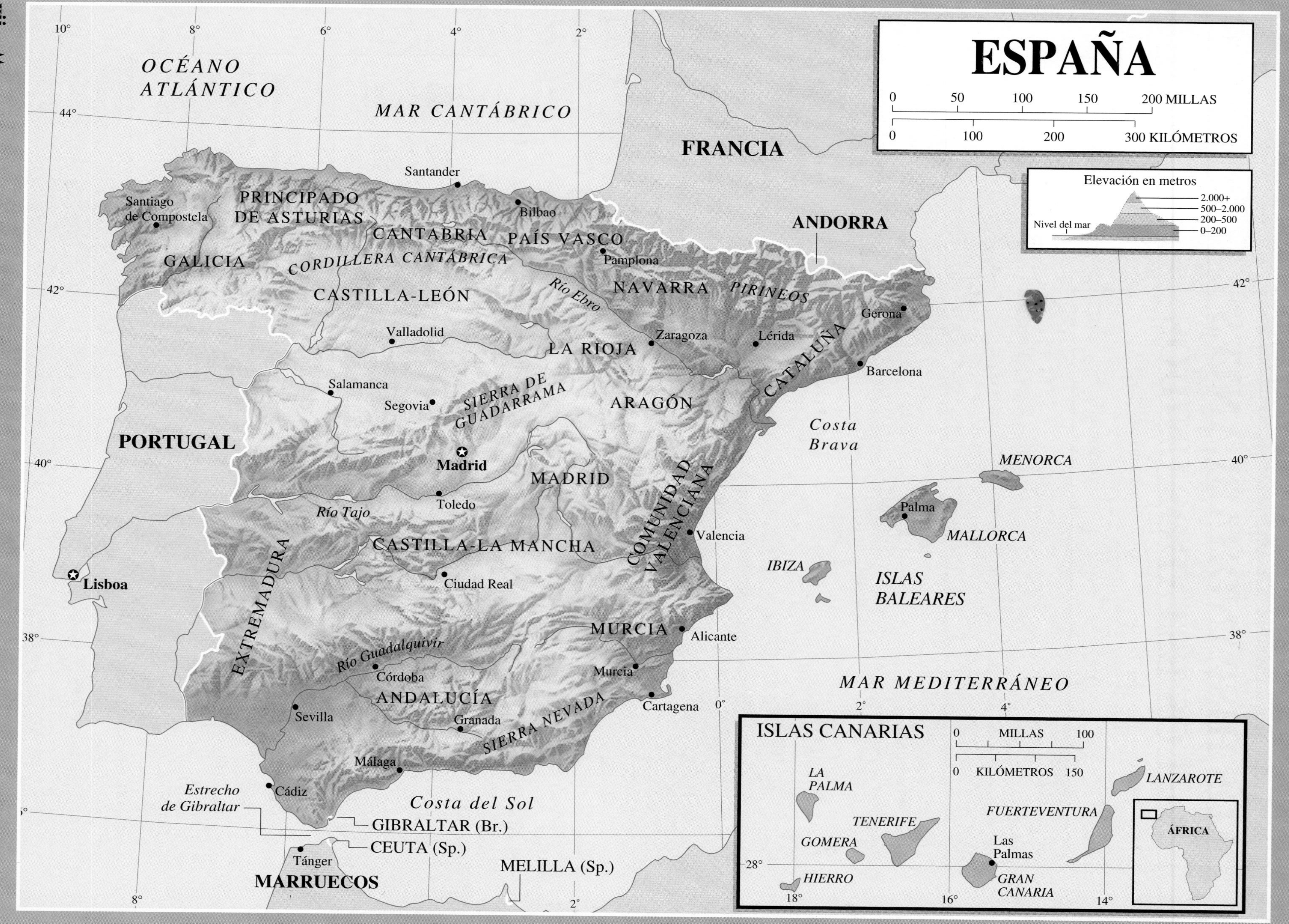

ESPAÑA
0 50 100 150 200 MILLAS
0 100 200 300 KILÓMETROS
Elevación en metros
2.000+
500–2.000
200–500
0–200
Nivel del mar
OCÉANO ATLÁNTICO
MAR CANTÁBRICO
FRANCIA
ANDORRA
PORTUGAL
MARRUECOS
MAR MEDITERRÁNEO
Costa Brava
Costa del Sol
GALICIA
PRINCIPADO DE ASTURIAS
CANTABRIA
PAÍS VASCO
NAVARRA
PIRINEOS
CORDILLERA CANTÁBRICA
CASTILLA-LEÓN
Río Ebro
LA RIOJA
ARAGÓN
CATALUÑA
SIERRA DE GUADARRAMA
MADRID
COMUNIDAD VALENCIANA
Río Tajo
CASTILLA-LA MANCHA
EXTREMADURA
MURCIA
Río Guadalquivir
ANDALUCÍA
SIERRA NEVADA
Santiago de Compostela
Santander
Bilbao
Pamplona
Zaragoza
Lérida
Gerona
Barcelona
Valladolid
Salamanca
Segovia
Madrid
Toledo
Ciudad Real
Valencia
Alicante
Murcia
Cartagena
Córdoba
Granada
Sevilla
Málaga
Cádiz
Lisboa
Tánger
Estrecho de Gibraltar
GIBRALTAR (Br.)
CEUTA (Sp.)
MELILLA (Sp.)
MENORCA
MALLORCA
Palma
IBIZA
ISLAS BALEARES
ISLAS CANARIAS
0 MILLAS 100
0 KILÓMETROS 150
LA PALMA
TENERIFE
GOMERA
HIERRO
Las Palmas
GRAN CANARIA
FUERTEVENTURA
LANZAROTE
ÁFRICA
10° 8° 6° 4° 2° 0° 2° 4°
44° 42° 40° 38°
28° 18° 16° 14°

To the Student ¡Bienvenidos!

Welcome to the world of the Spanish language and Hispanic cultures. Note the term *cultures.* Just as cultures vary for those who speak English (Ireland, the United States, Australia, Jamaica, South Africa, and so forth), there is no single Hispanic culture. Spanish is spoken in 21 countries by over 300 million people, including 22 million people in the United States. Each area of the Spanish-speaking world has its similarities as well as its unique cultural differences. With the *Así es* program, you will explore these cultures while learning Spanish. In addition to learning to communicate in Spanish with the *Así es* program, you will explore the variety of the Hispanic world and analyze some of yoiur own cultural beliefs.

How can Spanish help me?

Besides having 300 million extra people to talk to, you will learn that Spanish can be a real asset to your future. Did you know that if you are bilingual, you can command up to a twenty percent higher salary and that traveling can be more rewarding? As you learn Spanish, you will see that Hispanic cultures view reality in different ways, and that the languages are put together in different ways. As we say in Spanish, ¡Viva la diferencia! Or in another way, ¡Así es! (That's the way it is!)

How should I study Spanish?

The *Así es* program will help you to know what and how to study. Your instructor will undoubtedly give you lots of pointers on studying Spanish, and so will we, the authors of *Así es*. Pay special attention to the *«Guía para el estudio»* (study guide) sections in your *Student Activities Manual.*

But first, here is a brief list of general tips on how to approach the study of Spanish and succeed:

- Approach learning Spanish as you would learning to play a musical instrument or a sport. Communicating in a language requires daily practice in speaking and listening. Be willing to take every opportunity to use the language.
- Practice (out loud and with a friend, if possible) for many short, frequent sessions instead of one long marathon session.
- Be calm and relaxed. Don't panic if you don't understand a particular word.
- Listen for the general gist of meaning. Learn to make intelligent guesses. If a word in Spanish looks or sounds like one in English (e.g., grupo, información, pasaporte, etc.) it probably means the same thing. There are exceptions, but they are few. Be bold in (and out) of class. Volunteer. Participate. Don't be afraid to make mistakes. People who are fluent in a second language make lots of them—yet they communicate, and that is the key!

- Use your own style of learning, whether it be aural, visual, kinetic, computer oriented, and so forth. Use what works best for you. *Así es* has so many components that it addresses a variety of learning styles. Just remember to be regular in your practice.
- Expose yourself to the Spanish language. Listen to Spanish language radio and TV broadcasts. Go to or rent movies in Spanish.
- Listen to music CDs and tapes in Spanish , if for no other reason than to get the "rhythm" of the language. Practice your Spanish with other students.
- Above all, have FUN with the language and culture. If you try and practice, you will succeed. Así es.

The *Así es* Program Components

The *Así es* program has many components that will help you in your study of Spanish. They are:

- **Student Textbook with Free Audio CD.** The *Así es,* Third Edition student text with free accompanying audio compact disc is available for purchase.
- ***Student Activities Manual* (Workbook and Lab manual).** This component was written by the authors to ensure pedagogical consistency. The workbook-section exercises reinforce the grammar and vocabulary presented in the text in varied, easy-to-correct formats. Supplemental exercises, such as information-gap and tie-in activities to the *Así es Mariana* dialogues provide an additional opportunity for practice. The laboratory manual section, coordinated with the lab cassettes or CDs, provide the necessary listening comprehension opportunities that first-year students require in order to achieve a high level of aural comprehension.
- **Lab Cassettes or CDs.** This component is available for purchase, but it can also be used in a listening laboratory. The cassettes or CDs are to be used in conjunction with the laboratory manual section of the *Student Activities Manual.*
- **The *Así es* Text-Specific Integrated Video Program.** A multi-Emmy award-winning television product in conjunction with the author team have filmed a video that exposes you to the linguistic and cultural variety of the Hispanic world. The scripted *Así es Mariana* segments show you how to function in a variety of situations that you may encounter as you communicate in Spanish. In addition, the video contains cultural presentations, visits to interesting places throughout the Spanish-speaking world, performances, and interviews with many famous Hispanic personalities in the fields of politics, music, sports, film, literature, and more. Featured personalities include Enrique Iglesias, Gloria Estefan, Isabel Allende, the Gipsy Kings, Chi Chi Rodríguez, Carlos Santana, and many more. Both the scripted and unscripted segments accompany the eighteen lessons and six cultural *Gacetas* of the textbook.
- **Dasher™ Tutorial Software.** Available in Windows and Macintosh formats, this program features error analysis and is particularly suitable for extra practice

of specific problem structures, reviewing before a test, or learning a concept if you have been absent for some reason.

- **The *Así es* Interactive Multimedia CD-ROM.** The dual platform (Mac and Windows) interactive CD-ROM component has a four-skills and culture-based approach. This multimedia-based component is fully interactive and enables you to develop your listening and speaking skills and to develop your cultural awareness. The CD-ROM contains video, audio, activities, and games, as well as a voice recognition, record and compare feature, which allows you to work on improving your pronunciation.
- ***Así es* World WideWeb Site.** [www.hrwcollege.com/spanish/levy-konesky] *Así es* has its own home page. Correlated with each chapter of the text, the site has a section where you may access activities linked to and based on Web pages in the Hispanic world. In addition, there is access to resource materials, such as dictionaries, maps, and so forth.

Visual Icons Used Throughout the Text

In order for you to more easily recognize certain features of the *Así es* textbook, we have indicated with icons, or symbols, key features of the textbook:

The Group Work Icon is used throughout the textbook to help students and instructors readily identify activities designed for pair and small group work.

The Listening Icon is used with the *Escuchemos* sections in *Así es* to indicate that this section correlates with recorded material on the Student Listening CD which accompanies each textbook.

The Video Icon is used with the *Preparativos* and *Al ver el video* sections in each regular lesson and with the *Videocultura* section in the *Gacetas*. This icon indicates that these textbook sections are to be used with the *Así es* text-specific videocassette.

The Writing Icon is used to indicate those activities in *Así es* that are specifically designed to be writing activities.

The computer icon is used to identify writing exercises that simulate e-mail exchange.

The Reading icon is used to identify literary and cultural readings that are accompanied by pre- and post-reading strategies to facilitate comprehension.

ACKNOWLEDGMENTS

We wish to thank Phyllis Dobbins of Holt, Rinehart and Winston / Harcourt College Publishers for her support and for giving us the freedom to create. Thanks to Ken Kasee in HRW Marketing for his suggestions. We would also like to thank Jeff Gilbreath at HRW for his judgment, guidance, and skillful editing. We also wish to thank Angela Urquhart at HRW and Dee Josephson at TSI Graphics for pulling all the loose ends together at the eleventh hour. Thank you also to Sue Hart and the creative art department of HRW.

The following people contributed greatly in various forms to the creation of the third edition of the *Así es* program: Barbara Levy, Eliot Kraft, Nora McGillicuddy, Emma Sopeña Balordi, Vicente Galván Llopis, Jane Levy Reed, Jane Fields, Gladys Frontera, Natalie Colella, Ada and Oscar Ortiz, Gloria and Emilio Estefan, Enrique Iglesias, Andrés Salce and Fonvisa Records, Isabel Allende, Epic Records, Elena García, Charo Serrano, Irma Rodríguez, Román Cono, Juan Bautista and La Carreta Restaurant, the University of Miami, Carlos Santana and Kitsaun King, Luis Mayoral and the Texas Rangers baseball club, Kevin Shea and the Boston Red Sox, Peter Rodríguez, Martha Jiménez and the Mission Cultural Center, Doug Wheeler, WSBK-TV and Phoenix Communications, Eddie Palmeiri Jr., Pascal Imbert and the Gipsy Kings, Chi Chi Rodríguez, Electra Records, Sherman Wolf and the Great Woods Center for the Performing Arts, José Massó, Celia Cruz and Tito Puente, Amalia Barreda, Charles Grabau, Mary Sit, Alan Altman, United Farms Workers, Monkili Restaurant, Waldert Rivera and Centro Hispano, Tricia Reinus and Goya Foods, the Latin Empire, Ralph Mercado, Mago Franklin, pianista arreglista, Papa Colón y Su Orquesta, and John Kusiak at Anacrusis Productions.

A special thank you to TV Man/Riverview Productions for the brilliant videography of Paco Konesky, skilled sound recording of Jeff Spence, and masterful video editing of Steve Audette.

We also wish to express our appreciation for the work of the reviewers who provided us with insightful comments and constructive suggestions to help us improve the text and better meet the needs of our users:

Enrica J. Ardemagni, Indiana University/Purdue University Indianapolis
Melvin Arrington, University of Mississippi
Karen Berg, College of Charleston
Kathleen Boykin, Slippery Rock University
Fernanda Bueno, Southwest Texas State University
Beatriz Calvo, Auburn University at Montgomery
Irma Blanco Casey, Marist College

Isabel Cedeira, University of Kansas
John Chaston, University of New Hampshire
Francesca Colecchia, Duquesne University
Rafael Correa, California State University, San Bernadino
Judith Costello, Northern Arizona University
John Deveny, Oklahoma State University
Walberto Díaz, San Diego State University
Joseph A. Feustle, Jr., University of Toledo
Constance García-Barrio, West Chester University
Donald Gibbs, Creighton University
Kerry Gjerstad, The University of Iowa/Coe College
John Hall, Moorhead State University
Peggy Hartley, Appalachian State University
Magali Jerez, Bergen Community College
Vidal Martin, Everett Community College
Glenn Morocco, La Salle University
Mary O'Day, University of Kansas
Paul O'Donnell, University of Michigan at Flint
Federico Pérez-Piñeda, University of South Alabama
Rosalea Postma-Carttar, University of Kansas
Sandra Schreffler , University of Connecticut
Sharon Sieber, Idaho State University
Janet Snyder, University of Kansas
Suzanne Stewart, Daytona Beach Community College
Lourdes Torres, University of Kentucky
Lucia Varona, Santa Clara University
James Weckler, Moorhead State University

Nancy Levy-Konesky
Karen Daggett

Contents

UNIDAD PRELIMINAR *¡Bienvenidos al mundo hispano!*

Contents

UNIDAD 1 *Los años decisivos*

Contents

UNIDAD 2 *Estás en mi casa*

Contents

UNIDAD 3 *Las necesidades de la vida*

Contents

UNIDAD 4 *De viaje*

Contents

UNIDAD 5 *Cuidando el cuerpo*

Contents

UNIDAD 6 *¡Celebremos!*

Así es

Third Edition

UNIDAD PRELIMINAR

¡Bienvenidos al mundo hispano!

Valencia, España

Buenos Aires, Argentina

El Caribe

Humacao, Puerto Rico

Sección 

FUNCTION	Vocabulary building • Pronouncing Spanish • Expanding vocabulary with cognates
STRUCTURE	The Spanish alphabet • Spanish pronunciation • Stress and accentuation • Cognates
VOCABULARY	Days of the week • Cognates
CULTURE	Regional accents in the Hispanic world • The importance of learning Spanish
VIDEOCULTURA	Why learn Spanish? An asset to your future

Sección 

FUNCTION	Meeting and greeting people • Expressing **to be** •Asking questions • Counting to 20
STRUCTURE	Subject pronouns • The verbs ***ser*** and ***estar*** • Interrogative words
VOCABULARY	Greetings and introductions • Nationalities, capitals, and countries • Numbers 0–20
CULTURE	Greetings in the Hispanic world
DIÁLOGO Y VIDEO	Así es Mariana: ¡Bienvenidos! Saludos y presentaciones

Sección 

FUNCTION	Expressing **there is** and **there are** • Talking about the classroom • Expressing location • Expressing likes and dislikes
STRUCTURE	The expression ***hay*** • Definite articles •Indefinite articles • Nouns • The verb ***gustar***
VOCABULARY	In the classroom • Prepositions of location
CULTURE	¿Latino, hispano o… ? • The Hispanic World
VIDEOCULTURA	¿Latino, hispano o… ? • El mundo hispano: Rompiendo estereotipos

Where do you think this picture was taken?

There are many words in Spanish that are the same as or similar to words in English. These are called *cognates*. Look at the photograph above and make a list of words that you think are cognates. We found eleven. How many can you find?

AVISO CULTURAL

Hola, y bienvenidos al mundo hispano. Welcome to the Hispanic world. You probably aren't aware of words you already know that come from Spanish. Which of the following words do you commonly use or hear, and in what context do you hear them? What do they mean?

bronco	burro	canoe	chocolate	frito
guerrilla	hammock	hurricane	(*military*) junta	matador
patio	poncho	potato	rodeo	taco

Preparativos

As you begin to learn to speak Spanish, keep in mind that just as English varies in pronunciation from region to region, Spanish pronunciation varies also. Variations in the pronunciation of Spanish can be compared to the differences in the English spoken in England, Australia, New York, and Texas. Castillian Spanish, spoken in many parts of Spain, reflects the "th" pronunciation of the **c** before **e** or **i**, and of the **z**. Argentines are known for a special "zh" pronunciation of the **y** and **ll**. In parts of the Caribbean there is a notable African and Indigenous influence. These regional and cross-cultural differences make the study of languages even more interesting. Pronounce the following sentence as if you were from England, Texas, New York, and Boston: *I parked my car in Harvard yard.*

The Spanish Alphabet[1]

Letra *(Letter)*	Nombre *(Name)*	Ejemplo *(Example)*	
a	a	Alicia	Adrián
b	be	Bárbara	Benjamín
c[1]	ce	Carla	Carlos
d	de	Dora	Daniel
e	e	Elena	Enrique
f	efe	Flora	Felipe
g	ge	Gisela	Gonzalo
h	ache	Hilda	Hugo
i	i	Isabel	Iván
j	jota	Julia	Javier
k	ka	Karen	Kevin
l[1]	ele	Lidia	Luis
m	eme	Mariana	Miguel
n	ene	Natalia	Nelson
ñ	eñe	Begoña	Iñaki
o	o	Oriana	Octavio
p	pe	Paula	Pedro
q	cu	Quinta	Quintín
r	ere	Laura	Marco
rr	erre	Rebeca	Rubén
s	ese	Sandra	Santiago
t	te	Teresa	Timoteo
u	u	Úrsula	Ulises
v	ve (uve)	Verónica	Vicente
w	doble ve (doble uve)[2]	Wilma	Wilfredo
x	equis	Ximena	Xavier
y	i griega (ye)	Yolanda	Yayo
z	zeta	Zoraida	Zacarías

[1]In 1994 the Spanish Royal Academy officially removed the letter combinations **ch** and **ll** from the Spanish alphabet to accommodate the new computer-based technology.

[2]In Mexico this letter is called **doble u**.

Practiquemos

A **El alfabeto** (***The alphabet***). Fill in the missing letters of the Spanish alphabet. Then answer the questions that follow.

abc___ ef___ hi___ kl___ n___ op___ r___ stu___ wx___ z.

1. How many letters are in the Spanish alphabet?

2. What letters are in the Spanish alphabet that are not in the English alphabet?

B **Practique el alfabeto** ***(Practice the alphabet).*** Initials are often used to abbreviate the names of organizations, businesses, and equipment. They are also call letters for radio and television stations. Practice the names of Spanish letters by saying the following initials aloud.

1. de la A a la Z

2. COALICIÓN PNV-PSOE

3. HJCK F.M. Estéreo 89.9

4.

5.

6.

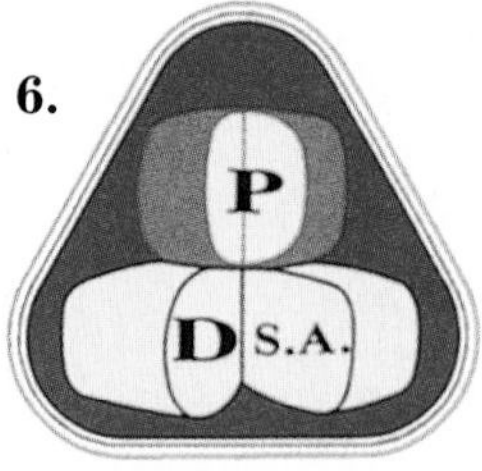

7. TVE

Now, make a list of familiar initials in English. Spell them with Spanish letters.

N B C = **Ene Be Ce**

C **¿Cómo se escribe... ?** ***(How do you spell . . . ?)*** Spell out the following information for a classmate. He or she will write down the letters and read the results. Change roles.

1. your first and last name

2. the name of your city of origin

3. the name of your high school

4. the name of your favorite actor or actress

D **Letras** ***(Letters).*** Spell the following with Spanish letters and see how quickly your classmates can recognize the words or names.

1. a movie you have recently seen

2. a fast-food restaurant

3. a musical group

4. your favorite book

5. your favorite television program

6. a country where Spanish is spoken

Spanish Pronunciation

The following pronunciation guide will help you to master the sounds of Spanish. Refer to these rules regularly, and be careful to imitate the models presented by your instructor and by the native speakers on the audio and videotapes, if you are using them. Spanish is often referred to as a "phonetic language" because it is usually pronounced as it is written and written as it is pronounced.

Vowels

Spanish vowels are short, clear, and clipped; they are never drawn out and their sounds are basically invariable. In order to produce accurate pronunciation of the Spanish vowels, the lips, tongue, and jaw muscles must be considerably tense and in a relatively constant position.

a, as in ah!	casa	ama	fama	Canadá
e, as in café	bebé	nene	este	mes
i, as in machine	sí	difícil	fin	Piri
o, as in no	loco	solo	como	poco
u, as in blue	tú	cultura	uno	cuna

Diphthongs

1. Spanish vowels fall into two categories: strong (**a**, **e** and **o**), and weak (**i** or **y** and **u**). A diphthong is the union of a strong vowel and a weak vowel which is pronounced as one syllable. Unlike many English diphthongs *(through, rough)*, the original sound of each vowel must be maintained.

   b**ai**le   tr**ei**nta   ag**ua**   c**au**sa   antig**uo**   h**ue**vo

2. When two weak vowels form a diphthong, the stress is always on the second vowel.

   b**ui**tre   c**iu**dad   v**iu**da   c**ui**dado

3. When two strong vowels are together, they are pronounced as separate syllables.

   cr**eo**   c**ao**s   mus**eo**   des**ea**mos

4. When the stress falls on the weak vowel in a two-vowel syllable, an accent mark is used to show that there is no diphthong, and the two vowels are pronounced as two syllables.

   día   país   hacía   baúl

Practiquemos

Los diptongos *(Diphthongs)*. Practice pronouncing these vowel combinations by repeating the words after your instructor.

1. ai	aire	**8.** iu	triunfo
2. au	Laura	**9.** oi	oigo
3. ei	reina	**10.** ua	cuatro
4. eu	Europa	**11.** ue	fuente
5. ia	piano	**12.** ui	Luisa
6. ie	siesta	**13.** uo	cuota
7. io	labio		

Consonants

b/v The Spanish **b** and **v** are identical in pronunciation. At the beginning of a word and after **m** and **n** they are pronounced like the English **b** in *boy*, though not as forcibly.

vamos bueno barco vecino hambre

Between two vowels, the **b** and **v** are pronounced with the lips slightly apart, creating more friction as the air passes, and producing a slightly muted sound.

automóvil nabo recibimos vivimos

c In Spanish America, **c** before **e** and **i** is pronounced like the English **s** in *Sam*. In many parts of Spain, **c** before **e** and **i** is pronounced like the English **th** in *thin*.

cena cero cereal gracias

In all other cases, the **c** in Spanish has the hard sound of the English **k**.

cama cortés cruz clase

ch The **ch** has the sound of **ch** in the word *church*.

chica choza coche marchar

d At the beginning of a word or after **n** and **l**, the **d** has a sound similar to the **d** in the word *dog*, although somewhat muted.

dos diente caldo cuando

At the end of a word or between two vowels it has a muted sound like the **th** in the word *although*.

cada hablado Granada todo Madrid ciudad medio universidad

g/j Before **e** and **i** the Spanish **g** has the same sound as the Spanish **j**—a strongly aspirated English **h**.

gitano género escoger jefe jota jarabe

In all other cases, **g** has the guttural sound of the English **g** in the word *gate*.

gato gracioso siglo algodón

h The **h** is always silent.

hotel ahora hospital almohada

ll The **ll** has a sound similar to the English **y** in the word *yes*.

llama amarillo llave valle

ñ The **ñ** has a sound similar to the English **ni** as in *onion*, or **ny** as in *canyon*.

niño mañana año señor

q **Q** is used only with **ue** and **ui**, and has the sound of **k** in English.

quiero que quinto riquísimo

r After **n**, **l**, and **s**, **r** is trilled or rolled.

Israel   Enrique   alrota   en resumen

At the beginning of a word, **r** has a very pronounced roll.

rápido   rima   renta   roto

In all other cases, the **r** sounds like the **dd** of *buddy*.

naranja   llorar   crema   aro

Sobre la arena el torero se prepara para torear.

rr This combination represents a very pronounced roll.

perro   querrá   carro   guerra

Rápido corren los carros del ferrocarril.

s The **s** always has the **s** sound of the word *saint*. It never has the **z** sound of the English word *rosy*.

sangre   vaso   televisión   sencilla   rosa   presente

x Before most consonants the **x** has the sound of the English **s**.

extra   experimento   experiencia

Between two vowels **x** has the sound of **cs** or **ks**, or even **gs**.

examen   exacto   existir   taxi

z In Spanish America, the **z** has the sound of **s**. It is never pronounced like the English **z** of *buzz*.

zapato   Arizona   lápiz   paz

In many regions of Spain, the **z** is pronounced like the **th** in the words *thin* and *thanks*.

Practiquemos

Trabalenguas *(Tongue twisters)*. Try reading the following tongue twisters aloud to practice your pronunciation. What letter or letters is each exercise emphasizing?

1. Don Daniel Durán, dentista, acusa al Doctor don Diego.
2. ¿Ves a los veinte vagos en el barrio de Víctor Vázquez?
3. Sin César, no es posible cazar cebras en la plaza sin cesar.
4. El jefe injusto se llama Jaime Jiménez.
5. La cucaracha charla y marcha con mucha chispa.
6. Agustín tiene una aguda gripe que lo agota. Toma pastillas de goma para curar su garganta.
7. Todo se halla callado y nos llega el perfume de la manzanilla.
8. Enrique rima romances de guerra y recita el de la rosa.

Stress and Accentuation

1. If a word has no written accent and ends in a vowel, **n** or **s**, the stress is on the second-to-last syllable.

   elegante pedimos pregunta examen considero

2. If a word has no written accent and ends in a consonant other than **n** or **s**, the stress is on the last syllable.

   final necesitar universidad reloj capaz

3. A word that carries a written accent is always stressed on the syllable that contains the accent. This accent indicates that the word does not follow the rules mentioned in 1 and 2 above.

   página capítulo fácil canción exámenes

4. Sometimes accents are used to help distinguish between words with identical forms but different meanings. Their presence does not affect the pronunciation of the word.

   si *if* el *the* tu *your* se *oneself* mi *my*
   sí *yes* él *he* tú *you* sé *I know* mí *me* (object of a preposition)

Practiquemos

A **Pronunciación.** Pronounce the following words. Explain why they do not have a written accent.

1. origen
2. lecciones
3. inglesa
4. feliz
5. clase
6. profesor
7. español
8. aprendemos
9. pared

B **Más *(more)* pronunciación.** Pronounce the following words. Explain why they have a written accent.

1. orígenes
2. lección
3. inglés
4. compañía
5. lápiz
6. república
7. él
8. águila
9. sí

C **¿Dónde están los acentos? *(Where are the accents?)*** Some of the following words are missing their written accents. Listen to your instructor pronounce them. Indicate which need an accent and where it is needed. Justify your answers according to the rules.

1. caracter
2. escribir
3. rapido
4. dificultad
5. aqui
6. interes
7. hablamos
8. matricula
9. papel

lunes	martes	miércoles	jueves	viernes	sábado	domingo
		1	2	3	4	5
6	7	8	9	10	11	12
13	14	15	16	17	18	19

D **Los días de la semana** ***(The days of the week).*** The following are the days of the week in Spanish. Which contain diphthongs? Pronounce them aloud and explain why some have written accents.

Los días de la semana[1] ***(The days of the week)***

lunes	*Monday*	viernes	*Friday*
martes	*Tuesday*	sábado	*Saturday*
miércoles	*Wednesday*	domingo	*Sunday*
jueves	*Thursday*		

Cognates

Many Spanish and English words have the same Latin root. These words, or *cognates*, are similar or identical in form and meaning. Learning to recognize and use cognates can help you to identify unfamiliar words and phrases and to get the general idea of a reading. It can also be a source of motivation and encouragement in your study of Spanish. Read this ad for Redder Appliances. They say they offer you more **(más).** What six things do they offer you more of?

.MÁS servicio, MÁS calidad, MÁS diversidad,
MÁS innovaciones, MÁS rapidez, MÁS soluciones.

10 años ofreciéndote MÁS

[1]Note that the days of the week in Spanish are not capitalized.

1. Some cognates have exactly the same spelling and meaning as their English equivalents.

   doctor terrible hospital musical cruel popular sentimental ideal

2. Most cognates have only minor differences.

   a. One such difference is a written accent mark.

      religión televisión región sofá Canadá visión América

   b. Another is the addition of a final vowel.

      novela dentista importante correcto restaurante presidente persona

3. There are several predictable patterns of cognates.

   a. Spanish nouns ending in **-ción** and **-sión** have English counterparts ending in **-tion** and **-sion.**

      participación conversación operación televisión conclusión explosión

   b. The Spanish ending **-dad** often corresponds to the English ending **-ty.**

      universidad popularidad curiosidad actividad autoridad realidad

   c. Spanish words that begin with **es-** + consonant often correspond to English words that begin with **s-** + consonant.

      España esnob estúpido especial espectacular

   d. In Spanish, doubling of the same consonant only occurs in the case of **cc, rr, ll,** and **nn.** An **nn** only occurs when the prefix **in-** (*un-*) is added to a word that begins with n (**innecesario**—unnecessary).

      posible profesor comercial dólar tenis atención clase

   e. The Spanish ending **-oso** often equals the English ending **-ous.**

      maravilloso famoso generoso curioso ambicioso

   f. The Spanish ending **-mente** often equals the English ending **-ly.**

      generalmente rápidamente posiblemente finalmente

   g. There are many cognates that follow no particular pattern but have only slight spelling changes.

      elefante tigre actriz examen teléfono automóvil

4. Some Spanish words are borrowed from English words.

   hamburguesa suéter fútbol béisbol boicoteo rosbif yanqui

5. Beware of false cognates. They look alike but their meanings are very different.

sano—*healthy*	suceso—*event*	arma—*weapon*
pariente—*relative*	embarazada—*pregnant*	lectura—*reading*
pastel—*cake, pastry*	librería—*bookstore*	sensible—*sensitive*
gracioso—*funny*	fábrica—*factory*	éxito—*success*

Practiquemos

A **Los cognados *(Cognates)*.** Refer to the previous lists of cognates and tell which words are:

1. positive personal qualities.
2. negative personal qualities.
3. useful in an emergency.

B **Sinónimos *(Synonyms)*.** A good way to build vocabulary is through association and contrast. Increase your vocabulary by matching the cognates in the first column with their synonyms in the second column. It may be helpful to repeat them after your instructor.

1. sección	**a.** atributo
2. inmenso	**b.** habilidad
3. característica	**c.** parte
4. tendencia	**d.** enorme
5. talento	**e.** inclinación

C **Antónimos *(Antonyms)*.** Now match the adjectives in the first column with their antonyms in the second column.

1. sincero	**a.** nervioso
2. inferior	**b.** realista
3. liberal	**c.** hipócrita
4. tranquilo	**d.** superior
5. idealista	**e.** conservador

D **Las reacciones *(Reactions)*.** What are the people saying in the following situations? Repeat each word or phrase after your instructor.

¡Qué *(How)* romántico! ¡Qué horror! Perdón.
¡Excelente! (¡Fantástico!) ¡Qué ridículo!

E **Lecturas *(Readings)*.** Read the following advertisements carefully. Make a list of all of the words that you recognize because of their similarity to English. What do you think the ads say? Then, answer the following questions about each ad.

1. Choose the correct answer based on the information in the car ad on page 12.

a. This ad is for a car . . .

1. wash. 2. dealership. 3. rental agency.

b. With this coupon the client receives . . .

1. a discount. 2. free transportation within Miami. 3. a credit card.

c. The ad indicates that you may pay by . . .

1. check. 2. cash. 3. credit card.

d. This company does not offer . . .

1. new cars. 2. hotel and airport transportation. 3. unlimited mileage anywhere in the U.S.

e. Two convenience factors of this company are that it . . .

1. is open all day long. 2. is on a main bus line. 3. has three locations.

2. This ad is from a Mexican newspaper. Read it carefully and tell:

a. who the candidate is.

b. what position he aspires to.

c. three things he hopes to achieve in his new position.

d. when the voting date is.

e. where the voting booths will be located.

PMS

VOTA

EN EL DISTRITO FEDERAL, QUE EL PUEBLO DECIDA

Ramón Sosamontes H.

Representante a la Asamblea del Distrito Federal

Para una ciudad digna y habitable:

Democracia y nuevo gobierno

Control popular a las autoridades

28 de febrero, casillas° en parques, delegaciones° y estaciones del Metro°.

booths
offices
subway

3. You can often guess the meaning of words from the context. Read the Quaker Oats Squares ad and guess the meaning of the following words:

Disfruta con **Quaker Cuadritos de Avena** lo más rico y nutritivo de la Avena, *el cereal más perfecto de la naturaleza.* El delicioso sabor que te ayuda a mejorar la digestión y a reducir los niveles de colesterol en tu cuerpo.

¡Cuadritos de Avena, naturalmente el más rico!

a. sabor	sauce	flavor	spoon
b. te ayuda	helps you	ails you	prevents you
c. niveles	novels	stress	levels
d. cuerpo	corpse	corporation	body

Based on the information in the ad . . .

a. find three adjectives that describe the cereal.

b. name three reasons why you should buy this cereal.

c. name one reason why the company wants you to call.

4. Now share your list of cognates from all three ads with the class.

Videocultura: *Why Learn Spanish? An Asset to Your Future*

Preparativos

1. Name three reasons why you think that it is important to know how to speak Spanish.
2. Name three professions that may require the use of Spanish.
3. Name three cities in the United States where Spanish is spoken by many people.

Al ver el video

After viewing the video, do the following activities.

1. Match the following people and their professions.

Amalia Barreda	cantautor *(singer/songwriter)*
Charles Grabau	doctor(a)
Alan Altman	reportero(a) para la televisión
Enrique Iglesias	periodista
José Massó	juez *(judge)*
Mary Sit	agente para atletas y actores

2. Give one reason why each of these professionals feels that knowledge of Spanish is an asset to their career.
3. Tell the class what impressed you most about these interviews.

Enrique Iglesias

Amalia Barreda

Alan Altman

Mary Sit

Charles Grabau

José Massó

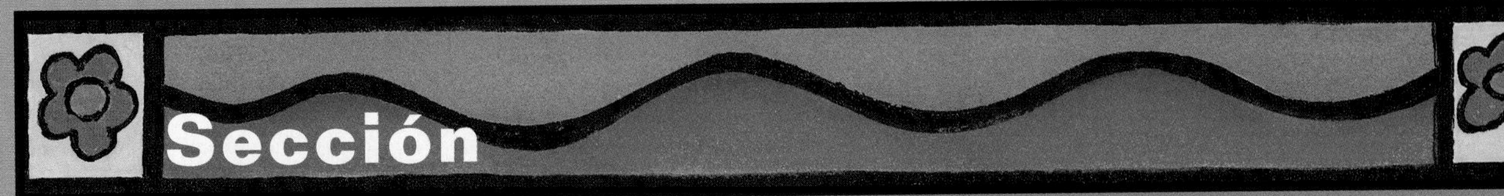

El profesor es fantástico.

AVISO CULTURAL

You have just met your friends in the student center. Name three ways you might greet them. In the Hispanic world it is common for a woman to greet a friend by kissing him or her on one or both cheeks. Men normally greet each other by shaking hands or embracing. Hispanics also tend to stand closer to the person they are addressing than do non-Hispanics.

Así es Mariana: Introducción al diálogo y video

Mariana Benavides

Alicia

Mariana Benavides es una estudiante en la Universidad de Miami. Es puertorriqueña. Su *(Her)* familia es de Puerto Rico pero ahora vive *(lives)* en Miami. Mariana vive en un apartamento en Miami con Alicia, una compañera *(friend)* de la universidad. Alicia es venezolana.

Luis Antonio

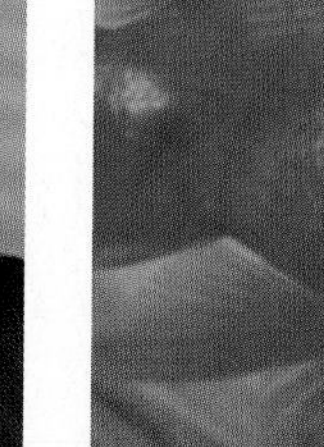

El General Zapata

Mariana tiene *(has)* un novio *(boyfriend)* que se llama Luis Antonio. Luis es mexicoamericano. Originalmente es de México, pero su familia vive en San Diego, California. Él también *(also)* es estudiante en la Universidad de Miami. El General Zapata es el pez de colores *(goldfish)* de Mariana. Es un regalo *(gift)* de Luis Antonio. Se llama Zapata al igual que un héroe de la Revolución Mexicana de 1910, el General Emiliano Zapata.

Carla

Octavio

Mariana es vicepresidenta del club de español. Ella tiene muchos amigos, como Carla y Octavio, que son de varios países *(countries)* hispanos, y todos son estudiantes y miembros del club. Mientras *(While)* Uds. estudian español, van a saber *(you are going to find out)* más de Mariana, su familia, sus amigos y su cultura. Buena suerte *(Good luck)*, y ¡qué se diviertan *(have fun)*!

Encantada, Octavio... Yo soy Mariana.

Preparativos

Review the vocabulary on pages 19–20 before viewing the video.

As you watch the video or read the following dialogue, look for cognates—words that are identical or similar in form and meaning to their English equivalents. Mariana's fish is called General Zapata. Do you know who he was? Mariana refers to her roommate as **"la princesa Alicia."** Why do you think that is? As you view the Spanish club segment, pay close attention to the different types of greetings that the students use. List them, or underline them in your book. Could a romantic triangle be developing so soon in the semester?

Así es Mariana: ¡Bienvenidos! Saludos y presentaciones

Mariana prepares to take a Polaroid picture of her goldfish swimming in his fishbowl.

Mariana: O.K. Zapata, smile . . . sonríe, Zapata.

Mariana: Ahh! ¡Hola! ¿Qué tal? Bienvenidos a la casa de Mariana... y del General Zapata.

Alicia, in jogging clothes and wearing a Walkman, jogs into the room looking for something.

Mariana: Y de la princesa Alicia.

Alicia finds the perfume she is looking for, sprays her neck, jogs back out the door, stopping to check herself out in the mirror.

Mariana: Alicia y yo somos estudiantes en la Universidad de Miami. Alicia es venezolana y yo soy puertorriqueña. Mi familia es de Puerto Rico, pero ahora estamos en Miami. ¿No es así, General Zapata? *(She looks at her watch)* Yikes! . . . It's the first Spanish Club meeting, and I'm already late . . . Let's go!

En la oficina del club de español de la Universidad de Miami hablan° Carla, Rubén, Tomás y Gonzalo. — *are talking*

Tomás: ¿Y la clase de historia?

Gonzalo: Excelente. El profesor es fantástico.

Mariana entra.° — *enters*

Rubén: Buenos días, Mariana. ¿Qué hay de nuevo?

Mariana: Nada en especial, Rubén. Y tú, Carla, ¿cómo estás?

Carla: ¡Fatal! Mañana hay un examen de biología muy difícil.

Entra Octavio, un estudiante nuevo.° — *new*

Octavio: Con permiso...

Rubén: ¿Sí?

Octavio: ¿Dónde está el club de español?

Carla: ¡Pues, aquí estamos!

Rubén: Bienvenido... eh... ¿Cómo te llamas, amigo?

Octavio: Me llamo Octavio. Mucho gusto.

Rubén: Igualmente. Soy Rubén.

Mariana: Encantada, Octavio... Yo soy Mariana, la vicepresidenta del club.

(continued)

Así es Mariana (cont'd)

Carla: *(Carla says flirtatiously)* Y yo soy Carla, la secretaria... El gusto es mío, señor Octavio.

Rubén: Oye, Mariana, ¿dónde está la presidenta?

Alicia entra.

Alicia: Pues, aquí estoy. Les presento a Octavio... ¡mi novio°!

boyfriend

Es decir

A Based on the dialogue, indicate if the following statements are true **(cierto)** or false **(falso).** Correct the false statements.

1. Mariana y Alicia son *(are)* artistas profesionales.

2. La mascota *(pet)* de Mariana es un perro *(dog).*

3. Mariana es puertorriqueña.

4. Alicia es de Venezuela.

B Match the questions or comments in the first column to the appropriate responses in the second column.

1. Buenos días, Mariana. ¿Qué hay de nuevo?	**a.** Me llamo Octavio. Mucho gusto.
2. Y tú, Carla, ¿cómo estás?	**b.** ¿Sí?
3. ¿Cómo te llamas, amigo?	**c.** Nada en especial, Rubén.
4. Con permiso.	**d.** ¡Fatal! Mañana hay un examen.

Al ver el video

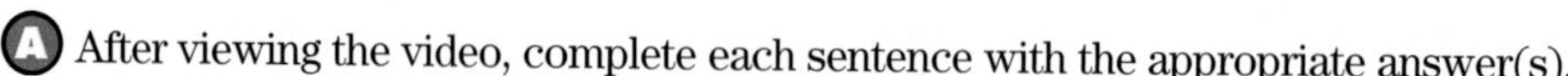

A After viewing the video, complete each sentence with the appropriate answer(s).

1. Mariana y Alicia están en...

a. una reunión de un club. b. el dormitorio *(bedroom)* de su apartamento.
c. la cafetería de la universidad.

2. Alicia practica...

a. tenis. b. jogging. c. fútbol.

3. Carla está muy mal hoy porque...

a. mañana hay un examen en la clase de historia.
b. mañana hay un examen en la clase de biología.
c. hay problemas en el club de español.

4. Alicia...

a. es la presidenta del club de español. b. es la novia de Octavio.
c. es la secretaria del club.

5. Carla está interesada en...

a. Rubén. b. Luis Antonio. c. Octavio.

B After viewing the video, do the following activities.

1. Find the title of your textbook in this dialogue. Consult the dictionary to find out what the title means in English.

2. Do the speakers address each other with **tú** or **usted?** Why do you think this is?

Greetings, Introductions, and Other Expressions

There are many different forms of greetings and ways of addressing people in Spanish.

¡Hola!	*Hi! Hello!*
Buenos días.	*Good morning.*
Buenas tardes. (Buenas.)	*Good afternoon. Good day.*
Buenas noches.	*Good evening. Good night.*
señor (Sr.), señora (Sra.), señorita (Srta.)	*Mister (Mr.), Misses (Mrs.), Miss*

To ask how someone is, you might use the following expressions.

¿Cómo está Ud? (¿Cómo estás tú?)	*How are you? (formal/informal)*
¿Qué tal?	*How are you? How's it going?*
¿Qué hay (de nuevo)?	*What's up? What's new?*

Some of the many responses to the questions, *"How are you?"* and *"What's new?"* are the following.

Bien, gracias. ¿Y usted? (¿Y tú?)	*Fine, thanks. And you? (formal/informal)*
No muy bien.	*Not very well.*
Bastante bien.	*O.K. (Well enough)*
Regular.	*Alright. Fair.*
Así así. (Más o menos.)	*So-so.*
¡Fenomenal! (¡Estupendo!)	*Great! (Fantastic!)*
Fatal.	*Terrible.*
No mucho.	*Not much (new).*
Nada en especial.	*Nothing special.*

The following phrases will help you get to know someone.

¿Cómo se llama Ud.? (¿Cómo te llamas tú?)	*What is your name? (formal/informal)*
Me llamo... (Mi nombre es...)	*My name is . . .*
Le(s) (Te) presento a...	*I introduce you to . . .*
Quiero presentarle(s)(te)...	*I want to introduce . . .*
Mucho gusto.	*It's a pleasure.*
El gusto es mío. (Igualmente).	*The pleasure is mine. (Same here.)*
Encantado(a).	*Delighted.*
Bienvenido(a).	*Welcome.*

Some expressions of courtesy are the following.

Sí, por favor.	*Yes, please.*
Muchas gracias.	*Thank you very much.*
No, gracias.	*No, thank you.*
De nada.	*You're welcome.*
Perdón.	*Pardon me.*
Con permiso.[1]	*Excuse me.*

[1] **Perdón** is often used when you interrupt, disrupt, or bump into someone, and when you want someone's attention. **Con permiso** is commonly used when you try to get through a crowd or reach for something. In some cases these exchanges are interchangeable.

Está bien.	*That's alright.*
No pasa nada.	*No problem.*

To take leave of someone you can say the following.

Adiós.	*Good-bye.*
Chau.	*Bye (informal, from the Italian,* ***Ciao****).*
Hasta luego (Hasta la vista).	*See you later.*
Hasta pronto.	*See you soon.*
Hasta mañana.	*See you tomorrow.*
Saludos a... (Recuerdos a...)	*Greetings to . . . (Remember me to . . .)*

Practiquemos

A Expresiones comunes *(Common expressions)*. Choose appropriate expressions from the list above (or on page 19) for the following situations.

1. 

2. 

3. 

4. 

5. 

6. 

B ¿Cómo responde Ud.? *(How do you answer?)* Respond in as many ways as possible to the following words and phrases. Turn to a classmate and have him or her respond in an original way.

1. ¿Qué tal?
2. Perdón.
3. Hola.
4. ¿Cómo te llamas?
5. Muchas gracias.
6. ¿Cómo está Ud.?
7. ¿Qué hay de nuevo?
8. Mucho gusto.

C **¿Cómo te llamas tú?** Get to know four people in your class using the following format.

1. Greet appropriately.
2. Identify yourself.
3. Find out his or her name.
4. Inquire as to his or her well-being.
5. Take leave of each other.

Subject Pronouns I

Forma

Subject Pronouns

	Singular		**Plural**	
first person	yo	*I*	nosotros	*we* (masculine)
			nosotras	*we* (feminine)
second person	tú	*you*	vosotros	*you* (masculine)
			vosotras	*you* (feminine)
third person	él	*he*	ellos	*they* (masculine)
	ella	*she*	ellas	*they* (feminine)
	usted (Ud.)	*you*	ustedes (Uds.)	*you*

1. **Tú** is the singular familiar form of *you* and is used with family members, friends, colleagues, children, and other informal relationships.
2. **Ud.** (abbreviated form of **usted**) is the singular formal form of *you* and is used with people you don't know well or with whom you have a formal relationship. It is also used to designate respect for an elder, a boss, a professor, and so forth.
3. **Vosotros** is the familiar plural form of *you* and is used only in Spain.[1]
4. **Uds. (ustedes)** is the plural form of **Ud.** It is used in Latin America with close friends as well as strangers. In Spain it is used only in formal situations.
5. **Nosotros, vosotros,** and **ellos** are used to refer to a masculine group or a group of mixed gender. **Nosotras, vosotras,** and **ellas** refer only to a group of females.

   Ana y Marta: ell**as** Ana y Pablo: ell**os** Juan y Pablo: ell**os**

[1]As **vosotros** is rarely used in the Spanish of Latin America and the United States, its use will not be emphasized in this text.

Practiquemos

A **Los pronombres personales *(Personal pronouns)*.** Give the appropriate subject pronouns.

1. Juan y yo
2. Marta y María
3. Leonor y Pascual
4. José
5. Elena
6. Tú y Fernando (en España)
7. Tú y Rosa (en Cuba)
8. Victoria, Rosaura, Anita, Susana y Carlos

B **¿Tú, usted, vosotros o ustedes?** Which form of *you* would you use when addressing the following people?

1. a professor
2. your Spanish friends
3. the Puerto Rican children for whom you baby-sit
4. a famous writer
5. your sister
6. your dog
7. your doctor
8. your husband or wife

The Verb *Ser*

You can begin to communicate in a meaningful way in Spanish by using forms of the verb **ser** *(to be)* and subject pronouns. Unlike English, Spanish has two verbs that express *to be*, but they vary greatly in usage. **Ser** is used to express nationality and profession, to describe and to define, and with the preposition **de** *(from, of)* to express origin and possession.

SER *(to be)*

Singular			Plural		
yo	**soy**	*I am*	nosotros(as)	**somos**	*we are*
tú	**eres**	*you are*	vosotros(as)	**sois**	*you are*
él	**es**	*he is*	ellos	**son**	*they are*
ella	**es**	*she is*	ellas	**son**	*they are*
usted	**es**	*you are*	ustedes	**son**	*you are*

Tú eres inteligente. — ***You are*** *intelligent.*

Yo soy profesora de español y **soy** de San José. — ***I am*** *a professor of Spanish and* ***I am*** *from San José.*

Es la clase de Pablo. — ***It is*** *Pablo's class.*

Practiquemos

A **Nacionalidades *(Nationalities).*** Fill in the blanks with the appropriate form of the verb **ser**. Notice the different endings on the adjectives **(-o, -a, -os, -as).** Why do you think these endings vary?

1. Yo _________ norteamericano.
2. Nosotros _________ chilenos.
3. Ella _________ mexicana.
4. Pablo y María_________ colombianos.
5. Tú _________ cubano.
6. Vosotros _________ españoles.

B **Entrevista *(Interview).*** Now interview five classmates to find out where their ancestors are from. Fill in the blank with various possibilities until you find the correct one.

francés   italiano   africano   irlandés *(Irish)*   alemán *(German)*
asiático *(Asian)*   hispano   ruso *(Russian)*   árabe   otro *(other)*

MODELO ¿Eres de origen ___?   ¿Eres de origen italiano?

C **Preguntas *(Questions).*** Ask a classmate the following questions. He or she will answer according to the cues.

MODELO ¿Uds. son tenistas? (futbolistas)
No, nosotros somos futbolistas.

1. ¿Ud. es profesor? (doctor)
2. ¿Juana es dentista? (artista)
3. ¿Tú eres presidente? (congresista)
4. ¿Vosotros sois astronautas? (atletas)
5. ¿Ellos son arquitectos? (pilotos)
6. ¿Uds. son actores? (arquitectos)

Interrogative Words

Now, let's speak Spanish. Here are some words that will be useful when asking questions. Notice the inverted question mark that begins each interrogative sentence.

Interrogative Words

¿Qué?	*What?*	¿Por qué?	*Why?*
¿Quién?	*Who?*	¿Cuánto (a, os, as)?	*How much? How many?*
¿Cómo?	*How?*[1]	¿(De) Dónde?	*(From) Where?*
¿Cuál?	*What? Which?*	¿Cuándo?	*When?*

[1]**¿Cómo?** can also be translated as *What?* when you did not hear what someone said.

Practice the following dialogues. Note the use of interrogative words and the use of the verb *ser*.

1. —¿Eres tú hispano?	*"Are you Hispanic?"*
—Sí.	*"Yes."*
—¿De dónde eres?	*"Where are you from?"*
—Soy de Texas.	*"I'm from Texas."*
2. —¿Quién es él?	*"Who is he?"*
—Es José Blanco.	*"He's José Blanco."*
—¿Ah, sí? Y, ¿cómo es?	*"Oh, really? What's he like?"*
—Es inteligente.	*"He's intelligent."*
—¿Es hispano?	*"Is he Hispanic?"*
—Sí, es colombiano.	*"Yes, he's Colombian."*
3. —¿Cuál es la profesión de Uds.?	*"What is your profession?"*
—Somos arquitectos.	*"We are architects."*
4. —¿Qué es esto?	*"What is this?"*
—Es una computadora.	*"It's a computer."*
—¿Y cuánto es?	*"And how much is it?"*
—Mil dólares.	*"A thousand dollars."*

The following Spanish nouns and adjectives are easy to recognize because their form is similar to their English equivalent.

Personas	**Características**	**Nacionalidades**
tenista	talentoso(a)	mexicano(a)
político(a)	famoso(a)	costarricense
músico(a)	inteligente	puertorriqueño(a)
autor(a)	importante	panameño(a)
astronauta	serio(a)	chileno(a)
beisbolista	apasionado(a)	norteamericano(a)
actor (actriz)	excelente	español(a)
estudiante *(student)*	ambicioso(a)	colombiano(a)

What general rule can you form regarding adjectives (columns 2 and 3 above) that end in **-o?** In **-a?** In **-e?** We will study more about number and gender of nouns and adjectives in the next section and in Lesson 2.

Practiquemos

A **Identifique *(Identify)*.** Use the words listed on page 24 and the appropriate forms of the verb **ser** to supply the necessary biographical information for each of the following people. If you have a choice of endings **(-o** or **-a)**, choose the **-o** for a male and the **-a** for a female.

MODELO Gabriel García Márquez—Colombia

Nombre:	**Mi nombre es Gabriel García Márquez.**
Nacionalidad:	**Soy colombiano... soy de Colombia.**
Profesión:	**Soy autor.**
Característica:	**Soy apasionado.**

Gabriel García Márquez, Colombia

1.

Rubén Blades, Panamá

2.

Arantxa Sánchez-Vicario, España

3.

Isabel Allende, Chile

4.

Franklin Chang-Díaz, Costa Rica

5.

Salma Hayek, México

6.

Rita Moreno, Puerto Rico

B **Responda *(Answer)*.** Answer the following questions with complete sentences.

1. ¿De dónde es Isabel Allende? ¿Es astronauta?
2. ¿De dónde es Rubén Blades? ¿Es autor?
3. ¿Quién es Franklin Chang-Díaz? ¿Es panameño?
4. ¿Quién es Arantxa Sánchez-Vicario? ¿Es talentosa?
5. ¿Es Rita Moreno mexicoamericana? ¿Es autora? ¿De dónde es ella?
6. ¿Quién es Ud.? ¿Es Ud. estudiante de italiano? ¿Es Ud. profesor(a) de historia? ¿De dónde es Ud.?

C **Información biográfica *(Biographical information)*.** What biographical information can you give about the following people?

1. Pedro Martínez
2. Gloria Estefan
3. Antonio Banderas

The Verb *Estar*

In addition to the verb **ser**, the verb **estar** also means *to be*. **Estar** is used to express location, and with adjectives that express conditions such as one's health.

ESTAR					
yo	**estoy**	*I am*	nosotros(as)	**estamos**	*we are*
tú	**estás**	*you are*	vosotros(as)	**estáis**	*you are*
él, ella, Ud.	**está**	*he, she is, you are*	ellos, ellas, Uds.	**están**	*they, you are*

Some common words that are used with **estar** to express conditions are:

bien	así así	cansado *(tired)*
mal	fatal	horrible
ocupado *(busy)*	regular	de lo más bien *(very well)*

Some common words used with **estar** to express location are:

allí *(there)*	en clase *(in class)*
aquí *(here)*	en la oficina *(at the office)*
en casa *(at home)*	en la universidad *(at the university)*
en casa de un amigo *(at a friend's house)*	

Subject Pronouns II

Función

1. Unlike English, verb endings in Spanish indicate the subject. Therefore, subject pronouns are often omitted.

   (Nosotros) est**amos** bien. — *We are well.*
   (Ellos) est**án** bien. — *They are well.*

2. Subject pronouns can be used to emphasize the person doing the action.

   Yo estoy bien pero **él** está mal. — ***I** am fine but **he** is ill.*

3. In a question, subject pronouns can precede or follow the verb.

¿Tú eres de Argentina? **¿Eres tú** de Argentina?	***Are you*** *from Argentina?*

4. The pronoun *it* is almost never expressed as the subject.

Es importante estudiar.	***It is*** *important to study.*
Es bueno hablar español.	***It is*** *good to speak Spanish.*

Practiquemos

A **Preguntas *(Questions).*** Ask a classmate the following questions. Refer to the expressions on pages 19 and 26.

1. ¿Cómo está Ud.? ¿Dónde está Ud.?
2. ¿Cómo está el (la) profesor(a)? ¿Dónde está el (la) profesor(a)?

B **Países y capitales *(Countries and capitals).*** Following the model, match the capitals to their countries and regions using the appropriate forms of **ser** and **estar.** If you need help, consult the maps in the front of the text.

MODELO Tegucigalpa es la capital de Honduras y está en Centroamérica.

Capital	**País *(Country)***	***Región***
Bogotá	España	
La Habana	la República Dominicana	
Ciudad de México	Nicaragua	Centroamérica
Buenos Aires	Bolivia	Sudamérica
San Salvador	El Salvador	el Caribe
Madrid	Colombia	Europa
Santo Domingo	Chile	Norteamérica
Managua	Argentina	
La Paz	México	
Santiago	Cuba	

The Numbers 0–20

Los números 0–20

cero	seis	once	dieciséis[1]
uno	siete	doce	diecisiete
dos	ocho	trece	dieciocho
tres	nueve	catorce	diecinueve
cuatro	diez	quince	veinte
cinco			

[1]Note the alternate form: **diez y seis, diez y siete,** and so forth.

Practiquemos

A **Ud., el (la) matemático(a)** ***(You, the mathematician).*** In Spanish the equivalents for *plus* and *minus* are **más** and **menos.** *Equals* is expressed by **son**. Follow the model to solve these problems.

4 + 5 =
Cuatro más cinco son nueve.

1. 0 + 15 =
2. 1 + 6 =
3. 17 + 3 =
4. 2 + 6 + 6 =
5. 3 + 5 + 11 =
6. 5 + 7 + 5 =
7. 7 + 12 =
8. 13 + 4 + 1 =

B **Más problemas** ***(More problems).*** Solve the following problems according to the model.

20 – 15 + 5 =
Veinte menos quince más cinco son diez.

1. 19 – 14 =
2. 14 – 8 =
3. 10 – 7 =
4. 16 – 9 =
5. 10 – 8 + 18 =
6. 13 + 2 – 10 =
7. 20 – 7 + 3 =
8. 18 – 9 + 6 =

C **Información personal** ***(Personal information).*** Interview a classmate and find out the following information.

NOMBRE (Name): ______
CALLE (Street): ______
CIUDAD (City): ______
ESTADO (State): ______
CÓDIGO POSTAL (Zip code): ______
NÚMERO DE TELÉFONO: ______
DIRECCIÓN DE CORREO ELECTRÓNICO: ______
NÚMERO DE FAX: ______
NÚMERO DE IDENTIDAD ESTUDIANTIL: ______

Calle Ocho, Miami, Florida

AVISO CULTURAL

Just as it is difficult to find one word to describe all of the people who speak English (English, Irish, Scottish, Australians, Canadians, citizens of the United States, and so forth), so is it equally difficult to find one term that describes people who speak Spanish. While some prefer the term **hispano,** others prefer **latino.** Many do not want to be labeled or placed in a category and would rather be referred to by their individual nationalities (Dominican, Cuban, Honduran, ...). There is a significant Mexican-American (U.S. citizens of Mexican descent) population in the West and Southwest who prefer the term **chicano.** What term or terms do you use to describe your nationality or ethnic heritage?

The Expression *Hay*

The word **hay** means both *there is* and *there are*, depending on the context of your sentence.

Hay un mapa en la clase.	***There is*** *one map in the class.*
¿Cuántos diccionarios **hay**?	*How many dictionaries* ***are there?***
Hay dos.	***There are*** *two.*

Practiquemos

A **¡Qué ridículo!** To practice the use of **hay** and **estar,** ask a classmate to answer these silly questions and correct them according to the cues. Note the cognates in this exercise.

¿Hay micrófonos en la cafetería? (laboratorio de lenguas)
No, no hay micrófonos en la cafetería. Los micrófonos están en el laboratorio de lenguas.

1. ¿Hay sandwiches en el laboratorio de lenguas? (la cafetería)
2. ¿Hay elefantes en la farmacia? (el zoológico)
3. ¿Hay estudiantes en la prisión? (la universidad)
4. ¿Hay antibióticos en el restaurante? (la farmacia)
5. ¿Hay ejercicios de gramática en el libro de biología? (el libro de español)
6. ¿Hay atletas en el hotel? (el gimnasio)
7. ¿Hay clientes en la universidad? (la oficina)
8. ¿Hay pacientes en la clase? (el hospital)

B **Diferencias en la sala de clase *(classroom).*** Study the following useful vocabulary. Then cover up drawing A on page 31. A classmate will cover up drawing B. Ask each other questions based on the drawing each of you has left uncovered. There are eleven differences. Can you find them all? Note: Spanish only.

EN LA SALA DE CLASE (el aula) *(In the classroom)*

1. el bolígrafo (el boli)	*ballpoint pen (pen)*	**12.** la luz	*light*
2. el calendario	*calendar*	**13.** el mapa	*map*
3. el cuaderno	*notebook*	**14.** el papel	*paper*[1]
4. la chica (la muchacha)	*girl*	**15.** la pared	*wall*
5. el chico (el muchacho)	*boy*	**16.** la pizarra	*blackboard*
6. el diccionario	*dictionary*	**17.** el profesor (el profe)	*professor (male) (prof)*
7. el escritorio	*desk*	**18.** la profesora	*professor (female)*
8. la estudiante (la alumna)	*student (female)*	**19.** la puerta	*door*
9. el estudiante (el alumno)	*student (male)*	**20.** el reloj	*clock, watch*
10. el lápiz	*pencil*	**21.** la silla (de ruedas)	*(wheel)chair*
11. el libro	*book*	**22.** la tiza	*chalk*
		23. la ventana	*window*

[1]Note that **papel** can also mean a role or part in a play.

Expressing Location with Prepositions			
debajo de	*under*	en	*in, on, at*
delante de	*in front of*	encima de	*on, over*
detrás de	*in back of, behind*		

Use the verbs **ser, estar** and **hay** to get the information that you need.

¿**Es** una clase de italiano?
¿Dónde **está** la tiza?
¿Cuántos[1] estudiantes **hay** en la clase?

A

B

Definite Articles

Although in English the definite article *the* remains constant, in Spanish it agrees in number (singular or plural) and gender (masculine or feminine) with the noun it modifies. The forms are given in the following chart.

Definite Articles

	Masculine	**Feminine**	
singular	el	la	*the*
plural	los	las	*the*

As you learn new nouns, try to learn the definite article that corresponds to them. This will help you to remember the gender.

el muchacho	***the*** *boy*	**la** muchacha	***the*** *girl*
los muchachos	***the*** *boys*[2]	**las** muchachas	***the*** *girls*

[1]Note that **cuánto** agrees in number and gender with the noun it is modifying.

[2]Note that the plural masculine form can also refer to a group of males and females. See page 34.

Indefinite Articles

The indefinite articles *a, an,* and *some,* like the definite articles, agree in number and gender with the nouns they modify.

Indefinite Articles

	Masculine	Feminine	
singular	un	una	*a, an*
plural	unos	unas	*some*

un muchacho	***a*** *boy*	**una** muchacha	***a*** *girl*
unos muchachos	***some*** *boys*[1]	**unas** muchachas	***some*** *girls*

Practiquemos

A **Los artículos.** Change the definite article **(el, la, los, las)** to the indefinite article **(un, una, unos, unas).**

1. el cuaderno
2. la puerta
3. las clases
4. los muchachos
5. el libro
6. los bolígrafos
7. las sillas
8. la pizarra
9. el estudiante
10. la pared

B **En español *(In Spanish).*** You learned so much in Spanish class and can't wait to tell your friend. Use the correct form of the verb **ser** and the indefinite article to form complete sentences and point to the various objects listed below as you say what they are.

libro
Es un libro.

1. escritorio
2. puerta
3. bolígrafo
4. silla
5. ventana
6. calendario
7. diccionario
8. estudiante *(feminine)*

Now repeat the exercise, making your sentences plural.

libro
Son unos libros.

Nouns

In Spanish, all nouns reflect gender, that is, they are either masculine or feminine. This does not mean that the speaker actually views these nouns as having masculine or feminine attributes. Rather the speaker merely knows the gender and will have all modifying articles and adjectives agree in both number and gender. Here are some general rules to help you learn the gender of certain nouns.

1. Masculine nouns include:

a. most nouns that end in **-o.**

el muchacho	*the boy*	el libro	*the book*

¡AVISO! Some common exceptions are **la mano** *(hand)* and **la foto** *(photograph)*, which is a shortened form of **la fotografía.**

b. those that refer to males, regardless of the ending.

el dentista	*the (male) dentist*	el policía	*the (male) police officer*
el hombre	*the man*	el profesor	*the (male) professor*
el juez	*the (male) judge*	el siquiatra	*the (male) psychiatrist*

¡AVISO! Nouns ending in **-ista** can be masculine or feminine. The definite article will determine the gender: **el artista** *the (male) artist*, **la artista** *the (female) artist.*

2. Feminine nouns include:

a. most nouns that end in **-a.**

la muchacha	*the girl*	la tiza	*the chalk*

¡AVISO! Nouns of Greek origin that end in **-ma, -pa,** and **-ta** are masculine **(el programa, el mapa, el planeta, el poeta).** Also, the word for *day* **(día)** is masculine.

b. those that refer to females, regardless of the ending.

la actriz	*the actress*	la juez	*the (female) judge*
la bebé	*the (female) baby*	la mujer	*the woman*
la cliente	*the (female) client*	la gerente	*the (female) manager*

c. most nouns that end in **-ión** and **-ad.**

la nación	*the nation*	la realidad	*the reality*
la televisión	*the television*	la universidad	*the university*

Pluralization of Nouns

1. To make a noun plural:

a. add **-s** to a noun ending in a vowel.

la silla	las silla**s**
el hombre	los hombre**s**

b. add **-es** to a noun ending in a consonant.

la pared	las pared**es**
el actor	los actor**es**

¡AVISO 1! If a noun ends in **-z,** it changes to **-ces.**

el lápiz	los lápi**ces**
la luz	las lu**ces**

¡AVISO 2! At times it is necessary to add or drop a written accent when a word is made plural. See rules for accentuation on page 8.

la nación	las naciones
el examen	los exámenes

2. Many words ending in **-es** and **-is** do not change in the plural.

el lunes	los lunes
la crisis	las crisis

3. The masculine plural form of the noun is used in Spanish to refer to a group of males and females.

el estudiante y la estudiante	**los** estudiantes
un muchacho y una muchacha	**unos** muchachos

Practiquemos

A **Los sustantivos (*nouns*) plurales.** Read each of the following words and add the definite article. Then give the plural forms.

profesor
el profesor, los profesores

1. profesora	**4.** nacionalidad	**7.** profesión	**10.** pared
2. hombre	**5.** ventana	**8.** luz	**11.** lápiz
3. bolígrafo	**6.** programa	**9.** actor	**12.** mano

B **Los artículos indefinidos.** Repeat Exercise A, replacing the definite article with the indefinite article.

profesor
un profesor, unos profesores

C **¿Quién es y dónde está?** Match each drawing with the corresponding profession and place from the list on page 35 to tell who and where each person is. Use the appropriate definite article and correct form of the verbs **ser** and **estar.** You may need to change the number or gender of the profession according to the subject.

MODELO atleta/gimnasio
Pedro Ortiz ________ ________ y ________ en ________. **Pedro Ortiz es atleta[1] y está en el gimnasio.**

Pedro Ortiz

1.

Ana Padilla

2.

Raquel Ramos

3.

Carmen y Rafa

4.

Nosotros

5.

Tomás

6.

Yo

Profesión		Lugar (Place)	
profesor	doctor	televisión	galería de arte
reportero	estudiante	hospital	oficina
ejecutivo	artista	clase	cafetería

[1]Note the omission of the indefinite article after the verb **ser** with unmodified nouns of profession.

Expressing Likes and Dislikes: The Verb *Gustar*

There is no verb in Spanish that literally means "to like." Instead, the verb **gustar**[1] *(to be pleasing to, to please)* is used. Look at the following examples.

Me gusta el español.	*Spanish is pleasing to me.*	*(I like Spanish.)*
Me gustan las matemáticas.	*Mathematics are pleasing to me.*	*(I like mathematics.)*

To ask someone if he or she likes something you say:

¿Te gusta la historia?	*Does history please you?*	*(Do you like history?)*
¿Te gustan los deportes?	*Do sports please you?*	*(Do you like sports?)*

To talk about a third person's likes you say:

Le gusta la historia.	*History pleases him/her.*	*(He/She likes history.)*
Le gustan los deportes.	*Sports please him/her.*	*(He/She likes sports.)*

Note that to include the proper name you put the preposition **a** before it.

A José le gusta la historia.	*History is pleasing to José.*	*José likes history.*
A María le gustan los deportes.	*Sports are pleasing to María.*	*María likes sports.*

¿Te gusta? Find out a classmate's likes and dislikes with the following survey. Choose six items from the list. Report to the class what you have learned about each other.

la música   el chocolate   el presidente de los Estados Unidos
las telenovelas *(soap operas)*   el arte   los animales   la clase de español
visitar al dentista   el tenis   el béisbol   las enchiladas   la pizza

¿Te gusta la clase de biología? ¿Te gustan las hamburguesas?
A Laura le gusta la clase de biología. No le gustan las hamburguesas.

	No me gusta(n)	Me gusta(n)	Me gusta(n) mucho
1. ¿Te gusta(n)... ?	___	___	___
2. ¿Te gusta(n)... ?	___	___	___
3. ¿Te gusta(n)... ?	___	___	___
4. ¿Te gusta(n)... ?	___	___	___
5. ¿Te gusta(n)... ?	___	___	___
6. ¿Te gusta(n)... ?	___	___	___

[1]**Gustar** and similar verbs are presented in depth in Lesson 7.

B **Preferencias.** A classmate will read a sentence from the first column. Choose a category in the second column that corresponds to his or her likes.

Me gustan el fútbol y los aeróbicos.
Ah... te gusta el ejercicio físico.

1. Me gustan las pinturas de Picasso y Dalí.	la literatura
2. Me gustan Arantxa Sánchez-Vicario y André Agassi.	la comida *(food)* española
3. Me gustan la salsa, el merengue, y el tango.	el arte contemporáneo
4. Me gustan la paella y el flan.	la música latina
5. Me gustan los poemas y las novelas.	el tenis

Preparativos

¿Latino, hispano o... ?

As mentioned in the **Aviso cultural,** there is a continuing debate regarding what to call the ever-increasing population of U.S. residents who are Spanish-speaking or of Spanish origin. The 1990 U.S. Census classifies this group as Spanish/Hispanic origin. The term **hispano** actually comes from the word the Phoenicians used to describe Spain during their occupation (*Hispania* meant "land of rabbits"). Opponents of this term feel that it is dated and exclusionary, ignoring the strong African and Indigenous elements prevalent in Latin America. They feel that the term **latino** more accurately encompasses all of these cultural influences. Opponents of the term **latino** feel that this term can be traced back even further than the Spaniards, to the Romans. They feel that they no longer reflect Latin or Mediterranean characteristics. In an effort to solve this semantic problem, a Latino National Political Survey was conducted in 1989–90. The results show that the majority of Mexicans, Cubans, and Puerto Ricans, whether they were born in the United States (on the mainland) or in Mexico, Cuba, or Puerto Rico, preferred to refer to themselves as Mexican, Cuban, and Puerto Rican (see the chart below).

We have done our own survey for *Así es* to find the term preferred by most for the sake of choosing a term that we could use consistently throughout the text.[1] The video segment for this *sección* shows you some of the participants and their reactions to our poll.

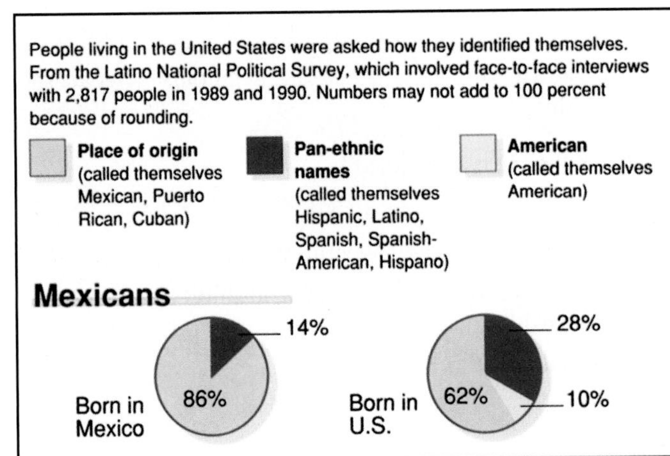

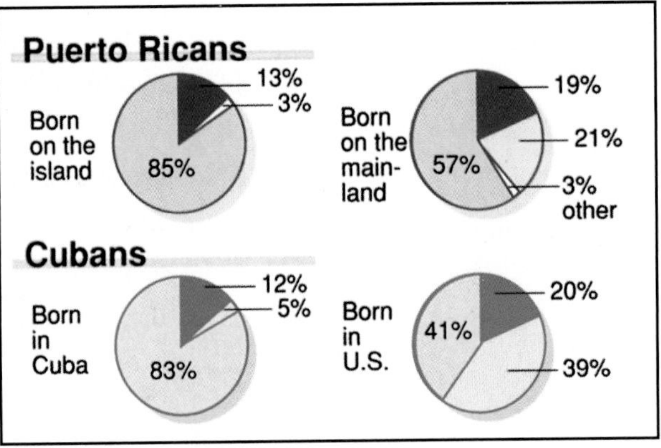

[1]In an effort to find a term which refers to Spaniards as well as all latino peoples, the word *Hispanic* is used frequently in *Así es*.

But perhaps *Hispanic* magazine addresses this controversy best. The management chose its most ridiculous issue.

MOST RIDICULOUS ISSUE:
Are we Hispanics, Latinos, Chicanos, Spanish, Mexican Americans, Cuban Americans, Puerto Ricans, etc., etc.? Who cares? Let's move on!

Al ver el video

As you watch the video, check off the term that each person prefers. Write in any original responses in the **Otro** column.

¿Qué término prefieren *(do they prefer)*?	**Latino**	**Hispano**	**Otro *(Other)***
José Massó— agente de atletas y actores/puertorriqueño	___	___	________
Charles Grabau— juez/cubanoamericano	___	___	________
Amalia Barreda— reportera/mexicoamericana	___	___	________
César Villalobos— músico/peruano	___	___	________
Iván Rodríguez— beisbolista/puertorriqueño	___	___	________
Tony Fossas— beisbolista/cubanoamericano	___	___	________
Chi Chi Rodríguez— golfista/puertorriqueño	___	___	________
Juan González— beisbolista/puertorriqueño	___	___	________
Carlos Santana— músico/mexicoamericano	___	___	________
Isabel Allende— escritora/chilena	___	___	________
Enrique Iglesias— cantautor/español	___	___	________

Preparativos

Now let's get to know more about the 392 million people who speak the language you are about to learn. Before you view the video segments or read the selection, do the following activities.

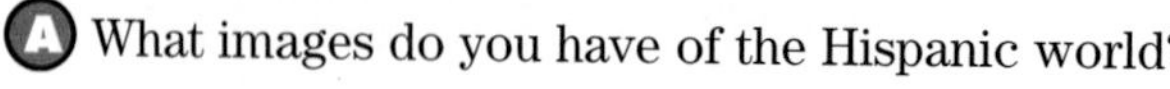

A What images do you have of the Hispanic world?

1. Name:

a. five things that you associate with the Hispanic world.

b. four cultural aspects of the Hispanic world that you think are different from the non-Hispanic world.

c. three cultural aspects that you think are similar.

2. Is the Hispanic world . . .

a. ancient or modern?

b. urban or rural?

c. provincial or cosmopolitan?

B Are the following statements true **(cierto)** or false **(falso)**? Explain.

1. A Puerto Rican is Spanish.
2. Hispanics are dark-haired.
3. Hispanic countries are tropical.
4. Hispanics commonly eat tacos and enchiladas.
5. The bullfight is a very popular Hispanic tradition.

Al ver el video

After viewing the video segments, correct your answers from the preceding exercises.

El mundo hispano: Rompiendo estereotipos *(Breaking stereotypes)*

We frequently tend to generalize—to put people and things into categories based on certain similar characteristics. Sometimes these generalizations can be useful in helping us to understand a very complex and diverse world. But often these same generalizations can be very deceiving, unjust, and even harmful. Let's examine some common generalizations regarding the Hispanic world.

1. **Un puertorriqueño es español.** ***(A Puerto Rican is Spanish.)*** **FALSO**
   Many people tend to use the word *Spanish* to refer to a Spanish-speaking person, regardless of their country of origin. Actually, the adjective *Spanish* is used only to designate a person or thing from Spain. Therefore, a Puerto Rican is not Spanish, but rather Hispanic. The dictionary defines *Hispanic* as "pertaining to the people of Spanish origin," or "Spanish-speaking person." Therefore, a boy from Chile is Chilean and Hispanic. People from Mexico, Colombia, and El Salvador are Mexican, Colombian, Salvadoran *and* Hispanic.[1]

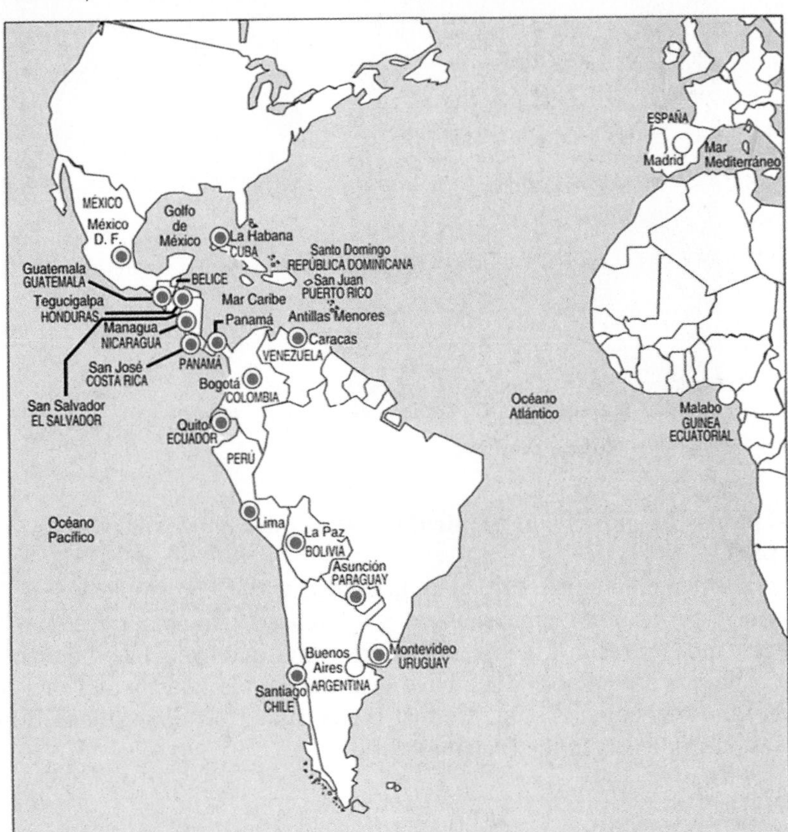

[1]Note that the term *Hispanic* is not used to refer to pure indigenous people.

It is very important to differentiate between the various Hispanic groups. The fact that English is spoken in the United States does not mean that the citizens are English. They may speak the same language but they have very definite cultural differences. Our customs and traditions and the way in which we interpret the world that surrounds us are the things that define us and give us our national identity.

2. **Los hispanos son morenos.** ***(Hispanics are dark-haired.)*** **FALSO**
On the contrary, the influence of various ethnic groups in many different combinations is clearly visible throughout the Hispanic world. In Spain, for example, there are many people of Northern European origin with blond hair and blue eyes, as well as dark-haired Spaniards of Arabic or Roman descent.

In Latin America this ethnic mix is even more diverse. While in some regions the European influence is dominant, in many other areas the indigenous element has combined with the European. And in much of the Caribbean a third element combines to enrich further the ethnic diversity—the black African. Therefore, a Hispanic can be black, white, or brown-skinned, with black, brown, blond, or even red hair, and have brown, blue, green, or hazel eyes.

Puerto Plata, República Dominicana

Quito, Ecuador

Mendoza, Argentina

3. **Los países hispanos son tropicales.** ***(Hispanic countries are tropical.)*** **FALSO**
Many Hispanic countries are, in fact, located within the tropical zone. These regions have beautiful white sandy beaches dotted with palm trees. They enjoy warm temperatures in which exotic plants thrive and fruits like the mango and the papaya are common. They have lush and fertile jungles and rain forests where the vegetation is so dense that roads cannot penetrate them. However, this is only one part of the Hispanic world.

Guayama, Puerto Rico

La Sierra Nevada, España

Palo Verde, Costa Rica

Many people think that Spain is a country of eternal sun and warmth. In reality, the winters in many parts of Spain are quite cold and snowy. Tierra del Fuego, Argentina, is one of the coldest regions in the world in spite of its deceiving name ("Land of Fire"). Even within the tropics the climate can vary. In Bogotá, the capital of Colombia, situated at an altitude of 8,500 feet above sea level, it rains frequently and the average temperature is only 57°F.

4. **Los hispanos suelen comer tacos y enchiladas.** ***(Hispanics commonly eat tacos and enchiladas.)*** **FALSO**
These dishes are typically Mexican. The foods from Hispanic countries are quite varied. While Mexican cuisine can be very spicy, incorporating a lot of peppers and hot salsa, Spanish food is cooked in olive oil with subtle seasonings like saffron and garlic. Caribbean cuisine incorporates many different kinds of beans—black, colored, and pigeon peas—with rice and plantains.

Even a food with the same name can vary from country to country. A Spanish **tortilla** is a type of omelette with potatoes and onions, while a Mexican **tortilla** is a thin pancake made from ground corn. Many countries have their own words for the same foods. **Habichuelas** are beans in Puerto Rico, while you would order **frijoles** in Cuba and **alubias** in other countries. If you were to ask for a **naranja** in Spain, you would be given an orange; however, you would need to request a **china** in Puerto Rico.

La comida caribeña *(Caribbean food)*

5. **La corrida de toros es una tradición hispana muy popular. *(The bullfight is a very popular Hispanic tradition.)* FALSO**
Bullfighting is a custom brought to Spain by the Romans in the first century B.C.[1] It is practiced only in Spain, Mexico, and, to a lesser degree, in a few other countries in Latin America, and is not a tradition of all Hispanic countries. Even within the countries where it is practiced, it is not frequented by all of the people. Just as in the United States, some people enjoy baseball whereas others choose to follow football or tennis, bullfighting has an appeal to a certain group of **aficionados** or fans, who tend to follow it regularly.

[1]For more information on the origin of bullfighting, see Lesson 18, page 530.

One of the most unifying attributes of the Hispanic world is the language. Spanish is spoken by 392 million people. It is the fourth most widely spoken language in the world after Mandarin, Hindi-Urdu, and English. It is spoken in 20 countries including the United States. Although these countries share the Spanish language, the accent and the vocabulary vary according to the region; Europeans, Indians, and Africans all contributed certain words, rhythms, and accents to the language.

It is projected that in this decade, Hispanics will become the largest minority group in the United States. The Hispanic population has increased by more than 60% in the last decade. Of the estimated 22 million Hispanics presently living in the United States, approximately 60% are of Mexican descent, 14% are Puerto Rican (with 2 million living on the mainland and 3 million on the island), 6% are of Cuban origin, and 20% are from Central or South America and other countries.

Of this Hispanic population the vast majority lives in the South and West, with another large concentration in the Northeast.

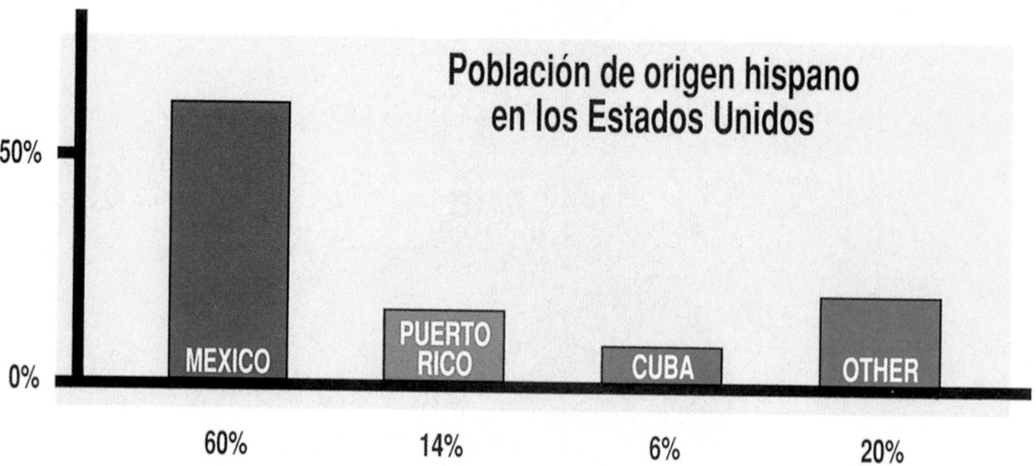

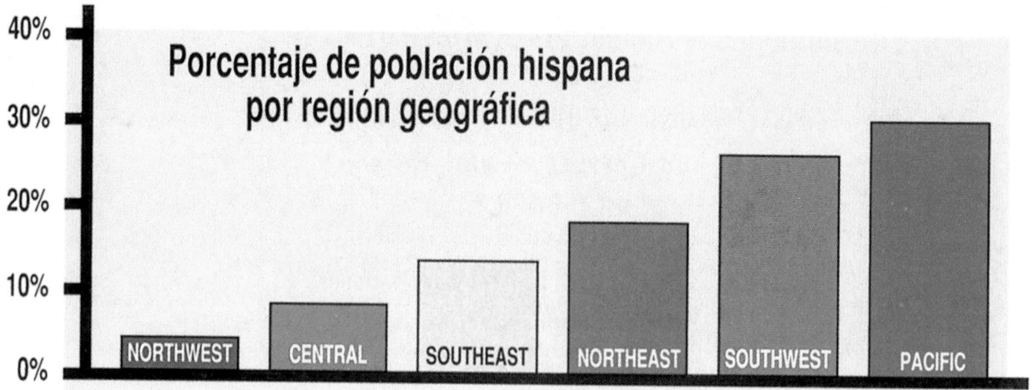

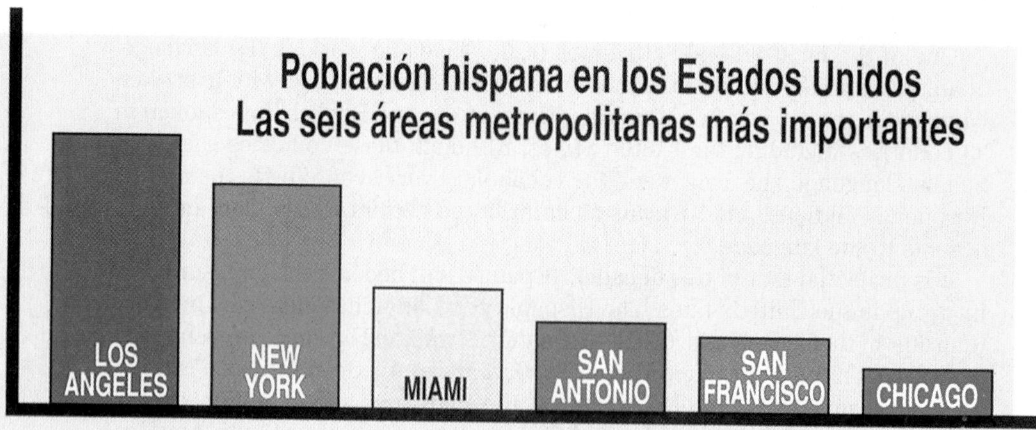

This Hispanic presence in the United States is becoming more evident in all aspects of society. There are Hispanic politicians such as current and former mayors of Miami, Denver, Tampa, and San Antonio, as well as Hispanic senators and members of Congress. There are more than 100 television stations and 200 radio stations that broadcast in Spanish. There are more than 30 newspapers in Spanish as well as numerous magazines in both Spanish and English that serve the Hispanic communities.

There are many Hispanic artists, journalists, athletes, and performers who are nationally and internationally famous, such as tennis champion Mary Jo Fernández, golf legend Chi Chi Rodríguez, and Major League Baseball players Sammy Sosa, Roberto Alomar, and Juan González. Actors and performers such as Jennifer López, Cameron Díaz, Jimmy Smits, Edward James Olmos, Andy García, Daisy Fuentes, John Leguizamo, Gloria Estefan, and Jon Secada continue to be among the most popular and best known in the country.

John Leguizamo

Mary Jo Fernández

Jennifer López

As you can see, it is not easy to define in just a few words a concept as broad as "Hispanic." Perhaps it is because the Hispanic world offers so many paradoxes and parallelisms, differences and similarities. It is the inexhaustible source of contrasts between the ancient and the modern, the rich and the poor, between highly technologically developed regions and regions that are still in development. In Spanish-speaking areas of the world, one can find rustic villages and cosmopolitan cities, straw huts and high-rise condos. While some people wear hand-woven ponchos and embroidered blouses, others prefer the *haute couture* directly from Europe. The Hispanic world indeed has a lot to offer.

24 HORAS AL DÍA EN ESPAÑOL

Practiquemos

A **¿Cuál es correcto?** ***(Which is correct?)*** Circle all correct answers.

1. A Hispanic can be from . . .
a. Puerto Rico. b. Uruguay. c. Spain.

2. A Hispanic can be . . .
a. black. b. white. c. brown-skinned.

3. The most dominant ethnic element(s) in the Caribbean is (are) . . .
a. the African. b. the Spanish. c. the Northern European.

4. There are more Spanish-speaking people in the world than people who speak . . .
a. French. b. Mandarin. c. Japanese.

5. The Mexican tortilla is made from . . .
a. corn. b. potatoes. c. eggs.

6. The climate in Hispanic countries can be . . .
a. tropical. b. cold. c. cool.

7. The bullfight is a custom of . . . origin.
a. South American b. Caribbean c. Roman

8. The largest Hispanic group in the United States is of . . . origin.
a. Puerto Rican b. Mexican c. Cuban

9. The Hispanic presence in the United States is evident in . . .
a. the arts. b. politics. c. the media.

B **Complete Ud.** ***(Complete).*** Complete the following sentences beginning with, "After reading this selection I learned that. . . ."

1. physically, Hispanics are . . .
2. the word *Spanish* means . . .
3. a Hispanic is . . .
4. in the United States there are . . .
5. the Hispanic world is . . .

C **Generalizaciones.** The following are generalizations about the United States. Do you agree with them? Explain. How do you suppose they originated?

In the United States everyone . . .

1. is inhospitable.
2. eats fast food.
3. chews gum.
4. thinks that everyone in the world speaks English.
5. is rich.

D **Falsedades** ***(Falsehoods).*** What are some other false generalizations about the United States?

UNIDAD

Los años decisivos

¡Vamos a España por Internet! **España!**

Experience the beauty, excitement, and diversity of Spain by browsing the World Wide Web and visiting the following addresses.

http://www.tourspain.es/ **http://www.cibercentro.com/** **http://www.ole.es/**

Since Internet addresses are subject to change, typing the following key words into most search engines will also get you to Spain.

España **Madrid** (or any Spanish city) **turismo en España**

To learn about Spanish art via the Internet, see page 120 of *Gaceta 1*.

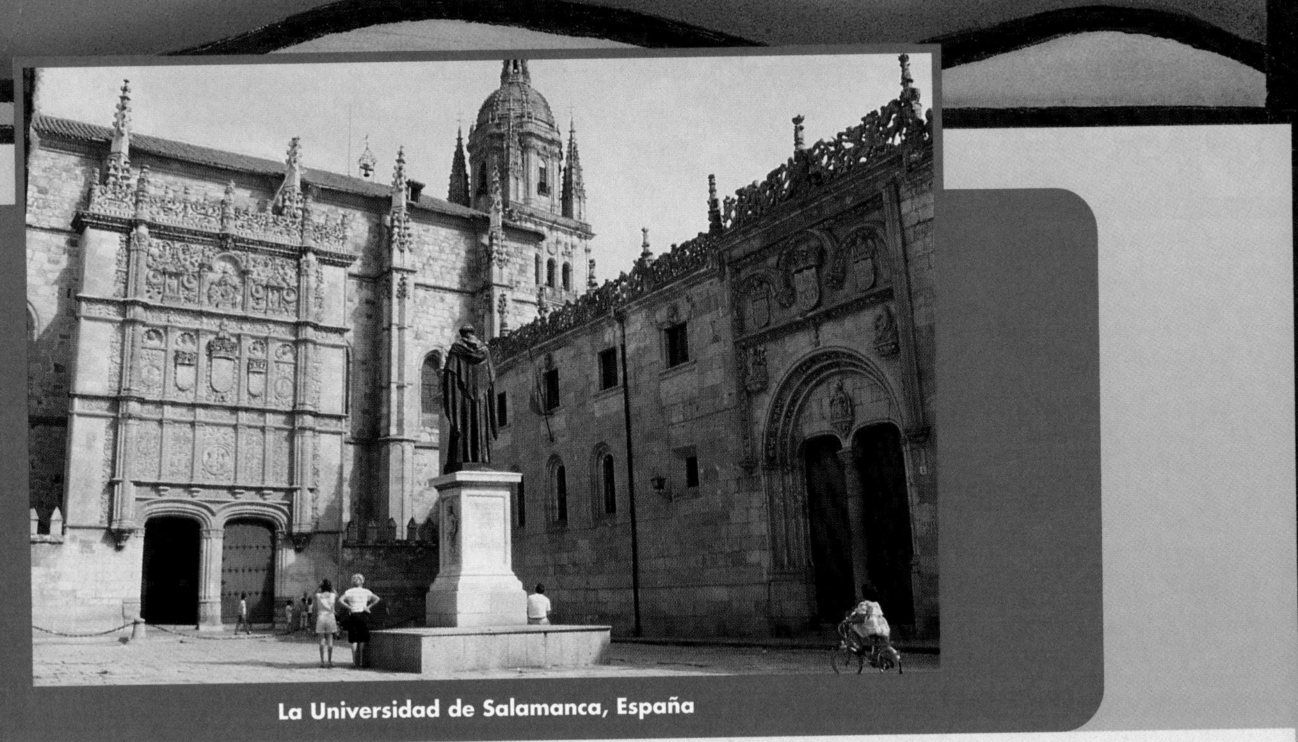

La Universidad de Salamanca, España

Lección 

FUNCTION	Expressing actions • Asking simple questions • Negating sentences • Counting to 100 • Telling time
STRUCTURE	The present indicative of ***-ar*** verbs, negative sentences, and forming simple questions • The verbs ***hacer*** and ***ir*** • The expression ***acabar de***
VOCABULARY	In school and on campus • ***-ar*** action verbs • Expressing disappointment and happiness • Numbers to 100
CULTURE	Student life and education in the Hispanic world
DIÁLOGO Y VIDEO	*Así es Mariana: En el campus*

Lección 

FUNCTION	Expressing actions • Describing people and things
STRUCTURE	The present indicative of ***-er*** and ***-ir*** verbs • Adjectives • ***Ser, estar,*** and ***hay*** • The contractions ***al*** and ***del***
VOCABULARY	In the classroom • Curriculum content • ***-ar, -er,*** and ***-ir*** action verbs
CULTURE	Graduation and university life
DIÁLOGO Y VIDEO	*Así es Mariana: La clase de Mariana*

Lección 

FUNCTION	Expressing actions • Expressing possession • Expressing indefinite and negative concepts
STRUCTURE	The present tense of ***e>ie*** and ***o>ue*** stem-changing verbs • The verbs ***tener*** and ***venir*** • Expressions with ***tener*** • Possessive adjectives • Indefinite and negative expressions
VOCABULARY	Professions • Locations • Action verbs
CULTURE	Finding a job
DIÁLOGO Y VIDEO	*Así es Mariana: El nuevo empleado*

Gaceta 

CULTURE	**Spain** Touring Spain • Faces in the News • Notes and Notables • Literature: Pedro Calderón de la Barca • Art
VIDEOCULTURA	La fiesta de los Reyes Magos • La Paella • La música contemporánea española

Lección 1

En la universidad

Hola, Verónica. Hola, Gonzalo.

AVISO CULTURAL

Where do you usually get together with your friends to talk and have a snack? You probably have several possibilities on campus: the cafeteria **(la cafetería),** the student center **(el centro estudiantil),** or the dorm **(la residencia).** In many Hispanic countries, universities do not have a central campus, and the concept of student dormitories does not exist. Since students live at home or in rooming houses **(pensiones),** they may get together in a local "cafetería"—not to be confused with the self-service restaurant that its name implies. In Hispanic countries "la cafetería" is a full-service café that serves complete meals and alcoholic beverages. The University of Madrid does have a campus and dormitories much like the universities in the United States. What are some advantages and disadvantages of living in an on-campus residence?

Preparativos

Review the vocabulary on pages 52–54 before viewing the video.

As you watch the video or read the following dialogue, pay close attention to the **-ar** verbs **tomar, estudiar, charlar, comprar,** and **necesitar.** Note their endings. Which person has an **-o** ending? Are the subject pronouns always used? Why or why not? **Estar** is also an **-ar** verb. How does it differ from the verbs above? Both of the "to be" verbs are presented in Unidad Preliminar. Do you remember the differences between them? What forms of **ser** and **estar** are in this dialogue? It's not good to make snap judgments about people, but . . . which of the following adjectives would you use to describe Mariana: **sociable, puntual, romántica, introvertida, optimista, tímida, activa?** Can you justify your choices?

Así es Mariana: En el campus

Mariana llega tarde al campus.

Luis Antonio: ¡Mariana! Son las diez y cuarto. Ya no hay tiempo para tomar un café y no hay tiempo para charlar. Vamos rápido a clase.

Mariana: Sí, ahora voy. Hola, Verónica. Hola, Gonzalo.

Gonzalo y Verónica: Hola, Mariana.

Mariana: ¿Cómo están? ¿Qué hay de nuevo?

Luis Antonio: ¡Mariana...es tarde!

Mariana: Bueno. ¡Vamos, chicos! ¡A la sala de clase! ¡Rápido!

Gonzalo: No, no voy a la clase con Uds. Voy a hablar con el profesor de matemáticas. Y después, voy a la librería. Necesito comprar libros, cuadernos, papel, bolígrafos...

Mariana: ¿Y tú, Verónica?

Verónica: Yo acabo de comprar los libros. Voy a la biblioteca porque necesito estudiar. Chau. Hasta luego.

Mariana: Adiós.

Es decir

A Based on the dialogue, match the questions or comments in the first column to the appropriate responses in the second column.

1. Hola.	**a.** Adiós.
2. Vamos rápido a clase.	**b.** ¿Qué hay de nuevo?
3. Chau. Hasta luego.	**c.** Sí, ahora voy.

B In the following sentences from the dialogue, fill in the blanks with the verbs from the list.

hablar   llega   estudiar   necesito   tomar   comprar

1. Mariana ___________ tarde al campus.
2. Ya no hay tiempo para ___________ un café.
3. Voy a ___________ con el profesor de matemáticas.
4. ___________ comprar libros, cuadernos...
5. Yo acabo de ___________ los libros.
6. Voy a la biblioteca porque necesito ___________.

C In pairs, ask your partner the following questions.

1. ¿Cómo se llaman los amigos de Mariana?
2. ¿Adónde va Mariana?
3. ¿Quién va a la librería? ¿Por qué?
4. ¿Qué acaba de comprar Verónica?

Al ver el video

A After viewing the video, answer the following questions.

1. ¿Dónde están los chicos? Están en...
   a. un restaurante. b. la universidad. c. una fiesta.
2. ¿Qué actividades no hacen los estudiantes (*do the students not do*)?
   a. no charlan. b. no toman café. c. no bailan.
3. ¿Qué frases *(sentences)* son falsas? Corríjalas *(Correct them)*.
   a. Mariana está sola (*alone*) en el apartamento.
   b. Mariana toma una clase de literatura italiana.
   c. Luis Antonio está impaciente con Mariana.

B Fill in the blanks with the adjectives that best describe Mariana and Luis Antonio. Note their endings. Pay close attention to the use of the verbs **ser** and **estar** in both sentences.

moren**o** (*dark-haired*) moren**a** frustrad**o**
activ**a** nervios**a** fabulos**o**

1. Mariana es __________, es __________ y está __________.
2. Luis Antonio es __________, es __________ y está __________.

C Match the questions or comments in the first column to the appropriate responses in the second column.

1. ¿Quién es Luis Antonio? **a.** ¿Ah, sí? ¿Por qué?
2. ¡Va a estar furioso! **b.** Sí, el amor es una cosa fabulosa.
3. ¡Qué romántico! **c.** Es el novio de Mariana.

D In pairs, ask your partner the following questions.

1. ¿Es romántica Mariana?
2. ¿De dónde es Luis?
3. ¿En qué universidad estudia él?
4. ¿Va a estar furioso Luis Antonio? ¿Por qué?

Verbos (-ar)

acabar (terminar)	*to finish*	llegar	*to arrive*
acabar de	*to have just ...*	mirar	*to look at, watch*
bailar	*to dance*	necesitar	*to need*
buscar	*to look for*	pagar	*to pay (for)*
comprar	*to buy*	pasar	*to pass; to happen; to spend (time)*
contestar	*to answer*	practicar	*to practice*
charlar	*to chat*	preguntar	*to ask*
desear	*to want, desire*	preparar	*to prepare*
enseñar	*to teach*	regresar	*to return*
escuchar	*to listen to*	tomar	*to take; to eat, drink*
estudiar	*to study*	trabajar	*to work*
hablar	*to speak, talk*	usar	*to use; to wear*
llamar	*to call*		

Verbos irregulares

hacer	*to do; to make*	ir	*to go*

Cosas *(Things)*

el dinero	*money*	el tiempo	*time; weather*
la tarea	*homework*		

¿A qué hora? *(At what time?)*

a tiempo	*on time*	la medianoche	*midnight*
ahora (mismo)	*(right) now*	el mediodía	*noon*
antes (de)	*before*	por la mañana (tarde, noche)	*in the morning (afternoon, evening)*
después (de)	*after*	tarde	*late*
en punto	*on the dot, exactly*	temprano	*early*
el fin de semana	*weekend*	toda la noche (esta noche)	*all night (tonight)*
la hora	*hour*	todo el día	*all day*
hoy	*today*		
más tarde	*later*		

Lugares *(Places)*

la biblioteca	*library*	el gimnasio	*gymnasium*
el centro estudiantil	*student center*	el laboratorio de lenguas	*language laboratory*
el dormitorio (cuarto)	*(bed)room*	la librería	*bookstore*
la escuela primaria (secundaria)	*elementary (high) school*	el recinto (campus)	*campus*
		la residencia	*dormitory*

Personas *(People)*

el (la) amigo(a)	*friend*	la mujer	*woman*
el (la) compañero(a) de cuarto	*roommate*	el (la) novio(a)	*boy (girl) friend*
el hombre	*man*		

Palabras útiles *(Useful words)*

a	*to, at*	para	*for, in order to*
allí	*there*	pero	*but*
aquí	*here*	poco	*few, (a) little*
bien	*well*	porque	*because*
con	*with*	si	*if*
de	*of, from*	sí	*yes*
mal	*badly, poorly*	siempre	*always*
más	*more*	sin	*without*
menos	*less, minus*	sobre	*about, on*
mucho	*much, many*	también	*also*
muy	*very*	y (e)[1]	*and*
nunca	*never*		

[1]Note that **e** instead of **y** is used to express *and* before a word that begins with **i-** or **hi-**: **José es sincero e inteligente.**

Vocabulario adicional

a eso de	*around, about (referring to time)*
a menudo (con frecuencia)	*often, frequently*
la cafetería	*cafe, cafeteria*
el cassette	*cassette*
el campo deportivo	*athletic field*
el colegio	*elementary or high school*
cómo no	*of course*
el despacho (la oficina)	*office*
el edificio	*building*
la fiesta	*party*
la máquina de escribir	*typewriter*
la matrícula	*tuition; enrollment*
el minuto	*minute*
presentar	*to present, introduce*
el segundo	*second*
el título	*degree; title*
todos los días	*every day*

Repasemos el vocabulario

A **Al contrario *(On the contrary)*.** Larisa has changed a lot since she's been away at college. Her mom corrects all of her dad's misconceptions about her. Change the following sentences, substituting antonyms for the underlined words or expressions to show how she has changed.

Papá: Larisa estudia <u>a eso de</u> las dos.
Mamá: **No, Larisa estudia a las dos <u>en punto</u>.**

1. Larisa estudia <u>con</u> los amigos.
2. Larisa trabaja <u>más</u> por la noche.
3. Larisa regresa a <u>mediodía</u>.
4. Larisa siempre llega <u>tarde</u>.
5. Larisa está <u>allí</u> ahora.
6. Larisa trabaja <u>toda la noche</u>.
7. Larisa escucha la radio <u>después de</u> la clase.
8. Larisa practica el piano <u>mucho</u>.

B **Nombre Ud. ... *(Name . . .)***

1. cuatro artículos necesarios para hacer la tarea.
2. tres lugares donde es posible estudiar.
3. dos cosas que Ud. compra en la librería.
4. un lugar para practicar el básquetbol.

C **En parejas *(In pairs)*.** Your classmate will ask you where certain people or articles can be found. Answer with a complete sentence. Then ask him or her the next question.

Estudiante 1: ¿Dónde está la profesora?
Estudiante 2: **La profesora está en el aula. ¿Dónde están los estudiantes? ...**

¿Dónde está(n)...

1. los estudiantes cuando desean charlar?
2. las enciclopedias?
3. el libro de texto para la clase de biología?
4. los estudiantes de diez años?
5. los atletas cuando practican básquetbol?
6. los dormitorios de los estudiantes?
7. las residencias de la universidad?
8. Ud. los sábados por la noche?

D **La lista.** In pairs, make a list of three things that you need to do and three things that you want to do. Your partner will report them to the class. Reverse roles.

Estudiante 1: Necesito trabajar mucho. Deseo bailar con Jaime.
Estudiante 2: **(Susana) necesita trabajar mucho. Desea bailar con Jaime.**

De uso común

Expressing Disappointment and Happiness

I was born on a sunny morning in April . . .

Desilusión *(Disappointment)*

¡Ay Dios! (¡Dios mío!)	*Oh, God! Oh, my God!*
¡Maldición!	*Curses!*
¡Me lo temía!	*I was afraid of that!*
¡Caramba!	*Darn!*
¡Rayos!	*Shucks!*

Alegría *(Happiness)*

¡Qué bien!	*How nice!*
¡Chévere![1] ¡Qué padre (guay)!	*Great! Awesome!*
¡Fenomenal!	*Super!*
¡Estupendo!	*Fantastic!*
¡Cuánto me alegro!	*I'm so pleased!*

Practiquemos

A Reacciones. In pairs, take turns listening to your partner's problem or situation. React, using the appropriate expression.

1. Recibo *(I receive)* una "D" en la clase de español.
2. Una amiga prepara una fiesta para mí.
3. Siempre llego tarde a clase.
4. Papá compra una computadora para mí.
5. Necesito estudiar toda la noche.
6. Deseo comprar un reloj pero necesito más dinero.

B Diálogos. In groups, write a dialogue incorporating expressions of disappointment and happiness. Share it with the class.

The Present Indicative of *-ar* Verbs

Papá, mamá, ¡gracias por enseñarme a conjugar en todas las formas el verbo ***amar!***

amar *(to love)*

Forma

In Spanish, verbs are divided into three categories: verbs that end in **-ar, -er,** and **-ir.** This form of the verb is called an infinitive. It is a verb that is not conjugated, that is, not given a subject that is performing the action. It is rather the expression of the possible action: *to speak, to eat, to think.* When you *conjugate* a verb, you designate a subject that will carry out the action of the verb: *I speak, you eat, he thinks.* In English, many verb conjugations are indistinguishable, thus the subject of the verb almost always accompanies the verb: *I speak, you speak, he speaks, she speaks, we speak, they speak.* In Spanish, each subject has a distinct verb ending. Study the verb **hablar.** Note that to conjugate the verb, you remove the infinitive ending **(-ar)** and add the appropriate personal endings.

[1]**¡Chévere!** is commonly used in Venezuela, Colombia, and other Latin American countries. **¡Qué padre!** is commonly used in Mexico, and **¡Qué guay!** is used in Spain.

HABLAR ***(to talk, to speak)***			
yo	hablo	nosotros(as)	hablamos
tú	hablas	vosotros(as)	habláis
él / ella / Ud.	habla	ellos / ellas / Uds.	hablan

1. Since the first- and second-person verb endings are distinct, the corresponding subject pronouns are rarely used.
2. Since the third-person verb endings can refer to multiple subjects, occasionally the pronouns are used to avoid confusion.

Él habla y **Ud.** escucha.	***He*** *speaks and* ***you*** *listen.*
Uds. estudian y **ellas** bailan.	***You*** *study and* ***they*** *dance.*

Función

1. The present tense is used to express various actions and ideas.

Yo hablo
- a. I speak
- b. I do speak
- c. I am speaking
- d. I will speak (in the immediate future)

a. This is the simple present tense. It can refer to present action or habitual action. *(I speak every day.)*
b. This form is an emphatic way to express action. *(I do in fact speak.)*
c. This reflects action in progress. *(I am in the process of speaking.)*
d. This form expresses future action only when referring to the immediate future. The listener knows from the context that this is future and not present action. [**Hoy estoy en el despacho hasta las 3:00.** *Today I am (I will be) in the office until 3:00.*]

2. To make a statement negative, place the word **no** before the conjugated verb.

José **no** estudia mucho.	*José* ***does not*** *study a lot.*
No hablamos inglés en clase.	*We* ***don't speak*** *English in class.*

¡AVISO! Note that although in English it is necessary to add the words *do* or *does*, in Spanish these forms do not exist.

3. There are two ways to form a simple question that requires a yes/no answer.

   a. Invert the subject and verb of your statement.

Ud. estudia mucho.	*You study a lot.*
¿Estudia Ud. mucho?	***Do you study*** *a lot?*

¡AVISO! Note the addition of an inverted question mark at the beginning of the question as well as the standard question mark at the end. Also note the omission of words like *do* and *are* that are necessary in English in order to form questions.

¿Habla Ud. italiano?	***Do you speak*** *Italian?*
¿Prepara Ud. la tarea ahora?	***Are you preparing*** *the homework now?*

   b. Change the intonation of your voice so that it rises at the end, forming a question.

statement: Ud. estudia mucho. ________\\.

question: ¿Ud. estudia mucho? ¿________/?

4. The infinitive is commonly used after a conjugated verb when there is no change of subject.

Deseo ser profesor de literatura.	***I want to be*** *a professor of literature.*
Necesitas estudiar más.	***You need to study*** *more.*

Practiquemos

A **Mis amigos Sara y Juan *(My friends, Sara and Juan).*** Fill in the blanks with the correct form of the verb in the present tense.

Sara y Juan son de Oviedo, España. Oviedo (estar) __________ en el norte *(north)* de España. Ellos (estudiar) __________ en la Universidad de Colorado porque ellos (desear) __________ hablar inglés bien. Yo (estudiar) __________ con Juan por la mañana. Él (hablar) __________ mucho y (preguntar) __________ mucho. Yo (contestar) __________ las preguntas. También, Sara y Juan (practicar) __________ en el laboratorio de lenguas. Sara (usar) __________ una computadora. Ella (pasar) __________ dos horas allí todos los días. Sara y yo (charlar) __________ por la tarde. Juan y Sara (regresar) __________ a Oviedo después de pasar un semestre aquí.

B **Preguntas personales *(Personal questions).*** Answer the following questions with complete sentences.

1. ¿Desea Ud. ir a una fiesta hoy?
2. ¿Habla Ud. bien o mal el español?
3. ¿Cuántas horas pasa Ud. en la biblioteca?
4. ¿Qué compra Ud. en la librería?
5. ¿Estudia Ud. por la mañana, por la tarde o por la noche?
6. ¿Termina Ud. la tarea todos los días?

Now change the questions to the **tú** form and interview a classmate.

C **¡No, no es verdad!** In pairs, correct your partner's exaggerations by responding negatively. After three statements, switch roles.

MODELO Estudiante 1: Yo soy un estudiante aplicado.
Estudiante 2: **¡No, no es verdad! Tú no eres un estudiante aplicado.**

1. Estudio ocho horas todos los días.
2. Charlo con la profesora después de la clase.
3. Contesto las preguntas en clase.
4. Bailo flamenco en clase.
5. Practico mucho en el laboratorio de lenguas.
6. Enseño las clases con frecuencia.

D **Clase de historia.** You and a classmate are working on a report about Spanish exploration and colonization of the United States. Arrange the following information chronologically by consulting *Un capítulo olvidado de la historia* in *Gaceta 1* on page 127. Use the correct form of the verbs in the present tense and share your information with the class.

1. ___ En San Agustín, los arqueólogos (acabar) ___________ de descubrir la fortaleza *(fort)* más antigua *(old)* de los Estados Unidos.
2. ___ Juan Ponce de León (llegar) ___________ a la Florida en 1513.
3. ___ Las exploraciones de los españoles (continuar) ___________ hasta el Pacífico.
4. ___ Ponce de León (formar) ___________ la ciudad *(city)* europea más antigua de los Estados Unidos.
5. ___ Pedro Menéndez de Avilés, otro español, (colonizar) ___________ San Agustín en 1565.

Continue to write the correct form of the verbs in parentheses in the present tense and answer the questions.

1. ¿Quiénes (llegar) ___________ a los Estados Unidos primero, los colonizadores españoles o los puritanos del Mayflower?
2. ¿Qué (buscar) ___________ Juan Ponce de León?
3. ¿Qué (estudiar) ___________ Ud. más, el pasado británico *(British past)* de los Estados Unidos o las exploraciones españolas?

The Numbers 20–100

Forma

Los números 21–100

veintiuno[1]	veintiséis	treinta y uno	sesenta
veintidós	veintisiete	treinta y dos	setenta
veintitrés	veintiocho	(tres, cuatro...)	ochenta
veinticuatro	veintinueve	cuarenta	noventa
veinticinco	treinta	cincuenta	cien

Función

1. Just as the number **uno** becomes **un** before a masculine noun, **veintiuno** becomes **veintiún, treinta y uno** becomes **treinta y un, cuarenta y uno** becomes **cuarenta y un,** and so on. The form preceding a feminine noun remains **una.**

   Hay **veintiún chicos** y **veintiuna** chicas. — *There are **twenty-one boys** and **twenty-one** girls.*

   Necesito **sesenta y un** libros y **cincuenta y una** sillas. — *I need **sixty-one books** and **fifty-one** chairs.*

2. Starting with the number 31, numbers in Spanish are expressed as separate words, with **y** between the multiple of ten and the ones.

   cuarenta **y** seis 46   ochenta **y** tres 83   noventa **y** siete 97

3. **Cien** is used in counting, before nouns, and when used alone. Note that the indefinite article (**un**) is never used with it.

   ¡Noventa y ocho, noventa y nueve, **cien!** — *Ninety-eight, ninety-nine, **one hundred!***

   Hay **cien** estudiantes en clase hoy. — *There are **one hundred** students in class today.*

   ¿Cuántos estudiantes hay? **Cien.** — *How many students are there? **One hundred.***

Practiquemos

A **¿Cuánto es?** ***(How much is it?)*** Use **dólar, dólares,** and **centavos** to tell how much the following items might cost.

1. unos blue jeans
2. un diccionario
3. una limonada
4. un radio
5. un cassette
6. un reloj
7. un sandwich en la cafetería
8. un bolígrafo

[1]Note the alternate form: **veinte y uno, veinte y dos,** and so forth.

B **Una encuesta *(A survey)*.** How many professionals responded to a recent survey? Express the numbers in Spanish.

1. 41 profesores	**4.** 73 artistas	**7.** 47 autores
2. 100 doctores	**5.** 22 atletas	**8.** 62 directores
3. 31 arquitectos	**6.** 88 dentistas	**9.** 99 actores

Telling Time

1.

Es (la) medianoche.

2.

Es la una (en punto).

3.

Es la una y media (de la mañana).

4.

Son las ocho menos cinco.

5.

Es (el) mediodía

6.

Son las doce y veinticinco

7.

Son las dos y cuarto (de la tarde).

8.

Son las once menos diez (de la noche).

1. To ask what time it is, the following expression is used.

   ¿Qué hora es?   *What time is it?*

2. To express the time, use **ser** + *definite article* + *hour*.

   a. Use **es** with **una,** since *one* is singular.

Es la una.	***It's*** *one o'clock.*
Es la una y media.	***It's*** *one thirty.*

b. **Son** is used with all other hours.

Son las diez en punto.	***It's*** *ten o'clock sharp.*
Son las dos y diez.	***It's*** *ten past two.*

c. The feminine definite articles **la** and **las** are always used before the hour since the word **hora** is feminine.

Es **la** una menos veinte.	*It's twenty of one.*
Son **las** ocho y media.	*It's eight thirty.*

d. To express time between the full hour and half past, add minutes to the hour with **y: es/son** + **la/las** + *hour* + **y** + *number of minutes.*

Es la una **y** diez.	*It's ten* ***after*** *one.*
Son las tres **y** veinte.	*It's three twenty.*

e. To express time after half past the hour, deduct minutes from the following hour with **menos: es/son** + **la/las** + *hour* + **menos** + *number of minutes.*

Es la una **menos** veinte y cinco.	*It's twenty five* ***of (to)*** *one.*
Son las nueve **menos** cinco.	*It's five* ***of*** *nine. (It's eight fifty-five).*

f. To express a quarter of an hour and a half hour, it is common to use the terms **cuarto** and **media,** respectively.

Son las dos menos **cuarto.**	*It's* ***a quarter*** *of two.*
Son las diez y **media.**	*It's ten* ***thirty.***

g. To ask at what time something is going to happen, use the expression **¿A qué hora?**

¿A qué hora es la clase?	***What time*** *is class?*

To reply, use **a la** or **a las** + *the time.*

La clase es **a las** nueve.	*Class is* ***at*** *nine.*

h. To express a specific time of the morning, afternoon, or evening, use **de la mañana** *(A.M.),* **de la tarde** *(P.M.),* **de la noche** *(P.M.).*

Llamo a mis padres a las ocho **de la mañana.**	*I call my parents at eight* ***in the morning.***

i. When no specific time is expressed, use **por la mañana, por la tarde,** and **por la noche.**

Por la mañana estudio y **por la tarde** trabajo.	***In the morning*** *I study and* ***in the afternoon*** *I work.*

j. Refer to the **¿A qué hora?** section of the vocabulary list on page 53 for words and expressions that will be useful in expressing time.

Practiquemos

A **¿Qué hora es?** Look at the clock drawings on page 63. As your instructor tells what time it is, write down the number of the corresponding clock.

MODELO Profesor(a): Son las tres de la tarde.

1. ___ **2.** ___ **3.** ___ **4.** ___

5. ___ **6.** ___ **7.** ___ **8.** ___

Now, listen as your professor tells you the wrong time for each clock. Correct him or her.

Profesor(a): Número 7. Son las doce y cuarto.
Estudiante: **No es cierto. Son las doce y media.**

1.

2.

3.

4.

5.

6.

7.

8.

Make a list of three activities you do at the times shown on clocks 3, 5, and 8. Use verbs from the vocabulary section on page 52. Compare with a classmate to find common activities.

B **No, no es posible.** Raúl wants to get together with Laura, but she's very busy. Role-play this exercise with a classmate. Laura tells where she is at each time. Follow the model.

MODELO 9:00/clase de español
Raúl: Laura... ¿a las nueve?
Laura: **No, Raúl, no es posible. A las nueve estoy en la clase de español.**

1. 10:15/biblioteca
2. a mediodía/cafetería
3. 2:30/laboratorio
4. 4:45/gimnasio
5. 7:25/fiesta para estudiantes internacionales
6. más tarde/residencia

C **¿Qué pasa?** ***(What's going on?)*** Complete these mini-monologues using time expressions from page 53.

1. "¿Estás loco *(crazy)*? ¡____________ las tres ____________ la mañana!"

2. "Vicente... son ____________ siete y la fiesta es ____________ las ____________. Es muy ____________."

3. "Manolo, es ____________ una y ____________. ¿Por qué llegas tan *(so)* ____________?"

D **¿Cuál es la pregunta?** Invent a question for each of the following answers.

1. No, la fiesta es a las nueve.
2. No, siempre estamos aquí a mediodía.
3. Son las dos menos cuarto.
4. No, mis amigos y yo estudiamos por la noche.
5. Al contrario, el profesor siempre llega tarde.
6. Trabajo a las ocho de la mañana.

The Verbs *Hacer* and *Ir*

1. As you will see in Lesson 2, **hacer** is conjugated as a regular **-er** verb, with the exception of the first-person singular **(yo)** form. (Refer to the **-er** verb chart on page 79.)

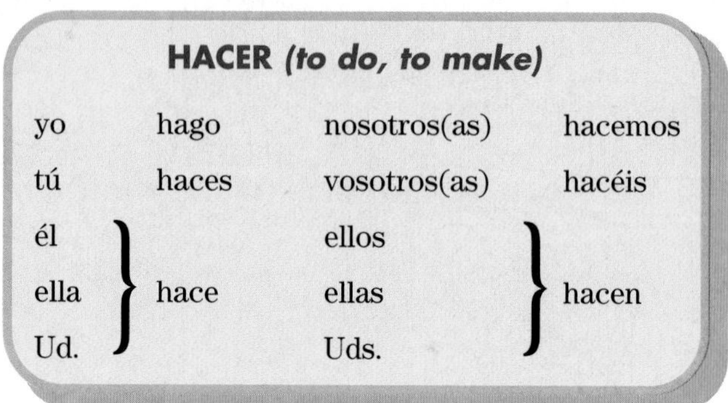

HACER ***(to do, to make)***

yo	hago	nosotros(as)	hacemos
tú	haces	vosotros(as)	hacéis
él / ella / Ud.	hace	ellos / ellas / Uds.	hacen

a. **Hacer** generally means *to do.*

¿Qué **hace** Rafael ahora?	*What's Rafael* ***doing*** *now?*
Prepara la tarea.	*He's preparing homework.*
El examen es mañana. **¿Qué hago?**	*The test is tomorrow.* ***What'll I do?***
Tú necesitas estudiar.	*You need to study.*
¿Qué **hacen** después de las clases?	*What do* ***they do*** *after class?*
Practican el fútbol.	*They practice soccer.*

b. **Hacer** can also mean *to make.*

¿Haces el café todos los días?	*Do you* ***make*** *the coffee every day?*
No, **hago** el café los lunes.[1]	*No, I* ***make*** the coffee on Mondays.

2. All forms of **ir** *(to go)* are irregular in the present tense.

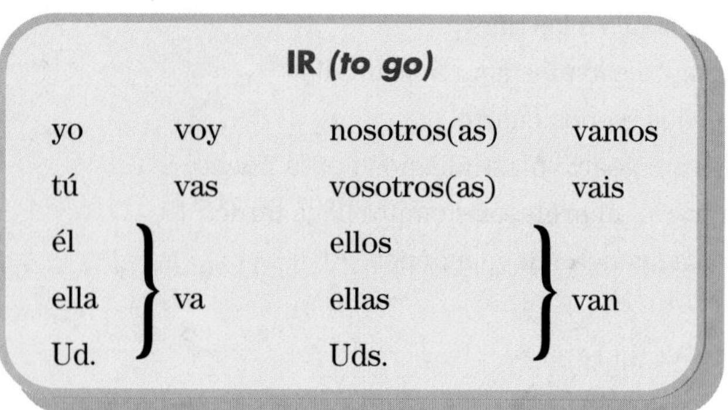

IR ***(to go)***

yo	voy	nosotros(as)	vamos
tú	vas	vosotros(as)	vais
él / ella / Ud.	va	ellos / ellas / Uds.	van

a. Note the use of the preposition **a** *(to)* when destination is expressed.

Voy a clase ahora, luego **voy a** la biblioteca y esta noche Marta y yo **vamos a** una fiesta.	***I'm going to*** *class now, then* ***I'm going to*** *the library, and tonight Marta and* ***I are going to*** *a party.*

[1]To express on a certain day or days, use **el** and **los: El lunes** *On Monday;* **Los lunes** *On Mondays.*

b. Note the use of **¿adónde?** to inquire about destination.

¿Adónde vas? — *(To)* ***Where** are you going?*

Voy a la clase de la profesora Vila. — *I'm going to Professor Vila's class.*

Ir + **a** + *infinitive* is used to express an action that will (is going to) take place in the future.

Vamos a estudiar en el centro estudiantil. — ***We are going to study** in the student center.*

Voy a practicar en el laboratorio. — ***I'm going to practice** in the laboratory.*

Practiquemos

A **El club de español.** The Spanish Club at the university is having a party. Ana, the president, tells which Spanish dish each member is making. Fill in the blanks with the correct form of the verb **hacer**.

Para la fiesta yo ___________ una sangría deliciosa. Como *(Since)* Carlos es de Valencia, él siempre ___________ la paella, y Silvia y Adela ___________ la tortilla de patatas. Isabel y yo ___________ tapas[1] *(Spanish appetizers)*. Ella ___________ croquetas y yo ___________ gambas al ajillo *(shrimp in garlic sauce)*. Yo pregunto a Elena, —Y tú, ¿qué ___________ para la fiesta? Ella contesta, —¡Yo ___________ mucho ruido *(noise)!*

B **La rutina diaria.** ***(Daily routine.)*** Interview four students to find out what they do **(¿qué hacen?)** in the following situations. Report the most common answer to the class.

¿Qué hace Ud....

1. si no desea estudiar?

___ No estudio. ___ Miro la televisión.
___ Escucho música. ___ ¿?

2. si el (la) profe llega tarde?

___ Regreso a la residencia. ___ Voy a la cafetería.
___ Espero. (*I wait.*) ___ ¿?

3. después de las clases?

___ Hago la tarea. ___ Charlo con amigos.
___ Trabajo. ___ ¿?

4. si hay una fiesta el lunes por la noche y un examen el martes por la mañana?

___ No voy a la fiesta. ___ Voy a la fiesta y no estudio.
___ Estudio en la fiesta. ___ ¿?

[1]For more information about **tapas**, complete exercise A on page 69.

C **Lugares *(Places)*.** In groups, practice using the verb **ir** by asking and answering the following questions. These words and phrases may be useful. Answer with complete sentences.

la oficina	la sala de clase	la cafetería	la librería
la residencia	la clase de español	la biblioteca	la fiesta de Rosa

¿Adónde...

1. va Ud. para bailar toda la noche?
2. vamos nosotros para comprar lápices y bolígrafos?
3. va José para charlar con María?
4. van Uds. para estudiar para el examen final?
5. va Ud. para hablar español?
6. va el profesor para preparar la clase?
7. va la profesora para enseñar?
8. van los estudiantes para escuchar la radio?

D **¿Adónde va? y ¿qué hace?** Using the model below, ask where the following people go and what they do there. Do this exercise with a classmate and follow the model.

MODELO Juan... fiesta/bailar
Estudiante 1: ¿Adónde va Juan?
Estudiante 2: **Va a la fiesta.**
Estudiante 1: ¿Qué hace allí?
Estudiante 2: **Baila.**

1. María... biblioteca/estudiar
2. Carlos y Pablo... oficina de la profe/hablar de la tarea
3. el profesor Martínez... España/trabajar
4. Uds.... librería/comprar papel
5. tú... cafetería/tomar una limonada
6. Juanita y Ud.... residencia/mirar un video

The Expression *Acabar de*

The expression **acabar de** + *infinitive* means *to have just done something.* Note that **de** is a preposition, and in Spanish the infinitive form of the verb always follows a preposition.

¿Qué **acabas de hacer?**	*What **have you just done?***
Acabo de estudiar para un examen.	***I have just studied** for an exam.*

Practiquemos

Problemas en la clase. José has a lot of problems in class although he tries everything. His friend Sofía suggests some solutions. Formulate questions and have a classmate answer using **acabar de** + *infinitive.* Follow the model.

MODELO estudiar la gramática
Sofía: ¿Necesitas estudiar la gramática?
José: **No, acabo de estudiar la gramática.**

1. hablar con el profesor
2. buscar un diccionario
3. usar la computadora
4. hacer las correcciones
5. ir a la librería
6. estudiar en la biblioteca
7. tomar una aspirina

Spend more time with Mariana and her friends while you review grammar and expand your cultural horizons.
See the **Así es Mariana** exercise in your workbook for this lesson.

En resumen

A **Vamos a tomar tapas.** Give the correct form of the verbs in parentheses and choose the appropriate word when two choices are given.

En España es costumbre *(customary)* "tomar tapas" (antes de, después de) trabajar. A eso de las 7:00 (por, de) la tarde, los españoles (ir) ______ a bares y restaurantes para (charlar) ______ con amigos, tomar una bebida y probar *(taste)* las muchas tapas que (estar) ______ en los mostradores *(counters)*. (Hay, Están) tapas típicas en cada *(each)* región, pero las tapas más populares son de gambas *(shrimp)*, tortilla *(omelette)*, albóndigas *(meatballs)* y aceitunas *(olives)*. ¿(Desear) ______ Ud. hacer una fiesta a la española? Pues, (necesitar) ______ (un, una) variedad de tapas, cerveza *(beer)* o un buen vino y compañeros, por supuesto *(of course)* . . . ¡Buen provecho!

B **Octavio, ¿por qué... ?** Octavio's little brother asks him a lot about university life. Answer his questions with complete sentences.

Rafaelito: Octavio, ¿por qué hay pizarras en las aulas?
Octavio: **Hay pizarras en las aulas porque los profesores usan las pizarras para enseñar la gramática.**

Octavio, ¿por qué...
1. escuchan cassettes los estudiantes?
2. no miras la televisión ahora?
3. va Juan Luis a la fiesta con Juliana?
4. están los estudiantes siempre en la biblioteca?
5. no habla inglés en clase el profesor?
6. no estudias hoy?
7. hablas mucho con las chicas?
8. tomas aspirinas ahora?

C La escuela secundaria en España. Isabel Serrano talks about what it is like to study in a **liceo.**[1] Give the correct form of the verbs in parentheses in the present tense and choose the appropriate word where two choices are given. These paragraphs contain structures presented in the preliminary sections as well as in Lesson 1. Before reading, scan the paragraphs and make a list of all the cognates that you recognize.

A excepción de la enseñanza *(education)* preescolar, (el, la) sistema educativo en España es diferente al sistema en los Estados Unidos. La enseñanza primaria (es, está) obligatoria, y gratuita *(free)*. Aquí nosotros (necesitar) ______ el título para entrar a la escuela secundaria y para obtener (un, una) trabajo *(job)*.

(Hay, Están) muchos tipos de escuelas secundarias en España; escuelas tecnológicas, escuelas militares y escuelas comerciales. Yo (estudiar) ______ en un liceo porque (desear) ______ estudiar en la universidad. (Tomar) ______ clases de historia, matemáticas y de italiano.

Nosotros (entrar) ______ a (los, las) ocho (de, por) la mañana. A las dos nosotros (ir) ______ a casa *(home)*, estamos con la familia y (regresar—nosotros) ______ a la escuela a las cuatro. (El, La) día escolar (terminar) ______ a las siete. El sistema es muy rígido. Todas las clases son obligatorias. También (hay, es) mucha tarea. En la escuela (los, las) estudiantes no (practicar) ______ deportes *(sports)* y no (participar) ______ en clubes, clases de arte, música, etc., porque, en general, no hay actividades extraescolares en las escuelas secundarias.

1. Choose the word in parentheses that best completes the sentence.
   a. En España, la enseñanza preescolar es (similar/diferente) a la enseñanza preescolar en los Estados Unidos.
   b. Hay varios tipos de escuelas (primarias/secundarias) en España.
   c. Isabel está en el liceo porque desea (estudiar en la universidad/trabajar) después de graduarse.
   d. El liceo es (rígido/flexible).
   e. A las dos de la tarde los estudiantes (regresan a la escuela/van a casa).
   f. En el liceo no hay (mucha tarea/muchas actividades después de las clases).

2. Carefully reread the paragraphs and find another way of expressing the following words or phrases.

a. inflexible	c. elemental	e. colegio
b. diploma	d. de educación	f. con la excepción de

D Una nota para los compañeros. In a paragraph of five to six sentences, leave a note for your roommates describing your agenda for today. Include eight activities that you are going to do, and at what time. Use the **ir** + **a** + *infinitive* construction and include as many details as you can.

[1]At the secondary level, a Spanish **liceo** is similar to a college preparatory high school.

E **Vamos a clase.** Translate the following dialogue to Spanish.

Raúl: See you later, Carlos. Paco and I are going now.

Carlos: But . . . class is at five, and it's four thirty.

Raúl: I need to speak with the professor before class. He always arrives early.

Carlos: Are you going to buy the books today?

Raúl: I've just returned from the bookstore, and the books are not there.

F **Una tarjeta postal.** Your friend Carmen sent you a postcard from the Parador Conde de Orgaz in Toledo, Spain. A **parador** is a hotel that combines the amenities of a luxury hotel with the intimate, regional atmosphere of a bed and breakfast. Many are restored castles, palaces, and monasteries set in picturesque locations. The first parador opened in 1926, and today there are about 83 across Spain. Don't forget to write back to Carmen and answer all her questions.

Escuchemos

A **¿Qué hace Juan?** You will hear a series of sentences that tell you what Juan is doing. Repeat each one, and then decide if the corresponding drawing matches the description. Write **cierto** or **falso** in the space below each drawing.

MODELO Juan toma café.
Falso

1. ______________________ **2.** ______________________ **3.** ______________________

4. ______________________ **5.** ______________________ **6.** ______________________

7. ______________________________ 8. ______________________________

B **Dictado *(Dictation)*.** You will hear a short narration about Hispanic universities. Listen carefully to the entire selection. Listen again and write each sentence during the pauses. You will hear the new word **difícil** *(difficult)*.

You will then hear a series of questions related to the dictation. Answer them with complete sentences. Refer to your dictation.

Lección 2

En clase

Repita la pregunta, por favor.

AVISO CULTURAL

In Spain and Latin America the universities are composed of **facultades** or *schools*, such as **la Facultad de Medicina, la Facultad de Derecho** *(law)*, and **la Facultad de Ingeniería** *(engineering)*. Unlike in the United States, entering students choose the facultad that corresponds to their **carrera** *(major)* and they take all of their classes there, most of which are in their specialized field. Since many universities do not have a campus, the facultades are often located in different areas of the city. If you were studying at a Hispanic university, in which facultad would you be enrolled?

Preparativos

Review the vocabulary on pages 76–78 before viewing the video.

As you watch the video or read the dialogue, try to identify the adjectives. With the exception of **bienvenidos,** all of the adjectives are in the singular form. Why? Note the final letter of each adjective. From previous observation, you may already know how to form the plural. If not, don't worry. In this lesson you'll practice forming and using adjectives. In this episode, Mariana handles herself pretty well for someone present in body but absent in spirit. Do you, like Mariana, ever "zone out" during class? Which of the following adjectives best describes the state of mind or body that causes you to daydream or fade out in class: **perezoso(a)** *(lazy)*, **cansado(a)** *(tired)*, **enfermo(a)** *(sick)*, **aburrido(a)** *(bored)*, **preocupado(a)** *(worried)?* What is Mariana's excuse?

Así es Mariana: La clase de Mariana

En la clase de literatura española. Mariana is daydreaming when the professor calls on her.

Profesora: ¡Mariana Benavides! *(Mariana no escucha.)* ¡Mariana Benavides!

Mariana: ¿Eh?... ¡Presente!, señora profesora.

Profesora: Buenos días, Mariana. Gracias por asistir a clase, pero "presente" no es la respuesta que buscamos.

Mariana: ¿Respuesta?... Repita la pregunta, por favor.

Profesora: ¡Ayyy, muchacha! Un momento eres una alumna aplicada, y al otro minuto, no sé dónde estás.

Mariana: Perdón, profesora.

Profesora: La pregunta es... en el libro, *El enfermo feliz*, ¿quién es la madre° real del doctor Sánchez?

Mariana: ¿La madre real? ¡Rayos! ¡Yo sé! Su° nombre es Juana. Es una buena actriz española. Es morena, delgada y muy perezosa. Ella vive con un maestro de arte encima de una montaña° alta.

Profesora: Muy bien. ¿Y cómo es el maestro de arte?

Mariana: El es... malo. Necesita un buen sicólogo, ¡pronto!

Profesora: ¿Y cómo sabe el doctor Sánchez que Juana es su madre real?

Mariana: En el capítulo diez, Juana está muy aburrida y decide hacer una fiesta grande. Luego, después de la medianoche, el doctor Sánchez abre la puerta del salón y pronto sabe los secretos de la familia Sánchez.

Profesora: ¡Fabuloso, Mariana! ¡Fabuloso!

Es decir

A The following sentences are false. Based on the dialogue, correct them.

1. Mariana asiste a una clase de historia.
2. Mariana escucha a la profesora.
3. En la clase, leen un libro sobre un actor español.
4. El maestro de arte es bueno.
5. A las 8:00, el doctor abre la puerta.
6. Mariana contesta mal la pregunta de la profesora.

B The following are comments that the professor makes to Mariana. Complete them with the correct form of the verb **ser** or **estar.**

1. Mariana, "presente" no ____________ la respuesta que buscamos.
2. Un momento (tú) ____________ una alumna aplicada, y al otro minuto, no sé dónde (tú) ____________.
3. En el libro, *El enfermo feliz*, ¿quién ____________ la madre real del doctor Sánchez?

C In pairs, create a new response to the question **"¿Quién es la madre real del doctor Sánchez?".** You can use Mariana's description as a model. Use the adjectives on page 83.

D Fill in the blanks with the prepositions **a** or **de.**

1. Vamos _______ hablar _______ la novela *Detrás _______ la luna, debajo _______ la mesa.*
2. Mariana, gracias por asistir _______ clase.
3. Es morena, delgada y muy perezosa y vive con un maestro _______ arte.
4. Viven encima _______ una montaña alta.

Al ver el video

After viewing the video, do the following activities.

A Not all of the sentences are true. Correct the false ones with complete sentences.

1. Mariana y Luis Antonio están solos *(alone)* en el aula.
2. La profesora es rubia *(blonde).*
3. La profesora está frustrada con Mariana.
4. La profesora está delante de los estudiantes.

B Refer to the list of adjectives on pages 77 and 83 to help you answer the following questions.

1. ¿Cómo es Mariana? *(What is Mariana like?)*
2. ¿Cómo es Luis Antonio?
3. ¿Cómo es la profesora?
4. ¿Cómo está Mariana en este episodio?

Vocabulario

Verbos

-ar

ayudar	*to help*	pronunciar	*to pronounce*
cambiar	*to change*	repasar	*to review*
llevar	*to carry; to take; to wear*		

-er

aprender	*to learn*	creer	*to believe; to think*
beber	*to drink*	deber	*ought to; must; to owe*
comer	*to eat*	leer	*to read*
comprender	*to understand*	vender	*to sell*

-ir

abrir	*to open*	escribir	*to write*
asistir (a)	*to attend*	insistir (en)	*to insist (on)*
consistir (en)	*to consist (of)*	recibir	*to receive*
decidir	*to decide*	vivir	*to live*

En la clase

el año	*year*	la pregunta	*question*
el examen	*test*	la prueba	*quiz*
el horario	*schedule*	la respuesta	*answer*
la nota	*grade*		

Personas

el (la) consejero(a)	*counselor*	el (la) maestro(a)	*teacher*
el (la) decano(a)	*dean*		

Materias (Asignaturas) *(Subjects)*

el alemán	*German*	el español	*Spanish*
el arte	*art*	el francés	*French*
la biología	*biology*	el idioma *m.* (la lengua)	*language*
el cálculo	*calculus*	el inglés	*English*
la ciencia política	*political science*	el italiano	*Italian*
las ciencias de computadora	*computer science*	las matemáticas	*mathematics*
la contabilidad	*accounting*	la medicina	*medicine*
el derecho	*law*	la química	*chemistry*
la economía	*economics*	la sicología	*psychology*
		la sociología	*sociology*

Adjetivos (See page 83 for additional useful adjectives)

aburrido	*bored, boring*	enfermo	*sick*
alegre (feliz)	*happy*	listo	*ready, clever*
aplicado	*applied, hardworking*	malo	*bad*
		otro[1]	*another, other*
bueno	*good, O.K.*	perezoso	*lazy*
cansado	*tired, tiresome*	preocupado	*worried*
		trabajador	*hardworking*
contento	*content*	triste	*sad*

Palabras y frases útiles — *Useful words and sentences*

¿Cómo se dice... ?	*How do you say . . . ?*
luego	*later, after*
por	*for, because, of, by*
Repita(n), por favor.	*Repeat, please.*
sólo (solamente)	*only*
Yo (no) sé.	*I (don't) know.*

[1]Note that **otro(a)** is never used with the singular indefinite article **un(a).**

Vocabulario adicional

la beca	*scholarship*	la literatura	*literature*
el capítulo	*chapter*	Otra vez, por favor.	*Again, please.*
¿Cómo se escribe... ?	*How do you write (spell) . . . ?*	por eso	*therefore*
		pronto	*soon, right away*
despacio (lento)	*slowly*		
entrar	*to enter*	el profesorado	*faculty*
la historia	*history*	¿Qué significa... ?	*What does . . . mean?*
la música	*music*		
la lección	*lesson*	el semestre	*semester*

Repasemos el vocabulario

A **¿Cuál no pertenece? *(Which doesn't belong?)*** Indicate which word does not belong and explain.

MODELO decano consejero instructor profesorado
Profesorado. Decano, instructor y consejero son personas individuales pero profesorado es un grupo de personas.

1. derecho	alemán	español	francés
2. cálculo	historia	contabilidad	matemáticas
3. aburrido	perezoso	trabajador	cansado
4. triste	horario	alegre	enfermo

B **¿Qué hacen los estudiantes allí?** Listen as your instructor mentions various places on campus. Choose an appropriate verb and form a complete sentence to tell what you do there.

biblioteca: estudiar
yo estudio en la biblioteca.

pronunciar beber vender aprender leer vivir

C **Palabras y frases útiles para la clase.** Spanish class is confusing for Mark because he rarely attends. Complete the dialogue with the correct vocabulary words from the list below.

asistes	debes	no sé	repita	cómo se dice
prueba	examen	preguntas	recibes	contenta

Profesora: Es hora de hacer la ______.

Mark: ¡Caramba! Profe, ¿______ "architect" en español?

Profesora: Ay, Mark, tú ______ asistir a clase. La palabra es *arquitecto*.

Mark: Profesora, ______, por favor. Hay mucho ruido *(noise)*. Pssssst, Ceci, ¿cuándo es el ______ final?

Sue: Yo ______, Mark. ¿Por qué no ______ a clase? Así, no necesitas hacer tantas *(so many)* ______, la profesora está ______ y tú ______ una nota buena en la clase.

D **En el futuro** ***(In the future).*** Tell what you need to study for the following professions. Complete the sentence five different ways, using the professions listed below in the second blank and the appropriate subjects from the vocabulary list in the first blank.

MODELO **Estudio derecho porque voy a ser juez *(judge).***

artista   sociólogo   doctor   presidente   sicólogo

Estudio ______ porque voy a ser ______.

E **¿Cómo están hoy?** Fill in the blanks with the correct form of the adjectives from the list below and complete the sentence in an original way.

triste	cansado	preocupado
aburrido	contento	enfermo

MODELO Hoy el maestro está **alegre** porque...
los estudiantes estudian mucho.

1. Hoy el profesor está ____________ porque...
2. Hoy los estudiantes están ____________ porque...
3. Hoy el muchacho perezoso está ____________ porque...
4. Hoy yo estoy ____________ porque...

The Present Indicative of *-er* and *-ir* Verbs

Forma

As with **-ar** verbs, to conjugate **-er** and **-ir** verbs you remove the infinitive endings and add the appropriate personal endings.

COMPRENDER *(to understand)*

yo	comprend**o**	nosotros(as)	comprend**emos**
tú	comprend**es**	vosotros(as)	comprend**éis**
él / ella / Ud.	comprend**e**	ellos / ellas / Uds.	comprend**en**

ASISTIR *(to attend)*

yo	asist**o**	nosotros(as)	asist**imos**
tú	asist**es**	vosotros(as)	asist**ís**
él / ella / Ud.	asist**e**	ellos / ellas / Uds.	asist**en**

Note that the endings for **-er** and **-ir** verbs are identical except for the **nosotros** and **vosotros** forms.

Función

As discussed in Lesson 1, the present tense in Spanish is used to express various actions and ideas.

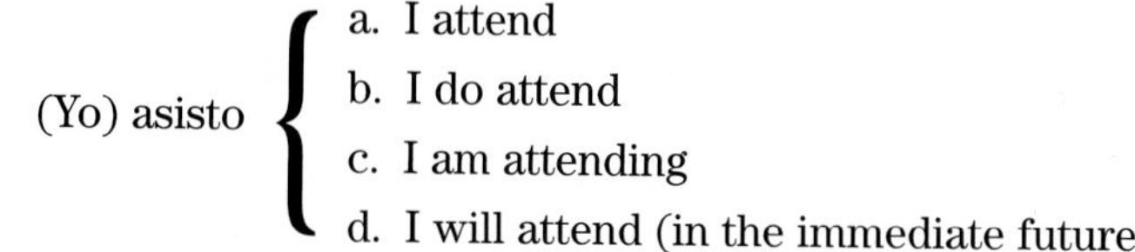

(Yo) asisto
- a. I attend
- b. I do attend
- c. I am attending
- d. I will attend (in the immediate future)

Some common **-er** and **-ir** verbs are:

-er		**-ir**	
aprender	*to learn*	abrir	*to open*
beber	*to drink*	consistir (en)	*to consist (of)*
comer	*to eat*	decidir	*to decide*
creer	*to believe*	escribir	*to write*
deber	*ought to, should; must; to owe*	insistir (en)	*to insist (on)*
leer	*to read*	recibir	*to receive*
vender	*to sell*	vivir	*to live*

Practiquemos

A **Las notas.** Refer to the grade form from the University of Valencia, Spain. Use the verb **recibir** to tell what grades Tomás receives in each of his classes.

Tomás recibe bien en la clase de inglés.

UNIVERSIDAD DE VALENCIA

Notas de: Tomás Moreno

	MATERIA	NOTA
1	español	sobresaliente
2	historia	muy bien
3	inglés	bien
4	cálculo	regular
5	economía	malo
6		

Now listen carefully as your instructor explains the reasons for the grades Tomás received. Indicate **cierto** if you agree, and **falso** if you disagree.

1. cierto/falso **3.** cierto/falso **5.** cierto/falso

2. cierto/falso **4.** cierto/falso

B **Problemas en clase.** Fill in the blanks with the correct form of the verb in parentheses in the present tense.

Victoria (ser) ______ una buena amiga. Nosotras (estudiar) ______ italiano y (estar) ______ en la clase de la profesora Licata. Pero, hay un problema. Nosotras (ser) ______ muy diferentes. Yo (creer) ______ que es importante estudiar. (Ser-yo) ______ muy aplicada y responsable. Yo (asistir) ______ a clase todos los días. Victoria no (asistir) ______ mucho y por eso ella (recibir) ______ malas notas. Los profesores (estar) ______ preocupados porque ella no (hacer) ______ la tarea.

Yo (aprender) ______ mucho en todas las clases y (recibir) ______ muy buenas notas. Yo no (comprender) ______ por qué ella no (leer) ______ las lecciones. Ella (deber) ______ repasar el vocabulario también. (Creer-yo) ______ que la educación es muy importante.

Now listen as your instructor asks you questions about what you just read.

C **¿Quién lo hace?** Listen carefully as your instructor reads a series of descriptions. Write the letter that corresponds to the description of the people in the following list.

a. la estudiante perezosa ______, ______
b. el consejero ______, ______
c. el estudiante enfermo ______, ______
d. la maestra ______, ______
e. los estudiantes aplicados ______, ______
f. los estudiantes de español ______, ______

D **Preguntas personales.** Answer the following questions.

1. ¿Qué días asiste Ud. a clase?
2. ¿Qué clases toma Ud.? ¿Qué notas recibe Ud. en las clases?
3. ¿Lee Ud. mucho? ¿Qué lee?
4. ¿Qué aprende en la clase de español?
5. ¿Qué debe Ud. hacer para recibir buenas notas?
6. ¿Por qué es importante hablar español?

Now change the questions to the **tú** form and interview a classmate.

Adjectives

Forma y función

Adjectives are used to describe or limit persons, places, and things.

juntos together

Agreement of Adjectives

1. Adjectives agree in number and gender with the nouns they modify. Adjectives that end in **-o** are masculine singular, and have a masculine plural, a feminine singular, and a feminine plural form.

	Masculine	**Feminine**
singular	el chico aplicado	la chica aplicada
plural	los chicos aplicados	las chicas aplicadas

2. Adjectives that end in **-e** or in a consonant other than **-n** or **-r** change only to agree in number with the noun they modify. They maintain the same form for masculine and feminine.

	Masculine	**Feminine**
singular	el muchacho alegre	la muchacha alegre
	el muchacho feliz	la muchacha feliz
plural	los muchachos alegres	las muchachas alegres
	los muchachos felices	las muchachas felices

3. Most adjectives of nationality have four forms, including those that end in a consonant.[1]

	Masculine		Feminine	
Singular	el profesor	mexicano español inglés	la profesora	mexicana española inglesa
Plural	los profesores	mexicanos españoles ingleses	las profesoras	mexicanas españolas inglesas

Other adjectives of nationality include: **chino** *(Chinese)*, **francés, irlandés** *(Irish)*, **japonés** *(Japanese)*, **ruso** *(Russian)*, **alemán.**

¡AVISO! Adjectives of nationality are not capitalized in Spanish, but the names of the countries are. **¿Es español? Sí, es de España.**

4. Adjectives whose masculine singular form ends in **-or** add **-a** for the feminine.

un muchacho trabajad**or** — una muchacha trabajador**a**

5. Adjectives are pluralized in the same way as nouns.
   a. Add **-s** to adjectives that end in a vowel.

      el estudiante aplicad**o** — los estudiantes aplicad**os**

      la chica perezos**a** — las chicas perezos**as**

   b. Add **-es** to adjectives that end in a consonant.

      el estudiante trabajad**or.** — los estudiantes trabajador**es**

   c. The verb **ser** is used with many adjectives to express basic qualities or characteristics of the noun or pronoun being modified.

      ¿Cómo **es** Alejandro? — *What **is** Alejandro like?*

      Alejandro **es inteligente** y **trabajador.** — *Alejandro **is intelligent** and* **hard-working.**

   The following are pairs of adjectives with opposite meanings that are commonly used with **ser.** Some of these you already know, but learn the new ones, as they are extremely common and useful.

aburrido/ interesante	*boring/ interesting*	inteligente/ estúpido	*intelligent/ stupid*
alto/bajo	*tall/short*	joven/viejo	*young/old*
bueno/malo	*good/bad*	rico/pobre	*rich/poor*
delgado/gordo	*slim/fat*	rubio/ moreno	*blond/ dark-haired*
difícil/fácil	*difficult/easy*	simpático/ antipático	*nice/ unpleasant*
grande/pequeño	*big/small*		
guapo (bonito)/feo	*handsome (pretty)/ugly*		

[1]Note that masculine singular adjectives of nationality that end in **-n** or **-s** have a written accent on the last syllable. The feminine singular form and the plural forms do not. See rules of accentuation on page 8.

6. The verb **estar** is used with some adjectives to express conditions or states of being of the noun or pronoun being modified.

Hoy es el examen y María **está preocupada.**	*Today is the test and María* ***is worried.***

Note the following adjectives commonly used with **estar.**[1]

aburrido	*bored*	enfermo	*sick*
cansado	*tired*	preocupado	*worried*
contento (alegre, feliz)	*happy*	triste	*sad*

Practiquemos

A **¿La novia ideal?** Refer to the cartoon on page 82. It seems that the parents have an impression of **"la novia"** that is, well, . . . a bit different from that of their son. Describe her from their point of view, using adjectives from this lesson. Begin with "**Es una chica**...."

B **¿Cómo están todos?** Change the following sentences to the plural.

El muchacho está nervioso.
Los muchachos están nerviosos.

1. El doctor está enfermo.
2. El decano está feliz.
3. El estudiante está aburrido.
4. El profesor está cansado.
5. El consejero está triste.
6. El maestro está preocupado.

Y ahora, el opuesto. In pairs, student 1 will change the sentences above to the plural form and will form questions from the statements. Student 2 will answer affirmatively, and will change the sentences to the feminine.

MODELO
Estudiante 1: ¿Están nerviosos los muchachos?
Estudiante 2: **Sí, y las muchachas están nerviosas también.**

C **Conclusiones.** Draw conclusions about people based on the descriptions that your instructor will read. Use the correct form of the following adjectives with the verb **ser.** Write complete sentences.

MODELO
Profesor(a): Marcos estudia seis horas todas las noches.
Estudiante: **Marcos es aplicado.**

rico inteligente simpático trabajador perezoso

1. Sandra... **2.** Roberto y yo... **3.** Uds.... **4.** Yo... **5.** Pablo y Rosa...

[1]Note that some adjectives (such as **aburrido**) change their meaning when used with **ser** and **estar.** **Cansado** is another example: **Ser cansado** = *to be tiresome.* **Estar cansado** = *to be tired.*

Now draw conclusions about the physical or emotional state of people using the verb **estar** and the adjectives below. Use complete sentences.

MODELO Profesor(a): Miguel y José deben tomar un examen mañana.
Estudiante: **Miguel y José están preocupados.**

contento triste enfermo feliz cansado

1. Anita... **2.** Uds.... **3.** Tú... **4.** Los chicos... **5.** Nosotros...

D **Sí, pero...** In pairs, student 1 will ask questions and student 2 will answer affirmatively, giving the antonym of the adjective in the original sentence. Reverse roles halfway through.

MODELO Estudiante 1: ¿Es **interesante** la conferencia? (las clases)
Estudiante 2: Sí, pero las clases son **aburridas.**

1. ¿Es fácil la química? (las matemáticas)
2. ¿Es grande el gimnasio? (las residencias)
3. ¿Es viejo Miguel? (Iván y Luis)
4. ¿Es alto Raúl? (José y Rafael)
5. ¿Es perezosa Carmen? (Ana y Rosa)
6. ¿Es simpática Alicia? (Marta y Ema)

Placement of Adjectives

1. Descriptive adjectives generally follow the nouns they modify.

una prueba **difícil**	*a **difficult** test*
unas clases **aburridas**	*some **boring** classes*

¡AVISO! Adjectives of nationality always follow the nouns they modify: **un chico francés** *(a French boy)*

2. Limiting or quantitative adjectives precede the nouns they modify.

tres profesores	***three** professors*
muchas/pocas becas	***many/few*** scholarships
¿Cuántas personas hay?	***How many** people are there?*
otro bolígrafo	***another** pen*

¡AVISO! With the exception of un(a), cardinal numbers **dos, cuatro,** and so forth, do not agree with the nouns they modify: **cuatro chicas.**

3. The adjectives **bueno** and **malo** may also precede the nouns they modify. When placed before a masculine singular noun, **bueno** is shortened to **buen** and **malo** to **mal.**

un hombre **bueno** *or* un **buen** hombre	*however:* una **buena** mujer
un hombre **malo** *or* un **mal** hombre	*however:* una **mala** mujer

4. **Grande** means *big* or *large* when it follows a noun, and *great* when it precedes a noun. **Grande** is shortened to **gran** when placed before a masculine or feminine singular noun.

un **gran** hombre	una **gran** mujer	un hombre **grande**
*a **great** man*	*a **great** woman*	*a **big** man*

Practiquemos

A **Al singular.** Change the sentences from plural to singular. Explain the position of the adjective.

MODELO unos secretarios alemanes
un secretario alemán. The adjective **alemán** *(German)* is an adjective of nationality and therefore always follows the noun it modifies.

1. unos buenos profesores
2. unos estudiantes franceses
3. unas muchachas guapas
4. unos años malos
5. unas grandes oportunidades

B **¿Quiénes son?** Use the nouns and adjectives below and any other necessary words to describe the following people.

MODELO Carlos Moya es un tenista bueno.

Personas	Sustantivos	Adjetivos
1. George Bush	actor	musical
2. Jerry Seinfeld	beisbolista	famoso
3. Roberto Alomar	ex presidente	republicano
4. Andy García	cómico	inteligente
5. Miami Sound Machine	grupo	fantástico

C **Más descripción, por favor.** Be more descriptive by inserting the adjectives in parentheses into the sentences.

Necesito una novela. (grande/francés)
Necesito una gran novela francesa.

1. Hay chicas aquí. (mucho/bonito)
2. Publican libros. (grande/histórico)
3. Busco un diccionario. (bueno/alemán)
4. Es un presidente. (grande/americano)
5. Hay tarea. (mucho/difícil)

D **Traducciones.** Translate the following phrases to Spanish.

1. a bad grade
2. another class
3. How many teachers?
4. the French faculty
5. a good year
6. a large campus
7. some difficult classes
8. many hardworking students
9. thirty little girls
10. a great Spanish president

Ser and *estar* used with adjectives

1. **Ser** is used with adjectives that express inherent qualities or characteristics of a person, place, or thing. For example: **alto, simpático, moreno, viejo, inteligente.**
2. **Estar** is used with adjectives that express a change in the usual states or conditions of a person or thing. It may reflect the state of an object or person described at a particular moment in time, for example: **nervioso, frío** *(cold)*, **cansado, enfermo. Estar** is also used with adjectives that express the result of a previous action, for example: **sorprendido** *(surprised)*, **roto** *(broken)*.
3. Both **ser** and **estar** can be used with many of the same adjectives; however, because of the nature of these verbs, the meanings will vary. Note the following examples:

Adjective	*Ser*	*Estar*
triste	La novela **es triste.**	Pablo **está triste.**
	The novel ***is sad.***	*Pablo* ***is (feeling) sad.***
guapo	Julio **es guapo.**	Julio **está guapo** hoy.
	Julio ***is handsome.***	*Julio* ***looks handsome today.***
aburrido	El programa **es aburrido.**	Yo **estoy aburrido.**
	The program ***is boring.***	***I'm bored.***
listo	La niña **es lista.**	La niña **está lista** para la clase.
	The girl ***is intelligent.***	*The girl* ***is ready*** *for class.*
rico	El doctor Moreno **es rico.**	El chocolate **está rico.**
	Doctor Moreno ***is rich (wealthy).***	*The chocolate* ***is delicious.***

The use of *hay*

Hay is an irregular form derived from the verb **haber. Haber** is mainly an auxiliary verb and means *to have,* in the sense of to have done something. **Hay,** however, does not vary in form and means ***there is*** as well as ***there are.*** Do not confuse this verb with either **ser** or **estar.** Compare the following forms.

hay: **there** is	es:	**it**, **he**, **she**, **you**	is/are	está	**it**, **he**, **she**, **you**	is/are
hay: **there** are	son:	**they**, **you**	are	están:	**they**, **you**	are

Hay un estudiante en la clase.	***There is*** *one student in class.*
Un estudiante **está** en la clase.	*One student* ***is*** *in class.*
Hay una clase de español a la una.	***There is*** *a Spanish class at one o'clock.*
Es una clase de español.	***It is*** *a Spanish class.*

Practiquemos

A Look at the following ads and headlines and tell why **ser, estar,** or **hay** is used.

1. **ESTAMOS UNIDOS**

2. Todos somos víctimas de las drogas

3. ***En Nicaragua hay realmente un conflicto***

4. **Si aquí está su banco ...**

5. Así soy yo

6. ¡Selena Está Aquí!

7. **¡Es un Vídeo!** **¡Es un Televisor!**

8. SÓLO HAY UNA FORMA DE LLEGAR A TIEMPO

B **Conteste, por favor.** Listen to the interrogative cues that your instructor gives you, and answer using **ser** or **estar.**

MODELO Profesor(a): ¿Pablo? ¿mexicano?
Estudiante: **Sí, Pablo es mexicano.**

C **¿Cuántas posibilidades?** Choose all of the possible answers for each sentence. Explain why certain answers are not correct.

1. El decano está...
   a. en su oficina.
   b. muy enfermo.
   c. con nosotros.
   d. profesor de arte también.

2. Somos...
   a. contentos ahora.
   b. muy inteligentes.
   c. españoles.
   d. en España.

3. Es…
   a. la una.
   b. tarde.
   c. fantástico.
   d. de metal.
4. Hay…
   a. muchas personas.
   b. un chico aquí.
   c. una fiesta en clase.
   d. poco dinero.
5. Antonio está…
   a. muy bien.
   b. aburrido.
   c. profesor.
   d. republicano.
6. El libro está…
   a. en la biblioteca.
   b. de Juan.
   c. fascinante.
   d. debajo de la mesa.
7. Tú eres…
   a. fantástico.
   b. trabajador.
   c. guapo.
   d. aplicado.
8. Son…
   a. detrás de él.
   b. las tres y media.
   c. con María.
   d. mexicanos.

D **Para terminar.** Finish each question in an original way. A classmate will answer your question.

MODELO ¿Qué hay… ?
Estudiante 1: ¿Qué hay en la biblioteca?
Estudiante 2: **Hay libros en la biblioteca.**

1. ¿Quién es… ?
2. ¿Qué es… ?
3. ¿Cómo es… ?
4. ¿Cómo está… ?
5. ¿Dónde está… ?
6. ¿Dónde es… ?
7. ¿Cuántos… hay… ?
8. ¿De quién es… ?

E **Lección de geografía.** You and a classmate are preparing for a trip to Spain during school break. You will read the partially correct list of facts about Spain's geography, and your partner will correct your errors (with complete sentences) by consulting the map in *Gaceta 1*, page 123. Choose the correct verb.

1. Alicante (es/está) muy cerca de Portugal.
2. Toledo (es/está) en la frontera *(border)* con Francia.
3. (Hay/Son) tres ciudades principales en el mar Mediterráneo.
4. Barcelona (es/está) la ciudad más grande de España.
5. Granada y Málaga (están/son) ciudades céntricas.

Barcelona, España

The Contractions *al* and *del*

In Spanish there are only two contractions: **al** and **del.**

a + el = al   de + el = del

1. The preposition **a** combines with the definite article **el** to form **al.**

   Vamos **al (a + el)** centro estudiantil.   *We're going to the student center.*

2. The preposition **de** combines with the definite article **el** to form **del.**

   Aquí está el lápiz **del (de + el)** profesor.   *Here's the professor's pencil.*

¡AVISO! No other definite articles **(la, las, los)** combine with **a** or with **de** to form contractions.

Vamos	a la residencia. a las clases. a los conciertos.	Aquí está el lápiz	de la profesora. de las profesoras. de los profesores.

Practiquemos

A **Todos hablan.** Answer the questions with complete sentences using the cues given. Follow the model.

MODELO ¿De qué habla el presidente? (la situación económica)
El presidente habla de la situación económica.

1. ¿De qué hablan Graciela y Rosita? (los muchachos)
2. ¿De qué habla el consejero? (el problema de Juan)
3. ¿De qué hablas tú? (la fiesta)
4. ¿De qué hablan Rita y el profesor? (las notas)
5. ¿De qué hablan Uds.? (el examen)

B **Preguntas y respuestas.** Fill in the blanks with: **al, a la, a los, a las, del, de la, de los,** or **de las.**

1. ¿Vas ______ gimnasio? No, voy ______ residencia ahora.
2. ¿Hablamos ______ fiesta, Bárbara? No, hablamos ______ notas.
3. ¿Los papeles son ______ maestro? No, son ______ estudiantes mexicanas.
4. ¿Vamos a comer antes ______ concierto? No, vamos a comer después ______ concierto. Vamos a comer ______ 11:00 ______ noche.
5. ¿Llegan ellos ______ recinto en taxi? No, pero llegan ______ colegios en taxi.
6. ¿Está Miguel delante ______ edificio? No, está detrás ______ cafetería.

Spend more time with Mariana and her friends while you review grammar and expand your cultural horizons.
See the **Así es Mariana** exercise in your workbook for this lesson.

En resumen

A **La historia del arte español.** The following exercise is an excerpt from a lecture on Spanish contemporary art. Fill in the blanks with the correct form of the verb in parentheses in the present tense. If there are two words, choose the most appropriate.

Pablo Ruiz Picasso (1891–1973) (es, está) el representante máximo (del, de la) "cubismo" y (el, la) artista más influyente del siglo *(century)* XX. En la pintura *(painting)* (usar) ______ las técnicas de «collage», y en la escultura *(sculpture)* (utilizar) ______ la fantasía para (transformar) ______ objetos reales en estructuras nuevas. En la obra *(work)* de Picasso (son, hay) varios períodos: «Azul», «Rosa», «Cubista» y «Clasicista», por ejemplo. Una obra (muy, mucho) famosa es *(La, El) destrucción de Guernica*, pintura que (representar) ______ el horror de la Guerra *(War)* Civil (español, española).

Joan Miró (1893–1983) y Salvador Dalí (1904–1989) (son, están) surrealistas por excelencia. La obra de ambos *(both)* (consistir) ______ en elementos de fantasía que (combinar) ______ con el realismo. En temperamento y estilo de vida *(lifestyle)* de Miró y Dalí (ser) ______ muy diferentes. Miró (llevar) ______ una vida convencional y (práctico, práctica), mientras *(while)* Dalí (vivir) ______ en un ambiente *(atmosphere)* de melancolía y horror. *La persistencia de la memoria* de Dalí es una de las obras más famosas del mundo *(world)*.

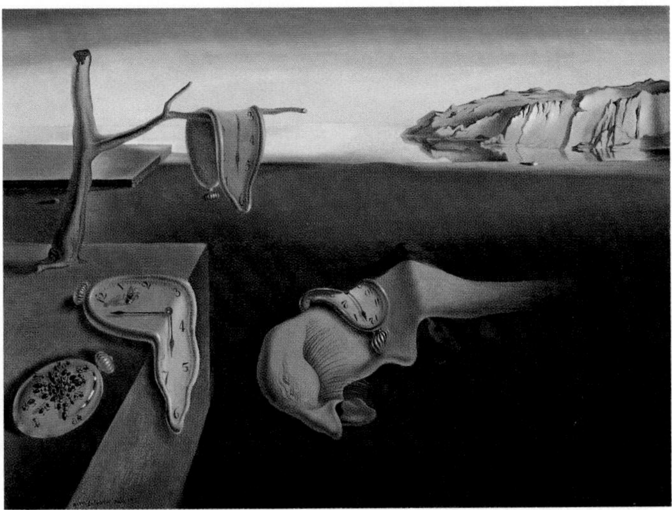

La persistencia de la memoria —Salvador Dalí

Ahora, conteste las preguntas.

1. ¿Qué objetos hay en el cuadro *(painting)*? ¿Qué observaciones o interpretaciones puede hacer Ud.?
2. ¿Qué piensa Ud. del arte surrealista? Explique. *(Explain)*.

B Ideales. Describe the ideal . . . Follow the model.

MODELO universidad
La universidad ideal es muy pequeña. Hay profesores muy simpáticos.
El recinto es bonito y en la residencia hay cuartos muy grandes.

1. compañero(a) de cuarto
2. profesor(a)
3. clase
4. amigo(a)

C ¿Cómo somos? How do you see yourself? How do others see you? Describe your physical appearance and your character or personality. Have a classmate describe you. Now compare the descriptions.

D Los anuncios *(The ads)*. Complete the following ads with your own descriptive words.

1.

comida *food*

2.

El nuevo coche deportivo
un coche muy _____ y _____.

coche *car*

E Mañana hay una prueba. Translate the following dialogue to Spanish.

Blas: Antonio, how do you say, *I'm worried* in French?
Antonio: I don't know. Why? Is there a quiz tomorrow?
Blas: Yes, and Professor Benet's quizzes are not easy! We ought to study all night.
Antonio: Why don't you review Lesson 2? I think I'm going to call Paulette Broussard.
Blas: Yes . . . she's the French student in sociology class.

F **Composición.** Write a brief composition using the verbs **ser, estar,** and the expression **hay** to describe one of the following things.

1. la residencia **3.** los compañeros de clase
2. Ud. **4.** el día de hoy

Escuchemos

A **¿Es lógico?** You will hear a series of sentences. Indicate if they are logical or not logical by placing a check on the appropriate line.

MODELO El estudiante perezoso estudia mucho.

________ Es lógico ✓ No es lógico

1. ________ Es lógico ________ No es lógico
2. ________ Es lógico ________ No es lógico
3. ________ Es lógico ________ No es lógico
4. ________ Es lógico ________ No es lógico
5. ________ Es lógico ________ No es lógico
6. ________ Es lógico ________ No es lógico
7. ________ Es lógico ________ No es lógico
8. ________ Es lógico ________ No es lógico

B **Dictado *(Dictation)*.** You will hear a short narration about Spanish universities. Listen carefully to the entire selection. Listen again and write each sentence during the pauses.

You will then hear a series of statements related to the dictation. Indicate whether they are true **(cierto)** or false **(falso).** Correct the false statements and answer with complete sentences. Refer to your dictation.

Lección 3

Necesito trabajar

¡Tiene que encontrar algo para mí!

AVISO CULTURAL

How do you choose a career? In addition to your aptitude and preferences, an important factor to consider is the future demand for a profession. In many Hispanic countries, engineering, architecture, and medicine continue to attract large numbers. Computer literacy is required in all areas of the business world. As in the United States, students interested in attending law school are encouraged to consider the emerging fields of law related to information technology, and law as it relates to rights in outer space.

Preparativos

Review the vocabulary on pages 98–100 before viewing the video.

As you watch the video or read the dialogue, note the use of the verb **tener** *(to have)* in certain expressions that in English require the verb *to be*. For example, Luis Antonio says, **"Tengo hambre"** to express *"I am hungry"* and **"Tengo miedo"** to express *"I am afraid."* What does Mariana mean when she says in the video, **"Algunas veces tengo ganas de...¡gritar!"**? Also, pay attention to these verbs: **tiene** *(tener)*, **sueña** *(soñar)*, **prefiero** *(preferir)*, **quieren** *(querer)*, **empieza** *(empezar)*, **entiendo** *(entender)*, and **puede** *(poder)*. What do they all have in common? They are all stem-changing verbs, that is, verbs that have a diphthong **(ie)** or **(ue)** in the root. In this episode we learn that Luis Antonio dreams of **(sueña con)** being a sports writer. Alicia thinks **(piensa)** that journalism is boring. **¿Qué piensa Ud.? ¿Es una profesión aburrida o interesante?** They say that opposites attract. **¿Qué tienen en común** *(common)* **Alicia y Mariana? ¿Cuáles son las diferencias?**

Así es Mariana: El nuevo empleado

En el dormitorio° de Mariana, Alicia mira una foto de Luis Antonio con traje° y corbata.°

bedroom
suit and tie

Alicia: ¡Qué guapo es tu hombre de negocios!

Mariana: Sí... es muy guapo. Está en su entrevista ahora mismo.

Alicia: ¿Una entrevista?... ¿Con quién?

Mariana: Con la agente de empleos de la universidad.

Alicia: ¿Tiene interés en un empleo en particular?

Mariana: Siempre sueña con ser periodista de deportes.

Alicia: ¿Periodista? ¡Qué profesión más aburrida! ¡Pobre Luis! Prefiero no comentar, pero con poca experiencia... no va a ser muy fácil.

En la oficina de empleos.

Agente: Hay un puesto como cocinero en un restaurante.

Luis Antonio: ¿Cocinero? No sé. Siempre tengo hambre cuando estoy en un restaurante. Prefiero algo diferente.

Agente: Todos quieren mucho dinero y poco trabajo. ¡Ajá! ¡Perfecto! Vendedor de zapatos.° El salario comienza a cuarenta dólares por día.

shoes

Luis Antonio: Tampoco quiero ser vendedor. Tengo miedo de los clientes difíciles.

Agente: ¡No entiendo! Ud. viene aquí porque busca un empleo. Tengo dos puestos muy buenos, pero Ud. no quiere ninguno.

Luis Antonio: ¿No hay otro? Por favor, señora. ¡Tiene que encontrar algo para mí!

Es decir

A Fill in the blanks with the correct form of the verb **tener: tengo** or **tiene.**

1. ¿Luis ______ interés en algún empleo en particular?
2. Algunas veces yo ______ ganas de... ¡gritar!
3. Siempre ______ hambre cuando estoy en un restaurante.
4. Tampoco quiero ser vendedor. ______ miedo de los clientes difíciles.
5. Por favor, señora. ¡______ que encontrar algo para mí!
6. Yo ______ dos puestos muy buenos.

B In pairs, correct the following false statements.

1. Mariana y Alicia están en clase.
2. La entrevista de Luis Antonio es en una tienda.
3. La agente de empleos no tiene ningún puesto para él.
4. Luis Antonio no tiene interés en trabajar.
5. Alicia mira una foto de Octavio.

C In pairs, write a dialogue in which Luis Antonio rejects yet another job offer from the employment agent. Share your dialogue with the class.

Al ver el video

After viewing the video, complete each sentence with the appropriate answer(s).

1. Algunas veces hay tensión entre Mariana y Alicia porque Alicia...
   a. comenta cuando no debe.
   b. no escucha bien
   c. no habla con Mariana.

2. En la agencia de empleos...
   a. hay muchos clientes.
   b. Luis Antonio habla con tres agentes.
   c. Luis Antonio ve un anuncio para el puesto de periodista.

3. Cuando la agente habla sobre el puesto de cocinero, Luis Antonio...
   a. está muy contento. b. acepta el puesto. c. miente un poco.

4. Luis Antonio imagina que en el restaurante él tiene...
   a. mucho éxito *(success)*.
   b. una experiencia positiva.
   c. un pequeño accidente.

5. Luis Antonio no quiere el puesto de vendedor de zapatos porque no le gusta...
   a. el gerente. b. el salario. c. el olor *(odor)*.

Vocabulario

Verbos (e–ie)	
cerrar	*to close*
comenzar (empezar)	*to begin*
entender	*to understand*
mentir	*to lie*
negar	*to deny*
nevar	*to snow*
pensar	*to think; to intend*
perder	*to lose*
preferir	*to prefer*
querer	*to want; to love*
recomendar	*to recommend*

Verbos (o–ue)	
almorzar	*to have lunch*
contar (con)	*to count (on); to tell*
costar	*to cost*
devolver	*to return (something)*
dormir	*to sleep*
encontrar	*to find; to meet*
llover	*to rain*
morir	*to die*
mostrar	*to show*
poder	*to be able to; can*
recordar	*to remember*
soñar (con)	*to dream (about)*
volver	*to return (to a place)*

Otros verbos	
dejar	*to leave (behind); to quit*
ganar	*to earn; to win*
jugar (ue)	*to play*
tener	*to have*
venir	*to come*

Profesiones	***Professions***
el (la) abogado(a)	*lawyer*
el (la) arquitecto(a)	*architect*
el (la) artista	*artist*
el (la) científico(a)	*scientist*
el (la) contador(a)	*accountant*
el (la) enfermero(a)	*nurse*
el (la) farmacéutico(a)	*pharmacist*
el hombre (la mujer) de negocios	*businessman(woman)*
el (la) ingeniero(a)	*engineer*
el (la) juez	*judge*
el (la) médico(a)	*doctor*
el (la) periodista	*journalist*
el (la) programador(a)	*programmer*
el (la) sicólogo(a)	*psychologist*

Oficios	***Occupations***
el (la) camarero(a)	*waiter, waitress*
el (la) cocinero(a)	*cook, chef*
el (la) mecánico	*mechanic*
el (la) vendedor(a)	*salesperson*

Palabras relacionadas con el trabajo	***Words related to work***
la carrera	*career*
la cita	*appointment, date*
el (la) cliente	*client*
la compañía (empresa)	*company, firm*
el (la) empleado(a)	*employee*
el empleo (puesto)	*position, job*
la entrevista	*interview*
la gente	*people*
el (la) gerente	*manager*
el (la) jefe(a)	*boss*
el (la) obrero(a) (trabajador/a)	*worker*
el periódico	*newspaper*
el salario (sueldo)	*salary*
la tienda	*store*

Palabras y expresiones útiles

algo	*something*
alguien	*someone*
mismo	*same*
nada	*nothing*
nadie	*no one*
nuevo	*new*
tampoco	*neither, either*

Vocabulario adicional

la agencia de empleos	*employment agency*
el almacén	*department store*
el anuncio	*advertisement*
el beneficio	*benefit*
el (la) candidato(a)	*candidate*
el currículum (vitae)	*resume*
la experiencia	*experience*
interesante	*interesting*
el (la) músico(a)	*musician*
el (la) secretario(a)	*secretary*
el (la) siquiatra	*psychiatrist*
solicitar	*to apply for*
la solicitud	*application*
tomar una decisión	*to make a decision*
el trabajo de medio tiempo (de tiempo completo)	*part-time (full-time) work*

Repasemos el vocabulario

A **Sinónimos y antónimos.** Look on the second line for the synonym of the following words.

sueldo	**empresa**	**trabajador**	**carrera**	**puesto**
profesión	salario	compañía	empleo	obrero

Now look on the second line for the antonym of the following words.

perder	**comenzar**	**cerrar**	**alguien**	**tampoco**	**algo**
nadie	encontrar	también	nada	terminar	abrir

B **¿Cuál no pertenece?** *(Which doesn't belong?)* Indicate which word does not belong and explain.

1. entrevista	profesión	oficio	carrera
2. obrero	jefe	trabajador	empleado
3. médico	farmacéutico	científico	periodista
4. nadie	también	nada	tampoco

C **¿Quién trabaja aquí?** Who works in the following places? There may be more than one possible answer.

Restaurante
La Tapatía

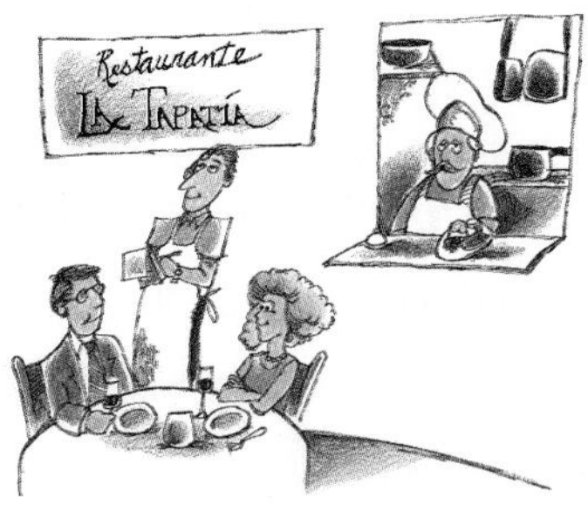

MODELO El cocinero trabaja en el restaurante.
También el camarero trabaja en el restaurante.

1.

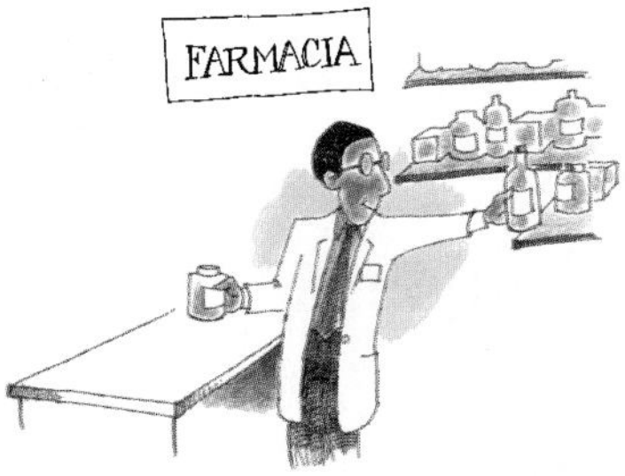
FARMACIA

2.

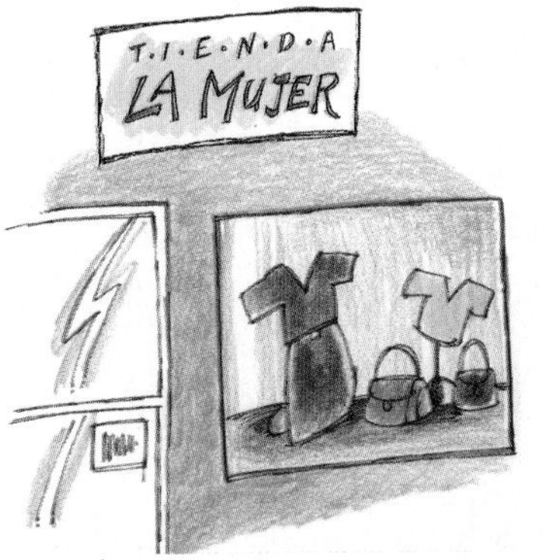
T·I·E·N·D·A
LA MUJER

3.

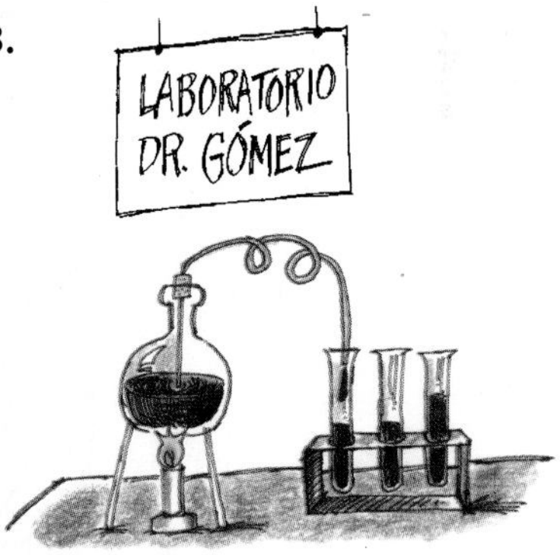
LABORATORIO
DR. GÓMEZ

4.

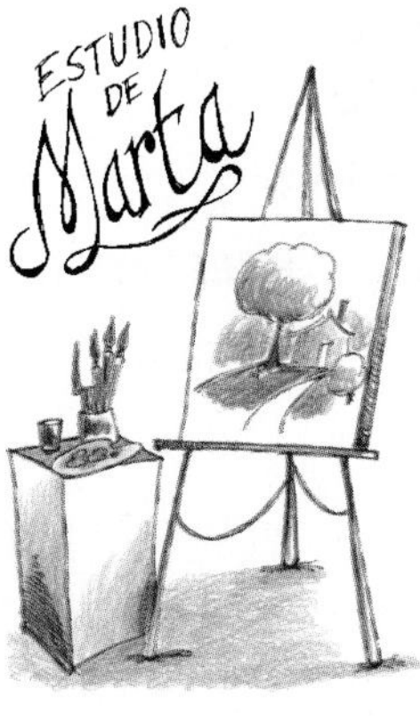
ESTUDIO
DE
Marta

5.

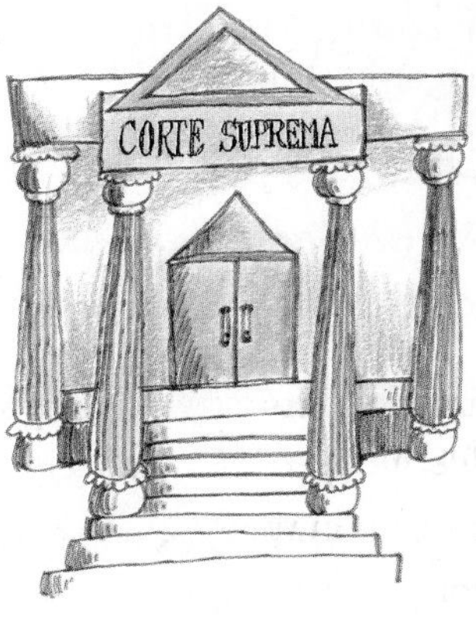
CORTE SUPREMA

6.

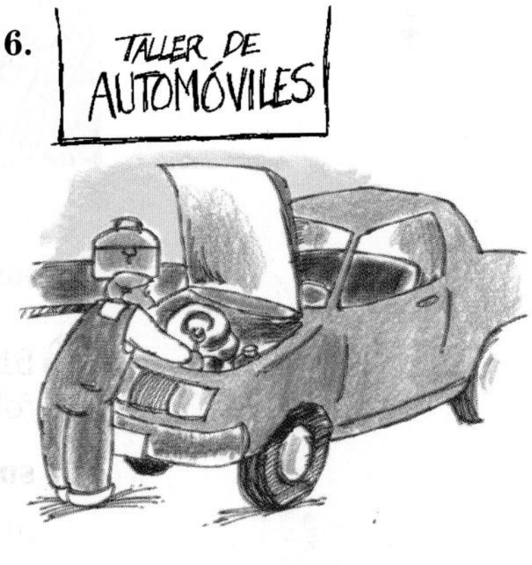
TALLER DE
AUTOMÓVILES

7.

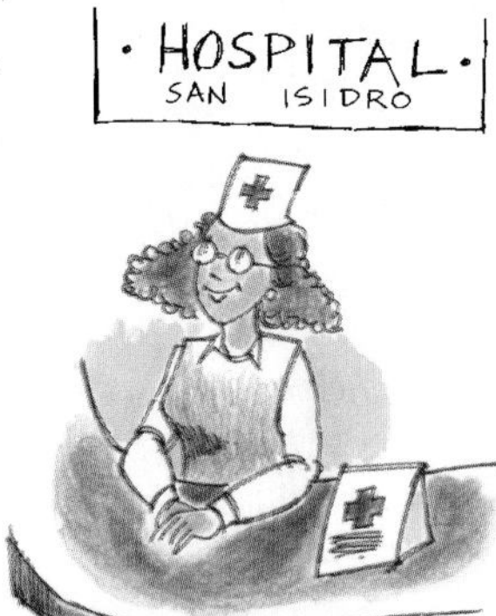
· HOSPITAL ·
SAN ISIDRO

8.

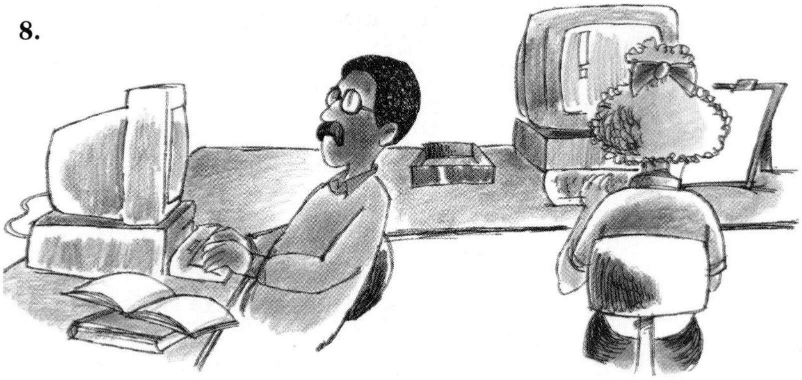

D **Preparativos.** Listen to your instructor read the activities of the following people as they prepare for their future. Complete each sentence with the appropriate profession.

MODELO Profesor(a): Inés lee libros sobre Dalí, Picasso y Miró.
Estudiante: **Inés quiere ser artista.**

1. Rosamelia... **3.** Cristóbal y Paula... **5.** Sebastián y Carlos...
2. Tomás... **4.** Celia y yo... **6.** Tú...

E **¿Qué profesiones... ?** Ask three classmates to name two professions that fit each of the following criteria. Share your results.

¿Cuáles son dos profesiones que...

1. pagan mucho dinero? ¿poco dinero?

2. necesitan muchos años de estudio?

3. son interesantes?

4. ofrecen muchos beneficios *(benefits)*? ¿pocos?

5. no necesitan un título *(degree)* universitario?

The Present Tense of *e* > *ie* Stem-changing Verbs

Forma

Certain verbs are called stem-changing because when stressed, the stem vowel **e** changes to **ie.** Since the stress does not fall on the stem in the first- and second-person plural forms **(nosotros** and **vosotros),** there is no stem change. The endings are regular in all forms.

EMPEZAR ***(to begin)***		**QUERER** ***(to want)***		**PREFERIR** ***(to prefer)***	
emp**ie**zo	empezamos	qu**ie**ro	queremos	pref**ie**ro	preferimos
emp**ie**zas	empezáis	qu**ie**res	queréis	pref**ie**res	preferís
emp**ie**za	emp**ie**zan	qu**ie**re	qu**ie**ren	pref**ie**re	pref**ie**ren

Some common **e** > **ie** stem-changing verbs are:

cerrar	*to close*	negar	*to deny*
comenzar (a)	*to begin (to)*	nevar	*to snow*
entender	*to understand*	pensar	*to think, to intend*
mentir	*to lie*	perder	*to lose*

¿Qué **quiere** la jefa? — *What does the boss **want**?*

Prefiere ver las solicitudes ahora. — *She **prefers** to see the applications now.*

¿A qué hora **empiezan** las entrevistas? — *At what time do the interviews **begin**?*

Función

1. The verbs **comenzar** and **empezar** take the preposition **a** before an infinitive.

Empieza **a** trabajar.	*He begins to work.*
Empieza el trabajo.	*He begins the work.*

2. The verb **pensar** followed by an infinitive means *to intend* or *plan* to do something. **Pensar** followed by **de** means *to think of* in the sense of to have an opinion about something or someone. **Pensar** followed by **en** means *to think of* or *about* in the sense of to have in mind.

Pienso ir a la oficina temprano.	***I plan** to go to the office early.*
¿Qué **piensas de** la compañía?	*What do you **think** of the company?*
Sólo **piensa en** el fin de semana.	*He only **thinks about** the weekend.*

3. The verb **nevar** is conjugated in the third-person singular only. The subject *it* is not expressed.

Nieva mucho en el norte de España.	***It snows** a lot in northern Spain.*

Practiquemos

A **¿Cuál no corresponde?** Underline the verb that does not logically or grammatically complete each sentence.

1. ...almorzar en la cafetería.
   a. Prefiero c. Pienso
   b. Empiezo d. Quiero
2. ¿Quién... la tarea?
   a. cierra c. comienza
   b. entiende d. empieza
3. No... el problema.
   a. niego c. entiendo
   b. pienso en d. miento
4. El menú es excelente. ¿Qué...
   a. quieres? c. pierdes?
   b. recomiendas? d. prefieres?

B **¿Qué piensas hacer en el futuro?** Fill in the blanks with the correct form of the verb **pensar.**

Susana ______ estudiar para ser arquitecta porque ella es muy creativa. Juan y Jorge ______ ser médicos porque quieren curar el cáncer. Paco y yo ______ estudiar diplomacia porque estamos interesados en la política y ya *(already)* hablamos varios idiomas. Víctor ______ trabajar con las computadoras porque es una profesión con muchas oportunidades. Y tú, ¿qué ______ hacer en el futuro?

C **Preguntas personales.** Interview a classmate to find out the following personal information. Use the **tú** form of the verb to form your questions.

1. ¿En qué situaciones...
   a. pierde la paciencia?
   b. miente?
   c. quiere dejar su trabajo?

2. ¿Qué...
   a. piensa del (de la) profesor(a) de español?
   b. quiere hacer después de clase?
   c. no entiende en la clase de español?

3. ¿A qué hora...
   a. empieza a estudiar los domingos?
   b. piensa ir a la biblioteca?
   c. prefiere ir a la cafetería?

The Present Tense of *o* > *ue* Stem-changing Verbs

Forma

Certain verbs change the stem vowel from **o** > **ue** in the present tense when the stem vowel is stressed. As with the **e** > **ie** stem-changing verbs, the **nosotros** and **vosotros** forms do not have this change, and the endings are regular in all forms.

ALMORZAR *(to eat lunch)*		**VOLVER** *(to return)*		**DORMIR** *(to sleep)*	
alm**ue**rzo	almorzamos	v**ue**lvo	volvemos	d**ue**rmo	dormimos
alm**ue**rzas	almorzáis	v**ue**lves	volvéis	d**ue**rmes	dormís
alm**ue**rza	alm**ue**rzan	v**ue**lve	v**ue**lven	d**ue**rme	d**ue**rmen

Some common **o** > **ue** stem-changing verbs are:

contar	*to count; to tell*	morir	*to die*
contar con	*to count on*	mostrar	*to show*
costar	*to cost*	poder	*to be able, can*
devolver	*to return (something)*	recordar	*to remember*
encontrar	*to find; to meet*	soñar (con)	*to dream (about)*
llover	*to rain*		

¿A qué hora **almuerzas?** — *What time do you **eat lunch?***

Puedo almorzar a la una si el jefe **vuelve.** — ***I can** eat lunch at one o'clock, if the boss **returns.***

Función

1. The verb **costar** is generally used in the third-person singular and plural forms only.

¿Cuánto **cuesta** la computadora nueva?	*How much does the new computer **cost?***
Todas las computadoras **cuestan** mucho.	*All of the computers **cost** a lot.*

2. The verb **llover**, like the verb **nevar**, is used in the third-person singular form only. The subject *it* is not expressed.

Llueve y por eso no podemos jugar al fútbol.	***It's raining** and therefore we can't play soccer.*

3. **Jugar** *(to play)* is the only verb in Spanish that changes its stem vowel **u** > **ue.** It is often followed by the preposition **a** before a game or a sport.

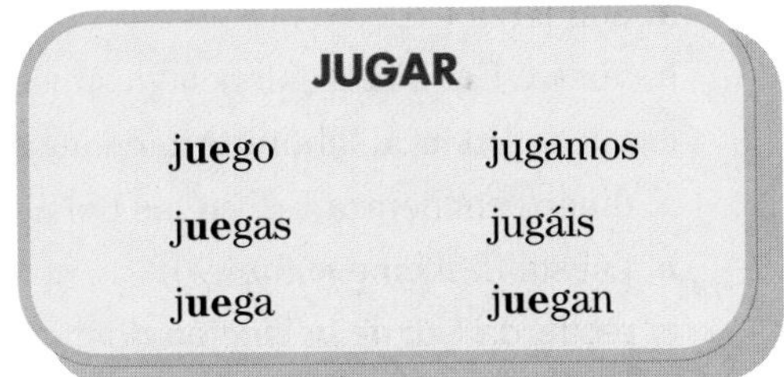

JUGAR	
juego	jugamos
juegas	jugáis
juega	**jue**gan

Laura **juega al** tenis con el jefe a menudo.	*Laura **plays** tennis with the boss often.*

Practiquemos

A **¿Cuál no corresponde?** Underline the verb that does not logically or grammatically complete each sentence.

1. Los estudiantes... los libros.
   a. pueden b. muestran c. recuerdan d. devuelven
2. Todos... a las doce.
   a. juegan b. almuerzan c. cuestan d. vuelven
3. ...ir al concierto de Los Gipsy Kings.
   a. Soñamos con b. Volvemos c. Podemos d. Contamos con
4. Yo nunca... el dinero.
   a. devuelvo b. vuelvo c. encuentro d. cuento

B **¿A qué hora vuelven del trabajo?** Fill in the blanks with the correct form of the verb **volver.**

Antonio ______ a las cinco porque la oficina cierra temprano. Marta y Paco ______ a eso de las nueve porque son médicos y trabajan muchas horas. Nosotros ______ a la una porque el trabajo es de medio tiempo. Sandra ______ a las ocho porque empieza a trabajar muy tarde en la mañana. Y tú, ¿a qué hora ______ del trabajo?

C **Plurales.** Complete the second sentence with the **nosotros** form of the underlined verb in the first sentence.

1. ¿Almuerzan Uds. con el presidente de la compañía? No, pero ______ con el jefe del departamento.
2. ¿Recuerdan Uds. la dirección del Sr. Robles? No, pero ______ el número de teléfono.
3. ¿Vuelven Uds. a la hora de comer? No, pero ______ a eso de las ocho.
4. ¿Duermen Uds. ocho horas cada *(each)* noche? No, pero ______ mucho los fines de semana.
5. ¿Pueden Uds. jugar al golf? No, pero ______ jugar al béisbol.

D **Preguntas personales.** Answer the following questions. Then interview a classmate using the **tú** form of the verbs.

1. ¿A qué hora... **a.** almuerza Ud.?
   b. vuelve Ud. a la residencia después de clase?
   c. puede Ud. ir al laboratorio de lenguas?
2. ¿Cuánto... **a.** dinero encuentra Ud. en los bolsillos *(pockets)?*
   b. cuesta ir al cine *(movies)?*
   c. recuerda Ud. de la lección dos?
3. ¿Con quién... **a.** cuenta Ud. para ayuda económica?
   b. sueña Ud.?
   c. juega Ud. al tenis?

E **¡El fin de semana!** In pairs, ask a classmate... **¿Con qué frecuencia haces las actividades?** *(How often do you do the activities?)* Use the correct form of the verb in parentheses and use complete sentences for the questions and the answers.

Possible answers are: **siempre** **nunca** **a veces** *(at times)*

1. (Dormir) ______ ocho horas.
2. (Almorzar) ______ en un restaurante.
3. (Volver) ______ a casa.
4. (Soñar) ______ con monstruos *(monsters)*.
5. (Jugar) ______ al básquetbol.
6. (Encontrar) ______ dinero en los bolsillos.

The Verbs *Tener* and *Venir*

The verbs **tener** *(to have)* and **venir** *(to come)* follow the pattern of change of other **e > ie** stem-changing verbs. Note, however, that the **yo** form is irregular. It ends in **-go.**

TENER ***(to have)***		**VENIR** ***(to come)***	
ten**go**	tenemos	ven**go**	venimos
t**ie**nes	tenéis	v**ie**nes	venís
t**ie**ne	t**ie**nen	v**ie**ne	v**ie**nen

Practiquemos

A **No, pero...** Your friends don't have exactly what you're asking for. Ask classmates for the following items. They will answer negatively, substituting the items they do have according to the cues.

MODELO lápiz/bolígrafo
Estudiante 1: ¿Tienes un lápiz?
Estudiante 2: **No, pero tengo un bolígrafo.**

1. libro de español/diccionario
2. computadora/máquina de escribir
3. 20 dólares/15 dólares
4. compañero(a) de cuarto simpático(a)/compañero(a) de cuarto inteligente
5. trabajo de medio tiempo/trabajo de tiempo completo

B **¿Por qué vienen?** Combine the words and phrases below to form sentences using the verbs **tener** and **venir.** Follow the model and supply any missing words.

MODELO Luisa y Carlos/universidad/clase
Luisa y Carlos vienen a la universidad porque tienen una clase.

1. nosotros/fiesta/discos compactos
2. Anita y Paco/España/amigos aquí
3. el Sr. García[1]/hospital/cita con el médico
4. yo/biblioteca/libros para devolver
5. Ud./oficina/entrevista con el gerente
6. Roberto y yo/almacén/cosas que comprar

[1]Note the use of the definite article **el** with Sr. García. The definite article is used with titles such as **señor(a), señorita, doctor(a), profesor(a),** and so forth when speaking about them. When they are addressed directly, the article is omitted. **El Sr. García está enfermo. Hola, Sr. García.**

Tener Expressions

Forma y función

1. Many idiomatic expressions in Spanish consist of the verb **tener** plus certain nouns. The English equivalent of these expressions is formed by the verb *to be* plus certain adjectives (*I am hungry, I am tired, I am hot,* and so forth).

La abuelita tiene 80 años y María tiene 20 años.

El Sr. Sánchez tiene calor pero la Sra Sánchez tiene frío.

Alberto tiene mucha hambre y Pedro tiene mucha sed.

Pablito tiene miedo.

Tienes sueño, Ana, ¿verdad?

Las chicas tienen prisa.

2. Some common **tener** expressions are:

tener... años	*to be . . . years old*
tener calor	*to be hot*
tener celos	*to be jealous*
tener cuidado	*to be careful*
tener éxito	*to be successful*
tener frío	*to be cold*
tener ganas de (+ *infinitive*)	*to feel like (doing something)*
tener hambre	*to be hungry*
tener miedo (de)	*to be afraid (of)*
tener prisa	*to be in a hurry*
tener que (+ *infinitive*)	*to have to (do something)*
(no) tener razón	*to be right (wrong)*
tener sed	*to be thirsty*
tener sueño	*to be sleepy*
tener suerte	*to be lucky*
tener vergüenza	*to be ashamed*

¿Cuántos **años tiene** Ud.? — *How **old are** you?*
Tengo 20 **años.** — ***I'm** twenty **years old.***
No tenemos frío. Tenemos calor. — ***We're not cold. We're hot.***
No debes **tener celos** de ella. — *You shouldn't **be jealous** of her.*

3. The adjectives **mucho** and **poco** are used to modify these nouns. They agree in number and gender with the nouns they modify.

No tengo **mucha** sed. — *I'm not **very** thirsty.*
Tenemos **pocas** ganas de ir al trabajo hoy. — *We have **little desire** to go to work today.*

4. **Tener que** + *infinitive* means to have to do something.

No puedo ir al gimnasio porque **tengo que** estudiar. — *I can't go to the gym because **I have to** study.*

Practiquemos

A **¿Quién tiene ganas de... ?** Look at the drawings on page 108 and tell who feels like doing the following activities, and why.

MODELO ¿Quién tiene ganas de buscar a mamá?
Pablito tiene ganas de buscar a mamá porque tiene miedo.

¿Quién tiene ganas de...

1. comer un sandwich?
2. celebrar?
3. buscar un suéter?
4. ir rápido?
5. dormir?
6. tomar una limonada fría?

B **¿Qué tienen?** Listen carefully as your instructor reads a series of activities. Write the number of the activities next to the corresponding **tener** expression.

a. ______ Tiene veinte años.
b. ______ Tengo mucha hambre.
c. ______ Tenemos prisa.
d. ______ Tengo frío.
e. ______ Tengo mucha suerte.
f. ______ Tienes razón, hijo *(son)*.
g. ______ Tenemos sed.
h. ______ Tengo sueño.
i. ______ Tiene miedo.

C **Encarna.** To solve all of your problems related to work, your love-life, or finances, read Encarna's newspaper column. Fill in the blanks with the correct form of one of the following expressions. You can use the verb **tener** more than once.

tener	tener razón
tener celos	tener miedo
tener éxito	tener cuidado
tener ganas	tener que

Querida Encarna...

Querida (*Dear*) Encarna,
______24 años de edad y soy programadora para una compañía internacional. ______ un problema en mi trabajo. Es mi jefa, Isabel. Ella es muy antipática y por eso yo no ________ de ir a la oficina. No entiendo. Soy responsable, inteligente y muy aplicada. El trabajo es interesante y hay posibilidades de ascenso. Quiero ________ en mi trabajo. ¿Qué debo hacer?

María del Carmen

Querida María,
Sí , Ud. ________. Es un problema. Es evidente que Isabel ________ de Ud. Es importante ________. Ella ________ de perder su autoridad en la oficina. Ud. ________ trabajar mucho pero Ud. debe recordar que Isabel ________ problemas también. No es fácil para ella.

Encarna

D Secretos. Complete the following sentences in an original way.

1. Tengo celos de... porque...
2. Tengo miedo de...
3. Los fines de semana el (la) profesor(a) tiene ganas de...
4. Yo tengo que... pero no quiero porque...
5. Nunca tengo... cuando...
6. Todos los estudiantes en la clase de español tienen...

Possessive Adjectives

Forma

Possessive Adjectives

mi, mis	*my*	nuestro (-a, -os, -as)	*our*
tu, tus	*your*	vuestro (-a, -os, -as)	*your*
su, sus	*your, his, her*	su, sus	*your, their*

Función

1. Unstressed possessive adjectives are placed before the nouns they modify. The endings of the adjectives **mi**, **tu,** and **su** agree in number with the items possessed, not with the possessor. **Nuestro** and **vuestro** agree with the items possessed in both number and gender.

¿Es ella **tu** jefa, Amalia?	*Is she **your** boss, Amalia?*
Sí, es **mi** jefa.	*Yes, she's **my** boss.*
¿Dónde están **nuestras** solicitudes?	*Where are **our** applications?*
Sus solicitudes están en **mi** escritorio.	***Your** applications are on **my** desk.*

2. Because **su** and **sus** mean many different things, the following constructions can be used for clarification.

su empleado	el empleado de él el empleado de ella el empleado de Ud. el empleado de ellos el empleado de ellas el empleado de Uds.
sus empleados	los empleados de él los empleados de ella los empleados de Ud. los empleados de ellos los empleados de ellas los empleados de Uds.

Su jefe es boliviano.
El jefe de ella es boliviano. } ***Her*** *boss is Bolivian.*

3. To ask to whom something belongs, use the expressions **¿De quién?** or **¿De quiénes**?

¿**De quién** son los periódicos?	***Whose*** *newspapers are they?*
Son **mis** periódicos.	*They're* ***my*** *newspapers.*
¿De quiénes es el coche?	***Whose*** *car is it?*
Es **nuestro** coche.	*It's* ***our*** *car.*

Practiquemos

A **¿Qué usan?** With what do the following people work?

el secretario/máquina de escribir
El secretario trabaja con su máquina de escribir.

1. el contador/números
2. el jefe/secretario
3. tú/arquitecto
4. los estudiantes/libros
5. yo/amigos
6. Juan Carlos y yo/compañero de cuarto
7. la gerente/empleados
8. nosotras/computadora

B **Diferencias.** Finish the sentence using the appropriate possessive adjective and the correct form of the verb.

Yo uso mi computadora pero Juan... (máquina de escribir)
Yo uso mi computadora pero Juan usa su máquina de escribir.

1. Rosa viene con sus amigos pero yo... (compañera de cuarto)
2. Arturo prefiere estar en su laboratorio pero tú... (oficina)
3. Ud. y José tienen su clase hoy pero nosotros... (cita)
4. El abogado almuerza con su cliente hoy pero la juez... (secretarias)
5. Tú cuentas con tu artista pero yo... (arquitectos)

C **Clarificaciones.** Iliana has missed the context of the following comments. Have a classmate play the role of Iliana. Look at the drawings and clarify the meaning of **su** in each case. The cues (checks) will tell you how to answer.

MODELO Su trabajo es fascinante.
Iliana: ¿Cuál? ¿El trabajo de él?
Ud: **No, el trabajo de ellas.**

1. 2.

Su pelota° es nueva. **Sus amigos son interesantes.**

°ball

3.

Su compañía es muy grande.

4.

Su compañero es presidente.

Indefinite and Negative Expressions

Forma

Indefinite and Negative Expressions

Affirmative		**Negative**	
algo	*something, anything*	nada	*nothing*
alguien	*someone, anyone*	nadie	*no one, nobody*
algún (alguno, a, os, as)	*some, any*	ningún (ninguno, a, os, as)	*none*
o... o	*either, or*	ni... ni	*neither, nor*
siempre	*always*	nunca/jamás	*never*
también	*also*	tampoco	*neither*

Función

1. You already know how to negate a sentence by placing the word **no** before the verb.

   Yo **no trabajo** con el Sr. Peña. — *I **don't work** with Mr. Peña.*

2. The negative words **nada, nadie, nunca, jamás,** and **tampoco** can either precede or follow the verb. The word **no** precedes the verb when another negative word follows the verb. In this case, the negative expression can always follow the verb directly and can at times be placed at the end of the sentence. When another negative word precedes the verb, the word **no** is not used.

   No trabajo **nunca** los fines de semana.
   No trabajo los fines de semana **nunca.**
   Nunca trabajo los fines de semana.
   } *I **never** work on weekends.*

   No viene **nadie** a la oficina hoy.
   Nadie viene a la oficina hoy.
   } ***Nobody** is coming to the office today.*

3. The adjectives **alguno** and **ninguno** drop the final **-o** before masculine singular nouns just as **uno** shortens to **un,** and **bueno** to **buen.** Note that the plural forms of **ninguno (ningunos** and **ningunas)** are rarely used.

   ¿Tienes algunas entrevistas hoy? — *Do you have any interviews today?*
   No, no tengo **ninguna.** — *No, I don't have **any.***

4. Note that the word **no** is repeated in some sentences to answer a question to which **no** is the appropriate response.

   ¿Vas al almacén con nosotros? — *Are you coming to the department store with us?*
   No, no voy al almacén con Uds. — ***No,** I'm **not** going to the department store with you.*

Practiquemos

A **Problemas en la oficina.** José complains to his wife, Ana, about his office problems. She shows him that he is wrong to worry. Play the role of Ana and change José's statements to the negative in two different ways if possible. Follow the model.

José: Mi secretaria siempre llega tarde.
Ana: **Tu secretaria nunca llega tarde.**
Tu secretaria no llega tarde nunca.

1. Pablo siempre duerme en la oficina.
2. Pablo almuerza en la oficina también.
3. Algunas secretarias beben café todo el día.
4. Alguien usa mi computadora.

B **¿Tienes algunos?** Sara always runs out of supplies. Her co-workers are tired of giving her theirs. Answer Sara's questions negatively. Remember that plural forms **ningunos(as)** will not be needed here.

MODELO
Sara: ¿Tienes algunos lápices?
Ud.: **No, no tengo ningún lápiz.**

1. ¿Tienes algunos cuadernos?
2. ¿Tienes algunos bolígrafos?
3. ¿Tienes algunas tizas?
4. ¿Tienes algunos cassettes?

C **No tengo interés.** Celia simply does not want a relationship with Rodolfo outside the office. With a partner, play the parts of Rodolfo and Celia, as he asks her the following questions. She always answers in the negative.

Rodolfo: ¿Siempre almuerzas a la una?
Celia: **No, nunca almuerzo a la una.**

1. ¿Juegas al tenis con alguien?
2. ¿Vas mucho al teatro?
3. ¿Quieres algo para beber?
4. ¿Siempre tomas el autobús por la mañana?
5. ¿Vas a algunas fiestas?
6. ¿Quieres ir a bailar o ir a un concierto?

D **Respuestas negativas.** Answer the following questions based on the illustrations.

1.

¿Qué hay en sus bolsillos *(pockets)*?

2.

¿Hay alguien en la oficina?

3. **4.**

¿Cuándo estudia Pedro?

Raúl no asiste a clase hoy, ¿y Marta?

5. **6.**

¿Hay algunos clientes en la tienda?

¿Llueve a menudo en el desierto?

Spend more time with Mariana and her friends while you review grammar and expand your cultural horizons.
See the **Así es Mariana** exercise in your workbook for this lesson.

En resumen

A **Éxito en la oficina.** An executive explains how he climbs the ladder of success. Fill in the blanks with the appropriate verb in the first-person singular *(yo)*.

empezar	tomar	tener
mostrar	asistir a	recordar

1. ______ decisiones.
2. ______ ideas nuevas.
3. ______ el día con energía y optimismo.
4. ______ todas las reuniones importantes.
5. ______ los nombres de todas las personas importantes.
6. ______ interés en las ideas de otras personas en la oficina.

B **Los títulos mienten.** Many professions seem fascinating but in fact involve boring tasks. In groups, list two routine daily activities of the following professionals.

1. médico
2. gerente
3. siquiatra
4. juez
5. presidente

C **Otra consulta con Encarna.** Encarna has another column with advice on how to cope with stress. Use the correct form of the verbs and choose the correct word in parentheses.

Medicina para la tensión

Según la Escuela de (Buen, Bueno) Humor en Valencia, España, hay (bueno buena) información para las personas que (querer) reducir la tensión que tienen en (su, sus) trabajo. Una dosis de humor es la mejor medicina para prevenir *(prevent)* la tensión. Pero, muchas personas no (recibir) la dosis mínima que los médicos (recomendar). Las investigaciones (mostrar) que las emociones positivas (poder) estimular las funciones inmunológicas de (nuestro, nuestros) organismo. Las personas que (tener) una actitud positiva no (estar) enfermas, (dormir) más y viven más años.

Entonces, si Ud. (pensar) unos segundos y no (recordar) un episodio cómico, pues Ud. (deber) empezar a reír *(laugh)* ahora. ¡Es bueno para Ud.!

D **Un día fatal.** Translate the following sentences to Spanish.

1. I'm in a hurry and the bus *(autobús)* isn't coming!
2. My interview is at nine and I don't want to arrive late.
3. I have to call a taxi *(taxi)*.
4. It costs a lot but that's alright.
5. Darn! No one is answering, and now it's starting to rain.

E **Minidrama.** You're a student at the Escuela de Buen Humor (see Exercise C). In groups, write a dialogue that represents a typical class. Share it with the class.

F **Composición.** What do you want in a job? Arrange the following in order of importance for you and explain your choices. Add any aspects that are not included. Then write a brief paragraph describing the type of job you want. Read it aloud to your classmates who will try to advise you.

1. un buen sueldo
2. gente simpática con quien trabajar
3. una oficina grande y elegante
4. ser mi propio *(own)* jefe
5. la oportunidad de expresar mi creatividad
6. buenos beneficios

Escuchemos

A **¿Cuál de los dos?** You will hear an incomplete sentence. Choose the word that best completes the sentence.

(almorzamos/encontramos)
Nosotros ______ en la cafetería. **almorzamos**
Nosotros almorzamos en la cafetería.

1. (cuenta/cuesta)
2. (cierra/empieza)
3. (jugar/llover)
4. (empresa/entrevista)
5. (gerente/cliente)
6. (dejar/nevar)
7. (periodista/periódico)
8. (algo/alguien)

B **Dictado.** You will hear a short narration about Elena's job interview. Listen carefully to the entire selection. Listen again and write each sentence during the pauses.

You will then hear a series of false statements related to the dictation. Correct each one with complete sentences. Refer to your dictation.

Gaceta 1 España

Puerta del Sol, Madrid

Una gira° turística por España

tour

Preparativos: Estrategias de prelectura

1. Before taking your tour of Spain, look at the **Es decir** section to help you anticipate the content of the text you are about to read. Which six cities will your tour include? Which feature mentioned in the exercise appeals to you most? When you read the passage you'll discover in which city you will find this feature.

2. Scan the paragraph about **Barcelona** to find synonyms for the following words:

   centro _____ moderna _____ separa _____ secciones _____

3. Scan the paragraph about **Sevilla** to find out if more tourists visit in the spring *(la primavera)*, in autumn *(el otoño)*, in summer *(el verano)*, or in winter *(el invierno)*.

Madrid, la capital de España, tiene una población de más de cuatro millones de personas y está situada en el centro de la península. La arquitectura de Madrid refleja° varias épocas históricas; la medieval, la barroca,° la neoclásica, la romántica y la moderna. En el famoso Museo° del Prado hay una magnífica colección de la pintura° española con obras° de El Greco, Velázquez, Murillo y Goya.

reflects
baroque
Museum; painting
works

Toledo, la antigua° capital de España, está a sólo 70 kilómetros de Madrid. Toledo se llama la «ciudad-museo»° por su gran valor° histórico y artístico.

former
museum-city; value

Barcelona es el puerto° más grande de España y su segunda° ciudad. Es el núcleo de la vida artística contemporánea y es la ciudad más europea del país. Las Ramblas, una avenida° bonita con flores° y cafés, divide la ciudad en dos partes. El Parque Güell del famoso

port; second
avenue; flowers

arquitecto Antonio Gaudí, combina la tradición gótica° con el surrealismo de sus compatriotas Joan Miró y Salvador Dalí.

Valencia, la tercera° ciudad de España, está situada en la costa del Mediterráneo. Es famosa por sus naranjas,° su cerámica exquisita, sus festivales y, sobre todo,° por la paella[1] deliciosa.

Granada, la ciudad del flamenco está en el sur° de España, en la región que se llama Andalucía. Allí está un monumento que es una de las maravillas° del mundo, La Alhambra. Este palacio, construido° en el siglo XII por los árabes,° es comparable sólo al Taj Mahal.

Sevilla, capital de Andalucía, simboliza la España romántica... de Carmen, de Don Juan, de los gitanos.° Turistas de todas partes del mundo visitan para mirar las procesiones solemnes de Semana Santa° y la catedral,° que es la tercera más grande después de San Pedro de Roma y San Pablo de Londres.

Gothic
third
oranges
above all
south
marvels; built
Arabs
gypsies
Holy Week (the week before Easter Sunday); cathedral

Toledo, España

La catedral de la Sagrada Familia, Barcelona, España

Es decir

Ciudades españolas (Spanish cities). Match the city with the appropriate description. Two cities are described twice.

Madrid	Barcelona	Granada
Toledo	Valencia	Sevilla

1. Es famosa por una celebración religiosa muy importante.
2. Está en el centro del país.
3. Allí bailan flamenco.
4. Si Ud. está en Madrid, es posible ir allí en auto en poco tiempo.
5. Es famosa por el arte moderno español.
6. Al igual que *(Like)* Granada, está en el sur *(south)* de España.
7. Hacen muy buena paella allí.
8. Es la ciudad más grande del país.

[1]Refer to page 133 for a description of **paella.**

La Alhambra, Granada, España

Procesión de Semana Santa, Sevilla, España

Practiquemos

Las playas *(beaches)* españolas. Read the following selection about Spain's famous coastline and beaches and do the exercises that follow.

De todas las playas de la **Costa Cantábrica,** la más famosa es La Concha.° Se llama La Concha porque tiene una forma semicircular. La **Costa Brava** empieza al norte de Barcelona y continúa hasta° Francia. Es una de las zonas más cosmopolitas del país. Un lugar favorito para las vacaciones es la **Costa Blanca.** Tiene playas bonitas, muchas actividades nocturnas° y paella muy deliciosa. Su ciudad principal es Valencia. La **Costa del Sol** se llama La Riviera española. Dos ciudades importantes son Málaga, la capital, y Marbella, el centro del jet-set internacional. La **Costa de la Luz** está en el sur del país, a poca distancia del norte de África.

The Shell
until
nighttime

A **El mapa.** Study the map on page 123. On the lines provided, write the names of Spain's five famous coastlines. Refer to the preceding reading.

B Based on the map and the reading selection, correct the following false statements.

1. Valencia está en la Costa Brava.
2. La Costa Cantábrica es el lugar favorito de los turistas jet-set.
3. Si Ud. va a pasar las vacaciones en la Costa Blanca puede ir a África también.
4. Barcelona está en la Costa de la Luz.
5. Si Ud. está en el norte *(north)* de la Costa Brava, Italia está a poca distancia.

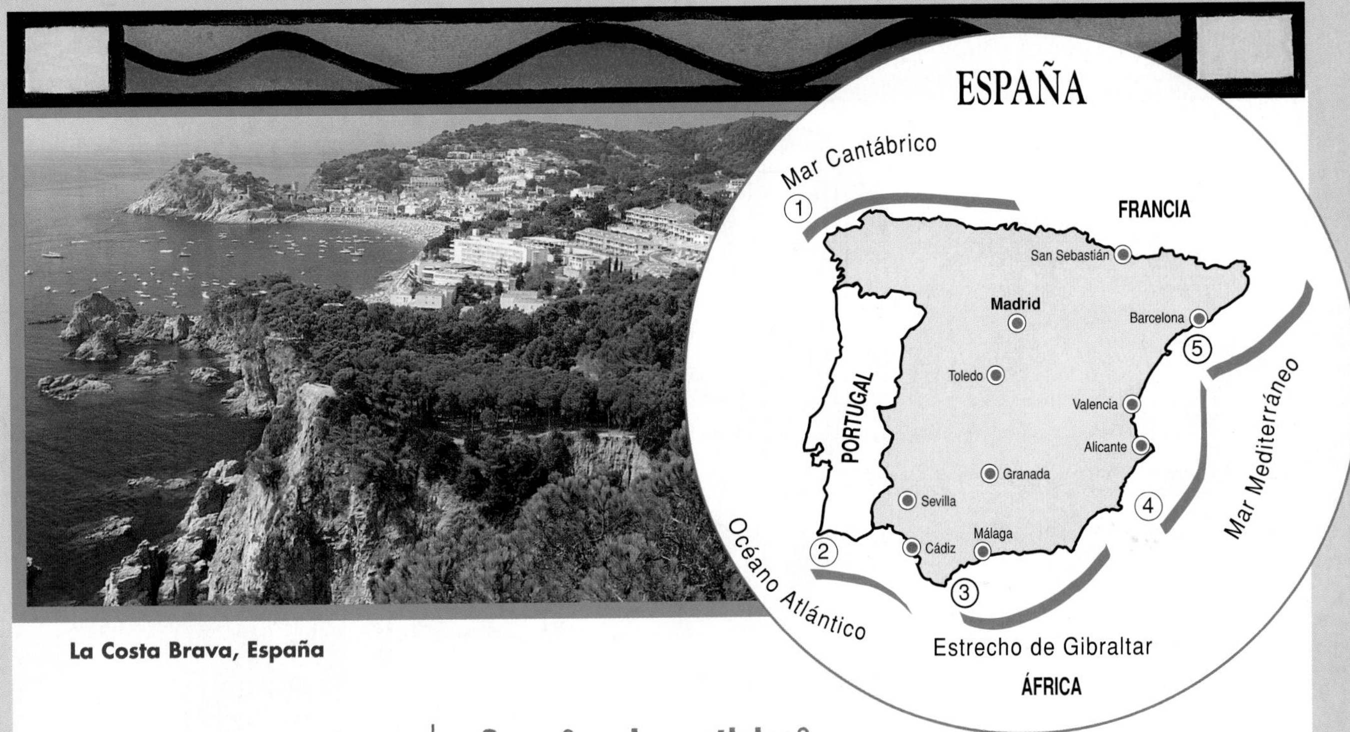

La Costa Brava, España

Caras° en las noticias°

Faces; news

Plácido Domingo

Plácido Domingo es uno de los nombres más importantes de la ópera internacional. Tiene un público° grande porque también canta° zarzuelas,[1] tangos y música folk y pop. Hace conciertos por todo el mundo con artistas famosos como José Carreras y Luciano Pavarotti. Entre sus muchas responsabilidades como director artístico de la ópera de Washington, Plácido dirige óperas, hace sus propias° producciones de música española y, por supuesto, canta. El famoso tenor está mencionado en el *Libro Guinness* por recibir un aplauso de una hora y cuarto de duración.

audience; he sings; own

[1]Spanish musical comedy

José María Aznar

Mecano

Antonio Banderas

En una entrevista, **José María Aznar,** presidente del Gobierno español desde 1996, revela que ser presidente es un honor y un privilegio, y que él está determinado en trabajar por el bien de su país. Admite que, aunque tiene más responsabilidades y obligaciones, no hay grandes alteraciones en su vida° privada y política. Es ahora, y siempre va a ser José María Aznar.

Antonio Banderas es probablemente el más internacional de todos los actores españoles. Actuó° en películas° del director español Pedro Almodóvar, y luego hizo° películas en los Estados Unidos como *Desperado* con Salma Hayek, *Philadelphia* con Tom Hanks, *Evita* con Madonna y en 1997 triunfó como el legendario héroe Zorro. Actúa en otros países pero dice que «los Estados Unidos es un país de posibilidades para los artistas.» Sin embargo, ama España y tiene lazos° fuertes con su familia, su gente y sus raíces.° Cuenta Banderas, «Yo soy latino y estoy orgulloso° de ello.»

Después de seis años de silencio, el popularísimo grupo musical, **Mecano,** decidió reunirse para grabar° un nuevo disco compacto con una combinación de canciones° nuevas y clásicas. Los tres artistas del grupo, Ana, José y Nacho, cantan° sobre temas° realistas y surrealistas; las drogas, la soledad,° el amor y la muerte.°

life

acted; movies
made

ties
roots
proud

tape
songs
sing; theme
loneliness; death

only; qualify bullfighting passed continues to grow; lately top ten	**Cristina Sánchez** no es la única° mujer en calificarse° como matadora de toros en la historia de la tauromaquia° española. Hay otras como Juanita Cruz (1940), y Morenita de Quindio (1968). Pero Cristina es la única que pasó° la última prueba llamada «la alternativa,» en España, donde los requisitos son más rigurosos y difíciles. Su popularidad sigue creciendo° por toda España y últimamente° se encuentra entre los primeros diez° matadores de España.

Cristina Sánchez

Enrique Iglesias

singer-songwriter

Enrique Iglesias, talentoso cantautor° español, acaba de recibir el título de «el hombre más sexy del mundo» de la revista *People en Español*. Pero esto no le afecta nada al joven cantante. Para él, la cosa más importante es la música y estar enfrente de su público. Una cosa cierta es que no necesita la ayuda de su famosísimo padre, Julio Iglesias, para tener éxito. Su talento natural y forma sincera de relacionarse con su público son los únicos requisitos. En 1997 Enrique ganó un «Grammy» por su primer álbum, y recibió dos nominaciones más. En 1999 ganó el «American Music Award» en la categoría de mejor artista latino. ¡Felicidades, Enrique!

Es decir

Frases incompletas. Choose the correct word(s) to complete each sentence.

1. Plácido Domingo canta...
   a. baladas. b. ópera solamente. c. varios tipos de música.
2. Mecano canta sobre...
   a. España. b. la fama. c. problemas personales y sociales.
3. José María Aznar...
   a. está contento de ser presidente.
   b. no quiere ser presidente.
   c. es el rey *(king)* de España.

4. Antonio Banderas...
   a. prefiere trabajar en España.
   b. no tiene familia en España.
   c. Tiene mucho contacto con España.

5. Cristina Sánchez...
   a. es la única matadora.
   b. se calificó en España.
   c. es menos popular porque es mujer.

6. Enrique Iglesias tiene éxito...
   a. por su talento musical.
   b. con la ayuda de su famoso padre.
   c. por su aspecto físico *(physical appearance)*.

Notas y notables

La familia real°

real: royal

Las responsabilidades de la familia real son muchas y variadas. Participan en las artes, asisten a conferencias y congresos, visitan a dignatarios internacionales y trabajan para un futuro mejor.° La **Reina**° **Sofía** muestra ternura° y caridad° por las personas débiles° e indefensas, y a través de la Fundación Reina Sofía ayuda a la gente necesitada. Participa en debates internacionales, viaja° a Asia y América y trabaja en los campos de refugiados en África. La labor humanitaria y filantrópica de la reina es muy admirable.

mejor: better; Reina: Queen; ternura: tenderness; caridad: charity; débiles: weak; viaja: travels

Siempre de interés es la vida privada de los hijos reales, el **Príncipe Felipe** y las Infantas Cristina y Elena. Los tres tienen una vida muy activa. Practican el esquí, son deportistas y navegantes° excelentes y son muy sociables. La **Infanta Cristina** vive en Barcelona con su esposo,° el Duque de Palma de Mallorca, Iñaki Urdangarín, quien es un jugador° del equipo Fútbol Club Barcelona. La **Infanta Elena** y su esposo Jaime de Marichalar ya son padres.°

navegantes: sailors; esposo: husband; jugador: player; padres: parents

Uno de los pasatiempos° nacionales de España es adivinar° quién va a ser la esposa del príncipe de Asturias. Don Felipe de Borbón es guapo, alto—6'5"—y tiene ojos muy azules.° Habla cinco lenguas y es brillante. Es serio, pero con sentido° del humor. No asiste mucho a corridas de toros y escucha la música clásica. Además de ser el heredero de la corona de España, es piloto, navegante, deportista, abogado y es considerado uno de los solteros° más elegibles del mundo... y con razón. Su madre, la Reina Sofía, prefiere un matrimonio real, aunque don Felipe admite que no necesita casarse con° una princesa.

pasatiempos: pastimes; adivinar: guess; azules: blue; sentido: sense; solteros: bachelors; casarse con: marry

(De izquierda a derecha) El Príncipe Felipe, el Rey Juan Carlos, la Reina Sofía, la Infanta Elena, la Infanta Cristina

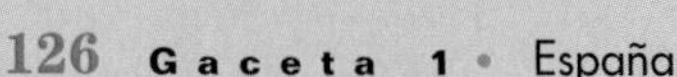

Un capítulo olvidado° de la historia

forgotten chapter
past
establishment
month; gold
silver; Fountain of Youth
coasts
decades
oldest European city
centuries
exciting
discover
fort; built
discovery
world

Hay mucho que aprender sobre la historia de los Estados Unidos. Estudiamos su pasado° colonial británico pero, ¿por qué ignoramos la importancia de las exploraciones españolas que ocurren mucho antes del establecimiento° de Virginia? Es un capítulo de la historia muy interesante y empieza en la Florida.

Es el mes° de abril de 1513. Con el motivo de encontrar oro,° plata° y la famosa fuente de la juventud,° Juan Ponce de León llega a las costas° de la Florida y toma posesión del territorio en nombre de España. En 1565—décadas° antes de llegar los puritanos del Mayflower—otro español, Pedro Menéndez de Avilés, llega a San Agustín, coloniza la región y establece la ciudad europea más antigua° de los Estados Unidos. Así empiezan tres siglos° de exploraciones que llegan hasta las costas del Pacífico.

Hoy, en San Agustín, ocurre otro momento emocionante° para la historia. Un grupo de arqueólogos acaban de descubrir° la primera fortaleza° de Avilés, construida° en 1565—16 años antes del Castillo de San Marcos,[1] la fortaleza más antigua del país. Los expertos están contentos. Creen que, con el nuevo descubrimiento,° el mundo° va a conocer y apreciar las contribuciones de los primeros exploradores.

Castillo San Marcos, San Agustín, Florida

La Calle St. George, San Agustín, Florida

[1]National historical monument in Saint Augustine, Florida

Pedro Almodóvar y el cine° español

cinema

Un símbolo del nuevo espíritu° artístico de la España posFranco es el cinematógrafo Pedro Almodóvar. Almodóvar tiene fama° internacional por sus películas° *Mujeres al borde de un ataque de nervios,*[1] *¡Átame!*[1] y *Tacones lejanos.*[1] *Kika,* con Peter Coyote y Victoria Abril es menos radical que sus películas anteriores.° Los temas de Almodóvar son la libertad, la muerte° y el amor.° Es un excelente observador de la vida moderna española, y es evidente que entiende la sicología femenina.

spirit
fame
movies

previous
death; love

Una de sus películas más recientes, *Carne trémula*[1] con Liberto Rabal y Francesca Neri, está basada en la novela de Ruth Rendell. En la película Almodóvar revela la vida trágica de varios protagonistas, y los celos° y la violencia que inspiran.

jealousy

Es decir

A La familia real. The following statements are false. Correct them using complete sentences.

1. La familia real no hace nada importante. Es sólo un símbolo del pasado *(past)* glorioso de España.
2. La reina Sofía pasa todo su tiempo en reuniones *(meetings)* oficiales.
3. Los reyes tienen dos hijos *(children)*.
4. Todos los hijos reales están casados *(married)*.
5. El esposo *(husband)* de Cristina es americano.
6. El príncipe Felipe es bajo, feo y tiene ojos verdes *(green)*. También es monolingüe, y prefiere la música pop.
7. Felipe es médico.
8. El príncipe no participa en actividades que no están relacionadas con su trabajo.

B ¿A qué lectura corresponden? To which of the previous readings do the following statements correspond? Readings may be mentioned more than once.

1. Es un director de cine famoso.
2. Hace mucho trabajo filantrópico.
3. Está en San Agustín, Florida.
4. Encuentran un monumento histórico nuevo.
5. Es un hombre con muchos talentos e intereses.
6. Es la familia más conocida *(known)* de España.
7. Conoce bien el carácter femenino.
8. Hay mucha influencia española en los Estados Unidos.

[1]Titles in English are: *Women on the Verge of a Nervous Breakdown; Tie Me Up, Tie Me Down; High Heels; Live Flesh.*

Practiquemos

El fenómeno del ciclismo (cycling) **español.** Miguel Indurain is one of the most talked-about athletes in Europe. Fill in the blanks with the correct verb from the list below.

es	creen	vive	pasa
están	se llama	hace	acaba

En España, algo fenomenal ______ en el mundo *(world)* de los deportes *(sports)*. El fenómeno ______ Miguel Indurain. Él ______ en la región de Navarra, en el norte *(north)* de España. Los españoles ______ locos *(crazy)* por él y sus adversarios ______ que es sobrehumano *(superhuman)*. Indurain ______ de triunfar *(triumph)* por tercera vez consecutiva *(the third consecutive time)* en el Tour de Francia y ______ considerado uno de los mejores *(best)* ciclistas de todos los tiempos. El éxito de Miguel Indurain ______ al ciclismo el deporte nacional del verano *(summer)* de España.

Pedro Calderón de la Barca

Enfoque literario

La vida es sueño por Pedro Calderón de la Barca

Preparativos: Estrategias de prelectura

Before reading the following literary selection, scan the biographical information below and complete the table with information that will help to set the scene for *La vida es sueño.*

About the author

Author's name: ____________ Place of birth: ______ Date of birth: ______

The play

Main themes: ______ ______ ______ Main characters: ______ ______

Astrologers' prediction: ________________________________

Keeping in mind the author's date of birth, when do you think this play takes place? What famous English playwright do you know who would be a contemporary of Calderón de la Barca? With this in mind, read a portion of *La vida es sueño.*

Pedro Calderón de la Barca (España, 1600–1681) es uno de los dramaturgos° españoles más famosos de todos los tiempos. Su obra maestra,° *La vida es sueño,*° combina los temas° filosóficos de la salvación, la predestinación y la vida transitoria. Las personas principales del drama son Basilio, rey° de Polonia,° y su hijo,° Segismundo. Los astrólogos predicen° que Segismundo va a ser un monstruo humano, incapaz° de ser rey. Poco después de su nacimiento,° Basilio mete° a su hijo en una prisión, donde vive por muchos años sin contacto con la gente. No comprende quién es y no puede diferenciar entre la realidad y el sueño. Un día Basilio, como° prueba, decide darle° su libertad. Segismundo llega al palacio y, de acuerdo con° la predicción de los astros, es como un animal salvaje° —cruel, brutal y despótico. Vuelve a la prisión. La agonía y la confusión de Segismundo son evidentes en sus palabras siguientes.°

dramatists
masterpiece; dream; themes
king; Poland; son
predict
incapable; birth
puts
as
to give him; in accordance with
savage
following

La vida es sueño *(fragmento)*

¿Qué es la vida? Un frenesí.°
¿Qué es la vida? Una ilusión,
una sombra,° una ficción,
y el mayor bien es pequeño;
que toda la vida es sueño,
y los sueños, sueños son.

frenzy

shadow

Es decir

Comprensión.

1. ¿Quién es Basilio?
2. ¿Quién es Segismundo?
3. ¿Por qué viven separados Basilio y Segismundo?
4. ¿Qué pasa cuando Segismundo va al palacio por primera vez *(for the first time)?*
5. Describa Ud. el estado *(state)* mental y emocional de Segismundo.
6. En los versos, Segismundo habla de dos cosas que son imaginarias. ¿Cuáles son?

Practiquemos

A El lenguaje *(language)* literario.

1. Calderón usa cuatro palabras para describir cómo es la vida. ¿Cuáles son?
2. Ahora, sustituya Ud. *(substitute)* las palabras con sus propias *(your own)* palabras para crear *(to create)* frases originales.

B Discusión. Explique Ud. *(Explain)* cómo el tema de la predestinación está representado en el drama.

C Reacción personal.

1. Nombre Ud. *(Name)* otras obras literarias que tienen el mismo *(the same)* tema.
2. ¿Cree Ud. en la predestinación? Explique.

Enfoque artístico... España

A. Visite Ud. el siguiente *(following)* sitio web y compare los tres museos.

http://www.munimadrid.es/ayuntamiento/htmlay/museos1.html

museos	Museo del Prado	Museo de Arte Reina Sofía	Museo de Ciencias Naturales
año de construcción			
tipo *(type)* de arte			
exhibiciones			
actividades/servicios			

B. En España hay una gran variedad de museos. Ud. puede visitar el sitio web

http://www.gti.ssr.upm.es/~vimp/SPAIN/indexES.html

para obtener una guía *(guidebook)* de todos los museos.

Since Internet addresses are subject to change, typing the following key words into most search engines will get you more information about Spanish art: **Museo del Prado, Picasso, Dalí, El Greco** (or

Videocultura

La fiesta de los Reyes Magos°

the Wise Kings

En España y en otras partes del mundo hispano, una parte de la celebración de la Navidad° es la fiesta de los Reyes Magos. En cada° ciudad° la tradición es diferente, pero en Valencia, el día cinco de enero° por la tarde los Reyes llegan al puerto° y cada uno sube° en una carroza.° Luego hay un desfile° que se llama «La Cabalgata de Reyes» del puerto a la plaza principal.

Christmas
each; city
January; port
gets on; float; parade

To find out more about the celebration of the Wise Kings, let's go to Valencia and join the parade. Watch the video and do the exercises that follow.

Palabras útiles

el país	*country*	la barba	*beard*
el niño	*child*	blanco	*white*
el regalo	*gift*	los padres	*parents*
el desfile	*parade*	pelirrojo	*red-haired*
la carroza	*float*	negro	*black*
la calle	*street*	el zapato	*shoe*
tirar	*to throw*	los abuelos	*grandparents*
el caramelo	*hard candy*	los parientes	*relatives*
el juguete	*toy*	el roscón de reyes	*King's cake*
tocar	*to play (music)*		

Es decir

A **¿Qué hay en el desfile?** Check off all of the things that you see in the parade.

1. ______ instrumentos musicales
2. ______ niños alegres
3. ______ Gaspar
4. ______ elefantes
5. ______ Melchor
6. ______ caballos *(horses)*
7. ______ niños tristes
8. ______ Baltasar
9. ______ perros *(dogs)*
10. ______ Santa Claus
11. ______ toros *(bulls)*
12. ______ luces bonitas

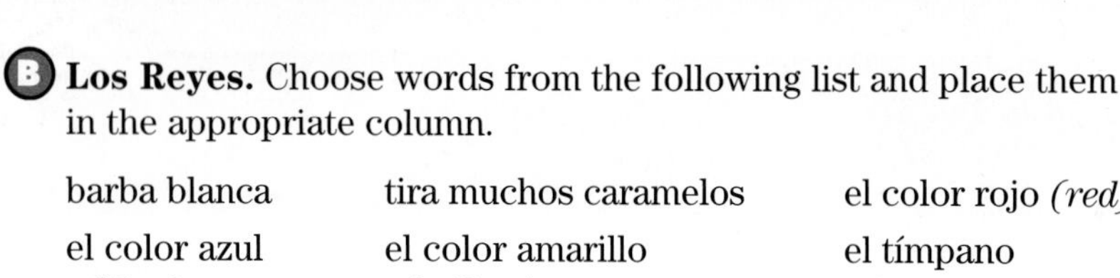

B **Los Reyes.** Choose words from the following list and place them in the appropriate column.

barba blanca	tira muchos caramelos	el color rojo *(red)*
el color azul *(blue)*	el color amarillo *(yellow)*	el tímpano *(kettledrum)*
hombre negro	va segundo *(second)*	

Melchor	**Gaspar**	**Baltasar**
______________	______________	______________
______________	______________	______________
______________	______________	______________

C **¿Cierto o falso?** Based on the video, circle **C** if the sentence is true **(cierto)** and **F** if the sentence is false **(falso).** Correct the false statements.

C F **1.** La fiesta de Reyes es el seis de enero.

C F **2.** Todas las ciudades celebran la fiesta de la misma *(same)* forma.

C F **3.** Hay cuatro Reyes Magos.

C F **4.** El desfile es por la mañana.

C F **5.** Los niños pueden dejar los zapatos en el balcón para recibir regalos.

D **¿Qué recuerda Ud.?** Based on the video, choose the correct answer.

1. En la fiesta hay...
   a. niños solamente.
   b. niños y sus padres.
   c. niños, padres, abuelos y parientes.

2. ¿Qué actividad no hacen en la fiesta?
   a. abrir regalos b. bailar c. jugar

3. ¿Dónde encuentran los niños sus regalos?
   a. en el dormitorio
   b. delante de la chimenea
   c. en el balcón

Practiquemos

A **¿Cómo celebra Ud.?** ¿Es el día de los Reyes una tradición en los Estados Unidos? ¿Cuándo celebra la gente la Navidad? ¿Cómo celebran?

Tres niños con los Reyes en el almacén Galerías Preciados en Valencia

B **Los Reyes.** Another custom is that of visiting the various department stores to have your picture taken with the Three Kings. Identify each King in the photo above. In groups, act out the following skit.

Un niño muy malo quiere recibir regalos de los Reyes. Él va a visitar a los Reyes en un almacén y empieza a mentir. Su mamá escucha todo.

La paella

Es en Valencia, España, donde Ud. puede encontrar el mejor° arroz.° Creen que es por° la experiencia y la tradición, y también por la clase° de arroz que los valencianos cultivan y por la clase de agua.° La paella es un plato° conocido° por todo el mundo.° Su nombre viene del tipo de recipiente° en que uno prepara el plato, que se llama una paellera. Hace muchos años° la paella era° un plato muy común° de trabajadores y campesinos° pobres. Las mujeres recogían° toda la comida° que sobraba° de la semana y se la echaban° al arroz y se la servían° a la familia. Hoy día° la paella es un plato que podemos encontrar en los restaurantes más elegantes del mundo.

best; rice
because of
type
water
dish; known
all over the world
receptacle
Many years ago; was
common
peasants
would collect; food; was left over
would add it
would serve it; Nowadays

To find out more about paella, let's visit Monkili, a well-known paella restaurant in Valencia. Watch the video and do the exercises that follow.

RESTAURANTE

MONKILI, C. B.

Avda. Neptuno, 52
Teléfono 371 00 39

46011 - VALENCIA

Palabras útiles

el cocinero	*cook*
la paella marinera	*seafood paella*
el arroz con azafrán o colorante alimenticio	*rice with saffron or food coloring*
las cigalas	*crayfish*
las gambas	*shrimp*
la sepia troceada	*cuttle-fish cut into pieces*
el perejil	*parsley*
el tomate frito	*fried tomato*
el caldo de pescado	*fish broth*
el aceite de oliva	*olive oil*
el ajo, la sal y otras especias	*garlic, salt and other spices*
el fuego	*fire, heat*
el horno	*oven*
¡Buen provecho!	*Bon appetit!*
el pan	*bread*
la ensalada	*salad*
los calamares a la romana	*fried squid*

Verbos activos

agregar	*to add*
cortar	*to cut*
limpiar	*to clean*
poner	*to put*

Es decir

A **Categorías.** Look at the list of ingredients and find as many words as you can that belong to each category.

mariscos *(seafood)*	**sazón y especias** *(seasoning and spices)*	**líquidos**
______	______	______
______	______	______
______	______	______
______	______	______

B **¿Qué agrega primero *(first)*?** In what order does the cook add the following ingredients? Number them accordingly, and then form complete sentences using the verb **agregar.**

MODELO _1_ el aceite de oliva
El cocinero agrega el aceite de oliva.

___ el colorante alimenticio
___ la sepia troceada
___ el caldo
___ las cigalas y las gambas
___ el tomate frito
___ la sal
___ el perejil
___ el arroz

C **¿En qué orden?** In what order does the cook do the following steps? Number them accordingly, and then form complete sentences.

MODELO _1_ encontrar una paellera
El cocinero encuentra una paellera.

___ poner la paella en el horno
___ cortar la sepia
___ llevar la paella a la mesa *(table)*
___ poner la paellera con el aceite al fuego
___ limpiar las cigalas y las gambas
___ poner todos los ingredientes en la paellera
___ preparar el fuego

D **¿Qué recuerda Ud.?** Based on the video, choose the correct answer.

1. El cocinero...
a. es gordo. b. es alto y rubio. c. es delgado y moreno.

2. El restaurante...
a. es muy moderno b. tiene un horno muy viejo.

3. En la mesa no hay...
a. pan c. ensalada.
b. vino d. salsa de tomate *(catsup).*

Practiquemos

A **Otros platos típicos.** ¿Cuáles son los platos típicos de su país *(country)*? ¿De su estado *(state)*? ¿En qué consisten?

B **Los turistas *(tourists)*.** In groups, act out the following skit.

En el restaurante Monkili, un grupo de turistas quieren saber *(to know)* qué es la paella. El camarero *(waiter)* intenta *(tries)* contestar todas sus preguntas ridículas *(ridiculous)*.

La música contemporánea española: Enrique Iglesias y Los Gipsy Kings

Enrique Iglesias, joven cantante español, sigue grabando discos, ganando premios y complaciendo a su público.

To find out more about Enrique Iglesias, listen to the following interview and then enjoy the concert! Watch the video and do the exercises that follow.

Palabras útiles

acostumbrarse a	*to get used to*	el principio	*the beginning*
antes de que me muera	*before I die*	el público	*the audience*
crecer	*to grow*	romper el corazón	*to break one's heart*
dentro de	*within*	la terapia	*therapy*
el disco	*record*	único	*unique*
enfrente de	*in front of*	valer la pena	*to be worth the trouble*
nacer	*to be born*	la vergüenza	*shame*
paré	*I stopped*	el viaje	*trip*

Es decir

A **Frases falsas.** The following statements are false. Correct them based on the video.

1. Enrique es de Miami originalmente.
2. Tiene 22 años.
3. Ahora vive en España.
4. Sólo habla español.
5. Escribe sobre los problemas de sus amigos.
6. No le gusta estar enfrente de su público.
7. Las personas que quieren aprender inglés deben comprar sus libros.

B **Números.** ¿Cuál es la importancia de los números siguientes?

1. 1975 **2.** 8 **3.** 14

C **¿Qué recuerda?** Choose the correct answer.

1. La madre de Enrique es (filipina/española).
2. El padre de Enrique es (americano/español).

3. El pasaporte de Enrique es de (los Estados Unidos/España).
4. Para Enrique, escribir canciones es una forma de (terapia/ejercicio).
5. Todo lo que escribe es como (una novela/un diario).

Practiquemos

Preguntas personales. Answer the following questions.

1. ¿Conoce Ud. la música de Enrique Iglesias? ¿Y de su padre, Julio? ¿Qué piensa de la música de Enrique?
2. Para Enrique, la música es una forma de terapia. ¿Qué usa Ud. como terapia? ¿Cuándo la necesita?
3. Enrique dice que es la persona más feliz del mundo cuando está enfrente de su público. ¿Cuándo es Ud. la persona más feliz πdel mundo?

La música de Los Gipsy Kings

Hay un nuevo sonido° en los Estados Unidos. Es un sonido muy contemporáneo pero encontramos el origen en la Edad Media.° Es una música apasionada° y percusiva, única° porque combina la tradición flamenca, el ritmo caliente° de la salsa caribeña° y el sonido más moderno del rock de los Rolling Stones, Sting y Prince. Se llama «Gypsy-rock» y el grupo musical europeo, Los Gipsy Kings, define la música.

El grupo, que consiste en seis músicos, empezó a cantar° en 1979, con la unión de dos familias° de gitanos.° Dos de los miembros del grupo, André y Nicolás Reyes, son los hijos° del famoso cantante° flamenco José Reyes. Los otros cuatro son de la familia Baliardo, y son primos° o cuñados° de la familia Reyes. Algunos de ellos viven en el sur° de Francia pero otros continúan la tradición gitana de viajar° en caravanas. Dice° Chico Bouchikhi, uno de los músicos: «Los lazos° familiares son muy importantes para nosotros, y

sound
Middle Ages; passionate; unique
hot rhythm;
Caribbean
began to sing
families; gypsies
sons
singer
cousins; brothers-in-law
south
to travel; Says
ties

también la tradición y el espíritu° de los gitanos. No podemos trabajar separados porque somos una familia, y nuestro lema° es libertad° y fe.°» Chico cree que los gitanos son discriminados pero su música ayuda a proyectar° una imagen° positiva.

Chico dice que su música no es una adaptación del flamenco, es una evolución. «Como gitanos, tenemos influencias de todo el mundo.° Nos gusta decir° que nuestra mano derecha° es gitana y la izquierda° es el resto del mundo.»

Sus álbumes son muy exitosos.° El grupo canta en una mezcla° de español, francés, catalán[1] y lenguas gitanas, pero la música realmente trasciende la lengua y el estilo° regional.

El siguiente° video muestra una entrevista con Chico Bouchikhi, uno de los músicos del famoso grupo. Él habla gitano y francés. La entrevista es en Massachusetts, donde ellos actuaron° delante de miles de fanáticos° norteamericanos.

spirit
slogan; freedom
faith
project; image
whole world
We like to say; right hand; left
successful; mixture
style
following
performed
fans

To find out more about the Gipsy Kings, let's listen to Chico. Watch the video and do the exercises that follow.

Es decir

A **Los Gipsy Kings.** Based on the reading, answer the following questions.

1. ¿Cómo es el sonido de los Gipsy Kings?
2. ¿En qué consiste el grupo?
3. ¿Quién es el padre de Nicolás y André?
4. ¿Dónde viven los músicos?
5. ¿En qué idiomas canta el grupo?

B **Más detalles *(More details)*.** Nombre Ud. *(Name)*...

1. las dos familias que forman los Gipsy Kings.
2. los dos conceptos que forman su lema.
3. los tres tipos de música que combinan para formar la música de los Gipsy Kings.

C **¿Qué recuerda Ud.?** After seeing the video, do the following activities.

1. The following sentences are false. Based on the video, correct them.
   a. Hay tres gitanos en el grupo.
   b. El instrumento musical principal es el piano.
   c. Chico dice *(says)* que su verdadera *(true)* lengua es el español.
2. Answer the following questions.
   a. ¿Por qué se llama su música «gypsy rock»?
   b. ¿Cómo son los fanáticos que van a sus conciertos?
   c. ¿Qué piensa Ud. de su música?

[1]El catalán es la lengua que se habla en la provincia española de Cataluña, cuya *(whose)* capital es Barcelona.

D **Djobi Djoba.** One of the most popular songs of the Gipsy Kings is *Djobi Djoba*, which in gypsy and **catalán** means **yo veo** *(I see)*, **yo voy** *(I go)*. Read the following lyrics and conjugate the verbs in parentheses in the present tense. As this song has a long oral tradition some of the lyrics do not have a literal meaning or a translation. Some of the words are a combination of a few languages. Even the Gipsy Kings themselves could not explain the meaning of all of the words.

Djobi Djoba

Ay niña
Yo te (encontrar) ______
solita° por la calle.
Yo me (sentir°) ______ amorado.°
Yo me (sentir) ______ triste solo.°
Ref: Djobi Djoba
Cada° día yo te (querer) ______ más.
Djobi Djobi, Djobi Djoba
Cada día yo te (querer) ______ más.
Djobi Djobi, Djobi Djoba
Cada día yo te (querer) ______ más.
Que no me importa°
que la distancia
ya nos separe.
Yo me (contentar°) ______, me retir.°
Y no me diga° ay
Para guarja ja.°
Ref: Djobi Djoba...

°solita: alone
°sentir: to feel; °amorado: in love
°solo: alone
°Cada: Each
°Que no me importa: It doesn't matter to me
°contentar: to be satisfied; °me retir: I leave
°no me diga: don't tell me
°guarja ja: (unknown expression)

Practiquemos

A **Los gitanos.** To know more about gypsies, fill in the blanks with the appropriate word from the following list.

danza capital larga independencia gitanos aproximadamente

Los gitanos tienen una ______ tradición en España. Hay ______ 500.000 (quinientos mil) gitanos en el mundo, y 200.000 (doscientos mil) viven en Andalucía (al sur de España) cerca de *(near)* Madrid, la ______ del país *(country)*, y Barcelona. Tradicionalmente los ______ llevaban *(used to lead)* una vida *(life)* nómada. Se conocen *(They are known)* por su ______, su fidelidad *(loyalty)* al grupo como *(as)* familia, y su gran habilidad para el canto y la ______. Contribuyen mucho a la cultura española.

UNIDAD

Estás en mi casa

Puerto Rico y la República Dominicana

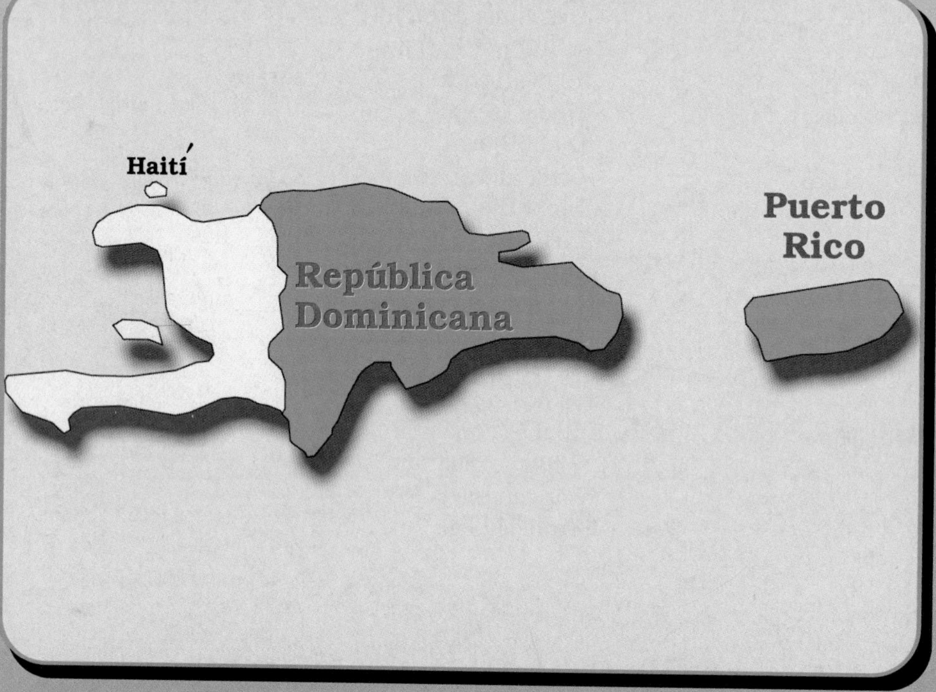

¡Vamos a Puerto Rico y la República Dominicana por Internet!

Experience the geographical and cultural diversity of Puerto Rico and the Dominican Republic by browsing the World Wide Web and visiting the following addresses.

http://www.latinworld.com/caribe/puertorico/
http://www.cibercentro.com/
http://www.coqui.com.IsladelEncanto.html

http://www.emely-tours.com/
http://www.latinworld.com/caribe/rdominicana/

Since Internet addresses are subject to change, typing the following key words into most search engines will also get you to Puerto Rico and the Dominican Republic.

Puerto Rico **San Juan, Ponce** (or any Puerto Rican city) **taíno** **borinquen**
Santo Domingo **Bayamón** (or any city in the Dominican Republic)

To learn about Puerto Rican art via the Internet, see page 225 of *Gaceta* 2.

Una casa en la República Dominicana

Lección 4 

FUNCTION Expressing actions • Expressing to know • Describing the weather • Counting above 100

STRUCTURE Irregular verbs in the present tense • The personal ***a*** • The verbs ***saber*** and ***conocer***

VOCABULARY Family members • Colors • Physical descriptions • Affirmative and negative expressions • Weather expressions • Seasons, months, and days • Numbers above 100

CULTURE Family names • The Hispanic family

DIÁLOGO Y VIDEO ***Así es Mariana: La familia de Mariana***

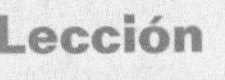 Lección 5

FUNCTION Expressing action in progress • Expressing actions • Pointing out people and things • Expressing **whom** or **what**

STRUCTURE Prepositional pronouns • The present progressive tense • The present tense of ***e>i*** stem-changing verbs • Demonstrative adjectives and pronouns • Direct object pronouns

VOCABULARY Parts of the house • Furniture and accessories

CULTURE Urban, suburban, and rural life • The Hispanic home

DIÁLOGO Y VIDEO ***Así es Mariana: La tarea doméstica***

Lección 6

FUNCTION Expressing **to whom** or **for whom** • Talking about the past

STRUCTURE Indirect object pronouns • Direct and indirect object pronouns together • The preterite tense of regular verbs • The preterite tense of the irregular verbs ***ir, ser, dar,*** and ***hacer***

VOCABULARY Diversions and pastimes • Technology • Sections of the newspaper • Reactions • Talking on the telephone

CULTURE Telephone etiquette • Hispanic newspapers

DIÁLOGO Y VIDEO ***Así es Mariana: La tecnología***

 Gaceta 2 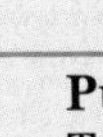

CULTURE **Puerto Rico and the Dominican Republic**
Touring Puerto Rico • Faces in the news • Notes and notables • Literature: Julia de Burgos • Art

VIDEOCULTURA Puerto Rico • Los beisbolistas caribeños • La música caribeña

Así es mi familia

¡Feliz cumpleaños!

AVISO CULTURAL

What is your last name? And your mother's? Your father's? Generally, Hispanics have two last names, that of their father and that of their mother. For example, Laura Vázquez Pérez has the last name of her father, Vázquez, and that of her mother, Pérez. If she marries Manuel Gómez Frontera, their children's last name will consist of the paternal last name from their father followed by the paternal last name from their mother. Thus their daughter will be named Ana Gómez Vázquez. How do you feel about this system? Read the two names below and tell what the last names of Emma's and Vicente's parents are. Emma and Vicente have a son named David. What are his last names?

A. EMMA SOPEÑA BALORDI
catedrática
Dep. Filología Francesa e
Italiana. E.U. Profesorado
Universidad de Valencia

Vicente Galvañ Llopis
DOCTOR ARQUITECTO
SUBDIRECTOR DE LA ESCUELA TECNICA SUPERIOR DE ARQUITECTURA
DE VALENCIA

TELS. 361 50 51 (EX. 393)
360 08 04
360 18 16

CAMINO DE VERA, S/N.
VALENCIA - 21

Preparativos

Review the vocabulary on pages 145–147 before viewing the video.

As you watch the video or read the following dialogue, note the use of the verbs **saber** and **conocer.** They both mean *to know*. For example, Luis Antonio doesn't know (isn't acquainted with) Mariana's family. In the video he says to Mariana, **"No conozco a tu familia."** Nor is he familiar with Puerto Rico. He says, **"No conozco Puerto Rico."** However, Mariana asks her father if he knows that it's windy outside. In the video she says, **"Sabes que hace viento aquí, papá?"** What do you think the difference is between the two verbs? In this episode Mariana is all nerves **("¡¡Qué nervios!!")**, afraid to introduce Luis Antonio to her family **("Tengo miedo de presentar a Luis a mi familia.")** at her brother's birthday party. How does Luis succeed in impressing Mr. and Mrs. Benavides? What feelings does Mariana experience at this family gathering?

Así es Mariana: La familia de Mariana

Mariana y Luis Antonio van a cenar a la casa de la familia Benavides. Sentados° a la mesa están Amparo y Ramón, los padres de Mariana, su hermano Miguelito, y sus tíos de Puerto Rico, Héctor y Celia. seated

Luis Antonio: Señora Benavides, la comida está muy rica. Ud. es una cocinera fabulosa.

Ramón: ¡Por supuesto! Mi esposa prepara la mejor° comida de Puerto Rico. best

Héctor: ¡Oye, Luis! ¿Conoces tú Puerto Rico?

Luis Antonio: No, no. No lo conozco. Uds. viven en San Juan, ¿no?

Celia: Sí. Mariana siempre pasa algunos días del verano en Puerto Rico con sus dos primos. ¿Quieres ver las fotos?

Mariana: ¡Ni modo! Tío, necesito ayuda, por favor.

Héctor: ¡En absoluto! Yo no digo nada.

Luis Antonio: Miguel, ¿cuántos años cumples hoy?

Miguelito: Doce, y para celebrar, ¡vamos para Puerto Rico! ¿Está bien, mamá? Puede ser un regalo muy bueno.

Amparo: ¡Sí, sí, claro, cómo no! ¡Vamos todos para Puerto Rico ahora mismo!

Mariana: Yo tengo muchos recuerdos de Puerto Rico. Las aguas azules del Caribe, el barrio del Viejo San Juan con sus casas coloniales, las calles pequeñas, los monumentos...

Luis Antonio: Veo que Puerto Rico es muy bonito.

Amparo: ¿Quién quiere más?

Ramón: Yo no. Estoy listo para comer el postre y contar chistes... una tradición en nuestra casa.

Amparo: Sí, sí, ahora traigo el postre.

Amparo trae la torta° de cumpleaños a la mesa. Todos cantan. cake

Todos: Cumpleaños feliz, cumpleaños feliz. Todos te deseamos, cumpleaños feliz.

Es decir

A Match the person in the first column with the description in the second column.

1. Mariana
2. Luis Antonio
3. Miguelito
4. Ramón
5. Amparo
6. Héctor
7. Celia

a. la mamá de Mariana
b. la esposa de Héctor
c. la hija de Ramón y Amparo
d. el hermano menor de Mariana
e. el tío de Mariana
f. el novio de Mariana
g. el esposo de Amparo

B Based on the dialogue, fill in the blanks with the correct infinitive from the second column.

1. ¿Quieres ______ las fotos?
2. Cumplo doce años, y para ______ vamos para Puerto Rico.
3. Estoy listo para ______ el postre y______ chistes.

a. comer
b. contar
c. celebrar
d. ver

C Based on the dialogue, choose a response from the second column that best responds to the sentence in the first column.

1. ¿Quién quiere más?
2. ¿Cuántos años cumples hoy?
3. Ud. es una cocinera fabulosa.
4. ¡Vamos para Puerto Rico! ¿Está bien, mamá?
5. Tío, necesito ayuda, por favor.

a. Doce.
b. ¡En absoluto! Yo no digo nada.
c. Sí, vamos todos para Puerto Rico ahora.
d. Yo no. Estoy listo para comer el postre.
e. Sí, mi esposa prepara la mejor comida de Puerto Rico.

Al ver el video

A **¿Quién(es)...?**

1. está avergonzado *(embarrassed)?*
2. quiere contar chistes?
3. llega a la fiesta un poco tarde?
4. canta *(sings)?*
5. trae regalos?
6. lleva un sombrero?
7. saca una foto?
8. limpia la mesa?
9. abre la puerta?

B In small groups, answer the following questions.

1. ¿Por qué está nerviosa Mariana? ¿Está Ud. nervioso(a) cuando presenta a sus amigos a su familia? ¿Por qué sí o no?
2. ¿Por qué está impresionado Ramón con Luis Antonio? ¿Está Ud. impresionado(a) con Luis? Explique.
3. ¿Qué sabe Ud. de la familia de Mariana?
4. ¿Conoce Ud. Puerto Rico? ¿Qué sabe de San Juan o de otra ciudad puertorriqueña?

C In groups of three, complete Mariana's sentence three different ways to explain why she's afraid to introduce Luis to her family. Share your sentences with the class: «**Pero tengo miedo de presentar a Luis a mi familia porque...**»

Vocabulario

Verbos

conducir (zc) (manejar)	*to drive*
conocer (zc)	*to know (be acquainted with); to meet*
dar	*to give*
decir	*to say, tell*
esperar	*to hope; to wait for*
invitar	*to invite*
llorar	*to cry*
ofrecer (zc)	*to offer*
oír	*to hear*
poner	*to put*
saber	*to know (how)*
salir	*to go out, leave*
traducir (zc)	*to translate*
traer	*to bring*
ver	*to see*
visitar	*to visit*

Adjetivos

amarillo	*yellow*
anaranjado	*orange*
azul	*blue*
barato	*cheap, inexpensive*
blanco	*white*
caro	*expensive*
casado	*married*
corto	*short (in length)*
divorciado	*divorced*
familiar	*pertaining to the family, familiar*
joven	*young*
largo	*long*
marrón	*brown*
mayor	*older, oldest*
menor	*younger, youngest*
negro	*black*

rojo	*red*
soltero	*unmarried*
verde	*green*
viejo	*old*

Los familiares	**Family members**
el (la) abuelo(a)	*grandfather(mother)*
los abuelos	*grandparents*
el (la) cuñado(a)	*brother(sister)-in-law*
la esposa (mujer)	*wife*
el esposo (marido)	*husband*
la familia	*family*
el (la) hermano(a)	*brother(sister)*
el (la) hijo(a)	*son(daughter)*
el (la) hijo(a) único(a)	*only child*
la madre (mamá)	*mother*
el (la) nieto(a)	*grandson(daughter)*
el (la) niño(a)	*child*
el padre (papá)	*father*
los padres	*parents*
el (la) pariente	*relative*
el (la) primo(a)	*cousin*
el (la) sobrino(a)	*nephew(niece)*
el (la) suegro(a)	*father(mother)-in-law*
el (la) tío(a)	*uncle(aunt)*
el (la) viudo(a)	*widower(widow)*

Expresiones (See pages 158–159 for dates, seasons, and weather)

contar chistes	*to tell jokes*
cumplir... años	*to become . . . years old*
estar de moda (onda)	*to be "in"*
¡Feliz cumpleaños!	*Happy Birthday!*
poner la mesa	*to set the table*
sacar fotos (fotografías)	*to take pictures*

Otras palabras	
el agua (*f.*)	*water*
el almuerzo	*lunch*
el apellido	*last name*
el barrio	*neighborhood*
la calle	*street*
la cena	*dinner, supper*
la ciudad	*city*

el coche (carro)	*car*
la comida	*food, meal*
el cumpleaños	*birthday*
el desayuno	*breakfast*
la fecha	*(calendar) date*
el pelo	*hair*
el postre	*dessert*
el regalo	*gift*
la vida	*life*

Vocabulario adicional

además	*besides*
el aniversario	*anniversary*
el árbol	*tree*
bien (mal) educado	*well-mannered (rude)*
el campo	*countryside*
crecer (zc)	*to grow*
gris	*gray*
el helado	*ice cream*
el juguete	*toy*
morado	*purple*
la muerte	*death*
el nacimiento	*birth*
producir (zc)	*to produce*
el recuerdo	*memory, souvenir*
reír[1]	*to laugh*
la reunión	*meeting, reunion*
rosa	*pink*
sin embargo	*nevertheless*

Repasemos el vocabulario

A Antónimos. Look in the second column for the antonym of the words in the first column.

1. casado	**a.** corto
2. barato	**b.** soltero
3. joven	**c.** menor
4. mayor	**d.** viejo
5. largo	**e.** caro

[1]Note the irregular conjugation of **reír, río, ríes, ríe, reímos, reís, ríen.**

B **¿Cuál no pertenece? *(Which doesn't belong?)*** Indicate which word does not belong, and explain.

1. hija	cuñada	abuela	madre
2. caro	verde	blanco	anaranjado
3. soltero	divorciado	viudo	regalo
4. almuerzo	postre	desayuno	cená
5. calle	apellido	ciudad	barrio

C **Los colores.** Ask classmates to name something they see or associate with the following colors. Follow the model. Be sure to give the correct form of the color. Note below the following things associated with a specific color.

MODELO Estudiante 1: Nombre Ud. algo blanco.
Estudiante 2: **La tiza es blanca.**

1. negro	**3.** rojo	**5.** anaranjado	**7.** marrón
2. azul	**4.** amarillo	**6.** blanco	**8.** verde

D **El árbol genealógico *(The family tree).*** Study the family tree and complete the sentences that follow.

[1]Although **medias** *(sox)* is feminine, the masculine definite article **los** is used, as it refers to **los peloteros** *(ballplayers)*.

1. Alfonso es el ______ de María.
2. Alfonso y María son los ______ de Saúl.
3. Rosa es la ______ de Saúl.
4. Juan, Carlos y Rosa son ______.
5. José es el ______ de Pedro.
6. Alfonso y María son los ______ de Manuela.
7. Raquel es la ______ de Pedro.
8. Raquel y Pedro son los ______ de Carlos.

Now listen as your instructor reads a series of descriptions. Indicate to whom the descriptions correspond. There may be more than one correct answer.

1. ________	3. ________	5. ________	7. ________
2. ________	4. ________	6. ________	8. ________

E **El sabelotodo *(The know-it-all)*.** Combine the phrases in both columns to form logical sentences.

MODELO **Sé *(I know)* que el regalo es caro porque es de Tiffany's.**

Sé que
1. ellos tienen niños pequeños...
2. es un día especial para la familia...
3. es la hora de almorzar...
4. son hispanos...
5. Ana tiene un novio simpático...
6. el señor es mayor...

porque
a. hoy cumple 99 años.
b. siempre compra regalos para ella.
c. su apellido es Martínez.
d. todos los parientes vienen a casa.
e. la abuela pone la mesa.
f. hay muchos juguetes en la casa.

De uso común

Reacting Affirmatively and Negatively

limpio *I clean*
pelota *ball*

Expresiones afirmativas	
¡Cómo no!	*Of course!*
¡Claro que sí!	*Of course, absolutely!*
¡Por supuesto!	*Of course!*
¡Desde luego!	*Of course!*
¡Correcto! ¡Cierto!	*Correct! Exactly!*

Expresiones negativas	
¡De ninguna manera!	*By no means!*
¡Ni modo!	*No way!*
¡En absoluto!	*Absolutely not!*
¡Ni hablar!	*Not a chance!*
¡Ni pensarlo!	*Don't even think about it!*

Practiquemos

A **Reacciones.** Using the preceding expressions, react to the following situations.

1. Su amigo(a) pregunta si quiere pasar todo el día en la biblioteca.
2. Su novio(a) pregunta si quiere comer en un restaurante muy elegante.
3. Gloria Estefan invita a Ud. y a todos sus amigos a su concierto.
4. En un restaurante el cocinero pregunta si Ud. quiere comer la especialidad... anguila *(eel)*.
5. Su profesor de español pregunta si Ud. aprende mucho en su clase.
6. Su jefe pregunta si Ud. quiere trabajar todo el fin de semana.

B **Más situaciones.** Describe more situations like those in the preceding exercise, and classmates will react appropriately.

More Irregular Verbs in the Present Tense

You have already learned that some verbs in Spanish do not follow the regular **-ar, -er, -ir** pattern of conjugation but rather have irregular forms. You have studied the irregular verbs **ser, estar, ir, hacer, tener,** and **venir** as well as stem-changing verbs. These irregular verbs should be learned well, since they are used frequently.

Forma

Some verbs have irregular forms only in the first-person singular **(yo)**.

CONOCER[1] *(to know)*		DAR *(to give)*		PONER *(to put, to place)*		SABER *(to know)*	
conozco	conocemos	**doy**	damos	**pongo**	ponemos	**sé**	sabemos
conoces	conocéis	das	dais	pones	ponéis	sabes	sabéis
conoce	conocen	da	dan	pone	ponen	sabe	saben

[1]Other verbs similar to **conocer** are **agradecer** *(to thank)*, **conducir, crecer** *(to grow)*, **merecer** *(to deserve)*, **obedecer** *(to obey)*, **ofrecer, producir, traducir.**

SALIR *(to leave)*		TRAER[1] *(to bring)*		VER *(to see)*	
salgo	salimos	**traigo**	traemos	**veo**	vemos
sales	salís	traes	traéis	ves	veis
sale	salen	trae	traen	ve	ven

Some verbs are irregular in more forms.

DECIR *(to say)*		OÍR *(to hear)*	
digo	decimos	**oigo**	oímos
dices	decís	**oyes**	oís
dice	**dicen**	**oye**	**oyen**

Practiquemos

A **¿Y tú?** Rosa has invited you to her home for a family reunion. You comment on the activities of some of her relatives, and ask her if she also does these things. In pairs, a classmate plays the role of Rosa and answers your questions affirmatively or negatively.

Ud.: Tus tíos oyen música caribeña. ¿Y tú?
Rosa: **No, yo no oigo música caribeña.**

1. Tu abuela conduce un coche deportivo. ¿Y tú?
2. Tu prima sabe bailar merengue. ¿Y tú?
3. Tu hermano juega dominó. ¿Y tú?
4. Tu prima sale con un actor famoso. ¿Y tú?
5. Tu primo trae comida a la fiesta. ¿Y tú?
6. Tu tío ve la televisión todos los días. ¿Y tú?

B **Muchas actividades.** Listen as your instructor reads the first part of a sentence. Find the logical ending from the following possibilities and write the number in the spaces below.

a. ___ pongo la mesa.
b. ___ veo a muchos actores.
c. ___ conduzco mi coche al trabajo.
d. ___ digo la verdad.
e. ___ no sé si puedo ir.
f. ___ traigo un regalo.
g. ___ conozco al presidente.
h. ___ salgo con mis amigos a bailar.

[1]Another verb similar to **traer** is **caer** *(to fall)*.

C **Mi celebración familiar favorita.** Fill in the blanks with the correct form of the verb in parentheses to find out how Carmen celebrates Christmas in Puerto Rico.

Yo (saber) ______ que la Navidad es especial en muchos lugares, pero en Puerto Rico, esta celebración no ______ (tener) igual. En diciembre, mis padres (poner) ______ el árbol *(tree)* de Navidad y el nacimiento *(nativity scene)*. Yo siempre (salir) ______ para las tiendas en el centro donde (ver) ______ todas las decoraciones. Allí yo (comprar) ______ regalos para mi familia. En las calles, (oír-yo) ______ los ritmos alegres de los «aguinaldos», que son canciones *(songs)* tradicionales de la Navidad en Puerto Rico.

El día 24, después de la Misa del gallo *(Midnight Mass)*, muchas personas (salir) ______ a restaurantes, pero nosotros (volver) ______ a casa y (hacer) ______ una cena especial; lechón asado *(roast pig)*, arroz con gandules *(rice with pidgeon peas)* y pasteles de plátano *(plantain pies)*. Yo siempre (decir) ______ que voy a comer todos los pasteles... pero sólo es un chiste. Para ayudar a mamá yo (poner) ______ la mesa. El 25 de diciembre, San Nicolás (dejar) ______ regalos para los niños. Pero, no es todo... el 6 de enero, los Reyes Magos *(Wise Men)* (venir) ______ y (traer) ______ más regalos.

Now, listen as your instructor reads statements about the passage you have just read. Write **C (cierto)** or **F (falso)** in the spaces.

1. ______ **2.** ______ **3.** ______ **4.** ______ **5.** ______

The Personal *a*

1. The personal **a** is used with direct objects that refer to people. The direct object receives the action of the verb and answers the question *what* or *whom*. In the sentence, *"I read the book," the book* answers the question, *"What do you read?"* and therefore is the direct object. In the sentence, *"I see Joe," Joe* answers the question, *"Whom do you see?"* and is therefore the direct object.
2. The personal **a** has no English equivalent and cannot be translated in English.

   Veo **a** los niños. *I see the children.*

3. The personal **a** comes immediately before the direct object of a sentence and is used in the following cases.

   a. when the direct object refers to a definite person or persons. It is not used when the direct object refers to things.

Llevo **a** mi prima a clase y luego llevo mis libros a la biblioteca.	*I take my cousin to class and then I take my books to the library.*

   However, when the direct object refers to an indefinite or unspecific person, the personal **a** is not used.

La abuela ve **a** un médico bueno.	*Grandmother sees a good doctor.*
La abuela necesita un médico bueno.	*Grandmother needs a good doctor.*

   b. with the indefinite pronouns **alguien** and **nadie** when they are used as direct objects.

No veo **a nadie** aquí.	*I don't see **anyone** here.*
Voy a visitar **a alguien** hoy.	*I'm going to visit **someone** today.*

   c. before the interrogative words **quién** and **quiénes** when they are used as direct objects.

¿A quién invitas a la reunión?	***Whom** are you inviting to the reunion?*
¿A quiénes llamas?	***Whom** are you calling?*

4. The following are commonly used verbs that require the personal **a.** Although in English these verbs require prepositions *(at, to, for)*, in Spanish the preposition is included in the verb.

mirar	*to look at*	buscar	*to look for*
escuchar	*to listen to*	esperar	*to wait for*

Busco a mi primo.	***I'm looking for** my cousin.*
Espero a mi tía. Vamos a **esperar** el autobús aquí.	***I'm waiting for** my aunt. We're going **to wait for** the bus here.*

¡AVISO! The personal **a** is usually omitted after the verb **tener.**

Tengo tres tíos.	*I have three uncles.*

Practiquemos

A **¿El objeto directo?** Find the direct object in the following sentences. Indicate if it answers the question *what* **(qué)** or *whom* **(a quién),** and if it requires the personal **a.** Then translate the sentences.

1. I don't know anyone here.
2. She finishes her homework.
3. Marta is taking her grandmother to the reunion.
4. We need more ice cream.
5. I see the children over there.

B **De visita en Puerto Rico.** Carmen Frontera is Puerto Rican but lives in New York now. She and her family are going to visit relatives on the island. Fill in the blanks with the personal **a** if it's necessary.

¡Vamos a Puerto Rico! En Manatí, un pueblo *(town)* pequeño en la costa, visitamos ______ mi abuela. Vamos a llevar ______ la abuela a Dorado, otro pueblo bonito, para ver ______ mis tíos. Quiero visitar ______ la Universidad de Puerto Rico que está en Río Piedras porque pienso estudiar allí. En San Juan, la capital, vamos a ver ______ los otros familiares. En las calles bonitas del Viejo San Juan, yo siempre miro ______ los turistas que compran ______ mucho en las tiendas. Finalmente, quiero visitar ______ un almacén y comprar regalos para mis amigos.

C **Los ídolos de los adolescentes.** According to a recent survey among university students in Puerto Rico, the following people are most admired. Form complete sentences by combining the person in the first column with the description in the second to tell why you admire each.

¿A QUIÉNES ADMIRAN NUESTROS MUCHACHOS?

Admiro a Marc Anthony porque es un cantante *(singer)* puertorriqueño fabuloso.

1. Juan González e Iván Rodríguez	**a.** porque a los 77 años volvió *(he returned)* al espacio.
2. John Glenn	**b.** porque fue *(she was)* una de las figuras humanitarias más importantes de nuestra época.
3. Michel Cousteau	**c.** porque son atletas excelentes.
4. la Madre Teresa	**d.** porque es una actriz talentosa.
5. Rita Moreno	**e.** porque el trabajo de él y su padre ayuda a conservar la vida submarina.

Now interview your classmates to find out whom they admire and why. Is there a common answer? Share your results.

The Verbs *Saber* and *Conocer*

Forma

Unlike English, Spanish has two verbs that express the concept of *to know:* **saber** and **conocer.**

SABER		CONOCER	
sé	sabemos	conozco	conocemos
sabes	sabéis	conoces	conocéis
sabe	saben	conoce	conocen

Función

Saber is used:

1. to express knowledge of facts or information.

Yo **sé** que Juan tiene dos hermanas menores.	*I **know** that Juan has two younger sisters.*
Ella **sabe** que Santo Domingo es la capital de la República Dominicana.	*She **knows** that Santo Domingo is the capital of the Dominican Republic.*
Tú **sabes** mucho de la historia del Caribe, ¿no?	*You **know** a lot about the history of the Caribbean, don't you?*

2. with an infinitive to indicate *to know how to do something.*

Mi abuelo no **sabe conducir.**	*My grandfather doesn't **know how to drive.***

Conocer is used:

1. to express familiarity or acquaintance with people, places, or things.

¿Conoces a mi marido?	***Do you know** my husband?*
Conozco bien la ciudad de Ponce.	***I know** the city of Ponce well.*
No conozco su restaurante. ¿Es bueno?	***I don't know** his restaurant. Is it good?*

2. to mean *to make someone's acquaintance* or *to meet* for the first time.

Voy a **conocer** a sus padres esta noche.	*I'm going **to meet** his parents tonight.*

Note the use of **saber** and **conocer** in the following sentences.

No sé mucho de la música de Juan Luis Guerra pero **conozco** su grupo, 4–40.	***I don't know** a lot about the music of Juan Luis Guerra but **I'm familiar with** his group, 4–40.*
Juan **no sabe** dónde vivo pero **conoce** mi calle.	*Juan **doesn't know** where I live but **he knows** my street.*

Practiquemos

A **¿Qué saben hacer estas personas?** Tell what the following people know how to do. Follow the model.

MODELO **Yo sé sacar fotos.**

1.

2.

3.

B **Mucho gusto en conocerlo.** Form complete sentences by using the verbs **conocer** and **saber** and by matching the people in the first column with the reasons why you want to meet them in the second column.

MODELO Rubén Blades
Quiero conocer a Rubén Blades porque sabe mucho de la historia de Panamá.

1. Sammy Sosa y Pedro Martínez	**a.** cantar *(to sing)* en inglés y español.
2. Pete Sampras	**b.** jugar al béisbol.
3. Gloria Estefan	**c.** mucho sobre la vida en Hollywood.
4. el presidente	**d.** mucho sobre el tenis.
5. Jimmy Smits	**e.** mucho de la política.

C **¿Saber o conocer?** Choose the answers that complete the sentences in a logical way. There is more than one correct answer.

1. ¿Sabes...
a. de quién es el coche?
b. preparar comida típica del Caribe *(Caribbean)?*
c. a Marta, la prima de Ramón?
d. a qué hora empieza el concierto?

2. Queremos conocer...
a. las tradiciones de Latinoamérica.
b. a los padres de Josefina.
c. a qué hora empieza nuestro programa de televisión.
d. el número de teléfono del dentista.

3. Sé...
a. su nombre.
b. al presidente personalmente.
c. que Alma sale con Jorge.
d. conducir bien.

4. ¿Cuándo vamos a conocer...
a. si abuela viene o no?
b. la respuesta?
c. a tu novio, Celia?
d. el arte caribeño?

D **Chismes *(Gossip)*.** Tell everything you know and everything you want to know about the following people, places, and things.

Juan Luis Guerra
Yo **sé** que tiene un grupo musical, que es de la República Dominicana, que es muy popular y que gana mucho dinero. **Quiero saber** si tiene novia y si viene a los Estados Unidos.

1. Jennifer López	**3.** Puerto Rico	**5.** la paella
2. Nueva York	**4.** el presidente	**6.** el Ratón *(mouse)* Mickey

Weather Expressions

Forma

¿Qué tiempo hace? *(What's the weather like?)*

Hace frío. *(It's cold.)*

Hace sol. Hace buen tiempo.
(It's sunny. The weather is nice.)

Hace calor. *(It's hot.)*

Está nublado. *(It's cloudy.)*

Hace fresco. *(It's cool.)*

Nieva. (nevar) *(It's snowing. [to snow])*

Hace viento. *(It's windy.)*

Llueve. (llover) Hace mal tiempo.
(It's raining. [to rain] The weather is bad.)

Función

1. Note that whereas in English the verb *to be* is used to describe many weather conditions, in Spanish the verb **hacer** is frequently used.
2. The adjectives **mucho** and **poco** are used to modify the nouns **frío, calor, fresco, sol,** and **viento.**

   Hace **mucho** viento pero **poco** frío. *It's **very** windy but **not very** cold.*

3. **Mucho** and **poco** are also used as adverbs with the verbs **nevar** and **llover**.

   Nieva mucho en enero y **llueve muy poco.** ***It snows a lot** in January and **rains very little.***

4. The adverb **muy** is used with **buen/mal tiempo**.

   Hace muy buen tiempo. ***The weather is very good.***

The Seasons, Months, and Days of the Week

Forma

Las estaciones *The seasons*

el invierno *winter*
la primavera *spring*
el verano *summer*
el otoño *fall*

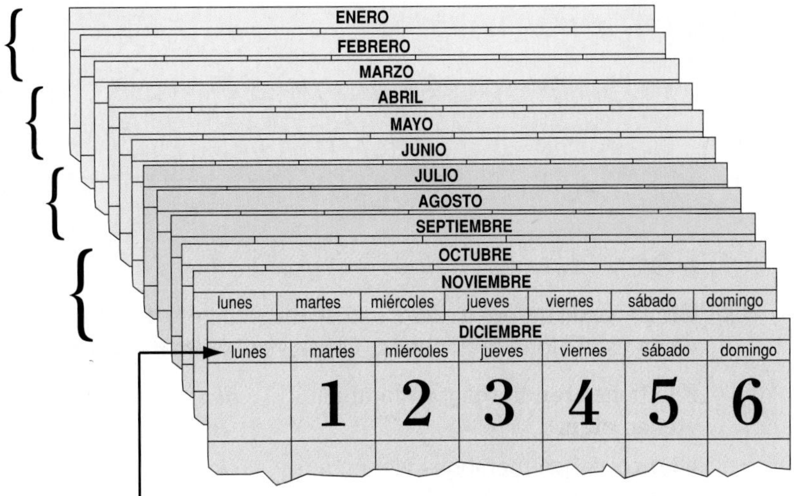

ENERO
FEBRERO
MARZO
ABRIL
MAYO
JUNIO
JULIO
AGOSTO
SEPTIEMBRE
OCTUBRE
NOVIEMBRE
lunes martes miércoles jueves viernes sábado domingo
DICIEMBRE
lunes martes miércoles jueves viernes sábado domingo
1 2 3 4 5 6

Los meses del año *The months of the year*

enero *January*
febrero *February*
marzo *March*
abril *April*
mayo *May*
junio *June*
julio *July*
agosto *August*
septiembre *September*
octubre *October*
noviembre *November*
diciembre *December*

Los días de la semana *The days of the week*

lunes *Monday*
martes *Tuesday*
miércoles *Wednesday*
jueves *Thursday*
viernes *Friday*
sábado *Saturday*
domingo *Sunday*

Función

1. Note that whereas the days of the week and the months of the year are capitalized in English, in Spanish they are not.
2. To express *on* a certain day you use only the definite article **el.** To express habitual action *on* a certain day you use only the definite article **los** with the plural form of the day.

El domingo voy a visitar al tío Pepe.	***On Sunday*** *I'm going to visit Uncle Pepe.*
Los domingos Susana no va a clase.	***On Sundays*** *Susan doesn't go to class.*

Numbers Above 100

Forma

Los números de cien a un millón

100	cien	400	cuatrocientos(as)	900	novecientos(as)
101	ciento uno	500	quinientos(as)	1.000	mil
102	ciento dos	600	seiscientos(as)	1.876	mil ochocientos setenta y seis
200	doscientos(as)	700	setecientos(as)	2.000	dos mil
201	doscientos(as) uno(a)	800	ochocientos(as)	1.000.000	un millón
300	trescientos(as)				

Función

1. **Cien** is used before a noun, before the numbers **mil** and **millón/millones,** and when used alone in counting. Otherwise, **ciento** is used.

Ella tiene **cien** libros y yo también tengo **cien.**	*She has* ***a hundred*** *books and I also have* ***a hundred.***
Ciento veinte personas vienen a la reunión.	***One hundred and twenty*** *people are coming to the meeting.*

2. Multiples of a hundred **(doscientos, trescientos...)** agree in gender with the nouns they modify.

Hay **novecientos** escritorios y **ochocientas** sillas.	*There are* ***nine hundred*** *desks and* ***eight hundred*** *chairs.*

3. **Mil** is used in the singular form.

Yo tengo **dos mil** centavos y ella tiene **tres mil.**	*I have* ***two thousand*** *pennies and she has* ***three thousand.***

¡AVISO! The indefinite article **un** is never used with **cien** and **mil. Cien** means *a* hundred and **mil** means *a* thousand.

4. To express the year, use the following form.

   1995 mil novecientos noventa y cinco

   1492 mil cuatrocientos noventa y dos

   1568 mil quinientos sesenta y ocho

   Note that in dates, multiples of a hundred are masculine since they refer to the word **año** *(year)*, which is masculine.

5. In dates, cardinal numbers are used, except to express *the first.*

Hoy **es el primero** de mayo y mañana **es el dos.**	*Today is May **first** and tomorrow is the **second.***

   To ask what the date is, use the expression: **¿Cuál es la fecha (de hoy)?**

   To express the complete date, use the form: **(Hoy) es el cuatro de abril de 1996.**

Practiquemos

A El calendario de Sofía. Tell when Sofía is going to do the following activities.

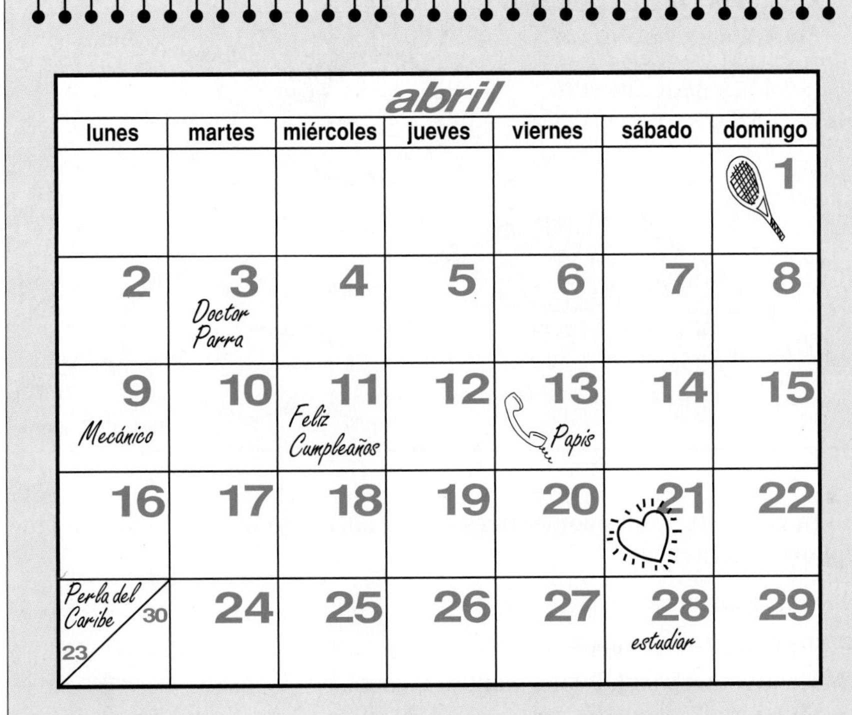

MODELO **Va a llevar el coche al mecánico el lunes, 8 de abril.**

1. comer en un restaurante puertorriqueño
2. salir con su novio
3. preparar la tarea
4. cumplir veinte años
5. ir al médico
6. jugar al tenis
7. llamar a sus padres

B **Fechas.** Read the following dates in Spanish.

1. January 1, 1518
2. October 8, 1952
3. August 12, 1492
4. September 30, 1883
5. December 25, 2001
6. April 2, 1776

C **Inventario en la librería.** Raúl needs to know what to order for the bookstore for the coming year. Help him count his inventory by reading him the following information.

Raúl, tú tienes...

1. 100 lápices
2. 250 cuadernos
3. 500 tizas
4. 125 bolígrafos
5. 300 libros de sicología
6. 200 botellas *(bottles)* de aspirina.

D **El tiempo en Puerto Rico.** Refer to the following weather map of Puerto Rico and tell what today's weather will be on various parts of the island.

E **Para traducir.** Grandmother likes to talk about the weather. Translate the following sentences.

1. What's the weather like today?
2. It's raining and it's windy.
3. The weather's bad. I don't want to go out.
4. I think (that) it's going to snow.
5. Aunt Larisa says that it's very hot in Santo Domingo.

F **La nueva máquina climática** ***(The new weather machine).*** You have just bought the climate control machine on page 163. Answer the following questions.

1. ¿Qué tiempo prefiere Ud. y por qué?
2. ¿Es un producto bueno? ¿Por qué sí o no?
3. ¿Qué pasa cuando la máquina no funciona *(doesn't function)* bien?

> Spend more time with Mariana and her friends while you review grammar and expand your cultural horizons.
>
> See the **Así es Mariana** exercise in your workbook for this lesson.

En resumen

(A) Los colores y la naturaleza *(nature)*. Read the ad and answer the following questions.

¿...Y de qué color son las latas° de su playa°...?

¿Doradas°? ¿rojas? ¿o azules?
No permita que las latas cubran la belleza° de su playa.
Deje° que el color y el calor de la arena° hagan° de ella un lugar más grato°.

latas *cans*
playa *beach*
Doradas *gold*
belleza *beauty*
deje *let*
arena *sand*
hagan *make*
lugar más grato *a nicer place*

1. ¿De qué color es esta playa? ¿De qué color debe ser la playa? Explique.
2. ¿De qué color es...
   a. un jardín *(garden)* en la primavera?
   b. un día de otoño?
   c. un arco iris *(rainbow)* después de llover?

B **El fascinante sol.** Read the following article and answer the questions that follow.

buenos ratos *good times*
nos ha hecho *has had us*
Tierra *Earth*
llega a alcanzar *reaches*
por 100 *% (percent)*

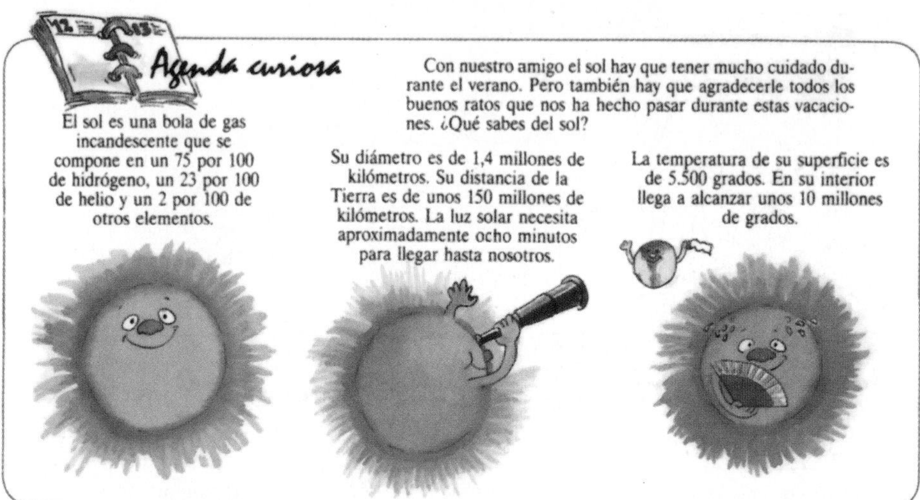

Agenda curiosa

Con nuestro amigo el sol hay que tener mucho cuidado durante el verano. Pero también hay que agradecerle todos los buenos ratos que nos ha hecho pasar durante estas vacaciones. ¿Qué sabes del sol?

El sol es una bola de gas incandescente que se compone en un 75 por 100 de hidrógeno, un 23 por 100 de helio y un 2 por 100 de otros elementos.

Su diámetro es de 1,4 millones de kilómetros. Su distancia de la Tierra es de unos 150 millones de kilómetros. La luz solar necesita aproximadamente ocho minutos para llegar hasta nosotros.

La temperatura de su superficie es de 5.500 grados. En su interior llega a alcanzar unos 10 millones de grados.

1. ¿Qué sabe Ud. del sol? ¿Qué piensa Ud. del sol?
2. ¿Por qué debe Ud. tener cuidado cuando hace sol?
3. ¿Qué usa Ud. para protección cuando hace mucho sol?

Una fiesta de quinceañera

C **La quinceañera.** Many Hispanics celebrate a girl's 15th birthday with a special party. The sentences in the following paragraphs are out of order. Arrange them to form a reading about the **quinceañera.** Then do the activities.

Párrafo 1

1. Puede ser una reunión íntima o una fiesta grande y elegante.
2. La celebración se llama **quinceañera** y significa que la muchacha ahora es una mujer y puede asistir a fiestas y salir con chicos.
3. En muchas familias hispanas, cuando una muchacha cumple quince años, hay una fiesta especial.

Párrafo 2

1. Hoy la quinceañera muestra la importancia de la familia en la cultura hispana.
2. Hay evidencias de algo similar en la antigua civilización azteca.
3. Nadie sabe cuál es el origen de la quinceañera.

Now, answer the following questions.

1. Tradicionalmente, ¿cómo celebra Ud. el cumpleaños?
2. ¿Cuáles son los cumpleaños importantes en su *(your)* cultura?
3. ¿Cómo es el cumpleaños ideal para Ud.?

D **La familia hispana.** Use the correct form of each verb and choose or give the correct form of the words in parentheses to find out about the Hispanic family.

La familia es muy importante en la cultura hispana. En los Estados Unidos, la familia (consistir) en el padre, la madre y (los, las) hijos. Para el hispano, el concepto de la familia es más (grande). Consiste en padres, hijos, abuelos, tíos, cuñados y primos. Los abuelos (tomar) una parte muy (activo) en la vida familiar, y con frecuencia viven con la familia. Los niños (aprender) a respetar (a, ______) la gente mayor.

Liliana, una joven puertorriqueña, dice: «Mi familia es muy unida. Yo (saber) que (ir-yo) a tener contacto íntimo con mis hermanos para toda la vida. Nosotros (mostrar) (nuestro) emociones. (También, Tampoco) respetamos mucho (a, ______) nuestros padres. Mis abuelos no viven con nosotros. Pero nosotros (ver) mucho a los abuelos porque nosotros (hacer) muchas fiestas y ellos siempre (venir) a comer».

Indicate if the following observations about Hispanic family life pertain to your culture as well and explain.

1. El aspecto más importante de la vida es la familia.
2. Muchas veces la familia extendida vive en una casa. Es decir, además de los padres y los hijos, también los abuelos viven con ellos, y posiblemente los tíos y primos.
3. El tener «novio» significa el matrimonio. Es decir, es una relación muy seria.

E **Carmen va a conocer a José.** Translate the following dialogue to Spanish.

Carmen: Raquel, do you know José Ortiz?

Raquel: Rosa's cousin? No, but I know that he attends the university. Why?

Carmen: Tomorrow I'm going to Rosa's house for lunch, and José is going to be there.

Raquel: He's single, he drives a black Ferrari, they say he's handsome, and he just turned twenty-five.

Carmen: Raquel, you know a lot. Do you want to meet José, too?

F **Composiciones breves.** Choose one of the following drawings and write a brief story about it. Include the following information.

1. ¿Quiénes son las personas?
2. ¿Cómo son y cómo están?
3. ¿Qué hacen ellos?
4. ¿Qué quieren hacer?
5. ¿Qué tiempo hace?
6. algo original

Escuchemos

A **¿Cuál de los dos?** You will hear an incomplete sentence. Choose the word that best completes the sentence.

(oye/trae)
Antonio ______ un regalo a la fiesta. trae.
Antonio trae un regalo a la fiesta.

1. (el desayuno/la cena)
2. (primo/tío)
3. (conducir/traducir)
4. (conoce/sabe)
5. (cuñados/abuelos)
6. (cuentan/crecen)
7. (suegra/nieta)
8. (anaranjado/verde)

B **Dictado *(Dictation)*.** You will hear a short narration about Liliana and her family. Listen carefully to the entire section. Listen again and write each sentence during the pauses.

You will then hear a series of false statements related to the dictation. Correct each one with complete sentences. Refer to your dictation.

Este lavaplatos es estupendo.

AVISO CULTURAL

(As a reading aid, refer to lesson vocabulary for new words.)

¿Viven sus padres cerca de su trabajo? En España, la idea de «*commuting*» es reciente *(recent)*. No hay una palabra en español para expresar la idea de ir en coche de su casa a su trabajo. Por lo general, las personas que viven en la ciudad también trabajan en la ciudad, y las personas que viven en el campo trabajan en el campo. La idea de «*suburbs*» es relativamente nueva en España, aunque ahora hay zonas residenciales o «*urbanizaciones*» en las afueras de algunas ciudades españolas. ¿Prefiere Ud. vivir en la ciudad, en las afueras o en el campo? ¿Por qué? ¿Quiere vivir cerca de su trabajo? ¿Cuáles son las ventajas *(advantages)* y desventajas de vivir y trabajar en el mismo lugar?

Preparativos

Review the vocabulary on pages 170–172 before viewing the video.

As you have learned in the preliminary sections, in Spanish the accent mark is used not only to tell you where the stress falls on words, but also to distinguish words that are spelled the same way but have different meanings. In the dialogue Amparo says, **"este lavaplatos...,"** and Celia says, **"un lavaplatos como éste...."** Both words are demonstratives, but one is an adjective and means "this," and the other is a pronoun and means "this one." Do you know which is which? You will also learn a new tense in this lesson—the present progressive tense, which is formed by joining the verb **estar** with a present participle (in English, the *-ing* form of the verb). Mariana thinks that the people in the kitchen **están**

chismeando *(are gossiping)* about her. Rather, they simply **"están charlando"** *(are chatting)* about housework. There are other examples of the present progressive tense in the dialogue, but the participle ends in **-iendo.** Can you guess why? In the following dialogue, Luis is at it again, impressing Mariana's family. What's he up to this time? Why do you think that he knows so little about dishwashers? Visiting Mariana's family is an education for him . . . in many ways!

Así es Mariana: La tarea doméstica

En la cocina, Luis Antonio ayuda a limpiar después de cenar.

Amparo: Según los expertos, este lavaplatos puede fregar y lavar más platos que veinte personas... y en muy poco tiempo.

Celia: En San Juan, un lavaplatos como éste cuesta alrededor de 500 dólares. Y fuera de la ciudad... ¡ni hablar!

Luis Antonio: Perdón, señora Benavides, pero... ¿no tiene que lavar los platos con jabón primero?

Amparo: Ya veo que sabes muy poco, hombre. Este lavaplatos es estupendo. Lava, seca... lo hace todo.

Celia: ¡Salvo limpiar los muebles, barrer el suelo y planchar la ropa!

Amparo: ¡Y darles de comer° a los gatos! *feed*

Entra Mariana.

Mariana: ¡Ajá! Están chismeando de mí.

Amparo: No, Mariana. Sólo estamos charlando de la tarea doméstica.

Mariana: ¡Qué horror! Hablar de cosas tan aburridas. *(A Luis Antonio)* Vamos al comedor...

Celia: Los voy a seguir. Quiero ver lo que están haciendo mi sobrino y mi cuñado.

Amparo: ¿Y tu marido?

Celia: ¿Mi marido?... no... ¡tu hermano! Lo cierto es que está durmiendo en el sillón delante de la tele.° *TV*

Es decir

A Basándose en el diálogo, escoja la respuesta incorrecta. *(Based on the dialogue, choose the answer that does not correctly complete each sentence.)*

1. Un lavaplatos... los platos.

a. friega b. seca c. barre d. lava

2. Un lavaplatos...

a. en San Juan cuesta menos que *(than)* en Miami.
b. fuera de San Juan cuesta más que en Miami.
c. en San Juan cuesta 500 dólares.
d. en San Juan es muy caro.

3. El lavaplatos no...

a. barre el suelo.
b. plancha la ropa.
c. limpia los muebles.
d. seca los platos.

B En parejas, escriban un breve diálogo original y represéntenlo. Mariana le pregunta a Luis Antonio: «¿Qué piensas de mi familia?» ¿Cuáles son algunas posibles respuestas? Después ella le pregunta: «¿Qué piensas de mi casa?» Luis contesta con muchos detalles. *(In pairs, write an original, brief scene and act it out. Mariana asks Luis what he thinks of her family. What are some possible answers? She also asks what he thinks of her house, and he gives detailed answers.)*

Al ver el video

A Después de ver el video, escoja *(choose)* la respuesta correcta.

1. En la cocina, Mariana...

a. ayuda a limpiar. b. saca una foto de Luis. c. habla con su papá.

2. Mariana cree que hacer la tarea doméstica...

a. es necesario. b. es interesante. c. es aburrido.

3. ¿Qué es lo que Luis no dice de la familia de Mariana?

a. Quiere pasar más tiempo con ellos.

b. No quiere estar solo con ellos.

c. Todos son muy simpáticos.

B ¿Por qué? Explique Ud. *(Explain.)* ¿Por qué...

1. dice Mariana que Luis hace «el error clásico» de seguir a su mamá a la cocina?

2. dice Mariana: «Vamos al comedor»?

3. dice Celia: «Los voy a seguir»?

4. no sabe Mariana qué hacer con Luis Antonio?

Vocabulario

Verbos

arreglar	*to arrange, put in order; to fix*
barrer	*to sweep*
cenar	*to have dinner, supper*
cocinar	*to cook*
compartir	*to share*
competir (i)	*to compete*
conseguir (i)	*to get, obtain*
corregir (i)	*to correct*
chismear	*to gossip*
desayunar	*to eat breakfast*
elegir (i)	*to elect; choose*
fregar (ie)	*to scrub*
lavar	*to wash*
limpiar	*to clean*

olvidar	*to forget*
pedir (i)	*to ask for, request; to order*
planchar	*to iron*
repetir (i)	*to repeat*
secar	*to dry*
seguir (i)	*to follow; to continue*
servir (i)	*to serve*

Partes de la casa	***Parts of the house***
la alcoba (el dormitorio)	*bedroom*
la cocina	*kitchen; cuisine*
el comedor	*dining room*
el cuarto (la habitación)	*room*
el cuarto de baño (baño)	*bathroom*
el jardín	*garden*
el piso	*floor (level of a building); condominium*
la sala (de estar)	*den*
el salón (la sala)	*living room*
el sótano	*basement*
el suelo	*floor*
el techo	*roof; ceiling*

Muebles y accesorios	***Furniture and accessories***
la alfombra	*rug*
la almohada	*pillow*
el armario (ropero)	*closet*
la bañera	*bathtub*
la cama (de agua, matrimonial)	*bed (waterbed, double bed)*
el cuadro	*painting*
la ducha	*shower*
el espejo	*mirror*
la estufa	*stove*
el horno	*oven*
el jabón	*soap*
el lavabo	*sink*
el lavaplatos	*dishwasher*
la manta	*blanket*
la mesa	*table*
el microondas	*microwave oven*
el mueble	*piece of furniture*
la plancha	*iron*
el radio	*radio (object)*
la radio	*radio (transmission)*
el refrigerador (la nevera)	*refrigerator*

la ropa	*clothing*
la sábana	*sheet*
la silla	*chair*
el sillón	*armchair*
el sofá	*sofa*
el televisor	*television set*

Adjetivos

cada	*each*
desordenado	*messy, disorderly*
limpio	*clean*
lleno	*full*
ordenado	*neat, orderly*
solo	*alone, lonely*
sucio	*dirty*
vacío	*empty*

Palabras y expresiones útiles
(Refer to page 177 for more useful prepositions)

adentro	*inside*
afuera	*outside*
las afueras	*outskirts, suburbs*
alrededor (de)	*around*
cerca (de)	*near*
dentro (de)	*inside (of)*
fuera (de)	*outside (of)*
el gato	*cat*
lejos (de)	*far away (from)*
pasar la aspiradora	*to vacuum*
el perro	*dog*
sacar la basura	*to take out the garbage*
la tarea doméstica	*housework*

Vocabulario adicional

alquilar	*to rent*
el alquiler	*rental fee*
aunque	*although*
el garaje	*garage*
el hogar	*home*
la lavadora	*washing machine*
el pájaro	*bird*
el patio	*patio*
la secadora	*clothes dryer*

Repasemos el vocabulario

A **Cuartos.** ¿Dónde hace Ud. las siguientes actividades? *Listen as your instructor reads a series of activities. Choose a room and form a complete sentence to tell where you do the activities.*

MODELO Profesor(a): escuchar la radio
Estudiante: **La alcoba. Escucho la radio en la alcoba.**

a. la cocina **b.** el dormitorio **c.** el sótano

d. el salón **e.** el comedor **f.** la sala

Nombre Ud. otra actividad que hace en cada cuarto mencionado arriba. *(Name another activity that you do in each of the rooms mentioned above.)*

B **Accesorios.** ¿Dónde encuentra Ud. los accesorios siguientes? *Refer to the drawings and tell where you find each accessory.*

MODELO **La bañera está en el cuarto de baño.**

a. **b.** **c.** **d.** **e.**

1. **2.** **3.** **4.** **5.**

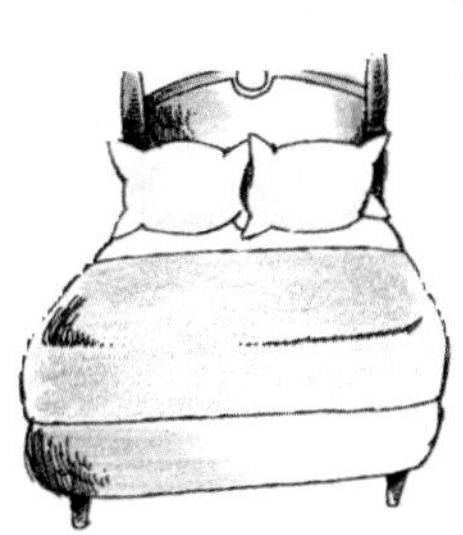

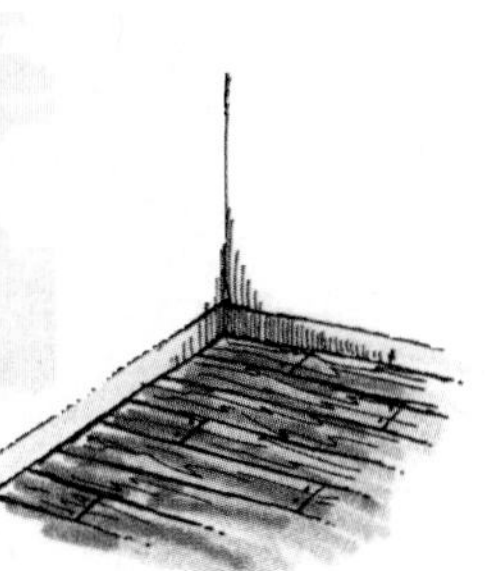

C **Relaciones.** Indique Ud. el accesorio que no está relacionado con el cuarto y explique. *(Indicate the accessory that is not related to the room and explain.)*

MODELO baño: bañera lavabo ducha cama
Cama no está relacionada porque está en la alcoba.

1. cocina:	lavaplatos	estufa	sillón	horno
2. dormitorio:	almohada	sábana	manta	lavabo
3. salón:	jabón	alfombra	cuadro	sofá
4. garaje:	ducha	coche	bicicleta	raqueta de tenis

D **¿Para qué?** Combine Ud. las palabras y frases en las tres columnas para formar frases completas. *(Combine the words and phrases in the three columns to tell why you do things.)*

MODELO **Pongo** *(I turn on)* **la luz para leer.**

1. Conducir	microondas	ayudar a mi madre
2. Barrer	platos	ir a las afueras
3. Lavar	sofacama	ayudar a mi padre
4. Abrir	coche	dormir
5. Usar	garaje	comer rápido

E **Preguntas personales.** Conteste Ud. las siguientes preguntas con frases completas. Luego, cambie las preguntas a la forma **tú** y entreviste a un(a) compañero(a). *(Answer the following questions with complete sentences. Then change to the **tú** form and interview a classmate.)*

1. ¿Cuántas tareas domésticas puede hacer en diez minutos? ¿Cuáles son?
2. ¿Prefiere cocinar o planchar? ¿Por qué?
3. ¿Qué tareas domésticas necesitan el uso de jabón?
4. ¿Usa Ud. un microondas? ¿Por qué sí o no?
5. ¿Cómo comparte Ud. las tareas domésticas con la(s) persona(s) con quien(es) vive?

F **Salones y salas.** Describa Ud. los cuartos siguientes. Un(a) compañero(a) va a identificar cada cuarto según su descripción. *(Describe the following rooms. A classmate will identify each according to your description.)*

1.

2.

3.

4.

5.

Ahora, conteste las preguntas siguientes.

1. ¿Qué muebles hay en el cuarto 1? ¿Y en el 3?
2. ¿Cuál de los cuartos es el más bonito? ¿el menos bonito? ¿el más contemporáneo? ¿el más tradicional? ¿Cuál tiene más colores? ¿Cuáles son los colores?
3. ¿Cuál de estos cuartos prefiere Ud.? ¿Por qué?

Prepositional Pronouns

Prepositions show relationships of time, location, and position between nouns and other words in a sentence. Some prepositions in English include: *to, at, for, from, near, by, on, under, after, behind, in,* and *before.* What are the Spanish equivalents of these words? Now study the following pronouns that are used with prepositions.

Forma

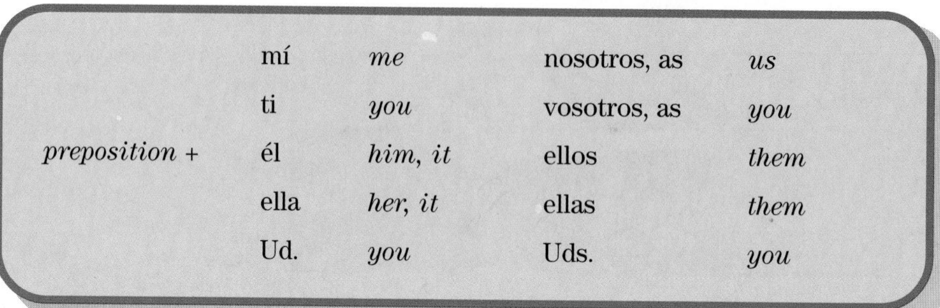

	mí	*me*	nosotros, as	*us*
	ti	*you*	vosotros, as	*you*
preposition +	él	*him, it*	ellos	*them*
	ella	*her, it*	ellas	*them*
	Ud.	*you*	Uds.	*you*

1. With the exception of the first- and second-person singular **(mí, ti),** prepositional pronouns have the same form as subject pronouns. Note the accent on the prepositional pronoun **mí** *(me)* to distinguish it from the possessive adjective, **mi** *(my).*
2. **Yo** and **tú** are used instead of **mí** and **ti** after the following prepositions.

entre	*between, among*	excepto	*except*
incluso	*including*	menos	*except*
según	*according to*	salvo	*except*

Entre tú y yo, creo que Tomás nunca limpia su cuarto. — ***Between you and me,*** *I think that Tomás never cleans his room.*

Todos ayudan a cocinar, **salvo tú.** — *Everyone is helping to cook* ***except you.***

3. The preposition **con** *(with)* has irregular forms when used with the first- and second-person singular pronouns.

¿Vienes **conmigo?** — *Are you coming* ***with me?***

Sí, voy **contigo.** — *Yes, I'm going* ***with you.***

Función

1. Prepositional pronouns are used with prepositions in place of nouns.

¿Sales antes de **José?** — *Are you going out before* ***José?***

No, salgo después de **él.** — *No, I'm going out after* ***him.***

2. Prepositional pronouns follow their corresponding prepositions.

para **ellos**   cerca de **nosotros**   por **ella**   de **mí**   a **Ud.**   en **tí**

Practiquemos

A **La cena familiar.** La familia Moreno acaba de preparar una cena deliciosa, pero no saben qué cosa es para quién. *Correct each statement according to the cues. Replace the name in the model with the appropriate prepositional pronoun.*

El sandwich es para Pepe. (mí)
No es para él. Es para mí.

1. La limonada es para Rosita. (ti)
2. Las pizzas son para Vicente y Javier. (nosotras)
3. El helado es para Susana. (Ud.)
4. Los tacos son para los tíos. (Uds.)
5. El café es para el abuelo. (mí)

B **¡Qué desastre!** La casa está muy desordenada y mamá vuelve en diez minutos. *Fill in the blanks with the correct prepositional pronoun to find out how the Gómez kids straighten up the house.*

Elena: Mamá vuelve en pocos minutos. Debemos limpiar todo para ______ *(her)*. Susana, cerca de ______ *(you)* está la aspiradora. Debes pasarla. Rafael, cerca de ______ *(me)* está el jabón. Tú vas a fregar el lavabo. Debes venir ______ *(with me)* a la cocina para poder empezar. Y Susana, tú debes venir con ______ *(us)* también, y puedes barrer el suelo primero.

Susana: Yo no quiero ir ___ *(with you two)*. Uds. deben limpiar todo dentro de la casa y yo voy a arreglar todo fuera de ___ *(it)*. El patio está muy sucio. ¡Y el garaje! Alrededor de ___ *(it)* Joselito tiene todos sus juguetes.

The Present Progressive Tense

To form the present progressive tense, use a form of the verb **estar** in the present tense with the present participle. A present participle is formed by removing the infinitive endings **-ar, -er, -ir** and adding **-ando** to **-ar** verbs and **-iendo** to **-er** and **-ir** verbs.

infinitive:	**LAVAR**	**BARRER**	**ESCRIBIR**
present participle:	lav + ando	barr + iendo	escrib + iendo
present progressive:	estoy lavando	estoy barriendo	estoy escribiendo

These participles are equivalent to the verb forms in English that end in **-ing: washing, sweeping, writing.**

1. When the root of an **-er** or **-ir** verb ends in a vowel, add **-yendo: leer → leyendo, creer → creyendo, traer → trayendo.**
2. With stem-changing verbs that end in **-ir,** the stem vowel **e** changes to **i** and **o** changes to **u: mentir → mintiendo, dormir → durmiendo.** Stem-changing verbs that end in **-ar** or **-er** do not change in this form: **fregar → fregando, volver → volviendo.**

Función

Whereas the present indicative can express many different actions,

Escribo
- *I write (in general)*
- *I do write (every day)*
- *I am writing (now)*
- *I will write (in the immediate future)*

the present progressive is very specific. It expresses an action that is in progress right now.

Estoy escribiendo. *I am writing (at this very moment).*

¡AVISO! The following verbs are rarely used in the progressive construction: **ir (yendo), venir, ser,** and **estar.**

Practiquemos

A **¿Qué está haciendo Ud.?** Usando el presente del progresivo, diga qué está haciendo en los siguientes lugares. *(Using the present progressive tense, tell what you are doing in the following places.)*

la sala de estar/charlar con amigos
Estoy charlando con mis amigos en la sala de estar.

1. la cama/dormir
2. el sótano/planchar ropa
3. el garaje/arreglar el carro
4. el sillón/leer un periódico
5. el comedor/servir la cena
6. la cocina/fregar el suelo
7. el jardín/barrer el patio
8. ¿?

Ahora nombre Ud. más lugares y un(a) compañero(a) va a decir qué está haciendo.

B **¿Qué está pasando?** Usando el presente del progresivo, diga qué está pasando en los siguientes dibujos. *(Using the present progressive tense, tell what is happening in the following drawings.)*

1.

2.

3.

4.

The Present Tense of *e > i* Stem-changing Verbs

Forma

Certain **-ir** verbs change the stem vowel from **e** > **i** in the present tense when the stem vowel is stressed. As with other stem-changing verbs you have already studied (**e** > **ie** and **o** > **ue**), the **nosotros** and **vosotros** forms do not have this change. The stem vowel **e** changes to **i** in the present participle of these verbs.

PEDIR *(to ask for)*		**REPETIR** *(to repeat)*	
p**i**do	pedimos	rep**i**to	repetimos
p**i**des	pedís	rep**i**tes	repetís
p**i**de	p**i**den	rep**i**te	rep**i**ten
p**i**diendo		repit**i**endo	

Some common **e** > **i** stem-changing verbs are:

competir	*to compete*	impedir	*to prevent*
conseguir	*to obtain*	seguir	*to continue; to follow*
corregir	*to correct*	servir	*to serve*
elegir	*to elect, choose*		

Mi papá **sirve** la cena esta noche.	*My dad* ***is serving*** *dinner tonight.*
Nosotros **elegimos** a un presidente mañana.	*We* ***are electing*** *a president tomorrow.*
Tú siempre **corriges** todos los errores.	*You always* ***correct*** *all of the mistakes.*

Función

1. **Pedir** means *to ask for*. It does not require a preposition since *for* is already included in the verb.

   Yo **pido** café todas las mañanas. — ***I ask for*** *coffee every morning.*

2. **Pedir** is used to request an object or an action, that is, to ask someone to give or to do something. When you use **pedir** you receive an object or action.

   Yo te **pido** el jabón. — ***I ask*** *you* ***for*** *the soap.* (The result: You give me the soap.)

   Yo te **pido** que laves[1] el suelo. — ***I ask*** *you to wash the floor.* (The result: You wash the floor.)

   To express *to ask* in the context of asking a question, you use the verb **preguntar.** When you use **preguntar** you receive an answer or information.

   Yo te **pregunto** dónde vive José. — ***I ask*** *you where José lives.* (Result: You tell me where José lives.)

3. The verbs **seguir** and **conseguir** (as well as other verbs that end in **-guir**) have an additional spelling change. The **u,** which is used to help maintain the hard **g** sound, is omitted in the first-person singular **(yo). Ge** and **gi** produce a soft **g** sound while **ga, go,** and **gu** produce a hard **g** sound.

   SEGUIR *(to follow)*

sigo	seguimos
sigues	seguís
sigue	siguen

   siguiendo

   Seguir is often used with the present participle to express a continuing action.

   José **sigue limpiando** su cuarto. — *José* ***continues cleaning*** *his room.*

4. The verbs **corregir** and **elegir** (as well as other verbs that end in **-gir** and **-ger**) have an additional spelling change. The **g** changes to **j** in the first-person singular **(yo)** in order to maintain the soft **g** sound. Remember that **ge** and **gi** produce a soft **g** sound while **ga, go,** and **gu** produce a hard **g** sound.

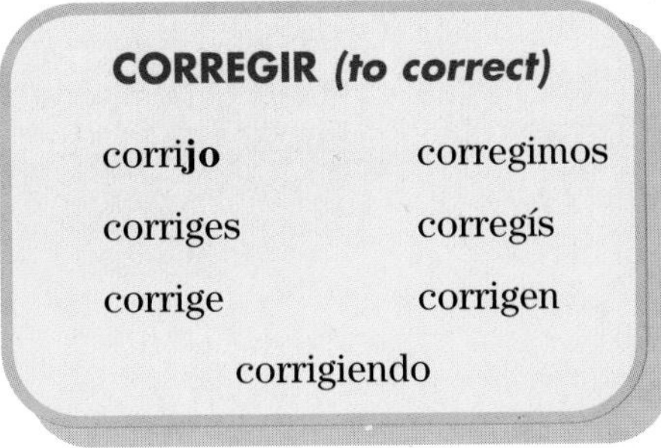

CORREGIR *(to correct)*

corri**jo**	corregimos
corriges	corregís
corrige	corrigen

corrigiendo

[1]The verb **lavar** here is used in the subjunctive. This will be presented later in Lesson 11.

Practiquemos

A **Servicio especial.** Complete el párrafo con la forma correcta del verbo **servir.** *(Complete the paragraph with the correct form of the verb* **servir.***)*

Cuando nuestros amigos vienen a comer, yo siempre ______ la comida y mi esposo ______ el vino. Pero él y yo ______ el postre. ¿Qué ______ tú para una cena especial?

B **Pedir y preguntar.** Forme Ud. frases usando los verbos **pedir** y **preguntar.** *(Form sentences using the verbs* **pedir** *and* **preguntar.***) Ask for the first item then ask about the second. Follow the model.*

MODELO vino/servir/tacos
Después de pedir vino voy a preguntar si sirven tacos.

1. jabón/vender/perfume
2. almohadas/tener/mantas
3. sábanas/vender/alfombras
4. sillas/tener/camas
5. café/servir/agua

C **Preguntas y respuestas.** Su compañero(a) va a contestar sus preguntas. *(Your classmate is going to answer your questions.)*

Pregúntele... *(Ask him/her . . .)*

1. quiénes generalmente sirven la cena en su casa y a qué hora.
2. cuántos cursos *(courses)* sigue este semestre.
3. qué pide en su restaurante favorito.
4. si va a conseguir trabajo para el verano.
5. si compite en el tenis.

Demonstrative Adjectives

Forma

Demonstrative Adjectives

	this, these	that, those *(nearby)*	that, those *(far away)*
masculine singular	este	ese	aquel
feminine singular	esta	esa	aquella
masculine plural	estos	esos	aquellos
feminine plural	estas	esas	aquellas

1. **Demostrar** in Spanish means *to show* or *demonstrate*. Demonstrative adjectives show or point out nouns—people, places, or things. The demonstrative adjective is more specific than the definite or indefinite article.

   la casa — ***the** house*
   una casa — ***a** house*
   esta casa — ***this** house*

   Las casas en mi barrio son bonitas, y hay unas casas grandes en mi calle, pero yo prefiero **esta** casa. — *The houses in my neighborhood are pretty, and there are some big houses on my street, but I prefer **this** house.*

2. Since they are adjectives, they agree in number and gender with the nouns they modify. Since they are a type of limiting adjective, they generally precede them.

   este refrigerador nuevo — ***this** new refrigerator*
   aquellas sábanas nuevas — ***those** new sheets (over there)*

3. Pay special attention to the masculine singular forms **este** and **ese.** Note that they end in **-e** although the plural forms end in **-os.**

   ese horno — ***that** oven*
   esos hornos — ***those** ovens*

4. **Este** and all its forms mean *this* or *these*, and indicate proximity to the speaker.

   Este espejo (que yo tengo) es de Ema. — ***This** mirror (that I have) is Ema's.*

   Ese and all its forms mean *that* or *those*, and often indicate proximity to the listener or *short* distance from the speaker.

   Ese cuadro (que tú tienes) es de José. — ***That** painting (that you have) is José's.*

   Aquel and all its forms mean *that* or *those*, and often indicate distance from both the speaker and listener or *long* distance from the speaker.

   Aquel jardín (en la otra calle) es bonito. — ***That** garden (on the other street) is pretty.*

Demonstrative Pronouns

Forma

Demonstrative Pronouns

	this, these	that, those *(nearby)*	that, those *(far away)*
masculine singular	éste	ése	aquél
feminine singular	ésta	ésa	aquélla
masculine plural	éstos	ésos	aquéllos
feminine plural	éstas	ésas	aquéllas
neuter	esto	eso	aquello

Función

1. A pronoun *(pro* = **por** = *in place of)* replaces a noun. Demonstrative pronouns have the same form as demonstrative adjectives, but they have written accents to help distinguish them from the adjectives.

Este lavaplatos es viejo pero **ése** es nuevo.	*This dishwasher is old but **that one** is new.*
Esos platos están sucios pero **éstos** están limpios.	*Those plates are dirty but **these** are clean.*

2. The neuter demonstrative pronouns **esto, eso,** and **aquello** are used to refer to abstract ideas, concepts, or situations, and undetermined or unidentified objects. Note that they have no written accent.

¿Qué es **esto?**	*What is **this?***
Eso es fácil de hacer.	***That's** easy to do.*
Aquello no es nada. Yo sé más.	***That's** nothing. I know more.*

Practiquemos

A **¿Cuál?** Practice agreement of demonstrative adjectives by substituting the words in parentheses for the underlined word in each sentence. Then replace each noun with the corresponding demonstrative pronoun.

MODELO Busco jabón en esa tienda.
Busco jabón en ésa.

1. Busco jabón en esa tienda. (ciudades, habitaciones, catálogos, cuarto de baño, casa).
2. Van a comprar aquel microondas. (estufa, camas, radio, muebles, televisor).
3. Estos cuadros son bonitos. (sillones, silla, alfombras, espejo, mesas).

B **¡¿Qué comprar?!** Mire Ud. el siguiente dibujo y complete Ud. las frases con el adjetivo demostrativo apropiado para saber qué quiere vender la vendedora. *(Look at the drawing and complete the sentences with the appropriate demonstrative adjective to find out what the saleswoman wants to sell.)*

«Señora, ______ microondas tiene reloj y ______ radios son excelentes, son del Japón. ______ sillas y ______ sillón son muy caros, pero ______ plancha no cuesta mucho. Pero, Ud. no puede pagar ______ jabón aquí porque viene del departamento de perfumes y cosméticos. ______ aspiradora no es para vender, sirve de modelo solamente. ______ sábanas cuestan $30.00. ¿Ves ______ lavaplatos? Es el modelo nuevo. ______ secadora *(dryer)* es eléctrica, ______ mesa es muy elegante y el cuadro, pues, no sé nada de ______ cuadros.»

C **El apartamento nuevo.** You are moving to a new apartment and your friend helps you pack. With a classmate, use demonstrative pronouns to help pack the correct items.

MODELO Ud.: Necesito esa plancha.
Su amigo(a): **¿Cuál, ésta?**
Ud.: **Sí, ésa.**

1. Voy a llevar ese televisor.
2. Ahora pongo esos libros.
3. Debes tener cuidado con ese espejo.
4. Quiero llevar esas sábanas.
5. Pienso llevar esos sillones.
6. Creo que necesito esas mantas.
7. Llevo esa mesa.
8. Dejo ese radio.

Direct Object Pronouns

Forma

Direct Object Pronouns

me	me	nos	us
te	*you (familiar, singular)*	os	*you (familiar, plural)*
lo	*him, you (formal, masc. sing.); it (masculine)*	los	*them, you (formal, masc. pl.)*
la	*her, you (formal, fem. sing.); it (feminine)*	las	*them, you (formal, fem. pl.)*

Función

1. Direct object pronouns, like direct object nouns, receive the action of the verb and answer the questions *what* and *whom*. They agree in number and gender with the nouns they replace. Direct object pronouns are placed before a conjugated verb.

   Lavo la manta y **la** seco. — *I wash the blanket and dry* ***it.***

   Compro otro televisor porque **lo** necesito. — *I'm buying another television set because I need* ***it.***

2. Direct object pronouns may follow and be attached to an infinitive or a present participle. There is absolutely no difference in the meaning or emphasis of the pronoun based on its placement before the conjugated verb or after the infinitive or present participle.

   La voy a lavar ahora.
   Voy a lavar**la** ahora. } *I'm going to wash* ***it*** *now.*

   La estoy lavando ahora.
   Estoy lavándo**la** ahora. } *I'm washing* ***it*** *now.*

   Note the addition of a written accent on the present participle when the pronoun is attached. It is needed to maintain the original stress on the syllable.

3. When a negative word precedes the verb, the direct object pronoun is placed between it and the verb.

   Yo no **lo** voy a comprar. — *I'm not going to buy* ***it.***

   Nunca **la** lavo. — *I never wash* ***it.***

   ¡AVISO! The neuter pronoun **lo** is often used with verbs like **ser, estar, creer**, and **saber** to refer to abstract ideas or situations. In English the pronoun is generally omitted.

   ¿Sabes que mañana viene José? Sí, **lo** sé. — *Do you know that tomorrow José is coming? Yes, I know.*

Practiquemos

A **Raúl, ¿tienes mi... ?** Andrés siempre acusa a su hermano menor, Raúl, de usar sus cosas y de no devolverlas. Complete Ud. las frases con la palabra apropiada de la lista. *(Andrés always accuses his younger brother of using his things and not returning them. Complete the sentences with the appropriate word from the list.)*

CD	suéter	videos
almohadas	bolígrafo	libro de cálculo

1. ¿Tienes mi ______? No, no lo tengo porque no lo comprendo.
2. ¿Tienes mi ______? No, jamás lo escucho.
3. ¿Tienes mis ______? No, nunca las uso para dormir.
4. ¿Tienes mi ______? No, ¿para qué lo quiero? Hace calor.
5. ¿Tienes mis ______? No. No tengo tiempo para verlos.
6. ¿Tienes mi ______? No. No quiero usarlo. Prefiero escribir con lápiz.

B **¿Qué hace Ud.?** Listen as your instructor reads a series of situations. Choose the correct verb and replace the nouns with the corresponding pronoun to tell what you would do.

MODELO Profesor(a): El lavabo está sucio. (fregar)
Estudiante: **Lo friego.**

barrer servir arreglar lavar hacer cocinar

1. ______ **2.** ______ **3.** ______ **4.** ______ **5.** ______ **6.** ______

Now tell what you are going to do, using the **ir** + **a** + *infinitive* construction.

MODELO Lo friego. **Lo voy a fregar. (Voy a fregarlo.)**

C **Tres hermanos.** En grupos de tres personas hagan los papeles de tres hermanos que no quieren hacer las tareas domésticas. Sigan el modelo. *(In groups of three, play the role of three brothers who do not want to do the household chores. Follow the model.)*

MODELO lavar el coche
Raúl: **No quiero lavar el coche.**
Andrés: **Yo no quiero lavarlo tampoco. (Yo no lo quiero lavar tampoco.)**
Julio: **Pues *(Well)*, yo no voy a lavarlo. (Yo no lo voy a lavar.)**

1. limpiar el garaje.
2. arreglar el sótano.
3. lavar el suelo.
4. planchar la ropa.
5. hacer las camas.
6. fregar los platos.

Spend more time with Mariana and her friends while you review grammar and expand your cultural horizons.
See the **Así es Mariana** exercise in your workbook for this lesson.

En resumen

A **Un dormitorio de niño(a).** Mire Ud. las siguientes fotos de tres dormitorios para niños y haga las actividades. *(Look at the following photos of three children's bedrooms and do the activities.)*

1. Llene Ud. los espacios con la palabra apropiada de la siguiente lista y diga a qué foto corresponde cada descripción. *(Fill in the blanks with the appropriate word from the following list and tell to which photo each description corresponds.)*

   cuadro pequeño este amarilla ventana camas azul armario dos

   a. En ______ dormitorio la alfombra es roja y encima de la cama hay una almohada roja, una almohada ______ y una almohada ______.

   b. Este ______ dormitorio es perfecto para la persona que tiene muy poco espacio. Un solo mueble combina dos ______ y un ______.

   c. Un dormitorio bonito para las niñas, con un ______ bonito detrás de las ______ camas y una ______ grande que deja entrar mucha luz.

2. ¿Cuál de estos tres dormitorios es para un niño? ¿para una niña? ¿Por qué?
3. ¿Cúal es similar al dormitorio de Ud. de niño(a)? ¿Cuáles son las similaridades? ¿las diferencias?

1.

2.

3.

B **Las casas del mundo hispano.** Read the selections about various living styles. Do the activity that follows.

Bogotá, Colombia: Lucy Villalobos

Mi casa es como muchas que hay por toda Latinoamérica. El estilo se llama **colonial** porque es del estilo de las casas en España de esa época. Es cuadrada *(square)*, de un piso, con un enorme patio sin techo en el centro. Éste es nuestro jardín. Generalmente no tenemos jardines en el frente *(front)* de la casa como en los Estados Unidos. Todos los cuartos dan *(open onto)* al patio. Casi todas las casas de mi barrio son blancas y de ladrillo *(brick)* pintado de cal *(lime)*.

Una casa colonial de Bogotá, Colombia

Córdoba, España: Silvia Augusto Cobos

Las rejas *(grillwork)* forman parte de la esencia de la típica casa española de la clase media *(middle class)*. Son de hierro *(iron)* y protegen *(protect)* las ventanas y decoran los balcones y las terrazas. La idea del patio viene de los romanos, y de los árabes tenemos la tradición de decorarlos con plantas, flores *(flowers)*, fuentes *(fountains)* y azulejos *(tiles)* de muchos colores. El patio es el centro de muchas actividades familiares.

Un patio de Córdoba, España

Madrid, España: Martín Castellano Núñez

Para una familia de nuestra economía, es imposible comprar una casa. Por eso, alquilamos *(we rent)* un piso en la ciudad. En las ciudades casi toda la gente vive en apartamentos, y generalmente los apartamentos están en edificios muy viejos. Nuestro piso es pequeño y el alquiler *(rent)* no es muy alto. Tenemos un jardín y un garaje comunal, y estamos cerca de las principales zonas comerciales.

Madrid, España

Ponce, Puerto Rico: Raquel Torres

La sala de estar es muy grande y está unida al comedor. Pero tenemos la cocina separada totalmente del comedor, cosa típica de la casa latinoamericana. Hace mucho calor durante el día y por eso generalmente cerramos las ventanas.

Una casa puertorriqueña

¿Cierto o falso? Si la frase es falsa, corríjala. *(If the sentence is false, correct it.)*

1. La típica casa colonial de Latinoamérica es de dos pisos y es azul.
2. El patio es de origen español.
3. Las rejas sirven de decoración solamente.
4. La idea de decorar el patio viene de los árabes.
5. En las ciudades españolas es más común *(common)* vivir en un apartamento que en una casa.
6. Una ventaja *(advantage)* de vivir en la ciudad es estar cerca de los almacenes y las tiendas.
7. En la casa puertorriqueña generalmente la cocina es una extensión del comedor.
8. No hace mucho calor en Puerto Rico y por eso nunca cierran las ventanas.

C **Residencial Tijerina.** In groups, look at the following floor plan of luxury condominiums in Seville, Spain. Answer the questions based on the floor plan.

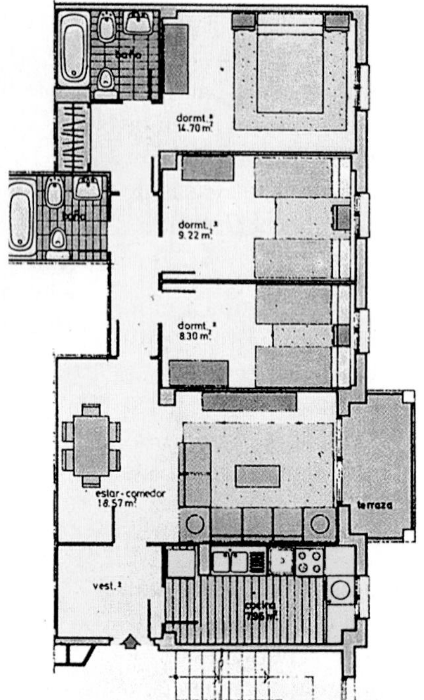

Residencial Tijerina

Por su excelente situación en el centro, la perfecta distribución de sus viviendas° y la financiación más adecuada a sus intereses, con diferentes variantes de las que a continuación° le presentamos una alternativa.

dwellings

following

Viviendas de 2-3 y 4 dormitorios
V.P.O.– Aparcamiento° Locales
Comerciales–Zonas ajardinadas°.

Parking
with gardens

1. ¿Dónde está la puerta principal?
2. ¿Cuántos dormitorios hay? ¿Cuál es el dormitorio de los padres? Explique.
3. ¿Cuántos baños hay? ¿Son diferentes a los baños en los Estados Unidos? Explique.
4. ¿Cuántas personas pueden comer fácilmente?
5. ¿Dónde puede comer la familia cuando hace mucho calor?
6. ¿Cuáles son dos aspectos del piso que son característicos de las viviendas *(dwellings)* hispanas? (Puede referirse a la lectura anterior.)

Answer the following questions based on the description of Residencial Tijerina.

7. ¿Está la Residencial Tijerina en el centro de Sevilla o en las afueras?
8. ¿Es posible conseguir un piso con sólo un dormitorio?
9. Las personas que viven allí, ¿tienen que dejar su coche en la calle?
10. ¿Está lejos de las tiendas?
11. ¿Por qué quiere o no quiere Ud. vivir allí?

D La abuela viene a visitar. Translate the following dialogue to Spanish.

Alberto: I'm going to have dinner in the city. Do you want to come with me?

Luisa: I can't. My grandmother arrives in an hour, and I'm fixing up the bedroom for her.

Alberto: Why doesn't your grandmother sleep in that room? It's neat and clean.

Luisa: She always requests this one because it's far from the cats.

Alberto: Fine. I'll help you. We can clean it in fifteen minutes.

E Minidrama. Ud. es una persona ordenada. La persona con la que vive—compañero(a) de cuarto, esposo(a), hermano(a), etc.—es super desordenada. *Act out a day in this odd couple's life.*

F Composición.

1. Ud. es arquitecto(a). Va a diseñar *(design)* una casa para una pareja *(couple)* joven, con poco dinero. *Convince them that they need the following features.*

   a. piscina *(pool)* b. jacuzzi c. terraza d. patio interior e. cinco alcobas

2. ***Ideas*** es una revista *(magazine)* que ofrece ideas decorativas para su estilo de vida. *Describe the ideas that this magazine offers for the following people.*

   a. un matrimonio *(married couple)* joven con dos hijos
   b. una muchacha soltera de 25 años con una economía limitada
   c. un matrimonio mayor

Escuchemos

A **¿Cierto o falso?** You will hear a series of statements. Look at the pictures and decide if the statement is true **(cierto)** or false **(falso).** If the statement is false, correct it.

MODELO Los niños están afuera.
Falso, los niños están adentro.

B **Dictado**. (Dictation). You will hear a short narration about Liliana's house. Listen carefully to the entire selection. Listen again and write each sentence during the pauses.

You will then hear a series of questions related to the dictation. Answer them with complete sentences. Refer to your dictation.

Lección 6

Pasando el día en casa

Con el módem podemos estar conectadas a la red mundial.

AVISO CULTURAL

(As a reading aid, refer to lesson vocabulary for new words.)

¿Tiene Ud. un teléfono en su coche? Aunque muchas personas están comprándolos, muchas no los tienen. Madrid es una ciudad famosa por sus problemas de tráfico, especialmente a la hora de ir y volver del trabajo. ¿Qué hacer cuando es tarde y uno está en su coche sin poder moverse por horas? Un grupo de vendedores muy listos pueden resolver su problema. Van de coche en coche por las calles de Madrid con teléfonos portátiles *(portable)* que alquilan por aproximadamente $2.88 dólares por 30 segundos, tiempo suficiente para decirle a su familia que Ud. va a llegar tarde.

¿Qué piensa Ud. de esta idea? ¿Es importante el teléfono en su vida? ¿Por qué sí o no? ¿Qué piensa de los teléfonos portátiles? Explique.

Preparativos

Review the vocabulary on pages 196–198 before viewing the video.

As you watch the video or read the following dialogue, pay close attention to the two telephone conversations. In the first, how does Mariana end a call that is not intended for her? In the second, why is Gonzalo unable to talk to Mariana? What two options does he have for speaking with her later? Why do you think that miscommunication, especially in a foreign language, occurs more frequently during a telephone conversation than when talking face to face?

In this episode you will learn one of the two simple past tenses in Spanish—the preterite. Mariana is very excited because something very special finally **"llegó"** *(arrived)*. **¿Qué llegó? Y, ¿qué accesorios llegaron también?**

Así es Mariana: La tecnología

Mariana y Alicia están en el dormitorio de Mariana mirando la computadora nueva.

Mariana: ¡Qué suerte! Llegó mi computadora nueva. Mis padres me la compraron hace tres semanas, y finalmente está aquí.

Alicia: ¡Uy... *(mira en la caja°)* cuántas cosas!... Pero, ¿quién sabe conectar todo eso?

Mariana saca° muchas cosas de las cajas.

Mariana: Es fácil, ¿ves? A ver° ...cables, el teclado, más cables, el ratón, unos cables más...

Alicia: Y esto, ¿qué es?

Mariana: Oh, es un módem. Nos permite estar contectadas y...

Suena el teléfono. Mariana contesta.

Mariana: ¿Aló?

Cocinero: Buenos días, señora. Habla el cocinero del restaurante La Carreta.

Mariana: Sí, diga, señor.

Cocinero: Ayer, Ud. me dio cuatro kilos de pollo pero yo necesito cuarenta kilos.

Mariana: Perdón, señor, pero tiene el número equivocado.

Mariana cuelga y sigue su conversación con Alicia.

Mariana: Bueno, ¿qué acabo de decir... ? Ah, sí, algo del módem. Pues, con el módem podemos estar conectadas a la red mundial. Podemos escribirles a todos nuestros amigos por correo electrónico...

Suena el teléfono otra vez. Mariana no quiere contestar y Alicia lo contesta.

Alicia: ¿Aló?

Gonzalo: ¿Está Mariana?

Alicia: ¿De parte de quién?

Mariana indica que no quiere hablar por teléfono ahora.

Gonzalo: Soy Gonzalo. ¿Alicia... eres tú?

Alicia: Sí, hola, Gonzalo. Mariana está ocupada ahora. ¿Quieres dejar un recado?

Gonzalo: No, está bien. Vuelvo a llamar más tarde.

Cuelgan y Mariana sigue hablando.

Mariana: Bueno, con el módem, también podemos tener un sitio web. Imagínate... Alicia...

Suena el teléfono otra vez. Mariana lo desconecta.

Mariana: Hay veces cuando es mejor desconectarse.

caja° box
saca° takes out
A ver° Let's see

Es decir

A Mariana le enseña a Alicia mucho sobre la computadora. ¿Qué aprendió ella? Busque la definición de las siguientes palabras.

el sitio web	el módem	el cable	el ratón
la red	el correo electrónico	el teclado	

1. el mecanismo que permite mover el cursor sobre la pantalla *(screen)*
2. el cordón para la conducción de la electricidad
3. la correspondencia con otros por el ciberespacio
4. la cosa que toca con los dedos *(fingers)* para escribir en la computadora
5. la Internet
6. nos permite estar conectadas a la red mediante las líneas telefónicas
7. la página en la red que tiene una persona o una compañía

B Busque en la segunda columna la respuesta que corresponde a la pregunta en la primera columna.

1. ¿Quién sabe conectar todo eso?	**a.** Soy Gonzalo.
2. Y esto, ¿qué es?	**b.** No, está bien. Vuelvo a llamar más tarde.
3. ¿De parte de quién?	**c.** Oh, es un módem.
4. ¿Quieres dejar un recado?	**d.** Es muy fácil, ¿ves?
5. ¿Aló?	**e.** Buenos días, señora. Habla el cocinero del restaurante La Carreta.

C Mariana intenta llamar a Luis Antonio para decirle que llegó la computadora. Use Ud. las palabras y frases siguientes para completar la conversación telefónica.

Habla	Luis no está	Vuelvo	¿Aló?
¿De parte de quién?	¿Quién habla?	dejar un recado	llegar

Mariana marca el número de Luis Antonio y espera el tono. Un muchacho contesta pero Mariana no sabe quién es. Rrrrrring...

Muchacho: ______

Mariana: ¿Está Luis Antonio?

Muchacho: ______

Mariana: ______ Mariana... Mariana Benavides, la novia de Luis. ______

Muchacho: Soy Roberto, el nuevo compañero de cuarto de Luis.

Mariana: Ah, sí. ¿Cuándo llegaste?

Muchacho: Acabo de ______. Lo siento pero ______ en este momento. ¿Quieres ______?

Mariana: No, gracias, Roberto. ______ a llamar más tarde. Adiós.

Al ver el video

Después de ver el video, haga las siguientes actividades.

A Diga si las siguientes actividades corresponden a **un teléfono** o a **una computadora**.

1. tener un sitio web
2. dejar un recado
3. volver a llamar
4. escribir por correo electrónico
5. tener un número equivocado
6. estar conectado a la red

B Mariana recibe otra llamada con el número equivocado. En parejas, escriban un diálogo original y represéntenlo.

Vocabulario

Verbos

apagar	*to turn off*
caminar	*to walk*
cantar	*to sing*
colgar (ue)	*to hang (up)*
construir	*to build*
dibujar	*to draw*
encender (ie)	*to turn on; to burn*
molestar	*to bother*
parecer (zc)	*to seem*
prestar	*to lend*
regalar	*to give a gift*
tocar	*to touch; to play an instrument*
tratar de (intentar)	*to try*

Sustantivos

la canción	*song*
la carta	*letter*
el cine	*movie theatre*
la guitarra	*guitar*
el juego	*game*
el pasatiempo	*hobby, pastime*
la película	*movie*
el refresco	*soft drink, refreshment*
la revista	*magazine*
la telenovela	*soap opera*
la vez	*time, occasion*

Reacciones	
¡Qué alegría (sorpresa, suerte)!	*What happiness (a surprise, luck)!*
¡Qué bien (gracioso, pesado)!	*How nice (funny, boring)!*
¡Qué lástima (pena)!	*What a shame!*
¡Qué va!	*Oh, go on!*

Por teléfono	On the telephone
¿Aló? ¿Bueno?	*Hello?*
¿De parte de quién?	*Who's calling?*
dejar un recado (mensaje)	*to leave a message*
¿Diga? ¿Dígame?	*Hello? (Spain)*
¿Está... ?	*Is . . . home?*
Están comunicando.	*The line is busy.*
hacer una llamada	*to make a telephone call*
marcar el número	*to dial the number*
el (la) operador(a) (telefonista)	*operator*
¿Quién habla?	*Who is it?*
Soy... (Habla...)	*It is . . .*
tener el número equivocado	*to have the wrong number*
volver a llamar	*to call back*

La informática	Computer science
el correo electrónico	*e-mail*
navegar la (el) Internet (la red)	*to surf the web*
el ratón	*mouse*
el sitio web	*Web site*
el teclado	*keyboard*

Otras expresiones	
anoche	*last night*
ayer	*yesterday*
¡Felicidades!	*Much happiness, All the best!*
¡Felicitaciones!	*Congratulations!*
hace[1] (+ *period of time*)	*ago*
jugar a las cartas	*to play cards*
Lo siento.	*I'm sorry.*
mejor	*better, best*
ocupado	*busy, occupied*
pasarlo bien (mal)	*to have a good (bad) time*
peor	*worse, worst*
ya	*already*

See page 212 of the **En Resumen** section for vocabulary related to the newspaper.

[1]For example: **hace una hora** = *an hour ago*; **hace una semana** = *a week ago*. For more uses of **hace** with time expressions see page 208.

Vocabulario adicional

agradecer (zc)	*to thank*
el cable	*cable*
el canal	*channel*
dar un paseo	*to take a walk*
destruir	*to destroy*
hacerle una pregunta a alguien	*to ask someone a question*
incluir	*to include*
el módem	*modem*
no sólo... sino también	*not only . . . but also*
el piano	*piano*
pintar	*to paint*
salir con	*to go out (on a date) with*
el violín	*violin*

Repasemos el vocabulario

(To reinforce previously presented vocabulary, the exercises will include words and expressions from past lessons.)

A **¿Cuál no pertenece?** Indique Ud. la palabra que no está relacionada con las otras y explique.

1. revista	periódico	libro	fotografía
2. regalar	dar	prestar	molestar
3. ¿Diga?	¿Aló?	¿Qué tal?	¿Bueno?
4. dejar un recado	colgar	hacer una llamada	pasarlo bien

B ¡Qué expresivo! Use Ud. expresiones de la lista de reacciones en la página 197 para saber qué dicen las siguientes personas.

C Reacciones. Su profesor(a) va a leer una serie de situaciones. Escuche y escriba la reacción apropiada.

1. ____
2. ____
3. ____
4. ____
5. ____

D **Actividades en la casa.** ¿Qué están haciendo las siguientes personas? *(Use the present progressive tense to tell what the following people are doing.)*

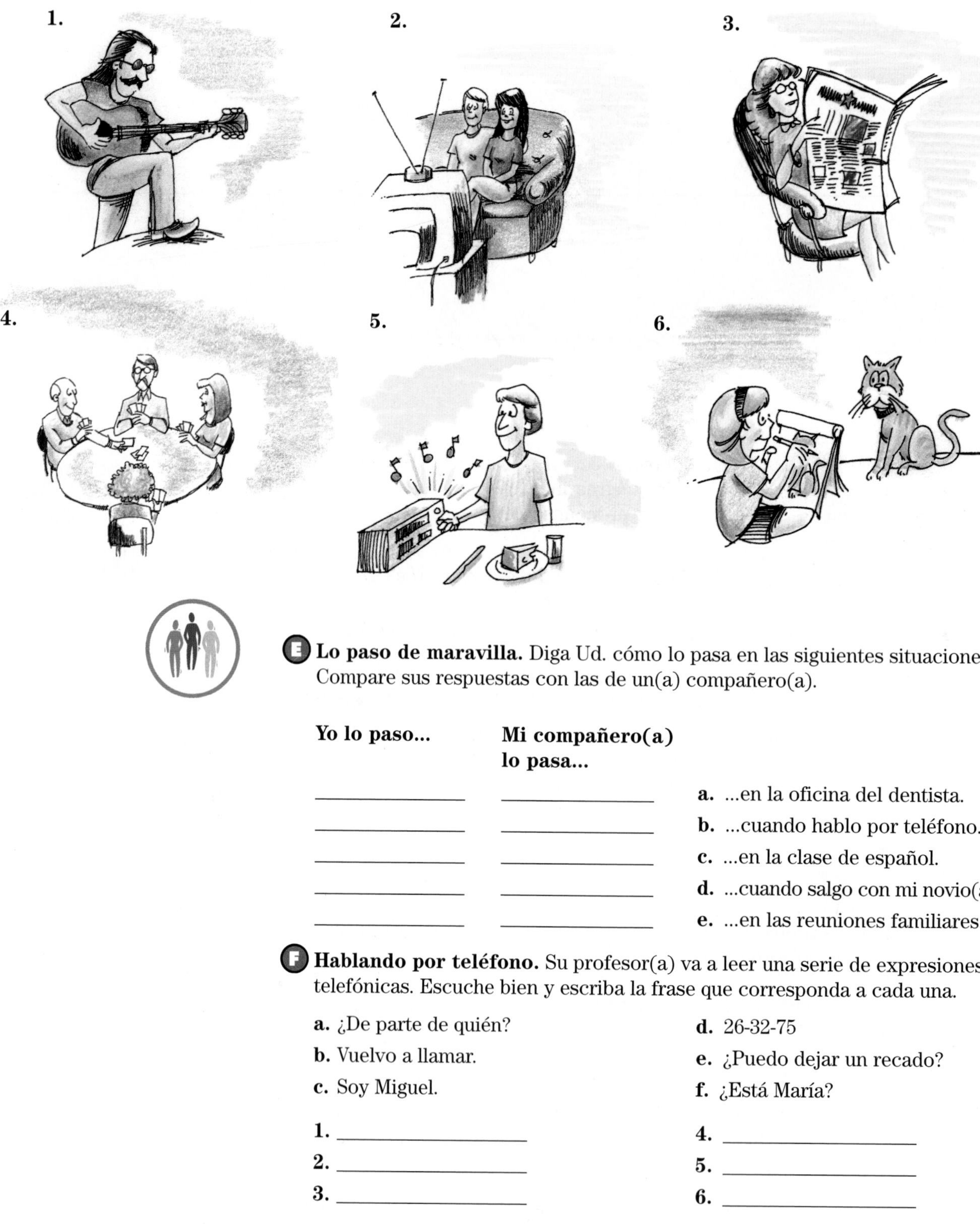

E **Lo paso de maravilla.** Diga Ud. cómo lo pasa en las siguientes situaciones. Compare sus respuestas con las de un(a) compañero(a).

Yo lo paso...	Mi compañero(a) lo pasa...	
______	______	**a.** ...en la oficina del dentista.
______	______	**b.** ...cuando hablo por teléfono.
______	______	**c.** ...en la clase de español.
______	______	**d.** ...cuando salgo con mi novio(a).
______	______	**e.** ...en las reuniones familiares.

F **Hablando por teléfono.** Su profesor(a) va a leer una serie de expresiones telefónicas. Escuche bien y escriba la frase que corresponda a cada una.

a. ¿De parte de quién?
b. Vuelvo a llamar.
c. Soy Miguel.
d. 26-32-75
e. ¿Puedo dejar un recado?
f. ¿Está María?

1. ______
2. ______
3. ______
4. ______
5. ______
6. ______

Indirect Object Pronouns

Forma

Indirect Object Pronouns

me	to, for me	**nos**	to, for us
te	to, for you (familiar singular)	**os**	to, for you (familiar plural)
le	to, for him to, for her to, for you (formal singular)	**les**	to, for them to, for you (formal plural)

Función

1. Indirect object pronouns, like indirect object nouns, indicate *to whom* or *for whom* an action is performed. They agree in number and person with the nouns they replace. Like direct object pronouns, they are placed before a conjugated verb.

   Mamá siempre **nos** lee el periódico. — *Mom always reads the newspaper **to us.***

   Susana **me** dice todos sus secretos. — *Susan tells all her secrets **to me.***

   ¡AVISO! Note that in English the word *to* is frequently omitted: *Mom always reads us the newspaper. Susana tells me all her secrets.*

2. Like direct object pronouns, indirect object pronouns may follow and be attached to an infinitive or a present participle. There is no difference in the meaning or emphasis of the pronoun based on its placement before the conjugated verb or after the infinitive or present participle.

   Carla **nos** va a cantar una canción caribeña.
   Carla va a cantar**nos** una canción caribeña. — *Carla is going to sing a Caribbean song **to us**.*

   Carla **nos** está cantando una canción caribeña.
   Carla está cantándo**nos** una canción caribeña. — *Carla is singing a Caribbean song **to us.***

   Note the addition of a written accent on the present participle when the pronoun is attached. It is needed to maintain the original stress.

3. When a negative word precedes the verb, the indirect object pronoun is placed between it and the verb.

   José no **te** va a comprar las revistas. — *José is not going to buy **you** the magazines.*

   Nunca **les** escribe. — *He never writes **to them.***

4. Since **le** (*to him, to her, to you* [s. formal]) and **les** (*to them, to you* [pl. formal]) refer to various people, a prepositional phrase (**a** + *prepositional pronoun*) is often used for clarification or emphasis.

Yo le escribo una carta **a ella (a él, a Ud.)**	*I write a letter* ***to her (to him, to you)***
Papi va a comprarles **a ellos (a ellas, a Uds.)** un piano.	*Daddy is going to buy a piano* ***for them*** *(m.),* ***(for them*** *[f.],* ***for you*** *[pl.]).*

5. The indirect object pronoun is almost always used in Spanish even when the indirect object noun is expressed in the sentence.

Paco siempre **le** dice buenos días **a la maestra.**	*Paco always says good morning* ***to the teacher.***
La abuela **les** manda muchos regalos **a sus nietos.**	*Grandmother sends a lot of presents* ***to her grandchildren.***

Practiquemos

A **¡Qué amigo más bueno!** Silvia está enferma y su amigo quiere ayudar. Con un(a) compañero(a) formen preguntas y respuestas según el modelo.

leer/libro
Amigo: **¿Puedo leerte un libro? (¿Te puedo leer un libro?)**
Silvia: **Sí, puedes leerme un libro. (Sí, me puedes leer un libro.)**

1. dar/medicina
2. hacer/café
3. contar/chistes
4. comprar/revistas
5. prestar/videos
6. cantar/canciones

B **¿A quién?** Ud. necesita las siguientes cosas. ¿A quién le va a pedir cada una? Conteste con frases completas, usando el pronombre del complemento indirecto apropiado.

un libro/mi profesora
Le voy a pedir un libro a mi profesora.

1. ayuda con la tarea/mis compañeros de clase
2. una "A" en el examen final/mi profesor
3. la dirección de correo electrónico/mi amiga Ana
4. el número de teléfono/el nuevo estudiante
5. una computadora nueva/mis padres
6. una cita/mi novio(a)

C **¿Qué regalar?** ¿Qué **no** va a regalarles Ud. a las siguientes personas? Explique.

MODELO **No voy a regalarle un juguete. (No le voy a regalar un juguete.) Ya tiene muchos.**

1.

2.

3.

4.

D **¿Por qué no... ?** Hágales las siguientes preguntas a sus compañeros. Ellos van a contestar de una forma original.

1. ¿Por qué no le haces una fiesta de cumpleaños a la profesora?
2. ¿Por qué no les traes regalos a tus compañeros de clase?
3. ¿Por qué no nos enseñas fotografías de tu familia?
4. ¿Por qué no me compras una computadora nueva?
5. ¿Por qué no le escribes una carta por correo electrónico a Bill Gates?
6. ¿Por qué no me prestas tu coche?

Direct and Indirect Object Pronouns Used Together

Función

Indirect Object Pronoun	Direct Object Pronoun
me	me
te	te
le → se	lo, la
nos	nos
os	os
les → se	los, las

1. When both direct and indirect object pronouns are used with a verb, the indirect object pronoun precedes the direct object pronoun. These may never be split. They are both placed either before the conjugated verb or they may follow and be attached to an infinitive or a present participle.

   ¿El desayuno? Mi mamá **me lo** prepara. — *Breakfast? My mom prepares **it for me.***

   ¿Las cartas? **Te las** voy a escribir. / Voy a escribír**telas.** — *The letters? I'm going to write **them to you.***

   ¿La revista? **Nos la** está leyendo. / Está leyéndo**nosla.** — *The magazine? He's reading **it to us.***

   Note the addition of a written accent on the infinitive and present participle when pronouns are attached.

2. When both the indirect **(le, les)** and direct object pronouns **(lo, la, los, las)** are in the third-person, the indirect object pronoun becomes **se.** Therefore **se** can have six different meanings.

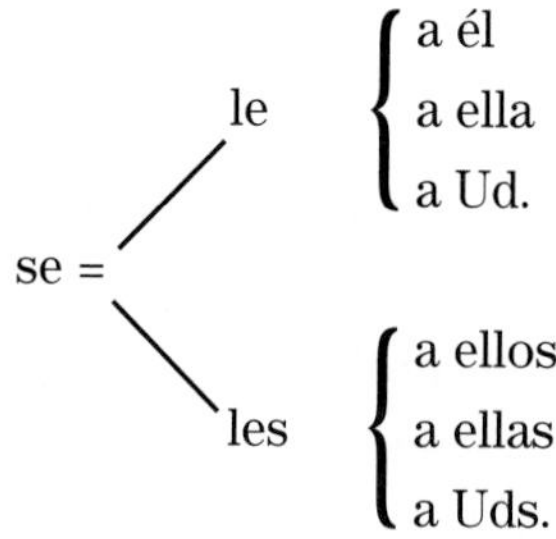

   José **se** la explica. — *José explains it **to him (to her, to you** [s. formal], **to them, to you** [pl. formal]).*

3. For clarification it is often necessary to add appropriate prepositional phrases (**a** + *prepositional pronoun*).

   José **se** la explica **a él.** — *José explains it **to him.***

   Voy a dár**se**lo **a ellos.** — *I'm going to give it **to them.***

Practiquemos

A **¿Cuándo lo haces?** Busque Ud. en la segunda columna la respuesta a las preguntas en la primera columna. *The verbs and pronouns are your clues.*

¿Cuándo...

1. nos muestran Uds. los videos?	**a.** Se lo doy ahora mismo.
2. nos da Ud. el regalo?	**b.** Me lo sirven a las tres.
3. me sirves el café?	**c.** Te las muestro esta noche.
4. me muestras las fotografías?	**d.** Te la doy más tarde en clase.
5. te sirven ellos el té?	**e.** Te lo sirvo después.
6. me das la información?	**f.** Se los mostramos el lunes.

B **¿A quién se lo traes?** Marta vuelve de unas vacaciones en el Caribe y trae regalos para todos. *With a classmate, find out what she brought to whom. Ask her the following questions, and answer them according to the cues. Change the nouns to pronouns, according to the model.*

Ud.: ¿A quién le traes el juego de dominó? (A Rafaelito)
Marta: **Se lo traigo a Rafaelito.**

1. ¿A quién le traes los cassettes de Chayanne? (a Juan y a Laura)
2. ¿A quién le traes el brazalete de ámbar *(amber bracelet)?* (a mamá)
3. ¿A quién le traes el ron *(rum)?* (a papá)
4. ¿A quién le traes los libros de la historia de Puerto Rico? (al profesor García)
5. ¿A quién le traes los periódicos y las revistas? (a los abuelos)
6. ¿A quién le traes las maracas? (a ti)

C **La niñera *(The baby-sitter)*.** Para ganar dinero, Ana ayuda a la señora Vargas con sus siete hijos. En parejas, hagan los papeles de Ana y la señora. *(In pairs, play the roles of Ana and Mrs. Vargas, and answer the many questions Ana asks.) Use the verb* **poder** *in the answers and replace the nouns with pronouns. Follow the model.*

Ana: ¿Les leo cuentos a los niños?
La señora Vargas: **Sí, puedes leérselos.**
(Sí, se los puedes leer.)

1. ¿Les preparo la cama a Carlitos y a Rosita?
2. ¿Le sirvo el postre a Sarita?
3. ¿Le muestro un video de Disney a Pedrín?
4. ¿Les cuento chistes a Tomás y a Teresa?
5. ¿Le canto una canción al bebé?

D **El amigo por correspondencia.** Iván le escribe a un amigo y contesta sus preguntas sobre la vida universitaria. *Answer all of the questions that Ivan's friend asks him about university life. Use the appropriate pronouns.*

MODELO Tus profesores:
¿Te ofrecen una variedad de clases? **Sí, me la ofrecen.**

Tus profesores

1. ¿Te dan mucha tarea? ____________
2. ¿Te dan buenas notas? ____________
3. ¿Te ofrecen muchas horas de consulta? ____________

Tu compañero de cuarto

1. ¿Te pide dinero? ____________
2. ¿Te presta su coche? ____________
3. ¿Te ofrece ayuda con la tarea? ____________

Tu novia

1. ¿Te escribe muchas cartas? ____________
2. ¿Te dice que te quiere mucho? ____________
3. ¿Te manda muchos regalos? ____________

The Preterite Tense of Regular Verbs

The preterite is one of the two simple past tenses in Spanish. A simple tense is one that does not need a helping or auxiliary verb. The other simple past tense is the imperfect, and will be presented in Lesson 8.

Forma

The preterite is formed by removing the infinitive endings **-ar, -er,** or **-ir** and adding the appropriate endings.

CAMINAR		**APRENDER**		**ESCRIBIR**	
camin**é**	*I walked*	aprend**í**	*I learned*	escrib**í**	*I wrote*
camin**aste**	*you walked*	aprend**iste**	*you learned*	escrib**iste**	*you wrote*
camin**ó**	*he, she, you walked*	aprend**ió**	*he, she, you learned*	escrib**ió**	*he, she, you wrote*
camin**amos**	*we walked*	aprend**imos**	*we learned*	escrib**imos**	*we wrote*
camin**asteis**	*you walked*	aprend**isteis**	*you learned*	escrib**isteis**	*you wrote*
camin**aron**	*they, you walked*	aprend**ieron**	*they, you learned*	escrib**ieron**	*they, you wrote*

1. The preterite endings of **-er** and **-ir** verbs are identical.
2. The first-person plural **(nosotros)** preterite form of **-ar** and **-ir** verbs is identical to that of the present indicative.
3. **-Ar** and **-er** stem-changing verbs have no stem change in the preterite tense.
4. The first- and third-person singular conjugations **(yo** and **él, ella, usted)** of the preterite require written accents. These accents determine the stress of the verb. It is important to differentiate between the verb **camino** *(I walk)* and **caminó** *(he walked)*, or between **¡camine!** *(walk!)* and **caminé** *(I walked)*.
5. Regular verbs that end in **-car, -gar,** and **-zar** have the following spelling changes in the first-person singular **(yo)** of the preterite, in order to preserve the sound of the infinitive.[1]

   c > qu buscar: yo bus**qué**, tú buscaste, él buscó, buscamos, buscasteis, buscaron

   g > gu pagar: yo pag**ué**, tú pagaste, él pagó, pagamos, pagasteis, pagaron

   z > c comenzar: yo comen**cé**, tú comenzaste, él comenzó, comenzamos, comenzasteis, comenzaron

   Other verbs in this category include: **sacar, secar, tocar, apagar, colgar, fregar, jugar, negar, almorzar, empezar.**
6. An unstressed **i** between two vowels changes to **y.** This occurs in the third-person singular and plural preterite of some **-er** and **-ir** verbs. Note that all forms have written accents, except the third-person plural **(ellos, ellas, Uds.).**

   leer: le**y**ó, le**y**eron

   oír: o**y**ó, o**y**eron

   Other verbs in this category include: **caer** *(to fall)*, **construir, contribuir** *(to contribute)*, **destruir, incluir.**

Función

1. The preterite tense is used to describe a completed past action or series of actions, or a change in a mental or emotional state. It is used to report the beginning or end of an action.

José **entró**, me **saludó, buscó** su libro y **salió.**	*José **entered, greeted** me, **looked for** his book, and **left.***
Susana **empezó** a tener miedo al oír las noticias.	*Susana **began** to be afraid upon hearing the news.*

2. The Spanish preterite has two meanings in English. For example, **hablé** means *I spoke* and *I did speak.* There is no Spanish equivalent for the auxiliary word *did.* Instead, the simple preterite form is used. Therefore, to form a question in the preterite, you simply invert the subject and verb or use the interrogative intonation.

   ¿Habló Ud.? }
   ¿Habló? } *Did you speak?*

[1]Remember that **c** and **g** before **e** and **i** produce a soft sound.

To express how long ago an action took place use the following formula:

Hace + **period of time** + **que** + verb in the preterite[1]

Hace una hora que Juan me llamó. *Juan called me* ***an hour ago.***

To ask how long ago an action took place use the following construction:

¿Cuánto tiempo + **hace** + **que** + verb in the preterite?

¿Cuánto tiempo hace que Juan te llamó? ***How long ago*** *did Juan call you?*

Practiquemos

A **¿Qué actividades?** Ask a classmate if he or she did the following activities yesterday, and check off the appropriate box. Use the correct form of the preterite. He or she will answer in complete sentences.

MODELO limpiar tu cuarto
Ud.: **¿Limpiaste tu cuarto ayer?**
Su compañero(a): **Sí, limpié mi cuarto ayer.**
(No, no limpié mi cuarto ayer.)

-ar

1. hablar por teléfono ____________
2. navegar la Internet ____________
3. practicar un deporte ____________
4. tocar un instrumento ____________

-er

1. comer en un restaurante ____________
2. ver un video ____________
3. volver a casa muy tarde ____________
4. beber café ____________

-ir

1. asistir a un concierto ____________
2. escribir por correo electrónico ____________
3. recibir un fax ____________
4. salir con amigos ____________

With your classmate, form a list of five activities that you think all of the students did yesterday. Use the **ellos** form of the verb in the preterite.

[1]An alternative construction is: verb in the preterite + **hace** + period of time **(Juan me llamó hace una hora).** Note that **hace** is used in the present even though past action is expressed.

B **La visita.** Paco y Pedro limpian su apartamento porque vienen invitados *(guests). Listen to your instructor play the role of Paco. Play the role of Pedro and answer in the preterite tense according to the cues.*

MODELO Paco: ¿Limpiaste la sala? (cuarto de baño)
Pedro: **No, pero limpié el cuarto de baño.**

1. (la bañera) ____________
2. (el suelo) ____________
3. (las sábanas) ____________
4. (el café) ____________
5. (la comida) ____________
6. (la puerta) ____________

C **¿Cómo pasó Ud. el día?** Interview a classmate to find out what he or she did yesterday and at what time. Report your findings to the class. You can use the following verbs.

llegar	comer	estudiar	almorzar	llamar
escribir	empezar	limpiar	salir	cenar

MODELO Estudiante 1: ¿Qué hiciste *(did you do)* a las 9:00 de la mañana?
Estudiante 2: A las nueve de la mañana yo llegué a mi clase.
Estudiante 1: *(A la clase)* A las nueve de la mañana el estudiante 2 llegó a su clase.

1. 9:00 de la mañana ____________
2. 11:00 de la mañana ____________
3. 1:00 de la tarde ____________
4. 3:00 de la tarde ____________
5. 6:00 de la tarde ____________
6. 8:00 de la noche ____________

D **La llamada telefónica.** Write a paragraph describing a telephone call you made yesterday. Include how you made it, and the conversation you had. Use the verbs below.

llamar marcar contestar hablar contar colgar

The Preterite of the Verbs *Ir, Ser, Dar,* and *Hacer*

The following verbs are irregular in the preterite tense. Note that **ir** and **ser** are identical in the preterite. The context helps to determine which verb is being used.

IR, SER	DAR[1]	HACER
fui	di	hice
fuiste	diste	hiciste
fue	dio	hizo
fuimos	dimos	hicimos
fuisteis	disteis	hicisteis
fueron	dieron	hicieron

Practiquemos

A **Selecciones.** Complete Ud. las frases con la forma del pretérito de los verbos: **ser, ir, dar** y **hacer.**

1. Yo no ___ nada ayer. ¡Qué pesado!
2. Oscar no me ___ la información.
3. Rocío y yo ___ el trabajo temprano por la mañana.
4. ¿A qué hora ___ Uds. al cine?
5. ¡ ___ una fiesta estupenda!
6. ¿Alguien te llamó a medianoche? No ___ yo.
7. Nosotros le ___ un microondas a mi mamá para su cumpleaños.
8. ¿Tú ___? ¿Con quién?
9. Ella ___ mi profesora de inglés el año pasado *(last)*.
10. ¿A quién le ___ Ud. la guitarra?

B **Ud. tiene correo *(You've got mail)*.** Ud. recibió una carta por correo electrónico de una amiga que está en Santo Domingo para visitar a su familia. *Read your e-mail and change the verbs to the preterite.*

Hola Carolina —Aquí la vida es muy tranquila. Nada de estrés *(stress)*. Ayer, por ejemplo, el día (empezar) ___ a las seis. Mamá (hacer) ___ el típico café dominicano —fuerte *(strong)* y delicioso—, y papá (ir) ___ a trabajar. Al mediodía, papá (volver) ___ y nosotros (almorzar) ___ en el patio. Yo (jugar) ___ al fútbol con mi hermano menor. Después, nosotros (caminar) ___ por la playa y (comer) ___ unos mangos jugosos *(juicy)*. Fue un día muy relajado, y yo lo (pasar) ___ de maravilla.

Escríbeme *(Write to me)* pronto. Celia.

Now, reply to your e-mail. Your life is anything but tranquil. Tell your friend what you did yesterday.

[1]**Ver** is conjugated in a similar way: **vi, viste, vio, vimos, visteis, vieron**.

C **Una gira *(tour)* por la isla de Puerto Rico.** Lea Ud. "Una gira turística por Puerto Rico" en la páginas 216–217 de la *Gaceta* 2 para poder completar la siguiente tarjeta postal *(postcard)*.

Querido Julio,

¡Puerto Rico es una maravilla!

1. Empecé la gira en...
2. Fue fantástico porque...
3. Por la tarde, pasé horas...
4. Al día siguiente, fui a... para contemplar la naturaleza *(nature)*.
5. El último día, hicimos un picnic y jugamos vólibol bajo el sol tropical en... ¡mi lugar favorito! Un abrazo *(hug)* de...

D **Buenas intenciones.** Lea Ud. la tira cómica *(comic strip)* y haga la actividad.

alégrate *be happy*

Llene Ud. el espacio con la forma correcta del verbo en el pretérito para contar la historia otra vez.

1. El pobre hombre (ir) ______ a darle una serenata a la vecina.
2. Cuando (volver) ______, su amigo le (preguntar) ______ si salió bien o mal.
3. El hombre le (contestar) ______ que (ser) ______ un desastre.
4. La vecina le (dar) ______ un golpe *(hit)* en la cabeza *(head)* con la guitarra.
5. Afortunadamente, dice el amigo, el hombre no (llevar) ______ un piano.

Spend more time with Mariana and her friends while you review grammar and expand your cultural horizons.

See the **Así es Mariana** exercise in your workbook for this lesson.

En resumen

A **En el periódico.** Read the index and do the activities. Refer to the list below for help.

Las secciones del periódico

los anuncios clasificados	*classified ads*
la cartelera	*entertainment section*
los deportes	*sports*
las noticias (inter)nacionales	*(inter)national news*
las noticias locales	*local news*
los obituarios	*obituary column*
la sección de cocina (de moda)	*cooking (fashion) section*
las tiras cómicas	*comic strips*

Cuando el Sr. Gaitán lee el periódico, siempre le comenta los artículos interesantes a su esposa. *Refer to the following index and tell to what section of the newspaper each comment applies. Change the verbs to the preterite.*

Índice

Centroamérica	Págs. 6A, 7A	El mundo de los Negocios	Pág. 8A
Clasificados	Págs. 7C, 8C, 9C, 10C, 11C, 12C	Horóscopo	Pág. 6C
Cocina	Págs. 5C, 1D, 2D, 3D, 4D, 6D	Locales	Págs. 1B, 2B, 3B, 4C
Crucigrama	Pág. 6C	Mujer	Págs. 1C, 2C
Defunciones	Pág. 3B	Puerto Rico	Pág. 3A
Deportes	Págs. 4B, 5B, 6B	Sociales	Pág. 3C
Editorial, Artículos y Comentarios	Págs. 4A, 5A	Tiras Cómicas	Pág. 6C

MODELO La nueva directora (abrir) **abrió** una clínica en la escuela primaria. **Locales**

1. a. La Universidad de Puerto Rico (ganar) ______ el campeonato *(championship)* de fútbol. ______
   b. El Chef Rondelé (dar) ______ una receta *(recipe)* para el Soufflé Alaska. ______
   c. Los Reyes *(King and Queen)* de España (ir) ______ a Alemania. ______
   d. La familia Piñero (cambiar) ______ la hora del velorio *(wake)*. ______
   e. La Fundación Kennedy (hacer) ______ una fiesta elegante anoche. ______
   f. La compañía OPTEC (construir) ______ un centro tecnológico en Japón.______
2. ¿A qué secciones del periódico corresponden los siguientes titulares *(headlines)?*

   a. El menú de la semana
   b. Tigres defienden el título
   c. Popurrí culinario
   d. Empresas y empresarios
   e. El feminismo en el año 2000

   Ahora, diga en qué sección Ud. encuentra a las personas, las palabras y las frases siguientes.

   a. viudo
   b. armas nucleares
   c. Sammy Sosa
   d. Buscamos secretaria
   e. Cine Gran Vía
   f. Martha Stewart

B Cortesía telefónica *(Telephone manners).* Haga las siguientes actividades.

1. Lea la lectura sobre la etiqueta telefónica y conteste las preguntas.

   - El teléfono no es para charlar. Su función principal es comunicar mensajes cortos y rápidos. Es decir, se usa para necesidades, especialmente en España donde cuesta hacer una llamada local. Si Ud. quiere charlar con un amigo, es mejor ir directamente a su casa si no vive muy lejos.
   - La manera de contestar el teléfono varía de país a país. En España se dice «Diga» o «Dígame»; en México, «¿Bueno?»; en la Argentina y el Perú, «Hable» u «Oigo»; en Cuba, «¿Qué hay?» en Puerto Rico, «Aló» y «Hola» y en Colombia, «¿A ver?».
   - Para iniciar una conversación, la persona que llama puede preguntar: «¿Está Antonio?».
   - Cuando la persona que contesta pregunta, «¿De parte de quién?», algunas posibles respuestas son: «Habla Francisco Madero» o «Soy Francisco».
   - Si Ud. tiene el número equivocado, es feo colgar sin decir: «Lo siento, tengo el número equivocado».
   - Cuando llama y contesta el contestador automático *(answering machine)*, es mejor ser breve y claro, y dejar su nombre y número de teléfono.

¿Qué hace Ud. si...

a. está en México y contesta el teléfono? ¿en Puerto Rico? ¿en España? ¿en el Perú?

b. Ud. llama y pregunta por Juan? Su mamá pregunta, ¿de parte de quién?

c. contesta el contestador automático?

2. **Conversaciones telefónicas.** Con un(a) compañero(a), complete Ud. el diálogo telefónico entre dos chicas colombianas.

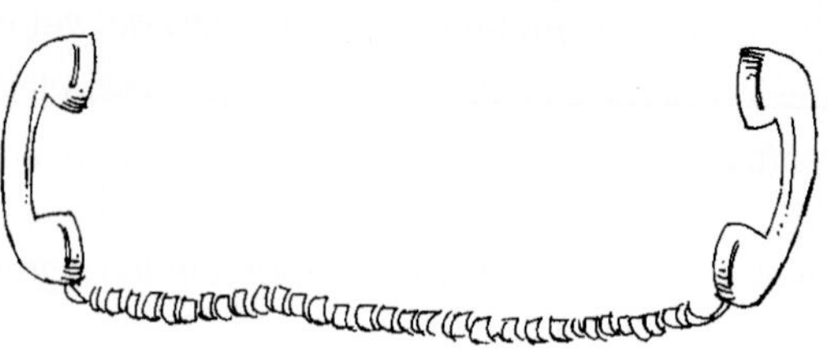

«¡¡¡Rrrrrrrring!!!!»

Carolina: ______

Teresa: ¿Está Carolina?

Carolina: ______

Teresa: Carolina, soy Teresa. ¿Qué tal?

Carolina: ______

Teresa: ______

Ahora escriban Uds. diálogos originales, incorporando los cambios siguientes.

a. La madre de Carolina contesta.

b. El novio de Carolina llama y el padre contesta.

C **El fin de semana.** Translate the following dialogue to Spanish.

Anita: How did you spend the weekend? Wasn't it Julio's birthday?

Paula: Yes. We had dinner at a nice restaurant and then we went to the movies.

Anita: What did you buy him?

Paula: Three cassettes. I gave them to him at the restaurant.

Anita: I went to Paquita's house. We watched TV and played cards.

D **Minidrama.**

1. Ud. es adicto(a) a la televisión y no sabe qué hacer. Sus amigos y familiares intentan resolver el problema.
2. Ud. trata de comunicarse con un amigo por teléfono pero es imposible porque siempre marca el número equivocado. Sin embargo *(however)*, resultan unas conversaciones telefónicas muy interesantes.

E **Composición.**

1. **Mi querido *(dear)* Ramón.** Todos los días Cecilia le escribe una carta a su novio Ramón pero exagera mucho las actividades de su día. *Write a letter from Cecilia to Ramón using the verbs below and any others to tell him about her unbelievable day. A classmate will write letter #2 from Julito, based on your letter.*

   ir   comprar   viajar   ver   escribir   dar   hacer   pintar

2. **La verdad *(The truth)*.** Julito, el hermano menor de Cecilia, sabe que Cecilia exagera. Él le escribe otra carta a Ramón y le dice la verdad de la vida de su hermana.

Escuchemos

A **¿Cuál de los dos?** You will hear an incomplete sentence. Choose the word that best completes the sentence.

(agradece/apaga)
Papá _______ la televisión. (apagar)
Papá apaga la televisión.

1. (caminar/dar)
2. (una película/un cine)
3. (prestar/dejar)
4. (tocar/jugar)
5. (deportes/obituarios)
6. (¿Diga?/¡Qué va!)
7. (el canal/la canción)
8. (encender/apagar)

B **Dictado.** You will hear a short narration about Liliana's weekend. Listen carefully to the entire selection. Listen again and write each sentence during the pauses.

You will then hear a series of questions related to the dictation. Answer them with complete sentences. Refer to your dictation.

La Playa de Luquillo en Puerto Rico

Una gira turística por Puerto Rico

Preparativos: Estrategias de prelectura

1. Before taking your tour of Puerto Rico, look at the **Es decir** section to help you anticipate the content of the text you are about to read. Which sites will your tour include?
2. Scan the reading to find synonyms for the following words:

   comenzar ________ conectada ________ viejas ________

   la historia ________ palacio ________ más importante ________

   muy grande ________ secreto ________
3. Scan the reading to find out the following information:

a. ¿Cuáles son los adjetivos que describen las calles, las casas y los patios en el Viejo San Juan?

b. ¿Cuántos bosques *(forests)* tropicales hay en los Estados Unidos?

c. ¿Cómo son las aguas de la Playa de Luquillo?

Para conocer la isla de Puerto Rico es bueno empezar en el *Viejo San Juan*. Fundado en 1521, es una isleta° que está unida a la isla por puentes.° Por todas partes de la ciudad hay calles pintorescas,° casas antiguas° y patios bonitos que recuerdan el pasado colonial español.

Hay varias fortalezas° en la isla. La construcción del Castillo de San Felipe del Morro, la fortaleza principal de la isla, empezó en

tiny island
bridges
picturesque; old

forts

1521 y no terminó hasta 1787. San Cristóbal es un edificio enorme que domina toda la ciudad. Los turistas pueden pasar horas explorando el misterioso interior de esta fortaleza.

El Yunque es el único bosque° tropical de los Estados Unidos. Tiene plantas y flores° tropicales y también un fabuloso bosque pluvioso.°

A unos 42 kilómetros de El Yunque está la famosa *Playa° de Luquillo*. Cada año turistas de todas partes del mundo van allí para pasar sus vacaciones en el sol tropical del Caribe.° Las aguas son muy claras y es posible ver hasta el fondo.°

forest
flowers
rain
Beach
Caribbean
bottom

El Castillo El Morro

Es decir

¿Cierto o falso? Si la frase es falsa, corríjala con una frase completa. *(If the statement is false, correct it with a complete sentence.)*

1. El Viejo San Juan está en el centro de Puerto Rico.
2. La arquitectura de San Juan muestra la influencia española en la isla.
3. La gente no puede entrar a San Cristóbal.
4. Para conocer las playas de Puerto Rico los turistas van a El Yunque.
5. La playa de Luquillo es famosa por sus plantas exóticas.

Practiquemos

A La historia de Puerto Rico. *Before the Spaniards arrived, the island of Puerto Rico was called Borikén, and it was populated by the Taíno Indians.* Para aprender más sobre la historia de Puerto Rico, busque en la segunda columna la terminación de la frase en la primera columna. Cambie los verbos al pretérito.

1. Cristóbal Colón (llegar)...	a. la guerra.
2. En 1508, Juan Ponce de León (comenzar)...	b. Puerto Rico, Cuba y las Filipinas.
3. Ponce de León (ser)...	c. el primer gobernador español de la isla.
4. La Guerra *(War)* Hispanoamericana (empezar)...	d. la colonización de la isla.
5. Los Estados Unidos (ganar)...	e. en la presente relación política de Estado Libre Asociado (ELA).
6. Los Estados Unidos (recibir)...	f. a la isla en 1493.
7. En 1952 Puerto Rico y los Estados Unidos (entrar)...	g. en 1898.

B **¿En qué orden?** *The paragraphs below contain information about Puerto Rico and the Dominican Republic.* Arregle Ud. las frases para formar dos párrafos lógicos.

Puerto Rico

1. La economía de la isla está basada en el cultivo de café, tabaco y frutas tropicales.
2. Puerto Rico es una de las 7.000 islas tropicales que hay en el Caribe y San Juan es la capital.
3. La manufactura de textiles es importante también.
4. Otras ciudades principales son Ponce, Mayagüez y Bayamón.

Santo Domingo, República Dominicana

La República Dominicana

1. Es una ciudad moderna pero tiene muchos edificios históricos.
2. Es más grande que Puerto Rico y llueve más, también.
3. Santo Domingo, la capital, es la ciudad más antigua de Hispanoamérica.
4. Otra isla del Caribe es la República Dominicana.

Caras en las noticias

Tito Puente es un puertorriqueño que creció en la ciudad de Nueva York. De niño tomó clases de piano. En los años 40, gracias a los conciertos que Tito dio en el Palladium de Nueva York, el público norteamericano empezó a conocer y a apreciar° la música hispanocaribeña. Hoy, con tres «Grammys» y 100 discos° Tito Puente es el rey° del Mambo, el rey de los Timbales° y un nombre máximo de la percusión,° el piano, el saxofón y la dirección de orquestas.

Tito Puente

appreciate
records
king; drums
percussion

Sammy Sosa

Marc Anthony

Y si Tito es el rey del Mambo, **Marc Anthony** es el rey de la salsa, y el que vende más discos de música tropical en el mundo. Y ahora va a empezar a cantar en inglés. Pero, para él la música no es suficiente. Apareció en la película *Big Night*, y en Broadway protagonizó° *The Capeman* de Paul Simon en 1997. Después, fue seleccionado por Martin Scorcese para su película° *Bringing Out the Dead*, con Nicolas Cage.

he starred
movie

El beisbolista dominicano, **Sammy Sosa**, figura entre los más grandes del deporte. En 1998 entró en una competencia de jonrones° contra° Mark McGwire, y aunque no ganó,° terminó con un total de 66 jonrones ese año. Sammy, casado y con cuatro hijos, es el símbolo de la esperanza° para su país.° El exlimpiabotas° ahora tiene un salario de casi 10 millones de dólares, y ayuda a construir una escuela de béisbol.

homerun competition
against, didn't win
hope; country; shoeshine

Rita Moreno, la gran artista puertorriqueña, lleva más de 50 años cantando, bailando y actuando.° Tiene el honor de ganar los cuatro premios° más importantes del mundo del espectáculo —un «Oscar» por su papel° de Anita en *West Side Story*, el «Tony» por su actuación en la comedia, *The Ritz*, el Emmy por su participación en la televisión y el «Grammy» por su música. Y recientemente salió en el programa de televisión *Oz*, en HBO.

acting
awards
role

Rita Moreno

«Mis recuerdos de *West side Story* son agradables», dice Moreno.

Juan Luis Guerra

Juan Luis Guerra asistió al Conservatorio Nacional de Música en su país, y estudió jazz en Berklee School of Music en Boston, Massachusetts. Fue en esa época cuando decidió dejar el jazz y volver a su música— el merengue.[1] Ahora dicen que el grupo musical Guerra 4–40 es el salvador° de la música merengue. El grupo dominicano combina los ritmos° del merengue tradicional, la poesía de Juan Luis Guerra y los estilos° musicales de los EE.UU., África y Latinoamérica. Sus álbumes más populares son *Acarreo y Mudanza, Mientras más lo pienso... tú, Ojalá que llueva café* y *Areito.*

saviour
rhythms
styles

El actor **Raúl Juliá** nació° en Puerto Rico y allí estudió derecho. En 1964 llegó a Nueva York y empezó su carrera artística. Juliá participó en obras° de teatro como *Man of La Mancha*, actuó en la Argentina e hizo películas en Hollywood. Fue famoso por *The Kiss of the Spider Woman, Romero, The Rookie, Havana* y *The Addams Family.* Raúl quería° ver más influencia hispana en el cine, y creía° que los hispanos debían° luchar° contra° los estereotipos de la gente hispana. Murió en octubre de 1994.

was born
plays
wanted
believed; should
fight; against

Raúl Juliá

El cantante puertorriqueño **Chayanne** entró en el mundo artístico a los diez años y hoy, con 28 discos de oro y 19 de platino, es muy popular en Europa, Latinoamérica y el mercado hispano de los Estados Unidos. Por su video *El ritmo se baila así*, Chayanne recibió la nominación al «Grammy» en la categoría de mejor cantante de pop latino, y en el verano de 1998 hizo su «crossover» al inglés con la película *Dance With Me.*

Chayanne

Es decir

¿Qué recuerda Ud.? ¿A quién se refiere cada frase?

1. Es la salvación del merengue.
2. Su nombre está en la sección de deportes de los periódicos.
3. Además de *(Aside from)* ser famoso por la música salsa, trabaja en Hollywood con los actores y directores más famosos.
4. Toca muchos instrumentos y también es director de orquesta.
5. Hace películas y también es famoso por el pop latino.
6. Ayudó a cambiar la imagen *(image)* de la gente hispana.
7. Es una artista con muchos talentos... puede bailar, cantar y actuar.

[1] Música típica de la República Dominicana.

Practiquemos

Una cara histórica. *Diego Colón is an important figure in the early history of the Dominican Republic, or La Española, as it was called in the fifteenth century.* Complete el párrafo con los verbos de la lista.

vinieron perdió tomó fue hizo vivió llegó

Diego Colón, el hijo mayor de Cristóbal Colón, ______ el segundo *(second)* gobernador *(governor)* de La Española. En Santo Domingo, la capital de la isla *(island)*, Colón ______ construir *(to construct)* El Alcázar, un palacio fabuloso donde él ______ por muchos años. Dicen que cuando Sir Francis Drake ______ a la isla, invadió el palacio y ______ todos los objetos de valor *(value)*. En esa época muchos africanos ______ a la isla para trabajar en los campos de azúcar *(sugarcane fields)*. Con el descubrimiento *(discovery)* del oro *(gold)* y la plata *(silver)* en México, Colombia y Perú, La Española ______ su importancia como colonia *(colony)* de España.

Notas y notables

Cristóbal Colón, ¿dónde estás?

¿EN SANTO DOMINGO, SEVILLA O LA HABANA?

Cristóbal Colón

Buscando a Cristóbal Colón

¿Dónde están los restos° de Cristóbal Colón? ¿En Sevilla, España? ¿En Santo Domingo, República Dominicana? ¿En la Habana, Cuba? Nadie sabe. Pero sí sabemos que su primera tumba° está en Valladolid, España, su segunda° tumba está en Sevilla y su tercera° está en la República Dominicana.

El problema es que nadie identificó la tumba. Muchos creen que en 1795 los restos de Colón llegaron a Cuba y que fueron divididos... Unos fueron a Santo Domingo y otros fueron a Sevilla. ¡Qué complicada es la cosa!

remains

tomb

second; third

Puerto Rico y los Estados Unidos... una relación única°

unique

El año 1952 es importante en la historia de Puerto Rico y los Estados Unidos. En este año Puerto Rico entró en una relación nueva con los Estados Unidos. Se llama Estado Libre Asociado° o ELA y es la relación que existe hoy en día. Los puertorriqueños son ciudadanos° de los Estados Unidos y usan el mismo sistema de dinero, aduana° y correos.° Tienen un gobernador° y votan en las elecciones locales. No pueden votar en las elecciones presidenciales de los Estados Unidos sin vivir en el continente por seis meses.

Free Associated State
citizens
customs; mail; governor

Hay conflicto en la isla sobre su situación política. Muchos puertorriqueños no están contentos con su status de ELA. Dicen que Puerto Rico no es un estado, no es libre pero sí está asociado con los Estados Unidos de una forma ambigua.° Para ellos ser estado es la solución. Otros quieren mantener el status de ELA porque tienen miedo de perder su cultura, su idioma y su identidad. Hay otros puertorriqueños que quieren la independencia completa. ¿Qué debe hacer Puerto Rico? ¿Mantener su status de ELA, ser estado de los Estados Unidos o conseguir la independencia?

ambiguous

Pedro Rosselló, gobernador de Puerto Rico

Pedro Rosselló, gobernador de Puerto Rico

La Fortaleza, situada en el Viejo San Juan y construida° en 1540, es la mansión ejecutiva más antigua en el hemisferio occidental.° Es la residencia del gobernador de Puerto Rico, Pedro Rosselló, su esposa Maga y sus tres hijos, Juan Oscar, Luis y Ricky. Rosselló asistió a las Universidades de Yale y Notre Dame, es médico, juega muy bien al tenis y cree en la importancia de la familia.

built
western

Rosselló quiere establecer nuevos programas de salud,° educación y justicia,° y lucha° contra el crimen que está relacionado con el narcotráfico. También hace mucho para unificar° a la gente puertorriqueña y para proteger° los recursos° naturales de la isla.° Es un hombre optimista y cree que la estadidad° es la esperanza° para el futuro de Puerto Rico.

health
justice; fights
unify
protect; resources; island
statehood; hope

Es decir

Preguntas. Basándose en los artículos, conteste Ud. las preguntas con frases completas.

1. ¿Quién sabe dónde están los restos de Cristóbal Colón?
2. ¿Dónde está la primera tumba de Colón?
3. ¿Cómo se llama la relación política que Puerto Rico tiene con los Estados Unidos?
4. ¿Cuándo pueden votar los puertorriqueños en las elecciones presidenciales?
5. ¿De qué tienen miedo muchos puertorriqueños?
6. ¿Quién es Pedro Rosselló?
7. ¿Qué quiere Rosselló para Puerto Rico, la estadidad o la independencia?
8. ¿Qué sabe Ud. de la vida personal de Pedro Rosselló?

Practiquemos

En Puerto Rico hay mucho que comprar. *Find out why it's fun to shop in Puerto Rico.* Use las palabras de la lista para completar el párrafo.

vienen	muebles	encontrar	mantas	hay
camina	venden	regalos	calles	

Comprar en Puerto Rico es una buena experiencia. Si Ud. ___________ por las ___________ de San Juan, va a ___________ muchas tiendas de ___________ y arte indígena. Puede comprar ___________ para la cama que ___________ de la India, y ___________ españoles para todas las habitaciones de la casa. También ___________ boutiques que ___________ la ropa tradicional de Puerto Rico.

Enfoque literario

Julia de Burgos

Preparativos: Estrategias de prelectura

Before reading the following literary selection, scan the biographical information below and complete the table with information that will help you understand the poem.

Julia de Burgos (Puerto Rico, 1916–1953) escribió poesías que no tienen igual en la lírica de Puerto Rico. Salió de la isla para estudiar en Nueva York, pero la experiencia urbana fue asfixiante° para ella. Muchos de sus poemas reflejan° la angustia° de su exilio y su deseo de volver a Puerto Rico. Otros temas incluyen el destino° personal, el amor y la muerte, y sus libros principales son *Poema en veinte surcos, Canción de la verdad sencilla* y *El mar y tú*, publicado después de su muerte.

suffocating
reflect; anguish
destiny

About the author

Author's name: ___________ Place of birth: ___________

Date of birth: ___________ Age at death: ___________

Main themes: ___________ ___________ ___________

___________ ___________

Major books of poetry: ___________ ___________ ___________

The poem

Cause of the poet's sorrow *(pena)*: ___________

Ay, ay, ay, de la grifa° negra *(second half)*

Dícenme° que mi abuelo fue el esclavo°
por quien el amo° dio treinta monedas.°
Ay, ay, ay, que el esclavo fue mi abuelo
es mi pena,° es mi pena.
Si hubiera sido° el amo,
sería° mi vergüenza°
que en los hombres, igual que° en las naciones,
si el ser el siervo° es no tener derechos,°
el ser el amo es no tener conciencia.
Ay, ay, ay, los pecados° del rey° blanco
lávelos° en perdón la reina° negra.
Ay, ay, ay, que la raza se me fuga°
y hacia° la raza blanca zumba° y vuela°
a hundirse° en su agua clara,
o tal vez° si la blanca se ensombrará° en la negra.
Ay, ay, ay, que mi negra raza huye°
y con la blanca corre° a ser trigueña°
¡a ser la del° futuro,
fraternidad° de América!

kinky-haired

They tell me; slave
master; coins

sorrow
he had been
it would be; shame
just as
servant; rights

sins; king
wash them; queen
escapes me
toward; buzzes; flies
sinks into
perhaps; will be enshrouded
flees
runs; light brown-skinned
that of
brotherhood

Es decir

Comprensión. Conteste Ud. las siguientes preguntas.

1. ¿Qué fue el abuelo de la poeta?
2. ¿Cómo consiguió el amo al abuelo de la poeta?
3. Hay algo que un esclavo no tiene. ¿Qué es?
4. Y hay algo que un amo no tiene. ¿Qué es?
5. En el poema hay evidencia de la ascendencia *(ancestry)* africana de la poeta. ¿Cuáles son algunos ejemplos?

Practiquemos

A El lenguaje *(language)* literario. Las palabras de la lista están en el poema. Arréglelas *(Arrange them)* según las siguientes categorías.

Esclavitud *(Slavery)*	Personas	Emociones	Colores

esclavo	siervo	negro	pena
vergüenza	hombres	trigueña	reina
blanco	ay, ay, ay	rey	
abuelo	amo	no tener derechos	

B Discusión. Haga Ud. las siguientes actividades.

1. ¿Cuál es el tema del poema? Explique su selección. Puede seleccionar más de uno.
   a. la esclavitud *(slavery)*
   b. el racismo
   c. la injusticia social
   d. la etnicidad *(ethnicity)*
   e. la cultura africana
2. En sus propias *(own)* palabras, explique Ud. el significado *(meaning)* del siguiente verso.
   «*Ay, ay, ay, que mi negra raza huye*
   y con la blanca corre a ser trigueña»
3. ¿Qué es la «fraternidad de América»?

C Reacción personal. Haga Ud. las siguientes actividades.

1. Describa *(Describe)* Ud. las emociones de la poeta.
2. ¿Es importante la etnicidad de una persona? Explique.

→ Enfoque artístico... Puerto Rico

Visite Ud. el sitio web,
http://www.spiderlink.net/coati/bio.htm, para conocer el arte de Eddrie Lorroig Ramos.

A Hojee *(Scan)* la biografía de Lorroig Ramos y diga *(tell)*...
1. cuántos años tiene.
2. qué medios artísticos usa.
3. cuáles son los temas *(themes)* de sus obras *(works)*.

B Mire las serigrafías y diga...
1. cómo reflejan *(reflect)* su estilo *(style)* artístico.
2. si son similares a las pinturas de otros artistas.
3. cuál le gusta más y por qué.

Since Internet addresses are subject to change, typing the following key words into most search engines will get you more information about Puerto Rican art.

Museos de Puerto Rico **Ponce, Museo Nacional de Puerto Rico**
Museo de las Américas

Videocultura

Puerto Rico

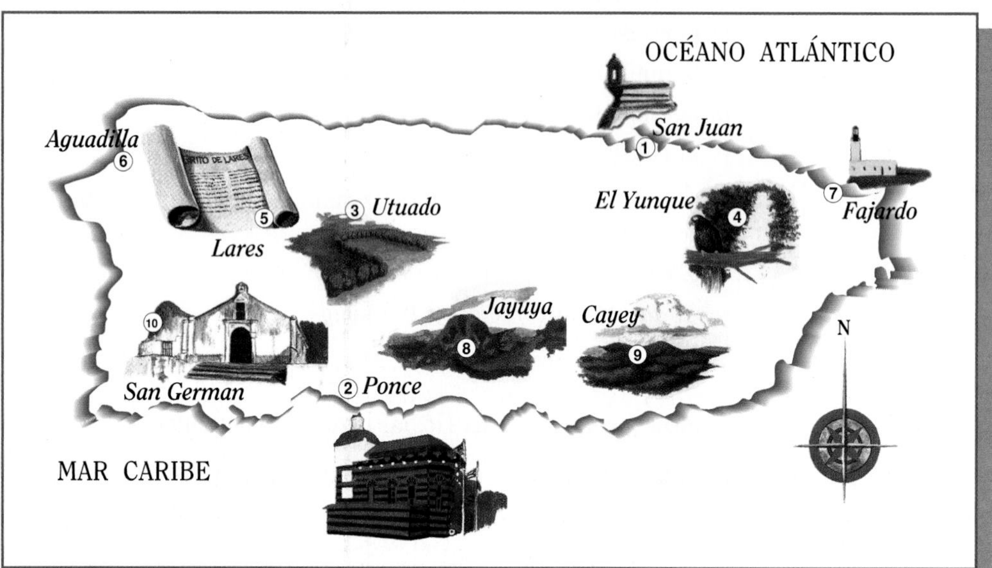

Le dicen *el pueblo arco iris*° para describir° a la gente de Puerto Rico, una combinación de tres ricas culturas: la europea, la taína° y la africana. Esta diversidad caracteriza también la geografía de la isla° con sus bonitas playas,° altas montañas° y ciudades cosmopolitas. También la futura política de Puerto Rico ofrece tres opciones: la independencia, la estadidad° o la situación actual° de Estado Libre Asociado.°

rainbow people; to describe

Tainan Indian

island; beaches; mountains

statehood; present

Commonwealth

Para conocer mejor a la gente y la isla, vamos a Puerto Rico. *(Watch the video and do the exercises that follow.)*

Palabras útiles

la isla	*island*
el castillo	*castle*
el ataque	*attack*
el pirata	*pirate*
la fortaleza	*fort*
la Garita del Diablo	*sentry box of the devil*
la estatua	*statue*
el gobernador	*governor*
la iglesia	*church*

el bosque (pluvioso)	*(rain) forest*
la playa	*beach*
la palmera	*palm tree*
el ciudadano	*citizen*
votar	*to vote*
el derecho	*right*
el estado	*state*
el partido (político)	*(political) party*
ha decidido (querido)	*has decided (wanted)*
propio	*own*
la estadidad	*statehood*
sea	*be*

Es decir

A Sitios de interés. What landmarks did you see in the video?

___ el Castillo San Felipe del Morro
___ la Garita del Diablo
___ la Fortaleza de San Jerónimo
___ el Castillo de San Cristóbal
___ la Catedral de San Juan
___ la Iglesia de San José
___ el Museo *(museum)* Taíno
___ Ponce de León
___ Cristóbal Colón
___ la Biblioteca de las Américas
___ el bosque tropical El Yunque
___ la Playa de Luquillo
___ San Juan
___ Ponce

B ¿Qué recuerda Ud.? Based on the video, tell if the following statements are true **(cierto)** or false **(falso)**. Correct the false statements.

1. Puerto Rico es una isla muy grande.
2. Todos los puertorriqueños son ciudadanos de los EE.UU.
3. Puerto Rico es un estado de los EE.UU.
4. No hay ciudades grandes en Puerto Rico.
5. Ponce es la capital de Puerto Rico.
6. En noviembre de 1993 la mayoría *(majority)* de los puertorriqueños votaron por la independencia.
7. El elemento africano está presente en la cultura puertorriqueña.
8. Hay mucha influencia india en la cultura puertorriqueña.

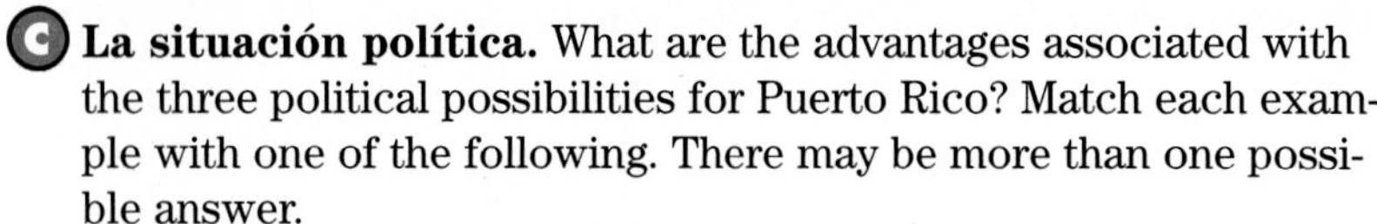

C **La situación política.** What are the advantages associated with the three political possibilities for Puerto Rico? Match each example with one of the following. There may be more than one possible answer.

E.L.A. (Estado Libre Asociado) Estadidad Independencia

1. Para poder recibir todos los beneficios *(benefits)* de ser ciudadano.
2. Para poder tomar sus propias decisiones.
3. Para poder seguir hablando español como idioma oficial de la isla.
4. Para mantener una relación con los EE.UU. y al mismo tiempo mantener su identidad latina.
5. Para tener votos y representación en el Congreso de los EE.UU.
6. Para poder votar por el presidente de los EE.UU.
7. Para determinar el tipo de gobierno *(government)* que la gente de Puerto Rico prefiere.
8. Para mantener su propia cultura y forma de vida pero también recibir protección y ayuda de los EE.UU.

Practiquemos

A **La bandera *(flag)* puertorriqueña.** This flag was adopted in 1952 as the official emblem of the **Estado Libre Asociado.** To learn about the Puerto Rican flag, match each symbol in the first column to its significance in the second column.

1. la estrella *(star)* blanca	**a.** la sangre *(blood)* vital que nutre *(nourishes)* un gobierno republicano
2. el triángulo azul	**b.** los derechos humanos
3. las tres franjas *(stripes)* rojas	**c.** sus tres ángulos representan los tres poderes *(powers)* del gobierno republicano: el legislativo, el ejecutivo y el judicial.
4. las dos franjas blancas	**d.** el símbolo de Estado Libre Asociado

B **El debate.** En tres grupos, representen un debate sobre el status político de Puerto Rico. Un grupo va a representar la independencia, otro grupo la estadidad y el tercer grupo el *status quo* (Estado Libre Asociado). Deben hablar de las ventajas *(advantages)* y desventajas de cada posibilidad.

Los beisbolistas° caribeños

El amor por el béisbol no es nuevo en Puerto Rico porque 300 años antes de la llegada° de Cristóbal Colón, los indios taínos jugaban° al batú, un juego° con un bate° y una pelota° de goma.° Hoy el béisbol sigue siendo el deporte° más popular de Puerto Rico y la República Dominicana. Algunos beisbolistas de las ligas mayores nos hablan de este fenómeno.

baseball players

arrival

used to play; game; bat; ball

rubber; sport

Juan González

Iván Rodríguez

To find out more about the importance of baseball in the Caribbean, watch the video and do the exercises that follow.

Palabras útiles

el receptor	*catcher*
los Medias Rojas	*the Red Sox*
el beisbolista (pelotero)	*ballplayer*
el ídolo	*idol*
único	*only*
el campo corto	*shortstop*
las ligas (mayores)	*(major) leagues*
el deporte	*sport*
el país	*country*
la isla	*island*
propio	*own*
la bandera	*flag*
pertenecer	*to belong*
orgulloso	*proud*
el coquí	*frog indigenous to Puerto Rico*
criado	*raised*
los campos	*fields*
echar hacia un lado	*to put aside*
los recuerdos	*memories*

Es decir

A **Entrevistas *(Interviews)*.** Listen carefully to the interviews with Tony Peña and Luis Rivera and fill in the missing words.

1. Tony dice:

Yo ______ que en mi país, pues, la ______ Dominicana, el béisbol es una cosa muy importante para ______. Siempre ______ un ídolo, siempre ___ ser como alguien que está delante de ______ cuando somos niños. Es una cosa muy ______. Yo creo que por eso es que el ______ es tan popular en la República ______.

2. Luis dice:

Yo me considero puertorriqueño. Yo nací en ______. Tenemos nuestra propia bandera, todavía pertenecemos a nuestro propio país, y ______ a Dios me considero y estoy muy orgulloso de ser ______.

B **Entrevistas *(Interviews)*.** Listen carefully to the interviews with Iván Rodríguez and Juan González and fill in the missing words.

1. Iván dice:

Mi ______ es Iván Rodríguez. Soy de ______, criado en Vega Baja, Puerto Rico, y mi ______ es el béisbol profesional.

2. Juan dice:

La diferencia es que en ______ países ______ no ______ estas oportunidades tan ______ como las que hay aquí en ______ Unidos.

C **¿De quién(es) hablan?** Based on the video, to which ballplayer(s) does each word or expression pertain? Form an original sentence for each one to describe the player. Some words may refer to more than one player.

Luis Rivera   Tony Peña   Iván Rodríguez   Juan González

1. República Dominicana
2. Puerto Rico
3. receptor
4. campo corto
5. 29 años
6. bigote *(mustache)*
7. Texas
8. Boston
9. la discriminación
10. el coquí
11. su papá
12. es importante tener un modelo

D **La discriminación.** Resuma Ud. *(Summarize)* los comentarios de Juan González sobre la discriminación. ¿Está Ud. de acuerdo *(in agreement)?* Explique.

Practiquemos

Los peloteros hispanos. To find out more about Hispanic ballplayers, fill in the spaces with the appropriate word from the following list.

control	bateó	brillantes	radio	perdió	ligas
béisbol	jugó	septiembre	hispano	víctimas	

La historia del ______ incluye los nombres de grandes latinoamericanos que jugaron un papel *(role)* importante en las grandes ______, nombres que todavía podemos oír en los parques de pelota *(ballparks)* entre los aficionados *(fans)*, y que la gente menciona repetidamente por la televisión y la ______ cuando hablan de los memorables jugadores del pasado.

Roberto Clemente de los Piratas de Pittsburgh fue uno de los peloteros más ______ en la historia del béisbol. En el mes de ______ de 1972 ______ su «hit» número 3000. Éste fue su último porque un poco después ______ su vida en un accidente de avión *(airplane)*. Iba *(He was going)* a Nicaragua para llevar provisiones a las ______ de un terremoto *(earthquake)* cuando chocó *(crashed)* su avión. El público nunca olvidó su talento y él fue el primer pelotero ______ en llegar al Salón de la Fama *(Hall of Fame)*.

Juan Marichal siguió a Clemente, consiguiendo fama por su «picheo» *(pitching)*. Marichal nació en la República Dominicana y ______ para los Gigantes de San Francisco. Combinó la velocidad con un ______ casi perfecto y ganó 243 juegos en 16 temporadas *(seasons)*. Podemos ver en el gráfico que sigue que hay una representación bastante grande de jugadores hispanos en las grandes ligas, y la lista sigue creciendo.

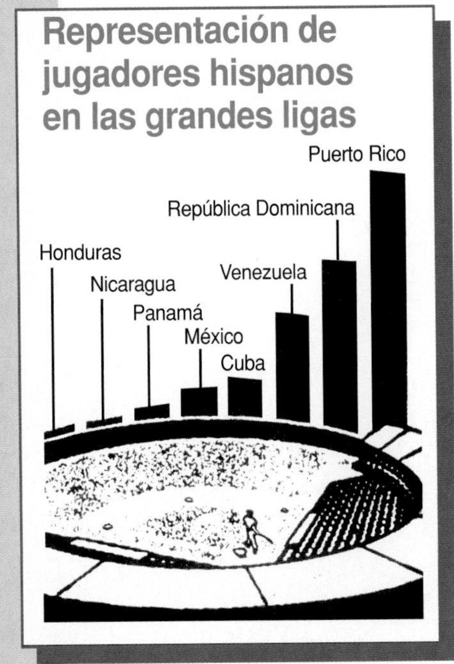

La música caribeña

La música del Caribe es tan diversa como° la gente. Tiene influencia indígena, europea y africana. La asociación política y económica que Puerto Rico tiene con los Estados Unidos desde 1898 también influye en la música. La influencia del jazz es evidente en la música salsa, y del rap americano salió el rap latino: el salsa-rap, el merengue-rap y el mambo-rap.

° *as diverse as*

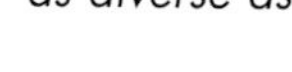

To hear the rich and rhythmic Caribbean beats and learn more about their origins, watch the video and do the exercises that follow.

Palabras útiles

el espíritu	*spirit*	enriquecer	*to enrich*
hispanocaribeño	*Hispanic-Caribbean*	se expresa	*is expressed*
la sensibilidad	*sensitivity*	étnico	*ethnic*
la barrera	*barrier*	calabazas secas	*dried gourds*
el mensaje	*message*	el sonido	*sound*
el ritmo	*rhythm*	el timbal	*kettle drum*
el corazón	*heart*	el orgullo	*pride*
la mezcla	*mixture*		

Vocabulario e identificaciones para la canción rap «Puerto Rican and Proud»

Pedro Navaja	*fictitious character in a famous Rubén Blades song*
Willie Colón	*Puerto Rican salsa musician*
Iris Chacón	*Cuban singer and popular icon*
Coco Rico	*coconut soft drink*
piragua	*snow cone*
coquito	*beverage made with rum and coconut liquor*
Bustelo, El Pico	*brands of Puerto Rican coffee*
el cuchifritos	*restaurant that serves Puerto Rican food*
carnicería	*butcher shop*
tontería	*foolishness*
porquería	*junk*

Es decir

A **Información musical.** Based on the video, choose the correct answer(s).

1. La música caribeña...
   a. es una rica combinación de muchos elementos culturales.
   b. tiene influencias de España solamente.
   c. sólo es popular en Puerto Rico.
2. Algunos tipos de música del Caribe son...
   a. la bomba de origen africano.
   b. el tango argentino.
   c. la danza de origen español.
3. Dos ritmos caribeños muy populares en los EE.UU. son...
   a. el flamenco y la conga.
   b. el merengue y el flamenco.
   c. el merengue y la salsa.

B **Identificaciones.** Which musical instrument(s) did each group contribute? Name each one.

1. los africanos **2.** los indios **3.** los españoles

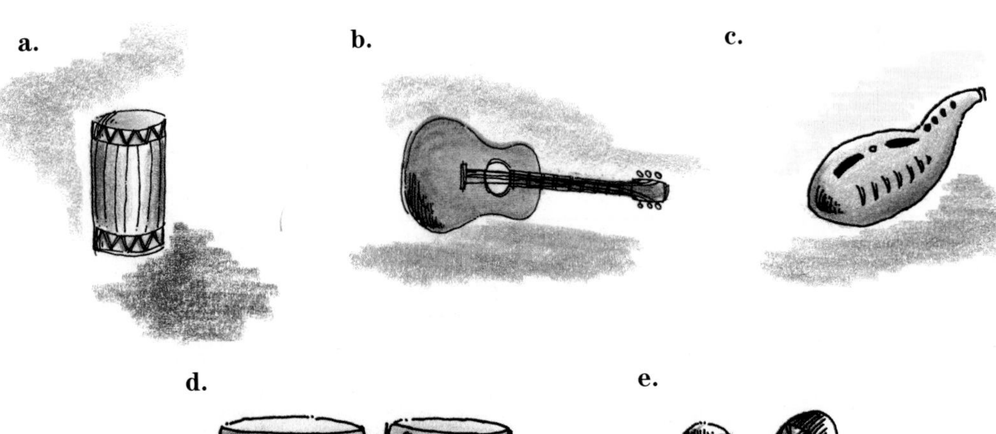

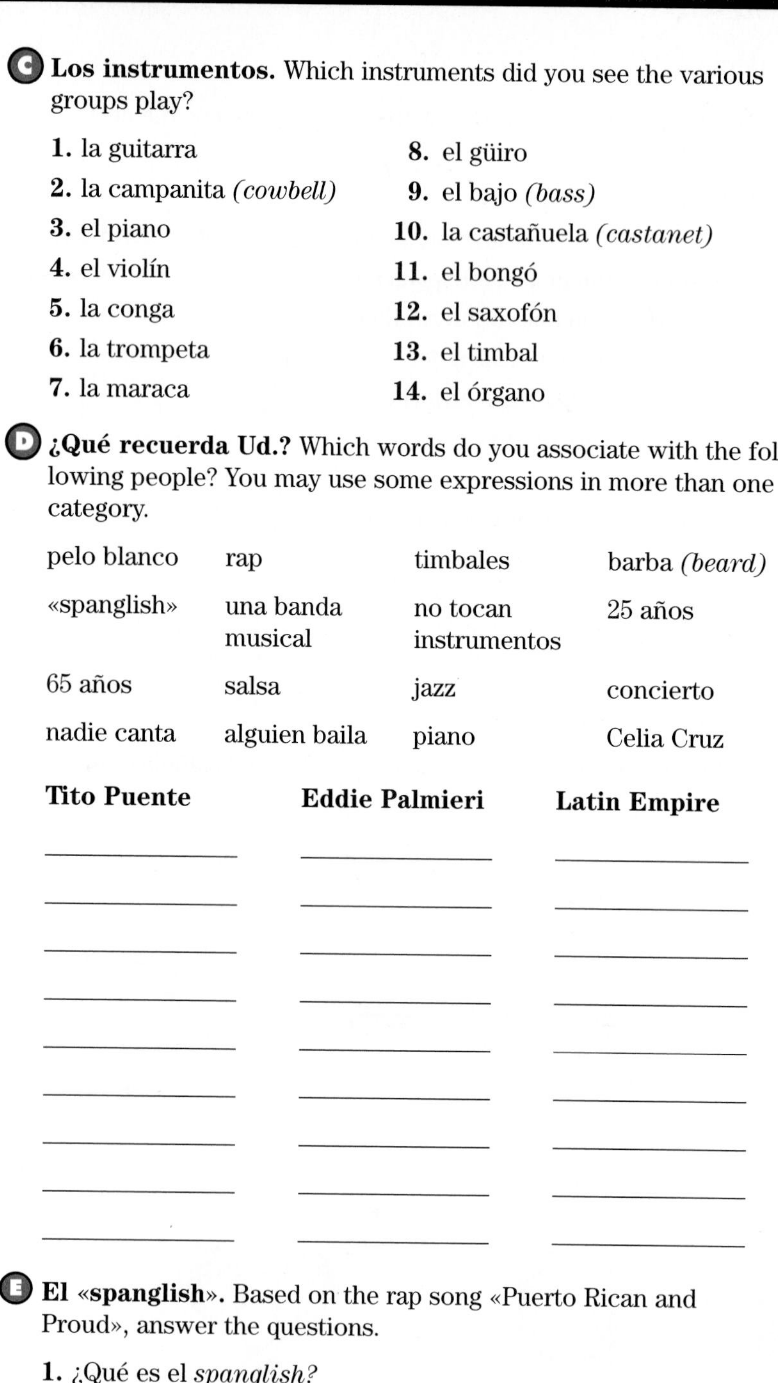

C **Los instrumentos.** Which instruments did you see the various groups play?

1. la guitarra
2. la campanita *(cowbell)*
3. el piano
4. el violín
5. la conga
6. la trompeta
7. la maraca
8. el güiro
9. el bajo *(bass)*
10. la castañuela *(castanet)*
11. el bongó
12. el saxofón
13. el timbal
14. el órgano

D **¿Qué recuerda Ud.?** Which words do you associate with the following people? You may use some expressions in more than one category.

pelo blanco	rap	timbales	barba *(beard)*
«spanglish»	una banda musical	no tocan instrumentos	25 años
65 años	salsa	jazz	concierto
nadie canta	alguien baila	piano	Celia Cruz

Tito Puente	**Eddie Palmieri**	**Latin Empire**
________	________	________
________	________	________
________	________	________
________	________	________
________	________	________
________	________	________
________	________	________
________	________	________
________	________	________

E **El «spanglish».** Based on the rap song «Puerto Rican and Proud», answer the questions.

1. ¿Qué es el *spanglish?*
2. ¿Cuáles son algunos ejemplos del *spanglish* en la canción?
3. ¿Cuándo usa el grupo el inglés y cuándo usa el español? ¿Por qué?
4. ¿Qué piensa Ud. del *spanglish*?

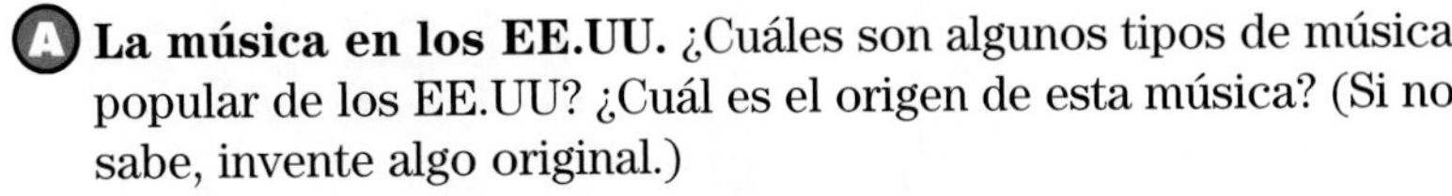

Practiquemos

A La música en los EE.UU. ¿Cuáles son algunos tipos de música popular de los EE.UU? ¿Cuál es el origen de esta música? (Si no sabe, invente algo original.)

B Minidrama. Ud. está de visita en la República Dominicana. Descríbale los bailes *(dances)* típicos de su país a un dominicano que no conoce los EE.UU.

UNIDAD

Las necesidades de la vida

Cuba y los cubanoamericanos

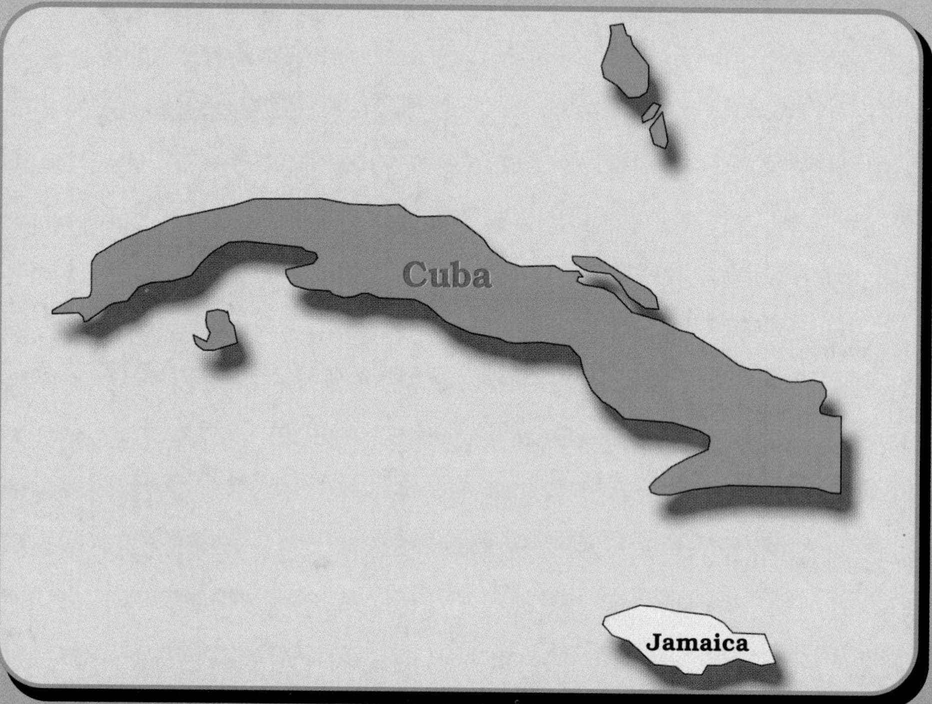

¡Vamos a Cuba por Internet!

Experience the mystery and splendor of Cuba, **«Perla del Caribe»**, by browsing the World Wide Web and visiting the following addresses.

http://www.latinworld.com/caribe/cuba/
http://www.latino.com/cubs1020.html
http://www.geocities.com/WallStreet/1568/
http://www.ceniai.inf.cu/turismo.html
http://www.generation.net/-minitur/cuatro.htm

Since Internet addresses are subject to change, typing the following key words into most search engines will also get you to Cuba.

Cuba **La Habana, Matanzas** (or any Cuban city) **Viajes a Cuba** **Turismo en Cuba**

To learn about Cuban art via the Internet, see page 311 of *Gaceta 3*.

Un mercado al aire libre

Lección  7

FUNCTION Expressing likes and dislikes • Talking about the past
STRUCTURE ***Gustar*** and similar verbs • The use of ***por*** and ***para*** • The preterite of irregular and stem-changing verbs
VOCABULARY At the restaurant • Ordering meals • Food preparation • Buying and selling
CULTURE Whom and where to tip • Hispanic culture
DIÁLOGO Y VIDEO ***Así es Mariana: Un plato cubano***

Lección  8

FUNCTION Describing and expressing habitual actions in the past • Expressing indefinite or unknown subjects (**one, they, you, the people**)
STRUCTURE The imperfect tense • The use of the preterite and the imperfect • ***Se*** to express an indefinite subject
VOCABULARY Food, measures, and quantity
CULTURE Regional food variations • The history of some favorite foods
DIÁLOGO Y VIDEO ***Así es Mariana: En el supermercado***

Lección  9

FUNCTION Expressing reflexive action (**-self, -selves**) • Giving orders
STRUCTURE Reflexive verbs • Commands: Formal and familiar • Commands with pronouns
VOCABULARY Clothing, materials, designs and sizes • Reflexive actions
CULTURE Attire in the Hispanic world
DIÁLOGO Y VIDEO ***Así es Mariana: Ropa y más ropa***

Gaceta  3

CULTURE **Cuba and Cuban-Americans**
Touring Cuba • Faces in the news • Notes and notables • Literature: José Martí • Art
VIDEOCULTURA Gloria Estefan y Miami Sound Machine: Una entrevista con la talentosa cantante • Una visita a la ciudad de Miami • La comida cubana

Lección 7

En el restaurante

¡Por fin! Alguien que me escucha.

AVISO CULTURAL

(As a reading aid, refer to lesson vocabulary for new words.)

La palabra <u>propina</u> viene del verbo latino *propinare* **(invitar a beber).** Es el dinero que dejamos para el camarero en un restaurante, y esta tradición varía mucho según el país. En España, por ejemplo, el servicio está incluido en la cuenta. Sin embargo, es recomendable dejar un diez por ciento (%) más en los restaurantes muy buenos. Además de darles propina a los camareros en España, también es costumbre darle propina al acomodador *(usher)* en el cine o el teatro, y al hombre que trabaja en la estación de gasolina. En los Estados Unidos, ¿a quién le damos propina? ¿Qué porcentaje (%) debemos dar si el servicio es bueno? ¿malo? ¿regular?

Preparativos

Review the vocabulary on pages 240–242 before viewing the video.

As you watch the video or read the following dialogue, pay close attention to the uses of the prepositions **por** and **para.** Although **por** often means *for*, it also has many other meanings. What do the expressions **por** primera vez, **por** fin, and **por** favor mean? **Para** also can mean *for*. Carla says, «Este festival es una buena oportunidad **para** nosotros». However, in the video Mariana says that the Spanish Club is meeting… «**para** hablar de mi tema favorito, la comida». What does **para** mean in this context? In the video Mariana warns us that the conversation may get «un poco picante». What might she mean by that? Is there a power struggle? Hurt feelings? Difference of opinion? You know how planning meetings can be—¡picantes!

Así es Mariana: Un plato cubano

Algunos de los estudiantes del club de español meriendan en el restaurante cubano La Carreta.

Alicia: Pero esto, sí es algo importante. Por primera vez el club de español está invitado a participar en el festival estudiantil.

Carla: No me gusta decirlo, pero la presidenta tiene razón. Este festival es una buena oportunidad para nosotros.

Alicia: ¡Por fin! Alguien que me escucha. Ahora, el festival nos permite escoger sólo una comida para el menú. Y yo quiero hacer un plato venezolano. A Octavio le encanta como cocino. *(Octavio indica que no le gusta nada su cocina. Alicia lo ve.)* ¡Octavio! Pensé que te gusta como cocino.

Octavio: Perdón, Alicia... no quise decírtelo.

El cocinero[1] viene y les sirve la comida. Todos indican quién pidió qué plato.

Cocinero: ¿El arroz con pollo?

Rubén: Aquí, señor.

Cocinero: ¿La sopa de frijoles negros?

Octavio: Aquí.

Cocinero: ¿El sandwich cubano?

Mariana: Aquí.

Cocinero: ¿El pollo asado? *(Nadie contesta. El cocinero repite.)* ¿El pollo asado?

Carla: Aquí. Gracias.

El cocinero le da los tostones° a Carla y los maduros° a Alicia, pero nadie lo ve.

fried salted plantains; fried sweet plantains

Carla: Ah, Octavio... tú eres cubano... ¿no? Pues, esta comida es muy sabrosa. ¿Por qué no preparamos una cena cubana? Te gustan estos platos, ¿no?

Octavio: Sí, Carlita... sobre todo los frijoles negros. Es la especialidad de mi madre. Me encantan.

Rubén: Además, la comida cubana es muy popular aquí en Miami. ¡Qué buena idea, Carla y Octavio!

Alicia: *(Alicia tiene celos.)* ¡Ay, claro! ¿Y mi cena venezolana? Y hablando de la cena... *(Alicia ve que no tiene lo que pidió).* Por favor, señor cocinero. Yo le pedí a Ud. tostones, como los que tiene Carla, y Ud. me trajo maduros.

Cocinero: Ah... ¿Ud. pidió tostones y yo le traje maduros? *(Él cambia su plato con el plato de Carla. Carla no está contenta pero Alicia está muy contenta ahora).* Pues, ya está.°

all set

Es decir

A Llene Ud. los espacios con **por** o **para.**

1. ______ primera vez el club está invitado a participar.
2. Este festival es una buena oportunidad ______ nosotros.
3. Nos permite escoger una comida ______ el menú.
4. ¡______ fin! Alguien que me escucha.
5. ______ favor, señor cocinero.

[1]En este restaurante pequeño, el cocinero también sirve de camarero.

B Sustituya *(Substitute)* las palabras subrayadas por una palabra similar de la lista.

preparar   está correcta   seleccionar   gusta mucho   deliciosa

1. El festival nos permite escoger sólo una comida.
2. Yo quiero hacer un plato venezolano.
3. A Octavio le encanta como cocino.
4. Esta comida es muy sabrosa.
5. La presidenta tiene razón.

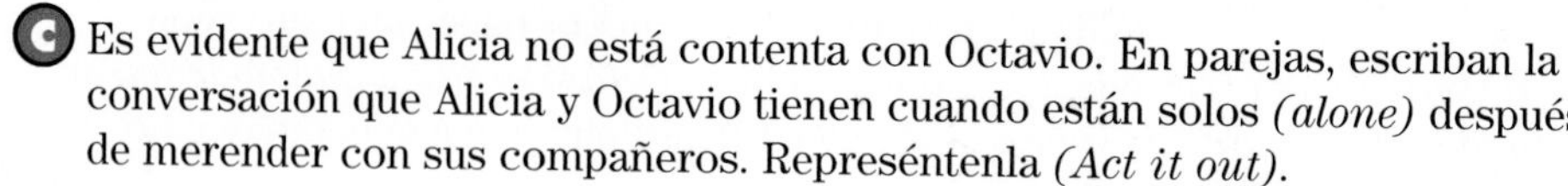

C Es evidente que Alicia no está contenta con Octavio. En parejas, escriban la conversación que Alicia y Octavio tienen cuando están solos *(alone)* después de merender con sus compañeros. Represéntenla *(Act it out)*.

Al ver el video

A En parejas, digan *(tell)* a quién(es) corresponden las siguientes descripciones.

Mariana   Alicia   Carla   Octavio   Rubén

1. Tiene celos.
2. Muestra mucho interés en el festival.
3. Escucha pero no participa.
4. Flirtea.
5. No está feliz.
6. Está avergonzado *(embarrassed)*.
7. Bebe Coca Cola.
8. Tiene mucha energía.

B En grupos pequeños, contesten las preguntas siguientes.

1. Mariana dice que no hay problemas en el club. ¿Está Ud. de acuerdo *(Do you agree)*? Explique.
2. De los platos que sirve el cocinero, ¿cuál le parece más delicioso? ¿Por qué? ¿Conoce Ud. la comida cubana? ¿Qué platos le gustan?
3. ¿Qué piensa Ud. de la actitud de Alicia? ¿Tiene ella razón? ¿Por qué?

Vocabulario

Verbos

andar	*to walk*
cortar	*to cut*
encantar	*to delight, charm*
escoger	*to choose*
faltar	*to lack, be missing*
gozar (de)	*to enjoy*
gustar	*to be pleasing*
hacer falta	*to be in need of*
importar	*to matter*
interesar	*to interest*
merendar (ie)	*to snack*

permitir	*to allow*
probar (ue)	*to taste, try*
soler (ue) (+ *infinitive*)	*to be accustomed to (doing something)*

Alimentos	***(Foods)***
el aceite (de oliva)	*(olive) oil*
la aceituna (oliva)	*olive*
el ajo	*garlic*
el arroz	*rice*
los camarones (las gambas)	*shrimp*
la carne (de res)	*meat (beef)*
la cebolla	*onion*
la ensalada	*salad*
el frijol	*bean (kidney, pinto)*
la lechuga	*lettuce*
el maíz	*corn*
los mariscos	*shellfish, seafood*
el pan	*bread*
el pastel	*pastry, pie*
el pescado	*fish*
la pimienta	*pepper (ground)*
la piña	*pineapple*
el pollo	*chicken*
el queso	*cheese*
la sal	*salt*
la sopa	*soup*
el tomate	*tomato*
la torta (tarta)	*cake*
la verdura (legumbre)	*vegetable*
la zanahoria	*carrot*

Bebidas	***(Drinks)***
el café	*coffee*
la cerveza	*beer*
el jugo	*juice*
la leche	*milk*
el té	*tea*
el vino (blanco, rosado, tinto)	*(white, rosé, red) wine*

Adjetivos	
asado	*roasted*
caliente	*hot (temperature)*
delicioso (rico, sabroso)	*delicious*
dulce	*sweet*

(continued)

Adjectivos *(Continued)*

frío	*cold*
frito	*fried*
picante	*hot, spicy*
salado	*salty*
sano (saludable)	*healthy (healthful)*
último	*last*
único	*only, unique*

En el restaurante	***(In the restaurant)***
la cocina	*cuisine; kitchen*
la copa	*goblet, wine glass*
la cuchara	*spoon*
el cuchillo	*knife*
la cuenta	*check, bill*
la lista (el menú)	*menu*
el plato	*plate; dish*
la propina	*tip*
la servilleta	*napkin*
la taza	*cup*
el tenedor	*fork*
el vaso	*glass*

(See p. 249 for expressions with **por**.)

Vocabulario adicional	
¡Buen provecho!	*Enjoy your meal!*
la costumbre	*custom*
la especialidad	*specialty*
el flan	*caramel custard*
la flor	*flower*
el ingrediente	*ingredient*
la merienda	*snack*
raro	*strange*
la receta	*recipe; prescription*
tomar una copa	*to have a drink (alcoholic beverage)*

Repasemos el vocabulario

A **¿Cuál no pertenece?** Indique Ud. la palabra que no está relacionada con las otras y explique.

1. cebolla	pescado	zanahoria	tomate
2. caliente	frito	último	asado
3. tenedor	propina	cuchillo	cuchara
4. sal	jugo	cerveza	leche

B **Especialidades.** ¿Cuál es la especialidad de... y ¿cuáles son los ingredientes?

1. la cafetería? **2.** Ud.? **3.** su restaurante preferido? **4.** su abuela?

C **Definiciones.** Su profesor(a) va a leer una serie de definiciones. Escoja *(Choose)* la palabra que corresponde a cada descripción.

el menú la propina la piña la cebolla la cuenta la cuchara

1. ________ **3.** ________ **5.** ________
2. ________ **4.** ________ **6.** ________

D **¿En qué orden?** Ud. prepara una cena para muchas personas. Diga *(Tell)* en qué orden va a hacer las siguientes actividades. Use la primera persona singular **(yo)** de los verbos.

MODELO escoger el menú
#1. Yo escojo el menú.

___ servir la cena
___ poner la mesa
___ llenar los vasos de agua
___ preparar la comida
___ probar la comida para ver si necesita sal o pimienta
___ saludar a los invitados

E **Costumbres culinarias.** Pregúntele a un(a) compañero(a) qué suele comer él (ella)...

1. cuando está nervioso(a).
2. cuando está triste.
3. antes de dormir.
4. en clase.
5. cuando sale con su novio(a).
6. después de hacer algún ejercicio físico.
7. cuando estudia para un examen.
8. en una fiesta.

De uso común

Buying and Selling

Dice el vendedor		**Dice el comprador**	
¿En qué puedo servirle?	*How may I help you?*	¿Cuánto es (vale, cuesta)... ? ¿A cuánto está?	*How much is (it) . . .*
		¿Cuál es el precio?	*What is the price?*
		¡Qué caro (barato)!	*How expensive (cheap)!*
Es una ganga (regalado).	*It's a bargain.*	Me costó un ojo de la cara (un dineral).	*It cost me a fortune.*
¿Algo más?	*Anything else?*	Nada más.	*Nothing else.*

Practiquemos

A **En un restaurante elegante.** You have chosen a restaurant too expensive for your budget. The waiter hands you a menu with no prices listed. You ask him the cost of various items and respond to the price. With a classmate, play the roles of the client and waiter.

MODELO **Cliente: ¿Cuánto cuesta la paella ($30.00)?**
Camarero: La paella cuesta treinta dólares.
Cliente: ¡Dios mío! Es muy cara.

¡Es regalado!	Es muy barato.	¡Cuesta un dineral!
Es muy caro.	¡Qué caro!	¡Dios mío!

1. ¿Cuánto cuesta el cóctel de gambas? ($15.00)
2. ¿Cuánto cuesta una copa de vino tinto? ($9.00)
3. ¿Cuánto cuesta la ensalada? ($2.00)
4. ¿Cuánto cuesta el flan? ($8.00)
5. ¿Cuánto cuesta la especialidad de la casa? ($50.00)
6. ¿Cuánto cuesta el pan? ($1.00)

B **Diálogos.** Complete Ud. el siguiente diálogo de una forma original.

En la frutería

Frutero: ¿En qué puedo servirle, señora?
Cliente: __________.
Frutero: Son 50 pesos por kilo.
Cliente: __________.
Frutero: Es porque no es la temporada *(season)*, señora.

Gustar and Similar Verbs

Forma y función

The verb **gustar** is used to express likes and dislikes.

Me gusta el café pero **no me gustan** las bebidas alcohólicas.	*I like coffee but I don't like alcoholic beverages.*

Since **gustar** does not mean literally *to like*, but rather *to be pleasing*, a different sentence structure is required. Look at the above example of **gustar.** Why do you think the first form of **gustar** is singular **(gusta),** but the second form is plural **(gustan)?** What is the subject of the verb in each case? Although in English the subject of the verb *like* is *I* in both cases, in Spanish the subject of the verb **gustar** is **café** in the first part of the sentence, and **bebidas alcohólicas** in the second part. Literally you say *"Coffee is pleasing to me but alcoholic beverages are not pleasing to me."* Note that the subject in the English sentence is the indirect object in the Spanish sentence, and the direct object in the English sentence (the thing liked) is the subject in the Spanish sentence.

subject	verb	direct object	=	indirect object	verb	subject
I	*like*	*coffee*	=	**Me**	**gusta**	**el café**

Note that it is common to place the subject after the verb with **gustar** and similar verbs, particularly when the subject is a thing or an infinitive. Study the following examples of the use of the Spanish verb (**gustar**—*to be pleasing)* and the English equivalent *(to like).*

Spanish	**English Equivalent**
Nos **gusta** la cocina cubana.	*We like Cuban cuisine.*
Le **gusta** preparar su especialidad.	*He likes to prepare his specialty.*
Te **gustan** los tostones.	*You like fried plantains.*

Study the following rules.

1. When **gustar** is followed by one or more infinitives, the third-person singular is used.

   Me gusta cantar, bailar y pasarlo bien. — *I like to sing, dance, and have fun.*

2. Even when the indirect object noun is expressed, the indirect object pronoun must be used.

   Al mozo no **le** gustó la propina que dejamos. — *The waiter didn't like the tip we left.*

   A ellos no **les** gusta este café. — *They don't like this coffee.*

3. A prepositional phrase is often used for clarification or emphasis.

   A él no le gusta este restaurante pero **a mí** me gusta mucho. — *He doesn't like this restaurant but I like it a lot.*

4. Although all forms of **gustar** can be used, it is most commonly used in the third-person singular and plural.[1]

   Nos gusta el arroz pero no nos **gustan** los tomates. — *We like rice but we don't like tomatoes.*

5. Some verbs similar to **gustar** are:

encantar	*to delight, charm (love)*	importar	*to matter*
faltar	*to lack, be missing*	interesar	*to interest*
fascinar	*to fascinate*	molestar	*to bother, annoy*
hacer falta[2]	*to be in need of*	parecer	*to seem*

6. To express degrees of like, you can use the following progression.

   Me gusta el flan. También me gusta **mucho** el helado. ¡Pero **me encantan** los pasteles! — *I like flan. I also like ice cream a lot. But I love pastries!*

[1]**Gustar: gusto, gustas, gusta, gustamos, gustáis, gustan. Tú me gustas.** *You are pleasing to me (I like you).* **Yo les gusto.** *I am pleasing to them (They like me).*

[2]Note that for this expression, ***hacer*** is conjugated but ***falta*** remains constant because it is used as a noun.

Identify the verbs used like **gustar** in the following ad. What are the subjects in each case?

trago *gulp*

sentir *to feel*

a todos lados *everywhere*

Practiquemos

A **Preferencias.** ¿Cuáles de las siguientes comidas le gustan (o no le gustan) a Ud.? Siga el modelo.

MODELO el maíz: **Me gusta el maíz.**
los mariscos: **No me gustan los mariscos.**

1. el flan
2. los frijoles
3. las aceitunas
4. los pasteles
5. el pescado
6. las zanahorias

B **La merienda.** Llene Ud. los espacios con la forma correcta del verbo **gustar** para saber cómo las siguientes personas pasan su tiempo libre.

Los fines de semana, a mí me ______ hacer muchas cosas. Me ______ los conciertos, me ______ participar en los deportes y me ______ las actividades culturales como ir a museos y al teatro. Pero lo que más me ______ es merendar en una cafetería con mis amigos Sandra y Carlos. A nosotros nos ______ las cafeterías al aire libre *(outdoors)*. A ellos les ______ comer flan con el café, pero a mí me ______ los pasteles. Nos ______ charlar y mirar a toda la gente.

C **Disgustos *(Dislikes)*.** Busque Ud. en la segunda columna la terminación de las frases en la primera columna para saber lo que no les gusta a las siguientes personas. Use la forma correcta del verbo **gustar** y el pronombre **le** o **les.**

MODELO Al camarero **no le gusta** servirle a una familia con seis niños pequeños.

1. A un cliente en un restaurante caro...
2. A los estudiantes universitarios...
3. A los niños pequeños...
4. A una persona que está a dieta...
5. A una persona nerviosa...

a. la cafeína.
b. ver tortas y pasteles.
c. las legumbres.
d. un menú sin precios.
e. la comida de la cafetería.

D **Reacciones.** Practique **gustar** y verbos similares. Describa los dibujos *(drawings)* según el modelo.

A Eduardo/hacer falta

MODELO A Eduardo le hace falta dinero para hacer una llamada telefónica.

1.

A mamá/molestar

2.

A nosotros/fascinar

3.

A Paula/encantar

4.

A mí/no gustar

5.

A Juan/gustar

6.

A ti/hacer falta

E **Gustos personales.** Indique Ud. cuánto le gustan (importan, interesan...) las siguientes cosas, y explique su selección. Luego, cambie las frases a preguntas, y hágaselas a dos compañeros.

Me interesa cocinar.
No me interesa nada cocinar porque es aburrido y no sé hacerlo.

	mucho	un poco	nada
1. Me gusta la comida picante.	______	______	______
2. Me importan las calorías.	______	______	______
3. Me gusta cenar en los restaurantes elegantes.	______	______	______
4. Me interesa saber qué ingredientes hay en las cosas que como.	______	______	______
5. Me importa tomar vitaminas.	______	______	______
6. Me interesa preparar comidas exóticas.	______	______	______
7. Me gustan los postres.	______	______	______

The Uses of *por* and *para*

Función

Although **por** and **para** can both mean *for* in English, they are not synonyms, but rather are used in very different contexts to express many different concepts. There is no one rule that tells you when to use **por** and **para**. In general, however, **por** may express reason or cause behind an action (having done something) while **para** may refer to an underlying goal, purpose, or use.

Lo compré **por** necesidad.	*I bought it* ***out of (because of)*** *necessity.*
Lo compré **para** regalárselo a mi hermana.	*I bought it* ***(in order) to*** *give it to my sister.*

Study some of the following meanings of **por** and **para**.

Por can mean:

1. *in exchange for*

Compré los tomates **por** 75 pesetas.	*I bought the tomatoes* ***for (in exchange for)*** *75 pesetas.*
Te doy mi helado **por** tu tarta.	*I'll give you my ice cream* ***for*** *your cake.*

2. *during* or *for* when referring to:

a. length of time

Tienes que cocinar el arroz **por** 45 minutos.	*You have to cook the rice* ***for*** *45 minutes.*

¡AVISO! Note that in this context, **por** is often omitted by native speakers, just as *for* is often omitted in English. **Tienes que cocinarlo 45 minutos.** *You have to cook it 45 minutes.*

b. general time *(in)*

Por la mañana el cocinero prepara el postre y **por** la tarde lo sirve.	***In*** *the morning the cook prepares the dessert and* ***in*** *the afternoon he serves it.*

¡AVISO! Remember that when a specific hour is mentioned, **de** is used instead of **por. A las 10:00 <u>de</u> la mañana estudio y a las 3:00 <u>de</u> la tarde voy a clase.**

3. *along, through, by*

Me gusta caminar **por** la calle.	*I like to walk* ***along*** *the street.*
Entramos **por** la puerta principal.	*We enter* ***through*** *the main door.*

4. *by (means of)*

Siempre van **por** avión (tren, barco).	*They always go* ***by*** *plane (train, boat).*
Rosita nos habla **por** teléfono cada semana.	*Rosita talks to us* ***by*** *phone every week.*
Ganó su fortuna **por** trabajar mucho.	*She earned her fortune* ***by*** *working a lot.*

5. *because of, on account of, for* (referring to cause or reason)

Estoy enferma **por** comer las gambas.	*I'm sick* ***because of*** *eating the shrimp.*
No vamos al restaurante **por** falta de dinero.	*We're not going to the restaurant* ***for*** *lack of money.*

6. *on behalf of, for the sake of, in place of*

Acepto el Premio Nobel **por** mi abuela.	*I accept the Nobel Prize* ***on behalf of*** *my grandmother.*
Lo hicieron **por** su amigo.	*They did it* ***for the sake of*** *their friend.*

7. **Por** is used in many idiomatic expressions such as the following.

por cierto	*for sure; by the way*	por lo menos	*at least*
por Dios	*for God's sake*	por otro lado	*on the other hand*
por ejemplo	*for example*	por primera (última) vez	*for the first (last) time*
por fin	*finally*	por supuesto	*of course*
por lo general	*generally*		

Para can mean:

1. *In order to, for the purpose of* (before an infinitive)

Juan toma una clase de cocina **para** poder preparar una cena para su novia.	*Juan takes a cooking class* ***in order*** *to be able to prepare a dinner for his girlfriend.*

2. *to* (referring to recipient)

Vamos **para** el mercado central.	*We're going* ***to*** *the main market.*
Ana va **para** Cuba en agosto.	*Ana is going* ***to*** *Cuba in August.*

3. *by* (referring to deadline)

Para el lunes Uds. deben leer la Lección 8.	***By*** *Monday you should read Lesson 8.*

4. *for*, to express the following concepts:

a. goal or recipient

El pescado es **para** papá y el pollo es **para** la abuela.	*The fish is* ***for*** *dad and the chicken is* ***for*** *grandmother.*

b. use or purpose

La copa es **para** vino y el vaso es **para** agua.	*The goblet is* ***for*** *wine and the glass is* ***for*** *water.*

c. employed by

Susana trabaja **para** el Café Cuba Libre.	*Susana works* ***for*** *Café Cuba Libre.*

Por and **para**

There are times when both **por** and **para** are grammatically correct to use in the same context, but very different concepts are expressed.

Yo preparé el flan **para** ti.	*I prepared the flan* ***for*** *you.* (you are the recipient)
Yo preparé el flan **por** ti.	*I prepared the flan* ***for*** *you.* (instead of you)
¿Vas **para** la Plaza José Martí?	*Are you going* ***to*** (destination) *José Martí Square?*
¿Vas **por** la Plaza José Martí?	*Are you going* ***by*** (through) *José Martí Square?*

Practiquemos

A **Las especialidades de la casa.** Forme frases completas y use **por** para indicar las especialidades de los siguientes restaurantes. Siga *(follow)* el modelo.

MODELO El restaurante Alí Babá es famoso **por** su cuscús.

1. Bella Italia	**a.** barbacoa
2. Perla del Caribe	**b.** enchiladas
3. Les Amis	**c.** lasaña y ravioles
4. Tejas	**d.** soufflés y patés
5. Acapulco	**e.** arroz con pollo y frijoles negros

B **Tiendas especializadas.** Muchas personas prefieren comprar en las pequeñas tiendas especializadas. Forme frases completas para indicar para qué fueron estas personas a las tiendas especializadas. Siga el modelo.

MODELO Mamá/pescadería *(fish market)*
Mamá fue a la pescadería para comprar pescado.

1. yo/pastelería
2. mis abuelos/carnicería
3. la tía/pizzería
4. nosotros/frutería
5. tú/panadería
6. Pepe y yo/heladería

C **¿Por dónde y para qué?** Diga Ud. cómo llegaron a su destino las siguientes personas. Use **por** y **para** y siga el modelo.

MODELO el estudiante/correr
El estudiante corrió por la calle para llegar a la escuela.

1.

los señores Álvarez/pasar

2.

Sara/caminar

3.

Javier/ir

4.

la doctora Torres/manejar

C **Comentarios culinarios.** Para saber los secretos de la buena cocina, complete Ud. las frases con **por** o **para.**

1. ______ preparar un auténtico plato cubano es necesario tener una buena receta.
2. ______ ejemplo, ______ cocinar sopa de frijoles negros, es necesario cocinar los frijoles ______ un mínimo de cuatro horas.
3. Mi mamá pone la sopa a cocinar ______ la mañana y está lista ______ la hora del almuerzo.
4. Siempre uso un plato pequeño ______ las cebollas que sirvo con la sopa.
5. En muchas de las recetas, Ud. puede sustituir leche ______ crema.
6. Si le falta algún ingrediente, es mejor llamar ______ teléfono al mercado ______ saber si lo tienen.
7. Pagué $10.00 ______ un libro de recetas caribeñas. Luego preparé una cena muy sabrosa ______ mi novia, Julia. Ella probó el arroz con pollo ______ primera vez, y le gustó mucho.
8. ______ fin, serví el postre, queso crema con guayaba *(guava jelly).* ______ supuesto, a Julia le encantó.

The Preterite of More Irregular Verbs

Forma

In Lesson 6 you studied the irregular preterite forms of the verbs **ir, ser, dar,** and **hacer.** The following are additional irregular verbs in the preterite tense that should be learned. They are verbs that are frequently used in daily conversation. The preterite of these verbs is formed by adding the appropriate endings to the irregular preterite stems.

Infinitive	Stem	Preterite Ending
andar	**anduv-**	
estar	**estuv-**	**e**
poder	**pud-**	**iste**
poner	**pus-**	**o**
querer	**quis-**	**imos**
saber	**sup-**	**isteis**
tener	**tuv-**	**ieron**
venir	**vin-**	

The following group of irregular stems that end in **-j** have no **i** in the third-person plural form.

Infinitive	Stem	Preterite Ending
conducir	**conduj-**	**e**
decir	**dij-**	**iste**
producir	**produj-**	**o**
traducir	**traduj-**	**imos**
traer	**traj-**	**isteis**
		eron

1. Unlike regular verbs in the preterite, the irregular verbs have no written accent on the first- and third-person singular forms **(yo, él, ella,** and **Ud.).**
2. The preterite form of **hay** *(there is, there are)*, is **hubo** *(there was, there were)*.
3. **Saber** in the preterite means *to find out.*

   Supe las noticias ayer. *I **found out** the news yesterday.*

Practiquemos

A **La cena.** Anoche organizamos una cena. Llene Ud. el primer espacio con la forma correcta del verbo **venir,** y el segundo *(second)* espacio con la forma correcta del verbo **traer** para saber quiénes vinieron y qué trajeron. Siga el modelo.

MODELO Yo **vine** a la cena y **traje** la sopa.

1. Mi novio y yo _______ a la cena y _______ los frijoles negros.
2. Mis padres _______ a la cena y _______ el vino.
3. Mi abuela _______ a la cena y _______ el flan.
4. Tú _______ a la cena y _______ los refrescos.
5. Mis primos _______ a la cena y _______ el helado.
6. Mi hermano Vicente _______ a la cena y _______ a su amigo Pepe.

B **¿Y tú?** Con un(a) compañero(a), hagan y contesten las siguientes preguntas.

MODELO ¿(Saber) _______ Uds. su nombre o su dirección?
Estudiante 1: **¿Supieron** Uds. su nombre o su dirección?
Estudiante 2: **Supimos** su nombre. ¿Qué **supiste** tú?
Estudiante 1: **Supe** su dirección.

1. ¿(Traer) _______ Uds. el vino o la cerveza?
2. ¿(Hacer) _______ Uds. los pasteles o el flan?
3. ¿(Poner) _______ Uds. sal o pimienta?
4. ¿(Poder) _______ Uds. pedir tacos o enchiladas?

C **El Café Caribe.** Anoche fue la inauguración *(opening)* del nuevo Café Caribe. Cambie Ud. los verbos entre paréntesis al pretérito para saber qué pasó.

Anoche yo (ir) _______ al Café Caribe por primera vez. Cuando yo (llegar) _______, (ver) _______ a muchos de mis amigos. No (tener-yo) _______ que esperar mucho. (Poder) _______ entrar inmediatamente. El camarero (venir) _______ pronto y me (dar) _______ el menú. Otro camarero (poner) _______ pan en la mesa y me (traer) _______ agua mineral. Después, él me (decir) _______ cuáles eran° las especialidades de la casa. Para mí, la decisión (ser) _______ muy difícil, pero por fin (decidir-yo) _______ probar el sandwich caribeño con tostones *(fried plantains)* y mermelada de mango. Todo (estar) _______ muy rico. Y el servicio (ser) _______ excelente. Cuando yo (salir), _______ (dejar) _______ una propina muy buena para los camareros.

°were

D **Ud. tiene correo *(You've got mail).*** Ud. recibió una carta por correo electrónico de un amigo que está en Miami para las vacaciones. Él cenó en un restaurante cubano por primera vez. Termine Ud. sus frases con la forma correcta de los verbos en el pretérito.

¡Qué comida más rica! Anoche yo (ir) _______ al restaurante La Carreta con mi novia, Linda. Primero, el camarero nos (traer) _______ el menú, pero como Linda no habla español, yo se lo (traducir) _______. Después, el camarero nos (leer) _______ la lista de las especialidades. Nosotros (decidir) ___ pedir el sandwich cubano y una ensalada. A Linda le (gustar) _______ todo y a mí también. Nosotros (comer) _______ tanto que no (querer) _______ comer postre. Después nosotros (andar) _______ por Miami Beach y luego (conducir) _______ a la Calle Ocho para tomar café.

Ahora, conteste Ud. la carta diciéndole lo que Ud. hizo anoche.

The Preterite of Stem-changing Verbs

Forma

Stem-changing verbs that end in **-ar** and **-er** have no stem change in the preterite tense.

PENSAR		**VOLVER**	
pensé	pensamos	volví	volvimos
pensaste	pensasteis	volviste	volvisteis
pensó	pensaron	volvió	volvieron

Stem-changing verbs that end in **-ir** have a stem change in the third-person singular and plural **(él, ella, Ud.** and **ellos, ellas, Uds.)**. The stem vowel **e** changes to **i** and the stem vowel **o** changes to **u.**

PREFIRIR		**DORMIR**		**PEDIR**	
preferí	preferimos	dormí	dormimos	pedí	pedimos
preferiste	preferisteis	dormiste	dormisteis	pediste	pedisteis
prefirió	prefirieron	durmió	durmieron	pidió	pidieron

Practiquemos

A **No cambian.** Las raíces *(stems)* de los siguientes verbos no cambian en el pretérito. Cambie Ud. los verbos entre paréntesis al pretérito y conteste las preguntas según el modelo.

MODELO **¿Recordaste** tú el número de teléfono o la dirección?
Yo **recordé** el número de teléfono. ¿Y mamá?
Mamá **recordó** la dirección.

1. ¿(Cerrar) _______ tú la puerta o la ventana? ¿Y ellos?
2. ¿(Volver) _______ tú el sábado o el domingo? ¿Y ella?
3. ¿(Probar) _______ tú el pescado o la carne de res? ¿Y tus amigos?
4. ¿(Almorzar) _______ tú antes o después? ¿Y Antonia?
5. ¿(Perder) _______ tú el dinero o los cheques? ¿Y papá?

B **Un almuerzo familiar.** Complete Ud. las frases con el verbo apropiado en el pretérito.

seguir pedir dormir servir repetir conseguir

1. El camarero ______ el café con el postre.
2. Los niños ______ tres veces: «No queremos beber leche».
3. Nosotros ______ la cuenta inmediatamente.
4. Los niños ______ gritando *(yelling):* «No queremos estudiar».
5. Después del almuerzo mis padres ______ la siesta.
6. Yo ______ el puesto de gerente del restaurante, porque el gerente renunció *(resigned).*

C **Preguntas y respuestas.** Cambie Ud. los verbos entre paréntesis al pretérito y forme preguntas. Un(a) compañero(a) va a encontrar las respuestas correctas en la segunda columna, y va a contestar con frases completas.

MODELO ¿(Seguir) Uds. al criminal? **¿Siguieron** Uds. al criminal?
Sí, ___ al criminal por la calle Florida.
Sí, **seguimos** al criminal por la calle Florida.

1. ¿(Dormir) Ud. bien anoche?
2. ¿Le (pedir) tú dinero a papá?
3. ¿(Servir) Uds. en la cocina?
4. ¿(Conseguir) Uds. un buen trabajo?
5. ¿(Repetir) yo todas las palabras?
6. ¿(Morir) el Sr. Contreras?

a. Sí, ___ diez dólares.
b. Sí, ___ de un ataque cardíaco.
c. No, ___ en el comedor.
d. Sí, ___ y con buena pronunciación.
e. No, ___ por el insomnio.
f. Sí, ___ en una compañía muy grande.

Spend more time with Mariana and her friends while you review grammar and expand your cultural horizons.
See the **Así es Mariana** exercise in your workbook for this lesson.

En resumen

A **En el pasado.** Cambie Ud. los verbos entre paréntesis al pretérito.

Ayer, Juan (ir) ______ a su restaurante favorito, (pedir) ______ la especialidad de la casa y la (probar) ______. Pero como no le (gustar) ______, le (decir) ______ al camarero: «¿Qué es esto?» El camarero le (contestar) ______: «La especialidad de la casa... pollo con aceitunas en salsa *(sauce)* de chocolate.» Juan (comentar) ______: «Cuando yo (probar) ___ este plato, casi (morirse) ______. Yo (venir) ______ a este restaurante porque la semana pasada (tener) ______ una cena maravillosa aquí. Yo (estar) ______ muy contento después de comerla. Por eso, (volver) ______ hoy. Pero, este plato que Ud. me (servir) ______ es un desastre». El camarero (ver) ______ la expresión rara en la cara *(face)* de Juan, y le (traer) ______ el menú. Juan (escoger) ______ otro plato que le (gustar) ______ mucho.

B **¿Qué cocinar?** Lea Ud. el índice de la revista *Cocina sabrosa en pocos minutos*. Luego, diga a qué secciones corresponden las siguientes situaciones.

Mamá está aburrida de preparar los mismos platos todos los días.
Mamá debe leer la sección «Variemos *(Let's vary)* el menú» para buscar platos diferentes.

COCINA SABROSA EN POCOS MINUTOS

huevos *eggs*
a la parrilla *grilled*
rellenos *stuffed*
toque *touch*
dórelos *brown them*
endulzando *sweetening*
mar *sea*
congelar *freeze*
especias *spices*

1. El presidente de la compañía viene a cenar a la casa de Ud. y Ud. necesita servirle algo elegante.
2. Ud. está a dieta. Quiere comer algo nutritivo y con pocas calorías.
3. A sus amigos les encanta la comida picante.
4. Su pasión son los postres de chocolate.
5. El equipo *(team)* de fútbol de su hijo viene a comer.

C **El Conde *(Count)* de Sandwich.** Complete Ud. la lectura *(reading)* siguiente con la forma correcta del verbo en el pretérito. Si hay dos palabras, escoja *(choose)* la más apropiada.

Nacido *(Born)* en 1718, el Conde de Sandwich (asistir) al colegio y a la universidad, pero no (lo,le) (interesar) la vida académica. (Ser) expulsado *(thrown out)* por robar pedazos *(pieces)* de pan y (por, para) hacer «experimentos raros» con ellos. En 1758, él (recibir) (un, una) comisión de la reina *(queen)* de Inglaterra *(England)* (por, para) preparar «algo especial» (por, para) el embajador *(ambassador)* de España. (Trabajar) noche y día, y (por, para) fin, a las 4:17 (de, por) la mañana (de la, del) 27 de (Abril, abril), (hacer) el primer sandwich—varias rebanadas *(slices)* de jamón *(ham)* encerradas *(enclosed)* por arriba y por abajo en dos rebanadas de pan de centeno *(rye)*. En (un, uno) momento de inspiración, le (poner-él) mostaza *(mustard)*. (Ser) un éxito inmediato.

El Conde (conseguir) más éxito. Todos los grandes hombres de la época (lo, la) (visitar): Haydn, Kant, Rousseau y Benjamin Franklin, y todos (pedir) (estos, estas) delicias (por, para) llevar a sus casas.

El Conde también (inventar) la hamburguesa. (Demostrar-él) cómo prepararla en las grandes ciudades de Europa. En Alemania, Goethe (recomendar) el uso del bollo *(roll)*. Al Conde le (encantar) la idea. En Londres (supervisar) la construcción del primer «sandwich héroe». Este famoso inventor (morir) en 1792, a los 74 años de edad. En su funeral, un poeta (decir) que el Conde de Sandwich (liberar) a la humanidad del almuerzo caliente.

D **El sandwich caribeño.** Lea Ud. los ingredientes de este sandwich. ¿Le gusta la combinación?

SANDWICH CARIBEÑO

Pan de cebolla
Plátano (banano, guineo) en rodajas°
Cerdo ahumado°
Mermelada de mango
Jugo de limón
Menta°

en rodajas *slices*
cerdo ahumado *smoked pork*
menta *mint*

¿Qué alimentos y condimentos va a poner en el sandwich... (use su imaginación)

a. mexicano?
b. francés?
c. estudiantil?
d. bostoniense?
e. tejano?
f. californiano?

E **Preguntas.** Entreviste Ud. a un(a) compañero(a) para saber sus gustos y costumbres.

1. ¿A ti te gusta la pizza? ¿Por qué? ¿Por qué es tan popular? ¿Cuándo sueles tú comerla?
2. ¿Qué preparas tú cuando muchas personas vienen a comer a tu casa? ¿Y cuando vienen pocas personas?
3. ¿Cuál es tu restaurante preferido? ¿Por qué te gusta tanto? Describe la comida, el ambiente *(atmosphere)* y la decoración.
4. Tú estás a dieta pero decides olvidarla por un día. ¿Qué vas a comer?

F **El restaurante.** Translate the following dialogue to Spanish.

Juan: Did you like the restaurant?
Sara: Yes . . . there was a small problem, but it didn't matter to us.
Juan: What happened?
Sara: Dad ordered shellfish paella and white wine for four. The waiter brought chicken paella and red wine. But it was delicious.
Juan: Ummm . . . I love a good paella. Let's go!

G **Minidrama.** En grupos, representen una de las siguientes escenas.

1. Ud. es adicto(a) a la «comida-chuchería» *(junk food)*, y sus padres están preocupados. Explíqueles cuáles son los beneficios de comer este tipo de comida.
2. Cuando las familias con niños pequeños salen a comer, suelen ir a lugares informales. Pero los Hernández decidieron cenar en un restaurante elegante con sus tres hijos de dos, cinco y ocho años.

H **Composición.** Ud. escribe artículos para la sección de cocina de un periódico. La semana pasada cenó en dos restaurantes nuevos en su ciudad. Uno fue fantástico, el otro fue un desastre. Escriba dos artículos, describiendo la comida, el ambiente y el servicio de los dos restaurantes.

Escuchemos

A **Un compañero lógico.** You will hear an incomplete sentence. Choose the object that logically accompanies the one in the sentence.

MODELO (pescado/helado)
A los niños les gusta comer torta y ___. helado
A los niños les gusta comer torta y helado.

1. (cebolla/cerveza)
2. (ensalada/sal)
3. (ajo/queso)
4. (té/jugo)
5. (recetas/tenedores)
6. (aceite/arroz)
7. (cuenta/pimienta)
8. (verduras/piña)

B **Dictado.** You will hear a short narration about the food that Cecilia's Cuban grandmother prepares. Listen carefully to the entire selection. Listen again and write each sentence during the pauses.

You will then hear a series of false statements related to the dictation. Correct each one with a complete sentence. Refer to your dictation.

Lección 8

¡Qué comida más fresca!

Leche, mantequilla, azúcar, huevos, una botella de vinagre...

AVISO CULTURAL

(As a reading aid, refer to lesson vocabulary for new words.)

Los nombres de los varios tipos de comida pueden variar mucho de país *(country)* **en país.** Por ejemplo, en España y México la palabra **plátano** significa *banana* pero en Puerto Rico significa **plantain.** Hay que pedir un **guineo** en Puerto Rico y una **banana** en algunos otros países de la América Latina. Los **frijoles** en Cuba son **habichuelas** en Puerto Rico. Una **china** en Puerto Rico es una **naranja** en España. Para pedir *peas* en el Perú, hay que pedir **alverjas,** pero son **petits pois** en Puerto Rico, **chícharos** en México y **guisantes** en muchos otros países, incluso *(including)* en España. ¿Cuáles son algunas palabras en inglés que pueden ser diferentes según la región o el país? ¿Cómo se dice papas fritas en inglés en los EE.UU.? ¿en Inglaterra?

Preparativos

Review the vocabulary on pages 263–264 before viewing the video.

As you watch the video or read the following dialogue, notice how Luis Antonio reminisces about his childhood while he and Mariana are grocery shopping. *When I was a little boy in Mexico…* **(Cuando yo era niño en México...)** *I used to like to go shopping…* **(me gustaba ir de compras).** *I always used to haggle…* **(Yo siempre regateaba el precio)** *and afterwards I would eat a dozen* **(y después me comía una docena).**" Luis uses the imperfect tense to describe his past and to relate habitual actions from his childhood. Look for other uses of the imperfect tense in the first part of the dialogue. **Era** is an irregular imperfect form. What is the infinitive? What do you think the imperfect endings are for regular **-er** verbs, like **comer?** Besides walking down memory lane in the grocery store, a lesson on interpersonal relations is taking place. Who is teaching what to whom?

Así es Mariana: En el supermercado

Mariana y Luis Antonio van de compras a un supermercado.

Luis Antonio: Mariana, me molesta mucho pasar tanto tiempo comprando comida. Aunque cuando era niño en México me gustaba ir de compras a los tianguis con mi abuela.

Mariana: ¿Tianguis? ¿Qué son tianguis?

Luis Antonio: En México los tianguis son mercados al aire libre.

Mariana: ¿Compraban el bistec al aire libre? Pero así no puede ser muy fresco.

Luis Antonio: No. Comprábamos la carne en la carnicería. Yo hablaba de las frutas y las verduras.

Mariana: Ah, sí. Las famosas frutas tropicales de México. Tú siempre hablas de las naranjas que comías de niño.

Luis Antonio: Sí, porque son muy dulces. Yo siempre regateaba el precio con el dependiente y después me comía una docena.

Mariana: Hablando de una docena... mira esas galletas... ¡Qué ricas! Pero debo evitarlas, o si no, voy a engordar.

Luis Antonio: Mariana, no estás a dieta. Estás muy delgada... Ya adelgazaste bastante.

Mariana: De acuerdo, pues sólo me compro unas cajas.

Ven a Octavio con una lista larga de cosas que comprar.

Octavio: Leche, mantequilla, azúcar, huevos, una botella de vinagre...

Mariana y Luis Antonio: Eh, Octavio... ¿qué haces aquí?

Octavio: ¡Ay... las cosas que Alicia me hace comprar! ¡Esto es demasiado!

Mariana: Pero Octavio, Alicia lo hace todo para ti... para hacerte feliz. Ella nunca fue cocinera pero no tiene miedo de probar algo nuevo.

Octavio: Sí, eso ya lo sé. Anoche me preparó sopa.

Luis Antonio: Bueno, pues muy bien. A todos nos gusta la sopa.

Octavio: ¿De atún?... Hombre, no lo creo.

Luis Antonio: Octavio, tú sabes, hay que tener paciencia con las mujeres.

Mariana: *(Molesta, le dice a Luis Antonio)* ¿Qué ibas a decir... bombón?

Luis Antonio: Ay... bueno... quería decir que las mujeres son más dulces que... *(busca una respuesta rápido, y ve las galletas)*... que las galletas.

Mariana: *(A Luis)* Sabía que eras un muchacho muy inteligente. *(A Octavio)* Bueno, hay que buscar las cosas, ¿no?

Octavio: Sí, en seguida. Pero, una cosa. Tengo hambre. Antes de volver a la cocina de Alicia, voy a prepararme bien. ¿Saben Uds. si por aquí hay una pizzería?

Es decir

A Basándose en el diálogo busque en la segunda columna la terminación de la frase en la primera columna. Note el uso del tiempo imperfecto para expresar una acción habitual o repetida en el pasado.

1. Cuando Luis era niño , vivía...	**a.** una docena.
2. Le gustaba mucho ir...	**b.** el precio de las naranjas.
3. Allí Luis y su abuela encontraban...	**c.** en México.
4. Luis siempre regateaba...	**d.** a los tianguis con su abuela.
5. Después él comía...	**e.** la carne en los tianguis.
6. Ellos no compraban...	**f.** naranjas muy dulces.

B El siguiente diálogo es un ejemplo de cómo Luis regateaba *(used to haggle)* cuando iba *(when he would go)* a los tianguis con su abuela. En parejas, completen el diálogo con palabras de la lista. Practíquenlo y represéntenlo.

voy a darte	más dulces	Cuánto cuestan
un precio muy bueno	voy a ver	un precio mejor

Dependiente: ¿En qué puedo servirle?

Luis Antonio: Buenos días, señor. ¿______ esas naranjas?

Dependiente: ¿Estas naranjas? Treinta pesos por kilo.

Luis Antonio: ¿No puede ofrecerme ______?

Dependiente: ¿Más bajo? ¡Caramba! Son las naranjas ______ de este mercado, pero para un muchacho como tú... veinte pesos.

Luis Antonio: Pues, ______ las naranjas en los otros puestos *(stands)*. Hasta luego.

Dependiente: Espera un momento. Como *(Since)* conozco bien a tu abuela, ______ un precio especial... quince pesos. ¿Qué te parece?

Luis Antonio: De acuerdo, señor. Me parece ______.

Al ver el video

Complete Ud. las frases con la respuesta correcta.

1. Luis y Mariana ven a Octavio en la sección de...
   a. frutas y verduras. b. carnes y pescado. c. galletas y café.

2. Octavio tiene sus compras (purchases) en...
   a. un carrito *(cart)*. b. una bolsa. c. una caja.

3. Antes de ver a Alicia, Octavio va a...
   a. comprarle un regalo. b. comer una pizza. c. preparar sopa.

4. Al final, Mariana...
   a. nos ofrece sus galletas. b. come una galleta. c. no quiere darnos sus galletas.

Vocabulario

Verbos	
adelgazar (zc)	*to lose weight, get thinner*
engordar	*to gain weight, get fatter*
evitar	*to avoid*
mezclar	*to mix*
recoger	*to gather, pick up*
regatear	*to bargain, haggle*
romper	*to break*

En el mercado	*(In the market)*
la bolsa	*bag*
la botella	*bottle*
la caja	*box*
la carnicería	*butcher shop*
el (la) dependiente	*clerk*
la docena	*dozen*
el kilo	*kilogram (approximately 2.2 pounds)*
la lata	*can*
la libra	*pound*
el litro	*liter*
la panadería	*bakery*
la pastelería	*pastry shop*
el precio	*price*
el (super)mercado	*(super)market*

Frutas y verduras	*(Fruits and vegetables)*
la fresa	*strawberry*
el limón	*lemon*
la manzana	*apple*
la naranja	*orange*
la papa (patata)	*potato*
el pepino	*cucumber*
la pera	*pear*
el plátano (la banana)	*banana*
la uva	*grape*

Otros alimentos	*(Other foods)*
el atún	*tuna fish*
el azúcar	*sugar*
el bistec	*steak*
el bombón	*chocolate candy, bonbon*

el caramelo	*hard candy, caramel*
el cerdo	*pork*
el chorizo	*sausage*
la galleta (salada)	*cookie (cracker)*
la hamburguesa	*hamburger*
el huevo	*egg*
el jamón	*ham*
la langosta	*lobster*
la mantequilla	*butter*
la mayonesa	*mayonnaise*
la mostaza	*mustard*
el pavo	*turkey*
el perro caliente[1]	*hot dog*
la salsa de tomate	*catsup*
el vinagre	*vinegar*

Adjetivos

bastante	*enough*
crudo	*raw*
delgado	*thin*
demasiado[2]	*too much, too many*
flaco	*skinny*
fresco	*fresh, cool*
gordo	*fat*
pesado	*heavy (boring)*

Otras palabras y expresiones

al aire libre	*open-air*
de acuerdo	*O.K., agreed*
en seguida	*right away*
estar a dieta (seguir un régimen)	*to be on a diet*
hay que (+ *infinitive*)	*one must (+ verb)*
ir de compras	*to go shopping*
mientras	*while*

Vocabulario adicional

el bocadillo	*sandwich on Spanish bread*
el(la) carnicero(a)	*butcher*
hervido	*boiled*
ligero	*light (referring to weight)*
el melocotón	*peach*
las papitas	*potato chips*
pesar	*to weigh*

[1]In Argentina **un pancho** is a hot dog. In Mexico one simply says *hot dog.*
[2]**Demasiado** is also an adverb and when used as such is invariable. **Sara es demasiado flaca.** *Sara is too skinny.*

Repasemos el vocabulario

A **¿Cuál no pertenece?** Indique Ud. la palabra que no está relacionada con las otras y explique.

1. langosta	atún	cerdo	camarones
2. botella	lata	fresa	caja
3. vinagre	chorizo	mostaza	mayonesa
4. pera	naranja	uva	pepino
5. pavo	galleta	bombón	caramelo

B **¿Qué hay de comer?** Aquí hay dos cenas diferentes. Tape Ud. *(Cover up)* la cena 1. Un(a) compañero(a) va a tapar la cena 2. Compare su dibujo *(drawing)* con el de su compañero(a). ¿Cuáles son las diferencias?

1.

2.

C **Parejas *(Pairs)*.** Su profesor(a) va a leer una serie de comidas. Forme parejas lógicas con las palabras de la lista.

a. ____________ y tomates	d. ____________ y huevos
b. ____________ y galletas	e. ____________ y mantequilla
c. ____________ y vinagre	f. ____________ y papas fritas

D **¿Cómo los venden?** ¿Cómo corresponden las medidas *(measures)* que lee su profesor(a) a los productos siguientes?

a. ____________ de vino	d. ____________ de atún
b. ____________ de huevos	e. ____________ de galletas saladas
c. ____________ de manzanas	f. ____________ de leche

E **¡Qué problema!** Ud. fue de compras pero no pudo encontrar nada. Escoja Ud. un lugar y un producto y diga qué pasó allí. Siga el modelo.

MODELO Fui a la **frutería** para comprar **uvas** pero **compré peras.**

panadería	langosta	no me gustaron
pastelería	queso	no las vi
pescadería	cerdo	decidí comprar camarones
carnicería	panecillos *(rolls)*	sólo encontré chorizo
lechería	galletas de chocolate	no lo pude encontrar

F **¿Es Ud. goloso(a)?** ***(Do you have a sweet tooth?)*** Lea Ud. *(Read)* el artículo y conteste las preguntas.

golosa *sweet tooth*
se trata de *it's about*
taza *cup*
Desde luego *of course*
sabor *flavor*
Almendras *Almonds*
Cerezas *Cherries*
Nueces *Walnuts*

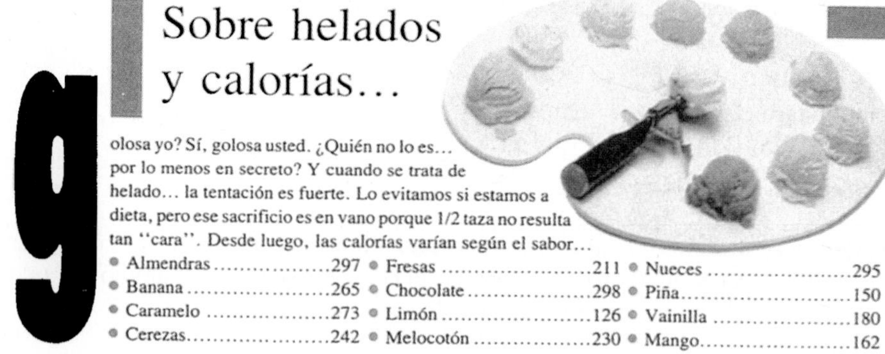

Sobre helados y calorías...

Golosa yo? Sí, golosa usted. ¿Quién no lo es... por lo menos en secreto? Y cuando se trata de helado... la tentación es fuerte. Lo evitamos si estamos a dieta, pero ese sacrificio es en vano porque 1/2 taza no resulta tan "cara". Desde luego, las calorías varían según el sabor...

Almendras	297	Fresas	211	Nueces	295
Banana	265	Chocolate	298	Piña	150
Caramelo	273	Limón	126	Vainilla	180
Cerezas	242	Melocotón	230	Mango	162

1. ¿Quiénes evitan el helado?
2. ¿Qué sabor(es) *(flavors)* de helados...
   - **a.** tiene(n) menos calorías?
   - **b.** tiene(n) más calorías?
   - **c.** le gusta(n) más a Ud.?
   - **d.** no le gusta(n) a Ud.?
   - **e.** es (son) tropical(es)?
   - **f.** es (son) cítrico(s)?
   - **g.** quiere Ud. probar?

The Imperfect Tense

You have learned to express past action by using the preterite tense: **Compré el chorizo y le dí el dinero al carnicero.** *(I bought the sausage and gave the money to the butcher.)* The imperfect tense also expresses past action but it is used in different contexts and focuses on the continuation of the action in the past.

Forma

To form the imperfect tense of **-ar** verbs remove the infinitive ending and add **-aba, -abas, -aba, -ábamos, -abais, -aban.** To form the imperfect of **-er** and **-ir** verbs, remove the infinitive endings and add **-ía, -ías, -ía, -íamos, -íais, -ían.**

HABLAR		**COMER**		**ESCRIBIR**	
hablaba	hablábamos	comía	comíamos	escribía	escribíamos
hablabas	hablabais	comías	comíais	escribías	escribíais
hablaba	hablaban	comía	comían	escribía	escribían

There are only three irregular verbs in the imperfect tense.

IR		**SER**		**VER**	
iba	íbamos	era	éramos	veía	veíamos
ibas	ibais	eras	erais	veías	veíais
iba	iban	era	eran	veía	veían

Función

1. The imperfect tense has several different meanings in English.

Yo **hablaba** con el carnicero.
- ***I spoke (repeatedly)*** *with the butcher.*
- ***I was (in the process of) speaking*** *with the butcher.*
- ***I used to (would) speak*** *with the butcher.*

¡AVISO! Note that the first example *(I spoke)* can also be expressed with the preterite tense. The tense is determined by whether the speaker wishes to convey completed action (preterite: **Yo hablé con el carnicero ayer.** *I spoke with the butcher yesterday.)* or repeated or ongoing action (imperfect: **Yo hablaba con el carnicero todos los días.** *I spoke with the butcher every day.)*

2. The imperfect tense is used:

a. to express time and age in the past.

Era tarde. **Eran** las tres de la mañana.	*It* ***was*** *late.* ***It was*** *three o'clock in the morning.*
José **tenía** trece años aquel verano.	*José* ***was*** *thirteen years old that summer.*

b. to describe a past action that was still going on at a certain time in the past, or an action whose beginning and end are not known or are not important. The English equivalent is *was* or *were + the present participle.*

Javier **miraba** los precios.	*Javier* ***was looking at*** *the prices.*
Susana y yo **regateábamos** en el mercado.	*Susana and I* ***were haggling*** *at the market.*

c. with the conjunction **mientras** *(while)* to describe two or more ongoing and simultaneous actions.

Vicente **bebía** su café **mientras** Ema **charlaba** con su madre.	*Vicente* ***was drinking*** *his coffee* ***while*** *Ema* ***was chatting*** *with her mother.*

d. to describe things or people in the past and to set the scene of past situations.

Era una noche bonita. **Había** mucha gente en el restaurante y todos lo **pasaban** bien.	*It* ***was*** *a lovely evening.* ***There were*** *a lot of people in the restaurant and everyone* ***was having*** *a good time.*
Paco **era** moreno, guapo y alto.	*Paco* ***was*** *dark, handsome, and tall.*

e. to describe ongoing physical, emotional or mental states and desires in the past.

Siempre **le gustaba** ir de compras y **estaba contento** de poder venir con nosotros.	*He always* ***liked*** *to go shopping and he* ***was happy*** *to be able to come with us.*

f. to express repeated or habitual past action. The English equivalent is *used to* or *would + verb.*

De niño, Roberto **tomaba** leche con todas las comidas y después siempre **pedía** postre.	*As a child Roberto* ***used to drink*** *milk with all his meals and afterwards he* ***would*** *always* ***ask*** *for dessert.*

¡AVISO! Certain expressions that reflect habitual or repeated action often accompany this use of the imperfect tense. Some of these are: **siempre, todos los días (meses, años...), con frecuencia, generalmente,** and **por lo general.**

Practiquemos

A De compras en la Pequeña Habana... ¡Recuerdos bonitos! Cambie Ud. los verbos subrayados *(underlined)* al imperfecto.

1. Todos los veranos <u>vamos</u> a Miami y <u>compramos</u> la comida en los mercados.
2. Me <u>gustan</u> más las frutas dulces que <u>encuentro</u> allí.
3. <u>Es</u> interesante mirar a todas las personas que <u>hacen</u> sus compras.
4. Siempre <u>busco</u> el pan más fresco que <u>venden</u> en las panaderías.
5. Cuando <u>tenemos</u> sed <u>tomamos</u> jugo de naranja que <u>compramos</u> en la frutería. ¡Qué rico!

B **Un restaurante ideal.** El Restaurante Camagüey ya no *(no longer)* existe pero sus clientes hablan de la comida y del servicio que ofrecía *(used to offer)*. Busque Ud. en la segunda columna la terminación de la frase en la primera columna. Cambie los verbos al imperfecto.

1. El restaurante (ser)...	**a.** precios muy buenos.
2. La orquesta siempre (tocar)...	**b.** ideal para una cena romántica.
3. El chef (preparar)...	**c.** margarina, sólo mantequilla.
4. Su carne siempre (estar)...	**d.** los platos.
5. El chef nunca (servir)...	**e.** música clásica.
6. Camagüey (ofrecer)...	**f.** muy fresca.
7. Los camareros nunca (romper)...	**g.** una sopa de frijoles negros excelente.

C **De compras.** La familia Benítez iba de compras todos los sábados. ¿Qué hacía cada persona? Cambie Ud. el verbo al imperfecto y forme frases completas según el modelo.

MODELO Susana/comprar
Susana compraba las legumbres en el mercado.

1.

nosotras/ir

2.

Paquito/recoger

3.

papá/pesar

4.

Raúl/romper

5.

mamá/regatear

6.

nosotros/volver

D **Preguntas.** Conteste Ud. las preguntas. Luego cambie las preguntas a la forma **tú** y entreviste *(interview)* a un(a) compañero(a).

1. De niño(a), ¿quién era su mejor amigo(a)? ¿Cómo era él(ella)? ¿Qué hacían Uds. los sábados por la noche?
2. De niño(a), ¿qué le gustaba hacer en el verano? ¿en el invierno?
3. ¿Qué hacía su familia los fines de semana?
4. Cuando era niño(a), ¿comía las mismas cosas que Ud. come hoy en día? ¿Qué frutas o legumbres no comía? ¿Cuáles prefería?

E **Así era mi vida.** Usando el imperfecto, nombre Ud. tres cosas que Ud. hacía...

1. en la escuela.
2. después de clase.
3. para ayudar en casa.

Ahora, comparta sus respuestas con la clase.

The Use of the Preterite and Imperfect

Función

In English there are many different ways to express past action. You, the speaker, choose which form best expresses the concepts you wish to convey. Note the difference in meaning in the following sentences because of the verb tenses used.[1]

1. I *ate* lunch at 12:30.
2. I *was eating* lunch at 12:30.
3. I *used to eat* lunch at 12:30.

Only one of these forms will accurately describe the particular situation that the speaker wishes to convey. Which of the previous sentences is the most appropriate response to the following questions?

a. What were you doing today at 12:30 when I called you?
b. Have you always eaten lunch at 1:00?
c. What time did you eat lunch yesterday?

This same concept is true in Spanish. Although there are times when only the preterite or the imperfect can be used (for example, to express time in the past you must use the imperfect), in other instances both past tenses may be grammatically correct in the same sentence, but they refer to different situations.

Review the following table of uses of the preterite and the imperfect. You may refer to Lesson 6 for a complete explanation of the preterite tense.

[1]Note the English structures and how they are expressed in Spanish:

English		Spanish
1. Simple past	→	Preterite
2. Past progressive	→	Imperfect
3. Auxiliary verb *used to* + verb	→	Imperfect

Uses of the Preterite and Imperfect

Preterite	**Imperfect**
1. to focus on the beginning or end of a past action.	**1.** to emphasize the action in progress.
Juan **caminó** por una hora y **volvió** a casa.	¿Qué **hacías** ayer a las tres?
*Juan **walked** for an hour and **returned** home.*	*What **were you doing** yesterday at three o'clock?*
2. to describe a series of past actions.	**2.** to describe habitual or continuous actions.
Entró a la tienda, **puso** algunas cosas en su bolsa, **miró** por todas partes y **salió** sin pagar.	Todos los sábados, **íbamos** al mercado y allí **comprábamos** frutas frescas.
*She **entered** the store, **put** a few things in her bag, **looked** all around, and **left** without paying.*	*Every Saturday, we **used to go** to the market and there we **would buy** fresh fruit.*
3. to describe a change in physical, emotional, and mental states and desires.	**3.** to describe physical, emotional, and mental states and desires; to set the scene; to express age and time in the past.
Juan **estuvo** furioso cuando **vio** su coche después del accidente.	Juan **era** un hombre alto y delgado. **Tenía** 29 años. Yo **sabía** que él **estaba** contento de pasar el verano con nosotros.
*Juan **was (became)** furious when he saw his car after the accident.*	*Juan **was** a tall, thin man. He **was** 29 years old. I **knew** that he **was** happy to spend the summer with us.*

Often the preterite and the imperfect will appear in the same sentence. The preterite action frequently interrupts the ongoing action of the imperfect.

Yo **cenaba** cuando Juan **llegó.** *I **was dining** when Juan **arrived.***

To see the preterite and imperfect in context, read the following excerpt from a short story by the Cuban author Reinaldo Arenas, entitled *Con los ojos cerrados (With Eyes Closed)*. Then read the English translation that follows and study the underlined past tense verb forms. In what contexts does the author choose to use the preterite? The imperfect?

«Seguí caminando con los ojos muy cerrados. Y llegué de nuevo a la dulcería. Pero como no podía comprarme ningún dulce porque gasté hasta la última peseta de la merienda, solamente los miré a través de la vidriera. Y estaba así mirándolos, cuando oí dos voces detrás del mostrador que me decían: —¿No quieres comerte algún dulce?— Y cuando levanté la cabeza vi que eran las dos viejitas. No sabía qué decir. Pero parece que adivinaron mis deseos y sacaron una torta grande de chocolate y almendras. Y me la pusieron en las manos.»

"I continued walking with my eyes tightly closed. And I arrived again at the pastry shop. But since I wasn't able to buy any sweets because I spent my last penny on snacks, I only looked at them through the glass case. And I was looking at them like that when I heard two voices behind the counter that were saying to me, "Don't you want to eat a pastry?" And when I raised my head I saw that it was the two old ladies. I didn't know what to say. But it seems that they guessed my desires and took out a large chocolate and almond torte. And they put it in my hands."

Verbs That Change Meaning in the Preterite and Imperfect

	Preterite	Imperfect
saber	to find out	to know
	Supe las noticias ayer.	**Sabía** que venía a Miami.
	*I **found out** the news yesterday.*	*I **knew** she was coming to Miami.*
conocer	to meet	to know, be acquainted with
	Conocí a mi esposo en 1980.	No lo **conocía** cuando vivía en Cuba.
	*I **met** my husband in 1980.*	*I didn't **know** him when I lived in Cuba.*
querer	to try	to want
	Quise comprar pan pero la panadería estaba cerrada.	**Quería** comprar pan pero no tenía bastante dinero.
	*I **tried** to buy bread but the bakery was closed.*	*I **wanted** to buy bread but I didn't have enough money.*
no querer	to refuse	not to want
	Pedrín **no quiso** beber la leche.	Elena **no quería** estudiar con nosotros.
	*Pedrín **refused** to drink the milk.*	*Elena **didn't want** to study with us.*
poder	to manage	to be able
	No pude hacer las compras.	**No podía** ir al cine porque tenía que trabajar.
	*I **didn't manage (failed)** to do the shopping.*	*I **wasn't able** to go to the movies because I had to work.*

Practiquemos

A **¿Pretérito o imperfecto?** En parejas, digan qué tiempo usan para expresar los siguientes conceptos, y den ejemplos.

para expresar la edad *(age)*; el imperfecto
Juan tenía trece años.

1. para expresar acción repetida o habitual
2. para expresar la hora
3. para expresar una acción o una serie de acciones terminadas
4. para enfatizar una acción continua
5. para enfatizar un cambio *(change)* de emociones
6. para expresar edad
7. para describir estados *(states)* físicos o mentales
8. para enfatizar el comienzo *(beginning)* de una acción

B **La cena romántica.** Javier quería tener una cena romántica con su novia, Elena, pero había muchas interrupciones. Cambie Ud. los verbos al pretérito o al imperfecto, según el contexto.

MODELO Los dos (bailar) ___________ cuando Elena (comenzar) ___________ a cantar.
Los dos bailaban cuando Elena comenzó a cantar.

1. Javier (declarar) ___________ su amor por Elena cuando la orquesta (empezar) ___________ a tocar un tango.
2. Los dos se (besar [*to kiss*]) ___________ cuando el camarero (llegar) ___________ a la mesa.
3. Javier le (dar) ___________ el anillo *(ring)* cuando Elena (romper) ___________ un vaso.
4. Javier le (pedir) ___________ la mano *(hand)* a Elena cuando el camarero (volver) ______ con la cena.
5. Elena (confesar) ___________ su amor por Javier cuando él (descubrir) ___________ que no tenía bastante dinero para pagar la cuenta.

C **¿Cuál fue la pregunta?** Ud. acaba de ir a Miami de vacaciones y le cuenta todo a un amigo. Él no oye bien, y necesita hacerle preguntas. En parejas, sigan el modelo.

MODELO Estudiante 1: **Fui a Miami.**
Estudiante 2: **¿Adónde fuiste?**

1. Fui con Tomás.
2. Eran las ocho cuando llegamos al hotel.
3. No, el hotel estaba cerca del centro.
4. El hotel era pequeño y bonito.
5. Sí, comimos en un restaurante cubano.
6. ¿Tostones? No, probamos los frijoles negros.

D **La historia de la piña.** Lea Ud. la selección y cambie los verbos entre paréntesis al pretérito o imperfecto.

En 1493, cuando Cristóbal Colón (llegar) __________ a Guadalupe en el Caribe, (encontrar) __________ una fruta rara. La gente que (cultivar) __________ esta fruta la (llamar) __________ «ananá», una palabra india que significa **fragancia.** La fruta (ser) __________ dulce aunque algunas veces (poder) __________ ser un poco ácida.

Cuando los españoles (ver) __________ la piña por primera vez, (pensar) __________ que la fruta (tener) __________ mucho en común con la piña del pino *(pine cone)*, y por eso le (dar) __________ el nombre de «piña de las Indias».

La piña (ganar) __________ fama por toda Europa en muy poco tiempo. A los reyes españoles, Fernando e Isabel, les (encantar) __________ la fruta en seguida. En Francia, los jardineros *(gardeners)* de Luis XIV (pagar) __________ mucho dinero para cultivar varios tipos de piña en Francia. Esta fruta dulce (empezar) __________ a ser muy popular y sigue siéndolo.

E **¿Qué aprendieron de la piña y la colonización?** En parejas, contesten las siguientes preguntas basándose en el ejercicio anterior.

1. ¿Cuándo llegó Colón a Guadalupe?
2. ¿Cuál era el nombre original de la fruta?
3. ¿Por qué llamaron los españoles la fruta «piña»?
4. ¿Cuál fue la reacción de Fernando e Isabel cuando la probaron?
5. ¿Hay piñas en Europa?

F **Ud. tiene correo.** Ud. recibió la siguiente carta de su amigo. Él acaba de cenar en un restaurante cubano por primera vez. Termine las frases de una forma original para saber qué pasó.

1. Anoche, mi amigo y yo...
2. Entramos en el restaurante y...
3. Después de ver el menú...
4. Con la cena...
5. Toda la noche...
6. Después de comer...

Se to Express an Indefinite Subject

Forma y función

In English when a sentence has no definite subject the following structures can be used:

People say *(It is* said) that milk is good for your health.

They eat *(One* eats) well in Miami.

You can find everything *you* need in that supermarket.

In Spanish, these impersonal subjects are often expressed by using the following construction.

se + verb in the third person singular

Se dice que la leche es buena para la salud.
Se come bien en Miami.
Se puede encontrar todo lo que **se necesita** en aquel supermercado.

Practiquemos

A **¿Quién lo hace?** Cambie Ud. el sujeto **la gente** por el uso del **se** impersonal, según el modelo.

MODELO En los EE.UU. la gente pica *(snack)* después de la cena.
En los EE.UU. se pica después de la cena.

1. En España la gente cena a las 10:00 de la noche.
2. En México la gente come tortilla de maíz.
3. En Argentina la gente suele comer mucha carne de res.
4. En Puerto Rico la gente dice que el jugo de mango es muy sabroso.
5. En Cuba la gente sabe que los frijoles negros tienen muchas vitaminas.
6. En los EE.UU. la gente empieza a comer de una forma más saludable.

B **Una prueba pequeña.** Para saber algo sobre la comida que comemos, forme Ud. preguntas según el modelo y contéstelas, buscando la información correcta en la segunda columna.

MODELO **¿Qué se sabe del plátano?**
Se sabe que tiene mucho potasio.

1. la langosta	a. engordamos si comemos muchos
2. las zanahorias	b. producen mucho en Cuba
3. las galletas	c. a la gente le gusta en los perros calientes
4. el azúcar	d. la Florida y Valencia, España son dos lugares famosos por estas frutas dulces
5. la mostaza	e. contienen mucha vitamina A
6. el atún	f. a los niños les gusta comerlas con leche
7. los bombones	g. es un tipo de marisco
8. las naranjas	h. es un pescado que se suele vender en lata

Ahora, hágales las mismas preguntas a sus compañeros. Ellos van a contestar de una forma original.

C ¿Qué se hace? Escoja Ud. *(Choose)* un verbo de la siguiente lista para decir qué se hace en cada lugar.

¿Qué se hace en una cafetería? (charlar)
Se charla en una cafetería.

engordar cenar regatear adelgazar comprar

1. ¿Qué se hace en un mercado al aire libre?
2. ¿Qué se hace en un comedor?
3. ¿Qué se hace en un supermercado?
4. ¿Qué se hace en una pastelería?
5. ¿Qué se hace en un gimnasio?

Spend more time with Mariana and her friends while you review grammar and expand your cultural horizons.
See the **Así es Mariana** exercise in your workbook for this lesson.

En resumen

A El café. ¿Cuánto sabe Ud. del café? Para saber la historia del café, lea la selección y cambie los verbos entre paréntesis al pretérito o imperfecto.

La Pequeña Habana, Miami

El uso del café como bebida se (originar) ______ en Etiopía hace más de 1.000 años. Allí la gente lo (beber) ______ todos los días. El café (pasar) ______ de Etiopía al Próximo Oriente *(Near East)* donde los musulmanes *(Muslims)* lo (adoptar) ______ como sustituto del alcohol que (ser) ______ prohibido por su religión. La palabra **café** viene de la palabra árabe «kaveh» que significa **vino.**

En el siglo *(century)* XVI la fama del café (llegar) ______ a Grecia y a Turquía. Los turcos (llevar) ______ el café con ellos a Europa a finales del siglo XVII. Pronto el café (empezar) ______ a ser una bebida muy popular por todo el continente. Los ingleses (llevar) ______ el café a América, donde sigue gozando de una popularidad enorme.

B **El vino.** Lea Ud. la lectura y haga el ejercicio.

No se sabe con seguridad cuándo se adquirió *(acquired)* el vino, pero desde el principio fue considerado como un regalo de los dioses *(gods)*. Hoy, el vino tiene importancia social, cultural y económica, y es la bebida más representativa de la cocina hispana. Se toma con muchas comidas, se usa en la cocina para preparar salsas para carne y pescado y es un elemento frecuente en la preparación de pasteles y postres. El vino, tomado en moderación, puede ser beneficioso para la digestión. Pero se sabe que el alcohol en exceso produce la dependencia.

Se dice que el champán es la bebida más refinada por excelencia. Se cree que un monje *(monk)* francés de la Abadía de Haut Villers inventó el champán. Cuando lo probó por primera vez exclamó: «¡Vengan, *(Come)*, estoy bebiendo estrellas *(stars)*!» En Francia este vino espumoso *(bubbly)* se llama «el único vino para las fiestas del corazón *(heart)*».

¿Cierto o falso? Si la frase es falsa, corríjala.

1. El vino no se bebe mucho en los países hispanos.
2. Es cierto que el vino se originó en 1823.
3. El vino puede ayudar al sistema digestivo.
4. Es costumbre tomar vino con las comidas.
5. El vino no se usa mucho en la preparación de las comidas.
6. El champán fue inventado en España.

C La sangría. Al ver la sangría en botella, un español dijo: «¡Dios mío, qué ironía!» Es decir, se debe beber la sangría fresca. Lea Ud. la siguiente receta para la sangría y arregle *(arrange)* las instrucciones en un orden lógico.

1 botella de vino tinto español

2 cucharadas de jugo de naranja

2 cucharadas de licor sabor de naranja como Grand Marnier

trozos *(pieces)* de melocotón, naranja y limón al gusto

canela *(cinnamon)*

1 cucharada de azúcar

1 taza de agua gaseosa *(seltzer)*

En una jarra *(pitcher)* de cristal alta.

1. se sirve en copas para vino.
2. se añade *(add)* el hielo.
3. se saca *(take out)* la canela antes de servir.
4. se combina todo, menos el hielo y se mezcla *(mix)* bien.
5. se bebe.
6. se pone en el refrigerador por unas horas.

D Recuerdos infantiles. Translate the following sentences to Spanish.

1. When I was a little girl, I went shopping with my grandmother every Monday.
2. At the pastry shop Grandma always bought me a bag of cookies.
3. One day I ate a dozen lemon cookies and a pound of chocolate candy.
4. I was sick for three days.
5. After that day I wasn't able to eat candy for a long time.

E Minidrama. En grupos, representen una de las siguientes escenas.

1. Ud aprendió las técnicas de regatear en los mercados al aire libre. Ahora Ud. intenta regatear en una tienda elegante donde los precios son fijos *(fixed)*.
2. Su cena es un desastre. Ud. preparó una comida muy especial para varias personas. Cuando llegan, Ud. descubre que uno es vegetariano, otro está a dieta y otro no toma alcohol. ¿Qué hace Ud.?

F Composición.

1. Escriba Ud. un diálogo entre una mujer y su esposo que están de compras en un supermercado. La señora quiere comprar la comida para toda la semana y su esposo desea comprar sólo lo necesario para la cena.
2. Escriba Ud. un régimen para...
   a. un(a) amigo(a) que quiere engordar.
   b. un(a) amigo(a) que es adicto(a) a la comida rápida y quiere dejar de comerla.

Escuchemos

A **La lista.** Sra. Álvarez is making her grocery list. You will hear a series of incomplete sentences from her list. Choose the word that best completes the sentence.

(uvas/huevos)
Es necesario comprar una docena de ___. huevos
Es necesario comprar una docena de huevos.

1. (mayonesa/bombones)
2. (limón/jamón)
3. (papitas/pavos)
4. (peras/mostaza)
5. (pepino/tomate)
6. (vinagre/mantequilla)
7. (azúcar/atún)
8. (langostas/galletas)

B **Dictado.** You will hear a short narration about Sra. Álvarez doing her grocery shopping. Listen carefully to the entire selection. Listen again and write each sentence during the pauses.

You will then hear a series of false statements related to the dictation. Correct each one with a complete sentence. Refer to your dictation.

Ocho camisetas, tres pantalones, dos cinturones, una cartera...

AVISO CULTURAL

(As a reading aid, refer to lesson vocabulary for new words.)

¿Cómo se viste un hispano? Esta pregunta es imposible de contestar. Es como preguntar, ¿cómo se viste un norteamericano? La forma de vestir depende de muchos factores, como la región, el nivel *(level)* socioeconómico y el clima *(climate)*. En España y en las capitales cosmopolitas de Latinoamérica, la gente suele vestirse de la última moda de Europa. En regiones más remotas de Latinoamérica se ve más la ropa tradicional: ropa bordada *(embroidered)* a mano *(by hand)* y de muchos colores. Los vestidos flamencos, las mantillas y los abanicos *(fans)* que solemos asociar con España, y los trajes multicolores y bordados de México no son para todos los días. Son para festivales tradicionales o folklóricos. En los EE.UU., ¿hay un traje típico que llevemos sólo para festivales tradicionales? ¿Cómo es? En los EE.UU., ¿se viste toda la gente de la misma forma? ¿Por qué creen muchos extranjeros *(foreigners)* que todos los americanos se visten de ropa de vaquero *(cowboy)*?

Preparativos

Review the vocabulary on pages 283–284 before viewing the video.

As you watch the video or read the following dialogue, pay close attention to the various *self/selves* verbs, that is, verbs whose subjects do the action to themselves. These are called *reflexive* verbs, because the action reflects back to the subject. Reflexive verbs are identifiable by the reflexive pronouns that accompany them. In the video Mariana says, "**Me levanté** *(I got myself up)*, **me bañé** *(I bathed* *myself)*, **me vestí** *(I got myself dressed)*. Mariana se despertó (woke up) a las 7:00 esta mañana. ¿A qué hora se despertó Ud.?

What personality traits are revealed about Mariana, Carla, and Luis Antonio in this episode? Who seems to be nurturing? Who seems assertive? Conciliatory? How are these traits expressed?

Así es Mariana: Ropa y más ropa

Luis Antonio está en casa de Mariana trabajando con la computadora. Mariana terminó su tarea y quiere ir al centro comercial.

Mariana: Luuiiis. Llévame al centro comercial. Hay que comprar ropa nueva.

Luis Antonio: ¿Ropa nueva? Pero fuiste de compras hace dos semanas.

Mariana: ¡Dos semanas! ¡Ay Dios! Mi ropa está pasada de moda. Vamos, Luis...

Luis Antonio: Ni modo. Tengo que estudiar. Y tú también. ¿No me dijiste que tienes un examen mañana... o estaba yo soñando?

Mariana: Ya estudié y ahora quiero divertirme. Escúchame, Luis. No seas perezoso. Ven. Hoy hay liquidaciones en todas las tiendas, y todos los nuevos estilos están en venta.

Carla llega y llama a Mariana.

Carla: Mariana.

Entra y ve que Luis Antonio usa la computadora.

Carla: ¡Rayos! Quería usar la computadora para escribir mi tarea de filosofía.

Mariana: ¡Perfecto! Luis y yo vamos de compras. (*A Luis*) Levántate. La señorita quiere sentarse.

Luis Antonio se levanta pero deja su suéter en la silla. Carla se lo da.

Carla: (*A Luis Antonio*) Ponte el suéter. Hace frío afuera.

Luis Antonio se porta (acts) como un niño.

Luis Antonio: Gracias, «mamá». ¿Y mis guantes? ¿Mi chaqueta?

Carla: ¡Vayan y diviértanse!

Unas horas más tarde Mariana y Luis Antonio vuelven con muchas bolsas.

Carla: ¡Cuántas bolsas! Se parecen a Santa Claus.

Luis Antonio: Mariana se probó todos los zapatos en Miami, pero no se compró ni un par.

Carla: Entonces, ¿qué hay en las bolsas?

Luis Antonio: ¿Qué tenemos? Ocho camisetas, tres pantalones, dos cinturones, una cartera...

Carla: ¿Nada más?

Mariana: ¡Por supuesto! Un traje de baño, una chaqueta de cuero, un impermeable y un paraguas.

Carla: Pero, Mariana... ¿tantas cosas? ¿Cómo vas a pagarlo todo?

Mariana: No me mires a mí. Pregúntaselo al «señor comprador». Yo compré el paraguas. La ropa es de Luis.

Es decir

A Busque Ud. en la segunda columna la terminación de la frase en la primera columna.

1. Mariana cree que su ropa está pasada de...	**a.** cuero.
2. Por eso, ella quiere ir de...	**b.** filosofía.
3. Se probó muchos, pero no compró ni un par de...	**c.** baño.
4. Carla quiere usar la computadora para su tarea de...	**d.** ropa.
5. Mariana y Luis volvieron con muchas bolsas llenas de...	**e.** compras.
6. Luis compró una chaqueta de...	**f.** zapatos.
7. También compró un traje de...	**g.** moda.

B Las siguientes frases contienen información falsa. En parejas, corrijan las frases.

1. Mariana fue de compras ayer.
2. Mariana estudió para un examen que tiene la próxima semana *(next week)*.
3. Alicia necesita usar la computadora para escribir su tarea de historia.
4. Luis no necesita ponerse el suéter porque hace calor afuera.
5. Mariana se probó una chaqueta de cuero.
6. Luis no compró nada, pero Mariana compró mucha ropa.

C En grupos, digan qué hay en las bolsas de los siguientes compradores *(shoppers)*.

1. Alicia **2.** El cocinero del restaurante La Carreta **3.** Ud.

Al ver el video

A Después de ver el video, termine Ud. las siguientes frases con la respuesta apropiada.

1. Luis Antonio dice: «Ni modo» porque...
   a. Carla quiere usar la computadora.
   b. no quiere ir de compras.
   c. no tiene ganas de estudiar.
2. Carla dice: «¡Rayos!» porque...
   a. está de mal humor.
   b. quiere ir de compras con Mariana pero no puede.
   c. Luis está usando la computadora.
3. Mariana dice: «¡Ay Dios!» porque...
   a. Luis no va de compras con ella.
   b. su ropa está pasada de moda.
   c. no estudió para su examen.
4. Carla dice: «¡Cuántas bolsas!» porque Luis y Mariana...
   a. compraron muchas bolsas.
   b. volvieron sin bolsas.
   c. entraron con muchas bolsas.

B En parejas, arreglen las actividades de Mariana en orden cronológico.

____ **a.** Salió de compras con Luis Antonio.
____ **b.** Volvió a su apartamento.
____ **c.** Se vistió.
____ **d.** Compró un paraguas.
____ **e.** Se levantó.
____ **f.** Se despertó.

C Mariana, en resumen... Ahora que Uds. han visto *(have seen)* la mitad *(half)* de los episodios de *Así es Mariana*, vamos a ver cuánto recuerdan. ¿A quién corresponden las siguientes descripciones?

Mariana Luis Antonio Carla Alicia Octavio

1. Pasó su niñez en México.
2. Es la novia de Octavio.
3. Sueña con ser periodista.
4. Su mamá prepara frijoles negros.
5. Es la presidenta del club de español.
6. Es secretaria del club.
7. No quiere engordar.
8. Es de Venezuela.
9. Flirtea con Octavio.
10. Iba a los tianguis con su abuela.
11. Tiene un hermano menor.
12. Es cubano.
13. Cocina muy mal.
14. Nació en Puerto Rico.
15. No tiene una computadora.

Vocabulario

Verbos (See pp. 289–290 for additional reflexive verbs)

acostarse (ue)	*to go to bed*
afeitarse	*to shave (oneself)*
bajar	*to go down; lower; get off*
bañarse	*to bathe, shower*
casarse (con)	*to marry, get married (to)*
despertarse (ie)	*to wake up*
divertirse (ie, i)	*to have a good time, amuse oneself*
levantarse	*to get up*
parecerse a (zc)	*to resemble*
ponerse	*to put on; to become*
probarse (ue)	*to try on*
quedarse	*to stay, remain*
quitarse	*to take off*
sentarse (ie)	*to sit down*
sentirse (ie, i)	*to feel*
subir	*to go up; to get on*
vestirse (i, i)	*to get dressed*

Ropa y accesorios	*(Clothing and accessories)*
el abrigo	*coat*
el anillo	*ring*
el arete	*earring*
los blue jeans (vaqueros)	*blue jeans*
la blusa	*blouse*
el bolso	*purse, pocketbook*
las botas	*boots*
el brazalete	*bracelet*
los calcetines	*socks*
la camisa	*shirt*
la camiseta	*T-shirt*
la cartera	*wallet*
el cinturón	*belt*
la corbata	*tie*
la chaqueta	*jacket*
la falda	*skirt*
los guantes	*gloves*
el impermeable	*raincoat*
las medias	*stockings*
los pantalones	*pants*
el paraguas	*umbrella*
el sombrero	*hat*
el suéter	*sweater*
el traje (de baño)	*(bathing) suit*
el vestido	*dress*
los zapatos (tenis)	*shoes (sneakers)*

Adjetivos	
abierto	*open*
ancho	*wide*
cerrado	*closed*
claro	*light (colored), clear*
(in)cómodo	*(un)comfortable*
elegante	*elegant, formal*
estrecho	*narrow, tight*
oscuro	*dark*

Otras palabras y expresiones

el algodón	*cotton*
el centro comercial	*shopping mall, shopping area (of a city)*
el cuero	*leather*
de buen (mal) gusto	*in good (bad) taste*
el estilo	*style*
estar de (en) venta	*to be on sale*
estar pasado de moda	*to be out of style*
hacer juego con	*to match*
la lana	*wool*
la liquidación	*sale*
el oro	*gold*
el par	*pair*
la plata	*silver*
el probador	*dressing room*
quedarle (bien, mal, perfecto, grande...)	*to fit (well, badly, perfectly, to be big . . .)*
la seda	*silk*
la talla	*size*
la tela	*material, fabric*

Vocabulario adicional

apretado	*tight*
atender (ie)	*to attend to, wait on*
durante	*during*
(in)formal	*(in)formal*
lindo	*pretty*
llamativo	*loud, gaudy*
la ropa interior	*underwear*
la variedad	*variety*
las zapatillas[1]	*slippers*

Repasemos el vocabulario

A **¿Cuál no pertenece?** Indique Ud. la palabra que no está relacionada con las otras y explique.

1. el abrigo	la chaqueta	el anillo	el impermeable
2. los calcetines	el paraguas	los zapatos	las medias
3. ancho	incómodo	estrecho	oro
4. claro	lana	seda	algodón
5. acostarse	probarse	ponerse	vestirse

[1]This means *high-heeled shoes* in Mexico. **Pantuflas** are *slippers*, and **zapatos tenis** are *sneakers*.

B **Antónimos.** Complete Ud. la frase con la forma correcta del antónimo de la palabra subrayada.

1. ¿El azul <u>claro</u>? No, no, tenemos. ¿Quiere probarse una blusa azul ______?
2. A las nueve las tiendas no están <u>cerradas</u>. Al contrario, están ______.
3. ¿<u>Subimos</u> al departamento de ropa para niños? No, nosotros ______ al departamento para mujeres.
4. Mamá, no están de moda las faldas <u>anchas</u>. Quiero comprar una falda ______.
5. Si vas a caminar mucho, necesitas zapatos <u>cómodos</u>. Tus botas parecen muy ______.

C **¡Me queda... estupendo!** ¿Qué dicen las siguientes personas? Use la construcción **quedarle + (bien, mal, grande...).**

MODELO Estos zapatos me quedan bonitos.

1.  tú

2. Ud.

3. Uds.

4. nosotros

5. ella

D **¿Hace juego?** Busque Ud. en el segundo grupo el artículo que hace juego con el artículo del primer grupo.

MODELO **La falda es anaranjada y hace juego con el suéter amarillo y anaranjado.**

1.

2.

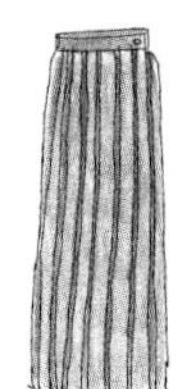

3.

4.

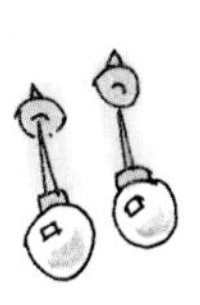

5.

a.

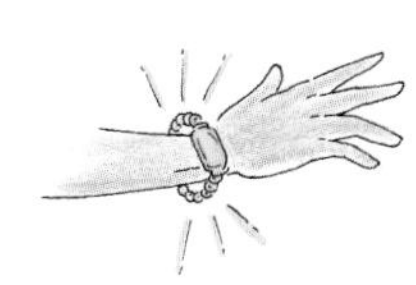

b.

c.

d.

e.

E **Definiciones.** Su profesor(a) va a leer una serie de definiciones. Escuche Ud. e indique la palabra que corresponde a cada definición.

el probador	la liquidación	el oro	vestirse
divertirse	el impermeable	el algodón	el dependiente

1. ____________ **3.** ____________ **5.** ____________ **7.** ____________

2. ____________ **4.** ____________ **6.** ____________ **8.** ____________

F **Tengo mis ideas.** Complete Ud. las siguientes frases de una forma original. Luego, entreviste *(interview)* a un(a) compañero(a). Compare sus respuestas.

¡Viva la moda!

1. Siempre llevo ____________ cuando voy al cine porque...
2. Cuando estoy en casa llevo ____________ porque...
3. Nunca salgo con un hombre (una mujer) que lleva...
4. Por lo general, los hombres (las mujeres) que llevan ____________ son...
5. Yo nunca llevo ____________ para ir ____________ porque...
6. Me gusta más la ropa de (verano, invierno, primavera, otoño) porque...

Reflexive Verbs

Forma

A reflexive verb is one in which the action reflects back to the subject. That is, the subject does the action of the verb to itself. The pronoun **se** at the end of an infinitive indicates that the verb can be used reflexively. When conjugated, the verb is accompanied by the following reflexive pronouns.

PROBARSE *(to try on)*

yo	**me** pruebo	nosotros(as)	**nos** probamos
tú	**te** pruebas	vosotros(as)	**os** probáis
él / ella / Ud.	**se** prueba	ellos / ellas / Uds.	**se** prueban

Reflexive pronouns, like direct and indirect object pronouns, precede a conjugated verb and can follow and be attached to an infinitive or present participle. Reflexive pronouns precede other object pronouns.

Me lo pruebo.	*I try it on.*
Me lo voy a probar. Voy a probár**me**lo.	*I'm going to try it on.*
Me lo estoy probando. Estoy probándo**me**lo.	*I'm trying it on.*

Función

1. Many Spanish verbs can be used reflexively and nonreflexively.

Yo **lavo** mi suéter. (nonreflexive)	*I **wash** my sweater.*
Yo **me lavo.** (reflexive)	***I wash (myself).***

2. In English, reflexive action is expressed in different ways:

a. by the use of the pronouns that end in *-self* and *-selves*.

Me corté.	***I cut myself.***
Ellos **se ven** en el espejo.	*They **see themselves** in the mirror.*

b. By using the auxiliary verb *to get.*

Nos levantamos, nos lavamos y nos vestimos.	*We **get up, get washed,** and **get dressed.***

c. Many verbs have reflexive meanings that are not expressed but rather understood.

Roberto **se baña** y **se afeita.**	*Roberto **bathes (himself)** and **shaves (himself).***

3. In a reflexive construction, the definite article rather than the possessive adjective is generally used with parts of the body and clothing. Since the reflexive expresses action that the subject does to itself, possession is understood.

Laura se lava **la** cara y se pone **el** sombrero.	*Laura washes **her** face and puts on **her** hat.*
Debes quitarte **la** chaqueta porque hace calor.	*You should take off **your** jacket because it's hot.*

4. Some common reflexive verbs are:

acostarse (ue)	*to go to bed*	lavarse	*to get washed*
afeitarse	*to shave*	levantarse	*to get up*
bañarse	*to bathe, shower*	llamarse	*to call oneself (be named)*
despertarse (ie)	*to wake up*	sentarse (ie)	*to sit down*
divertirse (ie, i)	*to have a good time*	vestirse (i, i)	*to get dressed*

5. Some verbs have slightly different meanings when used reflexively.

casar	*to marry (perform the ceremony)*	casarse	*to get married*
dormir (ue, u)	*to sleep*	dormirse (ue, u)	*to fall asleep*
ir	*to go*	irse	*to go away, leave*
poner	*to put*	ponerse[1]	*to put on*
probar (ue)	*to try, taste*	probarse (ue)	*to try on*
quedar	*to be located, be left*	quedarse	*to stay, remain*
quitar	*to take away*	quitarse	*to take off*
sentir (ie, i)	*to feel (sorry), regret*	sentirse (ie, i)	*to feel*

6. The verb **sentir(se)** *(to feel)* is used reflexively with an adjective and nonreflexively with a noun.

Pilar **se siente alegre** cuando piensa en Pablo. — *Pilar **feels happy** when she thinks about Pablo.*

Los niños **sienten** mucha **alegría.** — *The children **feel** much **happiness.***

Practiquemos

A **¿Qué hace Ud. primero?** Diga Ud. en qué orden hace las siguientes actividades. Forme frases completas.

¿comer o sentarse a la mesa?
Primero me siento a la mesa y luego como.

1. ¿despertarse o levantarse?
2. ¿bañarse o ponerse el suéter?
3. ¿acostarse o dormirse?
4. ¿quitarse los zapatos o acostarse?
5. ¿probarse los pantalones o comprar los pantalones?
6. ¿buscar una silla o sentarse?

[1]**Ponerse** can also express *to become* when referring to a change in emotion or mental state. **José se puso feliz cuando abrió el regalo.** *José became happy when he opened the present.*

B **Ud. tiene correo.** Ud. recibió una carta por correo electrónico de Dora, su amiga cubanoamericana que vive en Miami. Llene Ud. los espacios con la forma correcta de los verbos entre paréntesis en el tiempo presente. Conteste la carta, diciéndole cómo es un día típico para Ud.

¡Hola! Mucho tiempo sin escribirte! Lo siento, pero (tener-yo) ______ exámenes finales y hay mucha tarea. Como ya es mayo, quiero invitarte a pasar unas semanas con mi familia en Miami este verano. Lo vas a pasar muy bien. Por la mañana yo (despertarse) ______ a las nueve pero no (levantarse) ______ inmediatamente. (Quedarse-yo) ______ en la cama y (leer) ______ el *Nuevo Herald*, uno de nuestros periódicos en español. Después, (bañarse) ______, (vestirse) ______ y (prepararse) ______ el desayuno, café cubano, por supuesto y pan tostado o algo dulce. Luego (salir-yo)______ a ver a mis amigos. Nosotros siempre (divertirse) ______ porque hay mucho que hacer. Si hace sol, (ponerse-nosotros) ______ el traje de baño y vamos a la playa *(beach)* de South Beach. Allí (quedarse) ______ toda la mañana charlando y escuchando música. Yo siempre (dormirse) ______, pero mis amigos me (despertar) ______ a la hora de almorzar. Vamos a Lario's, el restaurante de Gloria Estefan y (sentarse) ______ afuera para poder mirar a toda la gente. Después, visitamos las boutiques y (probarse) ______ toda clase de ropa. Después, vuelvo a casa, (quitarse) ______ el traje de baño, (bañarse) ______ y (ponerse) ______ algo cómodo. Por la noche, hay más actividades —vamos a Coconut Grove para cenar o ver una película. ¡Yo nunca (acostarse) ______ antes de la medianoche! Pues, ¿cómo es un día típico para ti? Y dime *(tell me)* si puedes venir en julio.

Luego... Dora

C **Actividades reflexivas.** Use Ud. los siguientes verbos para decir lo que hacen las personas en las diferentes situaciones. Puede usar los mismos verbos más de una vez.

quitarse	quedarse	sentarse
ponerse	bañarse	acostarse
vestirse	despertarse	probarse

	en el invierno	**para ir a una fiesta**	**en casa**	**en el verano**
mi profesor(a)	se pone un suéter			
mis amigos				
yo				
mi hermano menor				

D **¿Qué pasó ayer?** Diga Ud. lo que hicieron las siguientes personas ayer. Use el pretérito de los siguientes verbos y la forma reflexiva si es necesario.

probar(se) dormir(se) acostar(se) poner(se) levantar(se)

MODELO Yo me probé el sombrero.

1.

nosotros

2.

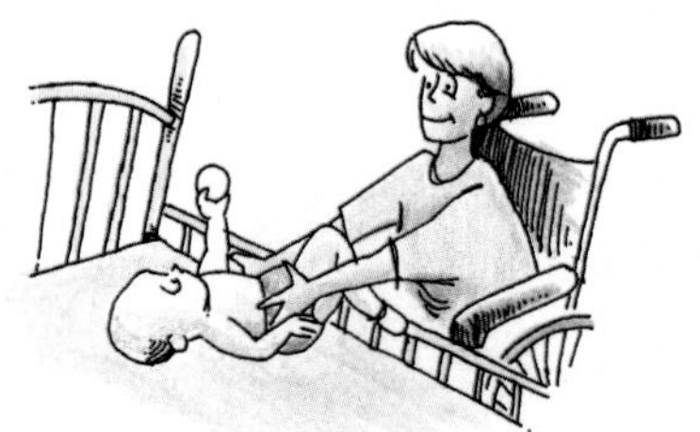

mamá

3.

los estudiantes

4.

el señor

5.

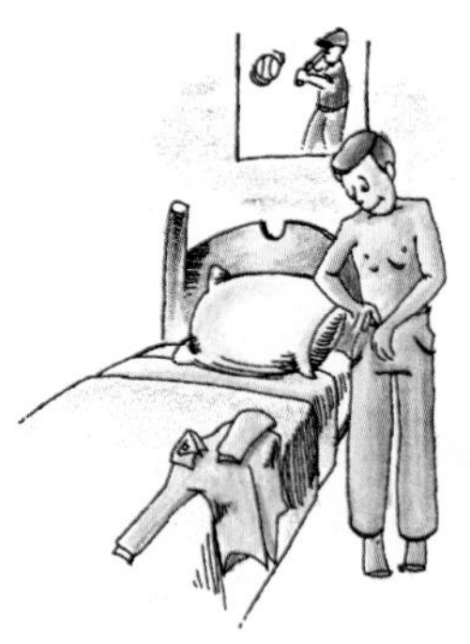

el niño

6.

tú

E **¿Por qué... ?** Termine Ud. las frases de una forma original.

Si una persona... es porque...

1. se duerme en clase
2. no se divierte en una fiesta
3. se despierta muy temprano en la mañana
4. se baña con frecuencia
5. no se prueba la ropa antes de comprarla
6. se acuesta muy tarde
7. se pone un impermeable
8. se quita la chaqueta y el suéter

Commands: Formal and Familiar

Forma y función

The command form of a verb is used to order someone to do something. It is used very frequently in daily speech. Think of how often you tell someone to do something. *Come in and sit down. Listen, put that down and try this on.*

In English and Spanish, commands can be directed at *you*, singular **(tú, Ud.)** as in *Take off your coat*, and *you*, plural **(vosotros, Uds.),** as in *Hand me your umbrellas.*

Commands with *Ud.* and *Uds.*

To form affirmative and negative **Ud.** and **Uds.** (formal) commands, take off the final **-o** from the first-person singular **(yo)** of the present indicative tense **(habl-o, com-o, escrib-o)** and add **-e** endings to **-ar** verbs and **-a** endings to **-er** and **-ir** verbs.

HABLAR		COMER		ESCRIBIR	
Hable. (Ud.)	*(Speak.)*	Coma. (Ud.)	*(Eat.)*	Escriba. (Ud.)	*(Write.)*
Hablen. (Uds.)	*(Speak.)*	Coman. (Uds.)	*(Eat.)*	Escriban. (Uds.)	*(Write.)*

1. Verbs that have irregular roots in the present indicative **yo** form maintain the irregular root in the command form.

CONOCER	TRAER	ESCOGER	CONSTRUIR	DECIR
conozca	traiga	escoja	construya	diga
conozcan	traigan	escojan	construyan	digan

2. Stem-changing verbs have the same stem changes as in the present indicative.

pensar: **pie**nse, **pie**nsen
dormir: d**ue**rma, d**ue**rman
sentir: **sie**nta, **sie**ntan
pedir: p**i**da, p**i**dan

3. Verbs that end in **-car, -gar,** and **-zar** have a spelling change in order to maintain the original sound of the consonant. These changes are: **-car** > **que, -gar** > **gue,** and **-zar** > **ce.**

buscar: bus**que**, bus**que**n
pagar: pa**gue**, pa**gue**n
comenzar: comien**ce**, comien**ce**n

4. There are five irregular command forms.

saber:	**sepa, sepan**
ser:	**sea, sean**
ir:	**vaya, vayan**
dar:	**dé, den**
estar:	**esté, estén**

5. Negative commands with **Ud.** and **Uds.** are formed by placing a negative word before the command.

No vuelva muy tarde.	***Don't return*** *very late.*
Nunca compren en aquel almacén.	***Never buy*** *in that department store.*

6. Although subject pronouns are rarely used with commands, they can be placed after the verb to strengthen the command or for courtesy.

Vuelvan **Uds.** a las 3:00.	*Come back at 3:00.*
Tome **Ud.** asiento.	*(Please) Sit down.*

Commands with *tú*

To form affirmative familiar **(tú)** commands, use the third-person singular present indicative verb form. The negative **tú** command is formed in the same manner as formal commands.[1]

Infinitive	Affirmative Command	Negative Command
HABLAR	habl**a**	no habl**es**
COMER	com**e**	no com**as**
BUSCAR	busc**a**	no busq**ues**
COMENZAR	comienz**a**	no comien**ces**

What are the negative forms of the following **tú** affirmative commands?

compra/no ___________ vuelve/no ___________

duerme/no ___________ escribe/no ___________

paga/no ___________

Explain why the following affirmative and negative **tú** commands have different roots.

trae/no traigas conoce/no conozcas escoge/no escojas oye/no oigas

[1]The affirmative **vosotros** command is formed by substituting **-d** for the final **-r** of the infinitive **(hablad, comed, venid).** The negative **vosotros** command is formed by removing the final **-o** from the first-person singular of the present indicative and adding **-e** endings to **-ar** verbs and **-a** endings to **-er** and **-ir** verbs **(no habléis, no comáis, no vengáis).**

1. The following **tú** commands are irregular in the affirmative. Except for **ir** and **ser,** their corresponding negative forms are formed in the same manner as the formal commands, by dropping the **-o** from the **yo** form of the present indicative tense and adding the opposite endings: **(-es** to **-ar** verbs and **-as** to **-er** and **-ir** verbs).

DECIR	**di**	no digas	TENER	**ten**	no tengas
HACER	**haz**	no hagas	VENIR	**ven**	no vengas
PONER	**pon**	no pongas	IR	**ve**	no vayas
SALIR	**sal**	no salgas	SER	**sé**	no seas

2. The verbs **dar, estar,** and **saber** have regular affirmative **tú** command forms, but have irregular negative command forms.

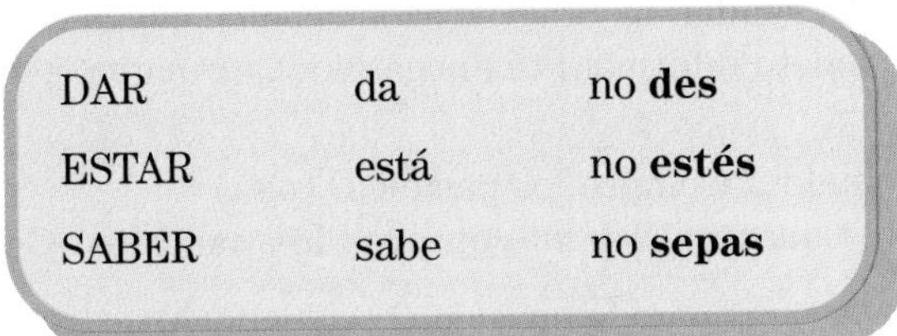

DAR	da	no **des**
ESTAR	está	no **estés**
SABER	sabe	no **sepas**

Practiquemos

A **De moda.** Para estar de moda, siga Ud. las recomendaciones. Cambie el verbo al mandato formal **(Ud.).**

1. (Aprender) ___________ a comprar bien. No (comprar) ___________ algo sólo porque le gusta.
2. (Buscar) ___________ en las revistas antes de ir al centro comercial.
3. (Escoger) ___________ el mejor color para Ud.
4. No (hacer) ___________ combinaciones ridículas, como zapatos negros con calcetines blancos.
5. (Conseguir) ___________ por lo menos una cosa de un color llamativo.
6. (Recordar) ___________ que los accesorios también son importantes.

En parejas, escriban cinco recomendaciones para su abuela. Ella va a empezar sus estudios universitarios y quiere estar de moda en el campus. Usen mandatos informales **(tú).**

B **Los consumidores ingenuos *(naive).*** Todos tenemos momentos vulnerables cuando vamos de compras. Aquí ofrecemos unas recomendaciones importantes. Cambie Ud. los verbos al mandato formal plural **(Uds.).**

1. No (ser) __________ impulsivos con el dinero.
2. (Ir) __________ a las tiendas que ya conocen bien.
3. No (salir) __________ a comprar cuando están tristes.
4. (Hacer) __________ sus compras más importantes con un(a) amigo(a).
5. (Leer) __________ las etiquetas *(labels)* con cuidado.
6. No (creer) __________ todos los anuncios que leen en el periódico.
7. (Tener) __________ cuidado con los vendedores en las calles.
8. (Tratar) __________ de combinar calidad *(quality)* y buenos precios.

C **En parejas.** Es el día después del Día de Acción de Gracias *(Thanksgiving)* y sus primos quieren empezar a hacer sus compras para la Navidad *(Christmas)* ahora. Denles cinco recomendaciones para poder sobrevivir *(survive)* la experiencia.

D **Alternativa.** Los Sres. Cabazos hacen una gran cena familiar. Los invitados *(guests)* quieren ayudar. La Sra. Cabazos les dice qué hacer. Cambie Ud. el verbo a un mandato informal **(tú)** negativo y afirmativo según el modelo.

MODELO Invitado: ¿Compro los pasteles? (pan)
Sra. Cabazos: **No, no compres los pasteles. Compra pan.**

1. ¿Corto los tomates para la ensalada? (la lechuga)
2. ¿Pongo platos en la mesa? (vasos)
3. ¿Sirvo el café? (el vino)
4. ¿Abro la botella de vino? (las botellas de cerveza)
5. ¿Traigo flores para la mesa? (tenedores)
6. ¿Vengo a las siete? (las seis y media)
7. ¿Voy a la pastelería? (la panadería)
8. ¿Lavo los platos? (los cuchillos)

Commands with Pronouns

Forma

1. Pronouns are always placed after and are attached to affirmative commands and must precede negative commands.

Ponte las botas. **No te pongas** las zapatillas.	***Put on*** *your boots.* ***Don't put on*** *your sneakers.*
Dígame la talla. **No me diga** el precio.	***Tell me*** *the size.* ***Don't tell me*** *the price.*

2. It is often necessary to add a written accent to an affirmative command when you add pronouns.[1]

Si hay una liquidación, **cómprame** dos camisetas y **tráemelas** esta noche.	*If there is a sale,* ***buy me*** *two T-shirts and* ***bring them to me*** *tonight.*

[1]See rules for stress and accentuation in *Unidad preliminar, Sección B.*

Practiquemos

A Una gira *(tour)* por la isla de Cuba. Parece increíble, pero Ud. tiene la oportunidad de visitar Cuba. Un agente de viajes *(travel agent)* le dice qué ver y hacer. Lea Ud. «Una gira turística por Cuba» en las páginas 302–303 de la *Gaceta 3*. Forme mandatos formales **(Ud.)** de los verbos entre paréntesis y busque en la segunda columna la terminación correcta de las frases.

En...

1. ...La Habana Vieja, (sacar)	**a.** una gira por las refinerías de azúcar.
2. ...La Rampa, (divertirse)	**b.** en un hotel elegante.
3. ...Coppelia, (probar)	**c.** bailando en las discotecas.
4. ...Santiago, (visitar)	**d.** una foto de la arquitectura colonial.
5. ...Camagüey, (hacer)	**e.** el famoso helado cubano.
6. ...Varadero, (quedarse)	**f.** las tumbas de los héroes políticos.

B Para relajarse *(relax)*. Alicia está muy tensa. Su amiga le da las siguientes recomendaciones. Forme Ud. mandatos informales **(tú)** de los verbos entre paréntesis.

1. (Despertarse) ____________ con música clásica. (Quedarse) ____________ en la cama por diez o quince minutos y luego, (levantarse) ____________ lentamente.
2. No (vestirse) ____________ en seguida. (Bajar) ____________ a la cocina primero y (prepararse) ____________ el desayuno.
3. Si hace sol, (sentarse) ____________ en el patio y (desayunar) ____________ allí. Pero, no (comer) ____________ rápido.
4. (Leer) ____________ el periódico, pero si hay noticias malas, no (leerlas) ____________.
5. Después, (subir) ____________ al baño y (lavarse) ____________ la cara. (Ponerse) ____________ ropa cómoda y zapatos de tenis.
6. (Salir) ____________ de la casa, (ir) ____________ al gimnasio y (hacer) ____________ algún ejercicio físico, pero no (hacer) ____________ demasiado.
7. (Bañarse) ____________ y (vestirse) ____________ para ir a la oficina. No (ir) ____________ al trabajo sin tener una actitud positiva.

C De compras en taxi. ¿Qué le dice Carolina a su chófer de taxi cuando va de compras a la ciudad de Nueva York? Cambie Ud. el verbo al mandato formal **(Ud.)** y busque en la segunda columna la terminación de la frase en la primera columna.

MODELO Recogerme/en el Hotel Plaza a las 9:00.
Recójame en el Hotel Plaza a las 9:00.

1. Llevarme	**a.** dos horas. Hay una liquidación en esta tienda.
2. No conducir	**b.** del taxi porque necesito ayuda con mis paquetes.
3. Darme el periódico	**c.** cuánto dinero le debo.
4. Bajar	**d.** tarde porque no me gusta esperar.
5. Apagar la radio	**e.** muy rápido.
6. Esperarme	**f.** a Tiffany's ahora.
7. No llegar	**g.** porque la música me molesta.
8. Decirme	**h.** porque quiero leer los anuncios comerciales.

Spend more time with Mariana and her friends while you review grammar and expand your cultural horizons.

See the **Así es Mariana** exercise in your workbook for this lesson.

En resumen

The clothes make the man.

A **El hábito sí hace al monje° *(monk).*** Haga las siguientes actividades.

1. Mire Ud. los dibujos y explique por qué la forma de vestir de cada persona no es apropiada (La falda le queda.... Ya no está de moda el...).
2. Use Ud. mandatos y diga lo que deben hacer las personas para estar bien vestidas *(dressed).*

B La moda.

1. Describa Ud. la forma de vestirse de...
   a. los «yuppies»
   b. los «preppies»
   c. los del estilo «grunge»
   d. los «jocks»
   e. los «nerds»
2. Describa la forma de vestir de alguna persona famosa (estrella de cine, músico, político...). La clase va a tratar de adivinar *(guess)* quién es.
3. Ud. es un(a) famoso(a) diseñador(a) *(designer)* de ropa. No le gusta la moda de hoy. Invente un estilo totalmente diferente. Descríbalo con detalles *(details)*.

C Para los hombres. Lea Ud. la selección sobre la guayabera y haga el ejercicio.

La guayabera

Para cierto hombre latino de raíces, o afinidades caribeñas, la guayabera clásica, de manga larga, de lino o algodón, es casi un uniforme. Esta prenda, descendiente de la túnica militar, imparte un aire de sobria disciplina, reemplazando al traje en ocasiones formales.

En su famosa **Casa de las Guayaberas de Miami (305-266-9683)** Ramón Puig, vende guayaberas hechas, o las corta para una selecta clientela de latinos y norteamericanos. Unos las prefieren ajustadas y otros más sueltas. Y a sus clientes que son policías, Puig les pregunta de que lado del torso cargan el arma para darles un poco más de tela y evitar un bulto sospechoso. ◆

raíces *roots*
caribeñas *Caribbean*
manga *sleeve*
lino *linen*
prenda *article of clothing*
sobria *sober*
reemplazando *replacing*
hechas *made*
ajustadas *tapered*
sueltas *loose*
lado *side*
cargan *carry*
bulto sospechoso *suspicious bulge*

Complete Ud. las frases.

1. A ___________ les gusta mucho la camisa guayabera.
2. La guayabera clásica está hecha *(made)* de ___________.
3. Para una ocasión formal, la guayabera puede sustituir al ___________.
4. En este país se pueden conseguir auténticas camisas guayaberas en ___________.
5. El señor Puig hace las camisas de una forma especial para sus clientes ___________.

D **Selecciones.** Complete Ud. la siguiente lectura *(reading)*.

Forme mandatos formales (Ud.) de los infinitivos entre paréntesis. Si hay dos palabras, escoja la más apropiada.

Cuidado cuando va (a, de) compras

Cuando Ud. va de compras (tomar) (estos, estas) precauciones. (Recordar) que, «no todo lo que brilla *(glitters)* es oro». Los letreros *(signs)* anuncian, «¡Gran venta!, ¡Fantásticas gangas! ¡Liquidación!» Pero, (tener) cuidado. (No creer) todo lo que lee. (Mirar) bien el artículo que piensa comprar porque muchas veces es inferior y cuesta un dineral. (Probarse) la ropa antes de comprarla. (No comprar-la) si le queda mal. También, (leer) todas las instrucciones (antes de, después de) comprar un producto. (Estar) alerta en las calles y en las tiendas. Si Ud. lleva varios paquetes en la mano, (recordar) guardar bien su bolso o su cartera.

E **En el almacén.** Translate the following dialogue to Spanish.

Silvia: Don't try on the dress. It's very dark for you. Put on the wool suit.

Carolina: O.K. Stay here for a minute. I see a blouse that matches the skirt.

Silvia: The suit fits you perfectly. Buy it.

Carolina: It's very expensive, and I know that there's going to be a sale at Casa Ramona.

Silvia: You don't need the black shoes. Return them, and don't buy a purse.

F **Minidrama.** En grupos representen la siguiente escena. Ud. es vendedor(a) y va de casa en casa *(from house to house)* vendiendo sus productos. Llame a la puerta de estas personas e intente venderles las siguientes cosas: una aspiradora, enciclopedias, revistas, cuchillos.

1. un famoso músico de rock
2. Batman o Superman
3. un actor (una actriz)
4. un(a) artista de fama internacional

G **Composición.**

1. Un hombre que Ud. conoce (padre, hijo, novio...) inventó un estilo nuevo. Escriba un artículo para una revista de moda para hombres. Incluya la siguiente información: quién es, su forma de vestir, qué personajes famosos van a seguir esta nueva moda, etc.
2. Ud. ganó veinte mil dólares en un concurso *(contest)*. Tenía que gastarlo *(spend it)* todo en 24 horas. ¿Qué hizo con el dinero?

Escuchemos

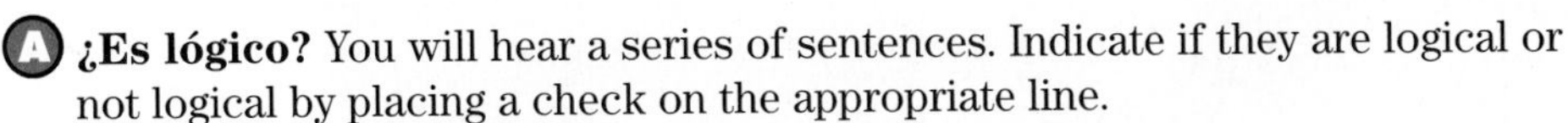

A **¿Es lógico?** You will hear a series of sentences. Indicate if they are logical or not logical by placing a check on the appropriate line.

MODELO Hace mucho frío y por eso me pongo el traje de baño.

_______ Es lógico	✓ No es lógico

	Es lógico	No es lógico
1.	_______	_______
2.	_______	_______
3.	_______	_______
4.	_______	_______
5.	_______	_______
6.	_______	_______
7.	_______	_______
8.	_______	_______

B **Dictado.** You will hear a short narration about a party that Cecilia attended and what some of the people were wearing. Listen carefully to the entire selection. Listen again and write each sentence during the pauses.

You will then hear a series of statements related to the dictation. Correct the false ones with complete sentences. Refer to your dictation.

Gaceta 3 Cuba y los cubanoamericanos

La Habana Vieja, Cuba

Una gira turística por la isla de Cuba

Preparativos: Estrategias de prelectura

1. Before taking your tour of Cuba, look at the **Es decir** section to help you anticipate the content of the text you are about to read. What sites and activities will your tour include?
2. Hojee Ud. la lectura *(Scan the reading)* para encontrar:
   a. dos cognados relacionados con la arquitectura de la isla.
   b. dos palabras que reflejen la historia o la política de la isla.
   c. dos sinónimos del verbo "muestran" en el segundo párrafo.
3. Hojee la lectura para saber: ¿Adónde va la gente...
   a. joven?
   b. que tiene interés en la historia?
   c. que quiere relajarse *(relax)*?

La Habana, la capital de Cuba, fue fundada en 1515 por el español Diego de Velázquez. Está a 90 millas° de Cayo Hueso *(Key West)*, Florida y tiene una población de unos dos millones de personas.

millas°: miles

En La Habana Vieja hay castillos,° plazas, patios y calles estrechas que recuerdan el pasado colonial español. Lugares como el Museo° de Arte Colonial, las fortalezas° antiguas y la Casa de José Martí enseñan la historia de la isla.

castillos°: castles
Museo°: Museum
fortalezas°: forts

La Habana moderna es una combinación de muchos estilos arquitectónicos, desde° el neoclásico hasta el arte deco. Allí está la Plaza, el centro político de la ciudad, el Parque° Lenin, la Universidad de La Habana y La Rampa, el centro de la vida nocturna.° Otro lugar de reunión social son las heladerías° Coppelia. El helado que venden es muy rico y muchas personas lo llaman la comida nacional de Cuba.

Santiago es la segunda° ciudad de la isla y la cuna° de la Revolución. Allí están las tumbas de José Martí y otros héroes de la independencia. La producción de azúcar es la industria principal de la isla. La ciudad de Camagüey está en el centro de la región azucarera° y, para los turistas que quieren aprender sobre esta industria, es un lugar muy interesante.

Las magníficas playas° son el centro turístico de la isla. La playa más popular es Varadero con casi veinte kilómetros de aguas cristalinas, hoteles elegantes y actividades culturales y recreativas.

from
Park
night
ice-cream shops
second; cradle
sugar (adj.)
beaches

Santiago, Cuba

Es decir

A **Descripciones de Cuba.** Busque Ud. en la segunda columna la frase que corresponde a las palabras en la primera columna.

1. azúcar	**a.** Describe la arquitectura de La Habana Vieja.
2. helado	**b.** No está muy lejos de Cuba.
3. La Rampa	**c.** Es importante para la economía de Cuba.
4. colonial	**d.** Hay que comerlo en La Habana.
5. playas	**e.** La gente va allí para divertirse por la noche.
6. el estado *(state)* de Florida	**f.** Son el centro turístico de la isla.

B **Lo pasé bien en Cuba.** Ud. acaba de pasar una semana de vacaciones en la isla de Cuba. Use frases completas y diga cuáles son...

1. cuatro cosas que Ud. aprendió sobre Cuba.
2. tres actividades que Ud. hizo.
3. dos lugares de interés que Ud. visitó.
4. una pregunta que Ud. quiere hacerle a un cubano sobre su país.

Practiquemos

¿Cuál es la pregunta? Las frases que siguen contienen más información sobre Cuba. Forme Ud. una pregunta que corresponda a cada respuesta. Hay más de una pregunta correcta.

MODELO el azúcar, las frutas cítricas, el cemento y el tabaco
¿Cuáles son las industrias de Cuba?

Palabras útiles

deporte *(sport)*	tiempo	presidente
comida	descubrir	población *(population)*

1. pescado, mariscos, platos de origen español, comidas preparadas con arroz
2. el béisbol, pero también el boxeo, el vólibol y el básquetbol
3. calor, todo el año
4. Cristóbal Colón *(Christopher Columbus)*
5. diez millones de personas
6. Fidel Castro

Alicia Alonso,
Ballet Nacional de Cuba

Caras en las noticias

Se dice que Cuba exporta tres productos principales: el tabaco, el azúcar y Alicia Alonso. **Alicia Alonso** es una bailarina del ballet clásico y es famosa por todo el mundo. Nació en La Habana en 1927. A los ocho años fue a España para aprender el baile flamenco, y el próximo° año volvió a Cuba para empezar a estudiar el ballet clásico.

following

A los 15 años fue a Nueva York con Fernando Alonso, hijo de la directora de su escuela de ballet, y poco después, los dos se casaron. En esa época Alicia empezó a perder la vista° y se quedó parcialmente ciega.° Eso no impidió su carrera. A los 19 años ya era una estrella° y bailaba por toda Europa y América. En 1959 volvió a La Habana, estableció el Ballet Nacional de Cuba y participó en la revolución de Fidel Castro. Alicia Alonso es la mujer más famosa de Cuba y la llaman la leyenda viva° del ballet.

sight
she remained partially blind
star
living legend

Andy García llegó a Miami desde° Cuba cuando tenía ocho años. Después de graduarse de la universidad, fue a Hollywood, donde, por ser latino, los únicos papeles° que le ofrecían eran los de drogadictos y criminales. García dijo: «Voy a ser actor y no sólo una selección racial». Hoy día García tiene talento, fama, premios° y muchas oportunidades para actuar° en películas importantes como *A Man and a Woman; Things to Do in Denver When You're Dead; Steal Big, Steal Little; The Disappearance of García Lorca,* and *Desperate Measures.*

from
roles
awards
to act

Andy García

El poeta **Nicolás Guillén** (1902–1989) nació en la provincia de Camagüey. Sus poemas son de temas° afrocubanos y muestran su profundo sentido° humano. Algunos de sus honores son: «Hijo Distinguido», «Profesor de Mérito» de la Universidad de La Habana y de la Universidad de Burdeos en París, «Doctor honoris causa». Es famoso por todo el mundo como el Poeta Nacional de Cuba. Sigue un segmento de su poema «Sensemayá (Canto para matar una culebra°)». La musicalidad, el ritmo° y la influencia africana son características de la obra° de Guillén y son evidentes en este poema.

themes
feeling
snake; rhythm
work

¡Mayombé—bombe—mayombé![1]
Sensemayá,[2] la culebra...
¡Mayombé—bombe—mayombé!
Sensemayá, no se mueve°...
¡Mayombé—bombe—mayombé!
Sensemayá, la culebra...
¡Mayombé—bombe—mayombé!
¡Sensemayá, se murió!

is not moving

Es decir

¿Cierto o falso? Si la frase es falsa, corríjala *(correct it)* con una frase completa.

1. Andy García no tiene mucha educación.
2. Alicia Alonso estudió en Cuba y en Europa.
3. Los temas de los poemas de Nicolás Guillén son políticos *(political)*.
4. Andy García vino a los Estados Unidos cuando era joven.
5. Alicia Alonso dejó de *(stopped)* bailar cuando perdió la vista.
6. La influencia de África es evidente en los poemas de Guillén.

Practiquemos

Figuras famosas. Las siguientes frases contienen más información sobre Alicia Alonso, Andy García y Nicolás Guillén. ¿A quién se refiere cada frase?

1. Sus primeros poemas se publicaron en una revista en 1920.
2. No tuvo que cambiar su nombre latino para actuar en Hollywood.
3. Fue presidente de la Unión Nacional de Escritores *(Writers)* de Cuba.
4. Muchas personas lo vieron en *El padrino III (The Godfather III)*.
5. Tiene más de 70 años y sigue bailando.
6. En Cuba todos la conocen.

[1]Las palabras tienen connotaciones musicales y mágicas. Reflejan *(They reflect)* la influencia africana.

[2]Esta palabra tiene un sonido *(sound)* musical.

Notas y notables

Novedades° de Fidel

Muy pocas personas saben que uno de los sueños° de **Fidel Castro** era el de ser lanzador° en las ligas mayores° de béisbol. De niño siempre era un buen atleta° y, en 1943, fue el mejor atleta de todas las escuelas de Cuba. Fidel siempre quería ganar pero no sabía perder. Si no le gustaba el partido° que jugaba, dejaba de° jugar y se iba para su casa. Cuando se hizo° presidente de la isla, empezó a jugar al béisbol con el equipo° los Barbudos,° el nombre del ejército° original de Castro. No era el mejor lanzador del equipo pero nunca lo sacaban° del juego.° ¿Quién se atrevería a quitarle el puesto a Fidel?[1] Dice un hombre que jugaba con Fidel cuando eran niños: «Si hubiéramos sabido que él quería ser dictador, lo habríamos hecho árbitro[2]».

news

dreams
pitcher, major leagues
athlete

game
he would stop; became
team
Bearded Ones; army
removed; game

Fidel Castro

[1]Who would dare to take the position away from Fidel?
[2]"If we had known that he wanted to be dictator, we would have made him umpire."

Celia Cruz

Celia Cruz... *¡Azúcar!*[1]

La quieren en el Japón, es una leyenda° en el Caribe,° triunfó en España y su nombre es mágico en América. Por más de 40 años, **Celia Cruz** es la Reina° de la Salsa, y nadie en el mundo de la música latina disputa este título. Celia creció en un barrio pobre de La Habana, y según ella, no sabía montar° en bicicleta, no sabía ni cocinar[2] ni patinar.° No sabía hacer nada excepto cantar. Este talento la sacó° de la pobreza° y para 1950 ya tenía fama en Cuba. En 1960, Celia salió de la isla y vino a vivir a los Estados Unidos.

Celia tiene más de 50 álbumes[3] y una estrella° en la acera° de Hollywood Boulevard. Cantó en el cine cubano, mexicano y norteamericano. Con frecuencia trabaja con otras grandes figuras de la música latina como Tito Puente,[4] Gloria Estefan y Jon Secada. Canta los ritmos° afrocaribeños y también los sonidos° nuevos del pop latino. *100% Azúcar! The Best of Celia Cruz*, es una colección de 19 canciones viejas, catorce grabadas° en Cuba en los años 50 y cinco grabadas en Nueva York una década más tarde. Con más de 70 años, Celia tiene más energía que nunca... ¡Azúcar!

legend; Caribbean
Queen
to ride
to skate
removed; poverty
star; sidewalk
rhythms; sounds
recorded

[1] Celia tiene la costumbre de gritar *(yell)* «¡Azúcar!» mientras canta.

[2] Ahora Celia sabe cocinar y muy bien, gracias a su esposo Pedro Knight, quien le enseñó a preparar los platos cubanos tradicionales.

[3] Algunos de sus álbumes son: *Recordando el ayer, Feliz encuentro, Grandes éxitos de Celia Cruz* y *La Reina del ritmo cubano.*

[4] Ud. puede leer sobre Tito Puente en la página 218 de *Gaceta 2*.

Es decir

Comprensión. Complete Ud. las frases con la palabra correcta de la lista siguiente. Diga a quién se refiere *(refers)* cada frase: Fidel Castro o Celia Cruz.

vivir sabía molestaba era jugaba

1. De niña __________ pobre.
2. Le __________ mucho perder.
3. Sólo __________ cantar.
4. __________ bien a los deportes *(sports)*.
5. Fue a __________ a los EE.UU.

Practiquemos

Más sobre Fidel. Lea Ud. *(Read)* la selección sobre Fidel Castro. Las frases que se encuentran después de la selección son falsas. Corríjalas con frases completas.

De padre español y madre cubana, Fidel Castro Ruz nació en 1927. Estudió para abogado y se graduó de la Universidad de La Habana. Castro y otros enemigos° del dictador° Fulgencio Batista fueron a la prisión por haber atacado el Cuartel° Moncada el 26 de julio de 1953, una fecha que los cubanos en la isla celebran con entusiasmo. En 1956, con un grupo de amigos, Castro hizo una serie de ataques° de guerrillas que pusieron fin al gobierno° de Batista en 1959. Más de 300.000 cubanos de la clase media y alta° salieron de la isla. Castro se declaró presidente por vida y buscó ayuda económica y política en Rusia. Hoy Fidel Castro es el jefe del partido° comunista, el único° partido político de Cuba.

enemies; dictator
Barracks
attacks; government
middle and upper class
party; only

1. Fidel Castro tiene 60 años.
2. Asistió a una universidad en España.
3. El gobierno de Batista terminó en 1956.
4. Después de la Revolución, miles de cubanos pobres salieron de la isla.
5. Después de declararse presidente, Castro le pidió dinero a Francia.
6. Castro sólo puede ser presidente por un máximo de 40 años.
7. Hay dos partidos políticos en Cuba.

José Martí, el apóstol de la independencia de Cuba

Enfoque literario

Versos sencillos por José Martí

Preparativos: Estrategias de prelectura

Before reading the following poem, *Versos sencillos* by the Cuban author José Martí, scan the biographical information in the text and list:

a. un sustantivo *(noun)* que refleja la meta *(goal)* política que Martí tenía para Cuba.

b. dos verbos que expresan lo que hizo Martí para realizar *(achieve)* su meta.

c. tres sustantivos que describen los muchos papeles *(roles)* de Martí.

d. cuatro productos de su prolífica actividad literaria.

Now scan the poem and tell with which economic class of people Martí identifies himself.

José Martí (Cuba, 1853–1895), poeta, ensayista° y autor de prosa muy variada. Martí tiene muchos títulos. Lo llaman poeta, profeta,° héroe, mártir° y apóstol... de la independencia de Cuba. Nació en La Habana y murió en 1895 en una batalla° en Dos Ríos, luchando contra° los españoles. Esta batalla siguió por tres años y terminó con el triunfo de Cuba. Es un momento irónico de la historia porque el próximo° año, 1898, los Estados Unidos ganó la Guerra° Hispanoamericana contra España, y los Estados Unidos ocupó la isla.°

Como resultado de° sus actividades revolucionarias, Martí estableció el Partido Revolucionario Cubano, unificó° a la gente cubana, pasó tiempo en la prisión y varias veces° dejó la isla para buscar refugio° en otros países.° Además de ser abogado y revolucionario, Martí fue un escritor° prolífico. Escribió novelas, poemas, obras de teatro,° ensayos° políticos, crónicas° y más. Su defensa de la gente pobre es evidente en este segmento de su poema «Versos sencillos°».

essayist
prophet
martyr
battle; fighting against
following
War
island
As a result of
unified
times
refuge; countries
writer
plays; essays; chronicles
simple

Versos sencillos (segmento)

Yo soy un hombre sincero
de donde crece la palma°;
y antes de morirme quiero
echar° mis versos del alma.°

Mi verso es de un verde claro
y de un carmín encendido°
mi verso es un ciervo herido°
que busca en el monte° amparo.°

Con los pobres de la tierra,°
quiero yo mi suerte echar°;
el arroyo° de la sierra°
me complace° más que el mar.°

palm tree
to pour out; soul
bright red
wounded deer
mountain; protection
land
share my future
brook; mountain chain
pleases me; sea

Es decir

Comprensión. Basándose en la lectura, conteste Ud. las siguientes preguntas.

1. ¿Qué tipo de hombre es el poeta?
2. ¿Qué quiere hacer antes de morirse?
3. ¿De qué color es su verso?
4. ¿Con qué compara su verso?
5. ¿Con quiénes se identifica el poeta?

Practiquemos

A **El lenguaje *(language)* literario.** Las palabras en la primera columna aparecen *(appear)* en el poema. Busque Ud. los sinónimos de las palabras en la segunda columna.

1. carmín	**a.** árbol tropical
2. sincero	**b.** poema
3. palma	**c.** humilde
4. verso	**d.** explorar
5. pobre	**e.** de color rojo
6. buscar	**f.** franco

B **Discusión.** Haga Ud. las actividades siguientes.

1. Nombre Ud. algunas de las referencias que el poeta hace a la naturaleza *(nature)*.
2. En sus propias *(own)* palabras, explique Ud. el significado *(meaning)* de las frases siguientes.

   Con los pobres de la tierra, quiero yo mi suerte echar;

   el arroyo de la sierra me complace más que el mar.
3. ¿Cuál es el significado de los colores verde y carmín?

C **Reacción personal.**

1. Termine Ud. las frases siguientes.
   a. Me gusta el poema porque...
   b. No me gusta el poema porque...
2. ¿Conoce Ud. un poema con un tema *(theme)* similar a éste? Explique.

Enfoque artístico... Cuba

A. Pocos norteamericanos viajan a la isla de Cuba, pero el sitio web, **http://www.cubanet.org/fotoindex.html**, ofrece la oportunidad de visitar esta isla poco conocida *(known)* por medio de una colección extraordinaria de fotografías. Mire Ud. las colecciones: «A Farmer in the Mountains», «Varadero Beach» y «A View of Havana». ¿Qué imagen de Cuba inspiran estas fotos?

B. En **http://www.cubanet.org/painters.html**, se encuentra una lista de pintores cubanos. Escoja *(Choose)* uno de los pintores, describa su vida y exprese su opinión de la pintura.

C. Since Internet addresses are subject to change, typing the following key words into most search engines will get you more information about Cuban art.

Museos de Cuba

Wilfredo Lam, Viredo or the name of any Cuban artist,

Videocultura

Gloria Estefan y Miami Sound Machine: Una entrevista con la talentosa cantante°

singer

Gloria y Emilio Estefan, del famoso grupo musical Miami Sound Machine, son excelentes ejemplos de la preservación de la cultura hispana. Los dos nacieron en Cuba y vinieron a los Estados Unidos en la década de 1960. Ellos se adaptaron a su nuevo país,° pero también pudieron mantener su cultura y su idioma. Su CD titulado *Mi tierra* refleja° sus raíces° afrocubanas.

country

reflects; roots

Para saber más sobre la vida, la música y la cultura de Gloria Estefan, vamos a uno de sus conciertos. Mire Ud. el video y haga los ejercicios que siguen.

Gloria Estefan

Palabras útiles

el fundador	*founder*
el sueño	*dream*
la libertad	*freedom*
los esfuerzos	*efforts*
ha conseguido	*has obtained*
ha mantenido	*has maintained*
fuerte	*strong*
criarse	*to be raised*
el ambiente	*atmosphere*
lo latino	*the Latin element*
el toquecito	*little touch*
suena	*it sounds*
se mantendrá igual	*will remain the same*
bilingüe	*bilingual*
sino	*but rather*
cualquier	*any*
la mente	*mind*
el punto de vista	*point of view*
el ser humano	*human being*

Es decir

A **Sobre los Estefan.** Basándose en el video, conteste Ud. las siguientes preguntas con frases completas.

1. ¿Cuándo vinieron las familias de Gloria y Emilio a los EE.UU.?
2. ¿Por qué vinieron?
3. ¿Por qué a Gloria le gusta Miami?
4. ¿Cuál fue el primer idioma de Gloria?
5. ¿Qué idioma habla Gloria mejor?
6. ¿Cómo es la familia de Gloria?
7. ¿Qué dice Gloria de lo latino?
8. Según Gloria, ¿por qué es importante ser bilingüe?

B **Sus canciones.** ¿Cuáles de las siguientes canciones canta Gloria en el video? ¿Las canta en inglés o en español?

1. «Primitive Love»
2. «Don't Wanna Lose You»
3. «Conga»
4. «Body to Body»
5. «Oye mi canto»
6. «The Rhythm Is Gonna Get You»

C **¿Qué recuerda Ud.?** ¿Qué cosas hace Gloria en el video?

1. Habla español.
2. Habla inglés.
3. Canta en inglés.
4. Canta en español.
5. Baila.
6. Lleva pantalones.
7. Lleva un vestido elegante.
8. Lleva botas.
9. Toca un instrumento musical.
10. Cuenta un chiste.
11. Presenta a su esposo, Emilio.
12. Le dedica una canción a su hijo, Nayib.
13. Lleva ropa de muchos colores brillantes.
14. Lleva aretes.

D **No quiero perderte *(Don't Wanna Lose You).*** Escuche Ud. bien la canción que Gloria canta y llene los espacios con las palabras apropiadas.

No quiero perderte

Por ______ vez, tenemos que ______.
Mejor que sea° ya, pues mi valor° me ______ faltar.°
Por más que traté, no te pude cambiar.
Tú que me entiendes bien, sabrás° que vi y nada te quiero ocultar.°

Pero tengo que ser... tengo que ser como ______.
Aunque te pierda a ti, seré° llena de ______.
Nadie dará° lo que te ______, por eso hoy...

Si voy a perderte ya, que sea por vez ______.
Si voy a perderte ya, es para siempre, ¿entiendes?
Que prefiero dejarte ir, y ______ a vivir sin ti,
Porque si voy a perderte ya, no ______.

Esperas° de mí, espero nada de ti.
Yo sólo quiero que seas feliz, aunque sé que puede ser que sea sin ______.
Pero mi corazón°, ya ______ puede más.
Si te vuelvo a perder tal vez° yo seré la que no vuelve jamás.
Ya no más.

Si voy a perderte ya, que sea por vez final.
Si voy a perderte ya, es para ______, ¿______?
Que ______ dejarte ir, y aprender ______ vivir sin ______.
Y si voy a perderte ya, no vuelvas, no vuelvas ______.
Si voy a perderte, perderte ya, que sea por vez final.
Si voy a perderte ya, si voy a perderte...

that it be; courage; may fail me
should know; hide
I will be
will give
You expect
heart
perhaps

Practiquemos

A **Preguntas personales.** Conteste Ud. las siguientes preguntas con frases completas.

1. ¿Conoce Ud. la música de Gloria y Miami Sound Machine? ¿Le gusta? ¿Por qué sí o no?
2. ¿Cree Ud. que es importante hablar más de un idioma? ¿Por qué sí o no?
3. ¿Cuáles son algunos de los idiomas que uno debe saber hablar? ¿Por qué?
4. Para la persona que estudia español, ¿es también importante conocer la cultura hispana? Explique.

B **Más sobre Gloria.** Llene Ud. los espacios con la forma correcta del verbo en el pretérito.

Gloria Estefan (crecer) ______ en un apartamento muy pequeño en Miami. Vivía modestamente con su madre. Su padre (participar) ______ en la invasión de la Bahía de Cochinos° en 1961, (ser) ______ capturado y (tener) ______ que ir a la prisión en Cuba. En 1963 fue liberado, (volver) ______ a Miami, (entrar) ______ en el ejército y (ir) ______ a Vietnam. Él (regresar) ______ muy enfermo y (morir) ______ en 1980.

Bay of Pigs

Para Gloria el escape de sus problemas era la música. Cantaba para su madre y amigas la siguiente canción que refleja la tristeza que los cubanos (sentir) ______ cuando (salir) ______ de Cuba.

Cuando salí de Cuba
Dejé mi vida, dejé mi amor
Cuando salí de Cuba
Dejé enterrado° mi corazón°

buried; heart

En 1975, Gloria (conocer) ______ a su esposo, Emilio, quien tenía una banda, Miami Latin Boys. Emilio (oír) ______ cantar a Gloria y la (invitar) ______ a ser parte del grupo. En 1976 ellos (cambiar) ______ el nombre del grupo a Miami Sound Machine, y en 1979 (casarse) ______.

Con su canción, «Conga», una canción afrocubana con letra° en inglés, ellos (hacer) ______ popular el sonido de Miami y (conseguir) ______ la fama internacional. En el invierno de 1990

words

el grupo (tener) ______ un accidente terrible y Gloria (romperse) ______ la espalda.° Ella (pasar) ______ un año de terapia física y (volver) ______ al escenario° en Miami el primero de marzo de 1991.

back

stage

Para Gloria, ser cubana es muy importante. Sin embargo, dice que no va a volver a la Cuba de Fidel Castro, y así lo expresa en sus propias palabras: «Sería como traicionar° a mi padre y no lo quiero hacer».

betray

Una visita a la ciudad de Miami

La Pequeña Habana, Miami

Miami es una ciudad muy animada. Tiene de todo —restaurantes excelentes, tiendas fabulosas, diez millas de playas° bonitas, un estilo de arquitectura «art-deco» muy único, un ambiente° internacional y un fuerte «sabor latino».

beaches

atmosphere

Para saber más sobre la ciudad de Miami, vamos a hacer un viaje a esta magnífica ciudad. Mire Ud. el video y haga los ejercicios que siguen.

Palabras útiles

el ajedrez	*chess*	dar un paseo	*to take a walk*
el batido	*milkshake*	el dueño	*owner*
el comercio	*business*	el puente	*bridge*

Es decir

A **¿A dónde va?** Basándose en el video, diga Ud. adónde va para hacer las siguientes actividades.

La Pequeña Habana   South Beach   Coconut Grove

1. Para ver una reproducción de un típico pueblo español.
2. Para jugar al dominó en el Parque Máximo Gómez.
3. Para comprar en una variedad de tiendas elegantes.
4. Para intentar conocer a los famosos dueños del restaurante Lario's.
5. Para probar la comida de una variedad de restaurantes hispanos como El Bodegón o Casa Juancho.
6. Para ver ejemplos de la arquitectura arte-deco.

B **¿Qué recuerda?** Nombre Ud. dos cosas que va a ver en los siguientes sitios.

1. La calle Ocho
2. El centro de Miami
3. El Parque Máximo Gómez
4. South Beach
5. Coconut Grove

Practiquemos

A **¿En qué orden?** Arregle Ud. en orden de preferencia tres lugares de Miami que Ud. quiere visitar. ¿Adónde va Ud. primero? ¿Qué hace allí? ¿Dónde va a almorzar? ¿Cómo va a pasar la tarde? ¿Qué cosas va a comprar?

B **En parejas.** Ud. está en Miami con un(a) compañero(a) que no quiere explorar la ciudad. Sólo le interesa dormir en la playa. En parejas, representen un minidrama en el que Ud. intenta convencer a su pareja de no pasar el día entero en la playa.

La comida cubana

La Carreta es un restaurante cubano muy popular en Miami. Hay varias localidades por todo Miami... en Key Biscayne, Miami Beach, la calle Ocho, y más. Allí preparan todos los platos cubanos más populares, como el arroz con pollo, la sopa de frijoles negros, los tostones y los plátanos maduros. Es una comida nutritiva y deliciosa, y por lo general, a precios muy razonables.

Para saber más sobre la comida cubana, vamos al restaurante La Carreta para hablar con Juan Bautista, mesero del restaurante en Key Biscayne. Mire Ud. el video y haga los ejercicios que siguen.

Palabras útiles

calentar	*to heat up*	freír	*to fry*
la caña de azúcar	*sugarcane*	el lechón	*pork*
el cañaveral	*sugar plantation*	la miel	*honey*
la carreta	*oxcart*	molido	*ground*
dorado	*golden*	el puñetazo	*punch*

Es decir

A **¿Qué son?** Basándose en el video, describa Ud. los siguientes platos.

1. un sandwich cubano
2. la sopa de frijoles negros
3. los tostones
4. los plátanos maduros

B **¿Cierto o falso?** Diga Ud. si las frases son ciertas o falsas. Si son falsas, corríjalas.

1. Juan Bautista es el cocinero del restaurante La Carreta.
2. Hay más de un restaurante en Miami, Dade County.
3. El nombre *La Carreta* se refiere a un pueblo de Cuba.
4. La comida cubana es muy popular porque es nutritiva, sabrosa y un poco cara.
5. No sirven postres en el restaurante.

Practiquemos

A **¿Qué plato?** Diga Ud., ¿qué plato le parece…

1. más nutritivo?
2. menos caro?
3. mejor para almorzar?
4. más dulce?
5. peor para un vegetariano?

B **Preguntas personales.**

1. ¿Qué le parece a Ud. la comida cubana? ¿Suele Ud. comer estos platos? ¿Por qué sí o no?
2. ¿Cómo es la comida típica de su casa? ¿Es más o menos nutritiva que la comida cubana? Explique.
3. Ud. va a abrir un restaurante. ¿Cómo se llama? ¿Por qué? ¿Dónde está el restaurante? ¿Qué tipo de comida sirve?

UNIDAD

De viaje

México y los mexicoamericanos

¡Vamos a México por Internet!

Experience the splendor of Mexico, one of the world's most popular tourist destinations, by browsing the World Wide Web and visiting the following addresses.

http://www.latinworld.com/
http://www.ceniai.inf.cu/turismo.html
http://www.mexicodesconocido.com.mx/vacation/editor.htm
http://www.edg.net.mx/otros/mexico.html

Since Internet addresses are subject to change, typing the following key words into most search engines will also get you to Mexico.

México   **Viajes a México**   **Turismo en México**   **México D.F.** (or any city in Mexico)

To learn about Mexican art via the Internet, see page 395 of *Gaceta 4*.

El aeropuerto de México, D.F.

Lección  10

FUNCTION	Expressing influence, emotions, and conjecture • Expressing **that, which** and **what**
STRUCTURE	The present subjunctive • The present subjunctive with impersonal expressions • Relative pronouns
VOCABULARY	At the airport • At the travel agency • Tourism • Getting around without getting lost
CULTURE	Getting to know Mexico • Mexican cuisine
DIÁLOGO Y VIDEO	***Así es Mariana: ¿Dónde está mi boleto?***

Lección  11

FUNCTION	Indicating uncertainty, feelings, and influence • Expressing the unexpected • Expressing "**Let's**" + action
STRUCTURE	The present subjunctive in noun clauses to express emotion, desire, doubt, and influence • ***Se*** to express unplanned occurences • Commands: ***nosotros***
VOCABULARY	Traveling by train, bus, boat, and car
CULTURE	Mexico's arts and crafts
DIÁLOGO Y VIDEO	***Así es Mariana: La llanta desinflada***

Lección  12

FUNCTION	Describing and expressing the indefinite or nonexistent • Describing and comparing
STRUCTURE	The present subjunctive in adjective clauses to express the indefinite and nonexistent • Comparatives and superlatives
VOCABULARY	In the hotel • Ordinal numbers
CULTURE	Hotels in Mexico • Mexican crafts • The Mayan culture • Facts about Mexico
DIÁLOGO Y VIDEO	***Así es Mariana: Una visita a México***

Gaceta  4

CULTURE	**Mexico and Mexican-Americans** Touring Mexico • Faces in the news • Notes and notables • Literature: Gregorio López y Fuentes • Art
VIDEOCULTURA	La vida del mexicoamericano: Una entrevista con el poeta chicano Tino Villanueva • Peter Rodríguez: El arte como reflejo de la cultura • La música de Carlos Santana

Aquí tienen sus boletos. Revísenlos, por favor.

Lección 10: En la agencia de viajes

AVISO CULTURAL

¿Qué sabe Ud. de México? Este país atrae a turistas de todo el mundo que van allí para gozar del clima *(climate)* fabuloso y del ambiente *(atmosphere)* histórico y cosmopolita. Al visitar sus museos y catedrales fascinantes se puede ver la influencia de sus tres grandes culturas importantes: la indígena, la española y la mestiza.[1] La Ciudad de México, capital del país, ofrece una vida nocturna *(night)* muy variada, desde los más típicos y populares «mariachis»[2] hasta los más sofisticados clubes nocturnos *(night clubs)*. Los turistas suelen visitar la famosa Zona Rosa para gozar de los restaurantes elegantes y de las discotecas que están abiertas hasta muy tarde. También el país cuenta con magníficas ruinas prehispánicas, artesanía *(crafts)* exquisita y playas *(beaches)* sin par. México tiene algo que ofrecerles a todos. ¿Conoce Ud. México? ¿Cuáles son otros lugares populares que los turistas suelen visitar? ¿Por qué son populares? ¿Cuáles son algunos problemas que suelen encontrar los turistas cuando viajan?

Preparativos

Review the vocabulary on pages 322–324 before viewing the video.

Al mirar el video o leer el siguiente diálogo, note Ud. el uso del modo subjuntivo. El subjuntivo refleja lo que piensa o lo que siente la persona que habla. Por ejemplo, ¿qué emoción expresa la agente de viajes cuando comenta: «**Es una lástima *(It's a shame)* que Uds. no tengan tiempo para hacer un viaje más largo.**»? O cuando Mariana dice: «**Es triste que no podamos pasar una semana allí...** »?

[1]**Mestizo** is a combination of Indigenous and European.

[2]**Mariachi** is a type of Mexican music and also refers to the musicians.

En este episodio Ud. va a aprender a formar el presente del subjuntivo, y va a ver uno de los muchos usos. Es evidente que Mariana y Luis Antonio están planeando un viaje. ¿Adónde van? ¿Cuál es el motivo principal de su viaje? ¿Dónde está el boleto de Mariana?

Así es Mariana: ¿Dónde está mi boleto?

Luis Antonio y Mariana están en la agencia de viajes. Van a visitar a la familia de Luis en San Diego.

Agente: Es una lástima que Uds. no tengan tiempo para hacer un viaje más largo. Hay una excursión especial para México y Centroamérica, a un precio muy bueno. Incluye el pasaje de ida y vuelta, el hotel y un guía turístico en cada ciudad. Pero, es necesario que Uds. pasen dos semanas allí.

Luis Antonio: Gracias, pero no es posible hacer un viaje largo ahora. Además, es dudoso que a mis padres les guste la idea.

Agente: ¿Y son ellos los que van a visitar en San Diego?

Luis Antonio: Sí, y también vamos a México a visitar a mi abuela. Pero vamos en coche porque no vive muy lejos de mis padres.

Mariana: ¡Ay, qué bien! ¡Cuánto me alegro de conocer México y California... y claro ...a tu familia también, Luisito!

Agente: Así es que, ¿Ud. no conoce California? Le va a gustar mucho. Lo que va a notar en seguida es la gran influencia mexicana, el clima estupendo y un paisaje° muy bonito. Mire, escoja algunos de estos folletos. Muestran todos los sitios de interés.

scenery

Mariana: Gracias. Es triste que no podamos pasar una semana allí, pero lo que más me interesa es ver todo lo posible en el poco tiempo que tenemos.

Agente: Aquí tienen sus boletos. Revísenlos, por favor, y no se olviden de confirmar el vuelo por lo menos un día antes de la salida. De esta forma, no tienen que hacer cola en el aeropuerto.

Luis Antonio: Perfecto, gracias. *(A Mariana)* Toma, para ti.

Mariana: No, gracias. Yo siempre pierdo todo. Guárdalo° tú. Es una cosa menos de la cual tengo que preocuparme.

Keep it.

Es decir

A Alicia quiere saber cuáles son los planes de Mariana. Conteste sus preguntas.

1. ¿Van a pasar mucho tiempo en California?
2. ¿Hay excursiones especiales?
3. ¿Dónde viven los padres de Luis?
4. ¿Por qué van a México?
5. ¿Es éste tu primer viaje a California?
6. ¿Qué dijo la agente sobre California?

B Basándose en el diálogo, termine Ud. la frase y diga quién la dijo.

1. Es una lástima...
2. Es necesario...
3. No es posible...
4. Es dudoso...
5. Es triste...

Al ver el video

Después de ver el video, haga las siguientes actividades.

A Mariana hizo muchos preparativos para su viaje. Busque en la segunda columna la terminación de la frase en la primera columna.

1. Le dio...	**a.** el periódico.
2. Hizo...	**b.** para California.
3. Canceló...	**c.** con la agente.
4. Salió...	**d.** al banco.
5. Tomó...	**e.** un taxi al aeropuerto.
6. Habló...	**f.** la maleta.
7. Fue...	**g.** su boleto a Luis.

B ¿Qué hay en su bolsa? Escriba **sí** en el espacio si Mariana sacó el artículo de su bolsa.

1. ______ calculadora	**5.** ______ periódico
2. ______ lápiz	**6.** ______ folleto
3. ______ boleto	**7.** ______ espejo
4. ______ cartera	**8.** ______ dinero

C En parejas, supongan *(suppose)* que Luis no tiene el boleto de Mariana. Terminen las frases de una forma original, explicando con detalles *(details)*, lo que pasa.

1. Mariana le explica a la agente de viajes lo que pasó y...
2. Mariana le dice a Luis que no puede encontrar su boleto y...
3. Mariana no descubre que no tiene el boleto hasta llegar al aeropuerto y...

Vocabulario

Verbos	
abordar	*to board*
abrochar(se)	*to fasten*
cancelar	*to cancel*
confirmar	*to confirm*
despedirse de (i, i)	*to say good-bye to, take leave of*
facturar	*to check (baggage)*
fumar	*to smoke*
meter	*to put into*
reservar	*to reserve*
revisar	*to examine*
viajar	*to travel*
volar (ue)	*to fly*

En el aeropuerto	***At the airport***
la aduana	*customs*
el aeromozo	*(male) flight attendant*

el asiento	*seat*
el avión	*plane*
la azafata	*(female) flight attendant*
el boleto (billete, pasaje)	*ticket*
el cinturón de seguridad	*seat belt*
la entrada	*entrance; ticket (to an event)*
el equipaje	*luggage*
la llegada	*arrival*
el (la) pasajero(a)	*passenger*
el pasaporte	*passport*
la puerta	*gate*
la sala de espera	*waiting room*
la salida	*exit; departure*
la tarjeta (postal)	*(post)card*
el viaje	*trip*
el (la) viajero(a)	*traveler*
el vuelo	*flight*

En la agencia de viajes	***At the travel agency***
el (la) agente	*agent*
la excursión (gira)	*tour*
el folleto turístico	*travel brochure*
el (la) guía turístico(a)	*tour guide*
el mundo	*world*
el país	*country*
la reservación (reserva)	*reservation*
el sitio (lugar)	*place*

Otras palabras y expresiones (See impersonal expressions on page 330)

al extranjero	*abroad*
la cámara (fotográfica)	*camera*
desde	*since, from*
estar atrasado (a tiempo)	*to be late (on time)*
estar de vacaciones	*to be on vacation*
extranjero	*foreign*
gratis (gratuito)	*free of charge*
hacer cola	*to stand in line*
hacer la maleta	*to pack a suitcase*
hacer un viaje	*to take a trip*
hasta	*until*
ida y vuelta	*round-trip*
libre	*free, unoccupied, at liberty*
más o menos	*more or less*

Vocabulario adicional

¡Buen viaje!	*Have a good trip!*
con destino a	*destined for*
extrañar	*to miss, long for*
el paquete	*package*
el pasillo	*aisle*
por desgracia	*unfortunately*
tardar en	*to delay in, take time*
todo el mundo	*everybody*
el (la) turista	*tourist*
verdadero	*true, genuine*

Repasemos el vocabulario

A **Formando nuevas palabras.** La lista de vocabulario incluye sustantivos *(nouns)* que corresponden a los siguientes verbos. ¿Cuáles son? Defina Ud. la palabra en español.

MODELO volver **la vuelta** **Cuando una persona regresa de un lugar.**

1. llegar ______ **4.** viajar ______ **7.** sentarse ______
2. entrar ______ **5.** esperar ______ **8.** reservar ______
3. volar ______ **6.** salir ______

B **¿Qué son?** Su profesor(a) va a leer una serie de definiciones. Busque la palabra que corresponda a cada definición.

a. la azafata c. el boleto e. el pasaporte
b. el asiento d. el pasajero f. el guía

1. ___ **2.** ___ **3.** ___ **4.** ___ **5.** ___ **6.** ___

C **¿En qué orden?** El Sr. Rivas acaba de volver de un viaje en avión. Él dice en qué orden hizo las siguientes actividades. Arregle Ud. las actividades lógicamente usando la primera persona singular **(yo)** del pretérito de los verbos.

buscar un taxi para ir al aeropuerto
Yo busqué un taxi para ir al aeropuerto.

1. abordar el avión
2. darle las gracias a la azafata por sus atenciones
3. abrocharse el cinturón de seguridad
4. despertarse unos minutos antes de llegar al destino
5. hacer cola en el aeropuerto
6. llegar al aeropuerto
7. pedir un asiento en la sección de no fumar
8. dormirse

Más actividades. Ahora, incluya Ud. cinco actividades lógicas que no mencionó el Sr. Rivas.

D **Expresiones con <u>hacer</u>.** Llene Ud. los espacios con una de las siguientes expresiones con **hacer** de esta lección y de las lecciones anteriores.

hacer + { preguntas, frío, cola, viaje, maleta, calor, llamada, juego }

1. Hace ______. Debemos encender el aire acondicionado.
2. Pásame el abrigo, por favor. Hace mucho ______ en este aeropuerto.
3. ¿Hay un teléfono aquí? Necesito hacer una ______.
4. Hay muchas personas delante de mí. Voy a tener que hacer ______ por una hora.
5. Juanito es muy curioso. Siempre me hace mil ______.
6. Estos zapatos rojos no hacen ______ con tu falda anaranjada.
7. La noche antes de viajar es mejor hacer la ______ y tener todo preparado.
8. No conozco México. Quiero hacer un ______ a Taxco y Acapulco algún día.

De uso común

Getting Around Without Getting Lost

Los turistas preguntan

¿Dónde queda... ? ¿Dónde está... ? ¿Dónde se encuentra... ?	*Where is . . . ?*
¿Cómo se llega a... ? ¿Por dónde se va a... ?	*How does one get to . . . ?*

Los ciudadanos *(citizens)* contestan

Siga Ud. derecho (recto).	*Go straight.*
Doble a la izquierda (derecha).	*Take a left (right).*
Baje (Suba) Ud. esta calle.	*Go down (Go up) this street.*
Queda en la esquina.	*It's on the corner.*
Camine Ud. dos cuadras (manzanas).	*Walk two blocks.*

Practiquemos

¿Dónde queda... ? Ud. es estudiante de primer año en esta universidad y no conoce bien ni el campus ni la ciudad. Otro(a) estudiante va a darle instrucciones a los siguientes lugares y Ud. tiene que identificarlos.

1. el mejor lugar para comer pizza
2. el mejor sitio para estudiar
3. la mejor residencia de la universidad
4. el mejor sitio para conocer a otros estudiantes

The Present Subjunctive: Form and Meaning

Forma

You are already familiar with various tenses of the indicative mood, such as the present, the present progressive, the preterite, and the imperfect. The tense is the time in which the action of the verb takes place. The *mood* (from *mode*, meaning *manner*) reflects the way the speaker feels about what he or she is saying. Is he or she feeling doubt or certainty, emotion or objectivity? The mood reflects these attitudes.

In Spanish there are two moods: the *indicative* and the *subjunctive*. Whereas the indicative mood has many different simple tenses,[1] the subjunctive has only two: the present and the imperfect (past). To form the present subjunctive, take off the final **-o** from the first-person singular **(yo)** of the present indicative conjugation **(habl -o, com -o, escrib -o)** and add **-e** endings to **-ar** verbs and **-a** endings to **-er** and **-ir** verbs.

[1]A simple tense consists of one main verb *(I ate)*. A compound tense consists of an auxiliary verb and a participle *(I have eaten)*.

HABLAR	**COMER**	**ESCRIBIR**
habl**e**	com**a**	escrib**a**
habl**es**	com**as**	escrib**as**
habl**e**	com**a**	escrib**a**
habl**emos**	com**amos**	escrib**amos**
habl**éis**	com**áis**	escrib**áis**
habl**en**	com**an**	escrib**an**

Why do you need to begin with the first-person singular form of the verb, rather than the infinitive? Study the subjunctive forms of the following verbs. Notice that the irregular form in the first-person singular is maintained throughout the entire conjugation.

tener:	tenga, tengas, tenga, tengamos, tengáis, tengan
decir:	diga, digas, diga, digamos, digáis, digan
traer:	traiga, traigas, traiga, traigamos, traigáis, traigan
conocer:	conozca, conozcas, conozca, conozcamos, conozcáis, conozcan
incluir:	incluya, incluyas, incluya, incluyamos, incluyáis, incluyan
escoger:	escoja, escojas, escoja, escojamos, escojáis, escojan

1. Stem-changing verbs that end in **-ar** and **-er** have the same stem changes as in the present indicative. Note that there is no stem change in the **nosotros** and **vosotros** forms.

pensar:	p**ie**nse, p**ie**nses, p**ie**nse, pensemos, penséis, p**ie**nsen
volver:	v**ue**lva, v**ue**lvas, v**ue**lva, volvamos, volváis, v**ue**lvan

2. Stem-changing verbs that end in **-ir** and have a diphthong **(e > ie, o > ue)** have an additional change **(e > i, o > u)** in the **nosotros** and **vosotros** forms.

sentir:	s**ie**nta, s**ie**ntas, s**ie**nta, s**i**ntamos, s**i**ntáis, s**ie**ntan
dormir:	d**ue**rma, d**ue**rmas, d**ue**rma, d**u**rmamos, d**u**rmáis, d**ue**rman

3. Stem-changing verbs that end in **-ir** and have an **e > i** change show the change throughout the entire conjugation.

pedir:	p**i**da, p**i**das, p**i**da, p**i**damos, p**i**dáis, p**i**dan

4. Verbs that end in **-car, -gar,** and **-zar** have a spelling change in the subjunctive in order to maintain the original sound of the consonant.

buscar:	bus**qu**e, bus**qu**es, bus**qu**e, bus**qu**emos, bus**qu**éis, bus**qu**en
pagar:	pa**gu**e, pa**gu**es, pa**gu**e, pa**gu**emos, pa**gu**éis, pa**gu**en
comenzar:	comien**c**e, comien**c**es, comien**c**e, comen**c**emos, comen**c**éis, comien**c**en

5. There are six irregular verbs in the present subjunctive.

saber:	sepa, sepas, sepa, sepamos, sepáis, sepan
ser:	sea, seas, sea, seamos, seáis, sean
ir:	vaya, vayas, vaya, vayamos, vayáis, vayan
haber:	haya, hayas, haya, hayamos, hayáis, hayan
dar:	dé, des, dé, demos, deis, den
estar:	esté, estés, esté, estemos, estéis, estén

¡AVISO! The subjunctive form is also used to express commands, as you have studied in Lesson 9. Review the following command table.

Subject	Affirmative Command	Negative Command
Ud.	subjunctive	subjunctive
Uds.	subjunctive	subjunctive
tú	third-person singular indicative	subjunctive

Función

The indicative mood is generally used to express certainty, reality, and objectivity and to report factual information.

I know that John **is** here.
It is true that the travel agency **is** closed today.
I'm sure that the airline **gives** special weekend rates.

The subjunctive mood is used to express conjecture, uncertainty, emotion, subjectivity, doubt, probability, influence, that which is as yet unknown, and that which you would like to happen.

I prefer that John **be** here early.
The travel agency **might be** closed today.
I insist that the airline **give** me their special weekend rate.

In Spanish the subjunctive is used much more frequently than in English. It is usually used in a sentence that has at least two clauses,[1] a main or independent clause and a subordinate or dependent clause. It is the verb in the main clause which determines the use of the subjunctive or the indicative in the subordinate clause. The most common conjunction used to join the two clauses is **que** *(that)*. Note that while in English the conjunction is often omitted, in Spanish it must always be expressed.

Espero que el avión llegue a tiempo.	***I hope (that) the plane arrives*** *on time.*
Dudo que podamos fumar en el avión.	***I doubt (that) we can*** *smoke on the plane.*

[1]A clause contains a subject and a verb. A main clause expresses a complete thought and can stand alone. A subordinate clause does not express a complete thought and cannot stand alone.

Generally the subject of the main clause is different from the subject of the subordinate clause. When the subject of both clauses is the same, the infinitive is used.

Yo espero que **tú** vayas.	*I hope that **you** go.*
Yo espero **ir.**	*I hope **to go**.*

Practiquemos

En avión. Indique si lo siguiente es importante cuando Ud. viaja. ¿Y qué piensan sus compañeros?

Es importante que...	sí	no
1. ...me siente cerca del pasillo *(aisle)*.	___	___
2. ...me siente cerca de la ventanilla.	___	___
3. ...sirvan una comida caliente durante el vuelo.	___	___
4. ...ofrezcan comida vegetariana durante el vuelo.	___	___
5. ...el avión llegue a tiempo.	___	___
6. ...haya una película durante el vuelo.	___	___
7. ...no pierdan mi equipaje.	___	___
8. ...el pasajero a mi lado *(next to me)* no hable mucho.	___	___

The Present Subjunctive with Impersonal Expressions

Función

An impersonal expression is an expression whose subject is not a specific person or thing, but rather is the impersonal (subject pronoun) *it*.

1. An impersonal expression reflects a generalization and is followed by an infinitive when the dependent verb has no expressed subject.

Es necesario **comprar** un pasaje de ida y vuelta.	*It is necessary **to buy** a round-trip ticket.*
Es preferible **viajar** en avión.	*It is preferable **to travel** by plane.*

2. When the dependent verb of an impersonal expression has an expressed subject, the subjunctive is used in the dependent (subordinate) clause.

Es necesario que **tú compres** un pasaje de ida y vuelta.	*It is necessary that **you buy** a round-trip ticket.*
Es preferible que **nosotros viajemos** en avión.	*It is preferable that **we travel** by plane.*

Some common impersonal expressions of this kind are:

es buena idea	*it is a good idea*	es malo	*it is bad*
es bueno	*it is good*	es mejor	*it is better*
es común	*it is common*	es necesario	*it is necessary*
es de esperar	*it is hopeful*	es preferible	*it is preferable*
es dudoso[1]	*it is doubtful*	es probable	*it is probable*
es importante	*it is important*	es ridículo	*it is ridiculous*
es (im)posible	*it is (im)possible*	es sorprendente	*it is surprising*
es (una) lástima	*it is a shame*	es terrible	*it is terrible*

3. When the impersonal expression indicates certainty and there is a specific subject, the indicative is used in the dependent clause. Some common impersonal expressions that require the indicative are:

es cierto	*it is certain*	es seguro	*it is certain*
es claro	*it is clear*	es verdad	*it is true*
es evidente	*it is evident*	no hay duda	*there is no doubt*
es obvio	*it is obvious*		

4. When you negate an impersonal expression of certainty, you express doubt or denial and therefore the subjunctive is used. When you negate an impersonal expression of doubt, you express certainty and therefore the indicative is used.

Es cierto que **vamos** a Guadalajara.	***It's certain*** *that* ***we're going*** *to Guadalajara.*
No es cierto que Pablo **venga** con nosotros.	***It's not certain*** *that Pablo* ***is coming*** *with us.*
No es dudoso que Pablo **viene** con nosotros.	***It's not doubtful*** *that Pablo* ***is coming*** *with us.*

¡AVISO! Only impersonal expressions of doubt and certainty are affected by negation. All other impersonal expressions require the subjunctive with a specified subject whether they are affirmative or negative. **Es posible que Pablo venga. No es posible que Pablo venga. Es necesario que vayamos a Guadalajara. No es necesario que vayamos a Guadalajara.**

[1]The expression **es dudoso** requires special consideration. See number 4 above.

Practiquemos

A **El nuevo agente de viajes.** Ricardo empieza a trabajar en la agencia Aviajar. ¿Qué le dice su jefe el primer día de trabajo? Llene Ud. los espacios con el infinitivo.

MODELO Es posible (hacer) ______ las reservaciones ahora.
Es posible hacer las reservaciones ahora.

1. Es importante (saber) ______ toda la información en nuestros folletos.
2. Es mejor (empezar) ______ a trabajar hoy mismo.
3. Es necesario (llegar) ______ a la oficina a las nueve en punto.
4. Es malo no (tener) ______ mucha experiencia.
5. Es bueno (ofrecer) ______ varias excursiones.

Ahora, cambie las frases, añadiendo *(adding)* el sujeto **Ud.** en la segunda cláusula, según el modelo.

MODELO Es posible hacer las reservaciones ahora. (Ud.)
Es posible que Ud. haga las reservaciones ahora.

B **El primer día.** Ricardo pasó su primer día en la agencia hablando con muchos clientes. Llene Ud. los espacios con la forma correcta del verbo en el indicativo o el subjuntivo.

1. Es cierto que (haber) ______ problemas políticos en ese país.
2. Es verdad que los inspectores (tener) ______ que revisar el equipaje.
3. No es cierto que el vuelo (estar) ______ lleno.
4. Es obvio que algunas personas (preferir) ______ sentarse cerca de la ventanilla.
5. No es verdad que los pasajeros (poder) ______ fumar en el avión.

C **¿Qué les dice?** Ricardo vuelve de su primer día de trabajo en la agencia de viajes, y su amigo le cuenta sus problemas. Con un(a) compañero(a), usen expresiones impersonales para formar sus recomendaciones.

MODELO Amigo: Cuando viajo no tengo dinero para comprar regalos para mi novia.
Ricardo: **No es necesario que le compres regalos caros. Es buena idea que le escribas muchas tarjetas postales.**

1. Mi hermano quiere ser aeromozo.
2. Mi compañero de cuarto tiene miedo de volar.
3. Yo me aburro durante los vuelos muy largos.
4. Mis padres viajan al extranjero pero no saben qué hacer para prepararse.

D **¿Cierto o dudoso?** Su profesor(a) va a leer algunas frases relacionadas con el viaje. Diga si Ud. cree que es cierto o es dudoso, y termine la frase usando la forma del indicativo o del subjuntivo, según el contexto.

Todos viajan durante el verano.
Es dudoso que todos viajen (Es cierto que todos viajan) durante el verano.

1. ______ **2.** ______ **3.** ______ **4.** ______ **5.** ______

Relative Pronouns

Forma y función

A relative pronoun replaces a noun or pronoun and often joins two clauses together. In English the four main relative pronouns are: *that, which, who*, and *whom*. In Spanish three common relative pronouns are: **que, quien(es),** and **lo que.**

Juana es la azafata. La conocí en el avión.	*Juana is the flight attendant. I met her on the plane.*
Juana es la azafata **que** conocí en el avión.	*Juana is the flight attendant* ***that*** *I met on the plane.*

1. **Que** can mean *that, which,* or *who.* It is the most common relative pronoun and can be used to refer to a person, place, or thing.

El agente **que** trabaja en esa oficina hizo las reservaciones.	*The agent* ***who*** *works in that office made the reservations.*
Los pasajes **que** dejé en la mesa son para ti.	*The tickets* ***that*** *I left on the table are for you.*

2. **Quien(es)** means *whom* when used after a preposition.

Paco es el agente **a quien** le diste el dinero.	*Paco is the agent* ***to whom*** *you gave the money.*
Los pilotos **de quienes** hablas te están escuchando.	*The pilots* ***about whom*** *you're speaking are listening to you.*

3. **Lo que** can mean *what* or *that which.* It is used to refer to abstract ideas, situations, actions, or concepts.

Lo que acabas de decir es fascinante.	***What*** *you just said is fascinating.*
No vamos a hacer **lo que** tú recomiendas.	*We're not going to do* ***what*** *you recommend.*

4. In English the relative pronoun is frequently omitted in daily speech. In Spanish, however, the relative pronoun must be expressed.

El viaje **que** hicimos el verano pasado fue maravilloso.	*The trip* ***(that)*** *we took last summer was marvelous.*
El hombre **que** conocimos en el avión es el hermano de Pilar.	*The man* ***(whom)*** *we met on the plane is Pilar's brother.*

5. In spoken English there is a tendency to end a sentence with a preposition *(John is the boy I'm going out with.)* rather than to express this same concept more formally *(John is the boy with whom I'm going out).* Only the formal English word order corresponds to correct Spanish word order: **Juan es el chico con quien salgo.**

Express the following in formal English and then in correct Spanish.

a. He is the tour guide you're writing to.

b. She is the flight attendant I was talking about.

c. They are the passengers we traveled with.

Practiquemos

A **Formando frases.** Forme Ud. frases lógicas, combinando las frases en las dos columnas con el pronombre relativo **que.** Cambie los verbos al imperfecto. Hay varias combinaciones posibles.

MODELO **Ése es el agente que planeaba el viaje.**

1. Ése es el pasajero...	**a.** (pedir) ______ información.
2. Ésos son los turistas...	**b.** (revisar) ______ las maletas.
3. Ésa es la azafata...	**c.** (traer) ______ la comida.
4. Ése es el inspector...	**d.** (sacar) ______ tantas fotos.
5. Ésos son los extranjeros...	**e.** (dormir) ______ durante el vuelo.

B **<u>Lo que</u>.** Traduzca Ud. los siguientes anuncios al inglés. Noten bien el uso de **lo que.**

1. LO QUE SÍ LO QUE NO

2. ¿Qué es lo que más me gusta?

3. *Sí, una revista completa en donde Ud. puede encontrar todo lo que le interesa.*

4. Sabemos lo que quieres,

5. Ven y visítanos para que descubras todo lo que tenemos para ti.

6. Lo que está in. Lo que está out.

7. **Lo que necesitas y más**

C **Ud. tiene correo.** Ud. recibió una carta por correo electrónico de su hermana y quiere saber cómo fue su viaje a Cancún, México. Llene Ud. los espacios con el pronombre relativo apropiado.

Hola Paco. Primero, gracias por las tarjetas postales ______ me mandaste. El viaje parece estupendo pero no me contaste todo. Por ejemplo, ¿con ______ fuiste por fin, con Pablo o Luis? ¿Qué es ______ más te gustó? ¿Hiciste todo ______ te recomendó el agente de viajes? La azafata de ______ escribiste parece muy simpática. Y finalmente..., ¿para ______ compraste regalos? Escríbeme.

Ahora, conteste la carta. Sea original.

D **Ud. decide.** Diga Ud. lo que necesitan las siguientes personas. Conteste con frases completas y dé por lo menos dos ideas.

MODELO Lo que esta mujer necesita es ayuda *(help)*.
Lo que esta mujer necesita son unas vacaciones.

1.

2.

3.

4.

E **Díganos.** Conteste Ud. las siguientes preguntas. Luego, cámbielas a la forma **tú** y entreviste a un(a) compañero(a).

¿Qué es lo que...

1. Ud. quiere más en el mundo?
2. Ud. hace mejor que nadie *(than anyone)?*
3. les fascina a sus padres?
4. le molesta a su profesor(a)?
5. está muy de moda entre los estudiantes de su universidad?

Spend more time with Mariana and her friends while you review grammar and expand your cultural horizons.
See the **Así es Mariana** exercise in your workbook for this lesson.

En resumen

A **La cocina de Yucatán.** Complete Ud. las frases con la forma correcta del verbo en el indicativo o el subjuntivo, con el infinitivo o con el mandato *(command)* **Ud.** cuando sea indicado.

Al hablar de la cocina de México, es común (mencionar) ______ platos como tacos y enchiladas, y las comidas fronterizas *(border)* como fajitas. Pero es una lástima que pocas personas (conocer) ______ la cocina de la península de Yucatán.[1] Es verdad que miles de viajeros (pasar) ______ sus vacaciones en Cancún, el balneario *(beach resort)* más popular de la península, sin probar ni un solo plato de esta cocina exquisita.

Querido viajero, no (ser) ______ como las masas. No (venir) ______ a este paraíso sólo para estar como en casa, comiendo sus hamburguesas y «bagels». (Desayunar) ______ **huevos motuleños,** (almorzar) ______ **poc chu** y a la hora de cenar, (buscar) ______ un verdadero restaurante mexicano y (probar) ______ la famosa y muy deliciosa **cochinita pibil.**[2]

No (irse) ______ de la zona sin visitar las ruinas mayas de Chichén Itzá y Tulum, y es importante que (viajar) ______ a la preciosa ciudad colonial de Mérida. Es seguro que Ud. nunca (ir) ______ a olvidar las vistas panorámicas, las playas maravillosas, los tesoros arqueológicos y los ricos sabores de este espléndido lugar.

B **La Primera de Mexicana.** Lea Ud. la descripción de la Primera Clase de Mexicana y nombre Ud....

1. dos cosas que se encuentran en la Primera Clase de Mexicana.
2. dos tipos de comida que sirven a bordo *(on board)*.
3. dos adjetivos para describir los asientos.
4. tres servicios en el aeropuerto que hacen la diferencia en Primera Clase.
5. el número de teléfono de la línea aérea *(airline)*.
6. la razón principal por la cual Ud. va a escoger la Primera Clase de Mexicana.

[1]Los estados de Yucatán, Campeche y Quintana Roo forman la Península de Yucatán.

[2]**Huevos motuleños** es un sandwich de huevos fritos, tortillas, frijoles, jamón, queso y salsa. **Poc chu** es un plato de cerdo y cebollas, preparado a la parrilla y servido con una salsa muy picante. **Cochinita pibil** es un lomo *(loin)* de cerdo preparado en una salsa de jugo de naranja y otras especias.

PRESENTAMOS CON ORGULLO LA PRIMERA CLASE DE MEXICANA.

Jorge Alberto Díaz y Araceli Caballero, sobrecargos de MEXICANA.

La tradicional hospitalidad MEXICANA y la más moderna tecnología, sólo se encuentran en nuestra Primera Clase* MEXICANA, la única en México y a la altura de las mejores del mundo.

Con amplios y cómodos asientos de piel, monitores individuales de televisión en estéreo, cocina nacional e internacional y las bebidas de su predilección. Además, mostradores exclusivos en todos los aeropuertos, recepción y entrega preferencial de su equipaje y la hospitalidad de nuestro personal que hacen la diferencia en Primera Clase.

* Actualmente disponible en nuestras rutas más importantes. Muy pronto en todos nuestros vuelos.
Consulte a su agente de viajes o llame a MEXICANA 325 09 90.

(Please note that although Mexicana Airlines no longer offers the "Primera Clase" program, the airline has many other excellent programs available.)

C **¡Qué aburrido!** Su vuelo es muy largo y no sabe qué hacer para divertirse. Haga los siguientes ejercicios.

1. Un pasajero le recomienda las siguientes actividades. Llene los espacios con un verbo apropiado en el presente del subjuntivo y arregle las actividades en orden de preferencia.

Es recomendable que Ud....

a. ______ un refresco. d. ______ la música.
b. ______ el almuerzo. e. ______ una carta.
c. ______ con la azafata. f. ______ la película.

2. Ud. hizo todas las actividades anteriores y todavía está aburrido(a).

a. Describa un juego que puede hacer solo(a) o con otra persona.
b. Describa tres cosas que Ud. trae para pasar el tiempo durante el vuelo.

D **De vacaciones.** Traduzca el siguiente diálogo al español.

Roberto: You're on vacation for four weeks. How nice! Are you planning to take a trip?

Pablo: It's possible that we'll go to Mexico, but I prefer to travel in August.

Roberto: It's a good idea to go to Mexico in April. The weather is nice, and the flights are cheap.

Pablo: You're right. Is it necessary for us to talk to a travel agent?

Roberto: Call Sandra Pardo. I am going to give you her number. She's the agent who helped us with our trip to Cancún. She's very good.

E **Minidrama.** En grupos, representen una de las siguientes escenas.

1. Ud. es aeromozo/azafata en un vuelo internacional. Uno de los pasajeros está causando problemas. Insiste en fumar en la sección de no fumar, no quiere abrocharse el cinturón de seguridad y sólo quiere comer la comida de los pasajeros de primera clase.

2. Ud. va a pasar por la aduana e inventa mil maneras para evitar que el aduanero revise su equipaje.

F **Composición.**

1. Ud. es de un país hispano pero pasó tres años en Nueva York. Sus amigos van a Nueva York por primera vez y le piden recomendaciones. Use expresiones impersonales y escriba una lista de diez recomendaciones. **(Es importante (que)..., Es necesario (que)..., etc.)**
2. Ud. es un(a) agente de viajes. Escriba un breve folleto turístico sobre los sitios de interés para visitar en México. Refiérase a la gira turística de México de la *Gaceta 4* en las páginas 380–382, y al ejercicio A de **En resumen** en la página 335. Use expresiones impersonales.

Escuchemos

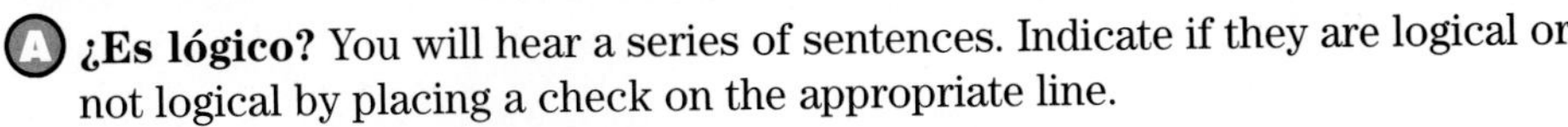

A **¿Es lógico?** You will hear a series of sentences. Indicate if they are logical or not logical by placing a check on the appropriate line.

MODELO Para sacar fotos el viajero necesita un buen folleto turístico.

________ Es lógico	✓ No es lógico

1. ________ Es lógico ________ No es lógico
2. ________ Es lógico ________ No es lógico
3. ________ Es lógico ________ No es lógico
4. ________ Es lógico ________ No es lógico
5. ________ Es lógico ________ No es lógico
6. ________ Es lógico ________ No es lógico
7. ________ Es lógico ________ No es lógico
8. ________ Es lógico ________ No es lógico

B **Dictado.** You will hear a short narration about Susan's travel plans. Listen carefully to the entire selection. Listen again and write each sentence during the pauses.

You will then hear a series of questions related to the dictation. Answer them with complete sentences. Refer to your dictation.

En la gasolinera

Espero que no sea la batería.

AVISO CULTURAL

(As a reading aid, refer to lesson vocabulary for new words.)

Por todas partes de México se vende una gran variedad de recuerdos que reflejan (reflect) la rica historia y cultura del país. Cada región o pueblo produce artículos de artesanía según los recursos *(resources)* naturales que hay. Son también de distintos colores, siendo espejo del paisaje regional. México tiene una gran selección de cerámica, de textiles, de artículos de madera *(wood)*, de vidrio *(glass)* y de cuero, juguetes y artículos de varios metales como hojalata *(tin)*, oro, cobre *(copper)* y plata. En Ensenada es muy posible que Mariana vaya a comprar cestos *(baskets)*, cerámicas, joyería de concha *(shell)* y, por lo menos, una blusa bordada *(embroidered)*. Y si no tiene tiempo para buscar estos artículos en México, seguramente puede encontrarlos en San Diego, por estar tan cerca de la frontera *(border)*. No hay duda de que ambos *(both)* Mariana y Luis Antonio no van a salir de Ensenada sin probar sus ricos y famosos tacos de pescado. ¿A Ud. le gusta comprar recuerdos cuando viaja? ¿Qué recuerdos suelen comprar los viajeros que vienen a los Estados Unidos?

Preparativos

Review the vocabulary on pages 342–343 before viewing the video.

Al mirar el video o leer el diálogo siguiente, note Ud. que cuando el verbo en la cláusula principal (la parte más importante de la frase) expresa emoción, deseo, duda o influencia, el verbo en la cláusula subordinada (la segunda [*second*] cláusula) se usa en el subjuntivo. Cuando hay un problema con el coche, Mariana dice: «Espero que no **sea** la batería». Luis dice: «No creo que **haya** una estación de gasolina cerca». Mariana contesta: «Sugiero que **busquemos** un taxi». ¿Qué les pasa a Luis y a Mariana en el camino *(on the way)* a México? ¿Quién tiene la culpa *(fault)?*

Así es Mariana: La llanta desinflada

Después de llegar a San Diego, Mariana y Luis Antonio deciden ir a México para visitar a la abuela de Luis. Por desgracia, tienen que salir de la autopista porque tienen un problema con el coche.

Mariana: ¡Ay Dios! Espero que no sea la batería.

Luis Antonio: Gracias, Mariana, pero no creo que sea la batería. ¿No oíste el ruido? Es cierto que tenemos una llanta desinflada.

Mariana: Pues, fenomenal. Esto es algo que podemos arreglar fácilmente. Mi padre me enseñó a cambiar las llantas cuando yo recibí mi licencia de conducir. Abre el maletero y saca otra llanta. Yo te la arreglo en seguida.

Luis Antonio: ¡Qué mujer! Qué talentosa eres tú. Y qué idiota soy yo.

Mariana: Luis... ¿Qué te pasa? Espero que no tengas malas noticias.

Luis Antonio: Es que no tengo otra llanta. La saqué y la dejé en casa de mis padres para poder llevar todo nuestro equipaje... y todos los recuerdos que tú vas a comprar en México. ¿Qué hacemos? No creo que haya una estación de gasolina cerca. Espero que mi abuela no se preocupe.

Mariana: Pues, no hay más remedio. Sugiero que busquemos un taxi. No estés triste, mi amor. Toma. *(Le da un caramelo).*

Es decir

A Para repasar la historia de la llanta desinflada, busque en la segunda columna la terminación de la frase en la primera columna.

1. Luis y Mariana oyeron...	**a.** un taxi.
2. Estacionaron...	**b.** el maletero.
3. El problema era...	**c.** una estación de gasolina por allí.
4. Luis abrió...	**d.** el coche.
5. Mariana dijo que sabía...	**e.** la llanta.
6. No había...	**f.** un ruido horrible.
7. Buscaron...	**g.** cambiar la llanta.

B Repase Ud. el diálogo y conteste las preguntas con frases completas.

1. ¿Qué espera Mariana? (dos cosas)
2. ¿Qué es lo que Luis no cree? (dos cosas)
3. ¿Qué espera Luis?
4. ¿Qué sugiere Mariana?

C En parejas, representen la siguiente escena. Mariana habla con su madre por teléfono y le cuenta lo que le pasó en la autopista. Su madre le hace muchas preguntas y comentarios.

Al ver el video

A Después de ver el video, diga Ud. si las frases son ciertas o falsas. Si son falsas, corríjalas.

1. Mariana nos recomienda que siempre viajemos con mucho dinero.
2. Mariana ya pasó una semana en San Diego con Luis y sus padres.
3. Ahora van a Ensenada, México para visitar a la abuela de Luis.
4. Mariana y Luis hablaban y comían cuando oyeron un ruido horrible.
5. Tuvieron que estacionar el coche en la autopista.
6. Mariana piensa que puede arreglar la llanta.
7. Luis recibió una multa por pasarse un semáforo en rojo.

B En grupos pequeños, escriban una breve descripción (cuatro frases) de cómo Mariana y Luis «pasaron dos días fabulosos» con los padres de Luis en San Diego. Usen su imaginación y cualquier *(any)* información que sepan sobre San Diego, porque Mariana no menciona nada todavía. Comparen su descripción con la de otro grupo, y combínenlas para formar una mejor.

Vocabulario

Verbos

aconsejar	*to advise*
alegrarse (de)	*to be happy (about)*
aprobar (ue)	*to approve*
aprovecharse de	*to take advantage of*
caer(se)	*to fall*
chocar con	*to collide with, hit*
descansar	*to rest*
estacionar (aparcar)	*to park*
frenar	*to brake*
gastar	*to spend, waste, use*
llenar	*to fill*
mandar	*to order; to send*
ordenar	*to order*
parar	*to stop*
pasearse (en coche)	*to take a walk (a drive)*
prohibir	*to forbid*
sugerir (ie, i)	*to suggest*
temer	*to fear*

El automóvil	*The automobile*
la autopista	*highway*
la batería	*battery*
el camino	*road*
el (la) conductor(a)	*driver*
la estación de gasolina (gasolinera)	*gas station*
el freno	*brake*
la licencia de conducir	*driver's license*
la llanta	*tire*
el maletero	*trunk*
la multa	*traffic fine*
el policía	*(police) officer*
la policía[1]	*police*
el ruido	*noise*
el semáforo	*traffic light*
el tanque	*tank*

Adjetivos	
(des)agradable	*(un)pleasant*
amable	*nice*
descompuesto (roto)	*broken*
desinflado (pinchado)	*deflated, flat*
peligroso	*dangerous*
ruidoso	*noisy*

Otras palabras y expresiones	
a menos que	*unless*
el autobús	*bus*
el barco	*boat*
la bicicleta (bici)	*bicycle (bike)*
el camión	*truck, bus (Mexico)*
el centro	*center, downtown*
el consejo	*advice*
cualquier(a)	*any*
hacer autostop	*to hitchhike*
el metro	*subway*
la motocicleta (moto)	*motorcycle*
no tener (hay) más remedio	*to have (there is) no other choice*
el norte (sur, este, oeste)	*north (south, east, west)*
ojalá	*it is hoped, I hope*
el paisaje	*countryside*
perder el tren (avión)	*to miss the train (plane)*
tal vez (quizás)	*maybe, perhaps*
la ventanilla	*ticket window, small window*

[1]**La policía** refers to *the police* collectively. A female police officer is often referred to as **la mujer policía.**

Vocabulario adicional

a lo mejor	*probably*
el andén	*railway platform*
la circulación (el tráfico)	*traffic*
el coche cama	*sleeping car (on a train)*
el coche comedor	*dining car (on a train)*
complicado	*complicated*
el gasto	*expense, waste*
la milla	*mile*
el motor	*engine*
¡Ojo!	*Careful!*
el taller	*repair shop, workshop*
la velocidad	*speed*

Repasemos el vocabulario

A **¿Cuál no pertenece?** Indique Ud. la palabra que no está relacionada con las otras y explique.

1. calle	autopista	metro	camino
2. este	sur	ojalá	oeste
3. maletero	freno	llanta	paisaje
4. avión	autobús	coche	motocicleta

B **Anatomía de un auto.** Nombre Ud. las partes del auto.

C **La respuesta correcta.** Su profesor(a) va a leer unas frases. Escoja Ud. la palabra que mejor termine la frase.

1. la estación/el maletero
2. arreglarlo/estacionarlo
3. a la ventanilla/al metro
4. un freno/una multa
5. frénelo/llénelo
6. semáforo/ruido

D **¿Cómo prefiere Ud. viajar?** Combine Ud. las palabras en la primera columna con las de la segunda columna para completar la frase lógicamente. Siga el modelo.

Voy en...
barco me encanta el mar.
Voy en barco porque me encanta el mar.

1. avión	**a.** gasta menos gasolina que el coche
2. bicicleta	**b.** me gusta conducir
3. coche	**c.** es buen ejercicio
4. motocicleta	**d.** es la forma más rápida de viajar
5. tren	**e.** quiero ver el paisaje
6. metro	**f.** es mejor que el autobús

E **Medios de transporte.** Pregúnteles a tres compañeros qué medio de transporte es más...

	coche	moto	bici	tren	barco	avión	metro
1. cómodo	___	___	___	___	___	___	___
2. incómodo	___	___	___	___	___	___	___
3. caro	___	___	___	___	___	___	___
4. romántico	___	___	___	___	___	___	___
5. aburrido	___	___	___	___	___	___	___
6. barato	___	___	___	___	___	___	___
7. divertido *(fun)*	___	___	___	___	___	___	___
8. peligroso	___	___	___	___	___	___	___

The Present Subjunctive in Noun Clauses to Express Emotion, Desire, Doubt, and Influence

As discussed in Lesson 10, the subjunctive is used to express conjecture, uncertainty, emotion, subjectivity, doubt, probability, and influence.

Sugiero que **él haga** reservaciones.	***I suggest*** *that* ***he make*** *reservations.*
Preferimos que **ella llegue** a tiempo.	***We prefer*** *that* ***she arrive*** *on time.*

As you can see in the preceding examples, the subjunctive is generally used in the subordinate clause. *He make* and *she arrive* are examples of the subjunctive form in English. The corresponding indicative forms are *he makes* and *she arrives*. The verb in the main clause determines the need for the subjunctive or the indicative in the subordinate clause. The conjunction **que** *(that)* joins the two clauses. Remember, if the subject of both clauses is the same, the infinitive is generally used.

Preferimos llegar a tiempo.	***We prefer to arrive*** *on time.*

The subjunctive is used in noun, adjective, and adverbial clauses. A noun clause is a clause that functions like a noun and serves as the direct object of the verb in the main clause. Identify the direct objects in the following sentences.

1. Yo prefiero un vuelo temprano.	*I prefer an early flight.*
2. Queremos un pasaje de ida y vuelta.	*We want a round-trip ticket.*
3. Ella recomienda el Hotel Astoria.	*She recommends the Astoria Hotel.*

Identify the noun clauses in the following sentences.

1. Yo prefiero que tomemos un vuelo temprano.	*I prefer that we take an early flight.*
2. Queremos que nos den un pasaje de ida y vuelta.	*We want them to give us a round-trip ticket.*
3. Ella recomienda que nos quedemos en el Hotel Astoria.	*She recommends that we stay in the Astoria Hotel.*

Función

1. The subjunctive is used in a subordinate noun clause when the verb in the main clause expresses emotion, hope, or desire.

Espero que ellos no **fumen** en el tren.	***I hope*** *(that) they don't* ***smoke*** *on the train.*
Está contenta de que tú **puedas** conducir.	***She's happy*** *that you* ***can*** *drive.*
Queremos que Ud. **descanse.**	***We want*** *you to* ***rest.***

Some other verbs and expressions that require the subjunctive for these reasons are:

alegrarse (de)	*to be happy (about)*
desear	*to desire, want*
estar feliz (triste, etc.)	*to be happy (sad, etc.)*
gustar	*to be pleasing*
ojalá[1]	*I hope*
preferir	*to prefer*
sentir	*to feel sorry, regret*
sorprenderse	*to be surprised*
tener miedo de (temer)	*to be afraid*

2. Verbs that indicate doubt, denial, and other expressions of uncertainty require the use of the subjunctive. When verbs and expressions of certainty are negated, they indicate doubt, and therefore require the subjunctive.

Dudo / **Niego** / **No creo**	que **haya** un tren a las 3:00.	***I doubt*** / ***I deny*** / ***I don't think***	*that* ***there is*** *a train at 3:00.*

When verbs of doubt are negated they indicate certainty, and therefore require the indicative.

No dudo / **No niego** / **Creo**	que **hay** un tren a las 3:00.	***I don't doubt*** / ***I don't deny*** / ***I think***	*that* ***there is*** *a train at 3:00.*

¡AVISO! Although the English equivalents of **creer** and **pensar** can indicate some uncertainty *(I think so, but I'm not sure)*, in Spanish these verbs express certainty. When a speaker says **Creo que hay un tren,** the speaker believes this to be true.

[1]**Ojalá (que)** is an expression of Arabic origin that literally means *Would to Allah (God)*. It is used to express hope or desire, and requires the subjunctive.

3. Verbs of influence require the use of the subjunctive in the subordinate clause. This category includes any verb that tries to influence the outcome of the action of the verb in the subordinate clause. These are verbs that command, suggest, advise, recommend, permit, allow, forbid, consent, oppose, request, or approve.

Yo **recomiendo (pido, permito, mando)** que tú **compres** el boleto.	*I **recommend (request, permit, order)** that you **buy** the ticket.*

Some other verbs that require the subjunctive for these reasons are:

aconsejar	*to advise*	insistir en	*to insist*
aprobar	*to approve*	ordenar	*to order*
decir	*to tell*	prohibir	*to forbid*
dejar	*to allow, let*	sugerir	*to suggest*
hacer	*to make*		

4. **Decir** and **insistir** are examples of verbs that can require either the subjunctive, when influence is expressed, or the indicative when information is communicated. Compare the following sentences.

José me **dice** que **salga** ahora.	*José **tells** me to **leave** now.*
José me **dice** que María **sale** ahora.	*José **tells** me that María **is leaving** now.*
Tú **insistes** en que Paco **esté** aquí.	*You **insist** that Paco **be** here.*
Tú **insistes** en que Paco **está** aquí.	*You **insist** that Paco **is** here.*

In the first sentence of each example the subject of the main clause is influencing the behavior of the subject of the subordinate clause by ordering that he or she do something. In the second sentence of each example the subject of the main clause is merely communicating information about the subject of the subordinate clause.

Practiquemos

A **Cómo hacer una maleta.** Para saber cómo hacer una maleta sin arrugar *(without wrinkling)* la ropa, siga las instrucciones. Cambie los verbos al subjuntivo.

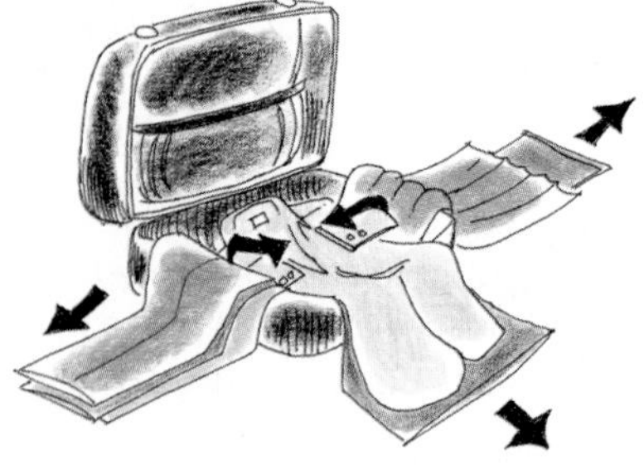

1. Recomendamos que Ud. (tener) ______ una maleta grande, y es preferible que (ser) ______ de buena calidad.
2. Ahora que tiene la maleta, queremos que Ud. la (llenar) ______ de la manera siguiente.
3. Sugerimos que (empezar) ______ con los zapatos, las blusas y la ropa interior.

4. Luego, es mejor que Ud. (poner) ______ los pantalones y las faldas sin doblarlos *(folding them)* por ahora. Vea el dibujo.
5. Preferimos que Ud. (meter) ______ las chaquetas y los vestidos boca arriba *(face up)*, y luego las camisas y los suéteres.
6. Ahora, con cuidado, aconsejamos que (doblar) ______ los pantalones y las faldas hacia adentro.
7. Finalmente, insistimos en que (llevar) ______ los cosméticos en una bolsa de mano.

B **Vacaciones... con hijos incluidos.** Marta habla con su agente sobre un viaje que quiere hacer con su familia. En parejas, llenen los espacios con la forma correcta del verbo en el indicativo, el subjuntivo o el infinitivo. Luego, representen el diálogo.

Marta: Quiero (pasar) ______ una semana de vacaciones en México. Tengo seis hijos de dos a quince años, y no creo que (ser) ______ posible (encontrar) ______ algo para todos. Es una lástima que yo no (conocer) ______ México.

El agente: Yo creo que nosotros (tener) ______ el plan ideal para Ud. Yo recomiendo que Uds. (ir) ______ al «Club Familia» en Ixtapa. Es verdad que ellos (tener) ______de todo. Por ejemplo, sugiero que los niños (participar) ______ en el «Mini Club». No dudo que les (ir) ______ a gustar.

Marta: ¿Y qué recomienda Ud. que mi marido y yo (hacer) ______?

El agente: Es importante que Uds. (tener) ______ tiempo para descansar, y para estar solos. Con seis hijos, yo dudo que Uds. (pasar) ______ mucho tiempo relajándose.

Marta tiene dudas. Combinen Uds. las expresiones en la primera columna con las de la segunda columna. Usen el subjuntivo o el indicativo. Hay varias combinaciones posibles.

1. Me molesta que...	**a.** a todos mis hijos les (gustar) el «Club Familia».
2. Me alegro de que...	**b.** Paquito no (divertirse) en el «Mini Club».
3. Ojalá que...	**c.** las actividades (incluir) el tenis y el golf.
4. Siento que...	**d.** no (haber) actividades para mi esposo.
5. Creo que...	**e.** nosotros (volver) aquí todos los años.

C **Preocupaciones.** Ud. es muy pesimista pero su amigo(a) es optimista. En parejas comenten las siguientes frases, usando **Yo dudo que** + *el subjuntivo* y **Yo creo que** + *el indicativo*, según el modelo.

MODELO Nuestro guía turístico sabe mucho sobre Guadalajara y Tepic.
Ud.: **Yo dudo que nuestro guía turístico sepa mucho sobre Guadalajara y Tepic.**
Su amigo(a): **Yo creo que nuestro guía turístico sabe mucho sobre Guadalajara y Tepic.**

1. Podemos comprar boletos de primera clase.
2. El tren va directamente a la Ciudad de México.
3. El tren sale a tiempo.
4. Sirven refrescos gratis.
5. Hay muchos asientos libres.
6. Llegamos temprano.

Se to Express Unplanned Occurrences

You have learned three uses of the pronoun **se** so far.

1. **Se** as a reflexive pronoun: **Él <u>se</u> lava la cara. Ellos <u>se</u> lavan las manos.**
2. **Se** as a third-person indirect object pronoun in place of **le** and **les** before a third-person direct object pronoun **(lo, la, los, las): Yo <u>se</u> lo doy a María.**
3. **Se** to express an indefinite subject with the verb in the third-person singular: **<u>Se</u> dice que el español es una lengua muy bonita.**

Se is also used to express unplanned occurrences, such as forgetting, losing, breaking, or dropping something. In English and Spanish, this type of action can be expressed two ways. By using an active construction, the subject takes responsibility for the mishap.

Yo rompí los vasos.	***I broke*** *the glasses.*
Tú siempre **pierdes** tu pasaporte.	***You*** *always* ***lose*** *your passport.*

Another common form of expressing these actions is by not having the subject be directly responsible for them. The subject becomes the victim; someone to whom these unfortunate actions happen rather than the perpetrator of them.

Se me rompieron los vasos.	*The glasses* ***got broken.***
Siempre **se te pierde** el pasaporte.	*Your passport always* ***gets lost.***

In Spanish, the object *(the glasses, the passport)* becomes the subject and does the action of the verb to the victim *(to me, to you).*

Spanish sentence	Literal English	English equivalent
Se me rompieron los vasos.	*The glasses broke (themselves) on me.*	*The glasses broke.*

The Spanish sentence is composed of:

Se + *indirect object pronoun* + *verb in the third person singular or plural* + *subject*

As with **gustar** and similar verbs the subject often follows the verb. If the indirect object noun is expressed or if clarification is desired, a prepositional phrase is used.

A Manuel se **le** rompieron los vasos.	***Manuel*** *broke the glasses.*
A Uds. se **les** olvidó ir a clase.[1]	***You*** *forgot to go to class.*
A nosotros se **nos** fue el tren.	***We*** *missed the train.*

This construction is commonly used with the following verbs.

acabar	ir	ocurrir	quedar
caer	olvidar	perder	romper

Se me **acaba** el dinero.	***I am running out*** *of money.*
Se nos **quedaron** los pasaportes en el avión.	***We left*** *our passports on the plane.*
A papá **se le ocurre** una idea fantástica.	*Dad* ***has*** *a fantastic idea.*

Practiquemos

A **Se me olvidó.** Para practicar el uso de **se** para expresar eventos inesperados *(unexpected events)*, llene Ud. los espacios con el pronombre del complemento indirecto *(indirect object pronoun)* apropiado, según el modelo. Traduzca las frases al inglés.

A ti, se te ocurrió una idea estupenda.
A great idea occurred to you. (You had a great idea.)

1. A Susana, se ______ rompió el vaso.
2. A los abuelos, se ______ olvidó llamarme.
3. A mí, se ______ acabó el dinero.
4. A Luis, se ______ perdieron los boletos.

Ahora, llene Ud. los espacios con la forma correcta del verbo entre paréntesis en el pretérito. Traduzca las frases al inglés.

A Juan, se le (romper) **rompió** la ventana.
John broke the window.

5. A nosotros, se nos (olvidar) ______ traer el vino.
6. A Marta, se le (perder) ______ los boletos.
7. A mis padres, se les (ir) ______ el autobús.
8. A Pedro, se le (caer) ______ la leche.

[1] If the subject is an infinitive, a singular verb is used.

B **¿Qué pasó?** Diga Ud. qué dicen las personas en las siguientes situaciones.

MODELO a Ud./caer/el dinero
A Ud. se le cayó el dinero.

1.

a mí/ir/el autobús

2.

a nosotros/quedar/los boletos

3.

¿a ti/perder/la licencia de conducir?

4.

a nosotros/olvidar/los regalos

5.

a Ud./romper/el zapato

C **Ud. tiene correo.** Ud. recibió una carta por correo electrónico de su amigo. Él le dice por qué Ud. no debe ir a recogerlo *(pick him up)* al aeropuerto esta noche. Cambie el verbo entre paréntesis al pretérito.

Espero que recibas este recado. ¡NO VAYAS AL AEROPUERTO!... Se me (ir) ______ el avión y no hay otro vuelo hasta mañana. Hoy fue un día fatal. Me desperté tarde, hice la maleta con prisa y salí corriendo. Corrí al coche pero se me (romper) ______ la maleta y se me (caer) ______ todas mis cosas en la calle. Además, se me (quedar) ______ las llaves del coche en mi cuarto. Finalmente subí al coche, pero en camino, se me (acabar) ______ la gasolina y no pude seguir. Se me (ocurrir) ______ llamar a mi compañero, pero se me (olvidar) ______ el número de su teléfono celular. En fin.... Llego mañana a las seis de la mañana. ¿Puedes recogerme?

Ahora, conteste Ud. su carta, usando por lo menos dos ejemplos del uso de "se."

Commands: *Nosotros*

Forma y función

You have already learned how to express formal and informal commands by using the subjunctive form of the verb. In English and Spanish, commands can be directed at *you*, singular **(tú, Ud.)** and plural **(vosotros, Uds.)** as in *Park the car over there*, and *us* **(nosotros),** as in *Let's fill the tank.*

To form affirmative and negative **nosotros** commands, take off the final **-o** from the first-person singular **(yo)** of the present indicative conjugation **(habl-o, com-o, escrib-o)** and add **-emos** to **-ar** verbs and **-amos** to **-er** and **-ir** verbs. The same orthographic and stem changes that occur when forming the subjunctive apply to the **nosotros** commands.

Nosotros commands

Infinitive	Affirmative and negative command
HABLAR	(no) hablemos
COMER	(no) comamos
BUSCAR	(no) busquemos
COMENZAR	(no) comencemos
DORMIR	(no) durmamos
SENTIR	(no) sintamos

1. There are five irregular command forms.

saber:	sepamos	dar:	demos
ser:	seamos	estar:	estemos
ir:	vayamos		

2. The affirmative **nosotros** command of **ir** is **vamos:** The negative command is **no vayamos.**

Vamos en tren y **no vayamos** en barco. — ***Let's go** by train and **let's not go** by boat.*

3. There are two other ways to express **nosotros** *(let's)* commands.

Vamos a descansar.
A descansar. — ***Let's rest.***

However, to express a negative **nosotros** command you must use the subjunctive form.

No descansemos ahora. — ***Let's not rest** now.*

4. When a **nosotros** affirmative command has a reflexive pronoun, the final **s** is dropped from the conjugated verb. Note the addition of a written accent when pronouns are added.

Levantémonos temprano, **vistámonos** rápido y **aprovechémonos** del buen tiempo. — ***Let's get up** early, **let's get dressed** quickly and **let's take advantage** of the nice weather.*

Practiquemos

A **Vámonos.** Para saber qué vamos a hacer hoy, forme Ud. mandatos con los verbos entre paréntesis en la primera persona plural **(nosotros).**

1. (Levantarse) ______ temprano, (bañarse) ______ , (desayunar) ______ y (vestirse) ______ , todo antes de las 8:00 de la mañana.
2. (Ponerse) ______ el abrigo y (salir) ______ de la casa a las 8:00 en punto.
3. (Subir) ______ al coche y (conducir) ______ al centro comercial.
4. (Llegar) ______ temprano y (buscar) ______ un sitio para aparcar el coche.
5. (Entrar) ______ en la tienda porque hay grandes liquidaciones.
6. (Probarse) ______ la ropa y (pagar) ______ todo con cheque.
7. (Irse) ______ a casa con nuestras compras.

Ahora, cambie todos los mandatos al negativo.

B **Un viaje al extranjero.** Con tres compañeros formen seis mandatos afirmativos y seis negativos para describir el viaje que Uds. quieren hacer. Consulten la lista del vocabulario.

Vamos a una agencia de viajes.
No hagamos los planes sin ayuda.

Spend more time with Mariana and her friends while you review grammar and expand your cultural horizons.
See the **Así es Mariana** exercise in your workbook for this lesson.

En resumen

A **Las emergencias en la autopista.** Un joven acaba de conseguir su licencia de conducir. Sus padres le dan consejos sobre qué hacer en caso de emergencia. Cambie los verbos entre paréntesis al subjuntivo o indicativo. Si hay dos palabras, escoja la más apropiada.

Si tú tienes un accidente es posible que un desconocido *(stranger)* (parar) para darte ayuda. Pero, hijo, no te recomendamos que (contar) con (el, la) bondad *(kindness)* de gente desconocida (por, para) ayudarte. Es mejor que les (dar) las gracias y les (pedir) que ellos (llamar) a la policía. Creemos que los policías (ser) capaces de ayudarte.

Si tienes un accidente de noche en la autopista, sugerimos que tú (subir) el capó *(hood)*, que (meterse) en tu coche y (cerrar) la puerta. Si una persona que no es policía te ofrece ayuda, queremos que (bajar) la ventanilla un poquito y que le (decir) que sólo necesitas un policía.

Una autopista en una noche cuando llueve no es el (mejor, peor) lugar (por, para) aprender a cambiar una llanta. Insistimos en que (aprender) hoy mismo a cambiarla. Pensamos que (ser) sumamente importante que tú (saber) hacer estas cosas. Es verdad que a veces una persona (poder) quedarse (sin, con) gasolina, pero esperamos que esto no te (pasar) (nunca, siempre) a ti.

B **El hombre o la mujer delante del volante *(steering wheel).*** ¿Quién maneja mejor? ¿Está Ud. de acuerdo con los siguientes comentarios? Defiéndase.

1. Hay una diferencia entre la manera en que manejan los hombres y las mujeres.
2. Las mujeres son «terrores al volante».
3. La mujer conduce con más cuidado que el hombre.
4. Los hombres son conductores agresivos.
5. Las mujeres son conductoras nerviosas.

C **Problemas en el camino.** Traduzca el siguiente diálogo al español.

Pablo: I ran out of gas. If I don't get to the station by five, I'm going to miss my train. What'll I do?

Julia: It's easy. I recommend that you hitchhike. Lots of people use this road.

Sara: No way! It's dangerous. I suggest that you take the subway to downtown and from there walk to the station.

Ramón: With all those suitcases . . . impossible! Allow me to take you in my car.

Sara: Be careful! You don't know him. I don't think it's a good idea.

D Minidrama. En grupos, representen una de las siguientes escenas.

1. Ud. viaja por tren. Tiene mucho sueño y sólo quiere dormir. El (La) pasajero(a) cerca de Ud. no quiere dejarlo(la) tranquilo(a). El (La) pasajero(a)...
   a. está nervioso(a) e inventa mil pretextos para hablar con Ud.
   b. ronca *(snores)* mucho.
   c. es un(a) niño(a) muy ruidoso(a).

2. Ud. y su amigo alquilaron un coche para hacer un viaje por todo México pero hay algunos problemas.
   a. Uds. se quedan sin gasolina.
   b. Uds. tienen una llanta desinflada.
   c. Ud. y su amigo descubren que no son compatibles.
   d. Invitan a una chica que hace autostop a subir al coche.
   e. Es de noche. Tienen un accidente. Un desconocido *(stranger)* les ofrece ayuda.

E Composición. Ud. y su prima, que vive en otra ciudad, quieren hacer un viaje. Ella prefiere volar y Ud. quiere ir en tren porque tiene miedo de volar. Escríbale una carta en la cual describe lo bueno de viajar en tren y lo malo de viajar en avión.

Escuchemos

A **¿Es lógico?** You will hear a series of sentences. Indicate if they are logical or not logical by placing a check on the appropriate line.

MODELO El maletero es donde meto las maletas.

✓	______
Es lógico	No es lógico

1. ______ Es lógico ______ No es lógico
2. ______ Es lógico ______ No es lógico
3. ______ Es lógico ______ No es lógico
4. ______ Es lógico ______ No es lógico
5. ______ Es lógico ______ No es lógico
6. ______ Es lógico ______ No es lógico
7. ______ Es lógico ______ No es lógico
8. ______ Es lógico ______ No es lógico

B **Dictado *(Dictation).*** You will hear a short narration about an accident Susan witnessed while on vacation in Mexico. Listen carefully to the entire selection. Listen again and write each sentence during the pauses.

You will then hear a series of false statements related to the dictation. Correct each one with a complete sentence. Refer to your dictation.

Busco un hotel que tenga...

Quiero una habitación que tenga aire acondicionado, que dé al jardín y que esté cerca de la piscina.

AVISO CULTURAL

(As a reading aid, refer to lesson vocabulary for new words.)

¿Busca Ud. un hotel en México? Va a encontrar todo lo que necesita, y más... México ofrece una gran variedad de alojamiento... balnearios *(spas)* elegantes, hoteles cosmopolitas y también una selección impresionante de ranchos, haciendas, misiones y conventos convertidos en hoteles lujosos con toda clase de servicios y comodidades. Para el viajero en Ensenada que quiera un hotel que tenga un verdadero sabor mexicano, el hotel ideal es Misión Santa Isabel. El estilo colonial, con su tradicional patio interior, recuerda el pasado español de Ensenada. Es posible que Mariana y Luis se queden en este hotel durante su estancia *(stay)* en México. ¿Qué tipo de hotel prefiere Ud.? ¿Qué servicios tiene que ofrecer? ¿Conoce Ud. un hotel que refleje la cultura y la historia de su región?

Preparativos

Review the vocabulary on pages 361–362 before viewing the video.

Al mirar el video o leer el diálogo siguiente, Ud. va a ver que Luis Antonio no es la única persona olvidadiza *(forgetful)*. A propósito *(By the way)*, ¿qué es lo que a Luis se le olvidó en el episodio anterior? Esta vez, a Mariana se le olvidó informarle a la abuela de Luis que venían a México a visitarla. Resulta que ella no está en casa cuando llegan. Deciden buscar un hotel y quedarse unos días.

Note el uso del subjuntivo cuando Mariana le dice al recepcionista del hotel que quiere una habitación que **sea** grande... que **tenga** jacuzzi... y que no **cueste** un dineral. Se usa el subjuntivo porque no es cierto que el hotel tenga una habitación con todas las comodidades que pide Mariana. En su opinión, ¿es razonable lo que ella pide? Explique.

Así es Mariana: Una visita a México

Luis Antonio y Mariana llegan a Ensenada, México y Luis llama a su abuela por teléfono, pero nadie contesta.

Luis Antonio: ¡Qué extraño! Es posible que yo me haya equivocado.° *I've made a mistake.*

Mariana: ¿Qué dijo el portero del apartamento de tu abuela?

Luis Antonio: Dijo que mi abuela fue de vacaciones a la ciudad de Guadalajara. No entiendo. Ella sabía que veníamos hoy. Le envié nuestro itinerario. Bueno, es decir, te lo di a ti. ¿No se lo enviaste?

Mariana: *(Mariana encuentra el itinerario en su bolso).* ¿Este itinerario?

Luis Antonio: ¡Pero, Mariana, no me digas que no lo mandaste!

Mariana: Ay, Luis, lo siento. Es que no pude encontrar un buzón, y después parece que me olvidé. Pero mira, ya que° estamos aquí, ¿por qué no vamos a ver la ciudad un poco? *since*

Luis Antonio: De acuerdo.

Los dos pasan unas horas paseando por las calles de Ensenada.

Mariana: Luis, México es muy bonito. ¿Nos podemos quedar aquí un día más? A ver si hay un hotel que no sea muy caro y que tenga dos habitaciones libres.

Luis Antonio: Sí, por qué no. Buena idea... Vamos.

Entran en un hotel.

Recepcionista: Dos habitaciones por una noche. Muy bien. ¿Qué tipo de habitación quieren?

Mariana: Pues, quiero una habitación que tenga aire acondicionado, que dé al jardín y que esté cerca de la piscina. También espero que sea muy grande, y que tenga un baño con jacuzzi. ¿Hay una así que no cueste un dineral?

Luis Antonio: Mariana... por favor. Dos habitaciones sencillas, por favor.

Recepcionista: Muy bien. Aquí tienen sus llaves. Están en el tercer piso, el 304 y el 305. Creo que les van a gustar mucho. Si quieren nadar, la alberca está abierta hasta las nueve de la noche, y pueden recoger toallas aquí en recepción. *(Le habla al botones.)* Botones.

Es decir

A Basándose en el diálogo, llene el espacio con la forma correcta del verbo **ser: es/sea.**

1. Espero que la habitación ______ grande.
2. Luis, México ______ muy bonito.
3. ______ que no pude encontrar un buzón.
4. A ver si hay un hotel que no ______ muy caro.
5. ______ posible que me haya equivocado.

B Llene Ud. el espacio con el número apropiado.

1. Mariana y Luis piden ______ habitaciones por ______ noche.
2. La alberca está abierta hasta las ______ de la noche.
3. Mariana quiere quedarse en México ______ día más.
4. Sus habitaciones están en el piso número ______.
5. El recepcionista les da las llaves para las habitaciones ______ y ______.

C Luis le dijo a Mariana: «¡Pero Mariana... no me digas que no lo mandaste!» ¿Cuándo se lo dijo y por qué? ¿Qué otros problemas pueden ocurrirles a Luis y a Mariana durante su viaje? En parejas, termine la frase de tres formas originales empezando con **¡Pero Mariana... no me digas que... !** Compare sus respuestas con las de sus compañeros.

Al ver el video

A Después de ver el video, termine las siguientes frases con la respuesta apropiada.

1. Mariana dice que México tiene
   a. restaurantes muy buenos. b. plazas antiguas. c. museos famosos.
2. Mariana compra...
   a. un refresco. b. una enchilada. c. un taco.
3. Luis llama a su abuela desde...
   a. el vestíbulo del hotel. b. una cabina telefónica en la calle. c. una gasolinera.
4. Mariana y Luis entran al hotel...
   a. sin equipaje. b. con una maleta. c. con muchas maletas.
5. Mariana espera que todas sus vacaciones...
   a. sean muy largas. b. tengan sorpresas agradables. c. incluyan viajes a México.

B ¿Qué vieron? Escriba **sí** en el espacio si Luis y Mariana vieron las siguientes cosas.

1. ___ una bandera *(flag)* enorme
2. ___ arquitectura española
3. ___ caballos *(horses)*
4. ___ el centro cívico
5. ___ jardines bonitos
6. ___ plantas exóticas
7. ___ restaurantes
8. ___ plazas bonitas
9. ___ estatuas de personas famosas
10. ___ el Instituto de Cultura
11. ___ tiendas
12. ___ barcos

C En parejas, supongan *(suppose)* que Luis y Mariana van a pasar un día en la ciudad donde Ud. vive. ¿Qué ven y qué hacen? Escriba una lista con seis actividades.

Vocabulario

Verbos

acordarse (ue) de	*to remember*
alojarse	*to stay, lodge*
cobrar	*to charge (money)*
(des)empacar	*to (un)pack*
firmar	*to sign*
funcionar	*to function, work*
nadar	*to swim*
permanecer (zc)	*to stay, remain*
prender	*to turn on*
relajarse	*to relax*
tomar el sol	*to sunbathe*

En el hotel

el aire acondicionado	*air-conditioning*
el ascensor	*elevator*
el balcón	*balcony*
el botones	*bellboy*
el (la) criado(a)	*servant, maid*
el cheque de viajero	*traveler's check*
las gafas (de sol)	*(sun)glasses*
el (la) huésped(a)	*guest*
la lavandería	*laundry*
la llave	*key*
la pensión	*rooming-house*
la piscina (alberca, Méx.)	*swimming pool*
la playa	*beach*
el portero	*doorman*
la recepción	*reception desk*
el (la) recepcionista	*receptionist*
la tarjeta de crédito	*credit card*
la toalla	*towel*
el vestíbulo	*lobby*
la vista	*view*

Adjetivos (See page 369 for ordinal numbers)	
antiguo	*old, antique, former*
bello	*beautiful*
doble	*double*
extraño	*strange*
(inter)nacional	*(inter)national*
lujoso	*luxurious*
moderno	*modern*
nocturno	*related to the night*
sencillo	*easy, simple; single (ref. to room)*
silencioso	*silent*
tranquilo	*tranquil*

Otras palabras y expresiones	
abajo	*down, downstairs*
arriba	*up, upstairs*
el buzón	*mailbox*
el correo	*post office; mail*
dar a	*to face, look out onto*
echar una carta	*to mail a letter*
el itinerario	*itinerary*
el mar	*sea, ocean*
el museo	*museum*
la parada (de taxi, de autobús)	*(taxi, bus) stop*
el quiosco	*kiosk, newsstand*
el sello (timbre)	*stamp*
el sobre	*envelope*

Vocabulario adicional	
a la vez	*at the same time*
al lado de	*next to*
el aparato	*apparatus, machine*
el castillo	*castle*
el cepillo	*brush*
el champú	*shampoo*
la escalera (mecánica)	*stairway (escalator)*
Me da lo mismo (igual).	*It's all the same to me.*
la pasta dental	*toothpaste*
salvar	*to save (people)*
todavía	*still, not yet*
tradicional	*traditional*

Repasemos el vocabulario

A **¿Dónde y adónde?** Su profesor(a) va a leer una serie de profesiones. Escuche y diga dónde trabajan.

MODELO Profesor(a): el cocinero
Ud.: **El cocinero trabaja en la cocina.**

restaurante	vestíbulo	recepción	museo	habitación	oficina
1. ______	**2.** ______	**3.** ______	**4.** ______	**5.** ______	**6.** ______

Ahora, su profesor(a) va a leer una serie de actividades. Diga Ud. adónde va para hacerlas. Use frases completas, según el modelo.

MODELO Profesor(a): ¿Adónde va Ud. para buscar al botones?
Ud.: **Voy al vestíbulo para buscar al botones.**

playa	pensión	lavandería	museo	quiosco
correo	piscina	recepción	ascensor	parada
1. ______	**3.** ______	**5.** ______	**7.** ______	**9.** ______
2. ______	**4.** ______	**6.** ______	**8.** ______	**10.** ______

B **Lo puedo encontrar en el hotel.** Ud. se queda en el hotel y necesita muchas cosas. El hotel tiene de todo. ¿Qué necesita Ud....

MODELO ...si quiere saber qué sitios visitar y a qué hora?
Necesito el itinerario.

1. ...si quiere abrir la puerta de su habitación?
2. ...si tiene que echar una carta?
3. ...si quiere comprar cosas pero no trajo dinero?
4. ...si quiere ver bien en la playa?
5. ...si quiere ver la vista desde su cuarto?
6. ...si acaba de salir de la piscina?

C **¿Cuál no pertenece?** ¿Qué palabras no corresponden a los siguientes lugares? Explique.

1. piscina:	gafas de sol	agua	toalla	ascensor
2. correo:	sellos	parada	tarjeta postal	buzón
3. habitación:	timbres	cama	toallas	balcón
4. vestíbulo:	recepcionista	botones	portero	playa

The Present Subjunctive in Adjective Clauses to Express the Indefinite and Nonexistent

The subjunctive is generally used in the subordinate clause when the verb in the main clause requires its use by expressing conjecture, uncertainty, emotion, subjectivity, doubt, probability, desire, or influence. You have studied the subjunctive in noun clauses, that is, clauses that act as nouns and serve as the direct object of the verb in the main clause.

The subjunctive is also used in adjective clauses. These are clauses that act as adjectives and modify a noun in the main clause.

Me quedo en	un hotel	lujoso.	*I'm staying in a*	*luxurious*	*hotel.*
	noun	**adjective**		**adjective**	**noun**
Me quedo en	un hotel	que es lujoso.	*I'm staying in a*	*hotel*	*that is luxurious.*
	noun	**adjective clause**		**noun**	**adjective clause**

In the preceding sentence, the entire clause (**que es lujoso** = *that is luxurious*) modifies the noun (**hotel** = *hotel*) in the main clause. The indicative is used in this example because the hotel is a definite, concrete object that exists, since I am staying there. Compare the following examples.

EL SUBJUNTIVO

Quiero quedarme en un hotel que **sea** lujoso.	*I want to stay in a hotel that* ***is*** *luxurious.*
Busco un hotel que **sea** lujoso.	*I am looking for a hotel that* ***is*** *luxurious.*
¿Hay un hotel que **sea** lujoso?	*Is there a hotel that* ***is*** *luxurious?*
No hay ningún hotel que **sea** lujoso.	*There is no hotel that* ***is*** *luxurious.*

EL INDICATIVO

Me quedo en un hotel que **es** lujoso.	*I'm staying in a hotel that* ***is*** *luxurious.*
Encontré un hotel que **es** lujoso.	*I found a hotel that* ***is*** *luxurious.*
Hay un hotel que **es** lujoso.	*There is a hotel that* ***is*** *luxurious.*
Hay muchos hoteles que **son** lujosos.	*There are many hotels that* ***are*** *luxurious.*

In the first set of sentences, the speaker either does not know that a luxury hotel exists, or thinks that it is nonexistent. In the second set of sentences the speaker is certain that a luxury hotel exists. What conclusions can you draw about the use of the subjunctive in adjective clauses?

Función

1. The subjunctive is used in the subordinate adjective clause when the antecedent (the noun or pronoun in the main clause that is modified by the adjective clause) is:

a. negative and therefore does not exist. You cannot assign the indicative mood since it reflects that which is concrete and definite.

No hay ningún cuarto que **tenga** vista al mar.	***There is no*** *room that* ***has*** *a view of the sea.*
No conozco a nadie que **tenga** un cuarto con vista al mar.	***I don't know anyone*** *who* ***has*** *a room with a view of the sea.*

b. indefinite. The speaker is not certain of its existence.

¿Hay un cuarto que **tenga** vista al mar?	***Is there*** *a room that* ***has*** *a view of the sea?*
Busco un cuarto que **tenga** vista al mar.	***I'm looking for*** *a room that* ***has*** *a view of the sea.*

2. The personal **a** is not used when the antecedent is indefinite. It is used with **alguien** and **nadie.**

Necesito una criada que **pueda** limpiar el cuarto ahora.	***I need a maid*** *who* ***can*** *clean the room now.*
Necesito a la criada que **limpia** el cuarto todos los días.	***I need the maid*** *who* ***cleans*** *the room every day.*
Necesito a alguien que **pueda** limpiar el cuarto.	***I need someone*** *who* ***can*** *clean the room.*

Practiquemos

A **Ud. tiene correo.** Ud. es el(la) gerente de un hotel y recibe una carta por correo electrónico de un cliente que quiere información sobre su hotel. Llene los espacios con la forma correcta del verbo en el subjuntivo para saber qué tipo de hotel quiere el cliente.

Estimado gerente:

Busco un hotel que (ofrecer) ______ las siguientes comodidades.

Quiero una cama que (ser) ______ grande y cómoda. Necesito un teléfono que (tener) ______ tres líneas diferentes. Prefiero una habitación que (dar) ______ a la calle. Quiero un balcón que (estar) ______ limpio porque me gusta desayunar allí. Necesito un criado que (poder) ______ ayudarme a desempacar y necesito un botones que (subir) ______ mi equipaje con mucho cuidado. Necesito un restaurante que (servir) ______ comida vegetariana y un quiosco que (vender) ______ periódicos de toda Latinoamérica .

Atentamente,

Sr. Juan Carlos Exigente

Ahora, conteste la carta del Sr. Exigente, diciéndole cuáles son las comodidades que tiene y no tiene su hotel.

B **Lo que tenemos y lo que queremos.** Cuando viajan, los García nunca están contentos. Llene Ud. los espacios con la forma apropiada del verbo entre paréntesis en el indicativo o en el subjuntivo.

1. Tenemos reservaciones en un hotel que (tener) ______ tres estrellas *(stars)* pero queremos hacer reservaciones en un hotel que (tener) ______ cinco estrellas.
2. Nos quedamos en un hotel que (ser) ______ muy antiguo pero queremos quedarnos en un hotel que (ser) ______ muy moderno.
3. Tenemos un cuarto que (dar) ______ a la piscina pero queremos un cuarto que (dar) ______ a la playa.

4. Nos alojamos en el hotel que (estar) ______ al lado de un museo pero queremos alojarnos en un hotel que (estar) ______ cerca de un castillo.
5. El restaurante en nuestro hotel (servir) ______ comida nacional pero buscamos un restaurante que (servir) ______ comida internacional.
6. Tenemos aire acondicionado que (hacer) ______ mucho ruido pero queremos aire acondicionado que no (hacer) ______ ruido.

C **Comprando en México.** Las siguientes personas están en México y quieren comprar objetos de artesanía *(crafts)* local. Un mexicano les dice dónde están los mejores sitios. Llene Ud. los espacios con la forma apropiada del verbo entre paréntesis en el subjuntivo. Con un(a) compañero(a), hagan los papeles *(roles)* de los turistas y del mexicano.

MODELO Estudiante 1: Quiero comprar un libro que (tener) **tenga** información sobre la artesanía.
Estudiante 2: Yo sugiero que Ud. (ir) **vaya** a una librería en Taxco.

1. Quiero unos aretes de plata que no (ser) ______ muy caros.
   Recomiendo que Ud. (ir) ______ a Taxco.
2. Buscamos una tienda que (vender) ______ productos de cuero.
   Sugiero que Uds. (comprarlos) ______ en la capital.
3. ¿Dónde encuentro cestos *(baskets)* que yo (poder) ______ usar para frutas y verduras?
   Aconsejo que Ud. (buscarlos) ______ en cualquier mercado popular.
4. ¿Conoce Ud. a un artesano que (hacer) ______ vasos de cerámica?
   Sí, recomiendo que Uds. (viajar) ______ a Guadalajara.
5. ¿Quién conoce un almacén que (tener) ______ ropa regional para niños?
   Yo, sí. Es necesario que Uds. (tomar) ______ el autobús para ir al centro de la ciudad.
6. Deseo comprar cristalería que ninguno de mis amigos (tener) ______.
   Pues, es importante que Ud. (visitar) ______ los talleres de cristalería en Guadalajara.

D **Un turista que exagera.** En los grupos de turistas, siempre hay uno que exagera mucho. Un(a) compañero(a) va a hacer el papel del turista que exagera. Dígale que Ud. no le cree. Use la frase **No hay ningún...**

MODELO Turista: Nuestro guía habla doce idiomas perfectamente.
Ud.: **No hay ningún guía que hable doce idiomas perfectamente.**

1. El hotel tiene veinte piscinas.
2. Mi cuarto cuesta diez dólares por noche.
3. El cocinero sabe cocinar mejor que Julia Child.
4. El criado limpia el cuarto cinco veces al día.
5. El quiosco vende revistas de todos los países del mundo.
6. El restaurante sirve tres postres gratis con cada comida.

E **Un hotel de lujo.** Lea Ud. el siguiente anuncio. Ud. es el (la) agente de viajes. Intente explicarle a un cliente que ningún hotel le ofrece los servicios que busca. Luego, basándose en el anuncio, dígale qué ofrece el Hotel Inter-Continental.

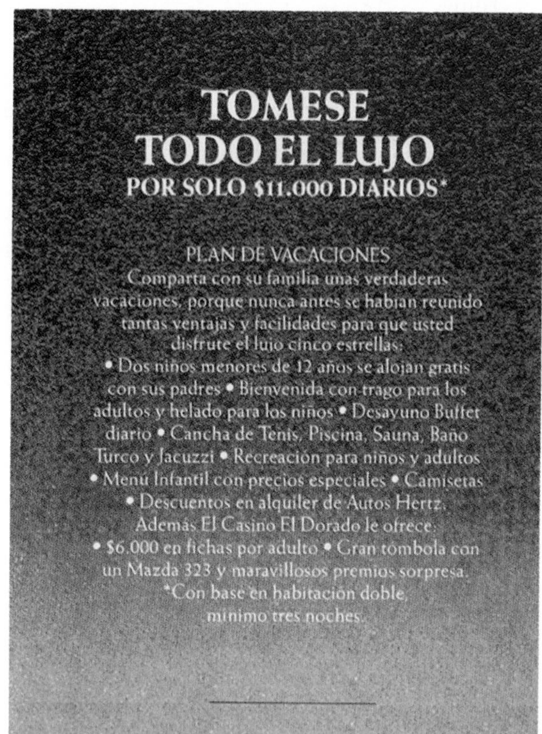

MODELO

Cliente: ¿Hay un hotel que (vender) **venda** sombreros especiales?
Agente: No, pero el Hotel Inter-continental (vender) **vende** camisetas.

1. ¿Hay un hotel que (tener) ______ cuatro canchas *(courts)* de tenis?
2. ¿Hay un hotel que (servir) ______ un almuerzo buffet diario?
3. ¿Hay un hotel que (organizar) ______ recreación para la gente mayor.
4. ¿Hay un hotel que (dar) ______ descuentos *(discounts)* en alquiler de Autos Avis?
5. ¿Hay un hotel que (ofrecer) ______ alojamiento gratis para tres niños?
6. ¿Hay un hotel que (regalar) ______ 10.000 en fichas *(tokens)* para el casino?

Ordinal Numbers

Forma

Función

1. Ordinal numbers are adjectives and therefore agree in number and gender with the nouns they modify.

Los dos primeros[1] **días** de la semana son lunes y martes.	***The first two days** of the week are Monday and Tuesday.*
La sexta casa a la derecha es de José.	***The sixth house** on the right is José's.*

2. **Primero** and **tercero** drop the final **-o** before a masculine singular noun.

Nos gustó el **primer** pueblo que visitamos.	*We liked the **first** town we visited.*
Vive en el **tercer** edificio a la derecha.	*She lives in the **third** building on the right.*

[1]Note that unlike English, in Spanish the cardinal number precedes the ordinal number.

Practiquemos

A **¿En qué orden?** Diga Ud. el orden de los diez primeros meses del año.

MODELO **Enero es el primer mes del año.**

B **Los ordinales.** Llene Ud. los espacios con el número ordinal apropiado.

1. George Washington fue el ______ presidente de los EE.UU.
2. En los EE.UU., el jueves es el ______ día de la semana.
3. Siete es el ______ número.
4. Enero, febrero y marzo son los tres ______ meses del año.
5. Según la canción, el ______ día la Navidad *(Christmas)* mi novio me regaló cinco anillos de oro.
6. Si Ud. es «*junior*» en una universidad en los EE.UU. éste es su ______ año de estudios.
7. El ______ mes del año es octubre.
8. La ______ comida del día es el almuerzo.

C **Una gira turística por México.** Lea Ud. «Una gira turística por México» en las páginas 380–382 de la *Gaceta 4*. Las siguientes personas piensan visitar México. En su opinión, ¿cuál es el primero, el segundo y el tercer lugar que deben visitar y por qué?

Comparatives and Superlatives

Forma

Comparatives allow you to compare equal and unequal degrees of qualities and characteristics.

Comparando adjetivos y adverbios

Inequality:	verb	+	**más (menos)**	+	adjective or adverb	+	**que**
Equality:	verb	+	**tan**	+	adjective or adverb	+	**como**

Función

1. Comparisons of unequal degrees in English are usually formed by adding **-er** to the end of an adjective or adverb to compare greater degrees, or by placing the word *less* before an adjective or adverb to compare lesser degrees. The word *than* is used in both comparisons.

   *Rosa is smart**er** **than** María but **less** creative **than** she.*

   *María drives fast**er** **than** Rosa.*

   In Spanish the words **más** *(more)* or **menos** *(less)* + **que** are used.

   Rosa es **más** inteligente **que** María pero **menos** creativa **que** ella.

   María conduce **más** rápidamente **que** Rosa.

2. Comparisons of equality in English are usually expressed with the construction *verb + as + adjective* or *adverb + as.*

   *Rosa is **as smart as** María.*

   *María drives **as fast as** Rosa.*

   In Spanish, the words **tan** *(as)* + **como** *(as)* are used.

   Rosa es **tan** inteligente **como** María.

   María conduce **tan** rápidamente **como** Rosa.

3. Certain comparative forms are irregular in Spanish.

bueno (adjective) *good*	**mejor** (adjective) *better*
bien (adverb) *well*	**mejor** (adverb) *better*
malo (adjective) *bad*	**peor** (adjective) *worse*
mal (adverb) *badly*	**peor** (adverb) *worse*
viejo (adjective) *old*	**mayor** (adjective) *older*[1]
joven (adjective) *young*	**menor** (adjective) *younger*[1]

   Yo bailo **mal** pero tú bailas **peor** que yo. — *I dance **poorly** but you dance **worse** than I.*

   Susana es **mayor** que yo. — *Susana is **older** than I.*

4. Superlatives express the highest or lowest degree of a comparison of more than two things. In English, superlatives are formed by adding the suffix **-est** to an adjective: *tallest, happiest, brightest,* and so forth. In Spanish the following construction is used:

   definite article + (noun) + **más (menos)** + adjective + **de**[2]

   María es **la estudiante más inteligente de** la clase. — *María is **the smartest student in** the class.*

   ¡AVISO! Note that the use of the noun is optional. It is correct to use the definite article when the subject is understood: **María es <u>la</u> más inteligente de la clase.**

[1]**Mayor** and **menor** are not used with inanimate objects.
[2]To form the superlative of adverbs use the following construction: *verb* + **lo** + **más (menos)** + *adverb* + **de. Él corre lo más rápidamente de todos** *(He runs the fastest of all).*

5. Certain superlative forms are irregular in Spanish.[1]

mejor *best*	**peor** *worst*	**mayor** *oldest*	**menor** *youngest*

Ellos son **los mayores de** todos sus amigos. — *They are **the oldest of** all their friends.*

Forma

Comparando sustantivos

Inequality:	verb	+	**más (menos)**	+	noun	+	**que**
Equality:	verb	+	**tanto(a, os, as)**	+	noun	+	**como**

Función

1. To compare nouns of inequality, place **más** or **menos** before the noun and **que** after the noun.

   Yo compré **más (menos)** recuerdos **que** tú. — *I bought **more (fewer)** souvenirs **than** you.*

2. To compare nouns of equality place a form of **tanto** before the noun and **como** after the noun. **Tanto** is an adjective and therefore agrees in number and gender with the noun it modifies.

   Irma compró **tantos** recuerdos **como** yo. — *Irma bought **as many** souvenirs **as** I.*

   Tú compraste **tantas** tarjetas postales **como** ella. — *You bought **as many** postcards **as** she.*

3. **De** is used with **más** or **menos** before a number.

   Leí **más de** diez libros durante el viaje. — *I read **more than** ten books during the trip.*

[1]Note that these are identical to the irregular comparative forms.

Practiquemos

A **Comparaciones.** Use Ud. los adjetivos para hacer dos comparaciones de las personas siguientes.

MODELO Susana va a muchas fiestas. Iris se queda en casa. (popular)
Susana es más popular que Iris.
Iris es menos popular que Susana.

1. Emilio recibió una A en la prueba. Oscar recibió una D. (aplicado)
2. Cristián siempre le da flores a su novia. Héctor olvida el cumpleaños de su novia. (romántico)
3. Ignacio escribe poesía y lee filosofía. Manuel baila la lambada. (serio)
4. Ramona juega al tenis, al golf y al béisbol. Felipe mira la tele. (atlético)
5. Amalia viaja a lugares exóticos. Rodolfo nunca viaja. (interesante)

B **Falso.** Corrija Ud. los errores de su amigo acerca de México usando **más de** o **menos de** y la información correcta entre paréntesis.

MODELO Hay sólo un famoso muralista mexicano, Diego Rivera. (David Siqueiros, José Clemente Orozco).
No tienes razón. Hay más de un famoso muralista mexicano.

1. México tiene 30 estados *(states)*. (32)
2. La Ciudad de México tiene 10 millones de habitantes. (17 millones)
3. Un 50 por ciento de los mexicanos trabajan en los campos. (30 por ciento)
4. Sólo hay un volcán *(volcano)* principal. Se llama Paricutín. (muchos)
5. En México un 50 por ciento de la gente tiene coche. (20 por ciento)
6. Hay una bebida tradicional, el tequila. (mezcal, atole, tepache, etc.)

C **En la estación de ferrocarriles.** Compare Ud. a las personas y las cosas en el dibujo.

MODELO **El padre es más gordo que la madre.**

D **Idénticos.** Su profesor(a) va a leer una serie de descripciones. Compare los adverbios según el modelo.

MODELO bien
Profesor(a): Eduardo baila bien y Pilar también.
Ud.: **Pilar baila tan bien como Eduardo.**

1. tarde **2.** temprano **3.** rápido **4.** mal **5.** lento

E **Todo igual *(equal)*.** Miguel no quiere que su hermano tenga más que él. Su madre le dice que todo es igual. Con un(a) compañero(a), hagan los papeles *(roles)* de Miguel y mamá y formen comparaciones según el modelo.

MODELO Miguel: Mamá, ¿come José más papitas que yo?
Mamá: **No, hijo. José come tantas papitas como tú.**

1. ¿Tiene más chocolate que yo?
2. ¿Juega con más juguetes que yo?
3. ¿Recibe más regalos que yo?
4. ¿Va a más fiestas que yo?
5. ¿Invita a más amigos que yo?
6. ¿Mira más programas de televisión que yo?

F **Gemelas *(Twins)*.** Inés y Carmela son gemelas. Sus posesiones son idénticas y hacen las mismas actividades. Forme Ud. comparaciones de igualdad *(equality)* según el modelo.

Inés lee tantos libros como Carmela.

1.

2.

3.

4.

5.

6.

Spend more time with Mariana and her friends while you review grammar and expand your cultural horizons.

See the **Así es Mariana** exercise in your workbook for this lesson.

En resumen

A **Las artesanías de Yucatán.** Complete Ud. la lectura con la forma correcta del verbo entre paréntesis. Si hay dos palabras, escoja la más apropiada.

Si Ud. (es, está) en Yucatán y busca un recuerdo que (ser) único, recomendamos que (ir) a un mercado mexicano y (comprar) ropa. (El, La) tradición de hacer y exportar ropa (venir) de la época de los indios aztecas. (Esta, Este) región es famosa (por, para) las guayaberas (vea la p. 299) y el huipil, que (es, está) una camisa (blanco/blanca) de algodón, bordada *(embroidered)* con muchos colores. También (es, hay) una (grande, gran) variedad de sombreros. No (irse) Ud. de Yucatán sin conseguir una «jipijapa», un sombrero muy cómodo y flexible. Aconsejamos que Ud. (comprar) muchos para regalarles a sus amigos. Es cierto que les (ir) a gustar.

Oaxaca, México

B **Un hotel ideal.** El Hotel Sol Azteca ofrece todo... hasta un abrelatas *(can opener)* para el cliente que quiere abrir una lata de atún. Combine Ud. las palabras de las dos columnas para formar palabras compuestas *(compound)*. Después, conteste las preguntas que siguen.

1. abre-	**a.** vidas
2. para-	**b.** corchos *(corks)*
3. saca-	**c.** sol
4. par(a)-	**d.** cartas
5. salva-	**e.** latas
6. abre-	**f.** aguas

Ahora, ¿qué necesita el cliente que quiere...

1. abrir una botella de vino?
2. leer una carta?
3. ir a la piscina pero no sabe nadar *(to swim)*?
4. pasearse cuando hace mucho sol?
5. comer sopa en lata?
6. salir a la calle cuando llueve mucho?

C **La civilización de los mayas.** Los mayas vivieron en México y Centroamérica durante mil años y tuvieron una de las culturas más importantes de América. Lea Ud. la lectura y cambie los verbos entre paréntesis al pretérito o imperfecto. Haga las actividades.

La cultura maya ya (existir) ______ mucho antes de llegar Cristóbal Colón. La arquitectura de los mayas es impresionante, con sus palacios *(palaces)*, pirámides *(pyramids)* y templos enormes. (Ser-ellos) ______ expertos en la astronomía. (Construir-ellos) ______ grandes observatorios con sus ventanas perfectamente orientadas *(facing)* hacia *(towards)* el sol y los planetas. Su calendario (tener) ______ un margen de error de sólo dos segundos mientras que en nuestro calendario el margen de error es de seis horas. Los mayas (practicar) ______ un sistema político muy sofisticado y (ser) ______ excelentes agricultores. (Usar-ellos) ______ el cero antes de las otras civilizaciones de su época. Su religión (ser) ______ mística y politeísta *(polytheist)*. (Desaparecer-ellos) ______ misteriosamente en el siglo *(century)* X. Cuando los españoles (llegar) ______, no había mucha evidencia de su existencia. Hoy todavía hay descendientes de esa gran civilización que preservan sus costumbres y su idioma. Algunos testimonios de su arquitectura y cultura son los sitios arqueológicos de Chichén Itzá, Uxmal (pronunciado «Ushmal»), Tulúm, Cobá y Palenque.

1. Basándose en la lectura *(reading)*, diga Ud. cómo sabe que los mayas...
   a. sabían medir *(measure)* el tiempo.
   b. tenían interés en la astronomía.
   c. usaban las matemáticas.
   d. creían en más de un dios *(god)*.
2. Basándose en la lectura diga cómo sabe que existía la antigua civilización maya. Ud. puede leer sobre otra gran civilización india, los aztecas, en la *Gaceta 4* en la página 383.

El templo de Kukulkán, Chichén Itzá, México

D **¿Qué hacemos?** Traduzca el siguiente diálogo al español.

Mónica: I can't believe it . . . two tranquil weeks in a luxurious hotel in Acapulco? What'll we do?

Luis: Go to the beach? Buy stamps? Unpack?

Mónica: I want to have dinner in a restaurant that serves fresh fish.

Luis: Fine, but first let's look for a kiosk that sells international newspapers.

Mónica: The receptionist told me that the hotel has as many newspapers as the kiosk.

E **Minidrama.** En grupos, representen una de las siguientes escenas.

1. Uds. son viajeros. Llegan a su destino muy cansados y sólo quieren pasar unas vacaciones tranquilas en su hotel de lujo. Pero, descubren que este «hotel de lujo» no es como la descripción en el folleto turístico.
2. Uds. son turistas «típicos», de los estereotipos... los que viajan al extranjero y esperan que todo sea igual que en su propio país. Representen una escena en un hotel en México.

F **Composición.**

1. Ud. es un(a) viajero(a) muy difícil de complacer *(please)*. Quiere que todo sea perfecto. Escríbale una carta al gerente de un hotel donde piensa quedarse durante un viaje. Pregúntele sobre los servicios que ofrece el hotel como piscina, restaurantes y otros aspectos.
2. Su estancia *(stay)* en un hotel muy caro y lujoso fue una experiencia horrible. Escríbale una carta al gerente del hotel, contándole todos los problemas y explicando por qué Ud. quiere que le devuelva su dinero.

Escuchemos

A **¿Qué hace Marcos?** You will hear a series of sentences that tell you what Marcos is doing. Repeat each one, and then decide if the corresponding drawing matches the description. Write **cierto** or **falso** in the space below each example.

MODELO Marcos pasa una noche tranquila en su habitación.
Falso

1.

2.

3.

4.

5.

6.

7.

8.

B **Dictado.** You will hear a short narration about Susan's hotel preferences. Listen carefully to the entire selection. Listen again and write each sentence during the pauses.

You will then hear a series of questions related to the dictation. Answer them with complete sentences. Refer to your dictation.

Gaceta 4 México y los mexicoamericanos

Mérida, México Guadalajara, México

Una gira turística por México

Preparativos: Estrategias de prelectura

1. Before taking your tour of Mexico, look at the **Es decir** section to help you anticipate the content of the text you are about to read. What thoughts about Mexico do the words **plata, arqueológico** and **vacaciones** evoke?
2. Hojee Ud. *(Scan)* la lectura para saber a qué se refieren los números y las expresiones siguientes:
   a. los números: 99.000.000, 2.280, 11.000, 800, 6.000.000.
   b. las expresiones: «México de los mexicanos» y «ciudad blanca».
3. Hojee la lectura para encontrar:
   a. un sustantivo en el primer párrafo que significa «un artista que pinta murales».
   b. un sustantivo en el último párrafo que expresa que México es un lugar popular para pasar las vacaciones.

México es una república con 31 estados° libres y un distrito federal, y tiene una población de casi 99.000.000 de personas. La Ciudad de México, con 2.280 metros de altitud, es la capital del país y la ciudad más grande del mundo hispano. El Palacio de Bellas Artes° contiene la famosa cortina de vidrio° de Tiffany y obras° de tres grandes muralistas mexicanos: José Clemente Orozco, Diego Rivera y David Alfaro Siqueiros. En el Parque° de

states

Fine Arts; glass
works
Park

Emperor

Chapultepec hay un zoológico y está el Castillo de Chapultepec, que fue la antigua residencia del Emperador° Maximiliano.[1] Hoy allí se encuentra el Museo Nacional de Historia. También en este parque está el Museo de Antropología con artículos de 11.000 sitios arqueológicos de México.

El Palacio de Bellas Artes, México, D.F.

pyramids
centuries
businesses
silversmith trade

Desde la capital se pueden hacer muchas excursiones de un día. En San Juan, Teotihuacán, a 48 kilómetros al norte, las pirámides° y ruinas datan de los primeros siglos° de la época cristiana. En Cuernavaca, la ciudad favorita de Maximiliano y Carlota, hay mansiones, calles típicas y jardines hermosos. El Palacio de Cortés tiene un fresco impresionante de Diego Rivera. Al sur de Cuernavaca está Taxco. Con su fabulosa arquitectura colonial y los 800 comercios° dedicados a la platería,° es un centro turístico muy popular.

Mexican cowboy
typical dance
charm
climate

Guadalajara, la ciudad del charro,° de la música de mariachi y del jarabe tapatío,° es la segunda ciudad del país. Es el «México de los mexicanos» porque tiene el encanto° y las tradiciones de su pasado colonial y también un ambiente cosmopolita con museos, tiendas y plazas elegantes. Tiene más de 6.000.000 de habitantes y el mejor clima° de Norteamérica.

Mayan
lost; jungle

Mérida es la «ciudad blanca» de México, la capital de Yucatán y un centro importante de la antigua civilización maya.° Desde allí hay excursiones a famosos sitios arqueológicos tales como Uxmal, Kabah, Chichén Itzá y las misteriosas ciudades perdidas° de la selva° de Yucatán.

bay; surrounded; mountains
water

¿Quién no conoce las magníficas playas de México? En una bahía° del Pacífico, rodeada° de montañas° está Acapulco, una de las playas más famosas del país. Los deportes acuáticos,° la intensa

[1]El francés Maximiliano de Habsburgo, con su esposa Carlota, gobernó México desde 1864 hasta 1867 cuando fue ejecutado por las fuerzas *(forces)* de Benito Juárez.

vida nocturna° y los clavadistas° de La Quebrada son sólo algunos de los atractivos de este paraíso.° Otro sitio muy bonito en el Pacífico es Puerto Vallarta, donde se puede apreciar un pueblo antiguo mexicano de pescadores.° En el Caribe hay importantes centros turísticos como Cancún y las islas° preciosas de Cozumel e Isla Mujeres. El clima, la abundancia de flores y frutas tropicales, los paisajes° fabulosos y la hospitalidad de la gente hacen de México un lugar ideal para pasar las vacaciones.

night; high divers
paradise
fishermen
islands
scenery

Es decir

A Conteste Ud.

1. ¿Cuántos habitantes tiene México?
2. ¿Quién es Diego Rivera?
3. ¿Dónde venden objetos de plata?
4. ¿Qué ciudad está cerca de la capital?
5. ¿Cuántos sitios arqueológicos hay en México?

B Nombre Ud....

1. cinco razones por las que muchas personas pasan sus vacaciones en México.
2. cuatro hechos *(facts)* referentes a la capital.
3. tres adjetivos que describen el país de México.
4. dos preguntas que Ud. quiere hacerle a una persona que acaba de volver de México.
5. un aspecto de México que Ud. quiere investigar.

La pirámide del Sol, Teotihuacán, México

Practiquemos

A **La civilización azteca.** Para aprender sobre la antigua civilización azteca, lea Ud. la siguiente lectura y conteste las preguntas.

Se cree que los aztecas, una tribu° de cazadores° y agricultores,° dejaron su tierra de Aztlán en el norte de México en 1168 y llegaron al Valle° de México en el año 1348. Conquistaron las tribus que vivían allí, construyeron su capital en Tenochtitlán y eligieron a Moctezuma I como jefe supremo. Para el siglo° XV, los aztecas eran muy poderosos° y su imperio° se extendía hasta el Pacífico.

La base de su economía era el cultivo° de maíz, frijol, cacao y algodón. De los indios toltecas aprendieron el arte de hacer ornamentos de oro. Interpretaban los astros,° calcularon el calendario, escribían poesía, tocaban música y construyeron grandes templos religiosos. Su escritura° era jeroglífica, y dos de sus dioses° fueron Quetzalcoatl y Tláloc. Creían que tenían que alimentar° a sus dioses con sangre° humana, especialmente al dios de la guerra,° Huitzilopochtli.

En el año 1519, el conquistador español Hernán Cortés llegó a México y, con la ayuda de las tribus enemigas,° destruyó por completo al imperio azteca.

tribe; hunters; farmers
valley
century
powerful; empire
cultivation
stars
writing; gods
feed; blood
war
enemy

1. ¿De dónde vinieron los aztecas?
2. ¿Cómo se llamaba su jefe?
3. ¿En qué estaba basada su economía?
4. ¿Cuáles son algunos aspectos culturales de la civilización azteca?
5. ¿Qué hacían los aztecas para satisfacer *(satisfy)* a sus dioses?
6. ¿Por cuántos años vivieron los indios aztecas en el Valle de México?

B **El origen de las piñatas.** A muchos turistas les gusta comprar piñatas en México. Para aprender sobre el origen de las piñatas, lea Ud. la siguiente lectura y haga el ejercicio.

Carmen Lomas Garza, «Cumpleaños de Lala y Tudi»

La historia de la piñata empezó en el siglo° XIII cuando el marinero Marco Polo volvió de un viaje a Asia y presentó las piñatas en la corte° italiana. Los cortesanos° iniciaron° la costumbre de romper las piñatas en sus fiestas elegantes. Sus piñatas no tenían frutas, juguetes ni bombones, sino monedas° de oro y piedras preciosas.° Las piñatas pasaron a España y formaron parte de las tradiciones religiosas de la Cuaresma.° Cuando llegaron a América con los conquistadores y colonizadores españoles se hicieron° parte importante de la celebración de la Navidad.° Hay piñatas multicolores en todos los mercados de México. La piñata clásica es la estrella° de papel plateado,° pero hoy día hay piñatas para todos los gustos—de flores, de aviones, de todo tipo de animales y de los héroes infantiles como Batman, Superman y las tortugas° Ninja.

century

court; courtesans; initiated

coins

precious stones

Lent

became

Christmas

star; silvery

turtles

Las siguientes frases son falsas. Corríjalas con frases completas.

1. En Italia la gente pobre rompía piñatas en sus fiestas.
2. Solamente en España las piñatas eran parte de las celebraciones religiosas.
3. La piñata llegó a América en el siglo XII.
4. La piñata más tradicional es la flor.
5. Para comprar una piñata en México hay que ir a una tienda elegante.

Carlos Fuentes

Luis Miguel

Thalía

Caras en las noticias

El historiador,°[1] diplomático, profesor y crítico literario, **Carlos Fuentes** es el novelista más famoso de México y uno de los autores más prolíficos de Latinoamérica. Nació en 1928 en México. De niño viajó mucho y así° conoció la gran diversidad cultural. La policultura y su impacto en la vida° norteamericana es un tema° común en sus conferencias. El autor cree que esta variedad cultural es algo muy positivo, y dice que todos deben aprender a vivir en un contexto multirracial.

historian
in this way
life; theme

Fuentes fue embajador° de México en Francia y profesor de literatura en las Universidades de Harvard y Oxford. Escribió *La región más transparente, Aura, Zona sagrada,°* y por su novela *La muerte de Artemio Cruz*, lo comparan con William Faulkner. Generalmente, sus novelas tratan temas mexicanos, pero su última novela, *La campaña,°* es sobre la independencia de Argentina.

ambassador
sacred
campaign

El presidente de la república mexicana, **Dr. Ernesto Zedillo Ponce de León** continúa el Tratado de Libre Comercio, o TLC *(North American Free Trade Agreement* [NAFTA]*)* con Canadá y los Estados Unidos.

Las principales fuentes económicas del país son la agricultura, la pesca,° la manufactura, y los diferentes servicios al consumidor, incluyendo el turismo.

fishing

No hay duda del por qué México continúa siendo un país muy atractivo para los inversionistas° extranjeros, quienes comentan que este país ofrece grandes oportunidades. Se espera que la economía del país siga aumentando,° creando nuevas oportunidades de trabajo.

investors
growing

La talentosa joven mexicana **Thalía** se sigue abriendo paso internacional. Su último disco llamado «En éxtasis» lo produjo Emilio Estefan. Con sus varias telenovelas° y discos su nombre poco a poco se escucha más en otros países fuera de México.

soap operas

[1]En honor del V Centenario, Carlos Fuentes escribió y presentó una serie para la BBC que se llama, *El espejo enterrado (The Broken Mirror): reflexiones sobre España y el Nuevo Mundo.*

Lo llaman enigmático, arrogante, evasivo, negativo, perfeccionista... y el encantador e «indiscutible monarca musical de México». **Luis Miguel**, cantante inigualado° de baladas y boleros, llegó al puesto número 14 en las listas musicales de los Estados Unidos con su álbum *Romances*, un logro° nunca realizado por ningún otro artista latino. Lo critican porque le gusta hacer las cosas a su manera, se niega a° hablar de su pasado y de su vida privada y prefiere manejar su carrera él mismo. A pesar de todos estos «defectos», los cuales Luis Miguel mismo admite tener, sigue siendo el ídolo de sus fanáticos. El mundo está esperando que cante en inglés, pero Luis Miguel no está seguro de que, por ahora, sea una buena idea.

unequaled

achievement

refuses

Es decir

¿Comprendió Ud.? Basándose en la lectura y en sus propias *(own)* palabras explique Ud. por qué...

1. Carlos Fuentes puede comprender y apreciar a personas de otras culturas.
2. México ofrece buenas oportunidades para inversionistas.
3. Luis Miguel es un enigma.

Practiquemos

Más figuras famosas. Para saber algo de Octavio Paz, Linda Ronstadt y Edward James Olmos, arregle Ud. las siguientes frases de cada grupo para formar párrafos lógicos.

Octavio Paz, escritor mexicano

Publicó su primer libro de poemas cuando tenía 19 años.

Otra gran figura de la literatura mexicana es el escritor *(writer)*, diplomático y filósofo Octavio Paz.

Paz murió en abril de 1998. El primer Premio Octavio Paz 1998 lo recibió el poeta chileno Gonzalo Rojas.

En 1990 recibió el Premio Nóbel de Literatura.

Cuando era joven, pasaba mucho tiempo en la biblioteca de su abuelo, y así empezó a interesarse *(to become interested)* en la literatura.

Linda Ronstadt, artista musical de origen mexicano

Su álbum *Frenesí* contiene música tropical y boleros, que son las canciones románticas que están muy de moda ahora.

Tiene una larga carrera cantando la música rock, disco, blues, nueva ola *(new wave)*, mexicana, pop y ópera.

Otro álbum es *Más canciones*, que canta con sus dos hermanos Mike y Pete.

Linda Ronstadt, la cantante norteamericana de origen mexicano, es una de las cantantes más versátiles de este país.

Edward James Olmos, actor chicano

Pero lo más importante es su orgullo de ser chicano y esto influye en todos los aspectos de su vida.

Este conocido actor ya tiene su estrella en la acera de Hollywood Boulevard además de muchos otros honores.

Aunque es un actor apasionado, el cine no es su única pasión. También le encanta el béisbol y cuando era joven, jugó como receptor en las ligas menores.

Por ejemplo, recibió el premio «Emmy» por su papel de Martín Castillo en la serie de televisión *Miami Vice*, una nominación al «Tony» por su participación en la obra teatral *Zoot Suit* y una nominación al «Oscar» en la categoría de Mejor Actor por la película *Stand and Deliver*.[1]

Edward James Olmos

[1]Otras películas de Edward James Olmos son *Blade Runner, The Ballad of Gregorio Cortez, Triumph of the Spirit, Talent for the Game* y *American Me*.

Notas y notables

El fenómeno de Frida Kahlo

Frida Kahlo

«Retrato de Luther Burbank» de Frida Kahlo

En los años setenta el interés en la obra° artística de Frida Kahlo renació° y Frida se hizo° un fenómeno. Veinte años más tarde la manía de Frida continúa. Venden sus cuadros por millones de dólares, publican su biografía[1] y hacen películas y obras de teatro° sobre su vida. Su popularidad viene de la originalidad de sus famosos autorretratos° y de su vida dura.° Para muchos, Frida Kahlo es un símbolo de la independencia y la liberación, y es la artista más celebrada de este siglo.°

De ascendencia° judía°europea, Frida nació en Coyoacán, México en 1910. A los seis años sufrió un ataque de poliomelitis, y a los 15 años tuvo un accidente terrible y quedó infértil y paralizada. Fue en esa época cuando empezó a pintar. A los 19 años se casó con el famoso artista Diego Rivera, ella por primera vez y él por tercera vez. El matrimonio fue complicado e inestable,° y le causó mucho sufrimiento.° Su dolor físico, sicológico y emocional está presente en la mayoría° de sus 200 cuadros. Según muchos críticos, la obra de Frida tiene las influencias del surrealismo porque combina los autorretratos con imágenes precolombinas y folklóricas. Sin embargo, Frida insistió en que no era surrealista sino° realista, y que estas imágenes eran «su propia realidad».

En honor a Frida, Diego Rivera le regaló a su país una casa extraordinaria. Hoy, la casa contiene el Museo Frida Kahlo, y está situada en Coyoacán, en las calles Allende y Londres. Se pueden ver los vestidos indígenas de Frida, sus cartas de amor y otros artículos personales, y de esta manera,° entrar un poco en la vida privada de Frida y Diego Rivera.

work
resurged; became
plays
self-portraits; difficult
century
ancestry; Jewish
unstable
suffering
majority
but rather
in this way

[1] *Frida Kahlo: An Open Life* de Raquel Tibol y *Frida Kahlo: Torment and Triumph in Her Life and Art* de Malka Drucker son dos biografías de la artista.

Los mexicoamericanos: Inmigrantes en su propia° tierra

own

En 1848, al terminar la Guerra Mexicoamericana, los Estados Unidos y México firmaron el Tratado de Guadalupe Hidalgo, y México perdió mucho de su país. California, Nevada y gran part de Nuevo México, Arizona y Utah pasaron a ser parte de los Estados Unidos por sólo 15 millones de dólares. El gobierno de los Estados Unidos les prometió a los 100.000 mexicanos que vivían en ese territorio sus derechos como ciudadanos norteamericanos y la preservación de su cultura y sus tierras. Pero las promesas° fueron falsas y estos primeros mexicoamericanos fueron explotados° y tratados como subordinados. Perdieron sus tierras, sus bienes° y sus derechos.°

promises
exploited
belongings
rights

En los años 40, para escaparse de la inestabilidad económica y política de su país, miles de mexicanos empezaron a trabajar en las minas, las fábricas y los campos norteamericanos. Irónicamente, estos «braceros»° se encontraron atrapados° en un ciclo de pobreza, sin salida y sin esperanza.° Hoy este ciclo continúa debido al° gran número de inmigrantes sin documentación que cruza la frontera entre México y los Estados Unidos en busca de un futuro mejor.

day laborers; trapped
hope; due to

El Legado° de César Chávez

¿Quién nos va a ayudar ahora? Ésta es la pregunta que se hacen muchos campesinos° chicanos° desde la muerte de César Chávez. Chávez, fundador° y presidente del Sindicato de Trabajadores Agrícolas o STA *(United Farm Workers of America, UFWA)*, murió el 23 de abril de 1993, y dejó un vacío° tremendo en el STA, y en la vida de muchas personas. Chávez dedicó toda su vida a la protección de los derechos° humanos del trabajador migratorio° y a la unificación política de la población chicana.

legacy

farmers; U.S. citizen of Mexican origin; founder

vacuum

rights; migrant

César Chávez

César Chávez nació en Arizona en 1927 y vivió allí hasta 1937, que fue cuando su familia perdió su finca° de 160 acres durante la Gran Crisis.° Tuvieron que viajar de pueblo en pueblo° buscando trabajo temporal. El joven César experimentó personalmente las condiciones miserables de los trabajadores migratorios: los salarios bajo el sueldo mínimo y la falta de casas, de beneficios médicos, de facilidades sanitarias y mucho más.

farm
Great Depression; town to town

En los años 50, Chávez empezó su trabajo de organizador sindical.° Para llamar la atención a su causa a nivel° nacional, sus estrategias° incluían el boicoteo° y la huelga de hambre.° Figuras famosas como Robert Kennedy, Rubén Blades y Edward James Olmos se unieron° a la causa y le dieron apoyo° a Chávez. En 1970, después de un boicoteo nacional de uvas, los rancheros firmaron un contrato con el sindicato. Sin embargo, para 1980 sólo uno de cada cinco campesinos recibía beneficios médicos y de trabajo.

union organizer
level; strategies
boycott; hunger strike
joined
support

En 1984, Chávez descubrió que un gran número de familias migratorias que trabajaban en regiones de California donde usaban ciertos pesticidas, contraía° cáncer. Empezó su nuevo boicoteo para impedir el uso de estos pesticidas. Chávez luchó° mucho por los campesinos chicanos y les consiguió mucho. Los miembros° del STA esperan que la gente no olvide el espíritu,° la dedicación y la generosidad de César Chávez y que siga luchando de la misma manera.

were getting
fought
members
spirit

El origen de «La Bamba»

Sólo el mundo hispano conocía la canción «La Bamba», hasta 1958, cuando un joven cantante chicano, Richard Valenzuela (Ritchie Valens) la hizo popular con los ritmos° de «rock and roll». Hoy, es muy probable que «La Bamba» sea la canción hispana más popular del mundo. El origen de la canción es interesante y está asociado con la ciudad mexicana de Veracruz.

En 1519, el español Hernán Cortés llegó a la costa° de México y empezó la colonización de Veracruz. En el siglo° XVII los españoles comenzaron a importar esclavos° africanos, y con ellos vinieron sus canciones y tradiciones. Según una teoría,° la canción y el baile «La Bamba» vinieron de Mbamba, un lugar en África. El baile se hizo muy popular en Veracruz y en los próximos° dos siglos llegó a conocerse° por todas partes del país.

ritmos: rhythms; costa: coast; siglo: century; esclavos: slaves; teoría: theory; próximos: next; llegó a conocerse: became known

Hay muchos versos de «La Bamba», pero el más famoso es:

Para bailar La Bamba
Para bailar La Bamba se necesita
una poca de gracia°
una poca de gracia y otra cosita°
ay arriba,° ay arriba.
Ay arriba, ay arriba, ay arriba iré°
Yo no soy marinero.°
Yo no soy marinero, por ti seré,°
por ti seré, por ti seré
(Una alternativa:
No soy marinero, soy capitán,
soy capitán, soy capitán)

gracia: grace; cosita: little thing; arriba: up; iré: I will go; marinero: seaman; por ti seré: for you I will be

¿Y qué significan los versos? Veracruz era un puerto° importante y allí siempre había marineros extranjeros que querían conocer a las mujeres de esa ciudad. Los hombres de Veracruz, compitiendo° por las atenciones de las mujeres, les cantaban a las mujeres «no soy marinero, pero por ti seré... o, mejor que marinero, soy capitán».

En los EE.UU., más de 150 artistas han grabado° «La Bamba»: Chuck Berry, Chubby Checker, The Mormon Tabernacle Choir, Harry Belafonte, Neil Diamond, Los Lobos y más. A algunos mexicanos no les gustan las versiones modernas o americanizadas. Dice Danny Valdez, asistente del productor de la película *La Bamba:* «Es como tocar un canto gregoriano en un sintetizador, pero prueba que la canción tiene vida y capacidad de trascender generaciones». Hay una versión que se llama «La Bamba Chicana» y dice así: «Para ser chicano se necesita un poquito de boicot».

puerto: port; compitiendo: competing; han grabado: have recorded

Es decir

¿Qué sabe Ud.? Diga Ud. por qué...

1. la vida y la obra artística de Frida Kahlo son tan populares.
2. muchos críticos creen que los cuadros de Frida Kahlo son surrealistas.
3. la canción «La Bamba» está asociada con África y con la ciudad mexicana de Veracruz.
4. muchas personas conocen la canción «La Bamba».
5. César Chávez conocía personalmente la vida del trabajador migratorio.
6. el trabajo de César Chávez debe continuar.
7. México era un país más grande antes de 1848.

Practiquemos

A El muralista *(muralist)* mexicano, Diego Rivera.[1] Para aprender algo sobre la vida y la carrera del artista Diego Rivera, complete Ud. la selección con el verbo apropiado de la lista. Hay varias posibilidades.

conoció	volvió	estudió	viajó	fue
murió	pintó	empezó	tuvo	

Diego Rivera, fundador *(founder)* del movimiento muralista mexicano, nació en 1886 en el pueblo *(town)* colonial de Guanajuato. La revolución de 1910 ______ mucha influencia en la vida del joven Rivera y despertó su patriotismo y su conciencia política. Rivera ______ por todo México y ______ los pueblos, los paisajes *(landscapes)*, el pasado precolombino y, lo más importante, la gente. A los 24 años ______ a París donde ______, ______ y ______ experimentar con otros estilos *(styles)* artísticos como el cubismo. ______ a México, y en el ambiente *(atmosphere)* de libertad y democracia, adornó *(he decorated)* la ciudad con murales que cuentan la historia del pueblo *(people)* mexicano. Rivera ______ en 1957, y le dejó a su país y al mundo miles de obras artísticas.

[1]José Clemente Orozco y David Alfaro Siqueiros son otros famosos muralistas mexicanos.

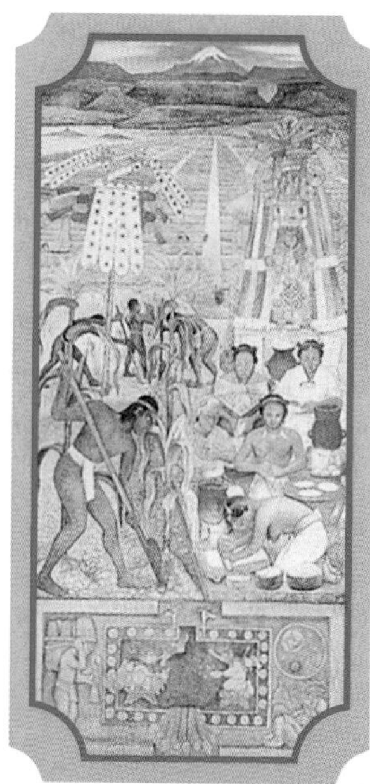

Un mural de Diego Rivera en el Palacio Nacional, México, D.F.

Ester Hernández, 1983

B **El arte chicano.** El siguiente cuadro *(painting)* forma parte de la exposición *(exhibition)* «Arte Chicano: Resistencia y Afirmación». Refleja *(It reflects)* con ironía los problemas que causan los pesticidas para la gente chicana. Mire Ud. el cuadro y conteste las preguntas. El siguiente vocabulario puede ayudar a contestar las preguntas.

esqueleto *skeleton* pasas *raisins* enojado *angry*

1. ¿Qué ve Ud. en este cuadro? Descríbalo.
2. ¿Cuál es el mensaje de este cuadro?

Enfoque literario

Una carta a Dios por Gregorio López y Fuentes

Preparativos: Estrategias de prelectura

Before reading the following segment from the story "Una carta a Dios" by the Mexican author Gregorio López Fuentes:

a. Scan the biographical information in the text (lines 1–4) and tell why the story poignantly and accurately depicts country life.
b. Scan lines 5–12 and list the main characters in the story.

Now read the last line of the story segment and tell what Lencho thought of the post office employees. After reading the segment and the background information, do you share Lencho's opinion?

Gregorio López y Fuentes (México, 1897–1966) creció en el campo de Veracruz donde se familiarizó con la vida agrícola,° un elemento importante en sus cuentos.° En el libro *Cuentos campesinos de México*, el autor escribió sobre las experiencias y las personalidades de su niñez.° Dice el autor: «No es un México perfecto ni un México ideal; es simplemente un México verídico°...». En el cuento «Una carta a Dios», hubo una gran tempestad° que destruyó todas las cosechas° de los campesinos del pueblo. Lencho, uno de los campesinos y un hombre de mucha fe,° le escribió una carta a Dios pidiéndole cien pesos.° Cuando el jefe de la oficina de correos vio la carta dirigida° a Dios, estuvo tan impresionado con la fe de ese hombre que reunió° sesenta pesos, se los puso en una carta dirigida a Lencho y firmó «Dios». Al día siguiente, Lencho volvió para ver si había una carta para él. Los empleados, escondidos° en la oficina, esperaban para ver su reacción.

agricultural; stories
childhood
real
storm
crops
faith
Mex. currency
destined for
gathered
hidden

Una carta a Dios (última parte, la reacción de Lencho)

Lencho no mostró la menor sorpresa° al ver° los billetes°—tanta° era su seguridad°—pero hizo un gesto de cólera° al contar el dinero... ¡Dios no podía haberse equivocado,° ni negar lo que se le había pedido!°

Inmediatamente, Lencho se acercó° a la ventanilla para pedir papel y tinta.° En la mesa destinada al público, se puso a° escribir... Al terminar, fue a pedir un timbre...

En cuanto° la carta cayó al buzón, el jefe de correos fue a recogerla. Decía: «Dios: Del dinero que te pedí sólo llegaron a mis manos° sesenta pesos. Mándame el resto, que me hace mucha falta, pero no me lo mandes por conducto° de la oficina de correos, porque los empleados son muy ladrones.° —Lencho».

surprise; upon seeing; bills; so much
confidence; anger
have made a mistake
had asked
approached
ink; he began

As soon as

hands
by means of
thieves

Es decir

Comprensión. Busque Ud. en la segunda columna la terminación de la frase en la primera columna.

1. Lencho no mostró	**a.** un timbre.
2. Lencho se acercó a	**b.** escribir.
3. Se puso a	**c.** la menor sorpresa.
4. Fue a pedir	**d.** muy ladrones.
5. Sólo llegaron a mis manos	**e.** la ventanilla.
6. Los empleados son	**f.** sesenta pesos.

Practiquemos

A **El lenguaje *(language)* literario.** En el segmento del cuento, busque Ud. las palabras que tienen el mismo significado *(same meaning)* que las siguientes palabras y frases.

1. el dinero	**4.** empezó a
2. para	**5.** solamente
3. ventana pequeña	**6.** no son muy honestos

B Discusión.

1. Describa Ud. { a Lencho. / al jefe de correos.

2. Explique Ud. { la situación económica de Lencho. / por qué Lencho le escribió una carta a Dios. / la reacción de Lencho cuando leyó la carta de Dios.

C Reacción personal.

El final del cuento puede ser cómico o triste, depende de su punto de vista *(point of view)*. ¿Qué piensa Ud.?

Enfoque artístico... México

A. Visite Ud. el sitio web del Museo de Arte Moderno,

http://www.arts-history.mx/museos/mam/escmex2.html.

B. Escoja *(Choose)* la colección de la Escuela Mexicana y lea las biografías de los famosos muralistas José Clemente Orozco, Diego Rivera y David Alfaro Siqueiros. Mire sus pinturas y complete la siguiente tabla.

muralistas	Orozco	Rivera	Siqueiros
fecha de nacimiento y de muerte			
estilo			
temas principales			
título de la pintura			
opinión personal de la pintura			

C. Since Internet addresses are subject to change, typing the following key words into most search engines will get you more information about Mexican art.

Museos de México **Museos del INBA** **Frida Kahlo**
Rufino Tamayo (or the name of any Mexican artist)

Videocultura

La vida del mexicoamericano: Una entrevista con el poeta chicano Tino Villanueva

Tino Villanueva

Tino Villanueva es profesor universitario en Boston,y también es escritor y poeta mexicoamericano. Escribe de la vida difícil del campesino° chicano, y de su experiencia personal de niño en los campos de algodón, pizcando° para los patrones.° La vida del trabajador migratorio° era una de constante cambio.

farm worker
picking; bosses
migrant worker

Tino tuvo la oportunidad de estudiar en la universidad gracias a becas que recibió del gobierno. Recibió su título universitario y luego su doctorado de Boston University. Su poesía chicana es conocida por todo el mundo.

Vamos a conocer al poeta. Mire Ud. el video y haga los ejercicios que siguen.

Palabras útiles

el trabajador migratorio	*migrant farmworker*
surgir	*to appear*
el campesino	*farmworker, person from the country*
la faena	*duty, task*
pizcar	*to pick (fruits and vegetables)*
la cosecha	*crop*
empaquetar	*to pack*
pertenecer	*to belong*
el patrón	*boss*
el cosechero	*owner of a crop*
explotado	*exploited*
el sindicato	*labor union*
el beneficio	*benefit*
la huelga	*strike*
la cereza	*cherry*
la voz	*voice*
la tierra	*land*

Es decir

A **La obra *(work)* poética.** Sigue una parte de su primer poema sobre la vida del chicano. Basándose en el video, llene Ud. los espacios con la palabra correcta.

Que hay otra voz°

voice	¡Y éntrale° otra vez con la frescura!
get to work (slang)	Éntrale a los surcos agridulces° más ______
bittersweet rows	que la vida misma:

plums / beans
______ / cotton
betabel° / pepinos°
pruning / ______
______ / apricots
chopping / plucking
soybeans / ______

no importa.
Que hay que comer, hacer pagos, sacar la ropa
del Lay-Away; '55 Chevy engine tune-up;
los niños en seventh-grade piden lápices
con futuro. Hay otra voz que ______.

Tú,
cómotellamas, mexicano, ______, Meskin,
skin, Mex-guy, Mex-Am, ______,
Mexican-American, Chicano,

tú,
de las manos diestras,° y la espalda°
empapada° desde que cruzó° tu ______ el Río.°

Las estaciones siguen en su madura marcha
de generación en ______, de mapa en ______,
de patrón en patrón, de surco en surco.
Surcos,
viñas,°
de donde ha brotado el grito audaz.°
las huelgas° siembran° un día ______.
El boycott es religión,
y la múltiple existencia se confirma en celdas.°

---

voice
get to work (slang)
bittersweet rows
beets; cucumbers
skilled; back
soaking wet; crossed; Río Grande River
vineyards
the bold cry has burst forth
strikes; are sowing
jail cells

B **¿Qué recuerda Ud.?** Basándose en el video, escoja Ud. *(choose)* la respuesta correcta.

1. La palabra «chicano» significa...
   a. latino
   b. español
   c. mexicoamericano
2. ¿De dónde es Tino?
   a. México
   b. Texas
   c. Boston
3. ¿Hasta qué edad *(age)* trabajó Tino en el campo?
   a. hasta los 17 años
   b. hasta los 13 años
   c. hasta los 20 años
4. Según Tino, ¿quiénes son los más explotados *(exploited)?*
   a. los patrones
   b. los campesinos
   c. los que trabajan en las ciudades
5. ¿Cuál fue la única defensa que tenían los trabajadores migratorios?
   a. buscar otros trabajos
   b. ir a la ciudad
   c. participar en un boycott
6. ¿Cuál es el tema del primer poema de Tino?
   a. el trabajo difícil de los campesinos
   b. César Chávez
   c. sus años en la universidad

C **¿Quién es? ¿Qué es?** En sus propias palabras, diga Ud....

1. ¿Quién es Tino Villanueva y cómo era su vida?
2. ¿Qué es el Ballet Folklórico de Aztlán?
3. ¿Qué significa la palabra **Aztlán**?

D **El ballet.** Conteste Ud. las preguntas con frases completas.

1. ¿Cómo son los trajes *(costumes)* que llevan los bailarines? ¿Por qué son diferentes para los dos bailes? ¿Qué reflejan *(reflect)* los trajes?
2. ¿Qué baile parece tener más influencia de los EE.UU.? ¿Y de México? Explique.

Practiquemos

A **¿Qué piensa Ud.?** Después de leer el poema «Que hay otra voz», conteste Ud. las preguntas.

1. ¿Por qué está el poema escrito *(written)* en inglés y en español?
2. ¿Cuál es el significado de las listas largas de cosechas y faenas que hacen los campesinos?
3. ¿Cuáles son algunos de los nombres que se usan para referirse a un chicano?
4. ¿Qué es un «lápiz con futuro»? ¿Qué es lo que quieren los niños?
5. ¿Es el poema optimista? Explique.

B **Actividades extraescolares.** Describa Ud. las actividades extraescolares y culturales que hay en su universidad. ¿Hay grupos de baile folklórico? ¿Participa Ud. en ellos? ¿Por qué sí o no?

Peter Rodríguez: El arte como reflejo de la cultura

Peter Rodríguez nació en California de padres mexicanos. Mantiene muy viva° su cultura mexicana en su arte personal y también como fundador° del Museo° Mexicano de San Francisco, un museo dedicado a la protección del arte mexicano y chicano en los EE.UU. Es un artista de mucho talento y expresa su creatividad por varios medios artísticos, pero siempre refleja el folklorismo mexicano.

alive
founder; Museum

Peter Rodríguez, «Self Portrait» (1975), Acrylic on canvas, 40" X 42".

Peter Rodríguez, «Santo Niño de Atocha» (1984)

Para ver la obra° artística de Peter Rodríguez, mire Ud. el video y haga los ejercicios que siguen.

work

Palabras útiles

la pintura	*painting*
la caja	*box*
el tapete	*small carpet*
surgir	*to appear*
utilizar	*to utilize*
el nopal	*prickly pear cactus (Mex.)*
el diseño	*design*
el tallador	*carver*
el sentido	*feeling, sense*
cotidiano	*daily*
el santo	*saint*
el homenaje	*homage*
cariñoso	*affectionate*
la guerra	*war*
el retrato; autorretrato	*portrait; self-portrait*
el soldado	*soldier*
el cofre	*coffin*
la bandera	*flag*
exhibir	*to exhibit*

Es decir

A **Uno es falso.** Basándose en la lectura *(reading)* y en el video, diga Ud. cuál de las respuestas es falsa.

1. Peter Rodríguez es...
   a. artista. b. autor. c. fundador de un museo.
2. Peter quiere preservar el arte...
   a. chicano. b. cubano. c. mexicano.
3. El arte chicano surgió en los...
   a. 80. b. 60. c. 70.
4. Peter hace...
   a. fotografía. b. video. c. cajas.
5. En la cultura de México, siempre utilizan...
   a. el taco. b. el nopal. c. el chile.

B **Las cajas.** Busque Ud. en la segunda columna la caja que corresponde al tema *(theme)* en la primera columna.

1. la política	**a.** Frida Kahlo
2. la vida cotidiana	**b.** el Sueño de Oaxaca
3. los personajes famosos	**c.** The Bottom Line

C **¿Qué recuerda Ud.?** ¿Cuáles de las siguientes cosas vio Ud. en el arte de Peter Rodríguez?

1. ______ la bandera de los EE.UU.

2. ______ la bandera de México

3. ______ una familia

4. ______ un esqueleto *(skeleton)*

5. ______ una bruja *(witch)*

6. ______ frutas

7. ______ luces brillantes

8. ______ un perro

9. ______ un árbol

10. ______ un revólver

11. ______ un avión

12. ______ un tren

Practiquemos

A **El mundo del arte.** Conteste Ud. las siguientes preguntas con frases completas.

1. ¿Cuáles son cuatro adjetivos que describen el arte de Peter Rodríguez?
2. ¿Qué piensa Ud. de la obra artística de Peter? Explique.
3. ¿Prefiere Ud. las sillas, las cajas o los retratos? ¿Por qué?

B **Las cajas de Ud.** En grupos, diseñen *(design)* dos cajas originales que representan la cultura de los EE.UU. Utilicen *(Use)* dos de los temas de Peter (la política, la religión, la vida cotidiana o los personajes famosos).

La música de Carlos Santana

Carlos Santana nació en Autlán en Jalisco, México el 20 de julio de 1947. Su familia fue a vivir a San Francisco en 1963, donde Carlos vive todavía. Es maestro de la guitarra «rock», y fue de los primeros guitarristas en combinar ritmos afrocaribeños con el rock. Pero, además de su fama y talento, Carlos le dedica mucho tiempo a la comunidad latina de San Francisco, especialmente al Centro Cultural de la Misión *(Mission Cultural Center)*.

Vamos a un concierto de Carlos Santana. Mire Ud. el video y haga las siguientes actividades.

Carlos Santana

Palabras útiles

complacer	*to please*
el corazón	*heart*
el sonido	*sound*
chiquito (chiquillo)	*tiny*
verdaderamente	*truly*
el vals	*waltz*
europeo	*European*
repugnar	*to repulse*

Es decir

A **La música.** Basándose en el video, llene Ud. los espacios con la palabra correcta.

1. Mi nombre es Carlos Santana y yo soy ______.
2. Quiero servir a la gente con el sonido de ______.
3. La música verdaderamente mexicana es la de los ______.
4. La música de mariachi es música ______.
5. La música ______ ha afectado mucho a América.

B **¿Qué recuerda Ud.?** Diga Ud. cuál es el significado de los siguientes términos. Forme Ud. frases completas.

1. Jalisco
2. San Francisco
3. la influencia africana
4. la siesta
5. un sombrero grande

Practiquemos

A **Otros personajes famosos de ascendencia mexicana.** Carlos habla más acerca de la influencia mexicana en los EE.UU. Llene Ud. los espacios con el nombre apropiado de la lista siguiente.

Olmos Tejas Los Lobos Plunket indio Nuevo Ronstadt

Para mí la influencia mexicana es la del ______. Este elemento se encuentra en gente como Jim ______ que era quarterback con los Raiders, en la música de ______, en la visión de Linda ______ y también en la obra del actor Edward James ______. Esta influencia está presente no sólo en California, sino también en ______ México y ______.

B **Los estereotipos.** En grupos, hagan una lista de cuatro estereotipos de la cultura de los EE.UU. Expliquen sus selecciones.

UNIDAD

Cuidando el cuerpo

Centroamérica

¡Vamos a Centroamérica por Internet!

Experience ecotourism and the topographical and cultural diversity of Central America by browsing the World Wide Web and visiting the following addresses.

http://www.latinworld.com/
http://www.tradepoint.org.gt/ingues/esinfosigh.html (Guatemala)
http://mars.cropsoil.uga.edu/trop-ag/guatem.htm (Guatemala)
http://www.tourism-costarica.com/ (Costa Rica)
http://www.expreso.co.cr/cr/areas.htm (Costa Rica)
http://www.virtualnet.com.sv/tourism/atracciones.htm (El Salvador)

Since Internet addresses are subject to change, typing the following key words into most search engines will also get you to Central America.

Turismo en Guatemala **Flora y fauna de Guatemala** **Los mayas** **Viajes a Guatemala** **San José** (or any city in Costa Rica) **Biodiversidad en Costa Rica** **Ecoturismo en Costa Rica**

To learn about Central American art via the Internet, see page 479 of *Gaceta 5*.

Unos jóvenes juegan al fútbol.

Lección  13

FUNCTION • Describing • Expressing what you **have** and **had done** • Expressing action when the subject is unknown

STRUCTURE • The past participle • The present and the pluperfect tenses • ***Se*** to express passive action

VOCABULARY • Parts of the body • Health • Symptoms and illnesses • At the doctor's office

CULTURE • Hispanic pharmacies • Health practices

DIÁLOGO Y VIDEO ***Así es Mariana: ¡Me duele todo!***

Lección  14

FUNCTION • Talking about the future • Describing actions: **how**, **when**, and **where** • Expressing future or pending action

STRUCTURE • The future tense • Adverbs • The present subjunctive in adverbial clauses of time

VOCABULARY • Sports and players • Equipment • Conjunctions

CULTURE • Sports and sports figures • A profile of Hispanic baseball players

DIÁLOGO Y VIDEO ***Así es Mariana: El gran campeón***

Lección  15

FUNCTION • Expressing influence, emotion, and uncertainty in the past • Expressing purpose and dependency

STRUCTURE • The imperfect subjunctive • The subjunctive in adverbial clauses of purpose and dependency • Sequence of tenses I: The present and past perfect subjunctive

VOCABULARY • Activities • Nature and camping • Animals

CULTURE • Facts about Central America • Recreation in Costa Rica and Panama • Profile of Guatemala

DIÁLOGO Y VIDEO ***Así es Mariana: San Diego y sus atracciones***

Gaceta  5

CULTURE **Central America**
Touring Central America • Faces in the news • Notes and notables • Literature: Rubén Darío • Art

VIDEOCULTURA Una visita a Costa Rica: Alajuela • Las Carretas de Sarchí y la Finca de Mariposas

¿Te has tomado la temperatura?

AVISO CULTURAL

(As a reading aid, refer to lesson vocabulary for new words.)

¿Qué se puede comprar en una farmacia en los EE.UU.? Nombre diez cosas. En las farmacias de España y de algunos países hispanoamericanos se venden casi exclusivamente medicinas. Para comprar champú y otros productos hay que ir a una perfumería. Muchas de las medicinas que en los EE.UU. requieren una receta médica (como los antibióticos), se pueden comprar sin receta. Cuando uno se siente enfermo es común ir a la farmacia en vez de llamar al médico, porque los farmacéuticos pueden poner inyecciones y recomendar tratamientos. Las «farmacias de guardia» son las farmacias que se quedan abiertas por la noche y los días de fiesta, y sus direcciones *(addresses)* y números de teléfono se publican en el periódico porque varían todas las semanas. ¿Cuál es su impresión de las farmacias y los farmacéuticos españoles? ¿Suelen los farmacéuticos en los EE.UU. recomendar tratamientos y poner inyecciones? Explique.

Preparativos

Review the vocabulary on pages 408–410 before viewing the video.

Al mirar el video o leer el diálogo siguiente, note bien las palabras de las diferentes partes del cuerpo de Luis Antonio: la boca, la lengua, el estómago, las orejas, los pies. Es fácil comprenderlas en el contexto del diálogo. ¿Alguna vez ha est**ado** Ud. *(have you been)* en la sala de emergencia? O ¿ha necesit**ado** una operación? O ¿ha com**ido** tanto que le duele el estómago? Parece que esto le ha pas**ado** a Luis. En este episodio Ud. va a aprender un nuevo tiempo *(tense)*, el presente perfecto. Es un tiempo compuesto *(compound)*, es decir, tiene dos partes... el verbo **haber** *(to have)* y el participio pasado. Pobre Luis. ¡Ojalá que no sea nada serio!

Así es Mariana: ¡Me duele todo!

Luis Antonio y Mariana han vuelto a San Diego, y el pobre Luis se ha enfermado. Van al consultorio del médico de la familia de Luis.

Doctor: Buenos días. Hola Luis. Mucho tiempo sin verte. ¿Cómo está la familia?

Luis Antonio: Bien, bien, gracias, doctor. Todos están muy bien, pero yo estoy...

Doctor: Ah sí, y esta joven estudiante de medicina debe de ser la famosa Mariana. *(A Mariana)* La mamá de Luis siempre habla de ti.

Mariana: Mucho gusto, doctor.

Doctor: Bueno, Luis. Cuéntame, ¿qué te pasa?

Luis Antonio: Bueno, pues me duele mucho el estómago. Mire, está muy hinchado.

Doctor: ¿Tienes fiebre? ¿Te has tomado la temperatura?

Mariana: Sí, hace unas horas pero no tiene fiebre.

Doctor: ¿Qué has comido hoy?

Luis Antonio: Pues, nada extraño. Cada día mi madre me prepara mis platos favoritos. Luego, insiste en que me los coma todos.

Mariana: Mire. *(Mira su reloj.)* Ahora son las tres de la tarde y ya se ha comido cinco enchiladas, tres tortillas, un plato de mole poblano, unas fajitas que encontró en la nevera y un perro caliente.

Doctor: Ahora entiendo. Pues, creo que he resuelto el problema. Realmente no es muy complicado. Te voy a recetar unas pastillas.

Luis Antonio: ¿Una receta? ¿Por qué? ¿Es grave? ¿Una reacción alérgica? ¿La gripe? ¿Necesito antibióticos?

Doctor: No, nada de eso. Te sugiero que compres bicarbonato y que en el futuro no comas tanto. Tu madre lo va a comprender.

Es decir

A Diga Ud. cuáles de los siguientes síntomas sufre Luis.

1. Tiene dolor de estómago.
2. Tiene una reacción alérgica.
3. Tiene el estómago hinchado.
4. No ha comido nada en todo el día.
5. Tiene fiebre.

B Para saber la causa de su dolor, diga qué comidas consumidas por Luis corresponden a los siguientes números.

1. cinco _____ **2.** unas _____ **3.** un _____ **4.** tres _____ **5.** un _____

C En grupos de tres, representen la siguiente escena. Como Luis se porta como un hipocondríaco, Mariana y el médico deciden hacerle una broma *(play a joke)*. Le dicen que tiene una enfermedad muy exótica y misteriosa y el doctor le describe un tratamiento un poco... raro.

Al ver el video

A Después de ver el video, busque en la segunda columna la terminación de las frases en la primera columna. ¿Quién lo dijo, Luis o Mariana?

1. Me duele todo, desde las orejas...	**a.** opinión.
2. Saca la...	**b.** boca.
3. Quiero una segunda...	**c.** con el doctor.
4. Pórtate bien...	**d.** lengua.
5. Abre la...	**e.** hasta los pies.

B El doctor conoce a Luis desde hace muchos años. Él empieza a contarle a Mariana algunas anécdotas vergonzosas *(embarrassing)* sobre cuando Luis era niño. En parejas, escriban una anécdota original sobre Luis.

C Luis vuelve al consultorio del médico el próximo día con más síntomas. Busque en la segunda columna la terminación de las frases del doctor en la primera columna.

1. Tengo que examinarte	**a.** urgente.
2. Está muy	**b.** el estómago.
3. Y tienes mucha	**c.** a la sala de emergencia.
4. Creo que he resuelto	**d.** hinchado.
5. Luis, tu caso es	**e.** una operación ahora mismo.
6. Necesitas	**f.** fiebre.
7. La ambulancia te lleva	**g.** el problema. Tienes apendicitis.

Vocabulario

Verbos

cuidar(se)	*to take care of (oneself)*
curar	*to cure*
doler (ue)	*to hurt*
enfermarse	*to get sick*

mantener	*to maintain, keep, support (financially)*
operar	*to operate*
portarse	*to behave*
preocuparse (de)	*to worry (about)*
quejarse (de)	*to complain (about)*
recetar	*to prescribe*
resfriarse	*to catch a cold*
respirar	*to breathe*
sufrir	*to suffer*
toser	*to cough*

El cuerpo humano	***(The human body)***
la boca	*mouth*
el brazo	*arm*
la cabeza	*head*
el cerebro	*brain*
el corazón	*heart*
el cuello	*neck*
el dedo (del pie)	*finger (toe)*
el diente	*tooth*
la espalda	*back*
el estómago	*stomach*
la garganta	*throat*
el labio	*lip*
la lengua	*tongue*
la mano	*hand*
la nariz	*nose*
el oído	*ear (inner)*
el ojo	*eye*
la oreja	*ear (outer)*
el pecho	*chest*
el pie	*foot*
la piel	*skin*
la pierna	*leg*
el pulmón	*lung*
la rodilla	*knee*
la sangre	*blood*
el tobillo	*ankle*

Adjetivos	
alérgico	*allergic*
doloroso	*painful*
embarazada	*pregnant*

grave (serio)	*serious*
hinchado	*swollen*
inflamado	*inflamed*
mareado	*dizzy, nauseated*

Medicamentos, síntomas y enfermedades	***(Medicines, symptoms and illnesses)***
el antibiótico	*antibiotic*
la apendicitis	*appendicitis*
la aspirina	*aspirin*
el catarro (resfriado)	*cold*
la cura	*cure*
el dolor	*pain*
la fiebre	*fever*
la gripe	*flu*
el jarabe	*syrup*
la medicina	*medicine*
la operación	*operation*
la pastilla (píldora)	*tablet (pill)*
la queja	*complaint*
la temperatura	*temperature*
el termómetro	*thermometer*
la tos	*cough*
el tratamiento	*treatment*

La salud	***(Health)***
la ambulancia	*ambulance*
el consultorio	*doctor's office*
el cuidado (médico)	*(health) care*
el (la) paciente	*patient*
la sala de emergencia	*emergency room*
el seguro (médico)	*(health) insurance*

Palabras y expresiones útiles	
a ver	*let's see*
apenas	*scarcely*
lo más pronto posible	*as soon as possible*
poner una inyección	*to give an injection*

Vocabulario adicional

aliviar	*to relieve, alleviate*
la caries	*cavity*
congestionado	*congested*
la farmacia	*pharmacy*
herido	*wounded*
hondo	*deep, (adv.) deeply*
el hueso	*bone*
pálido	*pale*
el peligro	*danger*
urgente	*urgent*
la vitamina	*vitamin*

MENTIRA MÉDICA NÚMERO 19

mentira *lie*

Repasemos el vocabulario

A **Relaciones.** Su profesor(a) va a leer una serie de frases o palabras. Busque la palabra de la siguiente lista que corresponde a cada una. Escriba la letra en los espacios.

1. ______ el antibiótico **3.** ______ la aspirina **5.** ______ las vitaminas

2. ______ la emergencia **4.** ______ la fiebre **6.** ______ la enfermedad

B **Los especialistas.** ¿En qué parte(s) del cuerpo se especializan los siguientes médicos?

1. la ortopedista **3.** la oftalmóloga **5.** el cardiólogo

2. el neurólogo **4.** el dentista **6.** la gastroenteróloga

C **¿Quién lo dijo?** Llene Ud. los espacios con la letra que corresponde a la persona que dijo las siguientes frases.

a. el paciente
b. el farmacéutico
c. la doctora
d. la recepcionista
e. la enfermera

_____ **1.** Le voy a tomar la temperatura mientras esperamos al doctor.
_____ **2.** Este jarabe cuesta 600 colones.[1]
_____ **3.** ¿Tiene Ud. seguro médico?
_____ **4.** Me duelen la cabeza y el estómago.
_____ **5.** A ver. ¿Cuál es el problema?
_____ **6.** Abra la boca y...
_____ **7.** ¡Aahhh!
_____ **8.** Lo siento, pero el doctor no está aquí.
_____ **9.** Esta medicina viene en pastillas o en cápsulas.
_____ **10.** Voy a recetarle un antibiótico.

Ahora en parejas, escriban un comentario original para cada persona en el ejercicio. La clase va a decir a quién corresponde cada uno.

D **Remedios y tratamientos.** Diga Ud. qué hace en las siguientes situaciones y luego entreviste a sus compañeros.

¿Qué hace Ud. cuando...

1. le duele la cabeza?
2. tiene un resfriado?
3. sufre de insomnio?
4. tiene fiebre?
5. está enfermo(a) y no puede conseguir una cita con el médico?

E **¿De acuerdo?** Indique Ud. si está de acuerdo con las siguientes ideas. Si no, explique por qué. Luego entreviste a sus compañeros.

	Estoy de acuerdo	**No estoy de acuerdo**
1. Se cura el dolor de cabeza con vitaminas.	_____	_____
2. Las farmacias deben quedarse abiertas toda la noche.	_____	_____
3. En los EE.UU. hay que tener una receta para comprar antibióticos.	_____	_____
4. Si sufre de insomnio es bueno tomar té antes de acostarse.	_____	_____
5. Es importante visitar al médico dos veces al año.	_____	_____
6. Una forma de protegerse de las enfermedades es lavarse las manos con frecuencia.	_____	_____

[1]Currency of Costa Rica. One U.S. dollar = 229 **colones.**

De uso común

At the Doctor's Office

—¡Curada! ¡Qué bien estar curada! Pero... ,
¿y de qué voy a hablar ahora?

El doctor pregunta:

¿Cómo se siente?	*How do you feel?*
¿Cómo está (se encuentra)?	*How are you?*
¿Qué le pasa?	*What's wrong with you?*
¿Tiene alguna molestia (algún dolor)?	*Do you have any pain?*
¿Le duele algo?	*Does something hurt you?*

El paciente contesta:

Me siento muy mal.	*I feel terrible.*
Estoy regular (más o menos; así, así).	*I'm O.K.*
Me encuentro fatal.	*I feel horrible.*
Tengo fiebre.	*I have a fever.*
Estoy cansado(a).	*I'm tired.*
Tengo el pie hinchado.	*My foot is swollen.*
Me duele la cabeza.	*My head hurts.*
Me duelen los pies.	*My feet hurt.*

El doctor recomienda:

Guarde cama.	*Stay in bed.*
No fume.	*Don't smoke.*
No se mueva.	*Don't move.*
Tome aspirina.	*Take aspirin.*

Practiquemos

A **Diferentes problemas.** ¿Qué le recomienda Ud. a la persona que...

1. tiene tos?
2. acaba de caerse?
3. acaba de tener una operación?
4. sufre de dolor de cabeza?

B **¡Ay! ¡Cuánto sufro!** Con un(a) compañero(a), hagan los papeles del médico y de la paciente hipocondríaca del dibujo en la página 413. Es su primera visita al consultorio y tiene muchos dolores y quejas.

The Past Participle

The past participle in English is often formed by adding *-ed* to the verb: *opened, closed, formed, pronounced, added.* Some past participles end in *-en: written, spoken, eaten;* many are completely irregular: *sung, seen, done, said.* The past participle is commonly used as an adjective as well as with a form of the verb *to have* to form the perfect tenses. *The doctor has prescribed penicillin and I have followed his advice.*

Forma

The participle in Spanish is formed by removing the infinitive endings **(-ar, -er, -ir)** and adding **-ado** to **-ar** verb stems and **-ido** to **-er** and **-ir** verb stems.

hablar habl**ado** comer com**ido** asistir asist**ido**

1. The past participles of stem-changing verbs show no stem change.

encontrar encontr**ado** sentir sent**ido** jugar jug**ado**
pedir ped**ido**

2. **-Er** and **-ir** verbs with stems that end in **a, e,** and **o** add a written accent to the **i** of the ending.

traer tra**ído** leer le**ído** oír o**ído**

3. The following verbs have irregular past participles.

abrir	**abierto**	hacer	**hecho**	romper	**roto**
(des)cubrir	**(des)cubierto**	morir	**muerto**	ver	**visto**
decir	**dicho**	poner	**puesto**	(de)volver	**(de)vuelto**
(d)escribir	**(d)escrito**	resolver	**resuelto**		

Note that the past participles of **ser (sido)** and **ir (ido)** are regular.

Función

1. The past participle used as an adjective agrees in number and gender with the noun it modifies.

Paco tiene un **brazo roto.**	*Paco has a* ***broken arm.***
También tiene las **piernas hinchadas.**	*He also has* ***swollen legs.***

2. The past participle is often used with the verb **estar** to express a condition that results from a previous action. The participle functions as an adjective, and must agree with the noun it modifies.

El médico escribió las recetas.	*The doctor wrote the prescriptions.*
Las recetas **están escritas.**	*The prescriptions* ***are written.***
El farmacéutico cerró la farmacia.	*The pharmacist closed the pharmacy.*
La farmacia **está cerrada.**	*The pharmacy* ***is closed.***

3. As with other adjectives, the past participle generally follows the noun it modifies.

Elena nos dio una **receta médica escrita.**	*Elena gave us a* ***written prescription.***

Practiquemos

A **Los participios pasados y la salud.** Forme Ud. el participio pasado de los siguientes infinitivos. Luego, úselos para describir el sustantivo *(noun)* indicado, y traduzca la frase al inglés. Siga el modelo.

recetar/jarabe
recetado. El jarabe recetado *(The prescribed syrup)*

1. hinchar/pierna
2. beber/té
3. sugerir/cura
4. escribir/recetas médicas
5. abrir/farmacias
6. resolver/problemas
7. poner/inyección
8. hacer/tratamientos

B **Ud. tiene correo.** Durante el verano Ud. trabaja para un médico. Él le escribe una carta por correo electrónico desde el hospital para saber si Ud. ha hecho *(have done)* todo su trabajo. Forme las preguntas del doctor usando los sustantivos y la forma correcta de **estar** + **el participio pasado.**

MODELO cuartos/arreglados. **¿Están arreglados los cuartos?**

1. computadora/apagar
2. suelos/barrer
3. baño/fregar
4. citas/hacer
5. receta médica/mandar
6. cartas/escribir

Ahora, conteste la carta diciéndole lo que está hecho y no está hecho.

C **No te preocupes, mamá.** La señora Rojas está enferma y tiene que guardar cama. Su hijo le contesta sus preguntas acerca de la casa. Mire Ud. los dibujos y conteste las preguntas.

MODELO ¿Cerraste la puerta?
Sí, mamá, la puerta está cerrada.

1. **¿Pusiste la mesa?**

2. **¿Limpiaste el baño?**

3. **¿Escribiste las cartas?**

4. **¿Barriste el suelo?**

5. **¿Apagaste el televisor?**
6. **¿Abriste las ventanas?**

The Present Perfect and the Pluperfect Tenses

As you've already seen, the past participle in English and Spanish can be used as an adjective *(the broken arm, the closed window)*. It can also be used with the auxiliary verb *to have* **(haber)** to form the perfect tenses. Note that **haber** and **tener** can both mean *to have*, but they are not interchangeable. **Tener** means to have in one's possession, whereas **haber** is an auxiliary verb used to express an action that one has done, had done, will have done, and so forth.

Forma

The perfect tenses are formed by combining the auxiliary verb **haber** in any tense with the past participle.[1]

HABER *(to have)*

present indicative *(have, has)*		present subjunctive *(have, has)*		imperfect *(had)*	
he	hemos	haya	hayamos	había	habíamos
has	habéis	hayas	hayáis	habías	habíais
ha	han	haya	hayan	había	habían

1. **Haber** in the present indicative combines with the past participle to form the present perfect tense. **Haber** in the present subjunctive combines with the past participle to form the present perfect subjunctive. **Haber** in the imperfect combines with the past participle to form the pluperfect tense.

   Yo sé que el doctor **ha llamado.** — *I know that the doctor **has called.***

   Espero que el doctor **haya llamado.** — *I hope that the doctor **has called.***

   Cuando llegué a casa, el doctor ya **había llamado.** — *When I arrived home, the doctor **had** already **called.***

2. When used to form a perfect tense, the past participle ends in **-o** and never changes in number or gender.

   Las pacientes **han ido** al hospital. — *The patients **have gone** to the hospital.*

   Nosotros **hemos venido** para ver al médico. — *We **have come** to see the doctor.*

3. The past participle immediately follows the form of **haber.**

   José **ha hecho** una cita con el dentista. — *José **has made** an appointment with the dentist.*

4. Negative expressions such as **no, nunca,** and **nadie,** and object and reflexive pronouns are always placed before the conjugated form of **haber.**

   No le han puesto la inyección todavía. — *They have **not** given **him** the shot yet.*

[1]The preterite forms of **haber** are not commonly used in perfect constructions.

Función

1. The present perfect indicative is used as its English equivalent to express a recently completed action.

   El farmacéutico nos **ha dado** las pastillas. — *The pharmacist **has given** us the tablets.*

2. The present perfect subjunctive is used to express a recently completed action in a context which requires the use of the subjunctive. Compare the following sentences.

   Present perfect indicative:

   Yo sé que tú **has ido** al consultorio del médico. — *I know that you **have been** to the doctor's office.*

   Present perfect subjunctive:

   Yo dudo que tú **hayas ido** al consultorio del médico. — *I doubt that you **have gone** to the doctor's office.*

3. The pluperfect tense is used to describe an action that took place prior to a more recent past action.

   Ya **había llamado** a su esposa cuando llegó la ambulancia. — *He **had** already **called** his wife when the ambulance arrived.*

4. Do not confuse the structure **acabar** + **de** that you learned in Lesson 1 with the perfect tenses. **Acabar** in the present tense + **de** reflects immediacy of a past action. Note the difference in meaning between the following structures.

   Acabo de comer. — *I have **just** eaten.*

   He comido. — *I have eaten.*

   Acabar in the imperfect tense + **de** means *had just.* Compare the following structures:

   Acababa de comer. — *I had **just** eaten.*

   Había comido. — *I had eaten.*

Practiquemos

A Ha hecho todo. En cada grupo hay un «sabelotodo» *(know-it-all).* Forme Ud. frases según el modelo. Un(a) compañero(a) va a hacer el papel *(play the role)* del sabelotodo.

hacer una gira por Centroamérica
Ud.: **Algún día quiero hacer una gira por Centroamérica.**
El sabelotodo: **Ya he hecho una gira por Centroamérica.**

1. leer los poemas de Rubén Darío.[1]
2. escuchar la música de Rubén Blades.[1]
3. ir de compras a los mercados de Chichicastenango.[1]
4. subir las pirámides de los mayas.
5. probar la comida guatemalteca.
6. visitar los bosques *(forests)* tropicales de Costa Rica.

[1]Para leer sobre Rubén Darío, Rubén Blades y el pueblo guatemalteco de Chichicastenango, vea las páginas 478, 472 y 476 de la *Gaceta 5.*

B **En el hospital.** Paquito está en el hospital. ¿Qué han hecho las siguientes personas?

yo

MODELO **Yo le he traído flores.**

1. la enfermera
2. nosotros
3. Paquito y el otro paciente

4. el médico
5. tú

C **Buenas intenciones.** Mamá (de la página 416) está mucho mejor después de una semana en la cama. Pero su casa es un desastre. Haga Ud. el papel de mamá y responda a las confesiones de su hijo, usando el pluscuamperfecto (pluperfect).

MODELO Hijo: Pero, mamá, yo iba a lavar los platos.
Mamá: **Y, ¿por qué me dijiste que los habías lavado?**

1. Pero, mamá, yo iba a pasar la aspiradora.
2. Pero, mamá, papá iba a sacar la basura.
3. Pero, mamá, íbamos a preparar la cena.
4. Pero, mamá, Pedrín y Rosita iban a hacer las camas.
5. Pero, mamá, papá iba a lavar el coche.
6. Pero, mamá, yo iba a limpiar el garaje.

D **Un episodio de «Hospital Típico».** Ud. mira la telenovela «Hospital Típico» por primera vez. Su amigo intenta explicarle quiénes son los personajes *(characters)* principales. Llene Ud. los espacios con la forma correcta del verbo **haber** en el presente del indicativo, el presente del subjuntivo o el imperfecto.

Este hombre es Juan, quien ______ sido siempre el enemigo *(enemy)* del Dr. Moreno. Hace dos semanas, parecía que Juan ______ muerto, pero resultó que sólo ______ fingido *(pretended)* para ver la reacción de Julia, su novia. Ahora, mucho ______ pasado entre los dos. El año pasado ellos ______ decidido casarse, pero cuando Julia supo lo que Juan ______ hecho, ella rompió con él. Ella ______ empezado a salir con Rogelio. Pero, la verdad es que me sorprende mucho que Rogelio ______ salido con ella porque él ______ dicho recientemente que va a dedicarse a su trabajo solamente.

Es interesante que el Dr. Moreno no ______ llamado a Julia todavía, porque él la quiere mucho. Aunque Julia ______ conocido al Dr. Moreno el verano pasado, no ______ podido salir con él. Además, hace dos años Juan le ______ dicho al Dr. Moreno que jamás quería verlo con Julia. El doctor nunca ______ olvidado eso. Es increíble que él ______ seguido trabajando en el mismo hospital.

Se to Express Passive Action

We have discussed various uses of the pronoun **se:** as a reflexive or indirect object pronoun, to express unplanned occurrences, as well as in the absence of a definite subject (the impersonal **se**). **Se** is used in another construction when the agent (person or thing doing the action) is indefinite or unknown.

Se venden vitaminas

SE PROHIBE FUMAR

SE HABLAN INGLÉS Y PORTUGUÉS

SE PROHIBE EL PASO

Se llenan recetas

Forma y función

se + verb in the third-person singular or plural + subject

Spanish	**English equivalent**
Se hace mucho trabajo.	*A lot of work* ***is done.***
Se hacen muchos ejercicios.	*A lot of exercises* ***are done.***

1. The verb always agrees with the subject. Thus, when the subject is singular **(trabajo)** the verb is singular **(hace)**; when the subject is plural **(ejercicios)** the verb is plural **(hacen)**.
2. Since *work* is an inanimate object and is not capable of performing the action of the verb to itself, it is understood that some unknown or unimportant agent is carrying out the action.[1]
3. An alternate form of expressing action when the agent is indefinite is to use the third-person plural subject *(they)*, as is used in English. Compare the following structures.

Hablan español en Guatemala.	***They speak*** *Spanish in Guatemala.*
Se habla español en Guatemala.	*Spanish* ***is spoken*** *in Guatemala.*

Practiquemos

A **Para ser un buen médico.** Complete Ud. la frase con uno de los verbos entre paréntesis.

1. Primero, se (toma, toman) muchos cursos de biología y química.
2. Se (necesita, necesitan) mucha paciencia.
3. No se (cobra, cobran) demasiado dinero por las consultas.
4. En el consultorio se (habla, hablan) por lo menos dos idiomas.
5. Se (ofrece, ofrecen) regalitos para los niños buenos.
6. Se (ve, ven) muchos títulos en las paredes de su consultorio de todas las universidades a las que ha asistido.

B **En el hospital.** El Dr. Suárez le explica a Ud. qué se hace en cada parte del hospital. Para practicar el uso del **se** pasivo, escriba los comentarios del doctor, según el modelo.

MODELO recetar/las medicinas
Aquí se recetan las medicinas.

1. tratar/las enfermedades de la sangre
2. hacer/los tratamientos de radiología
3. tomar/la temperatura de los pacientes
4. preparar/los jarabes
5. poner/las inyecciones
6. hacer/la evaluación siquiátrica
7. cocinar/la comida para los pacientes
8. escribir/la diagnosis
9. resolver/los problemas
10. buscar/las curas

[1]Refer to Appendix E for the true passive voice, in which the subject is expressed.

Spend more time with Mariana and her friends while you review grammar and expand your cultural horizons.

See the **Así es Mariana** exercise in your workbook for this lesson.

En resumen

A **El médico soy yo.** Fernando tiene sus propias ideas sobre lo que es la buena salud y cómo mantenerla. Aquí se ofrecen algunos ejemplos:

1. Cuando él se enferma, no va directamente al médico. ¿Qué hace él para curarse a sí mismo en los casos siguientes?
   a. la indigestión
   b. el insomnio
   c. el dolor de cabeza
   d. el hipo *(hiccups)*
2. Él cree que «ciudarse bien» es la mejor medicina. ¿Qué hace Fernando para no...
   a. tener caries *(cavities)?*
   b. resfriarse?
   c. engordar?
   d. tener arrugas *(wrinkles)?*
3. Sus ideas de la buena salud son únicas. Reaccione Ud. a las «ideas» siguientes.
   a. Comer chocolate y papas fritas es muy sano ya que *(since)* son elementos importantes en la dieta.
   b. El ejercicio físico no es necesario para los mayores de quince años. Puede causar daño *(harm)*.
   c. La comida más importante del día es la cena.
   d. Sin mucha tensión no nos sentimos bien y no podemos triunfar.

B **Para los «chocohólicos».** Lea Ud. la siguiente lectura y haga el ejercicio.

¡BUENAS NOTICIAS SOBRE EL CHOCOLATE!

¿Te parece que una pequeña dosis de chocolate te hace sentir bien? Probablemente. Los expertos en nutrición han llegado a la conclusión de que cuando comemos chocolate, nuestro cerebro responde segregando una sustancia química llamada serotonina, que controla algunas funciones de nuestro cuerpo… y nos hace sentir una sensación de felicidad.

Ahora bien, se dice que el chocolate, por otro lado, causa caries. ¡Falso! Lo que causa las caries es el azúcar contenido en el chocolate. Sin embargo, muchos chocolates contienen caseína (la proteína de la leche), que aparentemente evita las caries. Pero sí es cierto que el chocolate contiene alta cantidad de grasas saturadas, aunque el oscuro y amargo tiene más que el claro. Además, este último, al contener más azúcar, diluye la grasa y, por lo tanto, tiene menos calorías.

Una gran noticia: Se está fabricando una versión nueva del chocolate que es mucho más sana, y tiene como principal ingrediente el cacao.

por otro lado *on the other hand*

grasas *fats;* **amargo** *bitter*
diluye *dilutes*

¿Cierto o falso? Si la frase es falsa, corríjala.

1. El cacao es el ingrediente en el chocolate que causa caries.
2. El chocolate puede tener un efecto positivo en nuestro cerebro.
3. La caseína es una sustancia química contenida en el cerebro humano.
4. En general, el chocolate es muy bueno para la salud.
5. Las palabras, **claro, oscuro** y **amargo** describen tipos de chocolate.

C **Preguntas.** Conteste Ud. las siguientes preguntas. Luego, cámbielas a la forma **tu** y entreviste a un(a) compañero(a).

1. ¿Tiene Ud. buena salud? ¿Qué significa tener buena salud? ¿Qué se puede hacer para mantenerse en buenas condiciones?
2. ¿Cuáles son los alimentos que...
   a. son buenos para la salud?
   b. causan problemas dentales?
   c. son malos para el cuerpo?
3. ¿Mantiene Ud. un equilibrio *(balance)* entre el trabajo y el descanso? Explique. ¿Qué hace Ud. para controlar los nervios? ¿Qué hace Ud. para relajarse?
4. ¿Es Ud. hipocondríaco(a)? ¿Cuáles son algunas características del hipocondríaco?

D **Libros para la salud.** Lea Ud. los anuncios y haga las actividades.

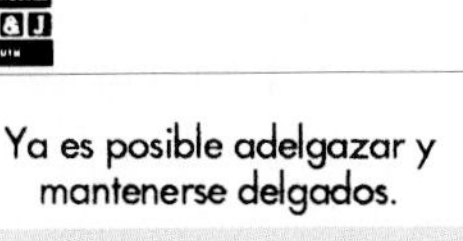
Ya es posible adelgazar y mantenerse delgados.

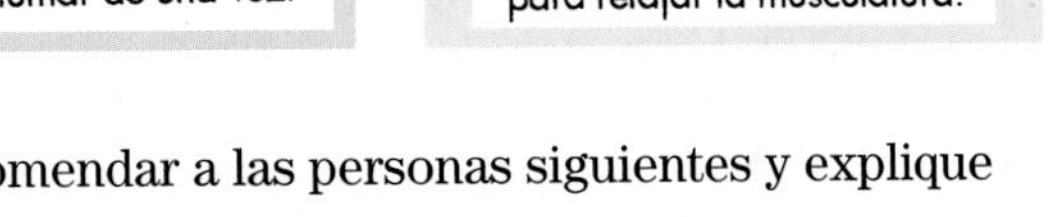
Finalmente, el método para dejar de fumar de una vez.

Práctica médica segura para relajar la musculatura.

El sistema más rápido y seguro contra el estrés.

1. Diga Ud. qué libro les va a recomendar a las personas siguientes y explique por qué.

   a. sus padres c. su novio(a)
   b. su profesor(a) d. su compañero(a) de cuarto

[1]«...**de una vez para siempre**» . . . *once and for all.*

2. ¿A qué libro corresponden las frases siguientes?
   a. Cuídela bien... es necesaria para la movilidad.
   b. Miles de personas deciden hacerlo cada año, pero no es fácil.
   c. Cómo llegar a la talla que quiere.
   d. La terapia *(therapy)* musical: una forma barata y rápida para aliviar las tensiones.
   e. Hágalo de repente *(instantly)* o gradualmente, pero hágalo.
   f. Aprenda Ud. a sentirse tranquilo.

E **Sea optimista y tenga buena salud.** Complete Ud. el párrafo con la forma correcta de la palabra entre paréntesis. Si hay dos palabras, escoja la más apropiada.

¿(Ha, Has) observado Ud. lo difícil que (es, está) encontrar personas enfermas entre aquéllas que tienen un carácter (optimista)? Pues, (este, esta) observación es (correcto). Según los estudios recientes, las personas que son más (tenso) tienen más tendencia a sufrir de enfermedades (crónico). Muchos médicos (hayan, han) llegado (al, a la) conclusión de que la mejor forma (por, para) evitar (los, las) enfermedades (es, está) evitar (los, las) tensiones. Recomiendan que la gente (vivir) en armonía con sus amigos y familiares y que (mantener) relaciones cordiales con los compañeros de trabajo. También aconsejan que todos (hacer) ejercicios, (controlar) las comidas y (buscar) un equilibrio *(balance)* entre el trabajo y el descanso.

F **Una visita al médico.** Traduzca las siguientes frases al español.

1. Doctor, my son has caught a lot of colds this winter.
2. My husband thinks that he's allergic to something in the house, like the cat.
3. But he had already gotten sick when we bought the cat.
4. He doesn't complain much, but I know that he doesn't feel well.
5. The pharmacist recommended this syrup for his cough, but it hasn't helped.

G **Minidrama.** En grupos, representen una de las siguientes escenas.

1. Ud. le tiene mucho miedo al dentista. El dentista trata de examinarle los dientes pero Ud. inventa mil pretextos para no abrir la boca.
2. Los participantes de un grupo de terapia están en el consultorio del sicólogo. Cada uno sufre de alguna forma de tensión mental o física. Comparen sus problemas y compartan soluciones.

H **Composición.**

1. Ud. es el (la) autor(a) de la siguiente sección de una revista popular. Escriba el artículo para esta semana.

2. En una revista popular está la siguiente sección dedicada a contestar las preguntas de los lectores. Ud. es el (la) Dr. (Dra.) Hernández y va a escribir un párrafo en el que contesta una de las siguientes cartas.
   a. Mi hijo le tiene miedo al doctor. No quiere ir. ¿Qué puedo hacer para aliviar su miedo?
   b. Paso todas las noches sin dormir. No quiero tomar pastillas pero, ¡necesito dormir! ¿Qué me recomienda, doctor?

Escuchemos

A **Ay, no me siento bien.** You will hear a series of incomplete statements that Dr. Sánchez makes as he examines a sick patient. Choose the word that best completes each sentence.

MODELO (garganta/lengua)
Abra Ud. la boca y saque la ___, por favor. **lengua.**
Abra Ud. la boca y saque la lengua, por favor.

1. (alérgico/herido)
2. (sangre/fiebre)
3. (mareada/inflamada)
4. (inyección/pastilla)
5. (peligro/jarabe)
6. (operar/aliviar)
7. (catarro/corazón)
8. (Cuídese/Quéjese)

B **Dictado.** You will hear a short narration about Elena's father's sudden illness. Listen carefully to the entire selection. Listen again and write each sentence during the pauses.

You will then hear a series of false statements related to the dictation. Correct each one with a complete sentence. Refer to your dictation.

Lección 14

La vida deportiva

En cuanto encuentre mi raqueta, saldré.

AVISO CULTURAL

(As a reading aid, refer to lesson vocabulary for new words.)

¿Cuál es el deporte nacional de los EE.UU.? El fútbol es un deporte que goza de una popularidad enorme en el mundo hispano. En España y en muchos países latinoamericanos es el deporte que se practica con más entusiasmo y se considera el deporte nacional. El fútbol profesional se juega todos los domingos de septiembre a junio. El jai alai, que es de origen vasco *(Basque)*, también es muy popular en el mundo hispano. El Caribe produce excelentes jugadores de béisbol como el dominicano Pedro Martínez, el cubano Liván Hernández y el puertorriqueño Iván Rodríguez. También hay famosos tenistas hispanos como Marcelo Ríos de Chile, Florencia Labat de Argentina y de España, Alex Corretja y Carlos Moya. ¿Cuál es el deporte favorito de Ud.? ¿Qué deportes asocia Ud. con los EE.UU.? ¿Inglaterra? ¿España? ¿Centroamérica? ¿Por qué tienen algunos países «deportes nacionales»?

Preparativos

Review the vocabulary on pages 428–430 before viewing the video.

Al mirar el video o leer el diálogo siguiente, Ud. **va a ver** varias maneras de expresar acción en el futuro. Ud. ya sabe la fórmula **ir a** + infinitivo como en la frase anterior. Note el uso del tiempo *(tense)* futuro. «¿Quién sabe cuándo **regresaré** a San Diego?,» dice Mariana. Luis dice: «Y mañana **tendremos** tiempo para ver la ciudad». ¿Cree Ud. que Mariana se divirtió en México? ¿**Se divertirá** de vuelta *(back)* en San Diego? Ya **veremos.**

Así es Mariana: El gran campeón

Luis Antonio está en el garaje de la casa de su madre, Teresa, y está buscando su raqueta de tenis. Le grita a su mamá.

Luis Antonio: Mamá, ¿dónde está mi raqueta de tenis?

Teresa: Ayer fuiste futbolista, hoy tenista y mañana qué serás, ¿ciclista?

Luis sigue buscando su raqueta, tirando cosas fuera del garaje.

Teresa: Luis, no voy a estar tranquila hasta que tú salgas de allí. Temo que te lastimes.

Luis Antonio: No te preocupes, mamá. En cuanto encuentre mi raqueta, saldré.

Luis encuentra una pelota vieja y empieza a jugar, y a narrar un partido imaginario.

Luis Antonio: Bienvenidos al gran estadio donde hoy se juega el campeonato de básquetbol. ¿Quién podrá vencerle a la estrella mexicana? Jorge tira la pelota... Luis la recibe y corre... se enfrenta contra Michael Jordan... quedan tres segundos... Tira la pelota... sube...

Luis lanza la pelota y se cae. Mariana lo encuentra en el suelo.

Luis Antonio: Eh, tan pronto como encuentre la raqueta, iremos a jugar... Y mañana tendremos tiempo para ver la ciudad.

Mariana: Ay no, Luisito. No quiero jugar tenis. ¿Quién sabe cuándo regresaré a San Diego? El desayuno estará listo en diez minutos. Y después de comer, tú me vas a llevar a ver la pintoresca ciudad de San Diego y el famoso zoológico.

Luis Antonio: Sí, señora... en seguida... como Ud. quiera...

Es decir

A El uso del infinitivo es importante en la formación de ciertas frases. Llene el espacio con el infinitivo correcto. Diga por qué se usa el infinitivo.

estar vencer ver llevar comer jugar

1. Después de ______, tú me vas a ______ a la pintoresca ciudad de San Diego.
2. No quiero ______ tenis.
3. Mañana tendremos tiempo para ______ la ciudad.
4. No voy a ______ tranquila hasta que tú salgas de allí.
5. ¿Quién podrá ______le a la estrella mexicana?

B Repase Ud. el diálogo y conteste las preguntas con frases completas.

1. ¿Qué busca Luis?
2. ¿Qué encuentra Luis?
3. ¿Qué teme su madre?
4. ¿Qué quiere Mariana?

C A Luis le gusta contarle a Mariana recuerdos especiales de su pasado. En parejas, escriban una conversación en la cual Luis describe sus mejores momentos con su equipo de fútbol. Usen las siguientes palabras y los tiempos pasados (el imperfecto y el pretérito).

equipo campeón pelota lastimado entrenador fútbol divertido

Al ver el video

A Después de ver el video, llene el espacio con el participio pasado apropiado.

interesado olvidado curado

Dice Mariana,

«Desde que Luis se ha ______ del dolor de estómago se ha ______ en los deportes y se ha ______ de mí.»

B Indique las cosas que hay en el garaje de Luis.

1. ___ unos cables
2. ___ una llanta
3. ___ un coche
4. ___ una bicicleta
5. ___ una pelota
6. ___ unos zapatos viejos
7. ___ unas aletas *(flippers)*
8. ___ una raqueta de tenis

C Para saber qué hay en el garaje de sus compañeros, haga una pequeña encuesta. Pregúnteles hasta que Ud. tenga una lista de las seis cosas más ridículas. Compare la lista con la clase.

Vocabulario

Verbos	
apoyar	*to support*
batear	*to hit, bat*
coger	*to catch*
correr	*to run*
dañar(se), (lastimarse)	*to harm (get hurt)*
desarrollar	*to develop*
enfrentarse con (contra)	*to face (go against)*
entrenar	*to train*
esquiar	*to ski*
lanzar	*to throw, pitch*
mejorar(se)	*to improve, get better*
patinar	*to skate*
tirar	*to throw*
vencer[1]	*to win, beat*

Deportes y jugadores	***(Sports and players)***
el básquetbol (baloncesto)	*basketball*
el béisbol	*baseball*
el (la) beisbolista (pelotero/a)	*baseball player*

[1]Note that the **c > z** before **a** and **o (venzo, venza).**

el ciclismo	*cycling*
el (la) ciclista	*cyclist*
el (la) entrenador(a)	*trainer, coach*
el equipo	*team, equipment*
el esquí	*skiing*
el fútbol	*soccer*
el fútbol americano	*football*
el (la) futbolista	*football (soccer) player*
el golf	*golf*
montar a caballo	*to ride a horse*
montar (andar) en bicicleta	*to ride a bicycle*
la natación	*swimming*
el tenis	*tennis*
el (la) tenista	*tennis player*

Sustantivos

el (la) aficionado(a)	*fan*
la anotación (el resultado)	*score*
el bate	*bat*
el campeón (la campeona)	*champion*
el campeonato	*championship*
la cancha	*(tennis) court*
la carrera	*race, contest*
la competencia	*competition*
el desarrollo	*development*
el (la) espectador(a)	*spectator*
los esquís	*skis*
el estadio	*stadium*
el fracaso	*failure*
el partido	*game, match*
la pelota	*ball*
la raqueta	*racket*
la red	*net*
la regla	*rule*
la temporada	*season*

Adjetivos

ágil	*agile*
débil	*weak*
divertido	*fun, amusing*
entusiasmado	*excited*
fuerte	*strong*
lastimado	*injured*
próximo	*next*

Conjunciones	(Conjunctions)
antes de que	*before*
después de que	*after*
en cuanto	*as soon as*
hasta que	*until*
tan pronto como	*as soon as*

Vocabulario adicional	
activo	*active*
animado	*spirited, full of life*
el año que viene	*next year*
el boxeo	*boxing*
el boxeador	*boxer*
la fuerza	*force, strength*
el (la) nadador(a)	*swimmer*
los ratos libres	*free time*
sonreír	*to smile*
tener lugar	*to take place*
típico	*typical*

Repasemos el vocabulario

A **¿Cuál no pertenece?** Indique Ud. la palabra que no está relacionada con las otras y explique.

1. coger	batear	patinar	tirar
2. aficionado	ciclista	tenista	pelotero
3. anotación	campo	cancha	estadio
4. pelota	raqueta	red	esquí
5. competencia	bate	carrera	partido

B **El mundo de los deportes.**

1. ¿Qué deporte(s) usa(n)...
   a. una pelota? c. un entrenador? e. unos guantes?
   b. un caballo? d. una red? f. un bate?
2. ¿Qué deporte(s) se practica(n) en...
   a. un estadio? c. un campo? e. un gimnasio?
   b. una cancha? d. una piscina?
3. ¿Qué deportes...
   a. necesitan sólo el cuerpo humano?
   b. cuestan mucho dinero si se practican con frecuencia?
   c. se asocian con los EE.UU.?
   d. se asocian con Europa y Latinoamérica?
   e. pueden ser peligrosos? Explique.

C **La cadena *(channel)* de los deportes.** Complete Ud. el anuncio con las palabras apropiadas de la lista.

deporte	lo que	deportivas
equipo	canchas	internacional

TODOS LOS DEPORTES
TODOS LOS DIAS
CON TODOS LOS QUE
SABEN DE DEPORTES

- Radio Deportes es la cadena especializada en transmisiones __1__. Está presente en todos los eventos deportivos a nivel nacional e __2__ que usted desea escuchar.
- Cuenta con el mejor __3__ de narradores y comentaristas especializados en cada __4__. Que le llevan toda la emoción. Todas las jugadas Todo __5__ sucede en las __6__. En las carreteras. En los escenarios deportivos.

nivel *level*
jugadas *plays*
sucede *happens*
carreteras *roads*

Formen grupos de tres o cuatro. Uds. son narradores de Radio Deportes. Escriban un segmento original en el cual comentan algún evento deportivo. Sean creativos.

D **Gustos y disgustos.** Termine Ud. las frases de una forma original.

1. En el invierno, me gusta mucho...
2. A muchos norteamericanos les encanta...
3. A mis amigos les gusta... pero a mí...
4. No me interesa... porque...
5. Siempre me ha gustado...
6. Me duele(n)... después de...

E **Los deportes y el clima.** Escoja Ud. una estación, un tipo de clima y un deporte y termine la frase de una forma original.

En <u>**el otoño**</u> cuando <u>**hace fresco**</u> me gusta <u>**ir a los partidos de fútbol**</u> porque... **(voy con mis amigos, nos divertimos mucho y después del partido hacemos una fiesta).**

LAS ESTACIONES	EL CLIMA	LOS DEPORTES
el invierno	hace frío	
la primavera	hace sol	
el verano	nieva	
el otoño	hace fresco	
	hace calor	

The Future Tense

So far you have learned two ways to express future action, the present tense and **ir** + **a** + infinitive.

1. The present tense can be used to express action taking place in the near future.

Estoy en casa todo el día hoy.	***I'll be*** *home all day today.*
Esta noche **tomo** una clase de aeróbicos.	*Tonight* ***I'm taking (I will take)*** an aerobics class.

2. The construction **ir** + **a** + *infinitive* is frequently used to express future action.

Vamos a jugar al vólibol mañana.	***We're going to play*** *volleyball tomorrow.*
El equipo **va a viajar** a Honduras el año que viene.	*The team* ***is going to travel*** *to Honduras next year.*

The future tense is also used to express future action.

Forma

The Future Tense

HABLAR		COMER		ESCRIBIR	
hablar**é**	hablar**emos**	comer**é**	comer**emos**	escribir**é**	escribir**emos**
hablar**ás**	hablar**éis**	comer**ás**	comer**éis**	escribir**ás**	escribir**éis**
hablar**á**	hablar**án**	comer**á**	comer**án**	escribir**á**	escribir**án**

1. To form the future tense, add the endings **-é, -ás, -á, -emos, -éis, -án** to the infinitive.[1]
2. The following verbs have irregular future stems. The future endings are added to these.

verb	stem	ending	Example: PONER	
decir	**dir-**		pondré	*I will put*
haber	**habr-**		pondrás	*you will put*
hacer	**har-**	é	pondrá	*he, she, you will put*
poder	**podr-**	ás	pondremos	*we will put*
poner	**pondr-**	á	pondréis	*you will put*
querer	**querr-**	emos	pondrán	*they, you will put*
saber	**sabr-**	éis		
salir	**saldr-**	án		
tener	**tendr-**			
venir	**vendr-**			

Yo le **diré** a Pablo que tú **vendrás** mañana. — ***I'll tell** Pablo that **you'll come** tomorrow.*

Habrá[2] treinta mil personas en el estadio. — ***There will be** thirty thousand people in the stadium.*

¡AVISO! Infinitives with written accents **(oír, sonreír)** drop the accents in the future tense **(oiré, sonreiremos).**

[1]It may be helpful to know that these endings come from the present indicative of the verb **haber:** h**e**, h**as**, h**a**, h**emos**, hab**éis**, h**an** (**hablar** he > **hablaré).**

[2]Note that **habrá** is used in the singular to express *there will be* for both singular and plural concepts.

Función

1. The future tense describes an action that will or shall take place. Although English requires the use of the auxiliary verbs *will* and *shall*, in Spanish only the simple future form is used.

   Iremos la semana que viene. — ***We will (shall)*** *go next week.*

2. To express willingness to do something the verbs **querer** or **desear** are used instead of the future tense.

   ¿Quiere Ud. acompañarme al partido? — ***Will you accompany me*** *to the game?*

3. Remember that future action is expressed by the present subjunctive in a sentence that requires the use of the subjunctive.

   Dudo que Jaime **lance** mañana. — *I doubt that Jaime* ***will pitch*** *tomorrow.*

4. The future tense can be used to express conjecture or probability in the present. Although in English special phrases are needed to indicate conjecture *(I wonder, I suppose, I guess, probably)*, in Spanish they are not necessary.

   ¿Dónde **estará** su mejor jugador? — *Where* ***do you suppose*** *their best player* ***is? (I wonder*** *where their best player* ***is.)***

   Estará lastimado. — ***He's probably*** *injured.*

Practiquemos

A **¿El futuro de los deportes?** Conteste Ud. las siguientes preguntas y explique sus respuestas. Luego entreviste a sus compañeros.

EN EL FUTURO...	SÍ	NO
1. ¿Jugarán las mujeres al fútbol americano profesional?	___	___
2. ¿Bajarán los salarios de los jugadores profesionales?	___	___
3. ¿Seguirá jugando al béisbol Mark McGwire?	___	___
4. ¿Será popular el esquí en la Florida?	___	___
5. ¿Participará Ud. en los Juegos Olímpicos?	___	___
6. ¿Practicará Ud. el boxeo algún día?	___	___
7. ¿Será Ud. aficionado(a) del ciclismo?	___	___
8. ¿Correrá Ud. en un maratón?	___	___

B **Una entrevista exclusiva.** Un periodista habla con un tenista antes de comenzar la Copa Davis, el famoso campeonato de tenis. Cambie Ud. los verbos al futuro.

Periodista: Ud. (jugar) ______ su primer partido de este campeonato en dos días. ¿(Sentirse) ______ nervioso? ¿Qué (hacer) ______ en las horas antes del partido?

Tenista: Yo (ver) ______ si tengo todo el equipo... raquetas, toallas, etc. (Hablar) ______ con los periodistas. (Tratar) ______ de estar muy tranquilo, pero eso (ser) ______ difícil porque (haber) ______ millones de televidentes *(viewers)* mirando el partido.

Periodista: Y, después del campeonato, ¿qué (hacer) ______ Ud.?

Tenista: Yo (seguir) ______ practicando todos los días y (empezar) ______ a entrenarme para el próximo campeonato. Mi hermano (jugar) ______ conmigo. Nosotros (practicar) ______ otros deportes como el básquetbol y la natación, y así me (mantener) ______ en buena forma.

C **En el partido de tenis.** Diga Ud. en qué orden van a pasar las siguientes actividades. Cambie los verbos al futuro.

1. Los amigos del campeón (ir) ______ a un club después para celebrar.
2. El primer jugador (servir) ______ la pelota.
3. Los jugadores (salir) ______ a la cancha.
4. Los jugadores (saludarse) ______ antes de empezar a jugar.
5. Ellos (jugar) ______ por dos horas, pero (haber) ______ sólo un campeón.
6. El partido (empezar) ______ a las cinco.
7. El mejor jugador (ganar) ______.
8. Los aficionados (sentarse) ______ en sus asientos.

Adverbs

Forma

1. Many adverbs in Spanish end in the suffix **-mente**, just as many in English end in **-ly** (for example, *easily, quickly, perfectly*). To form an adverb, add **-mente** to the feminine singular form of an adjective. Adverbs are invariable in form.

adjective	feminine form	adverb	English equivalent
rápido	rápida	**rápida**mente	*quickly*
fácil	fácil	**fácil**mente	*easily*
inteligente	inteligente	**inteligente**mente	*intelligently*

¡AVISO! When an adjective has a written accent, the adverb maintains the accent, as in **rápidamente** and **fácilmente.**

2. Many adverbs do not follow this pattern. Some commonly used adverbs are:

ahora	cada día (año...)	muy	siempre
allí, aquí	mal	nunca	todos los días
bien	mucho	poco	una vez (dos veces, a veces)

Función

1. Adverbs modify verbs, adjectives, and adverbs. They directly precede the adjective or adverb they modify and are placed after and close to the verb they modify.

Dora es **muy** fuerte y patina **muy rápidamente.**	*Dora is **very** strong and skates **very quickly.***

2. Adverbs can indicate:

a. quantity. They answer the question *how much?*

Él esquía **mucho** y patina **un poco.**	*He skis **a lot** and skates **a little.***

b. time. They answer the question *when?*

María llegará **temprano** pero Raúl no vendrá **hoy.**	*María will arrive **early** but Raúl won't come **today.***

c. place. They answer the question *where?*

Susana no vive **aquí** pero vive **cerca.**	*Susana doesn't live **here** but she lives **nearby.***

d. manner. They answer the question *how?*

El equipo jugó **muy bien.**	*The team played **very well.***

Practiquemos

A La sección de deportes del periódico. Cambie Ud. los adjetivos a adverbios.

1. En el partido, España tuvo problemas (principal) ______ contra Uruguay.
2. Los jugadores hondureños jugaron (ágil) ______ en el estadio.
3. (Técnico) ______ los brasileños son superiores, pero (físico) ______ los colombianos son los mejores.
4. El campeón habló (tranquilo) ______ y contestó las preguntas (honesto) ______.
5. René Higuida, el gran futbolista colombiano, pasó la pelota (fácil) ______.

B Al contrario. Conteste Ud. las preguntas de manera negativa, utilizando el antónimo de los adverbios subrayados.

1. ¿El tenista recibió el premio tristemente? (feliz)
2. ¿Los guatemaltecos ganaron el partido difícilmente? (fácil)
3. ¿Los boxeadores practicaron esporádicamente? (frecuente)
4. ¿Corrieron los peloteros lentamente? (rápido)
5. ¿Los jugadores hablaron nerviosamente? (tranquilo)

C La prognosis deportiva. Cambie Ud. los verbos entre paréntesis al futuro y termine las frases, formando adverbios de los adjetivos en la segunda columna.

1. Todos los peloteros (practicar) ______	**a.** fuerte
2. Iván Rodríguez (coger) ______	**b.** rápido
3. Los Medias Rojas (perder) ______	**c.** fácil
4. Sammy Sosa (batear) ______	**d.** perfecto
5. El Duque (lanzar) ______	**e.** frecuente
6. Roberto Alomar (tirar) ______	**f.** activo

Repaso: Cómo mantenerse en buenas condiciones

Para repasar la forma del presente del subjuntivo lea Ud. la siguiente selección y conteste las preguntas.

Es mejor que

- Coma despacio.
- Evite tentaciones. Saque los alimentos de alto contenido calórico del refrigerador y de la despensa. Tenga en casa únicamente lo que se propone comer en su dieta.
- Coma menos grasa. Use azúcares naturales de granos, frutas y verduras.
- Coma menos helado, queso, aderezos para ensaladas y aceites.
- Evite los bocadillos o tentenpies de paquete, las galletas y los postres con alto contenido en grasas.
- Use utensilios de teflón.
- Prepare las carnes al horno o a la parrilla, y las verduras al vapor, en lugar de freírlas en grasa o aceite.

- Coma productos lácteos desgrasados ("skim milk" en vez de leche entera).
- Haga ejercicio regularmente.
- Busque hacer actividades divertidas que no incluyan el comer (deportes, cultivar el jardín, etc).
- Acuda a terapia individual o de grupo si tiene dificultad para mantener su peso.

¿Por qué es mejor que Ud....

1. coma menos grasa (fat)?
2. haga ejercicios?
3. busque hacer actividades que no incluyan el comer?

The Present Subjunctive in Adverbial Clauses of Time

Forma y función

1. An adverbial clause is a clause (subject + verb) that modifies a verb in the main clause. Adverbial clauses are always introduced by conjunctions (words that join other words and phrases).

<u>Guatemala</u>	<u>ganó</u>	<u>fácilmente.</u>		*Guatemala won easily.*
subject	verb	adverb		
<u>Guatemala</u>	<u>ganó</u>	<u>después de que</u>	<u>Paco anotó el último gol.</u>	*Guatemala won after Paco made the last goal.*
subject	verb	conjunction	adverbial clause	

2. You already know the most common conjunction in Spanish: **que.** The subjunctive is used in an adverbial clause with the following conjunctions when future or pending actions are expressed or implied.

cuando	*when*	hasta que	*until*
después (de) que	*after*	mientras	*while*
en cuanto	*as soon as*	tan pronto como	*as soon as*

Iré a esquiar **en cuanto haya** suficiente nieve.	*I will go skiing* ***as soon as there's*** *enough snow.*
Sigan Uds. practicando **hasta que** el partido **empiece.**	*Continue practicing* ***until*** *the game* ***starts.***

The preceding sentences express an action in the main clause that will take place pending the completion of the action in the subordinate clause. You cannot be sure that these actions will occur since the future is uncertain. Will there ever be enough snow? Are you sure the game will start? Therefore, the subjunctive is used to indicate the uncertainty of the situation.

3. Many conjunctions are formed by adding **que** to a preposition (**después de que, hasta que**, and so on). Generally when there is no change of subject, the preposition is used with the infinitive. Compare the following sentences.

Después de patinar, voy a preparar chocolate caliente.	***After skating***, *I'm going to prepare hot chocolate.*
Después de que yo patine, mamá va a preparar chocolate caliente.	***After I skate***, *mom is going to prepare hot chocolate.*

4. The indicative is used after these conjunctions to indicate completed past action or to describe habitual action in the present.

Fui a esquiar **en cuanto hubo** suficiente nieve.	*I went skiing* ***as soon as there was*** *enough snow.*
Siempre voy a esquiar **en cuanto hay** suficiente nieve.	*I always go skiing* ***as soon as there is*** *enough snow.*

5. The subjunctive is always used with the conjunction **antes (de) que** *(before)*.

José siempre practica **antes de que lleguen** los otros jugadores.	*José always practices* ***before*** *the other players* ***arrive.***

Practiquemos

A **¡Excusas!** Un(a) amigo(a) quiere salir con Ud. pero Ud. no tiene interés y siempre le da una excusa. Cambie Ud. el verbo entre paréntesis al presente del subjuntivo. Siga el modelo.

MODELO No puedo jugar al tenis contigo hasta que mi madre me (comprar) **compre** una raqueta.

1. Sólo puedo ir al partido de fútbol contigo después de que mi padre (volver) ______ de la farmacia.
2. No puedo ir a esquiar contigo hasta que Luis me (devolver) ______ los esquís.
3. Iré a nadar contigo tan pronto como yo (encontrar) ______ un traje de baño.
4. No puedo hacer nada antes de que mi hermano me (dar) ______ dinero.
5. Puedo ir a un partido de básquetbol en cuanto yo (terminar) ______ toda la tarea.
6. Iré contigo a patinar cuando mi hermana me (prestar) ______ sus patines *(skates)* favoritos.

B **Listos para salir**. La familia Vasallo quiere ir a un partido de fútbol hoy pero no puede salir todavía por varias razones. Llene Ud. los espacios con la forma correcta del verbo entre paréntesis en el presente del subjuntivo.

MODELO No iremos hasta que todos (estar) **estén** listos.

1. Iremos al partido cuando mi papá (llegar) ______.
2. Saldremos en cuanto nosotros (encontrar) ______ las entradas.
3. No saldremos hasta que Susana (ponerse) ______ la chaqueta y los guantes.
4. Estaremos listos después de que mi mamá (preparar) ______ los sandwiches.
5. Te llamaremos tan pronto como nosotros (volver) ______ a casa.

Ahora, en el pasado. Por fin, la familia fue al partido. Llene los espacios con la forma correcta del verbo entre paréntesis en el pretérito. Compare las frases en el pasado con las frases en el futuro de la primera parte de este ejercicio.

MODELO No fuimos hasta que todos (estar) **estuvieron** listos.

1. Fuimos al partido cuando mi papá (llegar) ______.
2. Salimos en cuanto nosotros (encontrar) ______ las entradas.
3. No salimos hasta que Susana (ponerse) ______ la chaqueta y los guantes.
4. Estábamos listos después de que mi mamá (preparar) ______ los sandwiches.
5. Te llamamos tan pronto como nosotros (volver) ______ a casa.

C **Ud. tiene correo**. Ud. recibió una carta por correo electrónico de su amigo Carlos. Él comenta la participación de Ud. en el equipo universitario de béisbol. Busque en la segunda columna la terminación de las frases en la primera columna.

Querida Julia... Me alegro mucho de que juegues para tu equipo. Aquí te ofrezco algunas recomendaciones para tu primer partido.

1. Nada un poco antes de...	**a.** jugar el partido.
2. Empieza a correr en cuanto...	**b.** batees la pelota.
3. No empieces a correr hasta que...	**c.** el partido termine.
4. Báñate en agua caliente después de...	**d.** el lanzador tire la pelota.
5. Escríbeme por correo electrónico tan pronto como...	**e.** practicar.

Buena suerte. Carlos.

Ahora, conteste Ud. la carta, diciéndole qué pasó.

D **Papi, ¿cuándo... ?** Un padre lleva a su hijito a un partido de fútbol profesional por primera vez. Forme Ud. frases con las siguientes conjunciones adverbiales para contestar las preguntas del hijo. Con un(a) compañero(a), hagan los papeles del padre e hijo.

cuando   en cuanto   después de que   tan pronto como

MODELO Papi, ¿cuándo vamos a venir a otro partido? (tú/ser mayor)
Hijo, vamos a venir a otro partido cuando tú seas mayor.

1. Papi, ¿cuándo vas a comprarme un refresco? (tú/tener sed)
2. Papi, ¿cuándo va a empezar el partido? (los jugadores/estar preparados)
3. Papi, ¿cuándo voy a comer helado? (nosotros/terminar los perros calientes)
4. Papi, ¿cuándo van a sentarse los aficionados? (nuestro equipo/perder el partido)
5. Papi, ¿cuándo voy a hablar con los jugadores? (ellos/salir del campo)
6. Papi, ¿cuándo nos vamos a ir? Estoy aburrido. (el partido/terminar)

Spend more time with Mariana and her friends while you review grammar and expand your cultural horizons.
See the **Así es Mariana** exercise in your workbook for this lesson.

En resumen

A Los peloteros hispanos en los EE.UU. Escoja Ud. la palabra correcta entre paréntesis o forme un adverbio del adjetivo entre paréntesis.

Según los peloteros hispanos, para (llegar, llega) a las (gran, grandes) ligas hay que (saber, conocer) hablar inglés. Sin embargo, se (ha, han) notado un aumento *(increase)* en el número de jugadores puertorriqueños, cubanos, dominicanos, mexicanos, venezolanos y más. (Este, Esta) temporada ha (comenzada, comenzado) con más de 80 jugadores latinoamericanos. Dice el vicepresidente de los New York Mets: «Los de hoy son (tan, tantos) buenos (que, como) los de ayer». No hay duda que entre los más famosos (estén, están) el jardinero *(outfielder)* puertorriqueño, Juan González, el lanzador cubano, Liván Hernández, y el jardinero dominicano, el gran bateador, Sammy Sosa.

(Triste), es común que el latinoamericano que llegue aquí (sufra, sufre) del cambio de culturas y de idioma. Pero los equipos (ha, han) (comenzados, comenzado) a (preocuparse, se preocupan) por el pelotero hispano y ofrecen clases de inglés. Es probable que los jugadores (sabrán, sepan) hablar inglés (perfecto) en cuanto (empiece, empieza) la nueva temporada.

JUAN GONZÁLEZ
OUTFIELDER
TEXAS RANGERS

LIVAN FERNÁNDEZ
PITCHER
SAN FRANCISCO GIANTS

SAMMY SOSA
RIGHT FIELD
CHICAGO CUBS

B **Para estar siempre en forma**.

1. ¿Qué deporte practica este hombre? ¿Es éste un deporte realmente peligroso? Explique. ¿Qué otro deporte recomienda Ud. que él juegue? ¿Por qué?
2. Complete Ud. las frases para describir a este pobre pelotero.
   a. Le ______ la cabeza.
   b. Tiene la ______ rota.
   c. Le está sangrando *(bleeding)* la ______.
   d. Tiene el ______ hinchado.
   e. Ha perdido dos ______ de la boca.
3. En su opinión, ¿cuál es la mejor actividad física para desarrollar el cuerpo? ¿Participa Ud. en ella? Explique. ¿Qué actividades se consideran peligrosas? ¿Por qué?

C **El boxeo**. Complete Ud. el artículo con las palabras apropiadas de la lista.

guante	separarse	boxeador	boca
dientes	mano	edad *(age)*	

La 1_______ mínima para un 2_______ profesional es de 17 años cumplidos.

Cada 3_______ pesa 227 gramos. El protector de los 4_______ es de un material de caucho y mezcla de plástico blando que se hace sobre la medida de la 5_______ de cada boxeador.

El boxeador puede llevar en cada 6_______ una venda quirúrgica suave que no exceda de 2,5 metros de largo y 5 cms. de ancho.

La palabra Break quiere decir 7_______, Jab es un golpe de derecha realizado casi en línea recta al contendor.

caucho *rubber;* **blando** *soft*

venda quirúrgica *surgical bandage;* **suave** *soft*

D El esquí. Con un(a) compañero(a), lean Uds. el siguiente anuncio y hagan las actividades.

1. Arreglen Uds. los artículos de esquí mencionados en el anuncio y los que están en la siguiente lista en el orden de importancia para Ud.

las botas	los guantes	otros
los palos *(poles)*	la chaqueta	

anoraks *ski jackets*
gorros *caps*
fijaciones *bindings*
marcas *brands*

Este es el momento de equiparse para la práctica del esquí. En El Corte Inglés encontrará todo lo necesario: pantalones, anoraks, gorros, gafas, esquís, fijaciones... La mayor variedad de modelos de todas las grandes marcas.

FORME EQUIPO CON NOSOTROS Y LANCESE A DISFRUTAR SOBRE LA NIEVE

2. Uds. van a esquiar con sus amigos. Describan el viaje perfecto según el siguiente criterio.

a. el alojamiento	**d.** la condición de la pista *(course)*
b. las actividades sociales	**e.** la ropa
c. la comida y la bebida	**f.** el clima

E Un jugador pesimista. Traduzca Ud. el siguiente diálogo al español.

Paco: Don't worry. Next year our team will win the championship . . . easily.

Fernando: How do you know? Martínez is better than us now, and next year he'll be stronger.

Paco: But, we'll improve, too.

Fernando: Yeah, but as soon as the season ends, I have to get back to work, and classes will begin.

Paco: It doesn't matter. We'll train in our free time. You'll see.

F Minidrama. En grupos, representen una de las siguientes escenas.

1. Un hombre invita a una mujer a cenar en un restaurante y pasa toda la noche hablando sólo de los deportes. Ella intenta hablar de otra cosa pero resulta difícil.
2. Hágale Ud. una entrevista a un(a) atleta célebre.

G Composición.

1. Escriba Ud. un tema explicando por qué Ud. quiere o no quiere ser un(a) atleta profesional.
2. Escriba un artículo original sobre el (la)... del futuro.

a. cuidad	d. escuela o universidad
b. coche	e. comida
c. familia	f. deporte

Escuchemos

A **¡Los campeones!** Oscar comments on the success of last night's baseball game. His statements are incomplete. Choose the word that best completes each sentence.

MODELO (optimista/pesimista)
Siempre ganamos y por eso nuestro entrenador se siente muy _______. **optimista**
Siempre ganamos y por eso nuestro entrenador se siente muy optimista.

1. (rato/estadio)
2. (vencimos/entrenamos)
3. (animados/ágiles)
4. (fracaso/fuerte)
5. (batear/patinar)
6. (bateó/cogió)
7. (campeonato/campeón)
8. (equipo/partido)

B **Dictado**. You will hear a short narration about Anita and her feelings about tennis. Listen carefully to the entire selection. Listen again and write each sentence during the pauses.

You will then hear a series of questions related to the dictation. Answer them with complete sentences. Refer to your dictation.

No podemos volver a Miami sin que tú conozcas Old Town.

AVISO CULTURAL

(As a reading aid, refer to lesson vocabulary for new words.)

¿Qué sabe Ud. de los seis países centroamericanos de habla española? Guatemala: En el norte se encuentran las ruinas de Tikal, una antigua ciudad maya. Guatemala también es el país nativo del ganador del Premio *(prize)* Nóbel de literatura en 1967, Miguel Ángel Asturias y la ganadora del Premio Nóbel de la paz en 1992, Rigoberta Menchú. **El Salvador:** Aquí se encuentra la «Fuente de fuego *(fire)*», el volcán Izalco que produce una constante columna de fuego. **Honduras:** Es el único país de Centroamérica que no tiene volcán. **Nicaragua:** Es el país más grande de Centroamérica. La capital es Managua. **Costa Rica:** Es el único país de Centroamérica que no tiene ejército *(army)*. **Panamá:** Su moneda oficial lleva el nombre del descubridor del océano Pacífico, Balboa. El famoso sombrero llamado la jipijapa *(Panama hat)* se produce en Ecuador y no en Panamá. ¿Sabe Ud. a qué país corresponden las siguientes ciudades capitales? San Salvador, San José, Tegucigalpa, Panamá, Guatemala.

Preparativos

Review the vocabulary on pages 448–450 before viewing the video.

Al mirar el video o leer el diálogo siguiente, note Ud. el uso del modo subjuntivo. Ud. observará el uso del subjuntivo con conjunciones de propósito *(purpose)* y condición. Por ejemplo, Luis dice: «Iremos al famoso Bazaar del Mundo **para que puedas** comprar... » También dice: «No podemos volver a Miami **sin que conoz-**

cas... » Termine Ud. las dos frases anteriores de Luis y compárelas con las del diálogo. Parece que a Mariana le gusta mucho bromear *(joke)* con Luis. ¿Cuáles son dos ejemplos de bromas en este episodio?

Así es Mariana: San Diego y sus atracciones

Mariana y Luis Antonio acaban de visitar el zoológico de San Diego.

Mariana: ¡Cuánto me ha gustado el zoológico, Luis! Especialmente los tigres y los leones. Yo sé que son muy feroces, pero la verdad es que parecen gatitos.

Luis Antonio: Sí, sí, son muy impresionantes, pero los monos siempre han sido mis animales favoritos de aquí. Son muy cómicos. De niño le prometía a mi mamá portarme bien todo el día con tal que ella me llevara a ver los monos.

Mariana: Hmmmm. Pues, eso no me sorprende nada, con todo lo que tienes en común con ellos.

Luis Antonio: Muy chistoso.

Mariana: Bueno, y ahora, ¿qué? ¿Adónde vamos?

Luis Antonio: Bueno, no podemos volver a Miami sin que tú conozcas Old Town. Y claro, tienes que probar una de las deliciosas tortillas que se venden allí.

Mariana: Ah, otro recuerdo de tu niñez.

Luis Antonio: Sí... Old Town es precioso. Es la ciudad original de San Diego. Allí verás mucha influencia hispana. Iremos al famoso Bazaar del Mundo para que puedas comprar recuerdos para Alicia y Carla.

Los dos se pasean por Old Town, y finalmente se sientan para descansar.

Luis Antonio: Bueno, ahora... a buscar tortillas.

Mariana: Ay, Luis, no puedo más. Yo probaré tus tortillas con tal que tú me las traigas. Necesito descansar. Yo te espero aquí.

Luis Antonio: Bueno. Tú, tranquila... ahora vuelvo.

Él va y y vuelve con una tortilla.

Luis Antonio: Mariana... ¡Toma! Te va a gustar muchísimo.

Al ofrecerle la tortilla a Mariana, se le cae al suelo.

Es decir

A Relacione Ud. el adjetivo apropiado de la segunda columna con el sustantivo en la primera.

1. tigres y leones	**a.** hispana
2. monos	**b.** original
3. tortillas	**c.** cómicos
4. influencia	**d.** salvajes
5. ciudad	**e.** deliciosas

B En las siguientes frases, ¿hay que usar el indicativo o el subjuntivo?

1. Iremos al famoso Bazaar del Mundo para que tú (poder) ______ comprar recuerdos.
2. Probaré tus tortillas con tal que tú me las (traer) ______.
3. Sí, Old Town (ser) ______ precioso.
4. No podemos volver sin que tú (conocer) ______ Old Town.
5. Tienes que probar las deliciosas tortillas que se (vender) ______ allí.

C En grupos de tres, escriban dos versiones de cómo Luis y Mariana pasaron el día en San Diego.

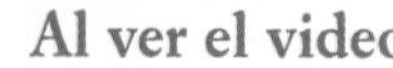

Al ver el video

A Después de ver el video, mencione Ud....

1. tres razones por las que a Mariana le gusta tanto el sur de California.
2. tres comidas que ha probado Mariana.
3. tres animales que Luis y Mariana vieron en el zoológico.
4. tres ejemplos de la influencia hispana en el sur de California.

B Ahora que han visto la belleza del sur de California, escriban un breve anuncio comercial, en el cual mencionen razones para visitar San Diego, y actividades que hay que hacer.

Vocabulario

Verbos

acampar (hacer cámping)	*to camp, go camping*
acercarse (a)	*to approach, come near (to)*
acompañar	*to accompany*
ahorrar	*to save (money, time . . .)*
alejarse (de)	*to withdraw, move away (from)*
atraer	*to attract*
disfrutar (de)	*to enjoy*
escalar	*to climb*
pescar	*to fish*

Adjetivos	
contaminado	*polluted, contaminated*
chistoso (cómico)	*funny*
feroz	*ferocious*
gracioso	*funny, entertaining; graceful*
indígena	*indigenous, native*
puro	*pure*
salvaje	*savage, wild*

Animales	
el elefante	*elephant*
el insecto	*insect*
el león	*lion*
el mono	*monkey*
el mosquito	*mosquito*
el oso	*bear*
el pez[1]	*fish*
la rana	*frog*
el tiburón	*shark*
el tigre	*tiger*
la tortuga	*turtle, tortoise*

La naturaleza	***(Nature)***
el aire	*air*
el ambiente	*environment, surroundings*
el bosque	*forest, woods*
el cielo	*sky*
el desierto	*desert*
la estrella	*star*
el lago	*lake*
la luna	*moon*
la montaña	*mountain*
el océano	*ocean*
la paz	*peace*
el río	*river*
la selva	*jungle, forest*
la tierra	*earth, land, soil, ground*
la tranquilidad	*tranquility*
el volcán	*volcano*

[1]Note that **pescado** also means *fish*, but refers to the fish when caught and prepared to be eaten.

Otras palabras y expresiones (Refer to conjunctions on p. 458)

el acuario	*aquarium*
el bote	*rowboat*
el circo	*circus*
como[1] (conj.)	*as; since; because*
el globo	*balloon*
la mochila	*knapsack, backpack*
el parque (de atracciones)	*(amusement) park*
el payaso	*clown*
el recreo	*recreation*
el saco de dormir	*sleeping bag*
la tienda de campaña	*tent*

Vocabulario adicional

estar de acuerdo	*to agree*
intenso	*intense*
junto	*together*
mundial	*universal, worldwide*
panorámico	*panoramic*
soleado	*sunny*
soñar despierto	*to daydream*
tomar (echar) una siesta	*to take a nap*

Repasemos el vocabulario

A **¿Cuál no corresponde?** Su profesor(a) va a leer una serie de palabras. Indique cuál no está relacionada con las siguientes palabras y explique.

La palabra...

1. ___ no está relacionada con un río porque...

2. ___ no está relacionada con el zoológico porque...

3. ___ no está relacionada con un circo porque...

4. ___ no está relacionada con la naturaleza porque...

5. ___ no está relacionada con hacer cámping porque...

[1]Note that **como** is used to mean **because** in the sense of *as* or *since*. **Como no tengo dinero, no puedo ir al circo.** *Because (As, Since) I don't have money, I can't go to the circus.*

B Nombre Ud. tres...

1. cosas que se necesitan para acampar.
2. cosas que hay en un circo.
3. sitios donde se puede nadar.
4. tipos de animales que hay en el acuario.
5. tipos de animales salvajes.

C Descripciones. Use Ud. adjetivos de esta lección y de las lecciones anteriores para describir las siguientes cosas.

1. un desierto
2. el cielo
3. la vista desde una montaña
4. un payaso
5. un volcán

D ¿Conoce Ud. los animales? Su profesor(a) va a leer una serie de descripciones. Identifique el animal.

a.

b.

c.

d.

e.

f.

E **Otros animales.** Nombre Ud. los siguientes animales. Descríbalos y diga todo lo que sabe de ellos.

1.

2.

3.

4.

Ahora con un(a) compañero(a) escriban definiciones originales de cinco palabras de la lista del vocabulario y la clase tiene que adivinarlas *(guess them)*.

F **Definiciones.** Complete Ud. las definiciones con las palabras apropiadas.

árboles	animales	puro	graciosas	tanque
pasearse	barco	nariz	parque	salvajes

1. bosque: Sitio lleno de ______ y aire ______.

2. bote: ______ pequeño que se usa para ______ en el agua.

3. zoológico: ______ donde se encuentran animales ______ o exóticos.

4. payaso: Cómico con una ______ grande y roja que hace cosas ______.

5. acuario: ______ destinado a la exhibición de ______ acuáticos.

Ahora, defina los términos siguientes:

6. selva

7. tienda de campaña

8. estrella

9. aire contaminado

The Imperfect Subjunctive

When studying the indicative and subjunctive moods, you learned that the indicative mood has many simple tenses whereas the subjunctive mood has only two.

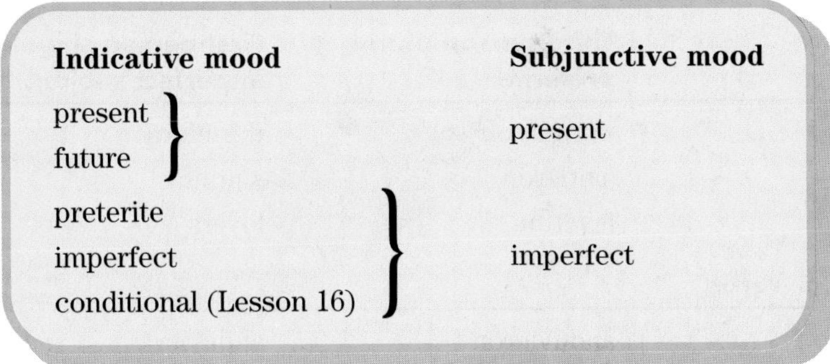

Indicative mood	Subjunctive mood
present future	present
preterite imperfect conditional (Lesson 16)	imperfect

As you know, the present subjunctive is used to express present or future action in a sentence that requires the use of the subjunctive.

Dudo que Juan **esté** aquí hoy. { *I doubt that Juan* ***is*** *here today.* / *I doubt that Juan* ***will be*** *here today.* }

In a sentence that requires the use of the subjunctive, the imperfect subjunctive is used to express both completed and habitual past action (preterite and imperfect meanings). It is also used to express conditional meaning (*would be*, *would do*, and so forth). The conditional tense is fully discussed in Lesson 16.

Forma

HABLAR		COMER		ESCRIBIR	
hablara	habl**áramos**	comiera	comi**éramos**	escribiera	escribi**éramos**
hablar**as**	hablar**ais**	comier**as**	comier**ais**	escribier**as**	escribier**ais**
hablara	hablar**an**	comiera	comier**an**	escribiera	escribier**an**

1. To form the imperfect subjunctive of regular **-ar, -er,** and **-ir** verbs remove the **-on** from the third-person plural **(ellos)** preterite form and add the endings **-a, -as, -a, -amos, -ais, -an.**[1] Note that the first-person plural **(nosotros)** form has a written accent **(compráramos, bebiéramos).**
2. There are no irregular verbs in the imperfect subjunctive because any stem change, spelling change, or irregularity already occurred in the preterite. All imperfect subjunctive verbs follow the rule of using the third-person plural preterite stem with imperfect subjunctive endings. Study the following verbs.

Infinitive	Third-person plural preterite	First-person singular imperfect subjunctive
dormir	durmieron	durmiera
sentir	sintieron	sintiera
leer	leyeron	leyera
Irregular verbs		
andar	anduvieron	anduviera
dar	dieron	diera
decir	dijeron	dijera
estar	estuvieron	estuviera
haber	hubieron	hubiera
hacer	hicieron	hiciera
ir	fueron	fuera
poder	pudieron	pudiera
poner	pusieron	pusiera
querer	quisieron	quisiera
saber	supieron	supiera
ser	fueron	fuera
tener	tuvieron	tuviera
venir	vinieron	viniera

[1]An alternative form is to remove the **-ron** from the third-person plural preterite and add the endings **-se, -ses, -se, -semos, -seis, -sen: habla-ron + se = hablase**.... These forms are used interchangeably with the -ra forms, primarily in Spain.

Función

1. The imperfect subjunctive is used in noun, adjective, and adverbial clauses to express past action in a sentence that requires the use of the subjunctive.
   - El presente: cláusula sustantiva

     Yo **no quiero que tú escales** los Himalayas. — *I **don't want you to climb** the Himalayas.*
   - El pasado: cláusula sustantiva

     Yo **no quería que tú escalaras** los Himalayas. — *I **didn't want you to climb** the Himalayas.*
   - El presente: cláusula adjetival

     Yo **quiero** escalar una montaña que **sea** alta. — *I **want** to climb a mountain that **is** tall.*
   - El pasado: cláusula adjetival

     Yo **quería** escalar una montaña que **fuera** alta. — *I **wanted** to climb a mountain that **was** tall.*
   - El presente: cláusula adverbial

     Yo **nadaré** en el río antes de que tú **escales** los Himalayas. — *I **will swim** in the river before you **climb** the Himalayas.*
   - El pasado: cláusula adverbial

     Yo **nadé** en el río **antes de que** tú **escalaras** los Himalayas. — *I **swam** in the river **before** you **climbed** the Himalayas.*

2. The imperfect subjunctive has various English equivalents according to the context in which it appears.

   Esperábamos que Juan **viniera** al lago. — *We hoped that Juan **would come** to the lake.*

   Era bueno que Juan **viniera** al lago. — *It was good that Juan **came** to the lake.*

   De niño me gustaba que Juan **viniera** al lago. — *As a child I liked that Juan **used to come*** to the lake.

3. The imperfect subjunctive of the verbs **querer, poder,** and **deber** can be used to indicate courtesy or to soften a request.

   ¿Pudiera pasarme la sal, por favor? — ***Could you** please pass me the salt?*

   Quisiera pedirte un favor. — ***I would like** to ask you a favor.*

   Debiera tener cuidado en el bosque. — ***You really should** be careful in the forest.*

Practiquemos

A De compras en Centroamérica. Ada nos dice lo que su guía turístico le aconsejó acerca de las compras en Guatemala. Llene Ud. los espacios con la forma correcta del verbo entre paréntesis en el imperfecto del subjuntivo.

El guía turístico me aconsejó que yo...

1. no les (dar) ______ propinas a los taxistas.
2. (buscar) ______ las pequeñas tiendas de artesanías. Son más baratas.
3. (conseguir) ______ un «huipil», que es la blusa típica de las indias.
4. no (pagar) ______ más de 20 dólares por una falda estilo maya.
5. no (comprar) ______ los productos farmacéuticos norteamericanos. Son caros.
6. (ir) ______ al Mercado Nacional de Artesanía.

B **Actividades variadas.** La familia de Ada prefiere hacer otras actividades. Mire Ud. los dibujos y diga qué sugirió el guía turístico que hicieran los familiares de Ada. Use el imperfecto del subjuntivo y termine la siguiente frase:

El guía turístico sugirió que...

Cecilia y Carlos/visitar

MODELO **El guía turístico sugirió que Cecilia y Carlos visitaran las ruinas mayas.**

1.

la abuela/descansar

2.

las jóvenes/ver

3.

papá/jugar

4.

Felipe/montar

5.

nosotros/comer

C **Ud. tiene correo.** Ud. recibió la siguiente carta por correo electrónico de sus amigos que están de vacaciones en San José. Llene los espacios con la forma correcta del verbo en el imperfecto del subjuntivo o del indicativo para saber cómo lo pasan.

Hola... Aquí estamos. Ayer hicimos muchas cosas. Por ejemplo...

1. Buscamos un club nocturno que (tener) ______ música rock.
2. Queríamos ver una película que no (poner) ______ subtítulos.
3. Conocimos a otro extranjero que no (saber) ______ hablar español.
4. No había ningún restaurante que (servir) ______ comida norteamericana.
5. Yo esperaba encontrar un museo que (ofrecer) ______ exhibiciones por la noche.
6. No vi ninguna taquilla *(box office)* que (vender) ______ entradas para el concierto.
7. Había varios autobuses que (poder) ______ llevarnos al centro.
8. Finalmente compramos un libro que (tener) ______ mucha información sobre la vida nocturna de esta ciudad.

Ahora, conteste la carta de sus amigos. Hágales tres preguntas sobre su viaje.

The Subjunctive in Adverbial Clauses of Purpose and Dependency

Función

You have learned that the subjunctive is used in the subordinate clause after conjunctions of time when future or pending actions are expressed or implied. When completed past action or habitual present action is indicated, the indicative is used.

The subjunctive is also used in adverbial clauses after conjunctions of purpose *(I will write to you in order that you may know what's happening)* and after conjunctions that express situations of dependency *(I will go to the movies provided that my check arrives).*

1. The following conjunctions reflect purpose or dependency. The subjunctive is always used in a subordinate clause that is introduced by these conjunctions.

a menos que	*unless*	en caso (de)[1] que	*in case that*
antes (de)[1] que	*before*	para que	*in order that*
con tal (de)[1] que	*provided that*	sin que	*without*

Iré con José **con tal que** él me invite.	*I'll go with José* ***provided that*** *he invites me.*
Fui al museo **antes de que** se cerrara.	*I went to the museum* ***before*** *it closed.*

2. Remember that when there is no change of subject the infinitive is used after the prepositions **antes, de, para**, and **sin.**

Vamos a las montañas **para descansar**.	*Let's go to the mountains* ***to rest.***
Vamos a las montañas **para que mi papá descanse**.	*Let's go to the mountains* ***so that my dad will rest.***
Dejé las llaves en casa **sin saberlo**.	*I left the keys at home* ***without knowing it.***
Dejé las llaves en casa **sin que mi mamá lo supiera.**	*I left the keys at home* ***without my mom knowing it.***

[1]Note that the use of the preposition **de** in these conjunctions is optional. Also note that **antes de que** is mentioned with adverbial conjunctions of time as well as of dependency. Although **antes de que** (before) does refer to time, it also reflects dependency in that one action must occur before another. For this reason, unlike adverbial conjunctions of time, **antes de que** always is followed by the subjunctive.

Practiquemos

A **Una gira turística por Centroamérica.** Lea Ud. «Una gira turística por Centroamérica» en las páginas 468–469 de la *Gaceta 5*. Su compañero y su familia se van para Centroamérica y Ud. les pregunta sobre su viaje. Complete las preguntas con la información apropiada de la lista. Su compañero va a formar respuestas con la información entre paréntesis. Siga el modelo.

MODELO Ud.: ¿Vas a Costa Rica para conocer **San José**? (todos/relajarse en la playa)
Su compañero: **Sí, y para que todos se relajen en la playa.**

las isletas — el famoso canal — en un Turicentro
de la arquitectura colonial — las pirámides

1. ¿Vas a Guatemala para sacar fotos ______? (mi esposa/comprar recuerdos)
2. ¿Vas a El Salvador para quedarte ______? (el abuelo/ver los volcanes)
3. ¿Vas a Honduras para escalar ______? (mis hijas/admirar los templos)
4. ¿Vas a Nicaragua para visitar ______? (mi hijo/pescar en el lago)
5. ¿Vas a Panamá para ver ______? (nosotros/disfrutar de su hospitalidad)

Su compañero ha vuelto de su viaje. Hágale las mismas preguntas en el pasado y él se las contestará en el pasado también.

MODELO Ud. ¿Fuiste a Costa Rica para conocer **San José**?
Sí, y para que todos se relajaran en la playa.

B **Conexiones con <u>a menos que</u> y <u>para que</u>.** Haga Ud. las siguientes actividades.

1. Busque Ud. en la segunda columna la terminación de la frase en la primera columna. Use la conjunción **a menos que** para unir *(unite)* las frases. Cambie el verbo al presente del subjuntivo. Luego, traduzca las frases al inglés.

Iremos al parque... papá (tener) que trabajar.
Iremos al parque a menos que papá tenga que trabajar.
We will go to the park unless dad has to work.

EL PARQUE DE ATRACCIONES

1. Juanito no quiere ir al parque de atracciones...	**a.** nos (doler) ___ el estómago.
2. Vamos a la montaña rusa *(roller coaster)*...	**b.** (llover) ___.
3. Podemos comprar perros calientes...	**c.** (haber) ___ caballitos *(carousel).*
4. De postre comeremos helado...	**d.** tú (tener) ___ miedo.
5. Pasaremos todo el día allí...	**e.** sólo se (vender) ___ hamburguesas.

2. Ahora, use Ud. la conjunción **para que** para unir las siguientes frases. Cambie Ud. el verbo al imperfecto de subjuntivo. Luego, traduzca las frases al inglés.

VIAJES DE RECREO

1. Papá volvió al hotel...	**a.** mi abuelo (respirar) ___ el aire puro.
2. Mis tíos fueron a Centroamérica...	**b.** nosotros (disfrutar) ___ de la vista.
3. Viajamos a la costa...	**c.** mamá (tomar) ___ una siesta.
4. Juan quería subir la montaña...	**d.** mis primos (ver) ___ los volcanes.
5. Mi abuela fue a Arizona...	**e.** mis hermanitos (divertirse) ___ en la playa.

C **Sólo el subjuntivo.** Complete Ud. las frases con la conjunción apropiada. Cambie los verbos al presente del subjuntivo. Puede usar algunas conjunciones más de una vez.

a menos que   con tal (de) que   para que   sin que   en caso (de) que

1. Vamos al acuario ______ los niños (asistir) ______ a una exhibición de tortugas gigantescas.
2. Compra tú otro boleto ______ Oscar (querer) ______ ir al circo, también.
3. Papá no va a las montañas ______ nosotros (poder) ______ pescar.
4. Voy al museo contigo ahora ______ tú (ir) ______ al mercado conmigo más tarde.
5. Prefiero subir las pirámides por la mañana ______ (hacer) ______ calor por la tarde.
6. Es imposible planear el viaje ______ ella lo (saber) ______.
7. Podemos conseguir las mochilas hoy ______ la tienda no (estar) ______ cerrada.
8. No quiero irme del país ______ mi mamá me (comprar) ______ un collar de jade.

Sequence of Tenses I: The Present and Present Perfect Subjunctive

Función

1. The present subjunctive and the present perfect subjunctive are used in the subordinate clause of a sentence that requires the subjunctive when the verb in the main clause is in the present tense, the future tense, or is a command.[1]

Main clause	**Subordinate clause**
present future command	present subjunctive present perfect subjunctive

Le **pido** a Roberto Le **pediré** a Roberto **Pídale Ud.** a Roberto	que traiga las mochilas.	***I ask*** *Robert* ***I will ask*** *Robert* ***Ask*** *Robert*	*to bring the backpacks.*

2. The present perfect subjunctive is used in the subordinate clause to express action that has already taken place in a context that requires the use of the present subjunctive.

Me alegro de que **tú hayas acampado** con nosotros. — ***I'm happy*** *that* ***you have camped*** *with us.*

Espero que **todos** lo **hayan pasado** bien. — ***I hope*** *that* ***everyone has had*** *a good time.*

Practiquemos

A **Costa Rica.** Ud. sabe mucho de este país centroamericano. Aconséjeles a las siguientes personas qué hacer allí. Use los verbos sugeridos *(suggested)* y cambie los infinitivos al subjuntivo.

El volcán Poás

MODELO Quiero nadar en Puntarenas. (recomiendo/Puerto Viejo)
Recomiendo que nades en Puerto Viejo.

1. Ramona quiere sacar fotos en San José. (será mejor/Cartago)
2. Queremos visitar Costa Rica en agosto. (sugiero/mayo)
3. Pedro tiene ganas de probar los frijoles de allí. (recomiendo/los tamales)
4. Los Ortiz van a alojarse en el Hotel Costa Rica. (insistiré en que/la Pensión Heredia)
5. Yo quiero pasar una semana en Alajuela. (aconsejo/la capital)
6. Los turistas desean ver el volcán Irazú. (dígales/el volcán Poás)

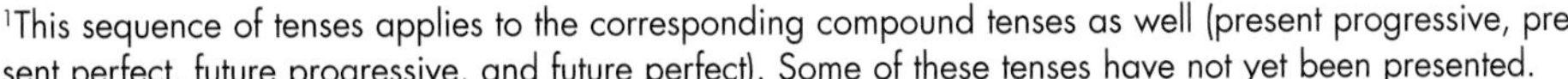
[1]This sequence of tenses applies to the corresponding compound tenses as well (present progressive, present perfect, future progressive, and future perfect). Some of these tenses have not yet been presented.

B **Unas vacaciones para todos.** Susana escribe un artículo cada semana para el periódico sobre qué hacer y adónde ir de vacaciones. Llene Ud. los espacios con la forma correcta del verbo en el subjuntivo, el indicativo o el infinitivo.

No es fácil (encontrar) ______ un sitio ideal para (pasar) ______ las vacaciones con la familia. Siempre buscamos un lugar que (ofrecer) ______ diversiones para los niños para que sus vacaciones (ser) ______ memorables. Pero es cierto que los padres también (necesitar) ______ actividades que (ser) ______ sólo para ellos. Pues, es verdad que yo (haber) ______ encontrado el sitio perfecto para Uds. Si Uds. quieren visitar una ciudad que (tener) ______ un ambiente tranquilo y cosmopolita, tienen que (visitar) ______ Antigua, Guatemala. Todos saben que Antigua (ser) ______ la antigua capital del país y que fue destruida *(destroyed)* casi por completo en 1773. También es verdad que Antigua (gozar) ______ de un clima muy bueno. ¿Qué pueden Uds. (hacer) ______ allí?

Antigua, Guatemala

1. Será mejor que Uds. (quedarse) ______ en un hotel que (tener) ______ piscina para los niños. Con el calor que hace, ellos podrán (pasar) ______ todos los días nadando.
2. Sugiero que todos (disfrutar) ______ de la gran variedad de artesanía que se encuentra en este gran centro artístico. Sé que a Uds. les (ir) ______ a gustar los tejidos *(weavings)*.
3. Antes de que Uds. (salir) ______, deben comprar un recuerdo único... el jade de Guatemala. Los mayas valoraban *(valued)* esta piedra *(stone)* preciosa mucho, y la usaban para crear excelentes obras *(works)* artísticas.

Espero que Uds. (haber) ______ escuchado mis consejos y les quiero (desear) ______ un buen viaje.

C **Decisiones.** Ud. y su amigo(a) planean un fin de semana divertido. Ud. tiene muchas ideas pero a su amigo(a) no le gusta ninguna. Terminen las frases de una forma original. Luego, escriban dos ideas más.

1. ¿Por qué no vamos al circo?
   No, porque no me gusta que...
2. Tengo ganas de ir al Jardín Botánico. ¿Y tú?
   Yo no. Prefiero buscar un parque que...
3. ¿Vamos al Museo de Antropología?
   En mi opinión, será mejor que...
4. Dicen que la feria *(fair)* de artesanías es interesante. ¿Quieres ir?
   No creo. Allí no hay nada que...
5. Me encantan los cafés al aire libre. ¿Me acompañas?
   Ahora no, a menos que...

> Spend more time with Mariana and her friends while you review grammar and expand your cultural horizons.
> See the **Así es Mariana** exercise in your workbook for this lesson.

En resumen

A **Centroamérica... un paraíso *(paradise)*.** Relacione Ud. los siguientes lugares centroamericanos con la descripción apropiada. Busque la «pista» *(clue)* en las descripciones.

Monteverde	Portobelo	la selva de Petén
el lago de Atitlán	islas *(islands)* de San Blas	

1. ______ es una densa jungla guatemalteca.
2. ______ en Panamá fue el puerto *(port)* más rico de la ruta entre España y América en el siglo *(century)* XVI.
3. ______ en Guatemala está rodeado *(surrounded)* de doce pueblos pequeños que son accesibles sólo por barco.
4. En las 368 ______ al norte de Panamá, viven los indios cunas que mantienen costumbres antiguas de hace más de mil años.
5. ______ es una reserva biológica situada en la parte montañosa de Costa Rica.

B **Si Ud. es deportista, vaya a Panamá.** Complete Ud. el párrafo con la forma apropiada del verbo entre paréntesis en el presente del indicativo, el presente del subjuntivo o el infinitivo.

Voy a hacer un viaje al extranjero. Todo el mundo recomienda que yo (ir) ______ a Panamá, un pequeño país situado entre Costa Rica en Centroamérica y Colombia en la América del Sur. Sugieren que yo (conseguir) ______ un pequeño bote para (pescar) ______ en los ríos. Es fácil (alquilar) ______ caballos y equipo para que nosotros (poder) ______ acampar. Quiero que mi hermano me (acompañar) ______, pero no creo que él (poder) ______ porque (querer) ______ ahorrar su dinero para ir a esquiar a Chile en julio. Como no quiero ir solo, llamaré a mi amigo Carlos para ver si él quiere (viajar) ______ conmigo. Yo dudo que él (poder) ______ conseguir el dinero en tan poco tiempo. Tengo muchas ganas de (ir) ______. Todos me aconsejan que yo (asistir) ______ a un partido de básquetbol, un deporte muy popular allí. ¡Qué emoción! Me muero de ganas de ir.

Ahora, en el pasado. Cambie Ud. el párrafo al pasado.

C **En Costa Rica.** Complete Ud. la lectura con la forma correcta de la palabra entre paréntesis. Si hay dos palabras, escoja la más apropiada. Traduzca las palabras subrayadas al español.

Costa Rica es uno de los (país) ______ más variados (del, en el) mundo. El Estado (has made) ______ un sistema (modelo) ______ de parques nacionales donde (one finds) ______ (un, una) variedad de flora y fauna: (volcán) ______ activos, jardines de orquídeas *(orchids)* y bosques tropicales. (It is interesting) ______ (ir) ______ de excursión al Parque Nacional Tortuguero que (is) ______ en la costa del Caribe. Allí (one can) ______ observar la naturaleza del trópico en su estado salvaje: (monkeys) ______, tortugas y (more) ______. (Esto, Este) parque fue creado (por, para) (el, la) protección de la tortuga verde, un animal importante y en (danger) ______ de extinción. (Otro) ______ excursión fascinante es (to the) ______ Parque Nacional del volcán Poás, un volcán moderadamente activo. Es recomendable que el viajero (llevar) ______ un abrigo porque (it's very cold) ______ allí.

D **Acampando en las montañas.** Traduzca Ud. el siguiente diálogo al español.

Raúl: Fresh air, peace, tranquility . . . You'll enjoy this place.

Ana: Frogs, insects, wild animals . . . I didn't want you to bring me here. You know that I don't like to camp. I insist that we go home right now.

Raúl: Ana, don't be that way. We can't leave without you seeing the moon and the stars and the mountains.

Ana: O.K., I'll stay for one day, provided that we go to the beach next year. All right?

Raúl: Yes. When I was a child I always wanted my parents to take me to the beautiful beaches of Costa Rica.

E **Minidrama.** En grupos, representen una de las siguientes escenas.

1. Ud. intenta planear un día de descanso para la familia pero resulta difícil. A su hijo de seis años no le gustan ni el circo ni el acuario. Él prefiere participar en otras actividades.
2. A Ud. le gusta la ciudad y a su amigo le gusta el campo. No saben qué hacer para pasarlo bien el próximo fin de semana.

F **Composición.**

1. Escriba Ud. sobre un día de descanso muy divertido (aburrido, fascinante, peligroso) que Ud. pasó cuando era niño(a).
2. Refiriéndose a los ejercicios que describen Centroamérica en esta lección, escríbale una carta breve a su amigo(a) en la cual Ud. habla de su viaje a algunos de estos lugares.

Escuchemos

A **¡Qué divertido es hacer cámping!** You will hear a series of statements that Roberto makes that describe what he and his family are doing during a camping trip. Repeat each one, and then decide if the corresponding drawing matches the description. Write **cierto** or **falso** in the space below each drawing.

MODELO Nosotros hacemos cámping en un desierto grande. **falso**

1.  ______________

2.  ______________

3.  ______________

4.  ______________

5.  ______________

6.  ______________

7.  ______________

8.  ______________

B **Dictado.** You will hear a short narration about Marta's afternoon at the circus with her little sister, Rosita. Listen carefully to the entire selection. Listen again and write each sentence during the pauses.

You will then hear a series of false statements related to the dictation. Correct each one with a complete sentence. Refer to your dictation.

Gaceta 5 Centroamérica

La catedral y un parque colonial en la ciudad de Guatemala

Una gira turística por Centroamérica

Preparativos: Estrategias de prelectura

1. Antes de hacer una gira por Centroamérica, mire Ud. la sección **Es decir** para ayudar a anticipar lo que va a leer. ¿Qué países va a visitar? ¿Cuáles son las capitales de esos países?
2. Hojee el párrafo sobre Guatemala para encontrar:
   a. un cognado relacionado con la naturaleza.
   b. un cognado relacionado con la ciudad.
   c. un cognado relacionado con la cultura indígena.
3. Hojee la lectura para saber a qué se refieren los números y las fechas siguientes:
   a. los números: 25, 310, 10 por ciento, 1 por ciento.
   b. las fechas: 1931, 1972.
4. En Centroamérica, ¿adónde va el turista que quiere ver...
   a. volcanes? b. pirámides? c. selvas? d. playas?

El volcán Izalco en El Salvador

Centroamérica une° América del Norte con América del Sur, y geográficamente se extiende desde el istmo° de Tehuantepec en el sur de México hasta el istmo de Panamá. Está cruzada° de norte a sur por la cadena° volcánica del océano Pacífico. En esta tierra, donde lo antiguo se combina con lo moderno, hay actividades diversas y atractivos° naturales que pueden satisfacer los gustos de todos.

unites
isthmus
crossed
chain
attractions

Guatemala es la tierra de la eterna primavera con lagos, volcanes y centros coloniales de mucho interés. Sus diversos grupos indígenas ofrecen un colorido° especial por sus bellos tejidos° y sus trabajos en plata. La Ciudad de Guatemala, la capital del país, es una metrópoli famosa por sus museos y sus mercados. La Antigua es una joya° de arquitectura colonial y es el centro de producción artesanal.° Las ruinas mayas de Tikal en la selva de Petén son admiradas por miles de turistas cada año. Todos los pueblos tienen su propio volcán, que da un toque° especial al paisaje guatemalteco. A unas horas de la capital está el lago de Atitlán, llamado «el lago más bello del mundo» por el escritor inglés Aldous Huxley.

El pequeño país de **El Salvador** tiene 25 volcanes, y los más importantes son Santa Ana, San Miguel e Izalco. Los mayas de El Salvador abandonaron el país cuando un volcán destruyó sus ciudades y las enterró° con cenizas.° Sus numerosas ruinas todavía están en un proceso de exploración. Es una nación de mucha industria, y muchos hogares° son pequeñas fábricas de ropa, tejidos, cerámica y joyería.° El país tiene diez parques naturales o «Turicentros» y uno de los más famosos está situado en el lago Ilopango, un inmenso lago volcánico.

En Copán, **Honduras,** está una de las ciudades mayas más grandes de su tiempo. Fundada en el siglo V, fue la primera capital del imperio maya. Allí hay pirámides, cortes, templos y otros tesoros° arqueológicos. Copán ha sido nombrada patrimonio° nacional para todo el continente.

Como Honduras, **Nicaragua** es una tierra de montañas y bosques. En 1931 y en 1972 Managua, la capital, sufrió terremotos° que destruyeron casi totalmente su aspecto colonial. La ciudad de Granada, un tesoro histórico-artístico, y el lago Nicaragua, con 310 isletas bonitas, son dos sitios que hay que visitar.

Costa Rica, por no tener un ejército° nacional, se llama la Suiza° de Centroamérica. A los costarricenses les gusta decir que sus cuarteles° se han convertido en escuelas, y sus soldados° en maestros. El nivel° de analfabetismo° es del 10 por ciento, uno de los más bajos de toda América. A diferencia de los otros países centroamericanos, la población indígena es sólo de 1 por ciento. San José, la capital y las playas hermosas son dos atractivos turísticos.

Panamá, un país lleno de bosques y selvas, es famoso por la hospitalidad de sus habitantes y por la exótica flora y fauna. Es interesante visitar la activa Zona del canal de Panamá para ver las enormes esclusas° y aprender sobre la historia del canal.

color; weavings
jewel; craft
touch
buried; ashes
homes; jewelry
treasures
heritage
earthquakes
army
Switzerland
barracks; soldiers
level; illiteracy
locks

El canal de Panamá

Es decir

A Los países centroamericanos. Comente Ud. sobre los países centroamericanos según el criterio siguiente.

Guatemala	El Salvador	Nicaragua
Honduras	Costa Rica	Panamá

1. paisaje
2. característica única
3. atractivos turísticos
4. influencia indígena
5. otro

B Lugares de interés en Centroamérica. Relacione Ud. el lugar en la primera columna con la información en la segunda columna. ¿A qué país corresponde cada lugar?

Las ruinas mayas de Copán, Honduras

1. Managua	**a.** volcán
2. Atitlán	**b.** centro de artesanía indígena
3. Zona del canal	**c.** capital de un país fundamentalmente pacífico
4. La Antigua	**d.** conexión entre el Atlántico y el Pacífico
5. Tikal	**e.** antigua capital de los mayas
6. Izalco	**f.** ciudad maya situada en la selva
7. Copán	**g.** el lago más bonito del mundo
8. San José	**h.** destruida dos veces

Practiquemos

La música de Centroamérica. Complete Ud. la lectura *(reading)* sobre la música de Centroamérica con las palabras apropiadas de la siguiente lista.

viene	han sido	instrumentos
vestirse	es	han traído
son	tocar	gusta

La música y la danza ______ parte del pueblo *(people)* centroamericano desde antes de la colonización.

La marimba, un instrumento musical de madera *(wood)*, similar al xilófono, ______ de los indígenas mayas. Varias personas se unen *(get together)* para ______ la marimba, y ______ común unir varias marimbas de tonalidades *(tones)* diferentes. La armonía que resulta es magnífica. La música de los garifunas[1] se caracteriza por el uso de varias clases de tambores *(drums)*, caracoles *(seashells)* y otros ______ de percusión. Su forma de ______ y sus melodías son únicas.

Los medios de comunicación —radio, televisión y cine— ______ a Centroamérica el baile y la música de otras partes del mundo. Actualmente *(presently)*, ______ muy populares los estilos de música de México, los EE.UU., Europa y las islas del Caribe. A muchos centroamericanos les ______ bailar salsa, merengue, reggae y lambada.

[1]Grupo de origen africano que ha mantenido su idioma y sus tradiciones.

Rigoberta Menchú

Rubén Blades

Caras en las noticias

En 1987, el ex presidente de Costa Rica, **Oscar Arias Sánchez,** recibió el Premio Nóbel de la paz por sus esfuerzos° por mantener la paz y la democracia en Centroamérica. Cuando aceptó el premio, Arias Sánchez dijo: «Yo recibo este premio como uno de los 27.000.000 de centroamericanos». Según él: «la paz no tiene línea final°».

Cinco años más tarde, otra centroamericana recibió el Premio Nóbel[1] por su trabajo constante de activar el interés en la pobreza° y la discriminación de los indígenas° de Guatemala y otras partes. **Rigoberta Menchú,** de Guatemala, es una joven indígena quiché[2] y es poco conocida comparada con otros ganadores° recientes del Premio Nóbel, como Mikhail Gorbachev (1990), Elie Wiesel (1986), Desmond Tutu (1984) y Lech Walesa (1983). En el libro *Me llamo Rigoberta Menchú y así me nació la conciencia*, Menchú describe su vida y su lucha política. Se le considera un símbolo de paz y reconciliación en su país y en el mundo.

¿Es **Rubén Blades** actor, abogado, cantante, director de orquestas o candidato presidencial de su país de Panamá? Es fácil ver por qué lo llaman «el camaleón». A pesar de° todas sus actividades, muy pocas personas realmente conocen a Rubén. El famoso autor colombiano Gabriel García Márquez le dijo una vez: «Tú eres el desconocido más popular que conozco. Todo el mundo sabe de ti pero nadie sabe cómo tú luces.° Saben tu nombre pero no saben tu cara. Saben tu cara pero no saben tu nombre». Y esto le gusta mucho a Rubén, quien más que nada está muy dedicado a la justicia social.

efforts

finishing line

poverty

Indigenous peoples

winners

In spite of

what you look like

[1]Otros latinoamericanos que han ganado el Premio Nóbel de la paz: Carlos Saavedra Lamas (Argentina, 1936) y Adolfo Pérez Esquivel (Argentina, 1976).

[2]Los indígenas quichés vinieron de la región El Quiché en las montañas de Guatemala. Se unieron con los mayas (siglos IV–IX, época cristiana) y desarrollaron una cultura notable.

En 1984, el famoso salsero,° pionero de la «nueva canción» (combinación de poesía, política y ritmos caribeños), dejó una exitosa° carrera musical para sacar la maestría en derecho en Harvard University. Después de graduarse volvió a la música (en 1997 ganó su tercer «Grammy») y también se dedicó al cine. Ha salido en muchas películas que incluyen: *Crossover Dreams, The Milagro Beanfield War, The Super, The Two Jakes, Fatal Beauty, Mo' Better Blues, Color of Night* y *The Devil's Own* con Harrison Ford.

Pero, como si todo esto no fuera° suficiente, Rubén también se dedicó a la situación política de su país. Volvió a Panamá y fundó un nuevo partido° político, Papá Egoró, nombre indígena que significa «tierra madre». En 1994 representó su partido político como candidato a la presidencia de Panamá, y aunque no ganó las elecciones, comentó: «Estoy creando mi infraestructura en Panamá». También sigue la lucha° por los derechos,° la unidad y la integración de la gente hispana en los EE.UU.

En 1998, Rubén hizo su primer papel estelar° en Broadway en *The Capeman*, una obra musical escrita por Paul Simon. ¿Sus esperanzas° para el futuro? Que el mundo sea un lugar donde lo que importe más sea el carácter de una persona, y donde el «corazón no necesite visa».

salsa singer / *successful* / *As if this weren't* / *party* / *struggle; rights* / *starring role* / *hopes*

Es decir

Díganos, por favor...

1. el título de un libro acerca de la vida de Rigoberta Menchú.
2. los nombres de dos personas de Centroamérica que han ganado el Premio Nóbel de la paz.
3. cuáles son tres elementos que combinan para formar la «nueva canción».
4. cuáles son cuatro profesiones de Rubén Blades.
5. cuáles son cinco aspectos de la vida política de Rubén Blades.

Practiquemos

Gente plástica. Lea Ud. estos versos de la canción «Plástico» de Rubén Blades. En el segundo verso, cambie Ud. el infinitivo al mandato informal **(tú).** Luego, conteste las preguntas.

Plástico

Era una pareja plástica, de esas que veo por ahí; él pensando siempre en dinero, ella, en la moda en París. Aparentando *(appearing to be)* lo que no son, viviendo en un mundo de pura ilusión, diciendo a su hijo de 5 años, no juegues con niños de color extraño *(strange)*, ahogados *(drowning)* en deudas *(debts)* para mantener su status social, en boda *(wedding)* o coctel.

(Oír) ______ latino (oír) ______ hermano, (oír) ______ amigo, nunca (vender) ______ tu destino *(destiny)* por el oro, ni la comodidad *(comfort)*; (aprender) ______, (estudiar) ______, pues nos falta andar bastante, marcha, siempre hacia adelante *(ahead)* para juntos acabar con la ignorancia que nos trae sugestionados *(influenced)*, con modelos importados que no son la solución.

No te dejes confundir *(let yourself be confused)*, (buscar) ______ el fondo *(the innermost part)* y su razón, (recordar) ______, se ven las caras y jamás el corazón.

1. Según Rubén, ¿en qué piensa el hombre plástico? ¿En qué piensa la mujer plástica?
2. ¿Por qué compara Rubén a estas personas con el plástico?
3. ¿Conoce Ud. a gente plástica? ¿Cómo son ellos?
4. ¿Qué es un mundo de ilusión? ¿Es el mundo de Ud. real o de ilusión? Explique.
5. ¿Qué consejos tiene Rubén para sus hermanos latinos?

Notas y notables

Datos de Centroamérica

- Centroamérica es una región muy montañosa con aproximadamente 75 volcanes, algunos todavía activos.
- Antes de 1881, Belice era una colonia inglesa.
- Panamá fue parte de Colombia hasta la construcción del canal de Panamá en 1903.
- La mayoría de la población centroamericana es mestiza, lo que es el resultado de la mezcla° de europeos con indígenas. Casi todos hablan español, pero en algunas regiones como en Belice y en las Islas de la Bahía en Honduras, el inglés es predominante.
- Centroamérica importa muchos de sus productos de consumo diario°; maquinaria, medicinas, productos químicos, fertilizantes, petróleo y aparatos eléctricos de tecnología avanzada.
- La comida centroamericana es variada, barata y rica en verduras, frutas exóticas, carnes y mariscos frescos. El maíz es el ingrediente más común en la comida diaria. En Guatemala, por ejemplo, la tortilla de maíz forma una parte integral en todas las comidas —el desayuno, el almuerzo y la cena.
- Nicaragua es el único país donde circulan simultáneamente tres monedas°: el córdoba oro, el córdoba corriente que se usa para pagar los salarios y el dólar, la única moneda a prueba de inflación y devaluación.°
- El lago de Nicaragua es el único lago de agua fresca del mundo que tiene tiburones.
- El béisbol es el deporte nacional de Nicaragua.
- Es común usar «tico» o «tica» para referirse a una persona de Costa Rica. Este apodo° viene de la costumbre que tienen los costarricenses de agregar° el sufijo° «tico» a muchas palabras. «Espera un momentico, por favor».

mixture

daily

currencies

inflation and devaluation-proof

nickname
add; suffix

Chichicastenango: Un pueblo pintoresco° de Guatemala

picturesque

Una mujer de Guatemala

La diosa Ixchel

En Guatemala, una excursión muy interesante es al pueblo maya[1] de Chichicastenango. Los jueves y domingos este pueblo pintoresco se llena de gente que viene de todas partes para ir al mercado más famoso del país. Los campesinos° de los pueblos vecinos° venden sus frutas, verduras, flores, cerámicas y telas.° Lo que más atrae° a los turistas es la variedad de tejidos.° Los colores brillantes de las telas y los dibujos° geométricos son simbólicos y describen historias antiguas y dioses mitológicos. El color de la guerra° es negro y el de la vida es rojo. El amarillo simboliza el dolor y el verde es la eternidad. Las rayas° representan los maizales° y los árboles que traen la buena suerte. Según la mitología maya-quiché, Ixchel, la diosa de la luna, era la patrona de la tejeduría.° La mujer indígena de hoy se sienta afuera de su casa y teje° exactamente como lo hacía Ixchel hace miles de años.

farmers
neighboring; cloth
attracts; weavings
designs
war
stripes; cornfields
weaving
she weaves

[1]Hay información sobre la antigua civilización maya en la página 376.

Es decir

¿Cierto o falso? Si la frase es falsa, corríjala.

1. Chichicastenango es una ciudad grande.
2. En el mercado de Chichicastenango, lo que más les gusta a los turistas son las frutas exóticas.
3. En los tejidos de los indígenas, el amarillo representa el dolor.
4. La carne de res es la comida más típica de Centroamérica.
5. Los productos químicos son una de las exportaciones principales de Centroamérica.
6. Panamá no formó parte de Centroamérica hasta el siglo *(century)* XX.

Practiquemos

El regateo *(bargaining)*. El arte de discutir con el vendedor el precio de una cosa es una costumbre muy típica en los mercados de Latinoamérica. Para aprender a regatear, arregle Ud. las frases siguientes en el orden apropiado para formar un párrafo lógico.

1. El mercado de Chichicastenango es el sitio perfecto para practicar el regateo.
2. Luego, Ud. debe ofrecer el precio más bajo posible.
3. El regateo sigue hasta que el comprador y el vendedor estén satisfechos.
4. La primera regla *(rule)* es no mostrar interés especial en el artículo.
5. Pero, esto se debe hacer sin insultar al artesano *(craftsman)*.

Enfoque literario

«Lo fatal» por Rubén Darío

Rubén Darío

Preparativos: Estrategias de prelectura

1. Before reading the following poem «Lo fatal» by the Nicaraguan author Rubén Darío, scan the biographical information in the text and:
   a. explain how Darío revolutionized poetic language.
   b. list three themes found in Darío's poetry.
   c. tell what themes appear in «Lo fatal».
2. Now read:
   a. the first two lines of the poem and explain why the tree and the rock are happy.
   b. the last two lines of the poem and tell why the author is not happy.

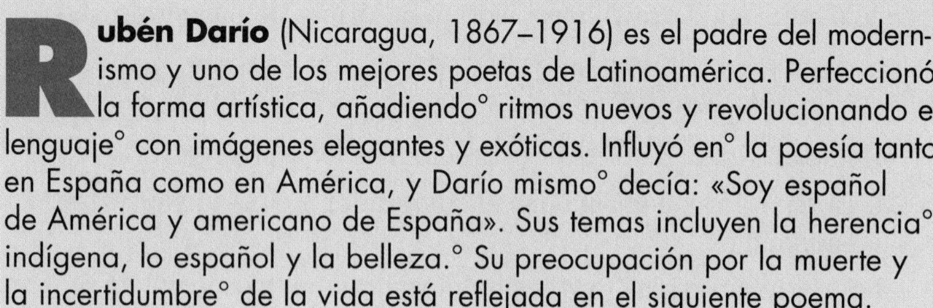

Rubén Darío (Nicaragua, 1867–1916) es el padre del modernismo y uno de los mejores poetas de Latinoamérica. Perfeccionó la forma artística, añadiendo° ritmos nuevos y revolucionando el lenguaje° con imágenes elegantes y exóticas. Influyó en° la poesía tanto en España como en América, y Darío mismo° decía: «Soy español de América y americano de España». Sus temas incluyen la herencia° indígena, lo español y la belleza.° Su preocupación por la muerte y la incertidumbre° de la vida está reflejada en el siguiente poema.

adding
language; He influenced
himself
heritage
beauty
uncertainty

Lo fatal

Dichoso° el árbol que es apenas sensitivo,
y más la piedra dura,° porque ésa ya no siente,
pues no hay dolor más grande que el dolor de ser vivo,°
ni mayor pesadumbre° que la vida consciente.
Ser, y no saber nada, y ser sin rumbo° cierto,
y el temor° de haber sido y un futuro terror...
y el espanto° seguro de estar mañana muerto,
y sufrir por la vida y por la sombra° y por
lo que no conocemos y apenas sospechamos,°
y la carne que tienta° con sus frescos racimos,°
y la tumba que aguarda° con sus fúnebres ramos,°
y no saber adónde vamos,
¡ni de dónde venimos... !

Happy
hard rock
alive
sorrow
direction
fear
fear
shadow
we scarcely suspect
tempts; branches
awaits; branches

Es decir

Comprensión. Conteste Ud. las siguientes preguntas.

1. ¿Qué imágenes de la naturaleza aparecen en los primeros versos?
2. ¿Qué es lo que sienten estas imágenes y por qué?
3. ¿Qué es lo que le duele a Darío?
4. ¿Cuál es el mayor dolor?
5. ¿Qué tienen en común el pasado y el futuro?

Practiquemos

A El lenguaje literario.

1. Darío tenía miedo de morir. ¿Qué palabras reflejan su intensa preocupación por la muerte?
2. Las palabras **pesadumbre, seguro** y **temor** aparecen en el poema. Busque Ud. en el poema sinónimos de estas palabras.

B Discusión.

1. ¿Por qué a Darío le duele tanto vivir?
2. Hay dos versos *(lines)* que reflejan muy bien la incertidumbre mortal de Darío. ¿Cuáles son?

C Reacción personal.

1. ¿Qué piensa Ud. de este poema? ¿Es pesimista? ¿Le gustó? Explique.
2. ¿Tiene Ud. las mismas preocupaciones que Darío? ¿Por qué sí o no?

→ Enfoque artístico... Costa Rica

A. Tomás Povedano de Arcos, pintor de la tradición moderna, fundó *(founded)* la Escuela Nacional de Bellas Artes en Costa Rica. Visite Ud. el sitio web

http://www.cr/arte/povedano/menup.html.

Lea la biografía de Povedano y describa sus contribuciones al mundo del arte.

B. Comente Ud. los tres temas principales de la obra de Povedano. Escoja una obra que represente cada categoría y descríbala.

Since Internet addresses are subject to change, typing the following key words into most search engines will get you more information about Costa Rican art.

Arte de Costa Rica **Museos de Costa Rica**

Videocultura

Una visita a Costa Rica: Alajuela

Xandari Plantation, Alajuela, Costa Rica

Costa Rica es un país pequeño situado en Centroamérica entre el océano Pacífico al oeste y el mar Caribe al este, con Nicaragua al norte y Panamá al sur. Tiene una geografía compleja: ríos, lagos, playas, montañas y valles. San José es la capital del país y la ciudad más grande, con una población de 300 mil habitantes. Goza de un clima extraordinario, y por eso se oye con frecuencia: ¡«En San José es primavera todo el año»!. Para escaparse de la vida metropolitana de la capital, a muchos costarricenses les gusta pasar un fin de semana en la bonita ciudad de Alajuela.

Para saber más sobre la ciudad de Alajuela, vamos a quedarnos en uno de sus lujosos hoteles, Xandari Plantation. Mire Ud. el video y haga los ejercicios que siguen.

Palabras útiles

la cascada	*waterfall*	el huerto	*vegetable garden*
el culantro	*coriander*	el rábano	*radish*
debido a	*due to*	el sendero	*footpath*
el dueño	*owner*	ubicado	*located*
espacioso	*spacious*	el valle	*valley*
la especia	*spice*		

Es decir

A Alajuela… ¿Qué recuerda? Escoja Ud. la respuesta correcta.

1. Alajuela es la (segunda/tercera) ciudad más grande de Costa Rica.
2. Está situada a sólo (30/40) minutos de la capital.
3. Más de (41/43) mil habitantes viven en Alajuela.
4. Alajuela es famosa por su ambiente (cosmopolita/tranquilo).
5. El parque central está lleno de árboles de (papaya/mango).

B Una experiencia única. Llene Ud. los espacios con la información correcta.

1. Marcela trabaja como jefe de ______. Xandari es un hotel ubicado ______, cerca del ______.
2. El hotel tiene vistas muy bonitas de ______ y ______.
3. Costa Rica es una buena opción para el norteamericano porque tiene ______ y______.

C Xandari. Describa Ud. con detalles los siguientes aspectos del Hotel Xandari Plantation.

1. las ultra villas
2. el diseño del hotel
3. formas de mantenerse en buenas condiciones
4. el restaurante del hotel
5. la naturaleza que se puede explorar

Practiquemos

Un día en el Hotel Xandari. En parejas, planeen un día fabuloso en el Hotel Xandari Plantation. ¿A qué hora se despiertan? ¿Qué hacen? ¿Qué ven? ¿Qué comen? ¿Cómo pasan la noche? Escriban un párrafo descriptivo.

Costa Rica: Las carretas de Sarchí y la Finca de Mariposas

Sarchí, Costa Rica

Costa Rica tiene mucho que ofrecer a cualquier turista que goce de un ambiente natural exquisito. Los costarricenses, (o «ticos» como se les llama por la costumbre de usar el sufijo «tico» al final de las palabras), suelen ser muy hospitalarios y comparten con orgullo sus ricas tradiciones.

Para experimentar la belleza de la artesanía y la naturaleza costarricense, mire el video y haga los ejercicios que siguen.

Palabras útiles

agrícola	*agricultural*	protegido	*protected*
el campesino	*farmer*	recurso	*resource*
la carreta	*oxcart*	reconocer	*to recognize*
la fachada	*facade*	el taller	*workshop*
el letrero	*sign*	el tesoro	*treasure*

Es decir

A **¿Qué es?** Después de ver el video, diga Ud. qué significan las siguientes palabras… ¡en español por favor!

1. un volcán
2. una cascada
3. la extinción
4. una mariposa
5. un taller
6. una carreta

B **Dos. ¿Cuáles son…**

1. dos cosas que los costarricenses hacen para conservar los recursos naturales?
2. dos razones para visitar Costa Rica?
3. dos características de las carretas de Sarchí?
4. dos adjetivos para describir el pueblo de Sarchí?
5. dos cosas que Ud. aprenderá en la Finca de Mariposas?

C **Ud., el (la) experto(a).** En sus propias palabras…

1. explique la historia y la importancia de las carretas de Sarchí.
2. explique por qué es importante conservar los recursos naturales.
3. describa la geografía de Costa Rica.

Practiquemos

La campaña publicitaria. En grupos, diseñen una campaña publicitaria para preservar los recursos naturales de Costa Rica. Escriban dos lemas *(slogans)* como los que ven en el video, y hagan un folleto en el que Uds. describen la belleza natural y cómo preservarla.

UNIDAD

¡Celebremos!

Sudamérica

¡Vamos a Sudamérica por Internet!

Experience lost civilizations, wonders of the world, and beauty that defies description in South America by browsing the World Wide Web and visiting the following addresses.

http://www.latinworld.com/
http://www.venezuelatuya.com/ (Venezuela)
http://www.cyberven.com/turismo/ (Venezuela)
http://www.segegob.cl/sernatur/inicio.html (Chile)
http://www.uniandes.edu.co/Colombia/Turismo/turismo.html (Colombia)
http://www.turismo.gub.uy/ (Uruguay)
http://www.sectur.gov.ar/e/menu.htm (Argentina)

Since Internet addresses are subject to change, typing the following key words into most search engines will also get you to South America.

Los Andes **La Selva Amazónica** **Viajes Argentina** **Turismo en Venezuela** **Machu Picchu** **Zipaquirá, Colombia** **Volcanes de Chile** **Galápagos**

To learn about South American art via the Internet, see page 548 of *Gaceta 6*.

Una boda sudamericana

Lección 

FUNCTION	Expressing what you **would do** • Expressing hypothetical situations
STRUCTURE	The conditional tense • Conditional **if-** clauses • Sequence of tenses II: The imperfect subjunctive
VOCABULARY	Dating, courting, and expressing affection • Stalling for time, filling in, and explaining more clearly
CULTURE	Meeting the opposite sex • Courtship and engagement in the Hispanic world
DIÁLOGO Y VIDEO	***Así es Mariana: La telenovela***

Lección 

FUNCTION	More descriptions • Expressing uncertainty, influence and feelings: A review • Expressing possession
STRUCTURE	Adjectives used as nouns • Review of the subjunctive mood • Possessive pronouns and the stressed form of possessive adjectives
VOCABULARY	Relationships • Male and female roles • Arguments and reconciliation
CULTURE	The engagement custom
DIÁLOGO Y VIDEO	***Así es Mariana: La pareja ideal***

Lección 

FUNCTION	Narrating in the past: A review • Expressing **each other**
STRUCTURE	Review of the use of the preterite and imperfect • Reciprocal actions with ***se***
VOCABULARY	Festivals • Celebrating • Religious holidays
CULTURE	Celebrations • Bullfights • Christmas traditions • ***Carnaval*** in Argentina • Birthday celebrations
DIÁLOGO Y VIDEO	***Así es Mariana: La fiesta de fin de año***

Gaceta 

CULTURE	**South America** Touring South America • Faces in the news • Notes and notables • Literature: Pablo Neruda • Art
VIDEOCULTURA	Las madres de la Plaza de Mayo • Isabel Allende • Inca Son

Con todo mi corazón

Luis... si tú quisieras ser útil, nos traerías más galletas.

AVISO CULTURAL

(As a reading aid, refer to lesson vocabulary for new words.)

En los EE.UU., ¿qué cosas les dicen los hombres a las mujeres que quieren conocer? Por las calles de algunos países hispanos es probable que se oigan «piropos» originales que dicen algunos hombres como forma de expresar su admiración por las mujeres. Ejemplos de unos piropos únicos son: «Si cocina como camina me como hasta la olla *(pot)*», «Que Dios bendiga *(bless)* el árbol que dio la madera *(wood)* con que hicieron la cama donde tú naciste». Las mujeres hispanas generalmente no reaccionan a estas expresiones. ¿Cuáles son algunas otras técnicas? ¿Es fácil conocer a personas nuevas hoy día? Explique.

Preparativos

Review the vocabulary on pages 488–490 before viewing the video.

Al mirar el video o leer el diálogo siguiente, Ud. verá que hay momentos de ironía en la vida de Mariana y Luis Antonio. Verá también que Mariana y Teresa tienen algo en común (claro, además de Luis). ¿Qué es? ¿Cuántas veces ha dicho Ud., «Si yo tuviera...» (*"If I had . . . "*), o «Si pudiera...» (*"If I could . . . "*), o «Si no fuera por...» (*"If it weren't for . . . "*)? Muchas veces, ¿verdad? Para expresar situaciones hipotéticas como éstas, se usan el imperfecto del subjuntivo y el tiempo condicional. Por ejemplo, si Mariana **tuviera** más tiempo y dinero, **se quedaría** *(she would stay)* en San Diego una semana más. Y Ud., si tuviera más tiempo y dinero, ¿qué haría? *(what would you do?)*

Así es Mariana: La telenovela

Teresa y Mariana están sentadas en el sofá mirando una telenovela y comiendo galletas.

Fabián: *Oye, mi amor, ¿me podrás perdonar por haber sido tan estúpido? Realmente me porté de una forma infantil.*

Laura: *Sí, claro que te perdono, cariño. Lo importante es que hayas aprendido a ser menos celoso y más maduro, ¿no?*

Mariana: Otro anuncio comercial... no lo creo.

Teresa: ¡Ay! Qué bien que Laura y Fabián hayan hecho las paces.

Mariana: Yo estoy de acuerdo. Yo sabía que si Fabían hiciera esfuerzos para respetar los deseos de Laura, todo saldría bien entre los dos.

Entra Luis Antonio, listo para jugar al tenis.

Luis Antonio: Encontré las raquetas. Vamos a jugar... ¿no?

Mariana y Teresa: ¡No!

Luis Antonio: ¿Cómo que no?... Tú querías que jugáramos a las dos. Son las dos. Vamos...

Mariana: Sí, sí... en unos minutos... Fabián acaba de admitirle a Laura que se ha portado muy mal con ella.

Luis Antonio: Perdón... ¿Fabián? ¿Laura? ¿Amigos tuyos, mamá?

Teresa: Hijo, déjanos tranquilas, por favor.

Mariana: ¿Viste cómo él miraba a Laura... ? Está completamente enamorado de ella.

Luis Antonio: Oh, ¡cuánto me alegro... ! Me preocupaba de que se rompieran... La verdad es que no entiendo cómo Uds. pueden ver esos programas tan sentimentales... tan ridículos... Mariana, ven... la cancha nos espera.

Teresa: Luis... si tú quisieras ser útil, nos traerías más galletas.

Mariana: Ay, sí, qué buena idea... vete a buscar galletas... y shhhh... el programa vuelve a empezar.

Fabián: *Laura, necesito confesarte algunas cosas más, querida.*

Laura: *¿Ah sí? ¿Por ejemplo?*

Fabián: *Pues, este, uhhh, Ema no es mi hermana como te había dicho. En realidad es mi ex novia... Y yo, no soy juez... soy dentista en un pueblo cerca de aquí, y...*

Mariana: Por favor... qué tonterías. Esto es demasiado.

Teresa: No lo entiendo. Todo era bonito y creíble... pero esto... esto es exagerado.

Mariana: Luis tiene razón... estos programas son ridículos. Vamos a jugar al tenis. Estoy lista.

Luis se ha interesado por la telenovela y no quiere irse.

Luis Antonio: Sí, sí, sí, voy ahora... voy...

Fabián: *Y mi nombre no es Fabián... es Raúl, y...*

Es decir

A ¿A quién se refieren las siguientes frases... a Luis Antonio, Teresa, Fabián o Laura?

1. Realmente se llama Raúl y es dentista.
2. Quiere jugar al tenis.
3. Quiere que Luis traiga más galletas.
4. Quiere que su novio sea menos celoso.
5. Cree que las telenovelas son ridículas.
6. Está contento(a) de que Laura haya perdonado a Fabián.

B Llene Ud. el espacio con **a** o **de.**

1. ¿Viste cómo miraba ______ Laura?
2. El programa vuelve ______ empezar.
3. Está enamorado ______ ella.
4. Acaba ______ admitirle a Laura.
5. Querías que jugáramos ______ las dos.
6. Estoy ______ acuerdo.
7. Vamos ______ jugar.
8. Me preocupaba ______ que se rompieran.

C En grupos de tres, inventen unas confesiones originales que Fabián le hace a Laura. ¿Cómo reacciona ella? Compártanlas *(Share them)* con la clase.

Al ver el video

Según Mariana, ¿qué cosas pueden pasar durante el breve periódo de treinta minutos? En parejas, escriban una lista de cinco cosas más que pueden ocurrir en una telenovela. Compártanlas con la clase.

Vocabulario

Verbos

abrazar	*to hug*
amar	*to love*
besar	*to kiss*
casarse (con)	*to marry*
comprometerse (hacerse novios)	*to become engaged*
disputar [reñir (i)]	*to argue*
divorciarse	*to get a divorce*
enamorarse (de)	*to fall in love (with)*

fracasar	*to fail*
negarse a (ie)	*to refuse to*
odiar	*to hate*
pelear (luchar)	*to fight*
resolver (ue)	*to resolve, solve*
reunir(se) (con)	*to gather, reunite (meet with)*

Adjetivos

cariñoso	*affectionate*
celoso	*jealous*
cortés	*courteous*
enamorado (de)	*in love (with)*
infantil	*childish, relating to childhood*
loco	*crazy, foolish*
maduro	*mature*

Sustantivos

el abrazo	*hug*
la amistad	*friendship*
el amor	*love*
el anillo de casado (de compromiso)	*wedding (engagement) ring*
la banda (el conjunto musical)	*band (musical group)*
el beso	*kiss*
la boda	*wedding*
el caballero	*gentleman*
el cariño	*affection*
los celos	*jealousy*
el compromiso	*engagement*
la disputa (riña)	*argument*
el divorcio	*divorce*
la iglesia	*church*
la luna de miel	*honeymoon*
el matrimonio	*matrimony, married couple*
el noviazgo	*courtship*
el (la) novio(a)	*boy(girl)friend, fiancé(e), groom (bride)*
la realidad	*reality*
la sinagoga	*synagogue*

Otras palabras y expresiones

cariño (cielo)	*sweetheart, honey*
hacer esfuerzos	*to make the effort*
hacer las paces	*to make up*
llevarse bien (mal)	*to get along well (badly)*
querido(a)	*dear, darling*
los recién casados	*newlyweds*
salir bien (mal)	*to turn out well (badly)*
el sentido del humor	*sense of humor*

Vocabulario adicional

contratar	*to hire*
de vez en cuando	*from time to time*
envidioso	*envious*
la invitación	*invitation*
el (la) invitado(a)	*guest*
la locura	*foolishness, nonsense*
la orquesta	*orchestra*
los preparativos	*preparations*
la recepción	*reception*
respetar	*to respect*
sobre todo	*above all, especially*
la soledad	*loneliness*

Repasemos el vocabulario

A **Sinónimos.** Su profesor(a) va a leer una serie de palabras. Busque el sinónimo apropiado.

a. reñir
b. conjunto
c. luchar
d. hacer esfuerzos
e. hacerse novios
f. amar

1. ______ **2.** ______ **3.** ______ **4.** ______ **5.** ______ **6.** ______

B **Problemas matrimoniales.** Lo siguiente es una conversación entre un(a) consejero(a) matrimonial y su cliente. Complete Ud. las frases con el antónimo de las palabras subrayadas.

1. ¿Anoche Uds. hicieron las paces? ¡Al contrario! Otra vez ______
2. ¿Su pareja le dijo que lo(la) quiere? ¡Ni hablar! Me dijo que me ______
3. ¿Se portó de una manera madura? ¡Claro que no! Es muy ______
4. ¿Es una persona cariñosa? ¡De ninguna manera! Es muy ______
5. ¿Es posible que todo vaya a salir bien? ¡En absoluto! El matrimonio va a ______

En su opinión, ¿qué tipo de persona es el(la) cliente? Use adjetivos para describirlo(la). Imagínese que Ud. es el(la) consejero(a). ¿Qué le recomienda a su cliente que haga?

C **Preparativos para la boda.** Ud. y su novio(a) planean su boda juntos. Con un(a) compañero(a) de clase, completen la lista de preparativos de la lista de vocabulario.

1. Un mes antes...

a. preparar la lista de ___________

b. escoger las ___________

c. planear la ___________ y hacer las reservaciones

d. ____

2. Dos semanas antes...

a. enviar el anuncio de la ___________ a los periódicos

b. solicitar la licencia de ___________

c. ____

d. ____

3. Tres días antes...

a. preparar el equipaje para la luna de miel

b. ____

c. ____

d. ____

4. La noche anterior...

a. ____

b. ____

D **Refranes amorosos *(Amorous sayings)*.** Un refrán es un proverbio que ofrece consejo. Los siguientes refranes hablan del amor. Busque Ud. en la segunda columna la terminación de la frase en la primera columna. Luego, tradúzcalos al inglés.

1. Antes que te cases...	**a.** es ciego *(blind)*.
2. Para el mal de amores...	**b.** hay dolor.
3. El amor...	**c.** mira lo que haces.
4. No firmes sin leer, no...	**d.** no hay doctores.
5. Donde hay amor...	**e.** te cases sin ver.

E **Pero, papá, lo quiero mucho.** A la madre le gusta mucho el novio de su hija, Juanita, pero al padre no le gusta nada. Para cada comentario positivo que hace la madre, forme Ud. un comentario negativo.

MODELO Madre: Este joven me encanta.
Padre: **A mí no me gusta nada.**

1. Madre: Es todo un caballero... muy cortés. En fin, es un amor.
   Padre: ______________________________
2. Madre: Y él es muy maduro, inteligente y guapo.
   Padre: ______________________________
3. Madre: Estoy segura que él la tratará muy bien.
   Padre: ______________________________
4. Madre: Espero que se casen pronto.
   Padre: ______________________________

De uso común

Stalling for Time, Filling in, and Clarifying

joyería *jewelry store*

kilates *karats*

este...	*umm . . .*	en otras palabras...	*in other words . . .*
sabe(s)...	*you know . . .*	Ya veo.	*I see.*
es decir...	*that is to say . . .*	ya, ya...	*uh huh, uh huh . . .*
o sea...	*that is . . .*		

Practiquemos

En situaciones tensas. Explíqueles a las siguientes personas qué pasó, incorporando algunas de las expresiones anteriores para darle a Ud. tiempo para pensar.

1. El padre de su novio(a) quiere saber por qué volvieron de su cita a las dos de la mañana.
2. El (La) profesor(a) quiere saber por qué no ha hecho su tarea para hoy.
3. Ud. perdió el dinero que su clase reunió para su fiesta de fin de año y la clase quiere saber dónde está.

The Conditional Tense

Forma

HABLAR		COMER		ESCRIBIR	
habla**ría**	habla**ríamos**	come**ría**	come**ríamos**	escribi**ría**	escribi**ríamos**
habla**rías**	habla**ríais**	come**rías**	come**ríais**	escribi**rías**	escribi**ríais**
habla**ría**	habla**rían**	come**ría**	come**rían**	escribi**ría**	escribi**rían**

1. To form the conditional tense, add the endings **-ía, -ías, -ía, -íamos, -íais, -ían** to the infinitive. These endings are identical to those used to form the imperfect indicative of **-er** and **-ir** verbs. Remember that the conditional is formed by adding these endings to the infinitive whereas the imperfect is formed by removing the **-er** and **-ir** infinitive endings first and then adding the **-ía** endings.

Pablo dijo que **comería** (conditional) después de la ceremonia.	*Pablo said that **he would eat** after the ceremony.*
Pablo **comía** (imperfect) cuando llegamos.	*Pablo **was eating** when we arrived.*

¡AVISO! Note that all forms have a written accent.

2. The following verbs have irregular conditional stems, identical to those used to form the future tense.

Verb	Stem	Ending	Example: PONER	
decir	**dir-**		pondría	*I would put*
haber	**habr-**		pondrías	*you would put*
hacer	**har-**	ía	pondría	*he, she, you would put*
poder	**podr-**	ías	pondríamos	*we would put*
poner	**pondr-**	ía	pondríais	*you would put*
querer	**querr-**	íamos	pondrían	*they, you would put*
saber	**sabr-**	íais		
salir	**saldr-**	ían		
tener	**tendr-**			
venir	**vendr-**			

El novio **tendría** que prepararse en el hotel. — *The groom* ***would have*** *to get ready at the hotel.*

La novia **podría** vestirse en la iglesia. — *The bride* ***could (would be able to)*** *get dressed at the church.*

Función

1. The conditional tense describes what you *would do* (under certain conditions). In English this concept is expressed with the auxiliary verb *would* + verb. In Spanish the simple conditional tense is used.

   Lo **invitaría** a la recepción. — *I* ***would invite*** *him to the reception.*

   Ana dijo que **asistiría** a la boda. — *Ana said that she* ***would attend*** *the wedding.*

2. The conditional tense is commonly used with the verbs **deber, gustar,** and **poder,** as well as with other verbs to reflect courtesy or to politely suggest something.

   Ud. **debería** comprar un regalo más elegante. — *You* ***really should*** *buy a more elegant gift.*

   ¿Podría ayudarme? — ***Could you (please)*** *help me?*

3. The conditional tense is not used to express *would* in the sense of past habitual action (an action that one used to do). The imperfect tense is used in this context.

   De niño, José **pasaba** todos los veranos en las montañas. — *As a child José* ***would spend*** *every summer in the mountains.*

4. The conditional tense can be used to express conjecture or probability in the past. Although in English special phrases are needed *(I wonder, I suppose, I guess, probably)*, in Spanish they are not necessary.

—¿Adónde **iría** el matrimonio después de la boda?	*Where **do you think** the couple **went** after the wedding?*
—**Irían** al aeropuerto.	***They probably went** to the airport.*

¿Qué le pasaría a la novia?
What do you suppose happened to the bride?

Practiquemos

A **Mi hermana la consejera.** En cuestiones de amor, mi hermana es experta. Comience Ud. cada frase con **Mi hermana me dijo que...** y cambie los verbos del tiempo futuro al condicional.

MODELO Conoceré a un hombre maravilloso.
Mi hermana me dijo que conocería a un hombre maravilloso.

1. Saldré con Marcos.
2. Nos llevaremos muy bien.
3. A mis padres les gustará mucho.
4. Lo querré mucho.
5. Estará muy celoso de mis antiguos novios.
6. Tendremos una riña.
7. Haremos las paces.
8. Nos casaremos.

B **Los invitados hablan de la boda.** Cambie Ud. las frases del presente al pasado de acuerdo con los verbos entre paréntesis.

MODELO Creo que la novia llevará un vestido blanco. (Creía)
Creía que la novia llevaría un vestido blanco.

1. Pienso que habrá mucha comida exótica. (Pensaba)
2. Creo que la orquesta tocará hasta la una. (Creía)
3. Estoy segura de que el vestido de la novia será elegante. (Estaba)
4. Me dicen que habrá más de 300 invitados en la boda. (dijeron)
5. Todos creen que los novios pasarán la luna de miel en Caracas. (creían)
6. Sé que ellos serán muy felices. (Sabía)

C **La luna de miel.** Hágale a un(a) compañero(a) las siguientes preguntas. Él (Ella) va a contestar de acuerdo con los dibujos. Usen el tiempo condicional para expresar probabilidad en el pasado.

MODELO ¿A qué hora empezaría la boda?
La boda empezaría a las dos.

1.

¿Qué hora sería cuando el matrimonio llegó al aeropuerto?

2.

¿Adónde irían los novios de luna de miel?

3.

¿Cómo llegarían al hotel?

4.

¿Cómo sería su habitación?

5.

¿Cómo pasarían su primer día de casados?

D **Situaciones.** En parejas, usen el tiempo condicional para decir lo que harían en las siguientes situaciones. Escojan una situación y represéntenla.

1. Ud. y su esposo(a) acaban de tener un bebé. Su suegra vino para ayudar. Ud. pensó que iba a quedarse por sólo dos semanas, pero han pasado tres meses y todavía está con Uds.
2. Ud. lleva a su novio(a) a conocer a sus padres y no les gusta.
3. Ud. descubre que su mejor amigo(a) está enamorado(a) de su novio(a).
4. Su novio(a) quiere casarse lo más pronto posible. Ud. prefiere esperar.
5. Ud. y su esposo(a) son recién casados. Él (Ella) anuncia que quiere un divorcio.

Conditional *if*- Clauses

Forma

To express what you do, will do, or would do (hypothetically) if certain conditions exist or were to exist, use the following formulas.

1. si + present indicative + { command / present indicative / future }

Si José te **llama,** { **sal** con él. / **puedes salir** con él. / **saldrás** con él. }

*If José **calls** you,* { ***go out** with him.* / ***you can go out** with him.* / ***you will go out** with him.* }

2. si + imperfect subjunctive + conditional

Si José te **llamara, saldrías** con él. — *If José **called (were to call)** you, **you would go out** with him.*

To express contrary-to-fact situations, use the following construction.

3. como si + imperfect subjunctive

Javier habla **como si conociera** bien a la pareja. — *Javier talks **as if he knew** the couple well.*

Función

1. When an *if*-clause expresses present action, **si** is followed by the present *indicative.* The present subjunctive is *never* used after **si.**

   Si tú llegas temprano, yo te veré. — ***If you arrive** early, I'll see you.*

2. When an *if*-clause expresses hypothetical or contrary-to-fact situations, **si** is followed by the imperfect subjunctive.

   Si llegaras temprano, yo te vería. — ***If you arrived (were to arrive)** early, I'd see you.*

3. Although the order of the clause may be reversed, the relationship to the verbs in each clause remains the same.

   Si **llegaras** temprano, yo te **vería.** — *If you **arrived** early, I **would see** you.*

   Yo te **vería** si **llegaras** temprano. — *I **would see** you if you **arrived** early.*

4. Since **como si** *(as if, as though)* expresses contrary-to-fact situations, it is followed by the imperfect subjunctive.

   Se porta **como si fuera** el novio. — *He acts **as if he were** the groom (but he's not).*

Practiquemos

A **¿Realidad o fantasía?** Vuelva Ud. a escribir *(Rewrite)* las frases cambiándolas al imperfecto del subjuntivo + el condicional para expresar una situación hipotética.

MODELO Si todo sale bien, pasaremos una luna de miel fantástica.
Si todo **saliera** bien, **pasaríamos** una luna de miel fantástica.

1. Si tenemos dinero, iremos a Buenos Aires después de la boda.
2. Si a mis padres no les gusta la idea, no me importará.
3. Si no es muy tarde, podremos salir esta noche.
4. Si el avión llega a tiempo, estaremos en Argentina a las seis.
5. Si no tenemos una reservación en el Hotel Astoria, nos quedaremos en el Hotel Inter-Continental.

B **Sueños *(Dreams)*.** Conteste Ud. las siguientes preguntas. Luego, cambie las preguntas a la forma **tú** y entreviste a un(a) compañero(a).

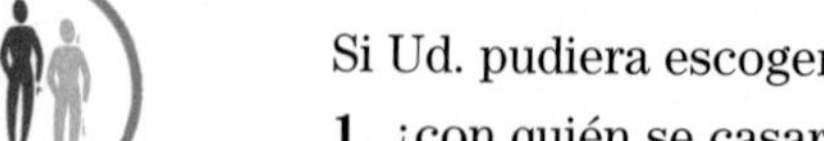

Si Ud. pudiera escoger...

1. ¿con quién se casaría?
2. ¿dónde celebraría su boda?
3. ¿cómo sería la boda?
4. ¿dónde pasaría su luna de miel?
5. ¿cómo sería su familia ideal?

C **La suegra.** Mire Ud. el dibujo y conteste las preguntas.

—¡Pepa, la comida estaba estupenda! ¿Es que ha venido mi madre?
(«Reveille»)

Si Ud. fuera la mujer de este hombre...

1. ¿cómo reaccionaría al escuchar su pregunta?
2. ¿qué le contestaría?
3. ¿qué haría para cambiar su situación?
4. ¿qué le prepararía para la próxima cena?

A propósito *(By the way)*, si Ud. pudiera tener la suegra ideal, ¿cómo sería?

D **Una gira turística por Sudamérica.** Lea Ud. «Una gira turística por Sudamérica» en las páginas 538–539 de la *Gaceta 6* y consulte el mapa en la página 540. Ud. y su novio(a) intentan planear su luna de miel, pero hay algunas «condiciones». Cambie los verbos entre paréntesis para expresar una situación hipotética y termine las frases basándose en la lectura. En algunos casos hay más de una terminación posible.

1. Si yo no (tener) miedo de las alturas *(heights)*...
2. Si a mi novio(a) le (interesar) la ecología...
3. Si mi novio(a) (querer) ver la arquitectura colonial...
4. Si no (estar) tan lejos...
5. Si nosotros no (ser) alérgicos al sol...

Sequence of Tenses II: The Imperfect Subjunctive

Función

1. The imperfect subjunctive[1] is used in the subordinate clause of a sentence that requires the subjunctive when the verb in the main clause is in the preterite tense, the imperfect indicative tense, or the conditional tense.[2]

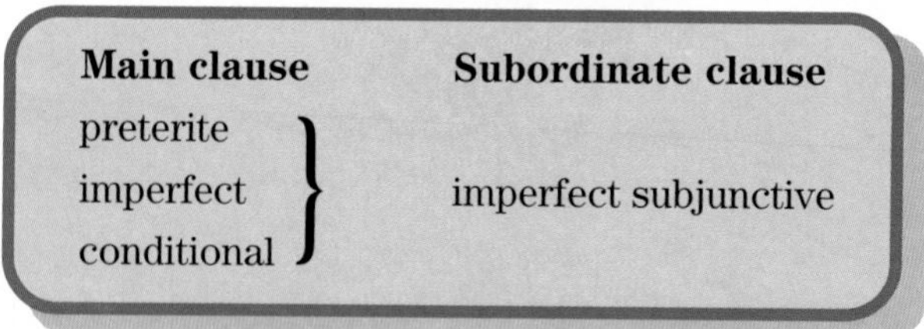

Main clause	Subordinate clause
preterite imperfect conditional	imperfect subjunctive

Le **dije** a Roberto / Le **decía** a Roberto / Le **diría** a Roberto } que **contratara** la orquesta.

*I **told** Robert / I **was telling** Robert / I **would tell** Robert* } ***to hire** the band.*

2. Remember that there are only two simple tenses in the subjunctive mood: the present and the imperfect. The present subjunctive can express present and future action. The imperfect subjunctive can express past and conditional action.

Tengo miedo de que el novio **esté** nervioso.
{ *I'm afraid that the groom **is** nervous.*
*I'm afraid that the groom **will be** nervous.*

Tenía miedo de que el novio **estuviera** nervioso.
{ *I was afraid that the groom **was** nervous.*
*I was afraid that the groom **would be** nervous.*

[1]The pluperfect subjunctive **(el pluscuamperfecto del subjuntivo)** can also be used in the subordinate clause of a sentence that requires the subjunctive. It describes an action that had previously taken place when a more recent past action occurred. The pluperfect subjunctive is formed by using the imperfect subjunctive of **haber (hubiera, hubieras...)** with the past participle.

[2]This sequence of tenses applies to the corresponding compound tenses as well (past progressive, pluperfect, conditional progressive, and conditional perfect). Some of these tenses have not yet been presented.

Practiquemos

A **Sería mejor así.** Pedro y Silvia hablan de su boda y de lo que preferirían. Forme Ud. frases nuevas comenzándolas con **Preferiríamos (que)...**

Mamá invitará a 300 personas. (100)
Preferiríamos que invitara a cien personas.

1. En la recepción servirán bistec. (langosta)
2. Habrá aperitivos fríos antes de la comida. (calientes)
3. Los fotógrafos sacarán fotos después de la ceremonia. (antes de)
4. El pastor nos casará a mediodía. (más tarde)
5. La madre del novio llevará un vestido verde. (azul)
6. La luna de miel empezará inmediatamente después de la boda. (dos días)

B **Comentarios sobre la boda.** Al día siguiente todos comentan la boda de Silvia y Pedro. Cambie Ud. los verbos de acuerdo con las palabras entre paréntesis.

Pedro estaba muy nervioso. (Teníamos miedo de)
Teníamos miedo de que Pedro estuviera muy nervioso.

1. Se casaron en junio. (Sus padres insistieron en)
2. Llovió todo el día. (Era una lástima)
3. Los niños pudieron participar en la ceremonia. (Me alegré de)
4. Tocaron música tradicional. (El padre de la novia insistió en)
5. Nadie lloró. (Yo no podía creer)
6. Se besaron al terminar la ceremonia. (El pastor les dijo)

C **Silvia tiene correo.** Ud. le escribió una carta por correo electrónico a Silvia, explicándole por qué Ud. no podía asistir a su boda. Termine Ud. las frases de una forma original para que ella sepa la razón.

Querida Silvia... Quería asistir a tu boda, pero era importante que yo... Y, no había nadie que... Además, mi hermano menor me pidió que... También, mi amigo Juan me dijo que... Finalmente necesitaba... Espero que me perdones.

Ahora, un(a) compañero(a) hará el papel de Silvia y reaccionará a las excusas con las siguientes expresiones.

Recibí tu carta en la cual me das muchas excusas. La verdad es que no creía que... Realmente me molestó mucho que... Tú sabes que no me importa que... Sin embargo, dudo que... Espero que la próxima vez que te invite... Hasta luego, Silvia.

Spend more time with Mariana and her friends while you review grammar and expand your cultural horizons.

See the **Así es Mariana** exercise in your workbook for this lesson.

En resumen

A **El noviazgo en el mundo hispano.** Complete Ud. la lectura con la forma correcta de la palabra entre paréntesis. Si hay dos palabras, escoja la más apropiada. Traduzca las palabras en inglés al español.

(Traditionally) ______ cuando las chicas estaban en edad casadera *(it was necessary)* ______ que (saber) ______ cocinar y hacer todo *(that which)* ______ correspondía a la casa. No se permitía que ellas (salir) ______ solas con un hombre sin que una persona mayor las (acompañar) ______. Los hombres podían visitarlas en las casas *(only)* ______ con el permiso de los padres.

Aunque las costumbres (del, de la) noviazgo en el mundo hispano *(have changed)* ______, *(especially)* ______ en las grandes ciudades, son diferentes a (los, las) tradiciones estadounidenses. La gente joven sale en grupos (por, para) ir (al, a la) cine o hacen (otro) ______ actividades. *(Generally)* ______ las señoritas empiezan a *(go out)* ______ solas de noche con los hombres a los 18 años. El concepto norteamericano de «girlfriend» o «boyfriend» no tiene equivalente en español. Cuando «se hacen novios» eso quiere decir que (el, la) relación es íntima y seria y que *(they will marry)* ______ en el futuro. En Argentina, por ejemplo, es común que el compromiso (hacerse) ______ formal «ante Dios» en una iglesia, reflejando (el, la) seriedad de (este, esta) costumbre.

B **Una telenovela *(soap opera)* fascinante.** Las fotos siguientes corresponden a algunos episodios de *Amor en silencio*, una telenovela hispana de «relaciones íntimas, brutales traiciones *(betrayals)* y amor puro que trasciende los peores obstáculos». Haga Ud. las actividades.

¿Qué dicen los actores?

1. Con un(a) compañero(a), escriban Uds. un diálogo original. Sean lógicos y creativos. Representen una breve escena delante de la clase.
2. Usen su imaginación y expliquen en breve la historia de cada personaje *(character)* en la foto.
3. ¿Qué opina Ud. de las telenovelas en general? ¿Cuáles son algunos de los temas comunes de las telenovelas norteamericanas? ¿A qué se debe su popularidad?

C **¡Cómo han cambiado las costumbres!** Mire Ud. el dibujo y haga el ejercicio.

1. En su opinión, ¿qué representa el dibujo?
2. Use mandatos formales y escriba cinco recomendaciones para el (la) soltero(a) que está a punto de *(about to)* casarse.

D **¿El matrimonio perfecto?** Traduzca Ud. el siguiente monólogo al español.

1. My boyfriend Jorge gets along well with my family, he respects me, and I love his sense of humor. But if I could, I'd change his infantile jealousy.
2. Everything would be perfect if he weren't so jealous.
3. Yesterday we fought a lot. He didn't want me to attend my cousin's wedding because Juan was going to be there. Do you believe it?
4. And he wanted us to become engaged last week! He's crazy!
5. I would make up with Jorge if he would make the effort to solve his problem.

E **Minidrama.** En grupos, representen una de las siguientes escenas.

1. Sus padres quieren que Ud. se case. Trate de convencerlos de las ventajas de ser soltero(a).
2. Con un(a) compañero(a), hagan los papeles de unos recién casados que tienen muchas dificultades en acostumbrarse a su vida nueva de casados.
3. Lean Uds. el anuncio y representen las siguientes escenas entre el (la) entrevistador(a) y el (la) candidato(a).

a. El (La) candidato(a) es norteamericano(a) y quiere conocer a una mujer (un hombre) latina(o).
b. El (La) candidato(a) se pone nervioso(a) y no quiere seguir con la entrevista.
c. El (La) entrevistador(a) invita a la (al) candidata(o) a salir.

F **Composición.**

1. Escríbale una carta al (a la) consejero(a) sentimental de un periódico. Pídale ayuda para tener más éxito con el sexo opuesto.
2. Ud. es un(a) consejero(a) sentimental para un periódico. Contéstele a la persona que le escribió pidiéndole ayuda para tener éxito con sus problemas amorosos. Dele recomendaciones originales.

Escuchemos

A **¿Es lógico?** You will hear a series of sentences. Indicate if they are logical or not logical by placing a check on the appropriate line.

MODELO Una mujer enamorada le muestra cariño a su novio.

___✓___ Es lógico   ________ No es lógico

1. ________ Es lógico   ________ No es lógico
2. ________ Es lógico   ________ No es lógico
3. ________ Es lógico   ________ No es lógico
4. ________ Es lógico   ________ No es lógico
5. ________ Es lógico   ________ No es lógico
6. ________ Es lógico   ________ No es lógico
7. ________ Es lógico   ________ No es lógico
8. ________ Es lógico   ________ No es lógico

B **Dictado.** Sandra attended her cousin Luisa's wedding yesterday. Listen carefully to the entire description of the wedding. Listen again and write each sentence during the pauses.

You will then hear a series of questions related to the dictation. Answer them with complete sentences. Refer to your dictation.

Lección 17

Problemas sentimentales

Lo importante es que las dos personas se quieran mucho.

AVISO CULTURAL

(As a reading aid, refer to lesson vocabulary for new words.)

En los EE.UU., cuando una pareja decide casarse, ¿qué cosa le da el hombre a la mujer? En España cuando los novios deciden casarse el hombre le compra una pulsera *(bracelet)* de oro a la mujer. A veces la pareja intercambia regalos. Después de casarse se lleva el anillo de casados en la mano izquierda. En muchos países hispanos los padres del novio ayudan a pagar la boda. En los EE.UU., ¿quién paga los gastos de la boda? ¿Cuál será el origen de esta costumbre? ¿Es justo?

Preparativos

Review the vocabulary on pages 508–509 before viewing the video.

Al mirar el video o leer el diálogo siguiente, verá muchos usos del modo subjuntivo. En este episodio Carla le cuenta a Luis sus problemas sentimentales con Octavio. ¿Cómo terminaría Ud. las frases siguientes de la conversación que tienen?

Carla: Sería inútil que yo... Nunca conoceré a alguien que...

Luis: Lo importante es que... Es necesario que el hombre... Una mujer tan complicada como Mariana necesita a un hombre que...

Ahora, compare sus frases con las frases en el diálogo. ¿Le gustan los consejos de Luis? Si Carla le pidiera consejos a Ud., ¿qué le diría?

Así es Mariana: La pareja ideal

Luis Antonio y Carla están sentados cerca de una piscina. Carla le cuenta sus problemas sentimentales.

Luis Antonio: No estés triste, Carla. ...Es que Alicia y Octavio están muy enamorados.

Carla: La verdad es que no lo entiendo, Luis. Parece que Alicia siempre provoca riñas con Octavio. Se opone a sus ideas y además, es bastante celosa. Por otro lado, Octavio casi nunca se enfada.

Luis Antonio: Tienes razón. Es un chico muy flexible. En el fondo Octavio quiere mucho a Alicia.

Carla: Sería inútil que yo fuera detrás de Octavio. Pero no sé cómo voy a poder olvidarlo. Nunca conoceré a alguien que me haga tan feliz como Octavio. Tú y Mariana son muy felices. ¿Cuál es el secreto?

Luis Antonio: Te digo una cosa, Carla. Mantener una relación nunca es fácil. Lo importante es que las dos personas se quieran mucho. Luego, es necesario que el hombre sea liberal, flexible y muy sensible, como lo soy yo... ¿no?

Mientras Luis habla, se le acerca un chico guapo a Carla y empieza a coquetear. Carla se levanta y va a sentarse con él, sin que Luis se dé cuenta de que se ha ido. Él sigue hablando.

Luis Antonio: Una mujer tan complicada como Mariana necesita un hombre que tenga mis cualidades... que sea maduro e inteligente, como lo soy yo... ¿no?... que sea fuerte y guapo pero también muy cariñoso... y sobre todo... que tenga un buen sentido del humor. Algún día, Carlita, conocerás al hombre de tus sueños, pero lo cierto es que... Carla... Carla... Ay, Carla.

Es decir

A Para repasar la conversación entre Carla y Luis, termine Ud. las siguientes frases.

1. Carla no entiende la relación entre Octavio y Alicia porque...
2. Luis sabe que en el fondo Octavio...
3. Es inútil que Carla...
4. Luis cree que Carla necesita a un hombre que...

B Es evidente que para Carla, Octavio es un amor imposible. ¿Qué recomienda Ud. que ella haga para olvidarse de él? Dé cuatro recomendaciones y compártalas con la clase.

C En grupos de tres, digan a quién(es) corresponden las siguientes cualidades. Justifiquen sus respuestas y comparen sus selecciones con las de sus compañeros.

Mariana Luis Antonio Octavio Alicia Carla

¿Quién es el (la) más... ?: celoso(a)? sensible? flexible? guapo(a)? maduro(a)? cariñoso(a)? cómico(a)?

Al ver el video

Después de ver el video, haga las siguientes actividades.

A Al principio del episodio, ¿qué es lo que Mariana no quiere que Luis sepa? Use su imaginación y termine la frase de cuatro formas: «**No quiere que Luis sepa que...** »

B En grupos, expliquen el significado de la última frase de Mariana: «**suerte, no... ¡industria!**»

Vocabulario

Verbos

combatir	*to combat, fight*
cooperar	*to cooperate*
criar	*to raise (children)*
discriminar	*to discriminate*
dominar	*to dominate*
enfadarse (enojarse)	*to become (get) angry*
obligar	*to oblige*
oponerse a	*to oppose*
provocar	*to provoke*
triunfar	*to triumph*
votar (por)	*to vote (for)*

Adjetivos

agresivo	*aggressive*
capaz	*capable*
conservador	*conservative*
coquetón(a)	*flirtatious*
enfadado (enojado)	*angry*
flexible	*flexible*
(in)útil	*useful (useless)*
liberado	*liberated*
liberal	*liberal*
machista	*macho*
obediente	*obedient*
pasivo	*passive*
rígido	*rigid*
sensible	*sensitive*
sociable	*sociable*

Sustantivos

el ama de casa (*f.*)	*housewife*
el deber	*duty*
el derecho	*right*
la discriminación	*discrimination*
el lazo	*tie, link*
la mitad	*half*
la pelea (lucha)	*fight (struggle)*
el prejuicio	*prejudice*

Palabras y expresiones

cumplir con	*to fulfill*
dar a luz	*to give birth*
la guardería infantil (el centro para niños)	*day care center*
hacer (jugar) un papel	*to play a role*
los demás	*the rest, everyone else*
llegar a un acuerdo	*to reach an agreement*

Vocabulario adicional

el comportamiento	*behavior*
contra	*against*
la dama	*lady*
en cuanto a	*as for, referring to*
la faena	*task*
el hecho de que	*the fact that*
el machismo	*exaggerated importance given to masculinity*
el macho	*male*
someter	*to subject*

Repasemos el vocabulario

A **Antónimos.** Su profesor(a) va a leer una serie de palabras. Busque el antónimo apropiado.

a. liberado b. flexible c. liberal d. útil e. pasivo

1. ______ **2.** ______ **3.** ______ **4.** ______ **5.** ______

B **Combinaciones.** Busque en la segunda línea las palabras asociadas con los verbos en la primera línea. Use la combinación en una frase original.

1. luchar por **2.** cooperar con **3.** llegar a **4.** combatir **5.** cumplir con

un acuerdo los deberes los demás los derechos los prejuicios

C **Formando frases.** Complete Ud. las frases con las palabras apropiadas de la lista de vocabulario.

1. Voy a ______ por ese candidato en las próximas elecciones.

2. Por la mañana los padres dejan al niño en la ______ y van a la oficina.

3. Una característica de las familias hispanas son los fuertes ______ familiares.

4. La razón por la cual ese hombre pelea tanto es para probar su ______.

5. Mi abuela no trabajaba. Se quedaba en casa para ______ a sus hijos.

D **Definiciones.** Busque Ud. en la segunda columna la definición de cada palabra de la primera columna. Complete las frases con las palabras apropiadas.

sentimental en unión se opone a inferioridad conocerlo

1. discriminar — **a.** prudente, moderado; a veces ______ las innovaciones
2. prejuicio — **b.** dar tratamiento de ______ a una persona o colectividad
3. conservador — **c.** trabajar ______ con otras personas
4. sensible — **d.** opinión sobre algo sin ______ de verdad
5. cooperar — **e.** fácil de conmover *(move emotionally)*, ______

E **¿Cómo son?** Dé Ud. una característica de los siguientes personajes. Un(a) compañero(a) va a dar un ejemplo de cada persona, nombrando a una persona famosa o de la clase.

MODELO un hombre coquetón
Intenta salir con muchas mujeres.
Don Juan era muy coquetón.

1. un hombre machista
2. una persona sensible
3. una persona rígida
4. una mujer coquetona
5. un político liberal
6. una persona sociable

Adjectives Used as Nouns

Forma y función

1. Adjectives can generally function as nouns when used with the corresponding definite article.

El hombre alto es mi esposo.	*The tall man is my husband.*
El alto es mi esposo.	***The tall one** is my husband.*
Los niños rubios viven cerca de mí.	*The blond children live near me.*
Los rubios viven cerca de mí.	***The blond ones** live near me.*

2. The neuter article **lo** is frequently used with the masculine singular form of the adjective to describe general characteristics and qualities as well as abstract ideas. This structure can be expressed in various ways in English.

Lo bueno es que la boda es en abril.	***The good thing (part, What's good)** is that the wedding is in April.*
Lo romántico es muy importante para un matrimonio.	***The romantic aspect** is **(Romantic things** are) very important for a marriage.*

Practiquemos

A La telenovela *Todo para Elena*. Esta telenovela es muy complicada porque hay muchos personajes diferentes. Reemplace Ud. el sustantivo subrayado *(underlined)* con la forma correcta del adjetivo.

La mujer rubia es Elena. **La rubia** es Elena.

1. La mujer morena está enamorada del hombre alto.
2. Pero, el hombre alto está enamorado de la mujer chilena.
3. El chico joven es el hijo de los señores argentinos.
4. La mujer anciana es la abuela de la niña mimada *(spoiled)*.
5. El hombre divorciado quiere salir con la mujer soltera, pero ella sale con el hombre rico.

B Hablando en serio. Forme Ud. oraciones originales con las frases de las dos líneas.

lo bueno ser soltero
Lo bueno de ser soltero es el tiempo libre que uno tiene y las posibilidades de viajar.

1. lo bueno **2.** lo malo **3.** lo difícil **4.** lo mejor **5.** lo importante

el divorcio el matrimonio ser soltero
casarse muy joven pelear con su novio(a)

C Hablando personalmente. Termine Ud. las frases con **lo... de mi vida** según el modelo.

Lo más fascinante de mi vida es que el año pasado hice un largo viaje por la Argentina y Chile.

1. lo más interesante
2. lo más triste
3. lo más importante
4. lo más cómico

Ahora, compare estos aspectos de su vida con los de sus compañeros. ¿Quién tiene el aspecto más interesante, cómico, triste e importante?

Review of the Subjunctive Mood

Función

1. The present subjunctive form is used to express all commands except the affirmative informal commands (**tú** and **vosotros**).

Vengan a la recepción pero **no traigan** al perro. — ***Come*** *to the reception but* ***don't bring*** *the dog.*

Comamos temprano porque la fiesta es a las seis. — ***Let's eat*** *early because the party is at 6:00.*

2. In noun clauses the subjunctive is used:

a. when the verb in the main clause expresses emotion, desire, doubt, petition, hope, obligation, insistence, approval, denial, conjecture, subjectivity, and other types of influence.

Espero que los novios **hagan** las paces antes de la boda. — ***I hope*** *the bride and groom* ***make up*** *before the wedding.*

b. after impersonal expressions that do not indicate certainty.

Es probable que vayan a Quito para la luna de miel. — ***It's probable that they'll go*** *to Quito for their honeymoon.*

3. In adjectival clauses the subjunctive is used when the antecedent is negative or indefinite.

Busco una orquesta que **sepa** tocar música latina. — ***I'm looking for an orchestra*** *that* ***knows*** *how to play Latin music.*

4. In adverbial clauses the subjunctive is used:

a. always after the conjunctions **antes de que, para que, sin que, en caso (de) que, con tal (de) que,** and **a menos que.**

Llegué **antes de que** la ceremonia **empezara.**	*I arrived **before** the ceremony **started**.*

b. with conjunctions of time to express pending or future actions.

Estaré aquí **hasta que** la ceremonia **empiece.**	*I will be here **until** the ceremony **starts.***

5. In conditional clauses the imperfect subjunctive is used to express hypothetical or contrary-to-fact ideas.

Si yo **fuera** tú, iría con Juan.	*If I **were** you, I'd go with Juan.*

6. In a sentence in which the subjunctive is required, the present subjunctive is used when the verb in the main clause expresses present or future action. The imperfect subjunctive is used when the verb in the main clause expresses past or conditional action.

Hoy **quiero** que tú me **acompañes** pero ayer **quería** que Javier me **acompañara.**	*Today I **want** you **to accompany** me but yesterday I **wanted** Javier **to accompany** me.*

Practiquemos

A **La riña justa *(fair)*.** Todos los matrimonios tienen riñas de vez en cuando. Aquí le explicamos cómo pelear y seguir amándose. Cambie Ud. los verbos a mandatos formales **(Ud.).**

1. (Resolver) ______ el conflicto en seguida; no (esperar) ______ mucho tiempo.
2. Nunca (atacar) ______ las debilidades *(weaknesses)* de su pareja.
3. (Respetar) ______ sus ideas. (Ser) ______ justo(a).
4. (Decirle) ______ exactamente lo que le molesta.
5. No (enojarse) ______ por errores que su pareja cometió en el pasado.
6. (Recordar) ______ que no hay vencedores ni vencidos *(winners or losers)*.

B **¿Riñiendo otra vez?** Ud. nunca ayuda en casa y esto provoca riñas con su compañero(a). En parejas, cambien el verbo entre paréntesis al subjuntivo. Luego, contesten con la forma correcta del mandato informal **(tú).**

MODELO El (La) compañero(a): Recomiendo que tú (barrer) **barras** el suelo.
Ud.: **¡Bárrelo tú!**

1. Insisto en que (sacar) ______ la basura.
2. Quiero que (hacer) ______ las camas.
3. Te digo que (fregar) ______ los platos.
4. Mando que (preparar) ______ la cena.
5. Prefiero que (poner) ______ la mesa.
6. Necesito que (arreglar) ______ el cuarto.

C **Con el consejero matrimonial.** Una pareja tiene una cita con un consejero. En grupos de tres, llenen los espacios con la forma correcta del verbo. Luego, escriban el papel del consejero y representen la escena.

La señora habla.

1. Hemos venido aquí para que Ud. nos (ayudar) ______.
2. No podemos pasar un día entero sin (reñir) ______.
3. Yo lo trataré mejor con tal que él me (dar) ______ amor y respeto.
4. Por ejemplo, anoche, después de que nosotros (cenar) ______ él se sentó delante de la tele sin (hacerme) ______ caso toda la noche... hasta (acostarse) ______.
5. Hasta que él (tener) ______ una actitud más abierta, no podremos comunicarnos.

El señor habla.

6. Yo la trataré con respeto en cuanto ella (dejar) ______ de criticarme.
7. A menos que ella (cumplir) ______ con sus deberes domésticos no podremos resolver nuestros problemas.
8. Cuando ella (entender) ______ mi punto de vista, habrá esperanza *(hope)* para nosotros.
9. Por ejemplo, anoche, después de (cenar) ______ yo estaba muy cansado y sólo quería mirar la tele sin que nadie me (molestar)______. Ella se enfadó.
10. Antes de que yo la (poder) ______ perdonar, necesito tiempo para pensar.

D **¿Una mujer agresiva?** Mire Ud. el dibujo y termine las siguientes frases.

1. La mujer quería que el hombre...
2. Ella creía que el hombre...
3. Por la expresión de la mujer, es evidente que ella...
4. Para poder salir con la mujer, es necesario que el hombre...
5. El perro del hombre se alegra de que...
6. Es dudoso que...
7. ¿Sería posible que... ?

EM– DISCULPE, ¿CREE USTED QUE MI PERRO PODRÍA OBTENER EL NÚMERO TELEFÓNICO DE SU PERRO?

Possessive Pronouns and the Stressed Form of Possessive Adjectives

Forma

Possessive Pronouns/Stressed Possessive Adjectives

mío (a, os, as)	*mine, my*	nuestro (a, os, as)	*ours, our*
tuyo (a, os, as)	*yours, your*	vuestro (a, os, as)	*yours, your*
suyo (a, os, as)	*his, his* *hers, her* *yours, your*	suyo (a, os, as)	*theirs, their* *yours, your*

Función

1. Possessive pronouns and stressed possessive adjectives have the same form.
2. The possessive pronoun and stressed form of the possessive adjective agree in number and gender with the nouns they replace or modify.

   Mi novio y **el tuyo** son guapos. — *My boyfriend and **yours** are handsome.*

   Una prima **mía** se casa en junio. — *A cousin **of mine** is getting married in June.*

3. Although possessive pronouns are generally used with the corresponding definite article, the article may be omitted after the verb **ser**.

   Tengo mi anillo y **el tuyo.** — *I have my ring and **yours.***

   ¿Es **tuyo** este anillo? — *Is this ring **yours?***

4. The stressed form of the possessive adjective follows the noun. The definite or indefinite article is always used. This form is used to express *of mine, of yours*, and so on, and to emphasize ownership. In English, emphasis is expressed with intonation.

   Un amigo **mío** vino a verme ayer. — *A friend **of mine** came to see me yesterday.*

   La familia **tuya** es muy simpática. — ***Your** family is very nice.*

Practiquemos

A **¿De quién es?** Ud. rompió con su novio(a) después de tres años saliendo juntos. Uds. tienen que decidir de quién son los siguientes artículos. Un(a) compañero(a) hará el papel de su novio(a). Usen los pronombres posesivos apropiados según el modelo.

MODELO Ud.: **Es mi disco compacto.**
Su novio(a): **No, no es tuyo. Es mío.**

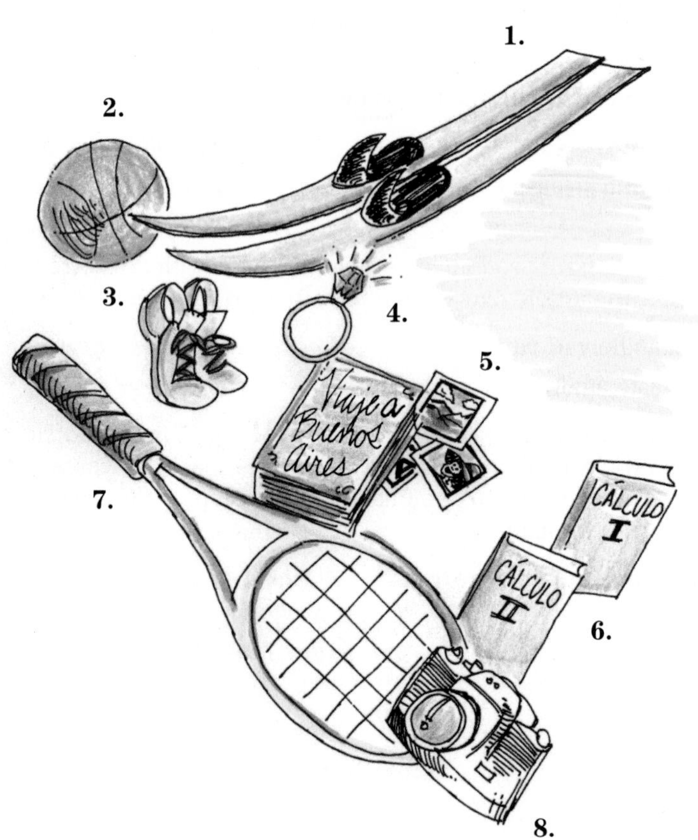

B **Ud. tiene correo.** Ud. acaba de recibir una carta por correo electrónico de su hermano quien necesita su ayuda. Está en casa limpiando el sótano y encuentra muchas cosas, pero no sabe de quiénes son. Conteste sus preguntas, usando la forma correcta del pronombre posesivo.

Hola. Perdona que te moleste durante los exámenes finales pero necesito ayuda. No sé de quiénes son todas las cosas que encontré en el sótano. Para que puedas contestar fácilmente te escribo esta lista. Escríbeme pronto porque mamá no me dejará salir hasta que todo esté limpio.

1. ¿Son tus esquís o son de Pilar? ______

2. ¿Es tu guitarra o es de José? ______

3. ¿Son tus libros o son de papá? ______

4. ¿Es tu guante de béisbol o es de Anita? ______

5. ¿Es tu mochila o es de Isabel? ______

6. ¿Son tus juegos electrónicos o son de Tomás? ______

C **Opuestos *(Opposites)*.** Forme Ud. una frase original con los siguientes adjetivos. Un(a) compañero(a) va a usar el pronombre posesivo apropiado y el antónimo para decir lo opuesto.

difícil
Ud.: Mi vida es muy **difícil**.
Su compañero(a): **La mía** es muy **fácil**.

1. liberal 2. pasivo 3. flexible 4. grande 5. útil

Spend more time with Mariana and her friends while you review grammar and expand your cultural horizons.

See the **Así es Mariana** exercise in your workbook for this lesson.

En resumen

A **Todo tiene solución.** Haga Ud. el papel de un(a) sicólogo(a) e intente ayudar a la señora del siguiente artículo a resolver su problema. Busque una terminación apropiada para las frases de la primera columna y use la forma apropiada de los verbos entre paréntesis en el indicativo o en el subjuntivo.

CELOSO DEL TRABAJO
Problema: Cada vez que regreso del trabajo, mi marido se porta como un niño celoso, acusándome de que le dedico mucho tiempo y atención a mi trabajo y no a él. ¿Qué puedo hacer?

1. La solución...	**a.** (saber) que Ud. le tiene amor y respeto.
2. Los celos de su marido...	**b.** (preferir) trabajar fuera de la casa.
3. Muchos hombres creen que son los únicos que...	**c.** (ir) a ser más fuerte que nunca.
4. Por eso, es importante que Ud. no...	**d.** (tener) raíces *(roots)* profundas.
5. Es necesario que él...	**e.** (poder) mantener a una familia.
6. Déjele saber que Ud....	**f.** (dañar) su ego.
7. Es verdad que su relación...	**g.** (ser) fácil.

B **Si Ud. fuera ella...** Mire Ud. el dibujo y haga los ejercicios.

La única vez que él me ha sacado es para venir aquí

1. ¿Cuál es... de esta situación?
   a. lo cómico c. lo bueno
   b. lo malo d. lo triste
2. Diga Ud. lo que está pensando cada persona en este momento.
3. Nombre Ud....
   a. dos quejas que el hombre tendrá de su mujer.
   b. dos quejas que la mujer tendrá de su marido.
   c. dos consejos que la consejera tendrá para esta pareja.

C **Cooperación matrimonial.** Traduzca Ud. el siguiente diálogo al español.

Antonia: My husband and I have reached an agreement: I'll work fewer hours provided that he cooperates more in the kitchen.

Silvia: I'd prefer my husband to play a more aggressive role with the children. He's very passive.

Antonia: Mine is passive, too, and then he gets angry when the children behave badly.

Silvia: The good thing is that neither your husband nor mine is rigid and macho.

D **Minidrama.** En grupos, representen una de las siguientes escenas.

1. Ud. es instructor(a) en un instituto que les enseña a los hombres a ser buenos amos de casa. Representen una clase típica con sus estudiantes.
2. Representen los problemas y obstáculos que encuentra una mujer ejecutiva con su jefe machista.

E **Composición.**

1. Ud. ha visto unas características en su novio que parecen ser un poco machistas y quiere hablar con él sobre la situación. Sus amigos le aconsejaron que Ud. escribiera una lista de sus quejas. Use los mandatos y el subjuntivo para formar la lista.

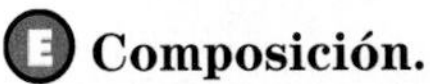

MODELO **No seas tan posesivo. Sé más sensible.**
No me gusta que tomes todas las decisiones nuestras.

2. Aparte de sus padres, ¿quién es la persona (hombre o mujer) que ha influido más en su vida? Escríbale una carta a esta persona, agradeciéndole su influencia y ayuda.

Escuchemos

A **Tome Ud. una decisión.** You will hear a series of incomplete sentences. From the list below choose the word that best completes each sentence.

MODELO Antes de ir al trabajo yo llevo a los niños a ___. (la guardería infantil)
Antes de ir al trabajo yo llevo a los niños a la guardería infantil.

se opone a	deber	lazos	se enojó
machista	dio a luz	liberal	mitad

B **Dictado.** You will hear a short narration about an incident that took place in the López family. Listen carefully to the entire selection. Listen again and write each sentence during the pauses.

You will then hear a series of questions related to the dictation. Answer them with complete sentences. Refer to your dictation.

Lección 18

Celebraciones

¡Feliz Navidad! ¡Feliz Jánuca! ¡Próspero Año Nuevo!

AVISO CULTURAL

(As a reading aid, refer to lesson vocabulary for new words.)

¿Le gustan a Ud. las fiestas y celebraciones? En muchos países hispanos no existe la gran división de generaciones que existe en los EE.UU. No es raro que en una fiesta los abuelos, los padres y los hijos celebren juntos. Tampoco hay una edad mínima para tomar bebidas alcohólicas. Además de las celebraciones de cumpleaños, del santo y del aniversario, la familia hispana suele celebrar muchas fiestas de carácter religioso. En muchos de los pueblos y ciudades de España se celebra un festival en honor del santo patrón. En Valencia se celebran las Fallas de San José en marzo. En Pamplona el 7 de julio empieza la fiesta de San Fermín, y Semana Santa en Sevilla empieza los días antes del domingo de la Resurrección.

¿Cuáles son algunas fiestas que se celebran en los EE.UU.? ¿Suele Ud. celebrarlas con sus amigos o con su familia? Explique. ¿A qué edad se puede comprar y tomar bebidas alcohólicas en los EE.UU.?

Preparativos

Review the vocabulary on pages 523–524 before viewing the video.

Al mirar el video o leer el diálogo siguiente, a ver si Ud. puede contestar las siguientes preguntas: ¿Por qué Alicia se siente feliz y triste a la vez? ¿Por qué no le importa tanto a Luis dejar a Mariana? ¿Por qué no celebra Carla la Navidad? ¿Por qué en España los niños no reciben sus regalos el 25 de diciembre? En este episodio, Luis tiene una oportunidad más para compartir recuerdos de su niñez con sus amigos. Y Ud. tiene una oportunidad más para practicar el uso del pretérito y el imperfecto. Adiós, y siga estudiando español... ¡Es muy importante!

Así es Mariana: La fiesta de fin de año

Todos están en una fiesta para celebrar el final del semestre y el Año Nuevo.

Mariana: Alicia, chica, es una fiesta, no un velorio... ¿Por qué estás tan solemne?

Alicia: En sólo diecisiete horas mi avión saldrá para Caracas. Claro, extraño a mis padres y a mi hermanita, y tengo ganas de estar con ellos, pero mi Octavio estará aquí en Miami, con... *(mira a Carla, sentada al lado de Octavio)* algunos de Uds.

Luis Antonio: Yo creí que Uds. ya habían resuelto todos esos problemas. No te preocupes, Alicia. Octavio te quiere mucho. Además, estará muy ocupado cuidando a Mariana mientras yo esté en San Diego.

Alicia: ¿Vuelves otra vez? Estabas allí hace poco con Mariana.

Luis Antonio: Yo lo sé, pero sólo voy por unos días, y después vuelvo. Yo nunca paso la Navidad fuera de casa. Es muy especial.

Alicia: ¿Por qué? ¿Cómo la celebran en tu casa?

Luis Antonio: Al estilo mexicano, por supuesto. Tenemos posadas. Nos juntamos un grupo de vecinos y vamos por las calles de la vecindad. Y todos llevamos velas encendidas. Llamamos a la puerta de cada uno de nuestros amigos pidiendo posada para María porque va a dar a luz al Niño Jesús. En una de las casas nos abren la puerta y nos invitan a pasar y allí festejamos todos. Hay comida tradicional, música, y claro, piñatas para los niños.

Mariana: En Puerto Rico la gente hace asaltos, que son similares a las posadas. O sea, vamos de casa en casa llamando a la puerta de nuestros amigos y vecinos y cantamos una plena° tradicional. Por fin nos dejan entrar y nos ofrecen galletas y bebidas. ¿Haces tú algo similar en Venezuela, Alicia?

type of Puerto Rican song

Alicia: No, no es una tradición, por lo menos en mi casa. En Venezuela los niños creen que el Niño Jesús trae los regalos en Nochebuena.

Tomás: En España, los niños reciben los regalos el Día de los Reyes Magos, el 6 de enero. Dejan sus zapatos en el balcón de su casa y según la tradición, si han sido buenos, los Reyes Magos los llenan de dulces y regalos. Pero si han sido muy malos, pues, sólo reciben carbón.

Mariana: Pues en Puerto Rico tenemos una costumbre similar. Los niños ponen una caja llena de hierba debajo de sus camitas.

Rubén: ¿Hierba? Pero, ¿para qué?

Mariana: Para dar de comer a los camellos de los Reyes Magos, por supuesto.

Carla: En mi casa no tenemos ninguna de estas tradiciones.

Mariana: ¿De veras? ¿Nada similar? ¿Cómo celebran Uds., entonces?

Carla: No celebramos la Navidad. Claro, es lógico... Soy judía.

Mariana: Claro, Carla. Me había olvidado. Lo importante es que todos estén juntos con su familia y amigos y ¡que tengamos un Año Nuevo próspero, sano y muy feliz!

Todos: ¡Feliz Navidad! ¡Feliz Jánuca! ¡Próspero Año Nuevo!

Es decir

A Para repasar cómo se expresa acción en el pasado, cambie Ud. al imperfecto la descripción de Luis Antonio de la celebración navideña. Empiece con **Cuando yo era pequeño...**

B Repase Ud. el diálogo y diga quién celebra la Navidad de las siguientes formas, y de dónde es.

1. Recibe los regalos en la Nochebuena.
2. Recibe los regalos el 6 de enero.
3. Deja hierba para los camellos.
4. Recibe carbón si ha sido malo.
5. Canta una plena tradicional.
6. Pide posada a la casa de sus vecinos.
7. Recibe galletas y bebidas en la casa de los vecinos.
8. Celebra con piñatas.

C En grupos, traten de animar a Alicia, quien todavía está triste y preocupada.

Al ver el video

Después de ver el video, haga las siguientes actividades.

A Termine Ud. la frase, basándose en el video.

1. La fecha es...
2. Todos se han reunido para...
3. Pronto, todos van a casa para...
4. Mariana espera que...
5. Mariana sacó fotos de todos sus amigos, menos...

B ¿Qué «ornamentos» llevan los amigos en la cabeza? ¿Cómo es el de Alicia? ¿Es apropiado? Explique.

C En el año 2010. En grupos, digan qué les habrá pasado a Mariana, Luis Antonio, Carla, Alicia y Octavio. Incluyan la información siguiente.

1. ¿Dónde estarán?
2. ¿Qué harán? (profesión, estudios, familia)
3. ¿Se verán (se escribirán, se visitarán) con frecuencia?

Vocabulario

Verbos

brindar	*to toast*
burlarse (de)	*to make fun (of)*
celebrar	*to celebrate*
disfrazarse (de)	*to disguise oneself (as), dress up*
enterrar (ie)	*to bury*
esconder	*to hide*
felicitar	*to congratulate*
festejar	*to have a party, celebrate*
juntar	*to gather, bring together*
rezar	*to pray*
suceder	*to happen*

Sustantivos

el alma (*f.*)	*soul*
el cementerio	*cemetery*
la corrida de toros	*bullfight*
el cura (sacerdote)	*priest*
el desfile	*parade*
el disfraz	*disguise*
el entierro	*funeral, burial*
el espíritu	*spirit*
la felicidad	*happiness*
la misa	*mass*
el (la) muerto(a)	*dead person*
el pastor	*minister*
el rabino	*rabbi*
la sorpresa	*surprise*
el velorio	*wake*
el villancico	*Christmas carol*

Adjetivos

católico	*Catholic*
cristiano	*Christian*
judío	*Jewish*
maravilloso (estupendo)	*marvellous (wonderful)*
protestante	*Protestant*
religioso	*religious*
sagrado	*sacred*
solemne	*solemn*

Días festivos y fechas importantes	(Holidays and important dates)
el Año Nuevo	*New Year*
el Día de los Muertos	*Day of the Dead*
el Día de (los) Reyes (Magos)	*Kings' Day (Epiphany)*
el día del santo	*Saint's Day*
Jánuca	*Chanukah*
la Misa del gallo	*Midnight Mass*
la Navidad	*Christmas*
la Nochebuena	*Christmas Eve*
la Noche vieja	*New Year's Eve*
la Pascua	*Passover*
la Pascua (Florida)	*Easter*
la Semana Santa	*Holy Week*

Palabras y expresiones útiles	
¡Enhorabuena!	*Congratulations!*
¡Feliz Navidad! (¡Felices Pascuas!)	*Merry Christmas!*
Mi más sincero pésame	*My condolences*
¡Próspero Año Nuevo!	*Happy New Year!*
¡Salud!	*Cheers!*

Vocabulario adicional	
el brindis	*toast*
Carnaval	*Carnival, Mardi Gras*
deprimente	*depressing*
la festividad	*festivity*
la religión	*religion*

Repasemos el vocabulario

A **¿Cuál no pertenece?** Indique Ud. la palabra que no está relacionada con las otras y explique.

1. velorio	desfile	cementerio	entierro
2. rabino	sorpresa	pastor	sacerdote
3. Misa del gallo	Jánuca	Navidad	Nochebuena
4. católico	judío	protestante	religioso
5. enterrar	celebrar	festejar	felicitar

B **Palabras cognadas.** Las palabras en la segunda columna no se encuentran en la lista de vocabulario de esta lección. Sin embargo, se pueden reconocer fácilmente por ser similares a sus equivalentes en inglés. Busque Ud. en la segunda columna dos palabras que corresponden a cada una de las palabras en la primera columna.

1. entierro	**a.** crucifijo
2. iglesia	**b.** procesiones
3. Navidad	**c.** máscara
4. Carnaval	**d.** San Nicolás
	e. tumba
	f. Polo Norte
	g. sepulcro
	h. altar

C **El Día de los Muertos... los mexicanos celebran la muerte.** El primero de noviembre es el Día de Todos los Santos, una fiesta importante para los hispanos católicos de todas partes del mundo. Pero, el dos de noviembre es un día aún más especial para los mexicanos. Complete Ud. los párrafos con las palabras apropiadas.

El Día de los Muertos, México, D.F.

celebran	recuerdan	pastelerías	festividad
rezar	espíritus	cementerio	almas
muerte	tumbas	preparan	

En México, el dos de noviembre se llama el «Día de los Muertos», y es una combinación curiosa de solemnidad y ______. En este día los mexicanos ______ a sus seres queridos. Van al ______ para llorar, ______ y decorar las ______ con flores. En las tiendas venden objetos relacionados con la muerte. En las panaderías y ______ venden panes, pasteles y dulces que tienen la forma de esqueletos *(skeletons)* y calaveras *(skulls)*. También se come el delicioso «pan de muertos».

En Pátzcuaro, un viejo pueblo colonial de México, los indios ______ ese día con mucho entusiasmo. Creen que las ______ de los muertos regresan cada año para visitar a sus seres queridos. Encienden velas *(candles)* para iluminar el camino a la tumba para los ______ de sus queridos y ______ las comidas y bebidas favoritas del muerto para mostrar su devoción. Estas costumbres reflejan una actitud de aceptación y resignación hacia la ______.

D Expresiones apropiadas. ¿Qué dice Ud. en las siguientes situaciones?

1. Está en la boda de su hermano y le piden que brinde por los recién casados.
2. Una pareja anuncia que se va a casar.
3. Va a un velorio. Habla con la viuda del hombre que acaba de morir.
4. Es el 25 de diciembre y ve al cura en la iglesia.
5. Se reúne con un grupo de amigos para despedir el año. Son las doce en punto.

E Definiciones. Busque Ud. en la lista de vocabulario las palabras que corresponden a las siguientes definiciones. Complete la definición con las palabras apropiadas.

religioso	cantar	año	muertos
beber	días	nacimiento	celebran

1. ______: Sitio donde entierran a los ______.
2. ______: Día en que se celebra el ______ de Jesucristo.
3. ______: Última noche del ______.
4. ______: Fiesta solemne que ______ los cristianos en memoria de la resurrección de Cristo.
5. ______: Fiesta que celebran los judíos que dura *(lasts)* ocho ______.
6. ______: Acción de ______ a la salud de una persona.
7. ______: Líder ______ de los católicos.
8. ______: Canción que se suele ______ en la Navidad.

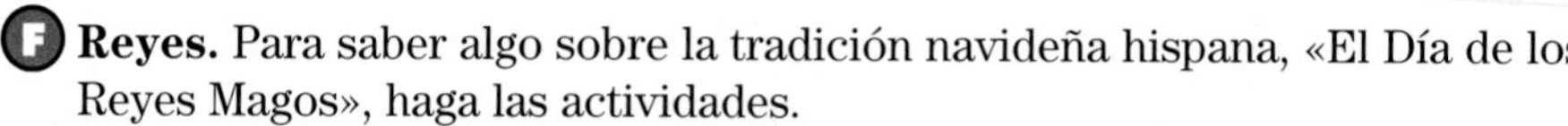

F Reyes. Para saber algo sobre la tradición navideña hispana, «El Día de los Reyes Magos», haga las actividades.

1. Lea Ud. la descripción de la fiesta de Reyes y conteste las preguntas.

   En muchos países hispanos los niños reciben sus regalos el 6 de enero. Este día se llama «Reyes» o el «Día de los Reyes Magos». Hace más de dos mil años Jesucristo nació en Belén. Los Reyes Magos lo visitaron y le trajeron regalos. Según la tradición, ellos se llamaban Gaspar, Melchor y Baltasar. Para celebrar la fiesta, algunos de los niños dejan sus zapatos debajo de la cama o en el balcón. Otros niños ponen cajas llenas de hierba *(grass)* debajo de la cama para dar de comer a los camellos de los Reyes. Si los niños han sido muy buenos, al día siguiente encuentran los regalos. Pero, si han sido muy malos, encuentran carbón *(coal)*. Muchas de las pastelerías venden un dulce que se parece mucho al carbón, pero en realidad es de azúcar. En la tarde toda la familia se reúne y hace una gran comida. En España, se suele comer el famoso «roscón de Reyes», que es una tarta especial que tiene un regalito y una haba *(bean)* escondidos adentro. La persona que encuentra el haba tiene que pagar el roscón. La persona que encuentra el regalito recibe una corona *(crown)* de papel.

   a. ¿Cuándo se celebra el Día de los Reyes Magos?
   b. ¿Cómo se llaman los tres Reyes?
   c. ¿Qué hacen los niños para celebrar la fiesta?
   d. ¿Qué encuentran los niños buenos al día siguiente?
   e. ¿Qué encuentran los niños malos?
   f. ¿Qué es el «roscón de Reyes»?

2. Lea Ud. el dibujo. ¿Con quién habla por teléfono el rey? Termine Ud. la conversación telefónica en este dibujo. ¿Qué más dice el rey y qué le dice la otra persona?

— *¿American Express? Mire, les llamo porque esta noche teníamos pensado salir de compras y...*

3. En muchos de los almacenes de España en la época de Reyes, les dan a los niños formularios especiales para escribirles cartas a los Reyes Magos. Escríbale una carta a los Reyes y un(a) compañero(a) contestará.

Los Reyes Magos llegaron a Cuenca a lomos de camellos

a lomos de camellos
on the back of camels

Queridos Reyes Magos:

Review of the Use of the Preterite and Imperfect

The preterite is used . . .

1. to describe or relate a completed action or a series of completed actions.

   Joselito **se despertó, se levantó** y **salió** al balcón para ver qué le **habían dejado** los Reyes. — *Joselito **woke up, got up,** and **went out** on the balcony to see what the Wise Men **had left** him.*

2. when a past action occurs a specific number of times.

   Fui a Sevilla para Semana Santa tres veces. — *I **went** to Seville for Holy Week three times.*

3. to indicate a change in a physical, emotional, or mental state at a specific time in the past.

   Al abrir el regalo el niño **estuvo** feliz. — *Upon opening the present the child **became** happy.*

4. to focus on the beginning or end of a past action.

   Laura **se rió** al ver a papá disfrazado de San Nicolás. — *Laura **laughed** upon seeing dad dressed up as Santa Claus.*

The imperfect is used . . .

1. to describe past action that was ongoing at a certain time in the past, or an action whose beginning or end is not indicated.

   Mamá **preparaba** la cena todo el día. — *Mom **was preparing** dinner all day long.*

2. to express repeated or habitual past action. The English equivalent is *used to* or *would* + verb.

   De pequeño siempre **íbamos** a la Misa del gallo. — *When I was a child we **would** always **go** to Midnight Mass.*

3. to express time and age in the past.

   Paco **tenía** tres años. — *Paco **was** three years old.*

   Eran las seis cuando llegamos a casa. — *It **was** six o'clock when we arrived home.*

4. to describe things or people in the past and to set the scene of past situations.

   Era un día muy bonito. El sol **brillaba** en el cielo y los pájaros **cantaban.** — *It **was** a beautiful day. The sun **was shining** in the sky and the birds **were singing.***

5. to describe ongoing physical, emotional, or mental states and desires in the past.

   Quería ir a la fiesta hoy pero **estaba** enfermo. — *He **wanted** to go to the party today but he **was** sick.*

   Often the preterite and the imperfect appear in the same sentence with the conjunction **cuando**. The preterite action frequently breaks up the ongoing action of the imperfect.

   Mamá **escondía** los regalos cuando los niños la **descubrieron.** — *Mom **was hiding** the presents when the children **found** her.*

Practiquemos

A **La corrida de toros.** La corrida de toros es considerada la «Fiesta nacional de España». También es popular en México, Perú, Ecuador, Colombia y Venezuela. En Lima, Perú siempre se celebra la corrida de toros más importante del año el Día de Navidad. Cambie Ud. los verbos al pretérito.

El año pasado yo (pasar) ______ el mes de diciembre en Lima, Perú. El día 25 yo (ir) ______ a una corrida de toros. Mis amigos y yo (sentarse) ______ en la sección de «sombra» *(shade)* y (esperar) ______ el comienzo del espectáculo. En cada corrida siempre hay tres matadores que lidian *(fight)* con dos toros cada uno. La corrida (empezar) ______ a las cinco en punto. Todos los participantes —los tres matadores y sus cuadrillas *(teams)*— (salir) ______ de paseo por la plaza. ¡(Ser) ______ magnífico!

Después, (seguir) ______ los tres segmentos de la corrida. En el primero, los «picadores», montados a caballo, (debilitar = *to weaken*) ______ el toro con picas *(lances)*. En el segundo, el «banderillero» (poner) ______ banderillas *(barbed darts)* en el cuello del toro para provocarlo. Luego (llegar) ______ «la faena», la parte más emocionante, en que el matador (demostrar) ______ sus artes y (matar) ______ el toro.

B **La Navidad en aquel entonces.** Octavia Gonzales Hurtado, una abuela colombiana, describe la Navidad que se celebraba en Colombia. Cambie Ud. los verbos al imperfecto.

Nosotros (celebrar) ______ la Navidad de una forma muy diferente cuando yo (ser) ______ pequeña. Los niños (soñar) ______ con la llegada del día e (imaginar) ______ cómo sería el día mágico. Nosotros no (tener) ______ televisión y por eso, no (ver) ______ los anuncios comerciales que intentaban venderle sus productos al público. Todos (esperar) ______ la Navidad. Los niños (creer) ______ que el Niño Dios (ser) ______ el responsable de todos los bonitos regalos que (encontrar) ______ debajo de sus almohadas.

Nosotros (adornar) ______ las casas con decoraciones que nosotros (hacer) ______. Los amigos (traer) ______ las comidas que cada uno (preparar) ______ para la ocasión. Los dulces y los tamales (llenar) ______ las mesas, y toda la casa (oler = *to smell*) ______ a Navidad.

Los niños de ayer (cambiar) ______ automáticamente en la época navideña. (Portarse) ______ como angelitos. (Soler) ______ escribirle cartas al Niño Dios, en las cuales (describir) ______ con detalle los regalos que (querer) ______ recibir... soldaditos de estaño *(tin soldiers)* o muñecas de trapo *(rag dolls)*. Y mi mamá (pasar) ______ meses preparando nuestros regalos que (ser) ______ todos hechos por su propia *(own)* mano.

C **Ud. tiene correo.** Ud tiene una «amiga por correspondencia electrónica» quien le escribe para hablar del Carnaval en su país natal de Argentina. Cambie los verbos al pretérito o al imperfecto. Luego, conteste la carta, describiendo una fiesta especial.

Hola. Pues, como yo sé cuánto te interesa aprender sobre las tradiciones de mi país, voy a describir el Carnaval, una fiesta que precede la Cuaresma *(Lent)*. Se celebra en febrero o marzo, y dura *(lasts)* unos cinco días.

A mí me (gustar) ______ el Carnaval. En las calles de Córdoba, mi ciudad, siempre (haber) ______ un ambiente festivo. La gente (disfrazarse) ______ con la ropa típica del Carnaval de Brasil y (haber) ______ bailes, desfiles, música, danza, comida y bebida hasta muy tarde. También (ser) ______ la costumbre llenar con agua unos globos pequeños y tirárselos a la gente.

Yo me acuerdo de una vez cuando (tener) ______ 16 años. Ese día mis amigos y yo (vestirse) ______ de payasos, (salir) ______ a la calle y (comer) ______ «choripán» *(bread with grilled sausage)* y «panchos» *(hot dogs)*, la comida típica de esa época. (Ser) ______ las cinco o las seis de la tarde. Nosotros (caminar) ______ por la calle cuando unos jóvenes, desde el séptimo piso de un edificio, nos (tirar) ______ un balde *(bucket)* de agua con jabón. Al principio yo (ponerse) ______ enojada, pues (tener) ______ la ropa mojada *(wet)*, pero después (reírse) ______. (Ser) ______ un día memorable.

Reciprocal Actions with *Se*

The reciprocal construction expresses *each other* or *one another*.

Forma

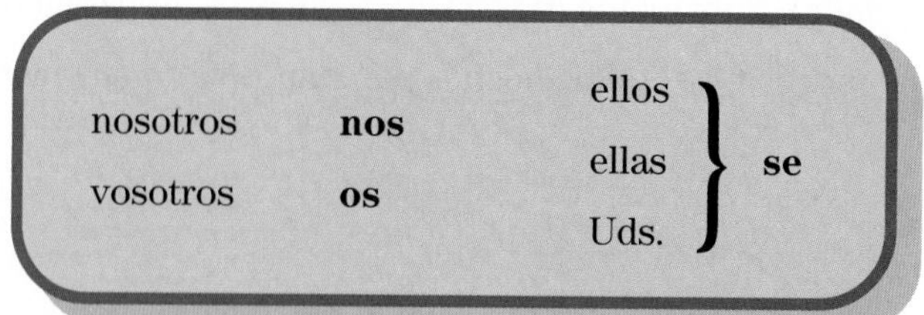

nosotros	**nos**	ellos	
vosotros	**os**	ellas	**se**
		Uds.	

Nos queremos mucho.	***We love each other*** *very much.*
¿Os conocéis?	***Do you know each other?***
Se ayudan siempre.	***They*** *always* ***help each other.***

Función

1. The plural reflexive pronouns can be used to express either reflexive or reciprocal action.

Magdalena y Laura **se ven.**	*Magdalena and Laura* ***see themselves.*** *Magdalena and Laura* ***see each other.***

2. It is generally clear from the context which concept is being expressed.

Jorge y Manolo **se escriben** a menudo.	*Jorge and Manolo* ***write to each other*** *often.*

Practiquemos

A **Distancias.** Gabriela vive muy lejos de su hermana. ¿Qué hacen las dos hermanas para mantener una relación íntima? Forme frases que muestran acción recíproca según el modelo.

MODELO mandar/muchas fotos
Se mandan muchas fotos.

1. llamar/por teléfono
2. escribir/cartas
3. visitar/cada mes
4. escuchar/cuando tienen problemas personales
5. contar/todos sus secretos

B **En mi familia todos celebramos.** Mi familia es muy grande y así celebramos la Navidad. Use Ud. el reflexivo recíproco de la primera persona plural **(nosotros)** y complete el párrafo con los verbos apropiados de la lista siguiente.

MODELO desear **Nos deseamos mucha felicidad en el año nuevo.**

contar	saludar	querer	preguntar
decir	ayudar	besar	abrazar
dar	mostrar		

Siempre celebramos la Navidad en la casa de mi abuela. Al llegar a la casa ______ cariñosamente y ______ «Feliz Navidad». Como es una cena muy grande, ______ con los preparativos. Después de comer, ______ fotos y ______ anécdotas sobre todos los eventos del año. ______ cómo están los niños y cómo van los trabajos, y ______ los regalos que hemos traído. Al salir ______ y ______. En mi familia ______ mucho.

Spend more time with Mariana and her friends while you review grammar and expand your cultural horizons.
See the **Así es Mariana** exercise in your workbook for this lesson.

En resumen

Una procesión de Semana Santa

A **Una tarjeta para cada ocasión.** Complete Ud. las tarjetas con las palabras apropiadas.

santa	corazón	seas	Navidad
felicito	Pascua Florida	abrazo	cariño
alegría	oraciones		

En el Día de tu Santo

En esta fecha tan grata
Te recuerdo cariñosamente
Y de todo ______ deseo
Que ______ muy feliz siempre

1. **El día del santo.** Si Ud. es hispano y se llama Juan, celebrará el día de su santo o su «santo» el 24 de junio. Es el día que la iglesia católica le ha dedicado a San Juan. Para algunos hispanos es un día de mucha celebración.

2. **Semana Santa** es la semana que precede el domingo de la Resurrección (Pascua Florida). En muchos países hispanos es la fiesta más larga y más espectacular. Hay grandes y solemnes procesiones de penitentes y pasos *(floats)* con magníficas imágenes religiosas. La semana entera se convierte en un teatro vivo de la pasión y muerte de Jesucristo. Las celebraciones de Sevilla, España y Antigua, Guatemala tienen fama mundial.

Que mis fervientes
____
se multipliquen este día
para que la
____
sea colmada de paz
y ________.

Una Plegaria
de Pascua Florida

QUERIDA
AMIGA

3. En la cultura hispana **la Nochebuena** es la culminación de todos los preparativos navideños. En muchos países hay grupos que van cantando villancicos de casa en casa. Hay procesiones religiosas y la gente asiste a fiestas y cenas elegantes y va a la Misa del gallo a medianoche. En algunos países se usan fuegos artificiales *(fireworks)* en esa noche tan especial.

¡Te_______ y te_______
Porque hoy es la_______!
Fecha gloriosa que marca
La_______ Natividad,
Y si es que en esta ocasión
El_______ hay que expresar,
Con mi más sincero afecto
Te dedico esta postal.

Bendiciones
en Navidad
y Año Nuevo

B **¡Feliz cumpleaños... al estilo hispano!** Complete Ud. la selección con la forma correcta de las palabras entre paréntesis. Si hay dos palabras, escoja la más apropiada. Traduzca las palabras en inglés al español y cambie los verbos al pretérito o al imperfecto.

En una familia grande como *(mine)*, no es posible que los padres festejen todos los cumpleaños de sus hijos a gran escala. Pero, (mi) padres me (festejar) los quince años. (Por, Para) una chica, los quince es la fiesta más importante que se hace. Yo (empezar) a asistir a las fiestas de quince años cuando (tener) catorce años y (terminar) a los dieciseis años —pues, tengo muchas amigas y todas me (invitar). (Por, Para) mi fiesta, yo (hacer) mi propia *(cake)* y los recuerdos, y mis hermanas me (ayudar) a hacer muchas cosas. Mi mamá (preparar) muchos platos. La fiesta no (ser) grande... *(only)* amigos. No (querer) invitar a mis parientes. La fiesta (terminar) a (los, las) siete (por, de) la mañana. Mi mamá (hacer) un (gran, grande) *(breakfast)* (por, para) todos los que (quedar) y después, todos (irse) (por, para) (su) casas.

C **¡Vamos al Carnaval!** Traduzca Ud. el siguiente diálogo al español.

Pablo: Your cousin in Argentina took this photo in 1962! How old were you?

María: Fifteen. I used to live in Córdoba, and Cecilia lived in Buenos Aires. We used to see each other every year during Carnaval.

Pablo: Look at this parade and these costumes! Paco told me that Carnaval was a very solemn time.

María: No way! We'd celebrate for many days. One year we celebrated Carnaval in Río de Janeiro in Brazil. It was fabulous!

D **Minidrama.** En grupos, representen una de las escenas siguientes.

1. Un encuentro entre los Reyes Magos y Santa Claus.
2. Un(a) niño(a) descubre a su papá vistiéndose de Santa Claus.

E **Composición.**

1. Su amigo es de Argentina donde la Navidad es en el verano. Imagine que Ud. es de Michigan. Escríbale a su amigo y dígale cómo Ud. celebra la Navidad durante el invierno norteamericano.
2. En la Noche vieja, cada persona tiene su propia forma de celebrar. En España, por ejemplo, la gente come doce uvas para simbolizar doce meses de buena suerte. ¿Cuál es su forma de celebrar? Describa Ud. con detalles tres formas originales e innovadoras de despedir el año.

TRES DELICIOSAS FORMAS DE ¡DESPEDIR EL AÑO!

Escuchemos

A **¿Qué palabra escoge Ud.?** You will hear a series of incomplete sentences. Choose the word that best completes each sentence.

El hombre judío quiere hablar con su ______ (rabino).
El hombre judío quiere hablar con su rabino.

1. (¡Salud!/¡Enhorabuena!)
2. (solemne/alegre)
3. (los Reyes Magos/la Misa del gallo)
4. (muerto/espíritu)
5. (sorpresa/desfile)
6. (Felices Pascuas/Mi más sincero pésame)
7. (Carnaval/Navidad)

B **Dictado.** Enrique was in South America during Carnaval time. Listen carefully to the entire description of Enrique's experience. Listen again and write each sentence during the pauses.

You will then hear a series of questions related to the dictation. Answer them with complete sentences. Refer to your dictation.

Gaceta 6 Sudamérica

Buenos Aires, Argentina

Una gira turística por Sudamérica

Preparativos: Estrategias de prelectura

1. Antes de hacer una gira por Sudamérica, mire Ud. la sección **Es decir** para ayudar a anticipar lo que va a leer. ¿Qué actividades y sitios de interés incluye la gira? ¿Qué países va a visitar? ¿Cuáles son las capitales de esos países?
2. Hojee la lectura para saber...
   a. ¿a qué país se refiere el segundo párrafo?
   b. ¿a qué países pertenecen las islas Galápagos, la isla de Pascua y la isla Margarita?
3. Hojee la lectura para saber a qué se refieren los siguientes números y fechas.
   a. los números: 112, 3.000, 500
   b. las fechas: el siglo XV, 1911, 1835, 1533

Las ruinas de Machu Picchu, Perú

En Sudamérica hay ciudades cosmopolitas y pequeños pueblos coloniales. Los muchos museos tienen tesoros° de arte contemporáneo y preciosos vestigios° de civilizaciones pasadas. Hay paisajes montañosos, selvas exóticas, valles, playas soleadas° y grandes plantaciones de café, cacao y bananas. En cuestiones de clima, de recreo, de cocina y de cultura... hay de todo en Sudamérica.

treasures
traces
sunny

astonishing; fortress	La asombrosa° ciudad-fortaleza° de los incas, Machu Picchu, está situada en los Andes peruanos a unos 112 kilómetros de Cuzco, la antigua capital incaica. Fue construida en el siglo XV y abandonada a la llegada de los conquistadores españoles.

Este santuario servía de refugio para los líderes de los incas en caso de peligro. Estaba tan escondido en las montañas que sólo unos campesinos° (*farmers*) sabían de su existencia hasta 1911 cuando fue «descubierto» por Hiram Bingham, un ex gobernador de Connecticut. Las ruinas que se han conservado son magníficas: templos, casas, palacios, una fortaleza, un cementerio, calles y avenidas. Es indudablemente° (*undoubtedly*) el espectáculo más impresionante de la América del Sur.

Diecisiete islas grandes, más de cien islotes° (*small barren islands*) y unos pueblos pequeños constituyen las islas Galápagos, una de las reservas ecológicas más importantes del mundo. A mil kilómetros de la costa del Ecuador, este parque nacional tiene tortugas gigantescas y reptiles antediluvianos. Fue aquí donde Charles Darwin, en 1835, empezó a formular su famosa teoría sobre la evolución.

En Chile, después de gozar del ambiente sofisticado de Santiago, su capital, y de la belleza de las playas increíbles de Viña del Mar y de la tranquilidad de los lagos plácidos de Puerto Montt, se debe hacer un viaje a la isla de Pascua,° (*Easter Island*) situada a unos 3.000 kilómetros de la costa. Por sus cráteres, volcanes, tumbas ceremoniales y sus 500 estatuas megalíticas° (*megalithic*) de origen misterioso, es llamada «el museo al aire libre».

Bolivia es el único país del continente que no tiene acceso al mar con la excepción de Paraguay. La Paz, la capital del país, y Potosí son dos ciudades pintorescas que han conservado casi intacta su antigua belleza colonial. Aquí se pueden probar comidas picantes, escuchar música regional en una peña° (*festive gathering*) folklórica y visitar museos interesantes. Cerca de la frontera entre Bolivia y Perú está el lago Titicaca, el lago navegable más alto del mundo.

Para los viajeros que quieren combinar playas fabulosas con un poco de historia, el lugar favorito es Cartagena de las Indias, la ciudad amurallada° (*walled*) de Colombia. Fundada en 1533, Cartagena guardaba las grandes riquezas del nuevo mundo antes de enviarlas a España. Fue la ciudad más rica de las Américas. Un lugar de veraneo que últimamente se ha hecho popular es Margarita, una isla que pertenece° (*belongs*) a Venezuela. Las playas de arena° (*sand*) fina y las aguas cristalinas son incomparables.

Es decir

A Atractivos turísticos. En Sudamérica, ¿adónde iría Ud. para...

1. navegar en un lago muy famoso?
2. hacer una variedad de actividades?
3. visitar un museo único?
4. pasar su luna de miel?
5. ver un verdadero museo de la vida incaica?
6. saber cómo era la vida colonial en la América del Sur?

B Lugares de interés. Identifique Ud. los siguientes lugares. Luego, encuéntrelos en el mapa.

1. un lugar de vacaciones «de moda»
2. la capital de Bolivia
3. el espectáculo más majestuoso del continente
4. el antiguo «puente» *(bridge)* que conectaba a España y a América
5. un lago de una altitud extraordinaria

Practiquemos

A **¿Qué sabe Ud. de Buenos Aires?** Para saber algo sobre la ciudad de Buenos Aires, busque Ud. en la segunda columna la terminación de las frases de la primera columna.

1. La segunda ciudad más grande de Sudamérica es...	**a.** artículos de piel *(leather)* y probar el «bife» *(beef).*
2. Tiene una población de...	**b.** el tango.
3. Los habitantes de esta ciudad se llaman...	**c.** una de las ciudades más interesantes del mundo.
4. La gente joven de Buenos Aires habla...	**d.** visitar «La Boca», un barrio italiano.
5. Buenos Aires es considerada...	**e.** Buenos Aires, la capital de la Argentina.
6. Una gira turística debe...	**f.** pocos edificios antiguos.
7. Si a Ud. le gustan los barrios internacionales hay que...	**g.** más de 10.000.000 de habitantes.
8. En esta zona nació el famoso baile...	**h.** «porteños».
9. Por las muchas renovaciones, hay...	**i.** un dialecto que se llama «lunfardo».
10. A los turistas les gusta comprar...	**j.** comenzar en el corazón de la ciudad, la Plaza de Mayo.

Ahora, conteste las preguntas. En Buenos Aires, ¿qué va Ud. a...

a. comer?	d. comprar?
b. ver?	e. bailar?
c. visitar?	f. oír hablar?

B **El imperio *(empire)* de los incas.** Arregle Ud. las siguientes frases en el orden apropiado para formar una lectura de tres párrafos sobre la civilización de los incas.

Párrafo 1

1. Eran una familia grande y poderosa *(powerful)* que venía de la región de Titicaca.
2. Los incas no eran una tribu *(tribe)*.
3. El gran imperio de los incas fue fundado en el siglo XII.

Párrafo 2

1. En esta época de esplendor, la civilización de los incas era un modelo de la organización social.
2. En su apogeo *(height)*, su dominio se extendía por los Andes desde el sur de Colombia hasta el norte de Chile y Argentina, y su capital era Cuzco.
3. La sociedad estaba dividida en tres clases: la nobleza *(nobility)*, el pueblo *(general population)* y los «yanacones», los servidores de los líderes.

Párrafo 3

1. Adoraban al sol, a la luna y a los fenómenos naturales.
2. Debilitado *(Weakened)* por una guerra civil, el imperio incaico fue destruido a principios del siglo XVI por Francisco Pizarro y sus soldados.
3. Su religión no era muy complicada.

Don Francisco

Gabriel García Márquez

Caras en las noticias

Parece increíble, pero cuando **Gabriel García Márquez** terminó su novela *Cien años de soledad* en 1967, tenía tan poco dinero que su esposa vendió su licuadora° para poder mandarle el manuscrito al redactor.° Hoy, *Cien años de soledad* es la novela hispana más conocida y más traducida (50 ediciones en español y traducciones en 27 idiomas) después de *Don Quijote*, y García Márquez es uno de los escritores más famosos de este siglo. Con una mezcla de ficción y realidad, dos elementos característicos de su obra, García Márquez cuenta la historia de Macondo, un pueblo imaginario que sintetiza la historia y la cultura de Latinoamérica.

blender
editor

Nació en 1928 en Aracataca, Colombia, uno de 16 hijos de un telegrafista. Ha trabajado de redactor, periodista y guionista° y publicó su primera novela, *La hojarasca*, en 1955. Este hombre humilde° de extraordinario talento literario, recibió el Premio Nóbel de literatura en 1982.

script writer
humble

Un día, un ingeniero peruano de origen japonés, **Alberto Fujimori,** decidió que quería hacer algo para sacar° a su país de la miseria racial y socioeconómica que sufría. Con la ayuda de amigos y sin ninguna experiencia política, Fujimori fundó un nuevo partido político, Cambio 90. Muy poco después, venció al otro candidato, el autor Mario Vargas Llosa, y se hizo° presidente de uno de los países más problemáticos de América.

remove
became

Quizás la cara más conocida en la televisión por toda la América Latina, incluso la televisión en los EE.UU., es la del chileno **don Francisco,** el «adorable inculto°» del programa *Sábado Gigante*. Este programa combina concursos,° entrevistas, cantantes y música, y llega a más de dos millones de hogares° en los EE.UU., Centro y Sudamérica. Dice él: «Yo tengo la suerte de Bolívar. Bolívar soñó hace 100 años con unificar a todos los países hispanos en un sólo país. Ése es mi sueño en la televisión. Unificar a todo el mundo en un programa de televisión».

clown
contests
homes

Es decir

Comprensión. Comente Ud....

1. la popularidad de la novela *Cien años de soledad* de Gabriel García Márquez.
2. la presidencia de Alberto Fujimori.
3. el sueño de don Francisco.

Practiquemos

A **Figuras famosas.** Las siguientes frases contienen más información sobre las personas o temas anteriores. ¿A cuál corresponde cada una?

1. Produce varias versiones de su programa debido a *(due to)* la variedad nacional de su público *(audience)*.
2. En 1939 sus padres huyeron de la Alemania *(Germany)* de los nazis y emigraron a Chile.
3. Es el primer descendiente de japoneses en llegar a ser presidente de un país latinoamericano.
4. Esta novela comenzó un período que se llama el «boom» de la literatura latinoamericana.
5. Aunque es considerado el colombiano más famoso de toda la historia, nunca se olvida de su pasado humilde.
6. Después de la segunda guerra mundial *(Second World War)* sus padres salieron del Japón y se establecieron en Perú.

B **Su opinión.** Conteste Ud. las preguntas con frases completas.

la televisión:

1. ¿A qué se debe la gran popularidad de programas como *Sábado Gigante*?
2. ¿Qué clase de programas de televisión le gusta a Ud.?

la literatura:

3. Combinar lo real con lo imaginario es una técnica literaria popular de García Márquez y otros escritores contemporáneos de Latinoamérica. ¿Por qué será tan popular esta técnica?
4. En su opinión, ¿en qué consiste una gran novela? ¿Ha leído Ud. *Cien años de soledad*? ¿Le gustó? Explique. ¿Cuál es su novela favorita? ¿Por qué le gusta?

la política:

5. ¿Qué cualidades o talentos debe tener un buen presidente?
6. ¿Cómo fue posible que un hombre sin experiencia política se hiciera presidente de Perú?

Notas y notables

Simón Bolívar: El Gran Libertador de Sudamérica

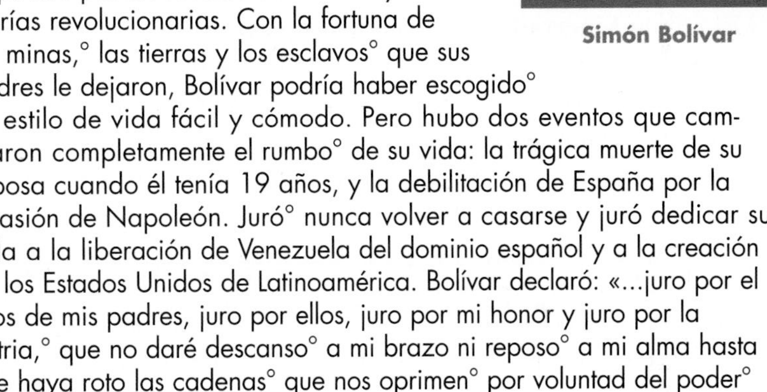

Simón Bolívar

Simón Bolívar —filósofo, orador, político extraordinario y genio° militar— llevó una vida que afectó el destino de millones de sudamericanos. Nació en 1783 en Caracas,[1] Venezuela, de una familia rica y aristocrática. De joven pasó mucho tiempo en Europa donde fue inspirado por los ideales de libertad y las teorías revolucionarias. Con la fortuna de las minas,° las tierras y los esclavos° que sus padres le dejaron, Bolívar podría haber escogido° un estilo de vida fácil y cómodo. Pero hubo dos eventos que cambiaron completamente el rumbo° de su vida: la trágica muerte de su esposa cuando él tenía 19 años, y la debilitación de España por la invasión de Napoleón. Juró° nunca volver a casarse y juró dedicar su vida a la liberación de Venezuela del dominio español y a la creación de los Estados Unidos de Latinoamérica. Bolívar declaró: «...juro por el Dios de mis padres, juro por ellos, juro por mi honor y juro por la patria,° que no daré descanso° a mi brazo ni reposo° a mi alma hasta que haya roto las cadenas° que nos oprimen° por voluntad del poder° español».

Bolívar cumplió con su palabra. Organizó un ejército,° y, durante más de diez años, batalló contra las tropas españolas. La lucha por la independencia fue larga y difícil, con grandes derrotas° y tropas mal entrenadas. En 1813, Bolívar fue proclamado «libertador» en Caracas, y en los próximos años recibió el mismo título en Bolivia, en Perú, en Colombia y en Ecuador. Pero sus esfuerzos por la unificación fracasaron, y los países entraron en un período de caos.° El libertador de cinco naciones murió en 1830 de tuberculosis, pobre y desilusionado.

Además de sus otros talentos, Bolívar fue un escritor prolífico. Siguen algunas de las palabras de Bolívar que expresan su pasión por una América fuerte, unida y libre:

- *Yo deseo más que otro alguno ver formar en América la más grande nación del mundo, menos por su extensión y riquezas° que por su libertad y gloria.*
- *Mi único amor siempre ha sido el de la Patria; mi única ambición, su libertad.*
- *Divididos, seremos más débiles, menos respetados de los enemigos y neutrales.*[2]

genius; mines; slaves; could have chosen; direction; He swore; nation; rest; repose; chains; oppress; power; army; defeats; chaos; riches

[1]En Caracas se puede visitar: La Plaza Bolívar, la Casa Natal *(birthplace)* de Bolívar, el Centro Simón Bolívar, el Museo Bolívar y el Panteón Nacional donde guardan los restos *(remains)* de este gran héroe. La moneda *(monetary unit)* de Venezuela es el **bolívar.**

[2]En su novela *El general en su laberinto*, Gabriel García Márquez examina los aspectos poco conocidos de la vida del legendario Simón Bolívar.

Es decir

Frases falsas. Las siguientes frases son falsas. Corríjalas, basándose en la lectura.

1. Bolívar pasó su vida entera como soltero.
2. Bolívar luchó para mantener separados los países de Sudamérica.
3. Bolívar nació en Bolivia y su familia era pobre.
4. Bolívar limitó su misión a su país natal *(native)*.
5. Bolívar murió en una batalla contra las tropas españolas.

Practiquemos

A El «Gran Libertador». Simón Bolívar era el «Gran Libertador» de Sudamérica. José Martí era «el Padre de la Independencia» de Cuba. ¿Qué otros títulos de personajes históricos sabe Ud.?

B ¿Héroe o villano? En grupos, escojan a un(a) héroe (heroína) o villano(a), y preparen una presentación breve sobre su vida.

Enfoque literario

Si tú me olvidas por Pablo Neruda

Pablo Neruda

Preparativos: Estrategias de prelectura

1. Antes de leer el poema, «Si tú me olvidas» por el autor chileno, Pablo Neruda, hojee la información biográfica en el texto y...
   a. describa la filosofía política de Neruda.
   b. diga cuáles son los temas literarios que reflejan esa filosofía.
   c. describa el estilo de sus poemas románticos.
2. Ahora, lea el título y el primer verso *(line)* del poema. ¿A quién le habla el poeta? En su opinión, ¿qué pasará si ella lo deja? ¿Qué quiere él que ella sepa? ¿Refleja el primer verso del poema el estilo del poeta? Explique.

Pablo Neruda (Chile, 1904–73) es considerado por muchos el mejor poeta del siglo XX. Fue diplomático en Asia, México y Europa. También fue una figura prominente en el movimiento comunista de Chile, y muchos de sus poemas reflejan su ideal marxista. Otros temas incluyen el indígena americano, la pobreza° y la injusticia social. Algunos de sus libros más populares son *Veinte poemas de amor y una canción desesperada*, *Residencia en la tierra*, *Odas elementales* y *Los versos del capitán*. En sus poemas de amor su estilo es fuerte y directo, como se puede ver en el siguiente poema.

poverty

Si tú me olvidas

Quiero que sepas
una cosa.

Tú sabes cómo es esto:
si miro
la luna de cristal, la rama° roja
del lento otoño en mi ventana,
si toco
junto al fuego°
la impalpable ceniza°
o el arrugado cuerpo de la leña,°
todo me lleva a ti,
como si todo lo que existe,
aromas, luz, metales,
fueran pequeños barcos que navegan
hacia las islas tuyas que me aguardan.°

Ahora bien,
si poco a poco dejas de° quererme
dejaré de quererte poco a poco.

Si de pronto°
me olvidas
no me busques,
que ya te habré olvidado.

Si consideras largo y loco
el viento de banderas°
que pasa por mi vida
y te decides
a dejarme a la orilla°
del corazón en que tengo raíces,°
piensa
que en ese día,
a esa hora
levantaré los brazos
y saldrán mis raíces
a buscar otra tierra.

Pero
si cada día,
cada hora,
sientes que a mí estás destinada
con dulzura implacable,
si cada día sube
una flor a tus labios a buscarme,
ay amor mío, ay mía,
en mí todo ese fuego se repite,
en mí todo ese fuego se repite,
en mí nada se apaga ni se olvida,
mi amor se nutre de° tu amor, amada,°
y mientras vivas estará en tus brazos
sin salir de los míos.

branch
fire
ashes
firewood
await me
you stop
suddenly
flags
shore
roots
feeds on; my love

Es decir

Comprensión. Basándose en el poema, diga Ud. qué hará el poeta si su amada...

1. deja de quererlo.
2. lo olvida.
3. decide dejarlo a «la orilla del corazón».
4. siente que está destinada a él.

Practiquemos

A El lenguaje literario.

1. ¿Qué objetos de la naturaleza aparecen en este poema?
2. ¿Qué otras imágenes hay?
3. Traduzca Ud. los siguientes versos:
   a. *Quiero que sepas una cosa.*
   b. *...como si todo lo que existe... fueran pequeños barcos.*

B Discusión.

1. ¿Qué sentimientos relacionados con el amor están representados en el poema?
   a. la felicidad
   b. la soledad *(loneliness)*
   c. el amor no correspondido *(unrequited love)*
   d. el dolor
   e. la pasión
2. En sus propias palabras, explique el significado de este verso: *...la luna de cristal, la rama roja... todo me lleva a ti.*

C Reacción personal.

1. Describa Ud. la actitud *(attitude)* del hombre. Si Ud. estuviera en su situación, ¿cómo reaccionaría?
2. ¿Qué otros poemas de amor conoce Ud.? ¿Qué sentimientos expresan? ¿Son similares a este poema? Explique.

→ Enfoque artístico... Sudamérica

A. Visite Ud. el sitio web **http://www.puc.cl./faba/ARTE/MUSEO/MuseoPintural.html** y dé un paseo por el Museo Nacional de Bellas Artes en Santiago, Chile. Mire las pinturas. Use su imaginación y cambie los títulos de las pinturas.

B. Escoja Ud. una pintura y diga qué es lo que el artista intenta comunicar.

C. ¿Qué estilos de arte están representados en esta colección de pinturas? ¿Cuál le gusta más y por qué?

Since Internet addresses are subject to change, typing the following key words into most search engines will get you more information about Chilean art.

Arte de Chile **Museos de Chile** **Museo Nacional de Chile**

Videocultura

Juana de Pergament y Mercedes Meroño (Las madres de la Plaza de Mayo)

Las madres de la Plaza de Mayo

military coup — *disappeared* — *disappeared ones* — *kerchiefs*

En 1976, como resultado de un golpe militar,° Argentina empezó un período de terror y terrorismo durante el cual desaparecieron° más de 30.000 personas—gente inocente nombrada «subversivos» por el gobierno. Las madres de los desaparecidos° se unieron para protestar.

Desde entonces, todos los jueves a las tres de la tarde, las madres van a la Plaza de Mayo, frente a la Casa de Gobierno en la capital de Buenos Aires. Allí, con los pañuelos° blancos puestos y con fotos de sus hijos desaparecidos, ellas continúan su marcha, año tras año, protestando los actos de brutalidad cometidos por su propio gobierno.

Para aprender más sobre la lucha por los derechos humanos de estas mujeres valientes, mire Ud. el video y haga las siguientes actividades.

Palabras útiles

la tesorera	*treasurer*	el refugio	*shelter*
copar el poder	*to seize power*	financiar	*to finance*
la desaparición	*disappearance*	infatigable	*untiring*
la guerra	*war*	la luchadora	*fighter (fem.)*
rechazar	*to reject*	el premio	*prize*
el enemigo	*enemy*	los derechos humanos	*human rights*
el arma	*weapon*	la cárcel	*prison*
lograr	*to achieve*		

Es decir

A **¿Juana o Mercedes?** ¿A cuál de las madres se refieren las siguientes frases?

1. Su hijo desapareció.
2. Su hija desapareció.
3. Es rubia.
4. Es la tesorera de la organización.
5. Pide la cárcel para los asesinos de todos los hijos.

B **¿Qué recuerda Ud.?** Conteste Ud. las siguientes preguntas con frases completas.

1. ¿Cuándo estuvieron las madres en Boston?
2. ¿Para qué fueron?
3. ¿Qué hicieron en Boston?
4. ¿Qué es Casa Myrna Vázquez?
5. ¿Para qué premio fueron nominadas las madres?
6. ¿Cómo financian su trabajo?

C **Nada de Guerra Sucia.** En sus propias palabras, explique Ud. por qué las madres se oponen categóricamente al término **Guerra Sucia.**

Practiquemos

A **Opiniones personales.** Conteste Ud. las siguientes preguntas con frases completas.

1. ¿Qué piensa Ud. de las madres de la Plaza de Mayo? ¿Qué haría Ud. en su situación?
2. ¿Merecen las madres el Premio Nóbel de la paz? ¿Por qué sí o por qué no?
3. ¿Ha perdido Ud. alguna vez sus derechos? Explique.

B **La represión.** En grupos, contesten las siguientes preguntas.

1. ¿En qué consiste la represión?
2. ¿Cuáles son ejemplos de gobiernos represivos?
3. ¿Existe la represión en los EE.UU.? Explique.
4. ¿Debe los EE.UU. intervenir en casos de gobiernos represivos?
5. ¿Qué organizaciones existen para proteger los derechos humanos? ¿Cómo funcionan estas organizaciones?

Isabel Allende

Isabel Allende

Seguramente la novelista latinoamericana más famosa del mundo, Isabel Allende combina su característica realidad mágica con los temas del amor, de la represión política y de la importancia de la tradiciones familiares, siempre con cierto sentido del humor e ironía. Sus libros han sido traducidos a más de 25 idiomas. Nacida en 1942, Isabel tuvo que salir de su país después del golpe militar que derrocó al gobierno y de la muerte controversial de su tío, Salvador Allende, el presidente de Chile durante esa época. Isabel Allende reside en California actualmente.

Para saber más sobre la vida y la obra literaria de Isabel Allende, mire Ud. el video y haga los siguientes ejercicios.

Palabras útiles

la arpillera	*small quilt made from sackcloth*
asesinar	*to assassinate*
la dictadura	*dictatorship*
la entretención (Am.)	*entertainment*
horrorizar	*to horrify*
el pedacito	*little piece*
el régimen	*regime*
suicidarse	*to commit suicide*
el vicio	*vice*

Es decir

A ¿Cómo termina? Basándose en el video, busque Ud. en la segunda columna la terminación de la frase en la primera.

1. Isabel Allende es una contadora...	**a.** bajo una dictadura.
2. Viene de una larga tradición...	**b.** murió.
3. Se enamoró...	**c.** de Chile.
4. Pasó la mayor parte de su vida fuera...	**d.** oral.
5. Salió de Chile porque no pudo vivir...	**e.** de cuentos.
6. El presidente de Chile, su tío, ...	**f.** de un gringo.

B ¿Puede Ud. nombrar... ? Basándose en el video, nombre Ud....

1. cuatro razones por las que Isabel dice que sus raíces culturales están en Chile.
2. tres títulos de libros que Isabel escribió.
3. dos profesiones de Isabel.
4. dos teorías sobre la muerte de su tío, el presidente Salvador Allende.
5. una expresión de la cultura chilena a través de las mujeres.
6. una razón por la que Isabel vino a los Estados Unidos.

C Fechas. ¿Cuál es el significado de las siguientes fechas en la vida de Isabel?

1. 1987 **2.** 1973 **3.** 1995

Practiquemos

A En sus propias palabras. Explique Ud....

1. ¿qué son las arpilleras que hacen las mujeres chilenas?
2. ¿cómo empezó el «vicio» de Isabel de contar cuentos?

B Formas de gobernar. En grupos, contesten las siguientes preguntas.

1. ¿Qué es una dictadura? ¿Y una democracia? ¿Qué otras formas de gobierno hay? Nombren por lo menos un país que tenga las formas de gobierno mencionadas. ¿Cuáles son algunas ventajas y desventajas de cada forma de gobierno?
2. ¿Qué diferencia habría en la vida de Uds. si vivieran bajo una dictadura? Describan un día típico y contrástenlo con su vida actual.

Inca Son

El grupo musical Inca Son

César Villalobos es el fundador y director del grupo musical Inca Son. Su música refleja los sonidos misteriosos de los Andes y muestra un profundo respeto por la naturaleza.

Para escuchar los sonidos mágicos de Inca Son, mire Ud. el video y haga los ejercicios que siguen.

Palabras útiles

andino	*Andean*
enriquecer	*to enrich*
incaica	*Incan*
alrededor	*around*
en la actualidad	*in the present, now*

Es decir

A **¿Cierto o falso?** Basándose en el video, diga Ud. si las frases son ciertas o falsas. Si son falsas, corríjalas.

1. César Villalobos es de Lima, Perú.
2. Vino a los EE.UU. para estudiar la música norteamericana.
3. Todos los músicos en su grupo son peruanos.
4. César usa instrumentos europeos.
5. El grupo toca música y también baila.
6. Todos se visten con auténticos trajes aztecas.

B **¿Qué sabe Ud. de la música andina?** Con la ayuda del video y de las siguientes pistas *(clues)*, identifique los instrumentos musicales.

quena:	se parece a la flauta
charango:	es un instrumento de cuerda
laquita:	tiene varias partes de diferentes tamaños
tambor:	es un instrumento de percusión

1.

2.

3.

4.

Practiquemos

A **Instrumentos regionales.** Ahora que ha oído la música de varias partes del mundo hispano, y ha visto el baile y los instrumentos, nombre Ud....

1. dos instrumentos que se usan para tocar la música española.
2. tres instrumentos que se usan parar tocar la música hispano-caribeña.
3. cuatro instrumentos que se usan para tocar la música andina.

B **Música regional.** Después de ver los videos que acompañan *Así es*, nombre Ud. dos características de la música o el baile de...

1. España.
2. Puerto Rico.
3. México.
4. los Andes.

APPENDIX A

Basic Grammar Terms in Spanish

The following are some Spanish grammar terms used in *Así es*. There are other terms you can recognize in context or with the help of your teacher or your classmates. You can also use the other appendices in this section and your dictionary.

acentuar to accentuate
añadir to add
cláusula clause
cláusula independiente o principal independent or principal clause
cláusula subordinada subordinate or dependent clause
complemento (in)directo (in)direct object
concordancia agreement
concordar to agree
deletrear to spell out
ejercicios exercises
frase sentence
género génder
intercambiable interchangeable
juntos together
literalmente literally
narrar to narrate
nombrar to name
ocurrir to occur, to happen
oración phrase or sentence
ortográfico orthographic, spelling
párrafo paragraph
pregunta question
pretérito preterite, past tense
principio beginning
pronombre pronoun
pronombre como complemento directo direct object pronoun
pronombre como complemento indirecto indirect object pronoun
raíz stem
referir(se) to refer to
relacionado related
requerir to require
respuesta answer
sentido meaning
serie series
significado meaning
siguiente following
sonido sound
subordinado subordinate
sujeto subject
subrayado underlined
sustantivo noun
tema theme
terminación ending
término term, word, expression
tiempo tense, time
título title
traducir to translate
vocal vowel

Glossary of Grammatical Terms Used in *Así es*

The following terms appear in the grammar explanations throughout the *Así es* textbook.

accent In Spanish, accent refers to the written mark that is used to show the stressed syllable of a word *(café)*. The accent mark is also used to distinguish words that are spelled the same but have different meanings. [*el* (the) / *él* (he); *de* (of, from) / *dé* (give)]

adjective An adjective is a word used to modify (describe, limit, qualify, or specify) a noun or a pronoun.

A **demonstrative adjective** points out which one(s).
(***this** street, **these** papers, **that** dog, **those** rocks*)

A **descriptive adjective** tells what kind.
(***black** slacks, **Italian** pastry, **strong** arms, **large** house*)

A **limiting adjective** indicates how many.
(***four** quizzes, **several** possibilities, **many** areas, a **thousand** times*)

A **possessive adjective** indicates possession, to whom something belongs.
(***my** notebook, **their** problem, **our** decision, **his** wallet)*

adverb An adverb is a word used to modify a verb. It generally expresses the time, place, manner, condition, or degree of the action of the verb.

*(She practices **daily** . . . **early** . . . **anywhere** . . . **vigorously**.)* Adverbs also modify adjectives (*He is an **extremely** competent teacher.*), and other adverbs (*They performed **very** well.*).

agree In grammatical terms, *to agree* means to correspond or to match. In a sentence, the subject and the verb always agree in person and number. In Spanish, adjectives correspond in gender and number with the nouns they modify; for example, if a noun is feminine and singular, the adjective must also be feminine and singular.

antonym An antonym is a word whose meaning is opposite to the meaning of another word in the same language. (*big / little, strong / weak)*

article An article is a word that is placed before a noun and whose function is to signal the noun and limit its use.

The **definite article** is specific. (***The*** *woman is my son's doctor.*)

The **indefinite articles** are nonspecific. (*I want **a** chance. Take* **an** *art class.*)

auxiliary The term auxiliary refers to those verbs that accompany and "help" the main verb express tense, mood, and voice. (*I **have** eaten. You **will** study! We **can** do it. He **has** accomplished a lot.*)

clause A clause is a group of words that contains a subject and a verb and forms part of a sentence.

A **main clause** can function alone if removed from the sentence. (***Mom had already gone to bed*** *when Dad came home.*)

A **subordinate clause** does not express a complete thought and therefore is always dependent upon the main clause. (*We want a yard **that has ample space.***)

An **adjectival clause** is a subordinate clause that modifies a noun or a pronoun in the main clause. (*There is no medicine **that can relieve her pain.***)

A **noun clause** is a subordinate clause that functions as a noun. (*They suggest **that the children leave the stadium.***)

An **adverbial clause** is a subordinate clause that modifies a verb, an adjective, or an adverb in the main clause. (*I'll buy the coat **as soon as I get paid.***)

conditional The term conditional refers to a tense or a clause that expresses a condition.

(*I **would love** to go to Madrid.* / conditional tense)
(*I **could go to Paris** if I had two weeks vacation.* / conditional clause)

conjugate To conjugate means to change a verb into different forms that correspond to person, number, tense, mood, and voice.

conjunction A conjunction is a word that connects words, groups of words, or sentences. (*Buy bread **and** milk. We'll **either** walk **or** ride our bikes. I wrote* **but** *he didn't write back.*)

gender Gender refers to the three classes (male, female, neuter) that distinguish nouns, pronouns, and their modifiers. In Spanish, nouns and their corresponding adjectives are either masculine or feminine.

indicative See ***mood, indicative***

infinitive An infinitive is a verb that is not conjugated, and therefore does not indicate person, number, or tense. It is used as a noun, a modifier, and in some verbal forms. In English it is usually preceded by *to.* (***To buy*** *a ticket, go to that window. They are hoping **to win** a trip to Acapulco.*)

mood Mood refers to the forms a verb takes to express the reality or probability of an indicated action or state, usually from the perspective of the speaker.

The **imperative mood** is used to express commands. (***Invest*** *in stocks.*)

The **indicative mood** is used to express actions or conditions that are objective, certain, or factual. Verbs are most often used in this mood. (*He **invests** in stocks.*)

The **subjunctive mood** is used to express hypothetical or contrary-to-fact actions or conditions, and to show wish or desire, doubt, influence, and subjectivity. (*I prefer that Jose **invest** in stocks. If I **were** you, I'd invest in municipal bonds.*)

noun A noun is a word that means a person, place, thing, quality, or action. In a sentence it is usually the subject or the object of a verb or a preposition. *(child, school, radio)*

number Number refers to the singularity or plurality of a word or group of words. *(song / songs; woman / women; I am / we are)*

object In a sentence, an object is a noun, a noun phrase, or a pronoun that is affected by the verb in some way.

A **direct object** receives the action of the verb. It answers the question "What?" or "Whom?" after the verb. [*Robert hit **the ball.*** (Hit what?); *We drove **Jean** to the station.* (Drove whom?)]

An **indirect object** generally answers the question "To whom?" or "For whom?" the action of the verb was done. [*My aunt gave **me** the address.* (To whom?); *We washed the car **for Dad.*** (For whom?)]

participle A participle is a verb form that is used as an adjective, an adverb, or with auxiliary verbs to express certain tenses.

The **present participle** ends in ***-ing*** (*They carried the **sobbing** child into the hospital. The witness **is sobbing** in the courthouse.*)

The **past participle** ends in **-d, -ed, -t, -en,** or **-n** *(taped, cooked, felt, written, been; The **written** examination is scheduled for next week. She **has written** a letter to the editor.)*

passive See ***voice, passive***

person Person is the form a subject pronoun or a verb takes to express the speaker *(first person: I, we)*, the person spoken to *(second person: you)*, and the person or thing spoken about (*third person: he, she, it, they)*.

preposition A preposition points out the relationship between a noun or pronoun to other words in the sentence. Some frequently used prepositions are *at, by, from, in, with. (The boat arrives **at** six.*)

pronoun A pronoun is a word that substitutes for a noun or a noun phrase.

A **demonstrative pronoun** points out persons or things. (***That one** is mine.*)

A **direct object pronoun** functions as a direct object. (*Did you see **her**?*)

An **indirect object pronoun** functions as an indirect object. (*Give **me** time.*)

An **interrogative pronoun** asks questions. (***Who** wants to swim?*)

A **personal (subject) pronoun** expresses a grammatical person (See ***person***), and functions as the subject of a sentence or clause. (***I** see; **he** does*).

A **possessive pronoun** expresses possession. (*The dog is **his.***)

A **prepositional pronoun** follows a preposition. (*He entered after **me.***)

A **reflexive pronoun** functions as an object that is the same as the subject of the sentence. (*They call **themselves** the Raging Raiders.*)

A **relative pronoun** introduces a clause. (*The athlete **who** won is from France.*)

syllable A syllable is the smallest part of a word, consisting of one or more letters. (*syl / la / ble; i / tal / ic*)

synonym A synonym is a word whose meaning is the same as or similar to the meaning of another word in the same language. (*happy / glad; fearful / afraid*)

tense Tense refers to the time indicated by the verb.

The **future tense** is formed with ***will*** or ***shall*** plus a verb, and expresses an action or an idea that will occur sometime in the future. (*We **will paint** the house tomorrow.*)

The **past tense** indicates an action that occurred in the past. (*I **shopped** at the mall.*)

The **past perfect tense** expresses an action that was completed in the past before some other past action or event occurred. It is formed with ***had*** and the past participle. (*The train **had** already **left** when I arrived at the station.*)

The **present tense** expresses an action that is occurring at the present time, that occurs habitually, or that will occur in the near future. (*I **study** on Mondays. Tomorrow I **am** in my office until 2:00.*)

The **present perfect tense** indicates an action that occurred at a nonspecific time in the past, or shows an action happening in the past and having bearing on the present or continuing in the future. It is formed with ***have*** and the past participle. (*We **have skated** here often. I **have attended** class for two months.*)

The **present progressive tense** expresses an action in progress. It is formed with the present tense of the verb ***to be*** and the present participle. (I ***am studying*** *now.*)

verb A verb is a word that expresses action or state of being. *(He **dropped** the vase. How **are** you? It **snows** a lot here.*)

voice Voice refers to the form a verb takes to indicate the relation between the subject and the action performed.

An **active voice verb** expresses an action performed by its subject. (*José **hit** the ball.*)

A **passive voice verb** indicates the subject as the receiver of its action. (*The ball **was hit** by José.*)

Appendix B

Accentuation

1. A word that carries a written accent is always stressed on the syllable that contains the accent.

   página ca**pí**tulo **fá**cil o**rí**genes can**ción**

2. If a word has no written accent and ends with a vowel, **n**, or **s**, the stress is on the second-to-last syllable.

   pre**gun**ta consi**de**ro o**ri**gen pe**di**mos computa**do**ras

3. If a word has no written accent and ends in a consonant other than **n** or **s,** the stress is on the last syllable.

   pa**pel** obli**gar** pa**red** re**loj** fe**liz**

Capitalization

Capital letters are used less in Spanish than in English. Capital letters are *not* used:

1. with the subject pronoun **yo** *(I)* unless it begins a sentence.

   Ellos quieren leer pero yo quiero bailar. — *They want to read, but I want to dance.*

2. with days of the week and months of the year.

   Hoy es lunes, el 25 de mayo. — *Today is Monday, May 25.*

3. with names of languages or adjectives and nouns of nationality.

   Son colombianos y por eso hablan español. — *They are Colombians, and therefore, they speak Spanish.*

4. with words in a title, except the first word and proper nouns.

   Historia de la isla de Cuba — *History of the Island of Cuba*
   Lo que el viento se llevó — *Gone with the Wind*

5. to express **usted, ustedes, señor, señora,** and **señorita,** except in their abbreviated forms: **Ud(s)., Vd(s)., Sr., Sra., Srta.**

Syllabification

To divide Spanish words into syllables, study the following guidelines.

1. All Spanish syllables contain only one vowel, diphthong, or triphthong.

   na-ción   co-piáis   vol-véis

   Note that two strong vowels (**a, e, o**) are divided.

   te-a-tro   le-o   po-e-ta

2. A single consonant (including **ch, ll, rr**) between two vowels begins a new syllable.

   ca-sa   ca-lle   ge-ne-ral
   co-che   ca-rro   mi-li-tar

3. Two consonants between vowels are generally divided.

   par-te   i-den-ti-dad   ár-bol
   cul-tu-ra   es-ta-do   car-tón

4. When **l** or **r** follow a consonant, they generally remain in the same syllable.

   li-bro   po-bla-ción
   es-cri-bir   an-glo

APPENDIX C

Review of Pronouns

Subject pronouns	Direct object pronouns	Indirect object pronouns	Reflexive pronouns	Prepositional pronouns
yo	me	me	me	mí (yo)[3]
tú	te	te	te	ti (tú)[3]
él, ella, Ud.	lo, la[1]	le (se)[2]	se	él, ella, Ud. (sí)[4]
nosotros, nosotras	nos	nos	nos	nosotros, nosotras
vosotros, vosotras	os	os	os	vosotros, vosotras
ellos, ellas, Uds.	los, las[1]	les (se)[2]	se	ellos, ellas, Uds.(sí)[4]

1. **Le** and **les** are used in Spain when the direct object pronoun refers to a masculine person or persons. **Conozco a José *y le* veo con frecuencia.**

2. **Se** is used when the direct and indirect object pronouns appear together and are both third person. ***Él le* escribe *la carta* a María. Él *se la* escribe.**

3. **Yo** and **tú** are used instead of **mí** and **ti** after **según, menos, salvo, excepto, incluso,** and **entre. Todos van salvo yo.**

4. **Sí** is used when the object of the preposition is reflexive *(himself, herself, themselves,* and so on). **José lo hace para sí** (*José does it for himself.*)

APPENDIX D

Time Expressions with *hacer*

Certain forms of the verb **hacer** (**hace** and **hacía**) are used to express the length of time an action took place. Note that although in English a very complex verb combination is required, in Spanish a simple tense with a form of **hacer** is used.

1. To express the length of time an action has been taking place use:

Hace + length of time + **que** + (**no** +) verb in the present tense

Hace tres horas que estudio para el examen. — *I have been studying for the test for three hours.*

2. To ask how long an action has been taking place use:

¿Cuánto tiempo + **hace** + **que** + (**no**+) verb in the present tense?

¿Cuánto tiempo hace que estudias para el examen? — *How long have you been studying for the test?*

3. To express the length of time an action had been taking place use:

Hacía + length of time + **que** + (**no** +) verb in the imperfect tense

Hacía tres horas que estudiaba para el examen cuando Juan llegó. — *I had been studying for the test for three hours when Juan arrived.*

4. To ask how long an action had been taking place use:

¿Cuánto tiempo + **hacía** + **que** + (**no**+) verb in the imperfect tense?

¿Cuánto tiempo hacía que estudiabas para el examen cuando Juan llegó? — *How long had you been studying for the test when Juan arrived?*

5. Remember that **hace** is used with the preterite tense to express how long ago an action took place.

Hace + length of time + **que** + (**no**+) verb in the preterite tense

Hace tres horas que estudié para el examen. — *I studied for the test three hours ago.*

APPENDIX E

The True Passive Voice

Form

Subject + form of **ser** + past participle used as an adjective + **por** + agent

In an active sentence, the subject *performs* the action of the verb. In a passive sentence, the subject *receives* the action of the verb.

ACTIVE:	Mamá preparó la cena.	*Mom prepared the dinner.*
PASSIVE:	La cena **fue preparada** por mamá.	*The dinner* ***was prepared*** *by mom.*

When the agent is not known, the passive **se** construction is often used.

Se preparó la cena. *The dinner was prepared.*

APPENDIX F

Verbs with Prepositions

Some verbs require prepositions before an infinitive or before an object. The following include common verbs that require the prepositions **a, de, en,** or **con.**

1. **a** before an infinitive

aprender	enseñar	Aprendo **a** hablar español.
ayudar	invitar	
comenzar	ir	
empezar	volver	

2. **a** before an object

acercarse	jugar *(optional)*	Llegamos **a** su casa.
asistir	llegar	
invitar	subir	
ir	volver	

3. **con** before an object

casarse	encontrarse	Sueña **con** su viaje a España.
consultar	soñar	
contar		

4. **de** before an infinitive

acabar	olvidarse	Acaba **de** volver de Madrid.
alegrarse	tratar	
dejar		

5. **de** before an object

bajar	enamorarse	José se enamoró **de** María.
burlarse	gozar	
depender	preocuparse	
despedirse	quejarse	
disfrutar	salir	

6. **en** before an infinitive

consistir insistir tardar	Insistimos **en** pagar la cuenta.

7. **en** before an object

entrar especializarse pensar	Piensas **en** tu familia.

Additional Perfect Tenses

The future and conditional perfect tenses

1. The future perfect tense is formed by combining the future form of the auxiliary verb **haber** with a past participle. As with all perfect tenses, the past participle remains constant, ending in **-o**.

Haber

habré	habremos		hablado
habrás	habréis	+	comido
habrá	habrán		vivido

The future perfect tense expresses an action that will have taken place at a future point in time, but is viewed from a past perspective.

Mañana yo **habré leído** todo el libro.	*Tomorrow **I will have read** the whole book.*
La semana que viene Susana **habrá terminado** todos sus exámenes.	*Next week Susan **will have finished** all of her exams.*

2. The conditional perfect tense is formed by combining the conditional form of the verb **haber** with a past participle.

Haber

habría	habríamos		hablado
habrías	habríais	+	comido
habría	habrían		vivido

The conditional perfect expresses an action that would have taken place.

Me habría gustado ir con Uds.	***I would have liked** to go with you.*
Ellos **habrían comprado** el coche rojo.	*They **would have bought** the red car.*

The present perfect and past perfect subjunctive tenses

1. The present perfect subjunctive is formed by combining the present subjunctive form of **haber** with a past participle.

Haber

haya	hayamos		hablado
hayas	hayáis	+	comido
haya	hayan		vivido

The present perfect subjunctive is used in a subordinate clause that requires the subjunctive to express an action that has taken place.

Espero que José **haya llegado** a tiempo.	*I hope that José **has arrived** on time.*
No creo que tú **hayas estado** en Madrid.	*I don't believe that you **have been** in Madrid.*

2. The past perfect subjunctive is formed by combining the imperfect subjunctive form of **haber** with a past participle.

Haber

hubiera	hubiéramos		hablado
hubieras	hubierais	+	comido
hubiera	hubieran		vivido

The past perfect subjunctive is used in a subordinate clause that requires the subjunctive to express an action that had taken place.

Esperaba que José **hubiera llegado** a tiempo.	*I hoped that José **had arrived** on time.*
No creía que tú **hubieras estado** en Madrid.	*I didn't believe that you **had been** in Madrid*

Appendix H

Stem-changing Verbs

1. First class: **-ar, -er** (**e > ie, o > ue**)

Pensar
present indicative: pienso, piensas, piensa, pensamos, pensáis, piensan
present subjunctive: piense, pienses, piense, pensemos, penséis, piensen
imperative: piensa tú, piense Ud., pensad vosotros, piensen Uds.

Volver
present indicative: vuelvo, vuelves, vuelve, volvemos, volvéis, vuelven
present subjunctive: vuelva, vuelvas, vuelva, volvamos, volváis, vuelvan
imperative: vuelve tú, vuelva Ud., volved vosotros, vuelvan Uds.
Other verbs in this category:

acordar(se)	costar	entender	recordar
acostar(se)	demostrar	llover	rogar
almorzar	despertar(se)	mostrar	sentar(se)
aprobar	devolver	mover	soler
cerrar	empezar	negar	sonar
comenzar	encender	perder	soñar
contar	encontrar	probar	volar

2. Second class: **-ir** (**e > ie** and **i, o > ue** and **u**)

Sentir
present indicative: siento, sientes, siente, sentimos, sentís, sienten
present subjunctive: sienta, sientas, sienta, sintamos, sintáis, sientan
preterite: sentí, sentiste, sintió, sentimos, sentisteis, sintieron
imperfect subjunctive: sintiera, sintieras, sintiera, sintiéramos, sintierais, sintieran
sintiese, sintieses, sintiese, sintiésemos, sintieseis, sintiesen
imperative: siente tú, sienta Ud., sentid vosotros, sientan Uds.
present participle: sintiendo

Dormir
present indicative: duermo, duermes, duerme, dormimos, dormís, duermen
present subjunctive: duerma, duermas, duerma, durmamos, durmáis, duerman
preterite: dormí, dormiste, durmió, dormimos, dormisteis, durmieron
imperfect subjunctive: durmiera, durmieras, durmiera, durmiéramos, durmierais, durmieran
durmiese, durmieses, durmiese, durmiésemos, durmieseis, durmiesen
imperative: duerme tú, duerma Ud., dormid vosotros, duerman Uds.
present participle: durmiendo
Other verbs in this category:

convertir	hervir	preferir	morir(se)
divertir(se)	mentir	referir(se)	sugerir

3. Third class: **-ir (e > i)**

Pedir

present indicative: pido, pides, pide, pedimos, pedís, piden
present subjunctive: pida, pidas, pida, pidamos, pidáis, pidan
preterite: pedí, pediste, pidió, pedimos, pedisteis, pidieron
imperfect subjunctive: pidiera, pidieras, pidiera, pidiéramos, pidierais, pidieran
pidiese, pidieses, pidiese, pidiésemos, pidieseis, pidiesen
imperative: pide tú, pida Ud., pedid vosotros, pidan Uds.
present participle: pidiendo
Other verbs in this category:

competir	despedir(se)	reñir	servir
conseguir	elegir	repetir	vestir(se)
corregir	reír(se)	seguir	

Appendix I

Verbs with Orthographic Changes

1. Verbs that end in **-car** (**c** > **qu** before **e**)

Buscar

preterite: busqué, buscaste, buscó, buscamos, buscasteis, buscaron
present subjunctive: busque, busques, busque, busquemos, busquéis, busquen
Other verbs in this category:

acercar(se)	explicar	sacar
comunicar	indicar	secar
dedicar	marcar	tocar

2. Verbs that end in **-gar** (**g** > **gu** before **e**)

Pagar

preterite: pagué, pagaste, pagó, pagamos, pagasteis, pagaron
present subjunctive: pague, pagues, pague, paguemos, paguéis, paguen
Other verbs in this category:

jugar llegar negar obligar rogar

3. Verbs that end in **-zar** (**z** > **c** before **e**)

Gozar

preterite: gocé, gozaste, gozó, gozamos, gozasteis, gozaron
present subjunctive: goce, goces, goce, gocemos, gocéis, gocen
Other verbs in this category:

almorzar comenzar cruzar empezar rezar

4. Verbs that end in **-cer** and **-cir** preceded by a vowel (**c** > **zc** before **a** and **o**)

Conocer

present indicative: conozco, conoces, conoce, conocemos, conocéis, conocen
present subjunctive: conozca, conozcas, conozca, conozcamos, conozcáis, conozcan
Other verbs in this category:

aparecer	establecer	obedecer	pertenecer
conducir	merecer	ofrecer	producir
crecer	nacer	parecer	traducir

(**Exceptions:** hacer, decir)

5. Verbs that end in **-ger** and **-gir** (**g** > **j** before **a** and **o**)

Coger
present indicative: cojo, coges, coge, cogemos, cogéis, cogen
present subjunctive: coja, cojas, coja, cojamos, cojáis, cojan
Other verbs in this category:

corregir	elegir	exigir	proteger
dirigir	escoger	fingir	recoger

6. Verbs that end in **-guir (gu** > **g** before **a** and **o)**
Seguir
present indicative: sigo, sigues, sigue, seguimos, seguís, siguen
present subjunctive: siga, sigas, siga, sigamos, sigáis, sigan
Other verbs in this category:

conseguir   distinguir   perseguir

7. Verbs that end in **-uir** (except **-guir** and **-quir**)

Huir
present indicative: huyo, huyes, huye, huimos, huís, huyen
preterite: huí, huiste, huyó, huimos, huisteis, huyeron
present subjunctive: huya, huyas, huya, huyamos, huyáis, huyan
imperfect subjunctive: huyera, huyeras, huyera, huyéramos, huyerais, huyeran
huyese, huyeses, huyese, huyésemos, huyeseis, huyesen
imperative: huye tú, huid vosotros
present participle: huyendo
Other verbs in this category:

atribuir	contribuir	distribuir	influir
concluir	destruir	excluir	instruir
constituir	disminuir	incluir	sustituir
construir			

8. Verbs that change unaccentuated **i** > **y**

Leer
preterite: leí, leíste, leyó, leímos, leísteis, leyeron
imperfect subjunctive: leyera, leyeras, leyera, leyéramos, leyerais, leyeran
leyese, leyeses, leyese, leyésemos, leyeseis, leyesen
present participle: leyendo
past participle: leído
Other verbs in this category:

caer(se)   creer   oír   poseer

Simple Tenses

hablar, comer, vivir

Infinitive	Present participle Past participle	Imperative	Indicative		
			Present	**Imperfect**	**Preterite**
hablar	hablando hablado	habla hablad	hablo hablas habla hablamos habláis hablan	hablaba hablabas hablaba hablábamos hablabais hablaban	hablé hablaste habló hablamos hablasteis hablaron
comer	comiendo comido	come comed	como comes come comemos coméis comen	comía comías comía comíamos comíais comían	comí comiste comió comimos comisteis comieron
vivir	viviendo vivido	vive vivid	vivo vives vive vivimos vivís viven	vivía vivías vivía vivíamos vivíais vivían	viví viviste vivió vivimos vivisteis vivieron

Compound Tenses

hablar

Indicative			
Present perfect	**Pluperfect**	**Future perfect**	**Conditional perfect**
he hablado has hablado ha hablado hemos hablado habéis hablado han hablado	había hablado habías hablado había hablado habíamos hablado habíais hablado habían hablado	habré hablado habrás hablado habrá hablado habremos hablado habréis hablado habrán hablado	habría hablado habrías hablado habría hablado habríamos hablado habríais hablado habrían hablado

Indicative		Subjunctive		
Future	Conditional	Present	Imperfect (-ra)	Imperfect (-se)
hablaré hablarás hablará hablaremos hablaréis hablarán	hablaría hablarías hablaría hablaríamos hablaríais hablarían	hable hables hable hablemos habléis hablen	hablara hablaras hablara habláramos hablarais hablaran	hablase hablases hablase hablásemos hablaseis hablasen
comeré comerás comerá comeremos comeréis comerán	comería comerías comería comeríamos comeríais comerían	coma comas coma comamos comáis coman	comiera comieras comiera comiéramos comierais comieran	comiese comieses comiese comiésemos comieseis comiesen
viviré vivirás vivirá viviremos viviréis vivirán	viviría vivirías viviría viviríamos viviríais vivirían	viva vivas viva vivamos viváis vivan	viviera vivieras viviera viviéramos vivierais vivieran	viviese vivieses viviese viviésemos vivieseis viviesen

Subjunctive		
Present Perfect	Pluperfect (-ra)	Pluperfect (-se)
haya hablado hayas hablado haya hablado hayamos hablado hayáis hablado hayan hablado	hubiera hablado hubieras hablado hubiera hablado hubiéramos hablado hubierais hablado hubieran hablado	hubiese hablado hubieses hablado hubiese hablado hubiésemos hablado hubieseis hablado hubiesen hablado

Irregular Verbs

Infinitive	Present participle Past participle	Imperative	Indicative Present	Indicative Imperfect	Indicative Preterite
andar *to walk; to go*	andando andado	anda andad			anduve anduviste anduvo anduvimos anduvisteis anduvieron
caber *to fit; to be contained in*	cabiendo cabido	cabe cabed	quepo cabes cabe cabemos cabéis caben		cupe cupiste cupo cupimos cupisteis cupieron
caer *to fall*	cayendo caído	cae caed	caigo caes cae caemos caéis caen		caí caíste cayó caímos caísteis cayeron
conducir *to lead; to drive*	conduciendo conducido	conduce conducid	conduzco conduces conduce conducimos conducís conducen		conduje condujiste condujo condujimos condujisteis condujeron
dar *to give*	dando dado	da dad	doy das da damos dais dan		di diste dio dimos disteis dieron
decir *to say, to tell*	diciendo dicho	di decid	digo dices dice decimos decís dicen		dije dijiste dijo dijimos dijisteis dijeron
estar *to be*	estando estado	está estad	estoy estás está estamos estáis están		estuve estuviste estuvo estuvimos estuvisteis estuvieron
haber *to have*	habiendo habido	he habed	he has ha hemos habéis han		hube hubiste hubo hubimos hubisteis hubieron

Indicative		Subjunctive		
Future	Conditional	Present	Imperfect (-ra)	Imperfect (-se)
			anduviera anduvieras anduviera anduviéramos anduvierais anduvieran	anduviese anduvieses anduviese anduviésemos anduvieseis anduviesen
cabré cabrás cabrá cabremos cabréis cabrán	cabría cabrías cabría cabríamos cabríais cabrían	quepa quepas quepa quepamos quepáis quepan	cupiera cupieras cupiera cupiéramos cupierais cupieran	cupiese cupieses cupiese cupiésemos cupieseis cupiesen
		caiga caigas caiga caigamos caigáis caigan	cayera cayeras cayera cayéramos cayerais cayeran	cayese cayeses cayese cayésemos cayeseis cayesen
		conduzca conduzcas conduzca conduzcamos conduzcáis conduzcan	condujera condujeras condujera condujéramos condujerais condujeran	condujese condujeses condujese condujésemos condujeseis condujesen
		dé des dé demos deis den	diera dieras diera diéramos dierais dieran	diese dieses diese diésemos dieseis diesen
diré dirás dirá diremos diréis dirán	diría dirías diría diríamos diríais dirían	diga digas diga digamos digáis digan	dijera dijeras dijera dijéramos dijerais dijeran	dijese dijeses dijese dijésemos dijeseis dijesen
		esté estés esté estemos estéis estén	estuviera estuvieras estuviera estuviéramos estuvierais estuvieran	estuviese estuvieses estuviese estuviésemos estuvieseis estuviesen
habré habrás habrá habremos habréis habrán	habría habrías habría habríamos habríais habrián	haya hayas haya hayamos hayáis hayan	hubiera hubieras hubiera hubiéramos hubierais hubieran	hubiese hubieses hubiese hubiésemos hubieseis hubiesen

Irregular Verbs *(continued)*

Infinitive	Present participle Past participle	Imperative	Indicative Present	 Imperfect	 Preterite
hacer *to do; to make*	haciendo hecho	haz haced	hago haces hace hacemos hacéis hacen		hice hiciste hizo hicimos hicisteis hicieron
ir *to go*	yendo ido	ve id	voy vas va vamos vais van	iba ibas iba íbamos ibais iban	fuí fuiste fué fuimos fuisteis fueron
oír *to hear*	oyendo oído	oye oíd	oigo oyes oye oímos oís oyen		oí oíste oyó oímos oísteis oyeron
oler *to smell*	oliendo olido	huele oled	huelo hueles huele olemos oléis huelen		
poder *to be able*	pudiendo podido		puedo puedes puede podemos podéis pueden		pude pudiste pudo pudimos pudisteis pudieron
poner *to put*	poniendo puesto	pon poned	pongo pones pone ponemos ponéis ponen		puse pusiste puso pusimos pusisteis pusieron
querer *to want; to love*	queriendo querido	quiere quered	quiero quieres quiere queremos queréis quieren		quise quisiste quiso quisimos quisisteis quisieron
reír *to laugh*	riendo reído	ríe reíd	río ríes ríe reímos reís ríen		reí reíste rió reímos reísteis rieron

Indicative		Subjunctive		
Future	**Conditional**	**Present**	**Imperfect (-ra)**	**Imperfect (-se)**
haré harás hará haremos haréis harán	haría harías haría haríamos haríais harían	haga hagas haga hagamos hagáis hagan	hiciera hicieras hiciera hiciéramos hicierais hicieran	hiciese hicieses hiciese hiciésemos hicieseis hiciesen
		vaya vayas vaya vayamos vayáis vayan	fuera fueras fuera fuéramos fuerais fueran	fuese fueses fuese fuésemos fueseis fuesen
		oiga oigas oiga oigamos oigáis oigan	oyera oyeras oyera oyéramos oyerais oyeran	oyese oyeses oyese oyésemos oyeseis oyesen
		huela huelas huela olamos oláis huelan		
podré podrás podrá podremos podréis podrán	podría podrías podría podríamos podríais podrían	pueda puedas pueda podamos podáis puedan	pudiera pudieras pudiera pudiéramos pudierais pudieran	pudiese pudieses pudiese pudiésemos pudieseis pudiesen
pondré pondrás pondrá pondremos pondréis pondrán	pondría pondrías pondría pondríamos pondríais pondrían	ponga pongas ponga pongamos pongáis pongan	pusiera pusieras pusiera pusiéramos pusierais pusieran	pusiese pusieses pusiese pusiésemos pusieseis pusiesen
querré querrás querrá querremos querréis querrán	querría querrías querría querríamos querríais querrían	quiera quieras quiera queramos queráis quieran	quisiera quisieras quisiera quisiéramos quisierais quisieran	quisiese quisieses quisiese quisiésemos quisieseis quisiesen
		ría rías ría riamos riáis rían		

Irregular Verbs *(continued)*

Infinitive	Present participle Past participle	Imperative	Indicative: Present	Indicative: Imperfect	Indicative: Preterite
saber *to know*	sabiendo sabido	sabe sabed	sé sabes sabe sabemos sabéis saben		supe supiste supo supimos supisteis supieron
salir *to go out*	saliendo salido	sal salid	salgo sales sale salimos salís salen		
ser *to be*	siendo sido	sé sed	soy eres es somos sois son	era eras era éramos erais eran	fui fuiste fue fuimos fuisteis fueron
tener *to have*	teniendo tenido	ten tened	tengo tienes tiene tenemos tenéis tienen		tuve tuviste tuvo tuvimos tuvisteis tuvieron
traer *to bring*	trayendo traído	trae traed	traigo traes trae traemos traéis traen		traje trajiste trajo trajimos trajisteis trajeron
valer *to be worth*	valiendo valido	val(e) valed	valgo vales vale valemos valéis valen		
venir *to come*	viniendo venido	ven venid	vengo vienes viene venimos venís vienen		vine viniste vino vinimos vinisteis vinieron
ver *to see*	viendo visto	ve ved	veo ves ve vemos veis ven	veía veías veía veíamos veíais veían	

Indicative		Subjunctive		
Future	Conditional	Present	Imperfect (-ra)	Imperfect (-se)
sabré sabrás sabrá sabremos sabréis sabrán	sabría sabrías sabría sabríamos sabríais sabrían	sepa sepas sepa sepamos sepáis sepan	supiera supieras supiera supiéramos supierais supieran	supiese supieses supiese supiésemos supieseis supiesen
saldré saldrás saldrá saldremos saldréis saldrán	saldría saldrías saldría saldríamos saldríais saldrían	salga salgas salga salgamos salgáis salgan		
		sea seas sea seamos seáis sean	fuera fueras fuera fuéramos fuerais fueran	fuese fueses fuese fuésemos fueseis fuesen
tendré tendrás tendrás tendremos tendréis tendrán	tendría tendrías tendría tendríamos tendríais tendrían	tenga tengas tenga tengamos tengáis tengan	tuviera tuvieras tuviera tuviéramos tuvierais tuvieran	tuviese tuvieses tuviese tuviésemos tuvieseis tuviesen
		traiga traigas traiga traigamos traigáis traigan	trajera trajeras trajera trajéramos trajerais trajeran	trajese trajeses trajese trajésemos trajeseis trajesen
valdré valdrás valdrá valdremos valdréis valdrán	valdría valdrías valdría valdríamos valdríais valdrían	valga valgas valga valgamos valgáis valgan		
vendré vendrás vendrá vendremos vendréis vendrán	vendría vendrías vendría vendríamos vendríais vendrían	venga vengas venga vengamos vengáis vengan	viniera vinieras viniera viniéramos vinierais vinieran	viniese vinieses viniese viniésemos vinieseis viniesen

Vocabularies

All words in the vocabulary lists and glossed words are given, as well as words necessary to the first-year Spanish students. Stem-changing words are indicated by **(e > ie), (o > ue)**. The gender of nouns is indicated except for masculine nouns ending in **-o** or referring to males, and feminine nouns ending in **-a, -dad,** and **-ión,** or referring to females.

Abbreviations

The following abbreviations are used in this glossary.

adj.	adjective	*interr.*	interrogative
adv.	adverb	*invar.*	invariable
conj.	conjunction	*m.*	masculine
def. art.	definite article	*n.*	noun
demons. adj.	demonstrative adjective	*obj.*	object
		p.p.	past participle
d. o.	direct object	*pl.*	plural
f.	feminine	*poss.*	possessive
fam.	familiar	*prep.*	preposition
form.	formal	*pron.*	pronoun
indef. art.	indefinite article	*refl. pron.*	reflexive pronoun
ind. obj.	indirect object	*sing.*	singular
inf.	infinitive	*subj. pron.*	subject pronoun
interj.	interjection	*v.*	verb

Spanish-English Vocabulary

A

a *prep.* to; at (*with time*) **1; a eso de** (*with time*) approximately **1; a la vez** at the same time **12; a lo mejor** probably **11; a menos que** *conj.* unless **11; a menudo** *adv.* often **1; a sus órdenes** at your service **12, in ex.; a tiempo** *adv.* on time **1; al lado de** *prep.* alongside of **12; al máximo** to the limit; **a veces** at times **7; a ver** let's see **13**
abajo *adv.* below **12**
abierto *p.p., adj.* open **9;** opened
abogado *n.* lawyer **3**
abordar *v.* to board **10**
abrazar *v.* to hug **16**
abrazo *n.* hug **16**
abrigo *n.* overcoat **9**
abril *n.* April **4**
abrir *v.* to open **2**
abrochar(se) *v.* to button **10;** to fasten
abuela *n.* grandmother **4**
abuelo *n.* grandfather **4; los abuelos** grandparents
aburrido *adj.* boring **2;** bored
acabar *v.* to finish **1; acabar de** + *inf.* to have just done (something)
acampar *v.* to camp **15**
accesorios *n.* accessories **5**
aceite *n.* oil **7**
aceituna *n.* olive **7**
acera *n.* sidewalk **Gac. 3**
acercarse (a) *v.* to approach **Gac. 4**
acompañar *v.* to accompany **15**
aconsejar *v.* to advise **11**
acordarse de (ue) *v.* to remember **12**
acostarse (ue) *v.* to go to bed, to lie down **9**
actitud *n.f.* attitude **3, in ex.**
activo *adj.* active **14**
actor *n.m.* actor **2, in ex.**
actriz *n.f.* actress **Sec. A**
actuar *v.* to act **Gac. 1**
acuario *n.* aquarium **15**
acuerdo *n.* agreement **8; estar de acuerdo** to agree **15, llegar a un acuerdo** to reach an agreement
adelgazar *v.* to lose weight **8**
además *adv.* besides **4**
adentro *adv.* inside **5**
adiós *interj.* goodbye **Sec. B**
adivinar *v.* to guess **Gac. 1**
adjetivo *n.* adjective **2**
aduana *n.* customs **Gac. 2; 10**
aeromozo *n.* flight attendant **10**
afeitarse *v.* to shave **9**
aficionado *n.* fan, supporter **14**
afortunadamente *adv.* fortunately **6, in ex.**
afuera *adv.* outside, outdoors **5; las afueras** the suburbs **5**
agencia de empleos *n.* employment agency **3**
agente *n.* agent **10**
ágil *adj.* agile **14**
agosto *n.* August **4**
agradable *adj.* pleasant, agreeable **11**
agradecer *v.* to be grateful for, to thank **6**
agregar *v.* to add **Gac. 1; 5**
agresivo *adj.* aggressive **17**
agrícola *adj.* agricultural **Gac. 4**
agricultor *n.* farmer **Gac. 4**
agua *n.* water **Sec. A; 3, in ex.; 4**
aguardar *v.* to await **Gac. 5**
ahora *adv.* now **1; ahora mismo** right away **1**
ahorrar *v.* to save money **15**
aire *n.m.* air **15; aire acondicionado** air conditioning **12; al aire libre** outside **8**
ajo *n.* garlic **7**
al contraction of **a** + **el** to the, at the **2**
alcoba *n.* bedroom **5**
alegrarse de *v.* to be happy **11**
alegre *adj.* happy **2**
alegría *n.* happiness **1**
alejarse (de) *v.* to go away, to keep away **15**
alemán *n.m., adj.* German **2**
alérgico *adj.* allergic **13**
alfombra *n.* rug **5**
algo *n., adv.* something, somewhat **3**
algo más *n.* something else **7**
algodón *n.m.* cotton **9**
alguien *n.* someone, anyone **3**

algún (alguno, a) *adj.* some **3**
alimentar *v.* to feed **Gac. 4**
alimento *n.* food **7**
aliviar *v.* to relieve, alleviate **13**
allí *adv.* there **1**
alma *n.* soul **Gac. 3**
almacén *n.m.* department store **3**
almeja *n.* oyster
almendra *n.* almond **7**
almohada *n.* pillow **5**
almorzar (o > ue) *v.* to eat lunch **3**
almuerzo *n.* lunch **4**
aló *interj.* hello (telephone, Puerto Rico) **6**
alojarse *v.* to lodge, stay **12**
alquilar *v.* to rent **5**
alquiler *n.m.* rent (payment) **5**
alrededor (de) *adv.* around **5**
alto *adj.* tall, high; *adv.* loudly **2**
alumno *n.* student **Sec. C**
ama de casa *n.* housewife, housekeeper **17**
amable *adj.* kind **11**
amado *n.* loved one **Gac. 6**
amar *v.* to love **1; 16**
amarillo *adj.* yellow **4**
ambicioso *adj.* ambitious **Sec. B**
ambiente *n.m.* environment, atmosphere **15**
ambiguo *adj.* ambiguous **Gac. 2**
ambos *adj.* both
ambulancia *n.* ambulance **13**
americano *n., adj.* American
amigo *n.* friend **1**
amistad *n.f.* friendship **16**
amo *n.* master **Gac. 3**
amor *n.m.* love **6; 16**
amparo *n.* protection **Gac. 3**
amurrallado *adj.* walled **Gac. 6**
analfabetismo *n.* illiteracy **Gac. 5**
analista de sistemas *n.* systems analyst
anaranjado *adj.* orange **4**
ancho *adj.* wide, broad **9**
andar *v.* to walk **7**
andén *n.m.* platform **11**
anfitrión *n.* host **9, in ex.**
angustia *n.* anguish **Gac. 2**
anillo *n.* ring **9; anillo de casado** wedding ring **16; anillo de compromiso** engagement ring **16**
animado *adj.* exciting **14**
aniversario *n.* anniversary **4**
anoche *adv.* last night **1, 6**
anotación *n.* score **14**
anterior *adj.* previous **Gac. 1**
antes *adv.* before **1; antes de** *prep.* before **1; antes de que** *conj.* before **14**
antibiótico *n.*antibiotic **Sec. C, 13 in ex.**
antiguo *adj.* old, ancient, former **8**
antipático *adj.* mean **2**; unpleasant
anuncio *n.* announcement, advertisement **3; anuncios clasificados** classified ads. **6**
añadir *v.* to add **8, in ex.**
año *n.* year **2; Año Nuevo** New Year **18; el año pasado** last year **18, in ex.; tener...años** to be...years old **3; el año que viene** next year **14**
apagar *v.* to turn off **6**
aparato *n.* apparatus, appliance **12**
aparcar *v.* to park **11**
aparecer *v.* to appear **Gac. 5**
apasionado *adj.* passionate **Sec. B**
apellido *n.* last name **4**
apenas *adv.* scarcely **13**
apendicitis *n.m.* appendicitis **13**
aplicado *adj.* studious, applied **2**
apodo *n.* nickname **Gac. 5**
apoyar *v.* to support **14**
apoyo *n.* support **Gac. 4**
apreciar *v.* to appreciate **Gac. 2**
aprender *v.* to learn **2; aprender de memoria** to learn by heart **2**
apretado *adj.* tight **9**
aprobar (o > ue) *v.* to approve **11**
apropiado *adj.* appropriate, correct **5, in ex.**
aprovechar *v.* to make good use of **11; aprovecharse de** to profit by, take advantage of
aquel *adj.* that **5**
aquí *adv.* here **1; aquí lo tiene** here you are
árabe *n.* Arab **Gac. 1**
árbitro *n.* umpire, referee **Gac. 3**
árbol *n.m.* tree **4**
arco iris *n.m.* rainbow **Gac. 2**
arena *n.* sand **Gac. 6**
arete *n.m.* earring **9**
argentino *adj.* Argentine **Sec. B**
armario *n.* clothes closet **5**
arquitecto *n.* architect **3**
arrancar *v.* to start (a motor)
arreglar *v.* to fix, to repair; to arrange **5**
arriba *adv.* up **12**
arroyo *n.* brook **Gac. 3**
arroz *n.m.* rice **7**
arte *n.* art **Sec. A; 2**
artista *n.m., f.* artist **Sec. B**
asado *adj.* roasted **7**
ascendencia *n.* ancestry **Gac. 4**
ascenso *n.* promotion **3**
ascensor *n.* elevator **12**
asfixiante *adj.* stifling **Gac. 2**
así *adv.* so, thus, like this **Sec. A; 16**
así así *adv.* so-so **Sec. B**
asiento *n.* seat **10**
asignatura *n.* subject **2**
asistencia *n.* attendance
asistir (a) *v.* to attend **2**
aspiradora *n.* vacuum cleaner **5**
aspirina *n.* aspirin **1, in ex. 13**
astro *n.* star **Gac. 4**
astronauta *n.m., f.* astronaut **Sec. B**
ataque *n.m.* attack **Gac. 3**
atender (e > ie) *v.* to wait on, attend to **9**
aterrizaje *n.m.* landing
aterrizar *v.* to land
atleta *n.* athlete **Gac. 3**
atractivo *n.* attraction **Gac. 5**
atraer *v.* to attract **15**
atrapado *adj., p.p.* trapped **Gac. 4**
atrasado *adj.* delayed, late, slow, backward **10; estar atrasado** to be late
atún *n.m.* tuna fish **8**
audaz *adj.* bold **Gac. 4**
aula *n.f.* classroom **Sec. C**
aumentar *v.* to increase **Gac. 4**
aumento *n.* increase **6, in ex.**
aún *adv.* still, yet **18; aún no** not yet
aunque *conj.* although, even if **5**
autobús *n.m.* bus **11**
automóvil *n.m.* automobile **Sec. A; 4**
autopista *n.* highway **11**
autor *n.m.* author **Sec. B**
autorretrato *n.* self-portrait **Gac. 4**
autostop, hacer *v.* to hitchhike **11**
avenida *n.* avenue **Gac. 1**
avión *n.m.* airplane **10**
aviso *n.m.* notice **1**
ayer *adv.* yesterday **6**
ayuda *n.* help, assistance **6, in ex.**
ayudar *v.* to help, aid **2**
azafata *n.* stewardess **10**
azúcar *n.m.* sugar **Gac. 2**
azul *adj.* blue **4**

B

bahía *n.* bay **Gac. 4**
bailar *v.* to dance **1**
bailarín *n.m.* dancer **bailarina** *n.f.* dancer **Gac. 3**
bajar *v.* to lower, to get out of **9**
bajo *adj.* short, low **2;** *adv.* under
balcón *n.m.* balcony **12**
baloncesto *n.* basketball **Gac. 2**
banana *n.* banana **Sec. A**
banco *n.* bank
banda *n.* band (musical) **16**
bandera *n.* flag **Gac. 6**
banquero *n.* banker
bañar *v.* to bathe **9; bañarse** *v.* to take a bath
bañera *n.* bathtub **5**
baño *n.* bathroom **5; cuarto de baño** bathroom
barato *adj.* inexpensive, cheap **4**
barco *n.* boat **11**
barrer *v.* to sweep **5**
barrio *n.* neighborhood **4**
barroco *adj.* baroque **Gac. 1**
básquetbol *n.m.* basketball **2, in ex.; 14**
bastante *adv.* enough **8; bastante bien** well enough **Sec. B**

batalla *n.* battle **Gac. 3**
bate *n.* baseball bat **14**
batear *v.* to bat **14**
batería *n.* drum set, battery (car) **11**
batido *n.* milkshake
bautismo *n.* baptism
bebé *n.* baby **Sec. C**
beber *v.* to drink **2**
bebida *n.* drink, beverage **7**
beca *n.* scholarship **2**
béisbol *n.m.* baseball (game) **3, in ex.; 14**
beisbolista *n.* baseball player **2 in ex.**
belleza *n.* beauty **Gac. 5**
bello *adj.* beautiful **12**
bendición *n.* blessing **18, in ex.**
beneficio *n.* benefit **3**
besar *v.* to kiss **Sec. B; 16**
beso *n.* kiss **1, in ex.; 16**
biblioteca *n.* library **1**
bibliotecario *n.* librarian
bicicleta *n.* bicycle **11**
bien *adv.* well **1; bien educado** well behaved **4; bien parecido** good-looking; **está bien** it's okay **Sec. B; muy bien** very well **Sec. B; pasarlo bien** to have a good time **6**
bienvenido *adj.* welcome **Sec. B**
bilingüe *adj.* bilingual **Gac. 3**
billete *n.m.* ticket **10**
biología *n.* biology **2**
bisabuela *n.* great grandmother
bisabuelo *n.* great grandfather
bistec *n.m.* steak **8**
blanco *adj.* white **4**
blue jeans *n.* blue jeans **1, in ex.; 9**
blusa *n.* blouse **9**
boca *n.* mouth **13**
bocadillo *n.* sandwich **8**
boda *n.* wedding **16**
boicoteo *n.* boycott **Gac. 4**
boleto *n.* ticket **10**
bolígrafo *n.* ballpoint pen **Sec. C**
bolsillo *n.* pocket **3**
bolso *n.* purse, pocketbook **9**
bombero *n.* firefighter
bombón *n.m.* chocolate candy **8**
bonito *adj.* pretty
bordado *adj.* embroidered **9**
boricua *n., adj.* Puerto Rican
borrar *v.* to erase
bosque *n.m.* forest **15**
bota *n.* boot **9**
bote *n.m.* boat **15**
botella *n.* bottle **4, in ex.; 8**
botones *n.* bellboy **12**
boxeador *n.* boxer **14**
boxeo *n.* boxing **14**
brazalete *n.m.* bracelet **9**
brazo *n.* arm **13**
breve *adj.* brief **6 in ex.**
brindar *v.* to toast **18**
brindis *n.m.* toast **18**
buen gusto good taste **8**
buen viaje good trip **10**
bueno *adj.* good **2;** *adv.* well, okay; **buenas noches** good evening, good night **Sec. B; buenas tardes** good afternoon **Sec. B; ¿Bueno?** Hello **6; buenos días** good morning **Sec. B**
buen provecho good appetite **7**
burlarse (de) *v.* to make fun (of) **18**
buscar *v.* to look for **1**
buzón *n.m.* mailbox **12**

C

caballero *n.* gentleman **16**
caballo *n.* horse **14**
cabeza *n.* head **13**
cada *adj., invar.* each, every **5**
cadena *n.* channel, network, chain **14, in ex.**
caer *v.* to fall; **caerse** *v.* to fall down **8, in ex.; 11**
café *n.m.* coffee; cafe **Sec. A7**
cafetería *n.* cafe **1**
caja *n.* box **8**
cajero *n.* cashier
calcetines *n.m.pl.* socks **9**
cálculo *n.* calculus **2**
calefacción *n.* heating
calendario *n.* calendar **Sec. C**
calentar (e > ie) to heat
caliente *adj.* hot **7**
calificarse *v.* to qualify **Gac. 1**
callado *adj.* silent, quiet
calle *n.f.* street **Sec. B**
calor *n.m.* heat; **hace calor** it's hot (weather) **4; tener calor** *v.* to be (feel) hot (warm) **3**
cama *n.* bed **5, in ex.; cama de agua** water bed **5; cama matrimonial** double bed **5**
cámara *n.* camera **10**
camarera *n.* waitress **3**
camarero *n.* waiter **3**
camarones *n.m.pl.* shrimp **7**
cambiar *v.* to change **2**
cambio *n.* change **16**
caminar *v.* to walk **6**
camino *n.* road **11**
camión *n.m.* truck **11**
camisa *n.* shirt **9**
camiseta *n.* T-shirt **9**
campaña *n.* campaign **Gac.1**
campeón *n.m.* champion **14**
campeona *n.f.* champion **14**
campeonato *n.* championship **14**
campesino *n.* peasant, country person **Gac. 4**
cámping *n.* campsite **15; hacer cámping** to go camping
campo *n.* country, field **4; campo deportivo** playing field **1**
campus *n.m.* campus **1**
canal *n.m.* channel **4, in ex.**
cancelar *v.* to cancel **10**
cancha *n.* court **14**
canción *n.* song **6**
candidato *n.* candidate **3**
cansado *adj.* tired, tiresome **2**
cantante *n.* singer **Gac. 4**
cantar *v.* to sing **6**
cantautor *n.* singer/songwriter **Gac. 1**
cantidad *n.* quantity **13, in ex.**
caos *n.m.* chaos **Gac. 6**
capaz *adj.* capable **11, in ex.**
capítulo *n.* chapter **2**
capó *n.* hood (of a car) **11, in ex.**
caprichoso *adj.* capricious, whimsical **Gac. 1**
cara *n.* face **Gac. 1**
¡caramba! gracious me! my goodness **1**
caramelo *n.* hard candy, caramel **8**
cárcel *n.f.* jail
caribe *n.m.* Caribbean **4**
caribeño *adj.* Caribbean **Gac. 1**
caridad *n.* charity **Gac. 1**
caries *n.f.* cavity **13**
cariño *n.* affection **16**
cariñoso *adj.* affectionate **16**
carnaval *n.m.* carnival **18**
carne *n.f.* meat **7**
carnicería *n.* butcher shop **7, in ex.**
carnicero *n.* butcher **8**
caro *adj.* expensive **4**
carpintero *n.* carpenter
carrera *n.* career, race **3**
carro *n.* car **4**
carroza *n.* float **Gac. 1**
carta *n.* letter, card, menu **6; echar una carta** to mail a letter **12**
cartas *n.* playing cards; **jugar a las cartas** to play cards **6**
cartel *n.m.* poster
cartelera *n.* T.V. section (newspaper) **6**
cartera *n.* wallet **9**
cartero *n.* mailman
casado *adj.* married **4; recién casado** newlywed **16**
casarse (con) *v.* to get married (to) **16**
casi *adv.* almost **5, in ex.**
cassette *n.m.* cassette **1**
castigo *n.* punishment
castillo *n.* castle **12**
catarro *n.* cold (health) **13**
catedral *n.f.* cathedral **Gac. 1**
católico *adj.* famous **Gac. 18**
cazador *n.* hunter **Gac. 4**
cebolla *n.* onion **7**
celda *n.* jail cell **Gac. 4**

célebre *adj.* famous **Gac. 6**
celos *n.* jealousy **16; tener celos** to be jealous **3**
celoso *adj.* jealous **16**
cementerio *n.* cemetery **18**
cena *n.* supper **4**
cenar *v.* to eat supper **5**
ceniza *n.* ash **Gac. 5**
centro *n.* center, downtown **Sec. B, in ex.; centro comercial** shopping center **9; centro estudiantil** student center **1; centro para niños** child care center **17**
cepillo *n.* brush **12**
cerca (de) *adv.* near, close **5**
cerdo *n.* pork **8**
cerebro *n.* brain **13**
cereza *n.* cherry **8, in ex.**
cero *n.* zero **Sec. B**
cerrado *adj.* closed **9**
cerrar (e > ie) *v.* to close **3**
cerveza *n.* beer **7**
chaleco *n.* vest
champú *n.m.* shampoo **12**
chaqueta *n.* jacket **9**
charlar *v.* to chat **1**
chau *interj.* goodbye **Sec. B**
cheque de viajero *n.* traveler's check **12**
chévere *adj.* great, awesome **1**
chica *n.* (little) girl **1 Sec. C**
chicano *n.* U.S. citizen of Mexican origin **Gac. 4**
chico *n.* (little) boy **1 Sec. C**
chileno *n., adj.* Chilean **Sec. B**
chisme *n.m.* gossip
chismear *v.* to gossip **5**
chiste *n.m.* joke; **contar chistes** to tell jokes **4**
chistoso *adj.* funny **15**
chocar (con) *v.* to run into, collide (with), hit **11**
chocolate *n.m.* chocolate **2, in ex.**
chorizo *n.* sausage **8**
ciclismo *n.* cyling **14**
ciclista *n.* cyclist **Gac. 1; 14**
ciego *adj.* blind **Gac. 3**
cielo *n.* sky, heaven **15;** sweetheart **16**
cien *adj.* one hundred **1**
ciencia *n.* science **2; ciencia política** political science; **ciencias de computadora/computación** computer science
científico *n.* scientist **3**
cierto *adj.* certain, sure **Sec. C; es cierto** that's right **10**
cine *n.m.* movie theater **6**
cinco *adj., n.m.* five **Sec. B**
cincuenta *adj., n.m.* fifty **1**
cinturón *n.m.* belt **9; cinturón de seguridad** seat belt **10**
circo *n.* circus **15**
circulación *n.* traffic **11**
cita *n.* date, appointment **3**
citar *v.* to make a date or appointment
ciudad *n.* city **Sec. B**
ciudadano *n.* citizen **10**
claro *adj.* clear **9 ¡Claro!** Of course! **4; es claro** it's clear **10; Claro que sí** Of course **4**
cliente *n.m., f.* client **Sec. C**
clima *n.m.* climate **9, in ex.**
cobrar *v.* to charge **12**
cocido *adj.* cooked
coche *n.m.* car **4; coche cama** sleeping car (train) **11; coche comedor** dining car (train) **11**
cocina *n.* kitchen **5**
cocinar *v.* to cook **5**
cocinero *n.* cook **3**
coger *v.* to grasp, seize, catch **14**
cola *n.* line, tail **10; hacer cola** to wait in line
coleccionar *v.* to collect
colegio *n.* school **1**
cólera *n.* anger **Gac. 4**
colgar *v.* to hang (up) **6**
colombiano *adj.* Colombian **Sec. B**
combatir *v.* to combat, fight **17**
comedor *n.m.* dining room **5**
comenzar (e > ie) *v.* to begin, start **3**
comer *v.* to eat **2**
comestibles *n.pl.m.* food
cómico *n.* comedian **2, in ex.;** *adj.* funny **15**
comida *n.* food, meal **4**
como *adv.* as, since **16; ¿cómo?** *interr.* how? **Sec. B;** what?, how's that again?; **¿Cómo anda?** How's it going?; **¿Cómo se dice ...?** How do you say ...? **6; ¿Cómo se escribe ...?** How do you spell **...? Sec. A; B; Cómo no** Of course **4; ¿Cómo está(s)?** How are you? **Sec. B; ¿Cómo se (te) llama(s)?** What's your name? **Sec. B**
cómodo *adj.* comfortable **9**
compañero *n.* friend, companion **1; compañero de clase** classmate; **compañero de cuarto** roommate
compañía *n.* company
compartir *v.* to share **5**
competencia *n.* competition **15**
competir *v.* to compete **5**
complacer *v.* to please **Gac. 3**
complicado *adj.* complicated **11**
comportamiento *n.* behavior **17**
comportarse *v.* to behave
comprar *v.* to buy **1**
compras, ir de to go shopping **8**
comprender *v.* to understand **2**
comprometerse *v.* to be engaged **16**
compromiso *n.* engagement **16**
computadora *n.* computer **Sec. B; 1**
común *adj.* common **Sec. B; 10, in ex.**
con *prep.* with **1; con destino a** destined for **10; con frecuencia** frequently **1; con tal de que** *conj.* provided that **15; conmigo** *prep.* with me **5; contigo** *prep.* with you **5**
concha *n.* shell **Gac. 1**
concurso *n.* contest **Gac. 6**
conducir *v.* to drive **4**
conductor *n.* driver **11**
conferencia *n.* lecture **Gac. 1**
confirmar *v.* to confirm **10**
congelador *n.m.* freezer
congestionado *adj.* congested **13**
conjunción *n.f.* conjunction **14**
conjunto musical *n.* band **16**
conocer *v.* to know; to meet **4**
conocido *adj., p.p.* known **Gac. 1**
conseguir (e > i) *v.* to get; to obtain **5**
consejero *n.* counselor, advisor **2**
consejo *n.* advice **9, in ex.**
conservador *n.* conservative **Sec. A**
conservar *v.* to keep, maintain **Gac. 6**
consistir (en) *v.* to consist (of) **2**
construir *v.* to build **6**
consultorio *n.* doctor's office **13**
contabilidad *n.* accounting **2**
contador *n.* accountant **3**
contaminado *adj.* contaminated, polluted **15**
contar (o > ue) *v.* to tell, count **3; contar chistes** to tell jokes; **contar con** to count on **3**
contento *adj.* content, happy **2**
contestar *v.* to answer **1**
contra *prep.* against **17**
contratar *v.* to hire **16**
cooperar *v.* to cooperate **17**
copa *n.* wine glass **7; tomar una copa** to have a drink **7**
coqueta *adj.* flirtatious **17**
corazón *n.m.* heart **13**
corbata *n.* tie **9**
correcto *adj., adv.* correct, exactly **4**
corregir (e > i) *v.* to correct **5**
correo *n.* post office **12**
correr *v.* to run **14**
corrida de toros *n.* bullfight **Sec. C**
cortar *v.* to cut **7**
corte *n.f.* court **4, in ex.**
cortés *adj.* polite, courteous **16**
cortina *n.* curtain
corto *adj.* short, brief **4**
cosa *n.* thing **1**
cosecha *n.* crop **Gac. 4**
costa *n.* coast **Gac. 1**
costar (o > ue) *v.* to cost **3**
costarricense *n., adj.* Costa Rican **Sec. B**
costumbre *n.f.* custom, habit **7**

crear *v.* to create **6, in ex.**
crecer *v.* to grow **4**
creer *v.* to believe, think **2**
criada *n.* maid **12**
criado *n.* servant **12**
criar *v.* to raise **17**
crisis *n.f.* crisis **Gac. 4**
cristiano *adj.* Christian **18**
crónica *n.* chronicle **Gac. 3**
crudo *adj.* raw **8**
cruz *n.f.* cross **18, in ex.**
cruzar *v.* to cross **Gac. 4**
cuaderno *n.* notebook **Sec. C**
cuadra *n.* block **10**
cuadro *n.* painting **5**
¿cuál? *interr.* what?, which? **Sec. B**
cualquier, cualquiera *adj.* any **11**
¿cuándo? *interr.* when? **Sec. B ¿cuánto?** *adj. interr.* how much? how many? **Sec. B; en cuanto** *conj.* as soon as **14**
cuarenta *adj., n.m.* forty **1**
Cuaresma *n.* Lent **Gac. 4, 18**
cuarto *n.* room; *adj.* fourth **5; cuarto de baño** bathroom **12; cuarto** (time) a quarter **1**
cuatro *adj., n.m.* four **Sec. B**
cuatrocientos *adj., n.m.* four hundred **4**
cubierto *p.p., adj.* covered **13**
cubrir *v.* to cover **13**
cuchara *n.* table or soup spoon **7**
cuchillo *n.* knife **7**
cuello *n.* neck **13**
cuenta *n.* check, bill **7; darse cuenta de** to realize **7**
cuento *n.* story **Gac. 4**
cuero *n.* leather **9**
cuidado *n.* care, caution **13; tener cuidado** to be careful **13; cuidado médico** *n.* medical care **13**
cuidar (de) *v.* to care for, to take care of; **cuidarse** *v.* to take care of oneself **13**
culebra *n.* snake **Gac. 3**
cultivar *v.* to cultivate **Gac. 4**
cumpleaños *n.m.* birthday **4; Feliz Cumpleaños** Happy Birthday
cumplir…años *v.* to turn…years of age **4**
cumplir (con) *v.* to fulfill **17**
cuna *n.* cradle **Gac. 3**
cuñada *n.* sister-in-law **4**
cuñado *n.* brother-in-law **4**
cura *n.m.* priest **18**
cura *n.f.* cure **13**
curar *v.* to cure **8, in ex.**
currículum (vitae) *n.* résumé **3**
curso *n.* course **5, in ex.**

D

dama *n.* lady **17**
dañar *v.* to harm, hurt **14**
daño *n.* harm; **hacer daño** to do harm
dar *v.* to give **4; dar a** to face **5, in ex.; dar a luz** to give birth **17; dar un paseo** to take a walk **6; dar la mano** to shake hands **Sec. B, in ex.**
de *prep.* of, from **1; de acuerdo** agreed **8; de buen (mal) gusto** in good (bad) taste **8; ¿De dónde es Ud.?** Where are you from? **Sec. B, in ex.; de nada** you're welcome **Sec. B; de ninguna manera** by no means **4; ¿De parte de quién?** Who's calling? **6; ¿De qué se trata?** What is it about? **6; ¿De quién…?** Whose…? **2; de vez en cuando** from time to time **16**
debajo (de) *prep.* under, below **Sec. C**
deber *n.m.* duty **17;** *v.* should, ought to **2**
débil *adj.* weak **14**
debilidad *n.f.* weakness **17, in ex.**
década *n.* decade **Gac. 1**
decano *n.* dean **2**
decidir *v.* to decide **2; decidirse a** to make up one's mind to
décimo *adj.* tenth **12**
decir (e > i) *v.* to say, to tell **4**
dedo *n.* finger **13; dedo del pie** toe
dejar *v.* to leave behind, to allow **3; dejar de** + *inf.* to stop **Gac. 3; 8, in ex.; dejar un mensaje (recado)** to leave a message **6**
del contraction of **de** and **el** of the **2**
delante (de) *prep.* before, in front of **Sec. C**
delgado *adj.* thin **2**
delicioso *adj.* delicious **7**
demás *adj.* (with **lo, la, los, las**) the other, the rest of the…**17**
demasiado *adj., adv.* too, too much **8**
dentista *n.m., f.* dentist **Sec. C**
dentro (de) *prep.* in, within **5**
dependiente *n.* clerk **8**
deporte *n.m.* sport **1, in ex.; 14**
deportivo *adj.* athletic **1; campo deportivo** athletic field
deprimente *adj.* depressing **18**
derecho *n.* right, privilege, law **Gac. 2;** *adv.* straight ahead; *adj.* right; **a la derecha** to the right **10**
derrota *n.* defeat **Gac. 6**
desagradable *adj.* unpleasant **11**
desaparecer *v.* to disappear **Gac. 6**
desaparecido *n.* missing person **Gac. 6**
desarrollar *v.* to develop **14**
desarrollo *n.* development **14**
desastre *n.m.* disaster **6, in ex.**
desayunar *v.* to have breakfast **5**
desayuno *n.* breakfast **4**
descansar *v.* to rest **11**
descanso *n.* rest **Gac. 6**
descompuesto *adj.* broken **11**
describir *v.* to describe **Gac. 2**
descubierto *p.p.* discovered **13**
descubrimiento *n.* discovery
descubrir *v.* to discover **13**
desde *adv.* since **10;** *prep.* from
desde luego of course **4**
desear *v.* to desire, want **1**
desempacar *v.* to unpack **12**
desempleo *n.* unemployment
deseo *n.* desire **Gac. 2**
desfile *n.m.* parade **18**
desierto *n.* desert **15**
desigualdad *n.* inequality
desilusión *n.f.* disappointment **1**
desinflado *adj.* flat **11; una llanta desinflada** a flat tire
desordenado *adj.* unorganized, messy **5**
despacho *n.* office **1**
despacio *adv.* slowly **2**
despedida *n.* farewell, parting, dismissal
despedirse (de) (e > i) *v.* to say goodbye to **10**
despertarse (e > ie) *v.* to wake up **9**
despierto *adj.* awake **15; soñar despierto** *v.* to daydream **15**
después *adv.* later, after **1; después de** *prep.* after; **después de que** *conj.* after **14**
destino *n.* destiny **10; con destino a** *prep.* destined for **10**
destruir *v.* to destroy **6**
detalle *n.* detail **9**
detrás de *prep.* behind, in back of **Sec. C**
devolver (o > ue) *v.* to return, to give back **3**
día *n.m.* day **1; hoy día** nowadays **Gac. 2**
Día de los Muertos Day of the Dead **18**
Día de los Reyes Magos King's Day **18**
día del santo Saint's Day **18**
diario *adj.* daily **Gac. 3;** diary **10**
dibujar *v.* to draw, sketch **6**
dibujo *n.* sketch, drawing **5, in ex.**
diccionario *n.* dictionary **Sec. C**
dicho *p.p.* said **13**
dichoso *adj.* happy, fortunate **Gac. 5**
diciembre *n.* December 4
dictador *n.* dictator **Gac. 3**
dieciséis *adj., n.m.* sixteen **Sec. B**
diente *n.m.* tooth **13**
diestro *adj.* skilled **Gac. 4**
dieta *n.* diet **8; estar a dieta** to be on a diet **8**
diez *adj., n.m.* ten **Sec. B**
difícil *adj.* difficult **2**
¡Diga! Hello (telephone, Spain) **6**
dineral *n.m.* large sum of money **7**
dinero *n.* money **1**
Dios *n.* God; **¡Dios mió!** My God!
dirección *n.* address, direction **Sec. B, in ex.**
dirigir *v.* to direct
disco *n.* record **Gac. 2**
discriminación *n.* discrimination **Gac. 2; 17**
discriminar *v.* to discriminate **17**
disfraz *n.m.* disguise **18**

disfrazarse (de) *v.* to disguise oneself (as), dress up (as) **18**
disfrutar (de) *v.* to enjoy **15**
disponible *adj.* available
disputa *n.* dispute, argument **16**
disputar *v.* to argue **16**
distinto *adj.* different **5**
diversión *n.* amusement
diverso *adj.* diverse **Gac. 2**
divertido *adj.* amusing **14**
divertirse (e > ie) *v.* to have a good time **9**
divorciado *adj.* divorced **4**
divorciarse *v.* to get divorced **16**
divorcio *n.* divorce **16**
doblar *v.* to turn a corner, fold **10**
doble *adj.* double **Sec. A**
doce *adj., n.m.* twelve **Sec. B**
docena *n.* dozen **8**
doctor *n.m.* doctor **Sec. A**
dólar *n.*m. dollar **Sec. A**
doler (o > ue) *v.* to hurt; to grieve **13**
dolor *n.m.* pain, grief **13**
doloroso *adj.* painful **13**
domicilio *n.* address **3, in ex.**
dominar *v.* to dominate **17**
domingo *n.* Sunday **Sec. A**
¿dónde? *interr.* where? **Sec B; ¿De dónde?** From where?
dorado *adj.* golden **4, in ex.**
dormir (o > ue) *v.* to sleep **3; dormirse** *v.* to fall asleep **9**
dormitorio *n.* bedroom **1**
dos *adj., n.m.* two **Sec. B**
dramaturgo *n.* dramatist **Gac. 1**
ducha *n.* shower **5**
ducharse *v.* to take a shower
duda *n.* doubt **10**
dudar *v.* to doubt **10**
dudoso *adj.* doubtful **10**
dueño *n.* owner
dulce *adj.* sweet **7**
durante *prep.* during **8**
duro *adj.* hard, difficult **Gac. 5**

E

e *conj.* and (instead of **y** before words that begin with **i** and **h) 1**
echar *v.* to throw **Gac. 3 echar de menos** to miss; **echar una carta** to mail a letter **2; echar una siesta** to take a nap **15**
economía *n.* economics
económico *adj.* economical **9**
edad *n.f.* age **8, in ex.**
edificio *n.* building **1**
EE.UU. U.S. **2, in ex.; Estados Unidos** United States
ejecutivo *n.* executive **Sec. C**
ejemplo *n.* example **7**
ejercicio *n.* exercise **5, in ex.**
ejército *m.* army **Gac. 3**
el *m. sing. def. art.* the **Sec. C**
él *subj. pron.* he **Sec. B;** *obj.* of *prep.* him **5**
electricista *n.* electrician
elefante *n.m.* elephant **Sec. A; 15**
elegante *adj.* elegant **Sec. A; 9**
elegir (e > i) *v.* to elect, choose
ella *subj. pron.* she **Sec. B;** *obj.* of *prep.* her **5**
ellas *f. subj. pron.* they **Sec. B;** *f. obj.* of *prep.* them **5**
ellos *m. subj. pron.* they **Sec. B;** *m. obj.* of *prep.* them **5**
embajador *n.* ambassador **Gac. 4**
embarazada *adj.* pregnant **13**
emocionante *adj.* exciting **Gac. 1**
empacar *v.* to pack **12**
emperador *n.* emperor **Gac. 4**
empezar (e > ie) *v.* to begin, start **3**
empleado *n.* employee **3**
empleo *n.* job, work **3**
empresa *m.* business, corporation **3**
en *prep.* in, on, at **Sec. C; en absoluto** absolutely not **4; en cambio** on the other hand **16; en cuanto** *conj.* as soon as **14; en otras palabras** in other words **16; en punto** on time **1; en seguida** right away **8; en vez de** instead of **11, in ex.**
enamorado *adj.* in love **16**
enamorarse *v.* to fall in love **16**
encantado *adj.* delighted **Sec. B**
encantar *v.* to delight, fascinate **7**
encanto *n.* charm **Gac. 4**
encender (e > ie) *v.* to light **6**
encima de *prep.* on top of, above, over, overhead **Sec. C**
encontrar (o > ue) *v.* to find **3**
enemigo *n.* enemy **Gac. 3**
enero *n.* January **4**
enfadarse *v.* to become angry **17**
enfermarse *v.* to become sick **13**
enfermedad *n.* illness, disease **13**
enfermero *n.* nurse **13**
enfermo *adj.* sick, ill **2**
enfrentarse (con) *v.* to face **14**
enfrente de *prep.* in front of
engordar *v.* to gain weight; to get fat **8**
enhorabuena *n.* congratulations **18**
enojado *adj.* angry **17**
enojarse *v.* to become angry **17**
ensalada *n.* salad **7**
ensayista *n.* essayist **Gac. 3**
ensayo *n.* essay **Gac. 3**
enseñar *v.* to teach **1**
entender (e > ie) *v.* to understand **3**
enterarse (de) *v.* to find out (about)
enterrar (e > ie) *v.* to bury **18**
entierro *n.* burial
entonces *adv.* then **4**
entrada *n.* entrance, ticket **10**
entrar *v.* to enter **2**
entre *prep.* between, among **5**
entregar *v.* to hand in
entrenador *n.* trainer **14**
entrenar *v.* to train **14**
entrevista *n.* interview **3**
entrevistar *v.* to interview
entusiasmado *adj.* excited **14**
enviar *v.* to send **6, in ex.**
envidioso *adj.* envious **16**
equipaje *n.m.* luggage **10**
equipo *n.* team **Gac. 3**
equivocado *adj.* wrong **6**
equivocarse *adj.* to make a mistake **Gac. 4**
esa *demons. adj.* that **5; ésa** *pron.* that one
escala *n.* stopover
escalar *n.* to climb, scale **15**
escaleras *n.pl.* stairs **12; escalera mecánica** escalator **12**
esclavo *n.* slave **Gac. 4**
escoba *n.* broom
escoger *v.* to choose **7**
esconder *v.* to hide **Gac. 4**
escribir *v.* to write **2; escribir a máquina** to type
escrito *p.p. adj.* written **13**
escritor *n.m.* writer **Gac. 3**
escritorio *n.* desk **Sec. C**
escritura *n.* writing **Gac. 4**
escuchar *v.* to listen to **1**
escuela *n.* school **1; escuela primaria** elementary school; **escuela secundaria** high school
es decir which is to say **1**
ese *demons. adj.* that **5; ése** *pron.* that one
esfuerzo *n.* effort **Gac. 5**
espalda *n.* back **13**
España *n.* Spain **Sec. A**
español *n.* Spanish (language) **Sec. B, in ex.;** *n.* Spaniard; *adj.* Spanish
especial *adj.* special **Sec. A**
especialidad *n.* specialty **7**
especialización *n.* major
especializarse (en) *v.* to major (in)
especialmente *adv.* especially **6, in ex.**
espectador *n.* spectator **14**
espejo *n.* mirror **5**
esperanza *n.* hope **Gac. 1**
esperar *v.* to wait for, expect, hope **4**
espíritu *n.* spirit **Gac. 3**
esposo *n.* spouse **4**
esquí *n.m.* ski, skiing **Gac. 1**
esquiar *v.* to ski **14**
esquina *n.* corner **10**
esquís *n.m.pl.* skis **14**
esta *demons. adj.* this **5; ésta** *pron.* this one; **esta noche** tonight **1**
establecimiento *n.* establishment **Gac. 1**
estación *n.* station, season **11**

estacionar *v.* to park **11**
estadidad *n.* statehood **Gac. 2**
estadio *n.* stadium **10, in ex.**
estado *n.* state **Gac. 4**
estar *v.* to be **Sec. B; está bien** it's okay, it's alright **Sec. B; estar a dieta** to be on a diet **8; estar atrasado** to be late **10; estar de acuerdo** to be in agreement **15; estar de moda (de onda)** to be in style **4; estar de vacaciones** to be on vacation **10; estar de venta** to be on sale **8; estar equivocado de número** to have a wrong number **6; estar loco** to be crazy
este *n.* east **11;** to stall for time **16**
este *demons. adj.* this **5; éste** *pron.* this one; **en este momento** right now
estilo *n.* style **Gac. 1; estilo de vida** lifestyle
estimulante *adj.* stimulating
estómago *n.* stomach **13**
estrecho *adj.* narrow, close **9**
estrella *n.* star **Gac. 1; Sec. B**
estudiante *n.* student **Sec. C**
estudiar *v.* to study **1**
estufa *n.* stove, heater **5**
estupendo *adj.* stupendous, wonderful **Sec. B**
estúpido *adj.* stupid **2**
europeo *adj.* European **Gac. 1**
evidente *adj.* evident **Gac.1**
evitar *v.* to avoid **8**
exagerar *v.* to exaggerate **6, in ex.**
examen *n.m.* exam **Sec. A**
excelente *adj.* excellent **Sec. A**
excepto *adv.* except **5**
exclamar *v.* to exclaim **8, in ex.**
excursión *n.* excursion, trip, tour **10**
exhibición *n.* exhibition, show **15, in ex.**
exhibir *v.* to exhibit, show
exigente *adj.* demanding
exigir *v.* to demand, require
existencia *n.* existence **12, in ex.**
existir *v.* to exist **Gac. 2**
éxito *n.* success; **tener éxito** to be successful **3**
exitoso *adj.* successful **Gac. 5**
experiencia *n.* experience **3**
explicar *v.* to explain **6, in ex.**
explotado *adj., p.p.* exploited **Gac. 4**
externo *adj.* external
extranjero *n.* foreigner **10;** *adj.* foreign, alien; **al extranjero** abroad
extrañar *v.* to miss, long for **10**
extraño *adj.* strange **12**
extraordinario *adj.* extraordinary **Gac. 6**

F

fabuloso *adj.* fabulous **Gac. 2**
fácil *adj.* easy **2**
facilidad *n.* ease, ability **Gac. 4**
factor *n.m.* factor **9**
facturar *v.* to check (luggage) **10**
facultad *n.f.* department, college school (of a university or college) **17**
faena *n.* task, duty **17;** death of the bull (bullfight)
falda *n.* skirt **9**
falso *adj.* false **1, in ex.**
falta *n.* lack, fault **7; sin falta** without fail; **hacer falta** to be in need of **7**
faltar *v.* to be lacking, miss **7**
fama *n.* fame **Gac. 1**
familia *n.* family **Gac. 1**
familiar *n.* relative, family member **4;** *adj.* pertaining to the family
famoso *adj.* famous **Sec. A**
fanático *n.* fan **Gac. 1**
fantástico *adj.* fantastic **Sec. A**
farmacéutico *n.* pharmacist **13**
farmacia *n.* pharmacy **13**
fascinante *adj.* fascinating **4, in ex.**
fascinar *v.* to fascinate **7**
fatal *adj.* terrible **Sec. B**
favor *n.m.* favor **6, in ex.; por favor** please
fe *n.f.* faith **Gac. 1**
febrero *n.* February **4**
fecha *n.* date **3, in ex.; 4**
felicidad *n.* happiness **18**
felicidades *n.* congratulations **6**
felicitaciones *n.f.* congratulations **6**
felicitar *v.* to congratulate **18**
feliz *adj.* happy **2; Feliz Cumpleaños** Happy Birthday
femenino *adj.* feminine
feminidad *n.* femininity **17**
fenomenal *adj.* phenomenal **Sec. C**
feo *adj.* ugly, unpleasant **2**
feroz *adj.* ferocious **15**
festejar *v.* to celebrate, entertain **18**
festividad *n.* festivity **18**
fichero *n.* card catalog
fiebre *n.f.* fever **13**
fiesta *n.* party **1; día de fiesta** holiday
fin *n.m.* end **1; fin de semana** weekend; **por fin** finally, at last **7**
final *adj.* final **6, in ex.**
finalmente *adv.* finally **Sec. A**
finca *n.* farm **Gac. 4**
firma *n.* signature
firmar *v.* to sign **12**
físico *adj.* physical **17, in ex.**
flaco *adj.* skinny, thin **8**
flan *n.m.* caramel custard **7**
flechazo *n.* hit with an arrow (love at first sight) **16**
flexible *adj.* flexible **17**
flojo *adj.* light, weak, lazy
flor *n.f.* flower **Gac. 1**
folleto *n.* brochure, pamphlet **10**
fondo *n.* bottom **Gac. 2**
formal *n.* formal **8**
formar *v.* to form **5, in ex.**
formidable *adj.* terrific
fortaleza *n.* fort **Gac. 1**
fotografía (foto) *n.f.* photograph **Sec. A; 4**
fracasar *v.* to fail **16**
fracaso *n.* failure **14**
francés *n.m.* French (language); *n.* French national; *adj.* French
Francia *n.* France **Sec. A**
frase *n.f.* sentence, phrase **2**
frecuente *adj.* frequent **8**
frecuentemente *adv.* frequently **13, in ex.**
fregar (e > ie) *v.* to scrub **5**
frenar *v.* to brake, to apply the brakes **11**
frenos *n.pl.* brakes **11**
fresa *n.* strawberry **8**
fresco *adj.* cool, fresh **4; hace fresco** it's cool (weather) **4**
frijol *n.m.* bean **7**
frío *adj.* cool, fresh **4; hace frío** it's cold (weather **4**); **tener frío** to be cold **3**
frito *adj.* fried **Sec. A; 7**
frontera *n.* frontier, border **Gac. 6**
fruta *n.* fruit **8**
fuego *n.* fire **Sec. C; 15**
fuente *n.* fountain **Gac. 1**
fuera *adv.* out, outside **5; fuera de** *prep.* out of
fuerte *adj.* strong; fort **Gac. 1; 8, in ex.**
fuerza *n.* force **14**
fumar *v.* to smoke **10**
función *n.* function, peformance, show **4**
funcionar *v.* to work, function, run **12**
furioso *adj.* furious, angry **8**
fútbol *n.m.* soccer **Sec. A; 14; fútbol americano** football
futbolista *n.* soccer player, football player **Sec. B., in ex.**
futuro *n. adj.* future **Gac. 2**

G

gafas *n.* eyeglasses **12; gafas de sol** sunglasses
galleta *n.* cookie **8**
galón *n.m.* gallon
gambas *n.pl.* shrimp **7**
ganador *n.* winner **Gac. 5**
ganar *v.* to earn, win **3**
ganas; tener ganas de to feel like, have the desire **3**
ganga *n.* bargain **7**
garaje *n.m.* garage **5**
garganta *n.* throat **13**
gaseosa *n.* soda **8, in ex.**
gasolina *n.* gasoline **11; estación de gasolina** gas station **11**

gasolinera *n.* gas station **11**
gastar *v.* to spend, use, waste **11**
gasto *n.* expense, waste **11**
gato *n.* cat **5**
gemelo *n.* twin
general *adj.* general **7; en general** in general; **por lo general** generally
generalmente *adv.* generally **Sec. A**
generoso *adj.* generous **Sec. A**
genio *n.* genius **Gac. 6**
gente *n.f.* people **3**
gerente *n.m.* manager **3**
gesto *n.* gesture **7, in ex.**
gimnasio *n.* gymnasium **1**
gira *n.* tour **10**
gitano *n.* gypsy **Gac. 1**
globo *n.* balloon **15**
gobernador *n.m.* governor **Gac. 2**
gobierno *n.* government **Gac. 3**
golf *n.* golf **14**
golpe *n.* blow **Gac. 6**
gordo *adj.* fat **Guía 2**
gótico *adj.* Gothic **Gac. 1**
gozar de *v.* to enjoy **7**
grabadora *n.* tape recorder
grabar *v.* to tape, record **Gac. 4**
gracia *n.* grace **Gac. 4**
gracias *n.* thanks, thank you **Sec. B; muchas gracias** thank you very much, many thanks
gracioso *adj.* funny **Sec. A**
grado *n.* degree (temperature) **13, in ex.**
graduarse *v.* to graduate **1, in ex.**
gramática *n.* grammar **6, in ex.**
grande (gran) *adj.* big, large, great **2**
gratis *adj.* free of charge **10**
gratuito *adj.* gratuitous **10**
grave *adj.* serious **13**
griego *n.* Greek (language) **8, in ex.;** *n.* Greek national; *adj.* Greek
gripe *n.f.* grippe, influenza **13**
gris *adj.* gray **4**
gritar *v.* to shout, yell
grupo *n.* group
guante *n.m.* glove **Sec. B, in ex.**
guapo *adj.* handsome, attractive **2**
guardar *v.* to keep, save **9, in ex.**
guarde cama *v.* stay in bed **13**
guardia *n.* guard
guardería infantil *n.* day-care center **17**
guerra *n.* war **4, in ex.**
guerrillero *n.* guerilla fighter **Gac. 5**
guía *n.m.f.* guide **10 guía turístico** tour guide
guisante *n.m.* pea **7**
guitarra *n.* guitar **6**
gustar *v.* to be pleasing **7**
gusto *n.* taste **8; mucho gusto** pleased to meet you **Sec. B; buen (mal) gusto** good (bad) taste **8**

H

haber *v.* to have (auxiliary verb) **13**
habichuela *n.* bean **8**
habitación *n.* room **5**
hablar *v.* to speak **1**
hacer *v.* to do, make **1; hacer autostop** to hitchhike **11; hacer cola** to stand in line **10; hacer el esfuerzo** to make the effort **16; hacer escala** to make a stopover; **hacer juego con** to match **9; hacer la maleta** to pack a suitcase **10; hacer las paces** to make up **16; hacerle caso a alguien** to pay attention to someone **6; hacerle una pregunta a alguien** to ask someone a question **6; hacer una cita** to make a date **8, in ex.; hacer una llamada** to make a call **6; hacer un papel** to play a role **17; hacerse novios** to get engaged **16; hacer calor** to be hot **4; hacer frío** to be cold **4; hacer viento** to be windy **4; hacer cámping** to go camping **15; hacer un viaje** to take a trip **10**
hacia *prep.* toward **11, in ex.**
hambre *n.f.* hunger **3; tener hambre** to be hungry
hamburguesa *n.* hamburger **Sec. A; 8**
hasta *prep.* until, up to **Sec. B; hasta que** *conj.* until **14; hasta luego** see you later **Sec. B; hasta mañana** see you tomorrow **Sec. B; hasta pronto** see you soon **Sec. B**
hay there is, there are **Sec. B; C; hay que** one must **8**
hecho *n.* fact, event **8, in ex.;** *p.p.* done, made **13; el hecho de que**… the fact that…**17**
heladería *n.* ice cream shop **7, in ex.**
helado *n.* ice cream **4**
helar (e > ie) *v.* to freeze
hembra *n.* female **15, in ex.**
hemisferio *n.* hemisphere **Gac. 2**
herencia *n.* heritage **Gac. 5**
herida *n.* injury, wound
herido *adj.* injured, wounded **13**
hermana *n.* sister **4**
hermano *n.* brother **4**
hermoso *adj.* beautiful **9**
héroe *n.m.* hero **8, in ex.**
hervido *adj.* boiled **8**
hervir *v.* to boil
hielo *n.* ice **8, in ex.**
hígado *n.* liver
hija *n.* daughter **4**
hijo *n.* son **4;** *pl.* children
hinchado *adj.* swollen **13**
hispánico *adj.* Hispanic **Sec. A**
hispano *n. adj.* Hispanic **Sec. C**
hispanoparlante *adj.* Spanish-speaking
historia *n.* history, story **2**
historiador *n.* historian **Gac. 4**
hogar *n.m.* home **5**
hoja *n.* leaf; **hoja de papel** sheet of paper
hola *interj., n.* hello, hi **Sec. A**
hombre *n.* man **Sec. C**
hondo *adj.* deep **13**
hongo *n.* mushroom **7**
hora *n.* hour, time **1; ¿A qué hora?** At what time?; **¿Qué hora es?** What time is it?
horario *n.* schedule **2**
horno *n.* oven **5**
horror *n.* horror **Sec. A**
hospital *n.m.* hospital **Sec. A; 13**
hotel *n.m.* hotel **Sec. A; 12; hotel de lujo** first-class (luxury) hotel
hoy *adv.* today **1; hoy día** nowadays
huelga *n.* strike **Gac. 4**
huésped *n.* guest **12**
huevo *n.* egg **8**
huir *v.* to flee **Gac. 2**
humano *adj.* human **Gac. 1; ser humano** *n.* human being
humilde *adj.* humble, modest **Gac. 6**
humor *n.* humor, mood **Sec. A; de buen (mal) humor** in a good (bad) mood
hundirse *v.* to sink **Gac. 2**

I

ida *n.* departure **10; ida y vuelta** round-trip
idea *n.* idea **Sec. A; 10**
ideal *adj.* ideal **Sec. A**
idioma *n.m.* language **2**
iglesia *n.* church **16**
igual *adj.* equal, same **4, in ex.; me da igual** it's all the same to me
igualdad *n.* equality **Gac. 2**
igualmente *adv.* equally **1**
ilusión *n.* illusion **Gac. 5**
imagen *n.f.* image **Gac. 2**
imaginación *n.* imagination **10, in ex.**
imaginar *v.* to imagine **18, in ex.**
impaciente *adj.* impatient
impedir (e > i) *v.* to prevent, impede **5**
imperfecto *adj.* imperfect **8**
imperio *n.* empire **Gac. 4**
impermeable *n.m.* raincoat **9**
imponer *v.* to impose
importancia *n.* importance **4, in ex.**
importante *adj.* important **Sec. A**
importar *v.* to import; to be important **7**
imposible *adj.* impossible **10**
impresión *n.* impression **2, in ex.; 12**
impresionante *adj.* impressive **12**
impresionar *v.* to impress
impuesto *n.* tax **Gac. 4**
incapaz *adj.* incapable **Gac. 1**
incendio *n.* fire
incertidumbre *n.* uncertainty **Gac. 5**
incluir *v.* to include **6**

incluso *prep.* including **5**
incómodo *adj.* uncomfortable **9**
incorporar *v.* to incorporate **18, in ex.**
independencia *n.* independence **Gac. 2**
independiente *adj.* independent
indígena *n.* native person **Gac. 2; 10** *adj.* indigenous
indio *n. adj.* Indian **12, in ex.**
indudablemente *adj.* undoubtedly **Gac. 6**
inesperado *adj.* unexpectedly **11, in ex.**
inestable *adj.* unstable **Gac. 4**
infancia *n.* childhood
infantil *adj.* childish, pertaining to children **Gac. 4; 16**
infeliz *adj.* unhappy
infinitivo *n.* infinitive **14, in ex.**
inflación *n.* inflation **Gac. 5**
inflamado *adj.* inflamed **13**
influencia *n.* influence **10**
influir (en) *v.* to influence **Gac. 4**
informal *adj.* informal **7, in ex.**
ingeniería *n.* engineering **2**
ingeniero *n.* engineer **Gac. 6**
Inglaterra *n.* England **8, in ex.**
inglés *n.m.* English (language) **4, in ex.;** *n.* English national; *adj.* English
ingrediente *n.m.* ingredient **7**
inicial *adj.* initial
iniciar *v.* to initiate **Gac. 4**
inigualado *adj.* unequaled **Gac. 4**
inmediatamente *adv.* immediately **16, in ex.**
inmigrante *n.* immigrant **Gac. 4**
inocente *adj.* innocent **16**
inolvidable *adj.* unforgettable **7, in ex.**
insecto *n.* insect **15**
insistir *v.* to insist **11**
instituto *n.* institute **Gac. 5**
instructor *n.* instructor **17, in ex.**
instrumento *n.* instrument **Gac. 3, in ex.**
insulto *n.* insult
inteligente *adj.* intelligent **Sec. B; 2**
intenso *adj.* intense **15**
intentar *v.* to try, attempt **6**
interés *n.m.* interest **3, in ex.**
interesado *adj.* interested
interesante *adj.* interesting **3**
interesar *v.* to interest **7**
interior *adj.* interior **4, in ex.; en el interior** on the inside
internacional *adj.* international **1, in ex.; 12**
interno *adj.* internal
intérprete *n.* interpreter
interrumpir *v.* to interrupt
íntimo *adj.* close, intimate **4, in ex.**
inútil *adj.* useless **17**
invención *n.* invention **17**
inventar *v.* to invent **8, in ex.**
investigar *v.* to investigate **Gac. 4, in ex.**
invierno *n.* winter **4**
invitación *n.* invitation **16**
invitado *n.* guest **9, in ex.; 16**
invitar *v.* to invite **4**
inyección *n.* injection, shot **13**
ir *v.* to go **1; ir de compras** to go shopping **8; ir de visita** to visit
irse *v.* to leave **9**
isla *n.* island **Gac. 2, in ex.**
Italia *n.* Italy **8, in ex.**
italiano *n.* Italian (language) **2;** *n.* Italian national; *adj.* Italian
itinerario *n.* itinerary **12**
izquierdo *adj.* left; **a la izquierda** on/to the left **10**

J

jabón *n.m.* soap **5**
jamás *adv.* never **3**
jamón *n.m.* ham **8**
Jánuca *n.* Chanukah **18**
jarabe *n.m.* syrup **13**
jardín *n.m.* garden **5; jardín zoológico** zoo **5**
jefe *n.* boss **3**
jornada *n.* working day
joven *n.* young person **2;** *adj.* young
joya *n.* jewel **Gac. 5**
joyería *n.* jewelry **Gac. 5**
judío *n.* Jew **18;** *adj.* Jewish
juego *n.* game **6; hacer juego** to match **9**
jueves *n.m.* Thursday **Sec. A**
juez *n.* judge **Sec. C; 3**
jugador *n.* player **Gac. 2; 14**
jugar (u > ue) *v.* to play **3; jugar a las cartas** to play cards **6; jugar un papel** to play a role **17**
jugo *n.* juice **7**
juguete *n.m.* toy **4**
julio *n.* July **4**
junio *n.* June **4**
juntar *v.* to join **18; juntarse** *v.* to get together
junto *adj.* together **15**
juntos *adv.* together **8**
jurar *v.* to swear **Gac. 6**
justicia *n.* justice **Gac. 2**
juvenil *adj.* youthful
juventud *n.f.* youth **Gac. 1**
juzgar *v.* to judge

K

kilo(gramo) *n.* kilogram (approx. **2.2** lbs.) **8**
kilómetro *n.* kilometer (approx. **0.62** miles) **Gac. 1**

L

la *f. sing. def. art.* the **Sec. C**
la *f. sing. d. o. pron.* her, you, it **5**
labio *n.* lip **13**
laboratorio *n.* laboratory **1; laboratorio de lenguas** language laboratory
lado *n.* side **Gac. 3; al lado de** *prep.* next to
ladrillo *n.* brick **5, in ex.**
ladrón *n.* thief, burglar **Gac. 3**
lago *n.* lake **15**
lámpara *n.* lamp
lana *n.* wool **9**
langosta *n.* lobster **8**
lanzador *n.* pitcher **14**
lanzar *v.* to throw **14**
lápiz *n.m.* pencil **Sec. C**
largo *adj.* long **4**
las *f. pl. def. art.* the **Sec. C**
las *f. sing. d. o. pron.* them, you **5**
lástima *n.* pity, shame **6; 10; ¡Qué lástima!** What a shame!
lastimado *adj.* hurt, injured **14**
lata *n.* can **8**
latín *n.m.* Latin (language)
latino *n., adj.* ref. to **latinoamericano Sec. C**
lavabo *n.* washbasin, bathroom sink **5**
lavadora *n.* washing machine **5**
lavandería *n.* laundry, laundromat **12**
lavaplatos *n.* dishwasher **5**
lavar *v.* to wash **5; lavarse** *v.* to wash oneself, get washed
lazo *n.* tie **Gac. 1; 17**
le *ind. obj. pron.* to or for him, her, you, it **6**
lección *n.* lesson **1**
leche *n.f.* milk **7**
lechuga *n.* lettuce **7**
lectura *n.* reading **Sec. A**
leer *v.* to read **2**
legado *n.* legacy **Gac. 4**
legumbre *n.f.* vegetable **7**
lejos *adv.* far **5; lejos de** *prep.* far away from
lema *n.m.* slogan, motto **Gac. 1**
lengua *n.* language, tongue **13**
lenguaje *n.* language **Gac. 5**
lento *adj.* slow **2;** *adv.* slowly
león *n.m.* lion **15**
les *ind. obj. pron.* to or for them, you **6**
letra *n.* letter (of the alphabet), lyrics **Sec. A**
levantar *v.* to raise, pick up **9; levantar pesas** to lift weights; **levantarse** *v.* to get up
ley *n.f.* law **Gac. 2**
leyenda *n.* legend **Gac. 3**
liberado *adj.* free, liberated **17**
liberal *adj.* liberal **Sec. A; 14**
libertad *n.f.* liberty **Gac. 1**
libra *n.* pound **8**
libre *adj.* free **10**
librería *n.* bookstore **Sec. A; 1**
libro *n.* book **Sec. C; 1**
licencia *n.* license **11; licencia de conducir** driver's license

licenciatura *n.* bachelor's degree; master's degree
liceo *n.* high school **1, in ex.**
liga *n.* league **Gac. 3**
ligero *adj.* light (weight) **8**
limitar *v.* to limit
límite *n.m.* limit
limón *n.m.* lemon **Sec. A; 8**
limonada *n.* lemonade **1, in ex.**
limpiar *v.* to clean **5**
limpio *adj.* clean **5**
lindo *adj.* pretty **Guía 1; 8**
línea *n.* line; **línea aérea** airline **16, in ex.**
liquidación *n.* sale **8**
lista *n.* list; menu **7**
listo *adj.*: **estar listo** to be ready; **ser listo** to be clever, smart **2**
litro *n.* liter **8**
llamada *n.f.* call **6**
llamar *v.* to call **1; llamarse** *v.* to be called **9; ¿Cómo se llama Ud.?** What is your name? **Sec. B; Me llamo**… My name is…**Sec. B**
llamativo *adj.* showy, attention-getting, "loud" **9**
llanta *n.* tire **11**
llave *n.f.* key **12**
llegada *n.* arrival **10**
llegar *v.* to arrive **1; llegar a ser** to become; **llegar a un acuerdo** to come to an agreement
llenar *v.* to fill **11**
lleno *adj.* full **5**
llevar *v.* to carry, take, wear **2; llevar una vida (feliz)** to lead a (happy) life
llevarse *v.* to carry off, take away; **llevarse bien (mal) con** to get along well (badly) with **16**
llorar *v.* to cry **4**
llover (o > ue) *v.* to rain **3**
lluvia *n.* rain **16**
lo *d. o. pron.* him, it **5; lo que** what, that which **2; 10; lo siento** I'm sorry **6; lo más pronto posible** as soon as possible **13**
loco *adj.* crazy **16**
locura *n.* madness, insanity, foolishness **16**
lógico *adj.* logical **2**
lograr *v.* to achieve, succeed, attain
logro *n.* achievement **Gac. 4**
los *m. pl. def. art.* the **Sec. C**
los *d. o. pron.* them, you **5**
lucha *n.* struggle, fight **14, 17**
luchar *v.* to fight **16**
luego *adv.* later, then **2; hasta luego** see you later **Sec. B**
lugar *n.m.* place **1; 14**
lujo *n.* luxury **12, in ex.**
lujoso *adj.* luxurious **12**
luna *n.* moon **15; luna de miel** *n.* honeymoon
lunes *n.m.* Monday **Sec. A**
luz *n.f.* light **Sec. C**

M

machista *adj.* macho **17**
macho *adj.* male **17**
madera *n.* wood **11**
madre *n.f.* mother **4**
madrina *n.* godmother
madurez *n.f.* maturity
maduro *adj.* mature, ripe **16**
maestría *n.* master's degree **Gac. 5**
maestro *n.* grade school teacher **2**
mágico *adj.* magic, magical **18, in ex.**
magnífico *adj.* magnificent
mago *n.* wizard, magician **4; 18; los Reyes Magos** the Magi, Wise Men **4; 18**
maíz *n.m.* corn **7**
mal *adv.* badly, poorly **1**
maleducado *adj.* ill-mannered, rude **4**
maleta *n.* suitcase **10**
maletero *n.* trunk of a car **11**
malo (mal) *adj.* bad, poor; **hace mal tiempo** the weather is bad **4**
maltrato *n.* mistreatment, abuse
mamá *n.* mom **4**
manchar *v.* to stain
mandamiento *n.* commandment
mandar *v.* to order, command, send **11**
manejar *v.* to drive **4**
manera *n.* way, manner **Gac. 4**
manifestación *n.* protest, demonstration
mano *n.f.* hand **Sec. B, in ex.; 13; darse la mano** to shake hands; **hecho a mano** handmade
manta *n.* blanket **5**
mantel *n.m.* tablecloth
mantener *v.* to maintain, support **Gac. 2; 13**
mantequilla *n.* butter **8**
manzana *n.* apple **8;** block (city) **10**
mañana *n.* morning **1**
mapa *n.m.* map **Sec. C**
maquillaje *n.* make-up
máquina *n.* machine **1; máquina de escribir** typewriter; **escribir a máquina** to type
mar *n.m., f.* sea **12**
maratón *n.* marathon
maravilla *n.* marvel, wonder **6**
maravilloso *adj.* marvellous **18**
marca *n.* brand
marcar *v.* to dial **6; marcar un número** to dial a number
mareado *adj.* dizzy, nauseated **13**
marido *n.* husband **4**
marinero *n.* seaman **Gac. 4**
mariscos *n.pl.* shellfish **7**
marrón *adj.* brown **4**
martes *n.m.* Tuesday **Sec. A**
mártir *n.* martyr **Gac. 3**
marzo *n.* March **4**
más *adv.* more **1; más o menos** more or less **10; más tarde** later **1**
mascota *n.* pet
masculinidad *n.f.* masculinity **17**
matar *v.* to kill **Gac. 3**
matemáticas *n.pl.* mathematics **2**
materno *adj.* maternal **17**
matrícula *n.* tuition **1**
matricularse *v.* to register, enroll **Gac. 4**
matrimonio *n.* matrimony, married couple **16**
máximo *adj.* maximum; **al máximo** to the limit **Gac. 1**
maya *adj.* Mayan **Gac. 4**
mayo *n.* May **4**
mayonesa *n.* mayonnaise **8**
mayor *adj.* older, oldest **4;** greater, greatest; **la mayor parte** the majority
mayoría *n.* majority **4**
me *dir., ind. obj. pron.* me **5; 6;** *refl. pron.* myself **9**
mecánico *n.* mechanic **3**
media *adj.* half (of the hour) **Son las dos y media** It is two thirty. **1**
medianoche *n.f.* midnight **1**
medias *n.pl.* stockings **9**
medicina *n.* medicine **2; 13; facultad de medicina** medical school
médico *n.* doctor **3**
medio *n.* middle, half **8;** *adj.* average; **medio ambiente** environment
mediodía *n.* noon **1**
medir (e > i) *v.* to measure **8**
mejor *adj.* better, best **6; es mejor** it's better, best **10**
mejorarse *v.* to improve **14**
melocotón *n.m.* peach **8**
memoria *n.* memory **18, in ex.**
menor *adj.* younger, youngest **4;** smaller, smallest
menos *prep.* less, minus, except **5**
mensaje *n.* message **6**
mensual *adj.* monthly
mente *n.f.* mind
mentir (e > ie) *v.* to lie **3**
mentira *n.* lie
menú *n.* menu **7**
menudo, a menudo *adv.* often **1**
mercado *n.* market **8**
merecer *v.* to deserve
merendar (e > ie) *v.* to snack **7**
merienda *n.* snack **7**
mes *n.m.* month **4**
mesa *n.* table **Gac. 1 in ex. 4; 5; poner la mesa** to set the table **4**

mesero *n.* waiter
mestizo *n., adj.* person of European and indigenous ancestry **10**
metal *n.m.* metal **9, in ex.**
meter *v.* to put into **Gac. 1; 10**
metro *n.* meter, subway **11**
mexicano *n.* Mexican (national) **2;** *adj.* Mexican
mexicanoamericano *n., adj.* Mexican-American **Sec. B**
México *n.* Mexico **Sec. B**
mezcla *n.* mixture, combination **8, in ex.**
mezclar *v.* to mix, combine **8**
mi(s) *poss. adj.* my **3**
mí *obj.* of *prep.* me **5**
microondas *n.m. sing.* microwave oven **5**
miedo *n.* fear **3; tener miedo** to be afraid
miel *n.f.* honey **16; luna de miel** honeymoon **16**
miembro *n.* member **Gac. 4**
mientras *adv.* while **8; mientras que** *conj.* while **14**
miércoles *n.m.* Wednesday **Sec. A**
migratorio *adj.* migratory **Gac. 4**
mil *n.* one (a) thousand **4**
milagro *n.* miracle **Gac. 5**
militar *adj.* militar **Gac. 6**
milla *n.* mile **11; millas por hora** miles per hour
millón *n.m.* million **4**
mimado *adj.* spoiled
mina *n.* mine **Gac. 6**
minoritario *adj.* minority
minuto *n.* minute **1**
mío *poss. adj., pron.* my, mine **17**
mirar *v.* to look at, watch **1**
misa *n.* Mass **18; Misa del gallo** midnight Mass (Christmas Eve)
mismo *adj.* same **3; me da lo mismo** it's all the same to me **17**
mitad *n.f.* half **17**
mito *n.* myth **17**
mochila *n.* knapsack **15**
moda *n.* fashion style **4; estar de moda** to be in style **9; fuera de moda** out of style **9**
modales *n.m.pl.* manners **9, in ex.**
modelo *n.* model **Sec. B, in ex.**
moderno *adj.* modern **Gac. 1; 12**
modo *n.* way, manner **4; de ningún modo** no way; **de todos modos** anyway
mojarse *v.* to get wet
molestar *v.* to bother, annoy **6**
molestia *n.* annoyance **13**
monarquía *n.* monarchy
moneda *n.* coin **Gac. 2**
mono *n.* monkey **15;** *adj.* cute
montaña *n.* mountain **15**
montañoso *adj.* mountainous **Gac. 6**
montar *v.* to ride **14; montar a caballo** to ride horseback; **montar en bicicleta** to ride a bicycle
monte *n.m.* mountain **Gac. 3**
montón *n.*m heap, pile
monumento *n.* monument **Gac. 1**
morado *adj.* purple **4**
moreno *adj.* brunette, dark-haired **2**
morir (o > ue) *v.* to die **3**
mosquito *n.* mosquito **Sec. A**
mostaza *n.* mustard **8**
mostrar (o > ue) *v.* to show **3**
motocicleta (moto) *n.f.* motorcycle **11**
motor *n.m.* motor, engine **11**
mover (o > ue) *v.* to move **6; no se mueva** don't move **13**
movimiento *n.* movement
mozo *n.* waiter **7**
muchacha *n.* girl **Sec. C; 1**
muchacho *n.* boy **Sec. C; 1**
mucho *adj.* many **1;** much; a lot of
mudanza *n.* move, change of residence **Gac. 2**
mudarse *v.* to move, to change residence **Gac. 4**
muebles *n.m.pl.* furniture **5**
muerte *n.f.* death **Gac. 1; 4**
muerto *n.* dead person **18;** *p.p.* dead
mujer *n.f.* woman **Sec. C; 1; mujer de negocios** business woman
multa *n.* fine, traffic ticket **11**
mundial *adj.* worldwide **15**
mundo *n.* world **Sec. C; 10**
muñeca *n.* doll **Gac. 6**
músculo *n.* muscle
museo *n.* museum **Gac. 1, 7, in ex.**
música *n.* music **2**
músico *n.* musician **Sec. B; 3**
muy *adv.* very **1; muy bien** very well **Sec. B**

N

nacer *v.* to be born
nacimiento *n.* birth **Gac. 1;4**
nación *n.* nation **Sec. C**
nacional *adj.* national **12**
nada *pron.* nothing **3; de nada** you're welcome **Sec. B; nada más** nothing else **7**
nadador *n.* swimmer **14**
nadar *v.* to swim **12**
nadie *pron.* no one, nobody **3**
naranja *n.* orange **Gac. 1, 8**
nariz *n.f.* nose **13**
natación *n.* swimming **14**
natural *adj.* natural **8, in ex.; recursos naturales** natural resources
naturaleza *n.* nature **4, in ex.; 15**
navegante *n.* sailor **Gac. 1**
Navidad *n.f.* Christmas **4, in ex.; 18; Feliz Navidad** Merry Christmas **18**
necesario *adj.* necessary **10**
necesidad *n.* necessity
necesitar *v.* to need **1**
negar (e > ie) *v.* to deny **3; negarse a** *v.* to refuse to **Gac. 4; 16**
negocio *n.* business **3; hombre (mujer) de negocios** businessman (woman)
negro *adj.* black **4**
nervioso *adj.* nervous **2, in ex.**
nevar (e > ie) *v.* to snow **3**
nevera *n.* refrigerator **5**
ni *conj.* neither, nor **3; ni siquiera** not even; **¡Ni hablar!** Not a chance! **4; ¡Ni modo!** No way! **4; ¡Ni pensarlo!** Don't even think of it! **4**
nicaragüense *n., adj.* Nicaraguan
niebla *n.* fog
nieto *n.* grandson **4;** *pl.* grandchildren
nieve *n.f.* snow **5**
ninguno (ningún) *adj.* no, none, not any **3**
niñera *n.* nursemaid, babysitter **6, in ex.**
niñez *n.f.* childhood, **Gac. 4**
niño *n.* child **4; de niño(a)** as a child
nivel *n.m.* level **Gac. 4**
no *adv.* no, not **Sec. A**
no sólo…sino también not only…but also **6**
nocturno *adj.* nighttime **Gac. 1**
noche *n.f.* night **1; anoche** last night **6; buenas noches** good evening, good night **Sec. B; de noche** at night; **esta noche** tonight **4, in ex.; 18; Nochebuena** Christmas Eve; **Noche vieja** New Year's Eve **18; por la noche** during the night; **todas las noches** every night **1**
nombrar *v.* to name **Gac. 1**
nombre *n.* name **Sec. B**
norte *n.* north **11**
norteamericano *n., adj.* North American **Sec. B**
nos *d.o. pron.* us **5;** *ind. obj. pron.* to or for us **6;** *refl. pron.* ourselves **9**
nosotros *subj. pron.* we **Sec. B;** *obj.* of *prep.* us
nota *n.* grade **2**
noticias *n.* news **6**
noticiero *n.* newscast
novela *n.* novel **Sec. A**
novecientos *adj., n.m.* nine hundred **4**
noveno *adj.* ninth **12**
noventa *adj., n.m.* ninety **1**
novia *n.* girlfriend, financée, bride **4; 16**
noviazgo *n.* courtship **16**
noviembre *n.* November **4**
novio *n.* boyfriend, fiancé, groom **4; 16**
nublado *adj.* cloudy **4**
nuestro *poss. adj., pron.* our, ours **3**
nueve *adj., n.m.* nine **Sec. B**
nuevo *adj.* new **3; de nuevo** again
nuez *n.f.* nut **8**

número *n.* number **Sec. B**
nunca *adv.* never **3**

O

o *conj.* or **3; o sea** that is...**16**
obedecer *v.* to obey
obediente *adj.* obedient **17**
obituarios *n.pl.* obituary column **6**
objeto *n.* object **4, in ex.**
obligación obligation **9, in ex.**
obligar (a) *v.* to oblige **17**
obra *n.* work (of art) **3, in ex.; obra maestra** *n.* masterpiece **Gac. 1**
obrero *n.* worker **3**
observación *n.* observation **13, in ex.**
observar *v.* to observe **4**
obstáculo *n.* obstacle **16, in ex.**
obtener *v.* to get, obtain **1**
obvio *adj.* obvious **10**
ocasión *n.* occasion **8**
occidental *adj.* western **Gac. 2**
océano *n.* ocean **Gac. 5**
ochenta eighty **1**
ocho *adj., n.m.* eight **Sec. B**
ochocientos *adj., n.m.* eight hundred **4**
octubre *n.* October **4**
ocupado *adj.* occupied, busy **6**
ocurrir *v.* to happen, occur **Gac. 1**
ocultar *v.* to hide **Gac. 3**
odiar *v.* to hate **16**
odio *n.* hate
oeste *n.m.* west **11**
ofender *v.* to offend, insult
oficial *adj.* official **11, in ex.**
oficina *n.* office **6**
ofrecer *v.* to offer **4**
oído *n.* (inner) ear **13**
oír *v.* to hear **4**
ojalá *interj.* I hope that **11**
ojo *n.* eye **Gac. 1; 13; ¡ojo!** be careful!
olvidar *v.* to forget **5**
once *adj., n.m.* eleven **Sec. B**
onda wave **estar de onda** to be "in" **4**
ópera *n.* opera **Gac. 1**
operación *n.* operation **Sec. A**
operador *n.* operator **6**
operar *v.* to operate **13**
oponerse (a) *v.* to oppose **17**
oportunidad *n.* opportunity **2, in ex.**
oprimir *v.* to oppress **Gac. 6**
optimista *n., adj.* optimist, optimistic **Gac. 1; 14**
orden *n.f.* order, command; *m.* order (sequence) **10**
ordenado *adj.* neat, orderly **5**
ordenador *n.* computer
ordenar *v.* to order **11**
oreja *n.* (outer) ear **13**
organizar *v.* to organize **12, in ex.**
orgullo *n.* pride
orgulloso *adj.* proud **Gac. 2**
origen *n.* origin **4, in ex.**
oro *n.* gold **Gac. 1; 9**
orquesta *n.* orchestra **Gac. 2; 16**
os *d.o. pron.* you **5;** *incl. obj. pron.* to or for you **6;** *refl. pron.* yourself **9**
oscurecer *v.* to grow dark
oscuro *adj.* dark **9**
oso *n.* bear **15**
otoño *n.* autumn, fall **4**
otro *adj.* other, another **2**
oye listen **4**

P

paciencia *n.* patience **13, in ex.**
paciente *n., adj.* patient **13**
padre *n.* father **4;** *pl.* parents
paella *n.* Spanish dish **Gac. 1; 7**
pagar *v.* to pay (for) **1**
página *n.* page **13, in ex.**
pago *n.* payment **Gac. 4**
país *n.m.* country **7; 10**
paisaje *n.m.* landscape, countryside **11**
pájaro *n.* bird **5**
palabra *n.* word **2**
palacio *n.* palace **Gac. 1**
pálido *adj.* pale **13**
palma *n.* palm tree **Gac. 6**
pan *n.m.* bread **7**
panadería *n.* bakery **7, in ex.; 8**
panameño *n., adj.* Panamanian **Sec. B**
panorámico *adj.* panoramic **15**
pantalones *n.m.pl.* pants **9**
pañuelo *n.* kerchief **Gac. 6**
papa *n.* potato **8; papas fritas** French fried potatoes
papá *n.m.* Dad **4**
papel *n.m.* paper **Sec. C;** role **Gac. 3; hacer un papel** to play a role **17; papel estelar** *n.* starring role **Gac. 5**
papitas *n.* potato chips **8**
paquete *n.m.* package, pack **10**
par *n.m.* pair **9**
para *prep.* for **1; para que** *conj.* in order that **15**
parada *n.* stop **12; parada de taxis** taxi stand; **parada de autobús** bus stop
paraguas *n.m. s.* and *pl.* umbrella **9**
paraíso *n.* paradise **Gac. 4; 18**
parar *v.* to stop **11**
pardo *adj.* brown
parecer *v.* to seem **6; parecerse a** *v.* to look like, resemble **9**
parecido *adj.* similar
pared *n.f.* wall **Sec. C**
pareja *n.* pair, couple, partner **1 in ex.; 15**
paréntesis *n.m. s.* and *pl.* parenthesis **10, in ex.**
pariente *n.m.* (family) relative **Sec. A; 4**
parque *n.m.* park **15; parque de atracciones** amusement park
párrafo *n.* paragraph **4, in ex.**
parte *n.f.* part **Gac. 1; 10; la mayor parte** the majority; **por todas partes** everywhere
participación *n.* participation **Sec. A**
participar *v.* to participate **1, in ex.**
participio *n.* participle **13; participio pasado** past participle; **participio presente** present participle
particular *adj.* private
partido *n.* party (political); game, match
pasado *n. adj.* past **Gac. 1; pasado mañana** the day after tomorrow; **pasado de moda** out of style **9**
pasaje *n.m.* ticket, passage **10**
pasajero *n.* passenger, traveler **10**
pasaporte *n.m.* passport **10**
pasar *v.* to pass **1;** to spend; to happen; **pasar la aspiradora** to vacuum **5; pasarlo bien** to have a good time **6**
pasatiempo *n.* pastime, diversion **6**
Pascua *n.* Passover **18; Pascua Florida** Easter
pasearse *v.* to stroll, take a walk **11; pasearse en coche** to take a drive
paseo *n.* stroll, walk; **dar un paseo** to take a walk
pasillo *n.* hall, corridor **10**
pasión *n.* passion **Gac. 1**
pasivo *adj.* passive **Sec. A; 17**
paso *n.* step **Gac. 4;** float (*parade*) **18 in ex.**
pasta dental *n.* toothpaste **12**
pastel *n.m.* pastry **Sec. A; 7**
pastelería *n.* pastry shop **7, in ex.; 8**
pastilla *n.* pill **13**
pastor *n.* minister **18**
patata *n.* potato **Sec. A; 8**
paterno *n.* paternal **17**
patinar *v.* to skate **14**
patio *n.* patio, backyard **Sec. A; 5**
pato *n.* duck
patria *n.* country, fatherland **Gac. 6**
patrón *n.* boss **Gac. 4**
pavo *n.* turkey **8**
payaso *n.* clown **15**
paz *n.f.* peace **15; hacer las paces** to make up **16**
pecado *n.* sin **Gac. 2**
pecho *n.* chest **13**
pedazo *n.* piece **7, in ex.**
pedir (e > i) *v.* to ask for, request **5;** order (*food*)
peinado *n.* hairdo
pelea *n.* fight **17**
pelear(se) *v.* to fight **16**
película *n.* movie, film **Gac. 1**

peligro *n.* danger **13**
peligroso *adj.* dangerous **11**
pelirrojo *adj.* red-haired **Gac. 1**
pelo *n.* hair **4**
pelota *n.* ball **14**
pelotero *n.* pitcher **Gac. 2; 14**
peluquero *n.* hairdresser
pena *n.* pain, suffering, sorrow, grief **Gac. 2; 6**
pensar (e > ie) *v.* to think **3; pensar** + *inf.* to plan to; **pensar de** to have an opinion about; **pensar en** to think about, have in mind; **¡Ni pensarlo!** Don't even think of it! **4**
pensión *n.f.* boarding house **12; pensión completa** room and board
peor *adj.* worse, worst **6**
pepino *n.* cucumber **8**
pequeño *adj.* small **2**
pera *n.* pear **8**
perder (e > ie) *v.* to lose, miss **3; perder un tren** to miss a train **11**
pérdida *n.* loss
perdón pardon, excuse me **Sec. A, in ex.**
perdonar *v.* to pardon, excuse **17**
perejil *n.m.* parsley
perezoso *adj.* lazy **2**
perfecto *adj.* perfect **4**
periódico *n.* newspaper **3**
periodista *n.* journalist **3**
permanecer *v.* to remain **12**
permanente *adj.* permanent
permiso *n.* permission **Sec. B; con permiso** pardon me, excuse me
permitir *v.* to permit **7**
pero but **1**
perro *n.* dog **5; perro caliente** hot dog **8**
persona *n.* person **Sec. A**
personalidad *n.* personality **15, in ex.**
pertenecer *v.* to belong **2, in ex.**
pesado *adj.* heavy, boring **6; 8**
pesar *v.* to weigh **8; a pesar de** in spite of
pescado *n.* fish (cooked) **7**
pescador *n.* fisherman **Gac. 4**
pescar *v.* to fish **15**
pesimista *n, adj.* pessimist, pessimistic **14**
pesado *adj.* heavy **8**
pésame *n.* condolences **18**
peseta *n.* unit of currency in Spain **7**
peso *n.* weight **8**
pez *n.m.* fish **15**
piano *n.* piano **6**
picante *adj.* spicy **7**
pie *n.m.* foot **13**
piedra *n.* rock **4, in ex.**
piel *n.f.* skin, fur **13**
pierna *n.* leg **13**
píldora *n.* pill **13**
piloto *n.* pilot **Sec. A, in ex.**
pimienta *n.* pepper (*the spice*) **7**
pimiento *n.* pepper (*the vegetable*)
pinchado *adj.* flat **11; una llanta pinchada** a flat tire
pintar *v.* to paint **6**
pintor *n.* painter
pintoresco *adj.* picturesque **Gac. 2**
pintura *n.* painting **Gac. 1**
piña *n.* pineapple **7**
pirámide *n.f.* pyramid **12, in ex.**
piscina *n.* swimming pool **12**
piso *n.* floor or level (*of a building*) **5**
pizarra *n.* blackboard **Sec. C**
placer *n.m.* pleasure **18**
plan *n.m.* plan **Gac. 1**
plancha *n.* iron **5**
planchar *v.* to iron **5**
planear *v.* to plan **10, in ex.**
planeta *n.m.* planet **Guía 1**
planta *n.* plant **4, in ex.**; floor of a building
plástico *n.* plastic **2**
plata *n.* silver **Gac. 1; 9**
plátano *n.* plantain, banana (Spain) **8**
plateado *adj.* silvery **Gac. 4**
plato *n.* plate **7**; dish
playa *n.* beach **Gac. 1; 12**
plaza *n.* square **Gac. 3**; place; **plaza de toros** bullring **18 (realia)**
plomero *n.* plumber
pluvioso *adj.* rainy **Gac. 2**
población *n.* population **Gac. 3**
pobre *adj.* poor, unfortunate **2**
pobreza *n.* poverty **Gac. 4**
poco *adj.* few, little **1**; *adv.* a little; **un poco** a little; **poco a poco** little by little
poder (o > ue) *v.* to be able to **3**
poderoso *adj.* powerful **Gac. 4**
poema *n.m.* poem **Gac. 2**
poeta *n.* poet **Gac. 4**
policía *n.m.* policeman **Sec. C; 1;** *n.f.* police force or department
política *n.* politics **Gac. 5**
político *n.* politician **Sec. B;** *adj.* political; **ciencia(s) política(s)** political science **2**
pollo *n.* chicken **7**
poner *v.* to put, place **4; poner la mesa** to set the table **4; poner la radio** to turn the radio on; **ponerse** *v.* to put on (clothing) **9**; to become; **poner una inyección** to give an injection **13**
poquito *n.* a very small quantity **11, in ex.**
por *prep.* for **2**; per; because of; on behalf of; on account of; during; through; by; **por cierto** for sure; **por Dios** for God's sake; **por completo** completely; **por ejemplo** for example **7; por eso** therefore **2; por favor** please **Sec. B; por la mañana** in the morning; **por lo general** generally **5; 7; por lo menos** at least **7; por medio de** by means of; **por otro lado** on the other hand; **por supuesto** of course **4; por teléfono** by phone **6; por último** lastly
porcentaje *n.m.* percentage
¿Por qué? *interr.* Why? **Sec. B**
porque *conj.* because **1**
portarse *v.* to behave **13**
portero *n.* doorman **12**
portugués *n.m.* and *adj.* Portuguese
posible *adj.* possible **Sec. A**
posibilidad *n.* possibility **Gac. 1**
posición *n.* position **Gac. 6**
posponer *v.* to postpone
postre *n.m.* dessert **4**
práctica *n.* practice **Gac. 2**
practicar *v.* to practice **1, in ex.**
práctico *adj.* practical
precio *n.* price **8**
precioso *adj.* precious, adorable **Gac. 4**
preciso *adj.* necessary
preferencia *n.* preference
preferible *adj.* preferable **10**
preferir (e > ie) *v.* to prefer **3**
pregunta *n.* question **Sec. B, in ex.; 2; hacer una pregunta** to ask a question **6**
preguntar *v.* to ask a question **1**
prejuicio *n.* prejudice **17**
premio *n.* prize **Gac. 2**
prenda de vestir *n.* article of clothing
prender *v.* to turn on **12**
prensa *n.* press
preocupación *n.* preoccupation, worry, care, concern **Gac. 5**
preocupado *adj.* worried, preoccupied, concerned **2**
preocuparse *v.* to worry **13**
preparar *v.* to prepare **1**
preparativos *n.pl.* preparations **16**
preposición *n.* preposition **Guía 4**
presentar *v.* to present **1**
presente *n.m.* present (*time, tense*) **15**
presidente *n.* president **Sec. A**
presión *n.* pressure tension
prestar *v.* to lend **6; prestar atención** to pay attention
prestigioso *n.* prestigious
pretérito *n.* preterite (tense) **6, in ex.**
primavera *n.* spring **4**
primero (primer) *adj.* first **4; de primera clase** first-class **41; por primera vez** for the first time; **primero** *adv.* firstly, first of all
primero *adj.* first **12**
primo *n.* cousin **4**
principio *n.* beginning
prisa *n.* haste **3; tener prisa** to be in a hurry
probable *adj.* probable **10**

probablemente *adv.* probably
probador *n.* dressing room **9**
probar *v.* to try, taste **7; probarse** *v.* to try on **9**
problema *n.m.* problem **Gac. 1**
procedente de *prep.* coming from
proceso *n.* process **10**
producir *v.* to produce **4**
profesión *n.* profession **3**
profesional *adj.* professional **Gac. 2**
profe *n.* prof
profesor *n.* professor **Sec. A; 1**
profesorado *n.* faculty **2**
profundo *adj.* profound, deep **Gac. 3**
programa *n.m.* program **Sec. C; programa de estudios** curriculum
programador *n.* programmer **3**
progresivo *adj.* progressive **5, in ex.**
progreso *n.* progress **Gac. 1**
prohibido *adj.* forbidden, prohibited **8, in ex.**
prohibir *v.* to forbid, prohibit **11**
promedio *n.* average
promesa *n.* promise **Gac. 4**
prometer *v.* to promise **6, in ex.**
pronto *adv.* soon **2; tan pronto como** *conj.* as soon as **14**
pronunciar *v.* to pronounce **2**
propiedad *n.* property
propina *n.* tip **7**
propio *adj.* appropriate, one's own **Gac. 1; 12, in ex.**
propósito *n.* purpose **Gac. 1; a propósito** by the way
próspero *adj.* prosperous **18**
protagonista *n.* main character **Gac. 2**
proteger *v.* to protect **Gac. 2**
protestante *n.* Protestant **18**
protestar *v.* to protest
provecho *n.* benefit; **buen provecho** enjoy your meal! (*typical greeting to a person who is eating*) **7**
provocar *v.* to provoke **16, in ex.; 17**
próximo *adj.* next **Gac. 3; 14; la próxima vez** the next time
prueba *n.* quiz **2**
(p)sicólogo *n.* psychologist **3**
(p)siquiatra *n.* psychiatrist **3**
público *n.* audience **Gac. 1;** *adj.* public
pueblo *n.* town **4, in ex.**
puente *n.m.* bridge **Gac. 2**
puerta *n.* door **Sec. C;** gate (at the airport) **10**
puerto *n.* port **Gac. 1**
pues *conj.* well...**16**
puesto *n.* job **3;** *p.p. adj.* placed, put
pulmón *n.m.* lung **13**
puntual *adj.* punctual
punto *n.* point **1; en punto** on the dot
puro *adj.* pure **15;** *n.* cigar

Q

que *conj., rel. pron.* that, who **10; lo que** what, that which **2; 10; ¿Qué?** What? **Sec. B; ¡Qué alegría!** What happiness! **6; ¡Qué bien!** How nice! **4; ¿Qué hay de nuevo?** What's new? **Guía 1; Sec. B; ¡Qué lástima!** What a shame! **6; ¡Qué suerte!** What luck! **6 ¿Qué tal?** How are you? **Sec. B; ¡Qué va!** Go on! No way! **6**
quedar *v.* to have left **8; quedarse** *v.* to stay, remain **9; quedarle (bien)** to fit (well) **9**
quehacer *n.m.* chore
queja *n.* complaint **13**
quejarse (de) *v.* to complain about **13**
quemar *v.* to burn
querer (e > ie) *v.* to want, wish; to love **3**
querido *adj.* dear **6, in ex. 16**
queso *n.* cheese **7**
quien *rel. pron.* who, whom **10; ¿quién?** *interr.* who? **Sec. B; ¿de quién?** whose? **2**
química *n.* chemistry **2**
químico *n.* chemist
quince *adj., n.m.* fifteen **Sec. B**
quinceañera *n.* celebration of fifteenth birthday (similar to Sweet 16) **4**
quinientos *adj., n.m.* five hundred **4**
quinto *adj.* fifth **12**
quiosco *n.* newsstand **12**
quitar *v.* to take away, remove **9; quitarse** *v.* to take off **9**
quizá(s) perhaps **11**

R

rabino *n.* rabbi **18**
radio *n.m.* radio apparatus, box **1, in ex.;** *n.f.* radio transmission, sound
raíz *n.f.* root **Gac. 1**
rana *n.* frog **15**
rápidamente *adv.* quickly **Sec. A**
rápido *adj.* fast, quick **2, in ex.;** *adv.* quickly
raqueta *n.* racket **14**
raro *adj.* strange, odd **7; raras veces** rarely
rascacielos *n.* skyscraper
rato *n.* short period of time **14; ratos libres** free time
raya *n.* stripe **Gac. 5**
rayo *n.* ray **1; rayos equis** X-rays; **¡rayos!** shucks! **1**
raza *n.* race **Gac. 2**
razón *n.f.* reason **3; (no) tener razón** to be right (wrong)
razonable *adj.* reasonable **17**
real *adj.* real; royal
realidad *n.* reality **Sec. A; 16**
realizar *v.* to accomplish, carry out
realmente *adv.* really
recado *n.* message **6**
recepción *n.* reception **12;** reception desk
recepcionista *n.* receptionist **12**
receta *n.* recipe **7;** prescription
recetar *v.* to prescribe **13**
rechazar *v.* to reject
recibir *v.* to receive, get **2**
recién *adv.* recently **16; recién casado** newlywed
reciente *adj.* recent **Gac. 5**
recinto *n.* campus **1**
recipiente *n.* receptacle **Gac. 1**
reclamar *v.* to claim
recoger *v.* to pick up, gather **8**
recomendar (e > ie) *v.* to recommend **3**
reconocer *v.* to recognize **18, in ex.**
recordar (o > ue) *v.* to remember, recall **3**
recreo *n.* recreation **15**
recuerdo *n.* memory, souvenir **4**
recuerdos a regards to **Sec. B**
recurso *n.* resource **Gac. 2**
red *n.f.* net **14;** network
redondo *adj.* round
referente a *prep.* concerning, regarding
referirse (e > ie) *v.* to refer **5, in ex.**
reflejar *v.* to reflect **Gac. 1**
reflexivo *adj.* reflexive **8, in ex.**
refresco *n.* refreshment, soft drink **6**
refrigerador *n.* refrigerator **5**
refugiado *n.* refugee **Gac. 5**
refugio *n.* refuge **Gac. 6**
regalar *v.* to give a gift **6**
regalo *n.* gift, present **4**
regañar *v.* to quarrel
regar (e > ie) *v.* to water
regatear *v.* to bargain, haggle **8**
régimen *n.* regime, diet **8**
región *n.* region **Sec. A**
registro *n.* register
regla *n.* rule **14;** ruler
regresar *v.* to return **1**
regular *adj.* alright, fair **Sec. B**
reina *n.* queen **Gac. 1**
reír(se) (e > i) *v.* to laugh; **reírse de** to laugh at, make fun of
relación *n.* relation **5, in ex.**
relajar relax **12**
relámpago *n.* lightning
religión *n.* religion **Sec. A; 18**
religioso *adj.* religious **Gac. 4; 18**
relleno *adj.* stuffed **7, in ex.**
reloj *n.m.* watch, clock **1**
remedio *n.* solution **11**
remordimiento *n.* remorse **16, in ex.**
renovado *adj.* renovated
renunciar *v.* to give up
reñir (e > i) *v.* to quarrel **16**
repasar *v.* to review **2**
repaso *n.* review

repetir (e > i) *v.* to repeat **5**
representar *v.* to represent **5, in ex.;** to put on
republicano *adj.* Republican **2, in ex.**
requerir (e > ie) *v.* to require
requisito *n.* requirement
reserva *n.* reservation **10**
reservación *n.* reservation **10**
reservar *v.* to reserve **10**
resfriado *n.* cold (health) **13**
resfriarse *v.* to catch cold **13**
residencia (estudiantil) *n.* dormitory **1**
resolver (o > ue) *v.* to solve **16**
respecto a *prep.* with respect to, with regard to, concerning
respetar *v.* to respect **16**
respeto *n.* respect, admiration **Gac. 2**
respirar *v.* to breathe **13**
responder *v.* to answer **Sec. B, in ex.**
responsabilidad *n.* responsibility **Gac. 1**
responsable *adj.* responsible **2, in ex.**
respuesta *n.* answer **2**
restaurante *n.m.* restaurant **Sec. A; 7**
resultado *n.* result **Gac. 1**
resumen *n.m.* summary **1**
retrasado *adj.* delayed
retraso *n.* tardiness, delay
reunión *n.* meeting **Gac. 1; 4**
reunir *v.* to unite **16; reunirse (con)** *v.* to get together (with)
revisar *v.* to inspect **10**
revista *n.* magazine **6**
rey *n.* king **Gac. 1**
rezar *v.* to pray **18**
rico *adj.* rich, delicious **2**
ridículo *adj.* ridiculous **Sec. A**
rígido *adj.* rigid, strict **1, in ex.**
rincón *n.m.* corner (of a room) **Gac. 2**
riña *n.* argument, fight **16**
río *n.* river **Gac. 3; 15**
riqueza *n.* wealth, richness **Gac. 6**
ritmo *n.* rhythm **4, in ex.**
robar *v.* to steal **7, in ex.**
robo *n.* robbery **16, in ex.**
rodeado *adj.* surrounded
rodilla *n.* knee **13; de rodillas** on one's knees
rogar (o > ue) *v.* to beg, plead
rojo *adj.* red **4**
romántico *adj.* romantic **Sec. A, in ex.**
romper *v.* to break, tear **8**
ropa *n.* clothing **5; ropa interior** underwear **9**
ropero *n.* clothes closet **5**
rosa *adj.* pink **4**
roto *adj. p.p.* broken **11**
rubio *adj.* blond **2**
ruido *n.* noise **11**
ruidoso *adj.* noisy **11**
rumbo *n.* direction **Gac. 5**
ruso *n.m. adj.* Russian **2**
ruta *n.* route
rutina *n.* routine **1, in ex.**

S

sábado *n.* Saturday **Sec. A**
sábana *n.* sheet **5**
saber *v.* to know, find out **4**
sabor *n.* taste **Gac. 1**
sabroso *adj.* delicious, tasty **7**
sacar *v.* to take out **10; sacar una foto** to take a picture **4; sacar la basura** to take out the garbage **5**
sacerdote *n.* priest **18**
saco de dormir *n.* sleeping bag **15**
sacrificar *v.* to sacrifice
sagrado *adj.* sacred, holy **18**
sal *n.f.* salt **7**
sala *n.* room **5; sala de clase** classroom **Sec. C; sala de estar** den; **sala de emergencias** emergency room **13; sala de espera** waiting room **10**
salado *adj.* salty
salario *n.* salary **3**
salida *n.* departure **10;** exit
salir *v.* to leave, go out **4; salir con alguien** to go out with someone **6**
salmón *n.m.* salmon
salón *n.m.* room **1; 5**
salsa *n.* sauce **8; salsa de tomate** catsup
salud *n.f.* health **Gac. 2; 13; ¡Salud!** To your health! (*toast*) **18**
saludable *adj.* healthy **7**
saludar *v.* to greet **Sec. B**
saludo *n.* greeting **Sec. B**
salvaje *adj.* savage **Gac. 1; 15**
salvar *v.* to save **12**
salvavidas *n.m.* lifesaver
salvo *prep.* except **5**
sandalia *n.* sandal
sandwich *n.* sandwich **1; 7**
sangre *n.f.* blood **Gac. 4; 13**
sano *adj.* healthy, fit **Sec. A; 7**
santo *n.* saint **18;** *adj.* holy, saintly
satisfecho *adj.* satisfied **Gac. 5**
secadora *n.* (clothes) dryer **5**
secar *v.* to dry **5; secarse** *v.* to dry oneself
sección *n.f.* section; **sección de cocina, de moda** cooking, fashion sections of a newspaper
seco *adj.* dry
secretario *n.* secretary **3**
sed *n.f.* thirst **3; tener sed** to be thirsty
seda *n.* silk **9**
seguir (e > i) *v.* to follow, continue **5; seguir un régimen** to follow a diet **8**
según *prep.* according to **3, in ex. 5**
segundo *adj.* second **1; 12**
seguridad *n.* security **Gac. 4**
seguro *adj.* certain, sure, safe **10; por seguro** for sure
seguro médico *n.* medical insurance
seis six **Sec. B**
selección *n.* selection, choice **Gac. 3**
seleccionar *v.* to select, choose
sello *n.* stamp **12**
selva *n.* jungle **Gac. 4; 15**
semáforo *n.* traffic signal
semana *n.* week **4; fin de semana** weekend; **Semana Santa** Holy Week **18**
semejante *adj.* similar
semejanza *n.* similarity
semestre *n.m.* semester **1, in ex.; 2**
semilla *n.* seed, nut
sencillez *n.f.* simplicity
sencillo *adj.* simple **Gac. 2**
sensible *adj.* sensitive **Sec. A; 17**
sentarse (e > ie) *v.* to sit down **9**
sentido *n.* sense, meaning **16; sentido del humor** sense of humor
sentimiento *n.* emotion, feeling
sentir (e > ie) *v.* to feel; to regret; **lo siento** I'm sorry; **sentirse** *v.* to feel **9**
señal *n.f.* sign, gesture **Sec. B, in ex.**
señalar *v.* to point out **Sec. B**
señor *n.* Mr., sir, gentleman **Sec. B**
señora *n.* Mrs., lady, ma'am **Sec. B**
señores *n.* Mr. and Mrs., gentlemen **Sec. B**
señorita *n.* Miss, young lady **Sec. B**
separación *n.* separation
separar *v.* to separate **Gac. 3**
septiembre *n.* September **4**
séptimo *adj.* seventh **12**
ser *v.* to be **Sec. B; 2; ser humano** human being
serenata *n.* serenade **6, in ex.**
serie *n.f.* series **Gac. 2**
serio *adj.* serious **Sec. B**
serpiente *n.f.* snake
servicio *n.* service **7**
servilleta *n.* napkin **7**
servir (e > i) *v.* to serve **5**
sesenta *adj., n.m.* sixty **1**
setecientos *adj., n.m.* seven hundred **4**
setenta *adj., n.m.* seventy **1**
sexo *n.* sex **12**
sexto *adj.* sixth **12**
si *conj.* if **1**
sí *adv.* yes **1**
sicología *n.* psychology **2**
sicólogo *n.* psychologist **3**
siempre *adv.* always **1**
sierra *n.* mountain chain **Gac. 3**
siesta *n.* nap, siesta **Sec. C; echar (tomar) una siesta** to take a nap
siglo *n.* century **Gac. 1**
significado *n.* meaning **Gac. 2**
significar *v.* to mean, signify **2**

siguiente *adj.* following **Sec. A**
sílaba *n.* syllable
silencio *n.* silence
silencioso *adj.* silent, quiet **12**
silla *n.* chair **Sec. C; 5**
sillón *n.m.* armchair **5**
simpático *adj.* nice **2**
simplemente *adv.* simply **Gac. 4**
sin *prep.* without **1; sin embargo** nevertheless **4; sin falta** without fail, **sin que** *conj.* without **15**
sinagoga *n.* synagogue **16**
sincero *adj.* sincere **18**
sino *conj.* but, rather **Gac. 4**
síntoma *n.m.* symptom **13**
siquiatra *n.m.f.* psychiatrist **Sec. C; 3**
sistema *n.m.* system **1, in ex.**
sitio *n.* place, location **12, in ex.**
situación *n.* situation **2**
situado *adj.* situated, located **Gac. 1**
sobrar *v.* to be left over **Gac. 1**
sobre *prep.* over, about, above, regarding **1; sobre todo** above all **16**
sobre *n.* envelope **12**
sobrepoblación *n.* over-population
sobrepoblado *adj.* over-populated
sobresaliente *adj.* outstanding **2**
sobresalir *v.* to excel
sobrevivir *v.* to survive
sobrino *n.* nephew **4**
sociable *adj.* sociable
sociedad *n.* society **17, in ex.**
sociología *n.* sociology **2**
sociólogo *n.* sociologist **2, in ex.**
sofá *n.* sofa **Sec. A; 5**
sol *n.m.* sun **4; hace sol** it's sunny **4; tomar el sol** to sunbathe **12**
solamente *adv.* only **2**
soldado *n.* soldier **Gac. 5**
soleado *adj.* sunny **15**
soledad *n.* solitude **Gac. 1, 16**
solemne *adj.* solemn **18**
soler (o > ue) *v.* to be in the habit of **7**
solicitar *v.* to solicit, ask for **3**
solicitud *n.f.* application **3**
solo *adj.* alone **5**
sólo *adv.* only **2**
soltero *n.* bachelor **4**
solución *n.* solution **Gac. 2**
solucionar *v.* to solve
sombra *n.* shadow **Gac. 1**
sombrero *n.* hat **9**
someter *v.* to submit, subdue **17**
sonar (o > ue) *v.* to sound, ring
sonido *n.* sound **Gac. 1**
sonreír (e > i) *v.* to smile **14**
sonriente *adj.* smiling
sonrisa *n.* smile
soñar (o > ue) *v.* to dream **3; soñar con** to dream about **3; soñar despierto** to daydream **15**
sopa *n.* soup **7**
soportar *v.* to bear, endure
sorpresa *n.* surprise **6; 18**
sospechar *v.* to suspect **Gac. 5**
sostener (e > ie) *v.* to support, sustain
sótano *n.* basement **5**
su *poss. adj.* his, her, your, their **3**
suave *adj.* soft, mild, gentle
subir *v.* to go up, climb **6, in ex.; 8**
subjuntivo *n.* subjunctive **10, in ex.**
suceder *v.* to happen **18**
suceso *n.* happening, event **Sec. A**
sucio *adj.* dirty **5**
suegra *n.* mother-in-law **4**
suegro *n.* father-in-law **4**
sueldo *n.* salary **3**
suelo *n.* floor **5**
sueño *n.* dream **3; tener sueño** to be sleepy
suerte *n.f.* luck **3; tener suerte** to be lucky; **¡Qué suerte!** What luck! **6**
suéter *n.m.* sweater **Sec. A; 9**
sufrimiento *n.* suffering **Gac. 4**
sufrir *v.* to suffer **13**
sugerencia *n.* suggestion
sugerir (e > ie) *v.* to suggest **11**
Suiza *n.* Switzerland **Gac. 5**
sujeto *n.* subject **15**
sumamente *adv.* extremely **11, in ex.**
sumiso *adj.* submissive
superar *v.* to overcome
supermercado *n.* supermarket **8**
suplicar *v.* to beg
sur *n.m.* south **Gac. 1; 11**
surgir *v.* to appear
suspender *v.* to suspend; to fail
sustantivo *n.* noun **Sec. A**
sustituto *n.* substitute
suyo *poss. adj., pron.* his, her, hers, your, yours, its **17**

T

tabaco *n.* tobacco **Gac. 2**
tal *adv.* so; *adj.* such; **tal vez** perhaps **11**
talentoso *adj.* talented **Sec. B**
talla *n.* size **9**
taller *n.m.* workshop **11**
tamaño *n.* size
también *adv.* also **1**
tambor *n.m.* drum
tampoco *adv.* neither, either **3**
tan *adv.* so, as **12; tan pronto como** *conj.* as soon as **14**
tanque *n.m.* tank **11**
tanto *adj.* so many **12**
tardar (en) *v.* to take time, delay **10**
tarde *n.f.* afternoon **1;** *adv.* late
tarea *n.* homework, task **1; tareas domésticas** housework **5**
tarjeta *n.* card **1, in ex.; tarjeta de crédito** credit card **12; tarjeta postal** postcard **10**
tarta *n.* cake **7**
tasa *n.* rate
taxi *n.m.* taxi **2, in ex.; 12**
taxista *n.* taxi driver
taza *n.* cup **7**
te d.o. *pron.* you **5;** *ind. obj. pron.* to you **6;** *refl. pron.* yourself **9**
té *n.m.* tea **1; 7**
teatro *n.* theatre **Gac. 4**
techo *n.* roof **5**
técnica *n.* technique **16**
tejer *v.* to weave **Gac. 5**
tejido *n.* weaving **Gac. 5**
tela *n.* cloth **Gac. 5**
teléfono *n.* telephone **Sec. A; 6**
telenovela *n.* soap opera **6**
televisión *n.* television **Sec. A**
televisor *n.* television set **5**
tema *n.m.* theme **Gac. 1**
temer *v.* to fear, be afraid of **11; Me lo temía** I was afraid of that **4**
temor *n.* fear **Gac. 5**
temperatura *n.* temperature
tempestad *n.* storm **Gac. 4**
temporada *n.* season **14**
temprano *adj.* early, young; *adv.* early **1**
tenedor *n.m.* fork **7**
tener *v.* to have, possess, hold **3; tener...años** to be...years old **3; tener celos** to be jealous **3; tener cuidado** to be careful **3; tener de todo** to have everything; **tener en cuenta** to keep in mind; **tener ganas de...** to feel like... **3; tener lugar** to take place **14; tener que** + *inf.* to have to **3; tener el número equivocado** to have the wrong number
tenis *n.m.* tennis **Sec. A; 14**
teoría *n.* theory **Gac. 4**
tercer, tercero *adj.* third **12**
terminación *n.* ending **Gac. 6**
terminar *v.* to end, finish **1**
termómetro *n.* thermometer **13**
ternera *n.* veal
ternura *n.* tenderness **Gac. 1**
terremoto *n.* earthquake **Gac. 5**
terrible *adj.* terrible **Sec. A; 10**
tesoro *n.* treasure **Gac. 6**
tía *n.* aunt **4**
tiburón *n.m.* shark **15**
tiempo *n.* tense **1;** time; weather **4; ¿Qué tiempo hace?** What's the weather like? **4**
tienda *n.* store **3; tienda de campaña** tent **15**
tierra *n.* land **Sec. C; 15;** earth
tigre *n.m.* tiger **Sec. A; 15**

timbre *n.m.* stamp **12**
tímido *adj.* timid, shy **2**
tinta *n.* ink **Gac. 4**
tío *n.* uncle **4;** *pl.* aunt and uncle
típico *adj.* typical **14**
tipo *n.* type **1, in ex.**
tirar *v.* to throw, fling **14**
tiras cómicas *n.pl.* comic strips, funnies **6**
título *n.* title, degree **1**
tiza *n.* chalk **Sec. C**
toalla *n.* towel **12**
tobillo *n.* ankle **13**
tocadiscos *n.m. s.* and *pl.* record player
tocar *v.* to touch, play **6**
tocino *n.* bacon
todavía *adv.* still, yet **12**
todo *adj.* all, every **1;** *n.* everything; **toda la noche** all night long **1; todos los días** every day **1; todo el mundo** everyone **10**
tolerante *adj.* tolerant
tomar *v.* to take, drink **1; tomar apuntes** to take notes; **tomar una decisión** to make a decision **3; tomar el sol** to sunbathe; **tomar una siesta** to take a nap **15; tomar una copa** to have a drink **7**
tomate *n.m.* tomato **7**
tontería *n.* foolishness, nonsense **16, in ex.**
tonto *adj.* stupid, silly, foolish
toque *n.m.* touch **Gac. 5**
toro *n.* bull **Sec. C; 18**
torta *n.* cake **7**
tortilla *n.* omelette, tortilla **Sec. C**
tortuga *n.* turtle, tortoise **Gac. 4; 15**
tos *n.f.* cough **13**
toser *v.* to cough **13**
tostado *adj.* toasted
trabajador *n.* worker **3;** *adj.* hard working **2; trabajador social** social worker
trabajar *v.* to work **1**
trabajo *n.* job, work **3; trabajo de medio tiempo** part-time job; **trabajo de tiempo completo** full-time job
tradicional *adj.* traditional **12**
traducción *n.* translation **7**
traducir *v.* to translate **4**
traductor *n.* translator
traer *v.* to bring **4**
tráfico *n.* traffic **6; 11**
trágico *adj.* tragic
trago *n.* gulp; drink **7**
traje *n.m.* suit **9;** outfit; **traje de baño** bathing suit **9**
tranquilidad *n.* tranquility **15**
tranquilo *adj.* tranquil, calm **Sec. A; 12**
trasladar(se) *v.* to move (house), transfer
tratado *n.* treaty **Gac. 4**
tratamiento *n.* treatment **13**
tratar *v.* to treat **6; tratar de** + *inf.* to try; **tratar de** + noun to deal with
trato *n.* deal, pact **14; trato hecho** it's a deal **14**
travieso *adj.* mischievous
trece thirteen **Sec. B**
treinta thirty **1**
tren *n.m.* train, **1, in ex.; 11**
trescientos *adj., n.m.* three hundred **4**
tribu *n.f.* tribe **Gac. 4**
triste *adj.* sad **2**
tristeza *n.* sadness
triunfar *v.* to triumph **15, in ex.; 17**
triunfo *n.* triumph **Gac. 3**
trucha *n.* trout **15, in ex.**
trueno *n.* thunder
tu *poss. adj.* your **3**
tú *subj. pron.* you **Sec. B**
tumba *n.* tomb **Gac. 2**
turista *n.* tourist **Gac. 1; 10**
tuyo *poss. adj., pron.* your, yours **17**

U

u *conj.* or (instead of **o** before words that begin with **o** or **ho) 3**
últimamente *adj.* lately **Gac. 1**
último *adj.* last **Gac. 1; 7; la última vez** the last time **Gac. 3; por último** lastly, finally
un, uno *indef. art., adj., pron.* one **Sec. B;** a, an **Sec. C**
único *adj.* only, sole **7;** unique
unido *adj.* united, close; **los Estados Unidos** the United States
unificar *v.* to unify **Gac. 2**
unión *n.* union **Sec. A**
unir *v.* to join **15**
universidad *n.* university **Sec. A**
universitario *adj.* pertaining to the university **3, in ex.**
urgente *adj.* urgent **13**
usar *v.* to use **1**
uso *n.* use, **in ex.**
usted(es) *sub. pron.* you **Sec. B;** *obj.* of *prep.* you
útil *adj.* useful **1; 17**
utilizar *v.* to use, utilize
uva *n.* grape **8**

V

vaca *n.f.* cow
vacaciones *n.pl.* vacation **Gac. 1; 10**
vacío *adj.* empty **5;** *n.* vacuum
valer *v.* to be worth **7; ¿Cuánto vale?** How much is it worth?
válido *adj.* valid
valientemente *adv.* bravely **15, in ex.**
valioso *adj.* valuable
valor *n.m.* value **Gac. 2**
valle *n.* valley **Gac. 4**
variar *v.* to vary **6, in ex.**
variedad *n.* variety **8**
varios *adj.* various, several **9, in ex.**
varón *n.* male
vasco *n.* Basque
vaso *n.* glass **7**
vecindad *n.* neighborhood
vecino *n.* neighbor **6, in ex.**
veinte twenty **Sec. B**
vejez *n.f.* old age
vela *n.* candle
velo *n.* veil **16, in ex.**
velocidad *n.* velocity, speed **11**
velorio *n.* wake **18**
vencer *v.* to defeat, expire **14**
vendedor *n.* seller, salesman **3**
vender *v.* to sell **2**
venezolano *n., adj.* Venezuelan
venir *v.* to come **3**
venta *n.* sale **9**
ventaja *n.* advantage **5, in ex.**
ventana *n.* window **Sec. C**
ventanilla *n.* (ticket, car, etc.) window **11**
ver *v.* to see **4; a ver** let's see **15; tener que ver con** to have to do with
verano *n.* summer **Gac. 1; 4**
verbo *n.* verb **1**
verdad *n.* truth **10; de verdad** really
verdadero *adj.* true, genuine **10**
verde *adj.* green **2; 4**
verduras *n.pl.* vegetables **7**
vergüenza *n.* shame, embarrassment **3; tener vergüenza** to be ashamed
verificar *v.* to verify
vestíbulo *n.* lobby **12**
vestido *n.* dress **9**
vestir (e > i) *v.* to dress **9; vestirse** *v.* to get dressed
vez *n.f.* time, instance **4; 6; una vez** once; **dos veces** twice **Gac. 5; a veces** at times **17; de vez en cuando** from time to time; **en vez de** instead of **11, in ex.; por primera vez** for the first time **7; tal vez** perhaps **11**
viajar *v.* to travel **10**
viaje *n.m.* trip **10; buen viaje** have a good trip; **de viaje** on a trip; **hacer un viaje** to take a trip
viajero *n.* traveler **10**
víctima *n.* victim
vida *n.* life **4**
vidrio *n.* glass **Gac. 4**
viejo *adj.* old **2;** *n.* old person
viento *n.* wind **4; hace viento** it's windy
viernes *n.m.* Friday **Sec. A**
villancico *n.* Christmas Carol **18**
vinagre *n.m.* vinegar **8**
vino *n.* wine **7**
violín *n.* violin **6**

visita *n.* visit; **hacer una visita** to pay a visit
visitante *n.* visitor
visitar *v.* to visit **Gac. 1; 4**
vista *n.* view **Gac. 3; punto de vista** point of view
vitamina *n.* vitamin **13**
viudo *n.* widow **4**
vivienda *n.* housing, dwelling **5**
vivir *v.* to live **2**
vivo *adj.* alive, lively **Gac. 4**
vocabulario *n.* vocabulary **1**
volar (o > ue) *v.* to fly **10**
volcán *n.m.* volcano **15**
voleibol *n.m.* volleyball **Gac. 3**
voluntad *n.f.* will, wish, desire **Gac. 6**
volver (o > ue) *v.* to return, come back **3; volverse** *v.* to become; **volver a** + *inf.* to do something again **6**
vosotros *subj. pron.* you **Sec. B;** *obj.* of *prep.* you
votar *v.* to vote **Gac. 2; 17**
voz *n.f.* voice **Gac. 4**
vuelo *n.* flight **10**
vuelta *n.* return **6**
vuestro *poss. adj., pron.* your, yours **3**

Y

y *conj.* and **1**
ya *adv.* already, right away **6; ya no** no longer; **ya que** since; **ya veo** I see **16; ya ya** uh huh, uh huh **16**
yo *subj. pron.* I **Sec. B**

Z

zanahoria *n.* carrot **7**
zapatería *n.* shoe store
zapatilla *n.* slipper, sneaker **9**
zapato *n.* shoe **9**
zona *n.* zone **Gac. 1**
zoológico *n.* zoo **Sec. C, in ex.; Gac. 4;** 15

English-Spanish Vocabulary

A

able, to be able poder (o > ue) **3**
about de, sobre **1**
above sobre, arriba **Gac. 1**
absent, to be absent (lacking) faltar **7**
accessories accesorios **5**
accompany acompañar **15**
accountant contador(a) **3**
accounting contabilidad *f.* **2**
acquainted, to be acquainted with conocer (zc) **4**
active activo(a) **14**
actor actor **2, in ex.**
ad anuncio **3**
address *n.* dirección *f.* **Sec. B, in ex.**
advertisement anuncio **3**
advice consejo **9, in ex.**
advise aconsejar **11**
advisor consejero(a) **2**
affection cariño **16**
affectionate cariñoso(a) **16**
afraid, to be afraid (of) tener miedo (de) **3**; **I was afraid of that.** Me lo temía.
after *prep.* **(with time)** después de; *conj.* después (de) que **14**
afternoon tarde *f.*: **Sec. B**: **good afternoon** buenas tardes; **in the afternoon** de/por la tarde **1**
afterwards después **1**
against contra **17**
age edad *f.* **3, in ex.**
agency agencia **3**; **employment agency** agencia de empleos
agent agente **10**
agile ágil *m., f.* **14**
ago, (two years) ago hace (dos años) **6**
agree estar de acuerdo **15**
agreement acuerdo **17; to come to an agreement** llegar a un acuerdo
aggressive agresivo(a) **Sec. A; 17**
air aire *m.* **15**
airplane avión *m.* **10**
airport aeropuerto **Sec. A, in ex.; 10**
all todo(a) **1**
allergic alérgico(a) **13**
alleviate aliviar **13**
allow permitir **7**
almond almendra **7**
alone solo(a) **5**
already ya **6**
also también **1**
although aunque **5**
always siempre **1**
ambitious ambicioso(a) **Sec. B**
ambulance ambulancia **13**
among entre **5**
amuse divertirse (e > ie, i) **9**
and y **1**
ancient antiguo **8, in ex.**
angry furioso(a), enfadado(a), enojado(a) **17; to get angry** enfadarse, enojarse **17**
ankle tobillo **13**
anniversary aniversario **4**
annoy molestar **6**
another otro(a) **2**
answer *v.* contestar **1**; *n.* respuesta **2**
antibiotic antibiótico **Sec. C, in ex.**; **13**
any algún **3**, alguno(a), cualquier(a) **11; not any** ningún, ninguno(a) **3**
anybody alguien; **not anybody** nadie **3**
anyone alguien; **not anyone** nadie **3**
anything, algo; **not anything** nada **3**
appendicitis apendicitis *f.* **13**
apple manzana **8**
appliance aparato **12**
application ***(form)*** solicitud *f.* **3**
apply solicitar **3**
appointment cita **3**
approach acercarse a **Gac. 4**
approve aprobar **11**
April abril *m.* **4**
aquarium acuario **15**
architect arquitecto(a) **3**
Argentine argentino(a) **Sec. B**
arm brazo **13**: **armchair** sillón *m.* **5**
arrival llegada **10**
arrive llegar (gu) **1**
art arte *m.* **Sec. A**; **2**
artist artista *m., f.* **Sec. B**
as como **16; as if** como si... (+ *past subj.);* **as soon as** en cuanto, tan pronto como **14**
ask preguntar **1**; **to ask for** pedir (e > i, i); **to ask a question** hacer una pregunta **6**
asleep, to fall asleep dormirse (o > ue, u) **9**
aspirin aspirina **1, in ex.; 13**
assistance ayuda **6, in ex.**
astronaut *m., f.* astronauta **Sec. B**
at en, a ***(with time)*** **Sec. C; at least** por lo menos **7**
attend asistir (a) **2**
attend to atender (e > ie) **9**
attract atraer **15**
attractive bien parecido(a)
August agosto **4**
aunt tía **4**
author autor(a) **Sec. B**
automobile automóvil **4**
autumn otoño **4**
avoid evitar **8**
awesome chévere **1**

B

baby bebé *m., f* **Sec. C**
bachelor soltero **4**
back espalda **13**
backpack mochila **15**
bacon tocino
bad mal, malo(a) **2; the weather's bad** hace mal tiempo **4; bad taste** mal gusto **8**
badly mal **2**
bag bolsa **9**
baggage equipaje *m.* **10**
bakery panadería **7, in ex.**; **8**
balcony balcón *m.* **12**
ball pelota **14**
balloon globo **15**
baptism bautismo
bargain *v.* regatear **8**, *n.* ganga **7**
baseball béisbol *m.* **3, in ex.**; **14**
baseball player beisbolista *m., f.* **2, in ex.**
basement sótano **5**
basketball básquetbol **m.**, baloncesto **2, in ex.; 14**
bat *v.* batear, *n.* bate **14**
bath baño **5; to take a bath** bañarse **9**
bathe bañar **9**
bathroom baño **5**
bathtub bañera **5**
battery batería **11**
be ser, estar **Sec. B; 2; to be (feel) hungry, thirsty** tener hambre, sed **3; to be . . . years old** tener...años **3**
beach playa **Gac. 1; 12**
bean frijol *m.* **7**
bear oso **15**
beautiful bello(a) **12**
because porque **1**
because of por **2**
become hacerse, ponerse **Gac. 2; 9**
bed cama **5; to go to bed** acostarse (o > ue) **9; to put to bed** acostar (o > ue) **9; to stay in bed** guardar cama **13**
bedroom alcoba, dormitorio **5**
beer cerveza **7**
before *prep.* antes de **1**; *conj.* antes (de) que **14**
begin empezar (e > ie) **3**; comenzar (e > ie)
behave (com)portarse **13**
behavior comportamiento **17**
behind detrás de **Sec. C**
believe (in) creer (e > y) (en) **2**
bellhop botones *m.s.* **12**
belt cinturón *m.* **9**
benefits beneficios **3**
besides además **4**
better mejor **6**

between entre **5**
beverage bebida **7**
bicycle bicicleta **11**
big gran, grande **2**
bike bicicleta **11; to ride a bike** montar (pasear) en bicicleta
bill cuenta **7**
bird pájaro **5**
birth nacimiento **Gac. 1**; **4**
birthday cumpleaños *m.s.* **4**
bit, a little bit un poco **1**
black negro(a) **4**
blackboard pizarra **Sec. C**
blanket manta **5**
blond(e) rubio(a) **2**
blouse blusa **9**
blue azul **4**
blue jeans blue jeans *m.* vaqueros **1, in ex.**; **9**
board abordar **10**
boardinghouse pensión *f.* **12**
boat barco, bote *m.* **11**
boiled hervido(a) **8**
bored aburrido(a) **2**
boring pesado(a), aburrido(a) **2**
boss jefe(a) **3**
bottle botella **4, in ex.**; **8**
box caja **8**
boxer boxeador(a) **14**
boxing boxeo **14**
boy niño **4**
boyfriend novio **4; 16**
bracelet brazalete *m.* **9**
brain cerebro **13**
brake ***(an automobile)*** *v.* frenar **11**; *n.pl.* **brakes** frenos
bread pan *m.* **4**
break romper **8**
breakfast desayuno **4; to have breakfast** desayunar **5**
breathe respirar **13**
brick ladrillo **5, in ex.**
bride novia **4;16**
bring traer **4**
broken roto(a), descompuesto(a) **11**
broom escoba
brother hermano **4**
brother-in-law cuñado **4**
brown pardo(a), café, marrón **4**
brunette moreno(a) **2**
brush cepillo **12**
build construir (i > y) **6**
building edificio **1**
bullfight corrida de toros **Sec. C**
burial entierro **18**
bury enterrar (e > ie) **18**
bus autobús *m.* **11**
bus station estación *f.* de autobuses **11**
bus stop parada de autobús **12**
business comercio, negocio, empresa **3**
businessman (woman) hombre *m.* mujer *f.* de negocios **3**
busy ocupado(a) **6**
but pero **1**
butcher shop carnicería **8**
butter mantequilla **8**
button abrochar **10**
buy comprar **1**
by no means de ninguna manera **4**

C

café café **Sec. A; 7**
cake pastel *m.* torta, tarta (Sp.) **Sec. A; 7**
calculus cálculo **2**
calendar calendario **Sec. C**
call llamar **1**; **be called, named** llamarse **9**
calm tranquilo(a) **Sec. A; 12**
calmness tranquilidad *f.* **15**
camp acampar **15; to go camping** hacer cámping
campus recinto **1**; campus
can *v.* poder (o > ue) **3**; *n.* lata **8**
cancel cancelar **10**
candidate candidato, aspirante *m., f.* **3**
candy dulce *m.* **18**; bombón **(chocolate candy) 8**
car automóvil *m.* carro, coche *m.* **4**
card tarjeta **1, in ex.; credit card** tarjeta de crédito **12**; **playing card** carta **6; post-card** tarjeta postal **10; to play cards** jugar a las cartas **6**
care cuidar **13; to take care of oneself** cuidarse
career carrera **3**
careful ¡Cuidado! **3**, ¡Ojo! **11; to be careful** tener cuidado **3**
carnival carnaval **18**
carrot zanahoria **7**
carry llevar **2**
castle castillo **12**
cat gato **5**
catch a cold resfriarse **13**
Catholic católico(a) **18**
cavity ***(tooth)*** caries *f.* **13**
celebrate celebrar, festejar **Gac. 3**
cemetery cementerio **18**
center centro **Sec. B, in ex.; shopping center** centro comercial **9**; **student center** centro estudiantil **1**
certain cierto(a) **Sec. C**
chair silla **Sec. C; 5**; **armchair** sillón *m.* **5**
chalkboard pizarra **Sec. C**
champion campeón (campeona) **14**
championship campeonato **14**
change cambiar **2**
channel ***(T.V.)*** canal *m.* **4, in ex.**
Chanukah Jánuca **18**
chapter capítulo **2**
charge ***(someone for an item or service)*** cobrar **12**
cheap barato(a) **4**
check *v.* revisar **10; to check baggage** facturar; *n.* cheque *m.* **7**; ***(restaurant)*** cuenta
cheese queso **7**
chemistry química **2**
cherry cereza **8, in ex.**
chicken pollo **7**
child niño(a), hijo(a) **4**
childbirth parto
Chilean chileno(a) **Sec. B**
chocolate chocolate *m.* **2, in ex.; chocolate candy** bombón *m.* **8**
choose elegir (e > i), escoger **5**
chore tarea, faena **1**
Christian cristiano(a) **18**
Christmas Navidad *f.* **4, in ex.; 18; Christmas Eve** Nochebuena **4, in ex.; 18; Christmas carol** villancico **18**; **Merry Christmas!** ¡Feliz Navidad! **18**
church iglesia **16**
cigar cigarro, puro **2, in ex.**
circus circo **15**
city ciudad *f.* **Sec. B**
class clase *f.* **Sec. B; first class** primera clase **10**; **tourist class** clase turística
classmate compañero(a) de clase **1**
clean *v.* limpiar **5;** *adj.* limpio(a)
cleaner (vacuum cleaner) aspiradora **5**
climate clima *m.* **9, in ex.**
climb escalar ***(mountains);*** subir **15**
clock reloj *m.* **1**
close *v.* cerrar (e > ie) **3**; prep. **close to** cerca de
closed cerrado(a) **9**
clothes closet armario, ropero **5**
clothing ropa **5**
cloudy nublado(a) **15**
clown payaso **15**
coach entrenador(a) **14**
coat abrigo **9**
coffee café *m.* **Sec. A; coffee shop** café
cold frío **3; It's cold (weather).** Hace frío **4**; **to be cold** tener frío **to catch a cold** resfriarse **13**; catarro **13**
Colombian colombiano(a) **Sec. B**
color color *m.* **4**
combat combatir **17**
come venir **3**
comfortable cómodo(a) **9**
comic strip tiras cómicas **6**
common común **Sec. B**; **10**
compact disc disco compacto *m.* **5**
company compañía **3**
compete competir (e > i, i) **5**
competition competencia **15**
complain (about) quejarse (de) **13**

computer computadora *(L.A.)* ordenador *m. (Sp.)* **Sec. B; 1**
computer science computación *f.*
conditioning ***(air conditioning)*** aire acondicionado *m.* **12**
condolence pésame *m.* **18; my most sincere condolences** mi más sincero pésame
confirm confirmar **10**
confront enfrentarse con **14**
congested congestionado(a) **13**
congratulations ¡felicidades!, ¡felicitaciones! **6**
conjunction conjunción **14**
conservative conservador(a) **Sec. A**
consist of consistir en **2**
contaminated contaminado(a) **15**
content contento(a) **2**
continue seguir (e > i, i) **5**
cook *v.* cocinar **5**; *n.* cocinero(a)
cooked cocido(a)
cookie galleta **8**
cool ***(weather)*** fresco **4; It's cool.** Hace fresco.
cooperate cooperar **17**
corn maíz *m.* **7**
correct correcto(a) **4**
cost costar (o > ue) **3**
costume disfraz *m.* **18**
cotton algodón *m.* **9**
cough *v.* toser **13**; *n.* tos *f.* **13; cough syrup** jarabe *m.*
country país m., nación *f.* **7; 10; countryside** campo **4**
course curso **5, in ex.**
court ***(tennis)*** cancha **14**
courteous cortés **16**
courtship noviazgo **16**
cousin primo(a) **4**
crash into chocar con **11**
craziness locura **16**
crazy loco(a) **16**
cream ***(ice cream)*** helado **4**
credit card tarjeta de crédito **12**
cross *v.* cruzar **Gac. 4**; *n.* cruz *f.*
cry llorar **4**
cucumber pepino **8**
cup taza **7**
cure curar **8, in ex.**; cura *n. f.* **13**
currency moneda **Gac. 4**
curtain cortina
custard flan *m.* **7**
customs ***(traditions)*** costumbres *f.* **7; *(duty)*** aduana **Gac. 2**
cyclist ciclista *m., f.* **Gac. 1; 14**

D

dad papá *m.* **4**
dance bailar **1**
dancer bailarín *m.* **Gac. 3;** bailarina *f.*
danger peligro **13**
dark oscuro(a) **9**
date ***(appointment)*** cita **3; *(calendar)*** fecha **4; make a date** citar
daughter hija **4**
day día *m.* **1; day after tomorrow** pasado mañana; **day before yesterday** anteayer; **every day** todos los días **1; Day of the Dead** Día de los Muertos; **Saint's Day** Día del Santo; **(Epiphany) Kings' Day** Día de los Reyes Magos (epifanía) **18**
day care center guardería infantil **17**
daydream soñar despierto(a) **15**
dead *adj.* muerto(a) **18; Day of the Dead** Día de los Muertos
dean decano **2**
dear ***(term of affection)*** querido(a) **6, in ex.; 16**
death muerte *f.* **Gac. 1; 4; death of the bull in a bullfight** faena **17**
December diciembre *m.* **4**
decide decidir **2**
deep hondo(a) **13**
defeat vencer (z) **14**
delay tardar **10**
delicious delicioso(a) , sabroso(a) , rico(a) **7**
delighted encantado(a) **Sec. B**
dentist dentista **Sec. C**
deny negar (e > ie) (gu) **3**
department store almacén *m.* **3**
departure salida **10**
desert desierto **15**
deserve merecer (zc)
desire desear **1**
desk escritorio **Sec. C; front desk *(hotel)*** recepción *f.*
dessert postre *m.* **4**
destined for con destino a **10**
destroy destruir (y) **6**
develop desarrollar **14**
development desarrollo **14**
dictionary diccionario **Sec. C**
die morir (o > ue, u) **3**
diet régimen *m.;* **to follow a diet** seguir un régimen; **to be on a diet** ester a dieta **8**
difficult difícil **2**
dining room comedor *m.* **5**
dinner cena **4; to have, eat dinner** cenar **5**
dirty sucio(a) **5**
disappointment desilusión **1**
discriminate discriminar **17**
discrimination discriminación *f.* **Gac 2; 17**
dish plato **7**
dishwasher lavaplatos *m.* s. **5**
divorce divorcio **16**
do hacer **1**
doctor ***(medical)*** médico(a) **3**
dog perro(a) **5**
door puerta **Sec. C**
doorman portero **12**
dormitory residencia **1**
dot ***(with time)*** **on the dot** en punto **1**
doubt dudar **10**; *n. f.* duda
downtown centro **Sec. B, in ex.**
dozen docena **8**
draw dibujar **6**
dream *n.* sueño, *v.* soñar **3**
dress *v.* vestir (e > i, i), *n.* vestido **9**
dressing room probador *m.* **9**
drink *v.* beber, tomar **1; 2;** *n.* bebida **7**
drive manejar, conducir **4**
driver conductor(a) **11**
drugstore farmacia **13**
dry secar **5**
dryer ***(clothes dryer)*** secadora **5**
during durante **8**
duty deber **17**

E

each cada **5**
ear oreja **13; inner ear** oído **13**
early temprano **1**
earn ganar **3**
earring arete *m.* **9**
east este *m.* **11**
Easter Pascua (Florida) **18**
easy fácil **2**
eat comer **2; eat breakfast** desayunar **5; eat lunch** almorzar (o > ue) **3; eat supper** cenar **5**
economical económico(a) **9**
education educación *f.* **1**
egg huevo **8**
eight ocho **Sec. B**
eighteen dieciocho **Sec. B**
eighth octavo(a) **12**
eighty ochenta **1**
either o **3; not either** tampoco
elect elegir (e > i) **5**
elegant elegante **Sec. A; 9**
elephant elefante *m.* **Sec. A; 15**
elevator ascensor, elevador *m.* **12**
eleven once **Sec. B**
embarrassed avergonzado(a)
employee empleado(a) **3**
employment empleo **3**
empty vacío(a) **5**
enchant encantar **7**
energy energía **3, in ex.**
engagement compromiso, noviazgo **16**
engineer ingeniero(a) **Gac. 6**
English *n., adj.* inglés *m.,* inglesa *f.* **4, in ex.; English language** inglés *m.*
enjoy gozar de (+ *inf.)* **7; to enjoy oneself** divertirse (e > ie) **9**
enroll ingresar
enter entrar (en, a) **2**
entertain divertir (e > ie, i) **9**
enthusiast aficionado(a) **14**
entrance entrada **10**

envious envidioso(a) **16**
environment ambiente *m.* **15**
Eve, Christmas Eve Nochebuena **4, in ex.; 18; New Year's Eve** Noche vieja **18**
evening tarde *f.*, noche *f.* **1; in the evening** de/por la tarde, noche
every *adj.* cada, todo(a) **5; every day** todos los días **1**
exaggerate exagerar **6, in ex.**
exam examen *m.*, prueba **Sec. A**
example ejemplo **7; for example** por ejemplo
excellent excelente **Sec. A**
except excepto, menos **5**
excited entusiasmado(a) **14**
exciting emocionante **Gac. 1**
excursion excursión *f.* **10**
excuse me perdón ***(to apologize)*** **Sec. B**; con permiso ***(to get through)***
exercise *v.* hacer ejercicios **5, in ex.**; *n.* ejercicio
expect esperar **4**
expense gasto **11**
expensive caro(a) **4**
experience experiencia **3**
explain explicar (qu) **6, ex.**
eye ojo **Gac. 1; 13**

F

fabulous fabuloso(a) **18**
faculty profesorado **2**
fail fracasar **16**
failure fracaso **14**
fall caer **8, in ex.; 11; to fall asleep** dormirse **9; to fall down** caerse; **fall in love with** enamorarse de **16**; *n.* ***(season)*** otoño **4**
family *n.* familia **4**; *adj.* familiar
famous famoso(a) **Sec. B**
fan aficionado(a) **14**
fantastic fantástico(a) **Sec. A**
far (from) lejos (de) **5**
fat gordo(a) **2**
father padre *m.* **4**
February febrero **4**
feel sentirse (e > ie, i) **9; to feel cold, warm, (hot)** tener frío, calor **3; to feel like *(doing something)*** tener ganas de *(+ inf.)* **3; to feel sorry** sentir (e > ie, i) **9**
fees, registration fees matrícula **1**
ferocious feroz **15**
fever fiebre *f.* **13**
fiancé(e) novio(a) **4; 16**
field, playing field campo **1**
fifteen quince **Sec. B**
fifth quinto(a) **12**
fifty cincuenta **1**
fight luchar, pelear **16**
fill (up) llenar **11; to fill out *(a form)*** llenar
filled relleno(a)
finally finalmente, por fin **Sec. A; 7**
find encontrar (o > ue) **3**
fine *n.* multa **11**; *adv.* (muy) bien; **It's fine.** Está bien. **Sec. B**
finish terminar, acabar **1**
first *n.* primero **4**; *adj.* primer, primero(a)
fish *(alive)* pez *m.* (*pl.* peces) **15**; ***(prepared as food)*** pescado; *v.* pescar **7**
five cinco **Sec. B**
fix arreglar **5;**
flashy llamativo(a) **9**
flavor sabor *m.* **Gac. 1**
flexible flexible **17**
flight vuelo **10**
flight attendant aeromozo(a) **10**
flirt coqueta **17**
floor suelo **5 *(building)*** piso; **ground floor** planta baja
follow seguir (e > i, i) (g) **5**
food comida **4; food** alimento **7**
foolish tonto(a) **17**
foot pie *m.* **13**
football fútbol norteamericano *m.* **Sec. A; 14**
for para **2**; por; **for example** por ejemplo **7**
forbid prohibir **11**
forbidden prohibido(a) **8, in ex.**
forget olvidar **5; to forget (about)** olvidarse (de)
fork tenedor *m.* **7**
formal formal **8**
forty cuarenta **1**
four cuatro **Sec. B**
four hundred cuatrocientos **4**
fourteen catorce **Sec. B**
fourth cuarto(a) **12**
free libre **10; free of charge** gratis
freeway autopista **11**
French *n., adj.* francés m., francesa *f.* **2; French language** francés *m.*
frequently con frecuencia **1**
fresh fresco(a) **4**
Friday viernes *m.* **Sec. A**
fried frito(a) **Sec. A; 7**
friend amigo(a) **1**
friendship amistad *f.* **16**
from de **1**
front, in front of delante de **Sec. C**
fruit fruta **8**
full lleno(a) **5**
function funcionar **12**
funny chistoso(a), gracioso(a) **15**
fur piel *f.* **9**
furniture muebles *m.pl.* **5**

G

gallon galón *m.*
game *(card, board)* juego **6; *(match)*** partido **14**
garage garaje *m.* **5**
garlic ajo **7**
gas gasolina **11; *(heating)*** gas *m.;* **gas station** gasolinera, estación de gasolina *f.*
gasoline gasolina **11**
German *n., adj.* alemán *m.*, alemana *f.* **2; German language** alemán *m.*
get *(obtain)* conseguir (e > i, i) (g) **5; get down (from)** bajar (de) **9; to get off (of)** bajar (de) **9; to get on *(a vehicle)*** subir (a) **9; to get up** levantarse **9**
gift regalo **4**
girl niña **4**
girlfriend novia **4; 16**
give dar **4; to give *(as a gift)*** regalar
glass vaso **7; wine glass** copa
glasses *(prescription)* gafas **12**
glove guante *m.* **9**
go ir **1**; **let's go to** vamos a; **to be going to *(do something)*** ir a (+ *inf.*) **1; to go away** irse **9; to go home** regresar a casa; **to go on vacation** ir de vacaciones **10; to go out** salir **4; to go to *(attend)*** asistir a **2; to go up** subir a **9**
God Dios *m.* **1**
gold oro **Gac. 1; 9**
golf golf *m.* **14**
good *adv.* bien **1**; *adj.* buen, bueno(a); **good afternoon/evening** buenas tardes **Sec. B**; **good evening/night** buenas noches **Sec. B; good morning** buenos días **Sec. B; It's good weather**. Hace buen tiempo. **4; good appetite** buen provecho **7; good taste** buen gusto **8; good trip** buen viaje **10; my goodness** caramba **1**
good-bye adiós **Sec. B; to say good-bye (to)** despedirse (e > i, i) (de)
good-looking guapo(a) **2**
gossip *n.* chisme *m. v.* chismear **5**
grade *(academic)* note **2; grade school teacher** maestro(a)
granddaughter nieta **4**
grandfather abuelo **4**
grandmother abuela **4**
grandparents abuelos **4**
grandson nieto **4**
grape uva **8**
gratuitous gratuito(a) **10**
gray gris **4**
great gran, grande **2**
great grandparents bisabuelos
green verde **4**
greet saludar **Sec. B**
grief dolor *m.* **13**
grill parrilla
groceries comestibles *m.pl.*
groom novio **16**
group grupo **2, in ex.**
grow crecer **4**
guest huésped(a) **12**

guide *n.* guía *m., f.* **10; guide book** guía *n.f.* **tour guide** guía turístico
guitar guitarra **6**
gymnasium gimnasio **1**

H

haggle regatear **8**
hair pelo **4**
hairdresser peluquero(a)
half medio(a) **8**; *n.* mitad; **It's half past *(time)*** Son las ***(give the hour)*** y media **1**
hall pasillo **10**; aisle
ham jamón *m.* **8**
hamburger hamburguesa **Sec. A; 8**
hand mano *f.* **Sec. B, in ex.; 13**
handsome guapo(a) **2**
hang colgar (o > ue) **6**
happen suceder **18**
happiness alegría **1**
happy alegre, contento(a), feliz *(pl.* felices) **2**
hardly apenas **13**
hard-working trabajador(a) **3**
hat sombrero **9**
hate odiar ***16***
have tener, haber **13; to have a good time** divertirse (e > ie, i) **9; to have just *(done something)*** acabar de (+ *inf.)* **1; to have to *(do something)*** tener que (+ *inf.)* **3**; **to have something to *(say, do)*** tener algo que *(decir, hacer)*
head cabeza **13**
health salud *f.* **13**
healthy sano(a) **Sec. A; 7**
hear oír **4**
heart corazón *m.* **13**
heaven cielo **15**
heavy pesado(a) **6; 8**
hello hola **Sec. B**; ***(phone)*** ¿aló?, ¿bueno(a)?, ¿diga?, ¿dígame? **6**
help *v.* ayudar **2**; *n.* ayuda **6, in ex.**
her *(possessive)* su(s) **3**
here aquí **1**
hi hola **Sec. B**
high alto(a) **Guía 1; 2**
high school escuela secundaria **1**
highway carretera, autopista **11**
his *(poss.)* su(s) **3**
history historia **2**
hitchhike hacer autostop **11**
hockey hockey *m.*
home casa, hogar **Sec. B; 5; at home** en casa
homework tarea **1**
honeymoon luna de miel **16**
hood *(car)* capó **11, in ex.**
hope *v.* esperar **4; I hope that** Ojalá que *(+ subj.)* **11**
horror horror **Sec. A**
horse caballo **14; to ride a horse** montar a caballo
hot *adj.* caliente **7; It's hot *(weather.)*** Hace calor. **4; to be/feel hot** tener calor **3**
hot dog perro caliente *m.* **8**
hotel hotel *m.* **Sec. A; 12**
hour hora **1**
house casa **Sec. B; 5**
housewife ama de case **17**
how? ¿cómo? **Sec. B; How are you?** ¿Cómo está(s)?, ¿Qué tal? **Sec. B; how many?** ¿cuántos (as)? **Sec. B; how much?** ¿cuánto(a)? **Sec. B**
hug *v.* abrazar **16**; *n.* abrazo
hungry, to be hungry tener hambre **3**
hurry, to be in a hurry tener prisa **3**
hurt doler (o > ue) **13**; *adj.* herido(a) **13**, lastimado(a) **14**
husband esposo **4**

I

ice cream helado **4**
if si **1**
illness enfermedad *f.* **13**
illusion ilusión *f.* **Gac. 5**
immediately en seguida **8**
importance importancia **4, in ex.**
important *adj.* importante **Sec. A; to be important** importar **7**
improve mejorarse **14**
in en **Sec. C; in (the morning, evening)** de/por (la mañana, la noche) **1**
inexpensive barato(a) **4**
information información *f.* **Sec. B**
inquire preguntar **1**
insist *(on doing something)* insistir (en + *inf.)* **11**
instead of en vez de **11, in ex.**
intelligent inteligente **Sec. B**; **2**
intend pensar (e > ie) (+ *inf.)* **3**
interesting interesante **2; to be interesting to *(someone)*** interesarle a *(uno)* **7**
interview v. entrevistar **3**; *n.* entrevista
invite invitar **4**
iron *v.* planchar **5**; *n.* plancha
Italian *n., adj.* italiano(a) **2; Italian language** italiano
itinerary itinerario **12**

J

jacket chaqueta **9**
January enero **4**
jealous estar celoso(a) **16**; tener celos **3**
jealousy celos *m.* **16**
jeans blue jeans *m.* vaqueros **1, in ex.; 9**
Jew judío(a) **18**
Jewish judío(a) **18**
job trabajo, puesto **3**
joke chiste *m.* **4**
journalist periodista *m., f.* **3**
judge juez *m., f.* **Sec. C; 3**
juice jugo, zumo *(Sp.)* **7**
July julio **4**
June junio **4**
jungle selva **Gac. 4; 15**
just, to have just *(done something)* acabar de (+ *inf.)* **1**

K

ketchup salsa de tomate **8**
key llave *f.* **12**
kilogram kilogramo
kilometer kilómetro **Gac. 1**
kind simpático(a), amable **2**
king rey **Gac. 1; Kings' Day (Epiphany)** Día de los Reyes Magos (epifanía) **4; 18**
kiosk quiosco **12**
kiss *v.* besar **Sec. B; 16;** *n.* beso **16**
kitchen cocina **5**
knapsack mochila **15**
knee rodilla **13**
knife cuchillo **7**
know *(a fact, how to)* saber **4; *(someone, to be acquainted with)*** conocer (zc)

L

laboratory laboratorio **1**
laborer obrero(a) **3**
lacking, to be lacking faltar **7**
ladder escalera **12**
lake lago **15**
lamp lámpara
land tierra **Gac. 3; 15**
landscape paisaje *m.* **11**
language lengua, idioma m; lenguaje *m.* **2**
large grande **2**
last *v.* durar; *adj.* ***(in time)*** pasado(a) **Gac. 1;** ***(in sequence)*** último(a), **at last** por fin **7**;
last night anoche **6**; **last name** apellido **4**
late *adj.* atrasado(a) **10**, *adv.* tarde **1**
later después **1; see you later** hasta luego **Sec. B**
latest último(a) **Gac. 1**; **7**
laugh (at) reírse (e i, > i) (de) **4**
laundry lavandería **12**
law ley *f.* **Gac. 2**
lawyer abogado(a) **3**
lazy perezoso(a) **2**
learn aprender **2**
least, at least por lo menos **7**
leather cuero **9**
leave irse, salir **9; to leave** dejar ***(behind)*** **3**
left, on/to the left a la izquierda **10**
leg pierna **13**
lemon limón *m.* **Sec. A; 8**
lend prestar **6**
lesson lección *f.* **1**
letter *(correspondence)* carta **6**

lettuce lechuga **7**
liberal liberal **Sec. A; 17**
liberated liberado(a) **17**
librarian bibliotecario(a)
library biblioteca **1**
license licencia **11; driver's license** licencia de conducir
life vida **4**
lifeguard salvavidas *m., f.*
lift levantar **9**
light *n.* luz *f. (pl.* luces) **Sec. C**; *adj.* ligero(a) **8**; ***(color)*** claro(a) **9**
like gustar **7; Do you like . . . ?** ¿Te (le) gusta(n)?; **No, I don't like . . .** No, no me gusta(n); **Yes, I like . . .** Sí, me gusta(n); **like that** *adv.* así **16**
likeable simpático(a) **2**
lips labios **13**
listen (to) escuchar **1**
liter litro **8**
little *adj.* poco(a) **1**; *adv.* poco; **a little bit** un poquito **11, in ex.**
live vivir **2**
living room sala **5**
lobby vestíbulo **12**
lobster langosta **8**
lodge alojarse **12**
long largo(a) **4**
look, to look at mirar **1; to look for** buscar (qu) **1**
lose perder (e > ie) **3; lose weight** adelgazar **8**
lot, a lot *adv.* mucho **1; a lot of** *adj.* mucho(a)
love *v.* amar **1, in ex.; 16;** querer (e > ie) **3**; *n.* amor *m.* **6; 16**
lovely bello(a) **12**
luck suerte *f.* *3*
luggage equipaje *m.* **10**
lunch almuerzo **4; to have, eat lunch** almorzar (o > ue) (c) **3**
lungs pulmones *m.* **13**

M

machine máquina **1**, aparato **12**; **washing machine** lavadora **5**
macho *adj.* machista **17**; machismo *n.*
magazine revista **6**
maid criada **12**
mailbox buzón *m.* **12**
make hacer **1; make fun of** burlarse de **18**
male macho
mall, shopping mall centro comercial **9**
man hombre *m.* **Sec. C**
manager gerente *m., f.* **3**
many muchos(as) **1**
map mapa *m.* **Sec. C**
March marzo **4**
market mercado **8**
marriage matrimonio **16**
married casado(a) **4**
marry casarse (con) **16**
masculinity masculinidad *f.* **17**
match ***(game)*** partido **14**
maternal materno(a) **17**
mathematics matemáticas **2**
matter *v.* **It doesn't matter (to me) (at all).** No (me) importa (nada). **7**
mature maduro(a) **16**
maturity madurez *f.*
May mayo **4**
mayonnaise mayonesa **8**
meal comida **4**
mean antipático(a) **2**
meat carne *f.* **7**
mechanic mecánico(a) **3**
medicine medicina **2**; **13**
meet ***(for the first time)*** conocer **3; *(at a predetermined place)*** reunirse **16**
memory ***(remembrance)*** recuerdo; ***(computer)*** memoria **18, in ex.**
menu menú *m.*, lista, carta **7**
Mexican *n., adj.* mexicano(a) **2**
Mexican-American mexicanoamericano(a) **Sec. B**
milk leche *f.* **7**
milkshake batido
minute minuto **1**; **free minute** rato libre **14**
mirror espejo **5**
mischievous travieso(a) **12**
miss señorita (Srta.) **Sec. B**
modern moderno(a) **Gac. 1**
mom mamá **4**
moment momento **6**; **at this very moment** en este momento
Monday lunes *m.* **Sec. A**
money dinero **1**; ***(currency)*** moneda
month mes *m.* **4**
more más **1; more or less** más o menos **10**
morning mañana **1; good morning** buenos días **Sec. B; in the morning** de/por la mañana **1**
mosquito mosquito **Sec. A**
mother madre *f.* **4**
motor motor *m.* **11**
motorcycle motocicleta **11**
mountain montaña **15**
mouth boca **13**
movie película **Gac. 1; movie theater** cine *m.* **6; movies** cine *m.*
Mr. señor (Sr.) **Sec. B**
Mrs. señora (Sra.) **Sec. B**
much *adj.* mucho(a) **1**; *adv.* mucho; **too much** demasiado
museum museo **7, in ex.; 13**
music música **2**
must deber (+ *inf.*) **2**
mustard mostaza **8**
my ***(possessive)*** mi(s) **3**

N

name nombre *m.* **Sec. B; last name** apellido; **My name is . . .** Me llamo... **Sec. B**; **What's your name?** ¿Cómo se (te) llama(s)? **Sec. B; nickname** apodo **Gac. 5**
named, to be named llamarse **9**
napkin servilleta **7**
nation país *m.* **Sec. C;** nación *f.*
national nacional **12**
nature naturaleza **4, in ex.**; **15**
nauseated mareado(a) **13**
near (to) *prep.* cerca de **5**
nearly casi **5, in ex.**
neat ***(orderly)*** ordenado(a) **5**
necessary necesario(a) **10; it is necessary** es necesario, es preciso; hay que (+ *inf.)*
neck cuello **13**
need necesitar **1**
neighbor vecino(a) **6, in ex.**
neighborhood barrio **4**
neither tampoco **3**
nephew sobrino **4**
nervous nervioso(a)
net red *f.* **14**
never jamás, nunca **3**
new nuevo(a) **3**
newspaper periódico **3**; diario
newlywed *adj., n.* recién casado(a) **16**
next *adj.* ***(in time)*** próximo(a) **14**; ***(in order)*** siguiente **Sec. B;** *adv.* luego **2**
nice simpático(a) **2**, amable **11; nice-looking** bien parecido(a), guapo(a) **2**
niece sobrina **4**
night noche *f.* **1; at night** de/por la noche **1; last night** anoche **6**; *adj.* nocturno(a)
nine nueve **Sec. B**
nine hundred novecientos **4**
nineteen diecinueve **Sec. B**
ninety noventa **1**
ninth noveno(a) **12**
no *adv.* no **Sec. A**; *adj.* ningún, ninguno(a); **no one** *pron.* nadie **3; no way** ni modo **4**
nobody nadie **3**
nocturnal nocturno(a) **Gac. 1; 12**
noise ruido **11**
noisy ruidoso(a) **11**
none ningún, ninguno(a) **3**
noon mediodía *m.* **1**
nor ni **3**
north norte *m.* **11**
nose nariz *f.* **13**
not no **3; not any** ningún, ninguno(a); **not anybody** nadie; **not anything** nada; **not at all** no... nada; **not a chance** ni hablar **4; not only . . . but also** no sólo . . . sino también **6**
nothing nada **3**
notice aviso **1**
November noviembre *m.* **4**

now ahora **1; right now** ahora mismo, en este momento **1**
number número **Sec. B; phone number** número de teléfono **Sec. B; dial a number** marcar un número; **wrong number** el número equivocado **6**
nurse enfermero(a) **13**
nut nuez *f.* **8**

O

obey obedecer (zc)
obituaries obituarios **6**
oblige obligar **17**
obtain conseguir (e > i) **5**
occupied ocupado(a) **6**
October octubre *m.* **4**
of de **1**
of course ¡Claro!, ¡Cómo no!, desde luego **4**
offer ofrecer (zc) **4**
office oficina **6**; ***(medical)*** consultorio **13**
often a menudo **1**
oil aceite *m.* **7**
okay, It's okay. Está bien. **Sec. B**
old viejo(a) **2**, antiguo(a) **8, in ex.**
older mayor **4**
olive aceituna *m.* **7**
once una vez **8**
one un, uno(a) **Sec. B**
one hundred cien **1**
onion cebolla **7**
only *adv.* sólo **2**; solamente
open abrir **2**
open(ed) *adj.* abierto(a) **9; open-air market** mercado al aire libre **8**
operate usar **5, in ex.; *(machine)*** manejar; ***(medical)*** operar **13**
operation *(medical)* operación *f.* **Sec. A**
operator operador(a) **6**; telefonista *m., f.*
oppose oponerse a **17**
optimistic optimista *m., f.* **Gac. 1; 14**
or o **3**
orange *n.* naranja **Gac. 1; 8**; *adj.* anaranjado(a) **4**
orchestra orquesta **Gac. 2; 16**
order *v.* mandar **11**, pedir (e > i, i) **5**; *prep.* **in order to** para **1**
orderly ordenado(a) **5**
other adj. otro(a) **2**; *pron.* **others** los demás **17**
ought deber (+ *inf.*) **2**
our *(poss.)* *adj.* nuestro(a)(s) **3**
outside *adv.* afuera **5**
oven horno **5**
overcast nublado(a)

P

pack, to pack one's suitcases hacer las maletas **10**
package paquete *m.* **10**
pain dolor *m.* **13**
paint pintar **6**
painting pintura, cuadro **5**
pair par *m.* **9**
palace palacio **Gac. 1**
pale pálido(a) **13**
panoramic panorámico(a) **15**
pants pantalones *m. pl.* **9**
paper papel *m.* **1**
pande desfile *m.* **18**
pardon perdón *m.* **Sec. 2; pardon me** perdóneme, discúlpeme
parents padres *m. pl.* **4**
park *v.* estacionar(se), aparcar **11**; *n.* parque *m.* **15**
part parte *f.* **Gac. 1; 10**
party fiesta **1; to give a party** hacer (dar) una fiesta
pass pasar **1**
passage *(ticket)* pasaje *m.* **10**
passenger pasajero(a) **10**
passive pasivo(a) **Sec. A; 17**
passport pasaporte *m.* **10**
past *adj.* pasado(a) **Gac. 1**
pastime pasatiempo **6**
pastry pastel *m.* **Sec. A; 7; pastry shop** pastelería **4, in ex.; 8**
paternal paterno(a) **17**
patient *adj.* paciente **Sec. C**; *n.* paciente *m., f.* **13**
patio patio **Sec. A; 5**
pay pagar (gu) **1**
peace paz *f.* **15**; **to make peace** hacer las paces **16**
peas guisantes *m. pl.* **7**
pen bolígrafo **Sec. C**; pluma
pencil lápiz *m.* **Sec. C**
people gente *f.* **3**
pepper *(spice)* pimienta **7; *(vegetable)*** pimiento
performance *(show)* función *f.* **4**
perhaps tal vez, quizá(s) **11**
permit permitir **7**
person persona *f.* **Sec. A**
pet mascota
pharmacist farmacéutico(a) **13**
phenomenal fenomenal **Sec. B**
photograph foto *f.* **4; to take pictures** sacar (qu) fotos
piano piano **6**
picture foto *f.* **4; to take pictures** sacar (qu) fotos
pie pastel *m.* **Sec. A; 7**
pill pastilla, píldora **13**
pink rosa **4**
pitcher *(baseball)* lanzador(a) **14**
place *v.* poner **4**; *n.* lugar *m.* **4; to take place** tener lugar **14**
plate plato **7**
platform andén *m.* **11**
play *(instrument)* tocar **6; *(sport)*** jugar **3; play cards** jugar a las cartas (naipes) **6**
player jugador(a) **Gac. 2; 14**
please por favor **Sec. B**
pleasing, to be pleasing gustar **7**
plumber plomero(a)
police officer policía *m.* **Sec. C; 1**
polluted contaminado(a) **15**
pool, swimming pool piscina **12**
poor pobre **2**
pork cerdo **8**
post office correo **12**
postcard tarjeta postal **10**
potato papa, patata **8; French fried potatos** papas fritas; **potato chips** papitas **8**
practice *v.* practicar **1**
pray rezar **18**
precious precioso(a) **Gac. 4**
pregnant embarazada **Guía 1**
prejudice prejucio **17**
prepare preparar **1**
prescribe recetar **13**
prescription receta; **7**
present *v.* presentar **1**; *n.* regalo
press prensa
pretty bonita, guapa **2**
priest cura, sacerdote *m., f.* **18**
produce producir **4**
profession profesión *f.*, carrera **3**
professor profesor(a) **Sec. A; 1**
prohibit prohibir **11**
promotion ascenso **3, ex.**
Protestant protestante **18**
provided (that) *conj.* con tal (que) **15**
provoke provocar **16, in ex.; 17**
psychiatrist (p)siquiatra *m., f.* **3**
psychologist (p)sicólogo(a) **3**
psychology (p)sicología **2**
pure puro(a) **15**
purple morado(a) **4**
purse bolso **9**
put poner **4; to put into** meter **Gac. 1; 10; to put on *(clothing)*** ponerse **9**

Q

quarter, It's a quarter after Son las ***(time)*** y cuarto **1**
question pregunta **1; *(matter)*** cuestión *f.* **1; to ask a question** hacer una pregunta **6**
quit dejar **3**

R

rabbi rabino(a) *m., f.* **18**
racket raqueta **14**
radio radio *f.* **1, in ex.; 5**
rain *v.* llover **3**; *n.* lluvia **16**
raincoat impermeable *m.* **9**
raise levantar **9**; ***(a family)*** criar **17**
rapidly rápido **2, in ex.**

raw crudo(a) **8**
read leer **2**
reality realidad *f.* **Sec. A; 16**
really de verdad **17, in ex.**
receive recibir **2**
recommend recomendar (e > ie) **3**
red rojo(a) **4**
refrigerator refrigerador *m.*, nevera **5**
register registro
regret sentir (e > ie, i) **9**
relative pariente *m.* **Sec. A; 4**
relax relajar **12**
religion religión *f.* **Sec. A; 18**
religious religioso(a) **Gac. 4; 18**
remain quedarse **9**
remember recorder (o > ue) **3**; acordarse (o > ue) de
remove quitar **9**
rent *v.* alquilar **5**; *n.* alquiler *m.* **5**
repair *v.* arreglar **5; repair shop** taller *m.* **11**
repeat repetir (e > i, i) **5**
reporter reportero(a)
Republican republicano(a) **2, in ex.**
requirement requisito
resemble parecerse a **9**
reservation *f.* reservación, reserve **10**
reserve reservar **10**
resign renunciar **3**
resolve resolver **16**
rest descansar **11; the rest** los demás **17**
restaurant restaurante *m.* **Sec. A; 7**
résumé currículum (vitae) *m.* **3**
return regresar **1**; volver (o > ue) **3; to return (something)** devolver (o > ue) **3**
review repasar **2**
rice arroz *m.* **7**
rich rico(a) **2**
ride, to ride a bike montar (pasear) en bicicleta; **to ride a horse** montar a caballo **14**
right *n.* ***(political)*** derecho; *adj.* derecho(a); **on/to the right of** a la derecha de **10; right?** ¿verdad?, ¿no?; **right now** ahora mismo, en este momento, en la actualidad **1; to be right** tener razón **3**
rigid rígido(a) **1, in ex.**
ring *v.* sonar; *n.* anillo **9; engagement ring** anillo de compromiso **16; wedding ring** anillo de casado **16**
river río **Gac. 3; 15**
road camino **11**
roof techo **5**
room cuarto, sala **5; *(hotel)*** habitación *f.*
roommate compañero(a) de cuarto **1**
round-trip *adj.* de ida y vuelta **10**
rug alfombra **5**
run correr **14; *(operate)*** funcionar **12**; **run into** chocar con **11; to run out of** acabarse

S

sacred sagrado(a) **18**
sad triste **2**
sadness pena **6**
safety belt cinturón de seguridad *m.* **10**
saint santo(a) **18; saint's day** día del santo *m.*
salad ensalada **7**
salary sueldo, salario **3**
salesperson vendedor(a) **3**
salt sal *f.* **7**
same mismo(a) **3**
sandwich sandwich *m.*, bocadillo *(Sp.)* **1; 7**
Saturday sábado **Sec. A**
sauce salsa **8; tomato sauce** salsa de tomate
sausage chorizo *(Sp.)* **8**
savage salvaje **Gac. 1; 15**
save *(money)* ahorrar **15**
say decir (e > i, i) **4; which is to say** es decir **1**
school escuela **1; grade school teacher** maestro(a)
science ciencia **2**
score anotación *f.* **14**
scrub fregar (e > ie) **5**
season *(weather)* estación *f.* **11**; ***(sports)*** temporada **14**
seat *v.* sentar (e > ie) **9**; *n.* asiento **10**
second segundo(a) **1**
secretary secretario(a) **3**
section sección; **T.V. section** cartelera; **cooking section** sección de cocina; **fashion section** sección de moda **6**
see ver **4; I see . . .** Ya veo **16**
seem parecer (zc) **6**
sell vender **2**
semester semestre *m.* **1, in ex.; 2**
send mandar **11**, enviar **6, in ex.**
sensitive sensible **Sec. A; 17**
September septiembre *m.* **4**
serious serio(a) **Sec. B**
servant criado(a) **12**
serve servir (e > i, i) **5**
set, to set the table poner la mesa **4**
seven siete **Sec. B**
seventeen diecisiete **Sec. B**
seventh séptimo(a) **12**
seventy setenta **1**
shame, It is a shame. lástima; Es una lástima. **10; What a shame!** ¡Qué lástima! **6**
shampoo champú *m.* **12**
share compartir **5**
shark tiburón *m.* **15**
shave afeitar(se) **9**
sheet sábana **5**
shellfish mariscos *m.pl.* **7**
ship barco **11**
shirt camisa **9; T-shirt** camiseta **9**
shoe zapato **9**
shop tienda **3; repair shop** taller *m.* **11**
shopping, to go shopping ir de compras **8; shopping mall** centro comercial **9**
short *(in height)* bajo(a) **2; *(in length)*** corto(a) **4**
should deber (+ *inf.)* **2**
shower ducha **5**
shrimp camarones *m.pl.* **7**
sick enfermo(a) **2; to get sick** enfermarse **13**
side lado **Gac. 3; along side of** al lado de
sign firmar **12**
signal, traffic signal semáforo **11**
silent silencioso(a) **12**
silk seda **9**
silly tonto(a); **silliness** tontería **16, in ex.**
simple sencillo(a) **Gac. 2**
sinagogue sinagoga **16**
since ya que; **ever since** desde que **Gac. 4**
sing cantar **6**
single *(not married)* soltero(a) **4**
sister hermana **4**
sit, to sit down sentarse (e > ie) **9**
six seis **Sec. B**
sixteen dieciséis **Sec. B**
sixth sexto(a) **12**
sixty sesenta **1**
size talla **9**
ski *v.* esquiar **14**; *n.* esquí *m.* **Gac. 1; *(equipment)*** esquís *m.pl.* **14**
skirt falda **9**
sleep dormir **3**
sleeping bag saco de dormir **15**
sleepy, to be sleepy tener sueño **3**
slender delgado(a) **2**
slipper zapatilla **9**
slow lento(a) **2**
small pequeño(a), chico(a) **2**
smart listo(a) **2**
smile *v.* sonreír **14**; *n.* sonrisa
smoke *v.* fumar **10**; *n.* humo
sneaker zapatilla **9**
snow *v.* nevar (e > ie) **3**; *n.* nieve *f.* ***5***
so *adv.* tan **Sec. B**; *conj.* **so that** para que **15; so-so** así así **Sec. B**
soap jabón *m.* **5**
soap opera telenovela **6**
soccer fútbol *m.* **Sec. A; 14**
sock calcetín *m.* **9**
sofa sofá *m.* **Sec. A; *5***
soft drink refresco **6**
soldier soldado **Gac. 5**
solemn solemne **18**
solitude soledad *f.* **16**
solve resolver (o > ue) **16**
some algún, alguno(a) **3**
someone alguien **3**
something algo **3; something else** algo más **7**

sometimes a veces **17**
somewhat algo
son hijo **4**
soon, as soon as en cuanto *conj.* **14**, tan pronto como *conj.* **14**, lo más pronto posible **13**
soul alma **18**
sound sonar
soup sopa **7**
south sur *m.* **11**
Spanish *n., adj.* español(a) **Sec. B, in ex.; 12; Spanish language** español *m.*
speak hablar **1**
specialty especialidad *f.* **7**
spectator espectador(a) **14**
spend *(money)* gastar **11; *(time)*** pasar **1**
spirit espíritu *m.* **Gac. 3**
spoon cuchara **7**
sport deporte *m.*, **1, in ex.**; *adj.* deportivo(a) **1**
spring primavera **4**
stadium estadio **10, in ex.**
stamp sello, estampilla **12**
start *(motor)* arrancar (qu)
station estación *f.* **11; bus station** estación de autobuses; **gas station** gasolinera, estación de gasolina
stay quedarse **9**
steak bistec *m.* **8**
still *adv.* todavía **12**
stimulating estimulante
stockings medias **9**
stomach estómago **13**
stop *v.* parar **11; to stop *(doing something)*** dejar de (+ *inf.*) **8, in ex.; Gac. 3; (to have) stopovers** (hacer) escalas
store tienda **3; department store** almacén *m.* **3**
stove estufa **3**
strange extraño(a) **12**, raro(a) **7**
street calle *f.* **Sec. B**, camino **11**
strength fuerza **14**
student estudiante m., *f.* **Sec. B**
student center centro estudiantil **1**
studious aplicado(a) **2**
study estudiar **1**
stupid estúpido(a) **2**
style estilo, modo **Gac. 1; 4; out of style** pasado(a) de moda **9**
subject *(school)* materia **2**
submit someter **17**
suburbs afueras **5**
subway metro **11**
suffer sufrir **13**
sugar azúcar *m.* **Gac. 2**
suggest sugerir (e > ie) **11**
suit traje *m.* **9**
suitcase maleta **10; to pack one's suitcases** hacer las maletas **10**
summer verano **4**
sunbathe tomar el sol **12**
sunny soleado(a) **15**
supermarket supermercado **8**
supper cena **4**
support apoyar **14**
surprise sorpresa *n.* **6; 18;** *v.* **(surprise)** sorprenderse
surprising sorprendente **10**
sweater suéter *m.* **Sec. A; 9**
sweep barrer **5**
sweets dulces *m.* **18**
swim nadar **12**
swimming natación *f.* **14; swimming pool** piscina **12**
swimsuit traje de baño *m.* **9**
swollen hinchado(a) **13**
systems analyst analista de sistemas *m.*

T

table mesa **4; 5; end table** mesita; **night table** mesita de noche
take tomar **1**, llevar **2; to take a trip** hacer un viaje **10; to take a walk** dar un paseo **6; to take away** quitar **9; to take off *(clothing)*** quitarse **9; to take out** sacar (qu) **10; to take photos** sacar fotos **4; to take advantage of** aprovecharse de **11**
talented talentoso(a) **Sec. B**
talk hablar **1**
tall alto(a) **2**
tank tanque *m.* **11**
taste gusto **8**
tea té *m.* **1; 7**
teach enseñar **1**
team equipo **Gac. 3**
teaspoon cucharita
teeth dientes *m.*, muelas **13**
telephone teléfono **Sec. A; 6; telephone number** número de teléfono
television set televisor *m.* **5**
tell decir **4**; contar **3**
temperature temperatura **13**
ten diez **Sec. B**
tennis tenis *m.* **Sec. A; 14**
tenth décimo(a) **12**
terrible fatal **Sec. B**
test examen *m.*, prueba **Sec. A**
textbook libro de texto **Sec. C; 1**
thank you gracias **Sec. B**; **thank you very much** muchas gracias
that *adj.* ese(a) **5; that *(over there)*** aquel, aquella; **that one** ése(a) eso; **that one *(over there)*** aquél, aquélla, aquello; *conj.* que; **that which** lo que **2; 10; that is . . .** o sea **16**
theater teatro **3, in ex.**
then luego **2; at that time** entonces **4**
there allí **1; there is** hay **Sec. B; there was** había; **there will be** habrá
thermometer termómetro **13**
these *adj.* estos(as) **5**; *pron.* éstos(as)
thin delgado(a) **Guía 1**
thing cosa **1**
think pensar, creer **3; Don't even think of it.** Ni pensarlo. **4**
third tercer, tercero(a) **12**
thirsty, to be thirsty tener sed **3**
thirteen trece **Sec. B**
thirty treinta **1**
this *adj.* este(a) **5**; *pron.* éste(a), esto
those *adj.* esos(as) **5; those (over there)** aquellos(as); pron. ésos(as), aquéllos(as)
thousand mil **4**
three tres **Sec. B**
three hundred trescientos **4**
throat garganta **13**
Thursday jueves *m.* **Sec. A**
thus así **16**
ticket boleto, billete *m.* ***(for a performance)*** entrada **10; *(fine)*** multa **11; *(passage)*** pasaje *m.*
tie corbata **9**; lazo
time hora **1**; tiempo; vez *f.* *(pl.* veces) **6**
tip propina **7**
tire llanta **11; flat tire** goma (llanta) pinchada (desinflada)
tired cansado(a) **2**
to a **1**
toast *v.* brindar **18**; brindis *m.*
today hoy **1**
toe dedo del pie **13**
together juntos(as) **8; to get together (with)** reunirse (con) **16**
toilet wáter, retrete *m.*
tomato tomate *m.* **7**
tomorrow mañana **Sec. B; day after tomorrow** pasado mañana; **until tomorrow** hasta mañana
tongue lengua **13**
tonight esta noche **1**
too much *adj.* demasiado(a), *adv.* demasiado **8**
toothpaste pasta dental **12**
top, on top of encima de **Sec. C**
tourist class clase turística *f.*
towel toalla **12**
toy juguete *m.* **4**
trade *(job)* oficio
traditional tradicional **12**
traffic tráfico, circulación *f.* **6**; **11; traffic signal** semáforo **11**
train tren *m.* **1, in ex.; 11 train station** estación del tren **11**
tranquil tranquilo(a) **Sec. A**; **12**
tranquility tranquilidad *f.* **15**
transportation transporte *m.*

travel viajar **10**
traveler viajero(a) **10**
treatment tratamiento **13**
tree árbol *m.* **4**
trip viaje *m.* **1, in ex.; 10; round trip** *adj.* de ida y vuelta **10; to take a trip** hacer un viaje; **Have a good trip!** ¡Buen viaje! **10**
triumph triunfar **15, in ex.; 17**
trunk ***(car)*** maletero **11**
try, to try to ***(to something)*** tratar de *(+ inf.)* **6**
T-shirt camiseta **9**
Tuesday martes *m.* **Sec. A**
tuna atún *m.* **8**
turkey pavo **8**
turn (a ***corner)*** doblar **10; to turn off (lights)** apagar (las luces) **6**
turtle tortuga **Gac. 4; 15**
TV televisor *m.* ***(set)*** **5**; televisión *f.* ***(concept)***; tele *f.*
twelve doce **Sec. B**
twenty veinte **Sec. B**
twice dos veces **Gac. 5**
two dos **Sec. B**
two hundred doscientos **4**
type escribir a máquina **1**
typewriter máquina de escribir **1**
typical típico(a) **14**

U

ugly feo(a) **2**
umbrella paraguas *m.* **9**
unbutton desabrochar
uncle tío **4**
uncomfortable incómodo(a) **9**
underneath debajo de **Sec. C**
understand comprender **2**
underwear ropa interior **9**
unique único(a) **7**
United States Estados Unidos *m.pl.* **2, in ex.**
university universidad *f.* **Sec. A**
unless a menos que **11**
unpack desempacar **12**
unpleasant antipático(a) **2**, desagradable **11**
until hasta que **14**
unusual extraño(a) **12**
urgent urgente **13**
use *v.* usar **1**, gastar **11**; *n.* uso **6, in ex.**
useful útil **1; 17**

V

vacation vacaciones *f.pl.* **to be on vacation** estar de vacaciones **Gac. 1; 10; to go on vacation** ir de vacaciones
vacuum *v.* pasar la aspiradora **5; vacuum cleaner** aspiradora
variety variedad *f.* **8**
VCR grabador de video *m.*
vegetable verdura, legumbre *f.* **7**
velocity velocidad *f.* **11**
very muy **1**
view vista **6, in ex.; point of view** punto de vista **Gac. 3**
vinegar vinagre *m.* **8**
violin violín *m.* **6**
visit *v.* visitar **4**
vitamin vitamina **13**
volcano volcán *m.* **15**
vote votar **Gac. 2; 17**
vowel vocal *f.*

W

wait (for) esperar **4**
waiter camarero, mesero, mozo **3**
waiting room sala de espera **10**
waitress camarera, mesera, moza **3**
wake despertar (e > ie) **9; to wake up** despertarse (e > íe); *n.* velorio
walk caminar **6; to take walk** dar un paseo; *n.* paseo
wallet cartera **9**
want desear **1**, querer (e > ie) **3**
warm, to be/feel warm tener calor **3; It's warm.** ***(weather)*** Hace calor. **4**
wash lavar **9**; ***(oneself)*** lavarse
washing machine lavadora **5**
watch *v.* mirar **1**; *n.* reloj *m.*
water agua *f.* **4; waterbed** cama de agua **4**
way, in that way así **16; one-way** de ida **10**
wear llevar **2**
weather tiempo **4; What's the weather like?** ¿Qué tiempo hace?
wedding boda **16**
Wednesday miércoles *m.* **Sec. A**
week semana **4; Holy Week** Semana Santa
weekend fin de semana *m.* **1**
weigh pesar **8**
weight peso **8**
welcome bienvenido(a) **Sec. B; you're welcome** de nada **Sec. B**
well bien **1; well** ***(now)*** pues **16; well enough** bastante bien **Sec. B**
west oeste **11**
what ***(that which)*** lo que **2; 10; what?** ¿qué? ¿cómo? **Sec. B; What a . . .!** ¡Qué *(+ n.)*! **6; What is . . . like?** ¿Cómo es...? **1**
when cuando **Sec. B; when?** ¿cuándo?
where donde **Sec. B; where?** ¿dónde?
which cual **Sec. B; which?** ¿cuál?; **that which** lo que **2; 10**
while mientras **8**
white blanco(a) **4**
who *rel. pron.* que **10**; *subj. and obj. pron.* quien; **who?** ¿quién? *pl.* ¿quiénes? **Sec. B**
whole entero(a) **17**
whom? ¿a quién? *pl.* ¿a quiénes? **Sec. B**
whose? ¿de quién(es)? **2**
why por qué **Sec. B; why?** ¿por qué? **that's why** por eso **2**
widow viuda **4**
widower viudo **4**
wife esposa **4**
win ganar **3**
wind viento **4**
window ventana **Sec. C**, ventanilla **11**
windy, It's windy. Hace viento. **4**
wine vino **7; red (white) wine** vino tinto (blanco)
winter invierno **4**
wish esperar **4; I wish that . . .** espero que... , ojalá que (+ *subj.)* **11**
with con **1; with me** conmigo; **with you** contigo, con Ud., con Uds. **5**
without sin **1**
woman mujer *f.* **Sec. C; 1**
wool lana **9**
word palabra **2**
work *v.* trabajar **1**, funcionar ***(machines)*** **12**; *n.* trabajo **3**
worker obrero(a), trabajador(a) **3**
workshop taller *m.* **11**
world mundo **Sec. C, 10**
worried preocupado(a) **2**
worry (about) preocuparse (por, de) **13**
worse peor **6**
wounded herido(a), lastimado(a) **13**
write escribir **2**

Y

yard patio **Sec. A**; **5**
year año **2; to be . . . years old** tener . . . años **3; New Year's Eve** Noche vieja **18; Happy New Year!** ¡Próspero Año Nuevo!
yellow amarillo(a) **4**
yes sí **1**
yesterday ayer **6**; **day before yesterday** anteayer
yet todavía **12**
you *subj. pron.* tú *(fam. sing.)* **Sec. B**; usted (Ud., Vd.) *(form. sing.)*; vosotros(as) *(fam. pl., Sp.)*; ustedes *(Uds., Vds.) (pl.)*; *d.o.* te, os, lo/la, los, las **5; to, for you** *ind. obj.* te, os, le les **6**; *obj. of prep.* ti, vosotros, Ud., Uds. **5**
young joven **2**
younger menor **4**
your (posessive) tu(s) *(fam. s.)* **3**; vuestro(a)(s) *(fam. pl., Sp.)*; su(s) *(form.)*
youth joven *m., f.* **2**

Z

zero cero **Sec. B**
zoo zoológico **Gac. 4; 15**

Index of Grammar

Photo Credits

p. xxvi: Valencia, Spain—George Levy; **p. xxvi:** Buenos Aires—Owen Franken/Stock Boston; **p. 1:** UMACO, P.R.—Nancy Levy-Konesky; **p. 2:** Street signs—Mark Ferri/ The Stock Market; **p. 14:** Video stills—Nancy Levy-Konesky / Frank Konesky; **p. 15:** Portraits—Nancy Levy-Konesky; **p. 14:** Enrique Iglesias—Buck Kelly/The Liaison Agency; **p. 16:** Video stills—Nancy Levy-Konesky / Frank Konesky; **p. 25:** Franklin Chang-Diaz—The Liaison Agency; **p. 25:** Salma Hayak—Barry King/The Liaison Agency; **p. 25:** Rita Moreno—Scapiro/The Liaison Agency; **p. 25:** Rubén Blades—Trapper/SYGMA; **p. 25:** Arantxa Sánchez-Vicario—Al Bello/Allsport; **p. 25:** Isabel Allende—Blake Little/SYGMA; **p. 25:** Gabriel García Márquez—Graziano Arici/SYGMA; **p. 29:** Calle Ocho—Stuart Cohen; **p. 40:** Young boy, Dominican Republic—Odyssey/Frerck/Chicago; **p. 40:** Portrait, woman—Odyssey/Frerck/Chicago; **p. 40:** Portrait, woman—Odyssey/Frerck/Chicago; **p. 41:** Rain forest, Costa Rica—Stuart Cohen; **p. 41:** Sailboat, P. R.—Thomas & Fletcher/Stock Boston; **p. 41:** Calahora Castle—Odyssey/Frerck/Chicago; **p. 42:** Caribbean food—Wolfgang Kaehler; **p. 45:** John Leguizamo—Mitch Gerber/Corbis; **p. 45:** Mary Jo Fernandez—Reuters/Corbis; **p. 45:** Jennifer López—Mitch Gerber/Corbis; **p. 49:** Univ. of Salamanca—Odyssey/Frerck/Chicago; **p. 50:** Video still—Nancy Levy-Konesky / Frank Konesky; **p. 74:** Video still—Nancy Levy-Konesky / Frank Konesky; **p. 91:** People in Barcelona—Odyssey/Frerck/Chicago; **p. 93:** "Persistence of Memory", 1931. Salvador Dalí Oil on canvas, 9.5x13″. MOMA, NY—Given anonymously. Photograph © 1999 MOMA, NY; **p. 96:** Video still—Nancy Levy-Konesky / Frank Konesky; **p. 120:** Puerto del Sol—Odyssey/Frerck/Chicago; **p. 121:** Sagrada Familia—Odyssey/Frerck/Chicago; **p. 121:** Toledo—Macduff Everton/The Image Works; **p. 122:** Alhambra—Mark Antman/The Image Works; **p. 122:** Parade float of Virgin de Macarena—Odyssey/Frerck/Chicago; **p. 123:** Domingo—No Credit; **p. 123:** La Costa Brava—Laura Elliott/COMSTOCK; **p. 124:** José Mariá Aznar—Cynthia Johnson/The Liaison Agency; **p. 124:** Mecano—Courtesy of BMG, U.S. Latin; **p. 124:** Antonio Banderas—Epipress/SYGMA; **p. 125:** Cristina Sánchez—Georges Merillon/The Liaison Agency; **p. 125:** Enrique Iglesias—Buck Kelly/the Liaison Agency; **p. 126:** Spain's Royal Family—Daniel Beltra/The Liaison Agency; **p. 127:** Castillo San Marcos—Odyssey/Frerck/Chicago; **p. 127:** St. George Street—William Johnson/Stock Boston; **p. 129:** Calderón—MAS; **p. 133:** Paella—Marcel Ehrhard/The Liaison Agency; **p. 133:** The 3 Kings with kids—Nancy Levy-Konesky; **p. 136:** Enrique Iglesias—Buck Kelly/The Liaison Agency; **p. 137:** The Gipsy Kings—deLaFosse/SYGMA; **p. 141:** House, D.R.—Mary Ann Hemphill/Photo Researchers Inc.; **p. 142:** Video still—Nancy Levy-Konesky / Frank Konesky; **p. 164:** Quinceañera—Stuart Cohen; **p. 168:** Video still—Nancy Levy-Konesky / Frank Konesky; **p. 189:** House, P.R.—Nancy Levy-Konesky; **p. 189:** Apartment, Madrid—Odyssey/Frerck/Chicago; **p. 189:** A colonial-style house—Odyssey/Frerck/Chicago; **p. 189:** Patio, Cordoba—Odyssey/Frerck/Chicago; **p. 193:** Video still—Nancy Levy-Konesky / Frank Konesky; **p. 216:** Beach, P.R.—Barbara Lewis/Monkmeyer Press Photo; **p. 217:** El Morro—David Frazier; **p. 218:** Santo Domingo—Hugh Rogers/Monkmeyer Press Photo; **p. 218:** Tito Puente—Jack Vartoogian; **p. 219:** Rito Moreno—Berliner/The Liaison Agency; **p. 219:** Rita Moreno in "West Side Story"—The Kobal Collection; **p. 219:** Marc Anthony—Evan Agostini/The Liaison Agency; **p. 219:** Sammy Sosa—Agence France Presse/Corbis-Bettmann; **p. 220:** Chayanne—The Kobal Collection; **p. 220:** Raúl Juliá—Barry King/The Liaison Agency; **p. 220:** Juan Luis Guerra—Courtesy of Karen Records; **p. 222:** Gov. Rossello—Larry Downing/Sygma; **p. 229:** Juan González—Courtesy of the Texas Rangers; **p. 236:** Mecano—Courtesy of BMG, U.S. Latin; **p. 237:** Open-air market—Jeff Gilbreath; **p. 238:** Video still—Nancy Levy-Konesky / Frank Konesky; **p. 260:** Video still—Nancy Levy-Konesky / Frank Konesky; **p. 276:** Little Havana, Miami—Donald Dietz/Stock Boston; **p. 280:** Video still—Nancy Levy-Konesky / Frank Konesky; **p. 299:** Guayabera—*Más* magazine; **p. 302:** Havana—Odyssey/Frerck/ Chicago; **p. 303:** Santiago, Cuba—G. Sioen/Rapho/The Liaison Agency; **p. 304:** Andy García—Greg Gorman/The Liaison Agency; **p. 304:** Alicia Alonso—Joe Picone/The Liaison Agency; **p. 306:** Castro—Pablo Ibarra/The Liaison Agency; **p. 307:** Celia Cruz—Christian Ducasse/The Liaison Agency; **p. 309:** José Martí—Courtesy of the OAS; **p. 311:** Gloria Estefan—P. F. Gero/SYGMA; **p. 315:** Little Havana, Miami—Odyssey/Frerck/Chicago; **p. 316:** Cuban food—Ulrike Welsch; **p. 319:** Airport—Ulrike Welsch; **p. 320:** Video still—Nancy Levy-Konesky / Frank Konesky; **p. 335:** Mayan woman preparing tortillas—Odyssey/Frerck/Chicago; **p. 340:** Video still—Nancy Levy-Konesky / Frank Konesky; **p. 358:** Video still—Nancy Levy-Konesky / Frank Konesky; **p. 375:** Mayan women—Odyssey/Frerck/Chicago; **p. 376:** Kukulkán temple, Chichén Itza—

Howard Dratch/The Image Works; **p. 380:** Mérida, Mexico—Ulrike Welsch; **p. 380:** People in Guadalajara—Odyssey/Frerck/Chicago; **p. 381:** Fine Arts Palace—Doug Bryant/DDB Stock Photo; **p. 382:** Uxmal ruins—Jeff Gilbreath; **p. 383:** Pyramid of the Sun—Craig Thompson/DDB Stock Photo; **p. 384:** "Cumpleaños de Lalay Tudi" Carmen Lomas Garza—Photo by Wolfgang Dietze; **p. 385:** Carlos Fuentes—Paolo Bosio/The Liaison Agency; **p. 385:** Luis Miguel—Mary Powell/Corbis; **p. 385:** Thalia—Ethan Miller/Corbis; **p. 387:** Edward James Olmos—D. Fineman/ SYGMA / **p. 388:** Kahlo—Corbis-Bettmann; **p. 388:** "Retrato de Luther Burbank" Frida Kahlo—Bob Schalkwijk/Art Resource; **p. 390:** César Chávez—Rod Lamkey, Jr./The Liaison Agency; **p. 392:** Rivera mural—Bob Schalkwijk/Art Resource; **p. 396:** Tito Villaneuva—Courtesy of Tito Villaneuva; **p. 399:** Peter Rodriguez "Self-Portrait—Courtesy of Peter Rodriguez; **p. 399:** "Santo Niño de Atocha" Peter Rodriguez—Courtesy of Peter Rodriguez; **p. 402:** Santana—Antonio Ribeiro/SYGMA; **p. 405:** Soccer—Chip & Rosa Maria de la Cueva Peterson; **p. 406:** Video still—Nancy Levy-Konesky / Frank Konesky; **p. 426:** Video still—Nancy Levy-Konesky / Frank Konesky; **p. 442:** Juan González—Courtesy of the Texas Rangers; **p. 442:** Livan Hernández of the Florida Marlins—Matthew Stockman/Allsport; **p. 442:** Sammy Sosa—Jean-Marc Giboux/The Liaison Agency; **p. 446:** Video still—Nancy Levy-Konesky / Frank Konesky; **p. 461:** Volcano Poás—John Mitchell/DDB Stock Photo; **p. 462:** Antigua, Guatemala—Odyssey/Frerck/Chicago; **p. 468:** Izalco Volcano—Chip & Rosa Maria de la Cueva Peterson; **p. 468:** Cathedral, Guatemala City—Odyssey/Frerck/Chicago; **p. 469:** Panama Canal—Wolfgang Kaehler; **p. 470:** Ruins at Copan—Bob Daemmrich/The Image Works; **p. 472:** Rigoberta Menchu—Gary Payne/The Liaison Agency; **p. 472:** Rubén Blades—Lynn Goldsmith/Corbis; **p. 476:** Woman weaving—Joe Cavanaugh/DDB Stock Photo; **p. 478:** Rubén Darío—Courtesy of the OAS; **p. 485:** Wedding—Arlene Collins/Monkmeyer Press Photo; **p. 486:** Video still—Nancy Levy-Konesky / Frank Konesky; **p. 506:** Video still—Nancy Levy-Konesky / Frank Konesky; **p. 520:** Video still—Nancy Levy-Konesky / Frank Konesky; **p. 526:** Day of the Dead candy—Peter Menzel/Stock Boston; **p. 534:** Semana Santa—Odyssey/Frerck/Chicago; **p. 538:** Machu Picchu—Odyssey/Frerck/Chicago; **p. 538:** Buenos Aires obelisk—Odyssey/Frerck/Chicago; **p. 543:** Don Francisco—Courtesy of UNIVISION; **p. 543:** Gabriel García Márquez—Gianfranco Gorgoni/SYGMA; **p. 545:** Bolívar—Courtesy of the OAS; **p. 546:** Neruda—Courtesy of the Americas Society; **p. 549:** Las madres—Nancy Levy-Konesky / Frank Konesky; **p. 551:** Isabel Allende—Nancy Levy-Konesky; **p. 553:** Inca Son